P9-DSW-523

WORKERS OF THE WHOLE WORLD, UNITE!

조선로동당 중앙위원회직속 당력사연구소

김 일 성
저작선집

1

조선로동당출판사
1975

THE PARTY HISTORY INSTITUTE OF THE
C. C. OF THE WORKERS' PARTY OF KOREA

KIM IL SUNG

SELECTED WORKS

I

FOREIGN LANGUAGES PUBLISHING HOUSE
PYONGYANG, KOREA
1976

ON THE OCCASION OF PUBLICATION OF THE TRANSLATED VERSION OF THE SECOND EDITION OF KIM IL SUNG'S *SELECTED WORKS*

In 1975 the Publishing House of the Workers' Party of Korea issued the second edition of Kim Il Sung's *Selected Works*, Volumes I-V.

This is its English version.

1976

CONTENTS

ON THE BUILDING OF NEW KOREA AND THE NATIONAL UNITED FRONT

Speech Addressed to the Responsible Functionaries of the Provincial Party Committees

October 13, 1945

Before going into the subject of the national united front, I should like first to refer to other countries' experience with the united front.

At the Seventh Congress of the Communist International in 1935, Comrade Dimitrov who read a report on "The Fascist Offensive and the Tasks of the Communist International in the Struggle for Working-Class Unity and against Fascism," advanced the line of forming broad anti-fascist popular fronts based on the unity and solidarity of the working class. At the time, Germany was under the sway of the most brutal fascist dictatorship of Hitler and in Italy Mussolini's fascist dictatorship was being further strengthened.

The fascists sought to enslave not only the people of their own countries but all mankind and to fascisticize the whole world. It was necessary to form popular fronts in many European countries to fight against the bloody dictatorships and aggressive policies of the fascists. Not only the working people, headed by the working class, but also those capitalists who were calling for liberty and democracy could participate in the popular fronts. The urgent need arose also to some capitalists, to say nothing of the workers, peasants and other working people, to fight back international fascism that was attempting to conquer the whole world and enslave all humanity. Fascist Italy's conquest of Ethiopia was a danger signal warning of the imminence of World War II. The question of the popular front was raised at the Seventh Congress of the Communist International to meet this crisis. The Congress recommended to the Communist Parties of various countries to form anti-fascist popular fronts. The French and Spanish Communist Parties were the first to adopt the tactical line on the formation of the popular front.

In the East, national united fronts were to be formed against Japanese imperialism, in view of the fact that the Japanese imperialists' aggressive schemes to conquer the Asian peoples were becoming ever more pronounced.

National united fronts were formed in countries fighting against imperialism's colonial rule for the elimination of the danger of colonization, and popular fronts were formed in countries like France and Spain which were confronted with the danger of being turned fascist. In essence, the popular front and the national united front were similar—in the sense that both were opposed to fascism and imperialist aggression—but the specific conditions of different countries gave rise to these two forms.

China affords us a good example of the national united front. When Japanese imperialism occupied Manchuria and extended its evil hand of aggression to the Chinese mainland, the Communist Party of China proposed that the Kuomintang and the Communist Party collaborate and come out in an anti-Japanese struggle for national salvation by rallying all forces of the nation. This proposal of the Communist Party was not accepted for a long time, owing to the obstinacy of the reactionary group of the Kuomintang, but the sincere and persistent efforts of the Communist Party of China gradually earned the support of the people throughout China. And, when the Sino-Japanese war broke out, the collaboration of the Communist Party and the Kuomintang crystallized at last, and the anti-Japanese national united front was formed. The reactionary group of the Kuomintang that had been so stubborn was forced to accept the proposal of the Communist Party under pressure of the unanimous demand of the Chinese people for national unity and resistance to Japan for national salvation.

World War II was a war of liberation for the democratic forces of the whole world against fascism. Thanks to the decisive role of the Soviet army in World War II, Germany, Italy and Japan were defeated, bringing liberation from the fascist yoke to many countries in Europe and Asia.

Which road should liberated Korea take? There is the most important, fundamental problem which we must take into account in deciding on the road to be followed by Korea. This is the fact that Korea was a colony of Japanese imperialism for a long time. Because of Japanese imperialist rule, the capitalist development of Korea was greatly retarded, and Korea's society remained colonial, retaining the vestiges of feudalism in a large measure. The feudal relations of exploitation are especially predominant in our countryside.

The Korean people, therefore, are today faced with the tasks of carrying out an anti-imperialist, anti-feudal, democratic revolution and building a Democratic People's Republic.

Who, then, is to lead this revolution: the working class, or the capitalist class? In the past, the capitalist class of Korea exploited and oppressed the Korean people and deceived the people with the slogans of "national reform" and "self-government of the nation" in collaboration with Japanese imperialism. Of course, we do not mean that there did not exist national capitalists at all who turned against Japanese imperialism.

It was the working class of Korea that fought courageously against Japanese imperialism to the bitter end. Though the Communist Party of Korea, founded in 1925, was dissolved in 1928 due to factional strife, that did not mean the end of the communist movement. From the 1930's on the Communists of Korea fought valiantly against Japanese imperialism, weapons in hand.

It goes without saying that the capitalist class of Korea that capitulated to Japanese imperialism and collaborated with it, is not entitled to lead the revolution. Only the working class that fought bravely against Japanese imperialism to the end can and must lead the Korean revolution.

In determining our course, we must also take into consideration the favourable international situation prevailing after World War II and, along with it, the fact that the armed forces of the United States, an imperialist country, and the Soviet Union, a socialist state, are stationed in the south and the north with the north 38th parallel as the demarcation line, and the fact that our Party is not yet strong enough.

To build a Democratic People's Republic, a united front should be formed of all the patriotic democratic forces including not only the working class and the peasantry but also the national capitalists. Only in the course of struggling—not in words but in deeds—for the founding of a People's Republic can we win over the masses to our side.

We must realize that the intellectuals, religious people, and capitalists, too, are now stirring, though not in an organized way. The stronger our organization and forces grow, the farther will they move forward gradually towards organizing themselves, forsaking their scattered traits. In this light, we cannot ignore the forces of the nationalists at the present stage and should not place obstacles in the way of the formation of the national united front by alienating them in an unprincipled manner.

Owing to the vicious propaganda launched against it by the Japanese imperialists and the harm done it by the factionalists in the past, the Communist Party does not yet have the support of the broad masses, and some sections of the masses who are not awakened politically still harbour illusions about the nationalists.

Needless to say, as our united front is a united front for the building of a Democratic People's Republic, a coalition with the lackeys of Japanese imperialism is utterly inconceivable. We can and should join hands with those conscientious national capitalists who want to build an independent and democratic state. Only the formation of a united front of this type will enable us to build a Democratic People's Republic and rally together the masses of the people in all walks of life.

The Communist Party must not be inert or passive in this struggle. In the struggle to establish a Democratic People's Republic the Communists should play the most active and positive role and should be at the head of the masses of the people and lead them forward. Only when they do so will the masses of the people follow the Communist Party.

The national capitalists may always waver in the course of the struggle to set up a Democratic People's Republic. Experience shows that they not infrequently deceive the masses or betray the national interests to look after their own narrow class interests. The national capitalists are afraid of the revolutionary advance of the masses and are apt to vacillate as the revolution forges ahead. We should, therefore, promote our unity with the national capitalists even when they fail to display enthusiasm and vacillate in the work of building a Democratic People's Republic and, on the other hand, should continuously expose and criticize their criminal acts and vacillating nature. Only by so doing can we bring the masses to see clearly the national capitalists in their true colours and, at the same time, to fully understand the policies of the Communist Party.

The Communist Party should co-operate unhesitatingly with the parties that advocate the reunification and independence of our country, but it should under no circumstances drag at their tail, much less be absorbed into another party. Working hand in hand with them, the Communist Party should always maintain its own identity.

At present, the Hanguk Democratic Party is vehemently opposed to our liquidation of the lackeys of Japanese imperialism. This is by no means an accident. The Hanguk Democratic Party is a grouping of landlords and comprador capitalists who until yesterday collaborated with the Japanese imperialists. With the defeat of Japanese imperialism, they suddenly turned pro-American and have come out seeking U.S. support in place of Japanese protection. Few of Korea's landlords and capitalists did not become minions of Japanese imperialism; the absolute majority of them, working at the beck and call of Japanese imperialism, exploited and oppressed the Korean people. This is an indisputable fact. It is, therefore, only reasonable that we should thoroughly liquidate those pro-Japanese landlords, comprador capitalists and traitors to the nation.

The national capitalists, too, are very much afraid of our struggle against the surviving elements of Japanese imperialism. For they, too, served Japanese imperialism more or less in the past. It is wrong to argue that we should not expose and criticize their criminal acts while calling for a national united front. In the united front we should adhere strictly to the principle of struggling while joining with them. This alone will heighten the political awareness of the working masses and make it possible to overcome the vacillating nature of the national capitalists.

There is a question which we should clarify in this regard. That is the question as to how to define the lackeys of Japanese imperialism. We cannot call a man a lackey of Japanese imperialism simply because he worked under a Japanese. Over a period of nearly 40 long years many Koreans found it impossible to make a living without entering the service of Japanese imperialist establishments. Needless to say, those who suppressed and murdered people deliberately in order to destroy the revolution, those who betrayed and sold out the national interests for the benefit of Japanese imperialism, and those elements that collaborated actively and intentionally with Japanese imperialism should be defined as lackeys. Such traitors to the nation must be liquidated through a mass struggle by arousing the masses to action. But those who were obliged to serve in the Japanese imperialist establishments in order to make a living or did so under pressure and the subordinate clerks who performed no more than a negative and passive role there cannot be labelled as lackeys. Those people should be educated and remoulded and the way should be open to them for regeneration.

Our immediate task is to found a Democratic People's Republic. We cannot skip over a stage in the development of the revolution; we must work out a correct strategy and tactics to carry out the tasks arising in the present stage of the revolution.

The immediate objects of our struggle are the lackeys of imperialism who are at pains to reintroduce the imperialist forces, and the feudal forces—that is, the landlords—that have allied themselves with them. In order to oppose the remnant forces of imperialism and the feudal forces and complete the democratic revolution, a Democratic People's Republic, a people's power led by the working class, must be built by forming a democratic united front of which the working class is the core and which embraces the broad sections of the peasantry and patriotic intellectuals, and even the national capitalists who have a national conscience.

The basic programme of the Party, which represents the strategic demands arising in the present stage of the revolution, is unalterable, but its action programme which represents the tactical demands is changeable on occasion. The basic programme of the Communist Party such as "Factories to the workers" or "Land to the peasants" is immutable, but its action programme should be drawn up in keeping with the changing situation to fit in with it. We should, therefore, bring forward an action programme most suited to the present situation and fight for it.

If we are to form a united front at present, we should first strengthen the alliance of the workers and the peasants and win over the broad sections of the peasantry to our side. And to defend the interests of the peasants and win them over, it is necessary to begin with the struggle for reducing the farm rents and, while carrying on the struggle for confiscating the lands of the Japanese imperialists and their minions, gradually unfold the struggle for confiscating the estates of all the landlords and dividing them among the peasants. In this way, the struggle should be extended gradually from smaller to larger targets.

If we want to win over the broad masses and weaken the

forces of the enemy, it is important more than anything else to strengthen the ranks of the Communist Party.

To begin with, we should fight against the opportunists who have wormed their way into the Party. The opportunists have no consistent principles and are seeking to destroy the unity of the Party, flitting from one side today to another tomorrow just like a bat. They are a set of people whom we should hate and guard against most.

Then, those whom we must watch for are lackeys of Japanese imperialism disguised as Communist Party members. To conceal their crimes, they pass themselves off as ardent Communists. They indulge in "ultra-Left" phraseology and actions and are clamouring as though they would overthrow the capitalist class and establish "soviet" power right away. However, their real aim is to bring the revolution to naught by wrecking the Communist Party and hoodwinking the working class. We should wage a merciless struggle against these alien elements that have sneaked into the Party.

Also, we should not neglect our own self-cultivation in order to keep ourselves from becoming dissolute and degenerated. It is not infrequent that even a simple, upright Communist is swayed by a desire for personal fame and gains and becomes dissolute and degenerated once he assumes power. This not only leads to his own ruin but also brings about the grave consequence of divorcing the Party from the masses. We Communists have no other objective than serving the people and working with devotion for their benefit.

If we Communists fight sincerely for the people, the people will open their hearts to us and even those who were hostile towards us, not knowing clearly what kind of people we are, will come to understand us.

Nowadays I often hear words such as popular rights and democracy. They are all fine words in the sense that they mean government granting rights to the people, government in which the sovereignty rests with the people. But "democracy" of a U.S. or British type does not fit today's Korea. West European "democracy" is already out of date and, moreover, if we adopted it, we would fail to attain our goal of achieving the country's independence and our country would be reduced again to a colony of foreign imperialism. It is, therefore, necessary to set up a new, progressive democratic system in Korea in keeping with its actual conditions.

Our task ahead is to quickly educate the masses who are not yet fully awakened and lead them to fight for genuine democracy for themselves. The masses are not clear as to who it is that defends and who it is that harms their interests. Therefore, we should do everything in our power to perseveringly publicize and explain our Party's assertions among the masses. We should not only educate the masses but also learn from them, and heed their voices and satisfy their demands.

The building of a new, democratic Korea is entirely dependent on whether or not we succeed in the work of strengthening the Communist Party, forming the national united front and rallying the broad masses around the Communist Party. Every Communist should wage an active struggle to constantly expand and strengthen the Party ranks, to co-operate in good faith with the friendly parties and win over the broad masses.

ON THE WORK OF THE ORGANIZATIONS AT ALL LEVELS OF THE COMMUNIST PARTY OF NORTH KOREA

Report to the Third Enlarged Executive Committee Meeting of the Central Organizing Committee of the Communist Party of North Korea

December 17, 1945

Comrades,

The Korean people have expelled the Japanese imperialists from the territory of our homeland and won freedom and independence with the help of the heroic Red Army of the Soviet Union. A broad avenue has now been opened to the liberated Korean people.

We will never forget the fraternal help given us by the great Soviet people, the Red Army and Comrade Stalin.

From the moment the Red Army entered Korean territory, the Communist Party began to be organized in north Korea. In the three months following liberation, the Communist Party did no small job in the way of organizational work. During these months the Communist Party grew rapidly and now has 4,530 members in its ranks.

Provincial, city and county Party committees have been organized, and Party cells have been formed in many districts. The Communist Party has five publications now. So, Party members have a basically correct understanding of the present political situation in north Korea. Many Party committees have already corrected the "Left" errors they committed in the early stage.

But, although the organizations at all levels of the Communist Party of North Korea have achieved considerable success in their work, they still have grave defects. These shortcomings are in evidence primarily in the organizational work of the Party. The formation of the Party is not yet organizationally complete.

Statistics on Party membership are not in proper shape, and uniform membership cards have not been issued to Party members.

Party committees have not yet been built up with best workers, and Party organizations have yet to be created in a large number of factories, enterprises and farm villages.

In local Party organizations, pro-Japanese and other hostile elements have managed to infiltrate our Party ranks, because procedures for admission to the Party have not been established. Those hostile elements attempt to damage the prestige of our Party in the eyes of the masses and wreck its unity. And such elements are to be found not only among the rank and file but also in the leading bodies of our Party.

A certain Kim, secretary of the Yangdok County Party Committee, for instance, was a police sergeant at the police station in that county during Japanese imperialist rule, yet he is now "directing" the Party organizations. A certain Kwon, chairman of the Yangdok County People's Committee, served as head of the pro-Japanese organization Iljin-hoe in that county before liberation, and now he is acting as a "Communist." Many other similar instances could be cited.

All these facts show that the ranks of our Communist Party are infested with pro-Japanese elements.

1. ON IMPROVING THE COMPOSITION OF THE PARTY

The present composition of our Communist Party is as follows:

Workers	30%
Peasants	34%
Intellectuals, tradesmen and others . . .	36%

We can see from these figures that the Party is not developing on a sound basis. The Party ranks consist primarily of peasants and intellectuals. Thus, the Party has failed to become truly a working-class party. A party with such a composition will not be able to carry out the will and demands of the working class to the full.

Comrade Stalin said, "The Party must be, first of all, the *advanced* detachment of the working class. The Party must absorb all the best elements of the working class, their experience, their revolutionary spirit, their selfless devotion to the cause of the proletariat." We have failed to observe this principle in our work.

How comes it that our Party ranks include many peasants and intellectuals and a small number of workers? Here is the reason:

First, our Party committees and functionaries have failed to maintain close ties with the working class and to work properly with it. Our Party functionaries do not go among the workers, but wait for the workers to come to them.

Second, Party cells have not yet been organized in many factories and enterprises.

Third, workers who want to join the Party have found it very difficult to do so owing to the stipulation that endorsers for admission to the Party must have more than a year's Party standing. This amounts to placing an artificial barrier in the way of the workers who desire to join the Party.

We cannot tolerate such a practice any longer. We must steer the right course in the growth of Party membership so that chiefly workers and advanced urban and rural working people may join the Party ranks.

2. ON STRENGTHENING PARTY UNITY AND DISCIPLINE

Another big defect in the work of the Party organizations is that Party unity is not strong enough and there is a lack of discipline. This is inconsistent with the spirit of the Communist Party and its organizational principles.

Various kinds of groupings have appeared within the Party organizations in Hwanghae, North Pyongan and South Hamgyong Provinces. This is a very dangerous phenomenon, one that weakens the unity of the Party and lowers its prestige.

Some local Party committees ignore or do not faithfully carry out the directives of the Central Organizing Committee. In so doing, they grossly violate the Party's principle of democratic centralism and weaken its discipline.

Some provincial Party committees do not deem it their duty to report regularly to the Central Organizing Committee on their work and the work of their Party organizations. There was even an instance that when we sent a comrade working in the Central Organizing Committee to South Hamgyong Province, the Provincial Party Committee did not accept him. In that province, the Young Communist League has not yet been reorganized into the Democratic Youth League in spite of repeated instructions from the Central Organizing Committee.

We must consider such behaviour of some provincial Party committees that disregard the instructions of the Central Organizing Committee acts of liberalism incompatible with the organizational principles of the Marxist Party. Lenin once said, "...the Communist Party will be able to perform its duty only if it is organized in the most centralized manner, if iron discipline bordering on military discipline prevails in it, and if its Party centre is a powerful and authoritative organ, wielding wide powers and enjoying the universal confidence of the members of the Party." "Whoever weakens in the least the iron discipline of the Party of the proletariat (especially during the time of its dictatorship), actually aids the bourgeoisie against the proletariat." Many of our functionaries are oblivious of this dictum of Lenin's.

We should not forget even for one moment that not a few pro-Japanese elements who have sneaked into our Party will resort to every conceivable scheme to disrupt its ranks.

If we want to have a powerful and dignified Communist Party, we must strive with might and main to strengthen discipline in the Party and preserve its unity.

3. ON STRENGTHENING OUR TIES WITH THE MASSES

Our Party now shows a very small number of workers in its membership. This is so because the ties between the Party and the masses are weak.

Party bodies fail to carry out their organizational and educational work properly among the masses, and leading functionaries do not visit the factories, enterprises, coal mines and farm villages. They are not, therefore, well acquainted with the actual conditions of the local areas and are ignorant of the mood of the masses. As a result, there occurred an untoward incident in Sinuiju in which middle-school boys armed themselves and raided the provincial Party headquarters at the instigation of the national socialists. A similar incident took place in another region as well.

Communists have failed to mobilize the masses actively to tackle the immediate tasks arising in all spheres of political and economic life in north Korea, such as rehabilitating production enterprises, putting railway transport in order and securing voluntary deliveries of farm produce. Leading functionaries of the Party do not deem it their duty to go to the factories and talk to the workers, listen to their demands, explain the present situation in our country to them, settle difficulties that crop up in their work and set them concrete tasks.

If, instead of going among the masses, we only shut ourselves away in our offices, we will not be able to win over the masses, and the people will not follow us; and, thus, we will find ourselves divorced from the masses of the people. If we do not continually strengthen our ties with the masses, if we do not lend an ear to the voices of the masses, teach them, and, in addition, learn from them, the Communist Party, a working-class party, will not be able to become a truly mass party, competent to lead the entire working people.

If a party always approaches the broad working masses and maintains close ties with them, that party will be ever-victorious. In contrast, if a party is isolated from the masses and falls captive to bureaucracy, that party will become impotent and ruined. Comrade Stalin said, "We may take it as the rule that as long as the Bolsheviks maintain connection with the broad masses of the people they will be invincible. And, on the contrary, as soon as the Bolsheviks sever themselves from the masses and lose their connection with them, as soon as they become covered with bureaucratic rust, they will lose all their strength and become a mere cipher." Some of our Party functionaries do not fulfil this basic requirement, and many local Party organizations ignore it.

4. ON THE GUIDANCE OF THE TRADE UNIONS

Leading Party bodies pay little attention to the guidance of the trade unions. As a result, the trade unions fail to mobilize workers, technicians and office employees fully for the work of rehabilitating and putting factories and enterprises back into operation, raising labour productivity and strengthening labour discipline.

Provincial and city Party committees have underestimated their guidance of the trade unions, which has resulted in many non-Party people coming to hold leading posts in these unions and Communists making up but a small portion of the trade union membership.

Some trade union committees, far from helping the management in its work, offer obstacles to its running of the enterprise. For example, workers in a certain production enterprise in Sadong (which has a trade union) raised an unlawful demand under the "guidance" of a Party member, organized something like a strike and went so far as to beat up the manager and engineers. The workers, though their wages were higher than they had ever been in the years of Japanese imperialist rule, came out with a strong demand for a wage increase. It should be realized that the economic situation in the country does not allow us to grant large wage increases. In order to effect a large wage raise, a quick readjustment and operation of all the production enterprises and an increase in labour productivity are needed.

In guiding the trade unions, we should not focus attention merely on the question of improving the immediate living conditions of the working class without taking into consideration the long-range interests of the development of the national economy. It is important to make the trade unions enlist the patriotic zeal and creative activity of the working people in the struggle for the rehabilitation and construction of the national economy. Only by so doing can we steadily improve the living standards of the working people.

The Party is not an ordinary organization; it is the highest form of organization of the working class, and an organization that leads all other organizations of the working class. As regards the leadership of the Communist Party over the trade unions and other social organizations, Comrade Stalin said as follows: "It only means that the members of the Party who belong to these organizations and are doubtlessly influential in them should do all they can to persuade these non-Party organizations to draw nearer to the Party of the proletariat in their work and voluntarily accept its political leadership." **This statement of Comrade Stalin should be made the guide to our Party's work in the trade unions.**

Some comrades assert that the direction of the trade unions is none of the Communist Party's business and that the trade unions need not function under the leadership of the Party. This is a view quite contradictory to Marxism-Leninism. We should relentlessly combat these wrong tendencies.

5. ON THE TRAINING OF CADRES AND ALLOCATION OF PARTY FORCES

Our Communist Party is very short on leading cadres who are tested and seasoned in practical work, for it is a young party.

Moreover, it cannot be said that the few cadres in its service are all doing their jobs well and working devotedly for the interests of the people. Some leading personnel who are Communists neglect their duties and fail in their self-improvement while only seeking high posts, and feather their own nests by taking advantage of their positions. The security chief of North Pyongan Province, for instance, was a fast liver who had several mistresses; he occupied a number of houses and misappropriated a stupendous amount of confiscated Japanese property. Upon learning of this fact, of course, we dismissed him at once.

We also have Party members who refuse to go to work at a lower level when they are told to do so and consider it shameful to work at the lower level.

One of the big defects found in some of our leading Party workers is that, in selecting and assigning personnel, they do not observe the principle of personnel management, but display favouritism and partiality for their friends and relatives. Such functionaries are eager to surround themselves with their relations and close friends.

As you see, we are short of cadres and, moreover, those cadres we do have are still very immature. Despite this, the provincial Party committees do not pay close attention to the training and education of cadres, and, after they assign personnel, fail to give them any assistance.

We should always remember the following words of Comrade Stalin with regard to personnel: "After a correct political line has been worked out and tested in practice, the Party cadres become the decisive force in the work of guiding the Party and the state. A correct political line is, of course, the primary and most important thing. But that in itself is not enough. A correct political line is not needed as a declaration, but as something to be carried into effect. But in order to carry a correct political line into effect, we must have cadres, people who understand the political line of the Party, who accept it as their own line, who are prepared to carry it into effect, who are able to put it into practice and are capable of answering for it, defending it and fighting for it. Failing this, a correct political line runs the risk of being purely nominal."

We **should train cadres, assign them properly, teach them in practical work, check up on their work, give them help** when **needed and keep exact statistics on them.**

We are now in dire need of competent newspapermen. As

a result, our Party publications are doing very unsatisfactory work and fail to perform properly the task of explaining and popularizing the line of our Party.

The **Central Organizing Committee of our Party must strengthen the work of training and educating cadres so as to ease their shortage and raise their qualifications.**

6. ON THE WORK OF ISSUING PARTY MEMBERSHIP CARDS AND PREPARING MEMBERSHIP STATISTICS

A serious defect in the work of provincial and city Party committees is that they do not keep accurate statistics on their Party organizations and members. They have no set forms for registering and keeping statistics on Party members, and monthly statistics on their membership are not compiled.

Party members do not have uniform Party membership cards as yet. This is fraught with the danger of enabling the hostile elements to forge Party cards and pass themselves off **as Party members. Now the Central Organizing Committee has prepared uniform Party cards. We will issue them soon to Party** members. Great vigilance should be exercised to avoid Party cards falling into the hands of hostile elements when they are issued to Party members. Issuing membership cards, we should check the Party members and expel the alien elements that have insinuated themselves into the Party from its ranks.

7. ON THE QUESTION OF THE UNITED FRONT

Our Party is not working as well as it might do in establishing a united front with the democratic political parties.

Some of our comrades, instead of trying to solve weighty problems facing the Party and the people in co-operation with the friendly parties, provoke unnecessary friction. This places great obstacles in the way of forming a united front with the democratic political parties and social organizations.

In local districts, it is not uncommon that Communists antagonize members of the democratic political parties and vice versa. We cannot tolerate such practices.

Why do we need a united front? It is needed to unite the entire people; to put the political and economic life at home quickly in order; and to build our country into a unified, independent and democratic state. The Communist Party cannot carry out this great task singlehandedly. Only in unity with all the democratic political parties and social organizations at home and with the entire people can we realize the cause of building a unified, independent and democratic state.

Comrades,

What is at the bottom of the mistakes and defects discovered in the work of the organizations of the Communist Party of North **Korea? Unsatisfactory work of the Central Organizing Committee.**

Now then, can we eliminate all these shortcomings? Yes, of course. In order to eliminate the deficiencies in our work, we should, first of all, strive to preserve the unity of our Party ranks and establish iron discipline within the Party. Without this, we cannot do anything, nor can we strengthen and develop our Party into an invincible party.

8. OUR TASKS

What, then, are our Party's immediate tasks?

First, the political line of our Party at the present stage is to establish a unified, democratic government in our country based on an alliance with all the democratic political parties and social organizations, and transform north Korea into a powerful democratic base for the building of a unified, independent and democratic state. We, therefore, should rouse the labouring masses in the urban and rural areas to struggle for the speedy democratization of the political, economic and cultural life in north Korea on the one hand and, on the other, form a united front with all the democratic political parties and social organizations in north and south Korea, and strengthen it in every way.

Second, the issuance of Party membership cards should be carried on with scrupulous care. This has a great political significance. Party cards should be issued only to those who have really joined the Party. We should not regard the work of issuing Party cards merely as a technical matter, but should consider it a task of closing the Party ranks, a political task of purging them of reactionary elements, office seekers and other unsound elements that do harm to Party work.

Third, the *Chongno* newspaper staff should be enlarged and competent workers be assigned there so that the quality of the newspaper may be improved and its circulation boosted to 50,000 copies. At the same time, the newspaper should be made a daily publication. In this way, we must see to it that our newspaper becomes a collective propagandist and organizer.

Fourth, the growth of the Party should be properly regulated. The finest of the toiling people in urban and rural areas, particularly the advanced workers, should be drawn into the Party ranks.

Fifth, disorderly practices should be eliminated in the work of compiling statistics on Party membership. Every Party organization should enforce the system of taking and settling monthly statistics on the Party members and see that Party members take good care of their membership cards.

Sixth, Party cells should be formed in the factories and enterprises, and should be strengthened organizationally.

Seventh, the Party bodies should direct special attention to the training, assignment and education of Party cadres, and organize Party schools and short courses to train them at provincial, city, county and *myon* levels.

Eighth, Party conferences should be held at the provincial, city, county and *myon* Party committees to discuss questions pertaining to the immediate tasks of the Communist Party.

I am convinced that our Party organizations will successfully carry out the above-mentioned tasks set before them.

ON THE PRESENT POLITICAL SITUATION IN KOREA AND THE ORGANIZATION OF THE PROVISIONAL PEOPLE'S COMMITTEE OF NORTH KOREA

Report to a Consultative Meeting of Representatives of the Democratic Political Parties and Social Organizations, Administrative Bureaus and People's Committees of North Korea

February 8, 1946

Esteemed representatives,

We are gathered here today to solve important problems on the political, economic and cultural development of north Korea.

Five months have already elapsed since our people were liberated from Japanese imperialist colonial rule. Even though five months is a short period of time, it has witnessed great changes in north Korea. North Korea has confidently taken the road of truly democratic development.

Only five months ago Korea was a colony of Japanese imperialism. Nearly half a century of colonial rule by Japanese imperialism has left our nation with a distorted industry and transport, backward agriculture and ignorance and poverty for millions. Japanese imperialism deliberately hampered the economic development of Korea. The consequences of the rule by the Japanese aggressors may be seen clearly in all the state of affairs in different provinces of north Korea.

In the elaboration of their plans for the invasion of the

continent, the Japanese imperialists began industrial construction in north Korea several years ago. The factories, mines and hydroelectric power stations built by the Japanese aggressors were intended for Japanese imperialism's production of war supplies, but not for our country's economic development nor the improvement of the Korean people's living standard. Year after year Japanese imperialism robbed Korea of a huge amount of industrial raw materials and grain. Thus, Korea supplied Japan's war industry with raw materials and fed her rapacious armies.

Though Korea has favourable conditions for developing a modern industry, the aggressive policy of Japanese imperialism rendered it impossible to develop her national industry and also left her agriculture in a terribly backward state.

The long-drawn war plunged the Korean people, particularly the peasants, into abject poverty. The predatory policy of Japanese imperialism in the countryside left the majority of the peasants landless. As a result, 80 per cent of Korea's peasantry were tenant farmers, semi-tenant farmers and farm hands. By maintaining the feudal system of tenancy, the Japanese imperialist aggressors greatly retarded the development of the agricultural productive forces and forced millions of peasants to suffer from poverty and hunger.

The Japanese held a monopoly of industry and trade. The Koreans accounted for only 5 per cent of the total industrial capital, and 85 per cent of the commercial capital belonged to the Japanese.

All powers were completely in the hands of the Japanese robbers.

The Koreans were subjected to outrageous national oppression and humiliation. Special laws and special trials were applied to them and they were paid lower wages than the Japanese.

More than half of our children could not afford to go to school. Universities and specialized technical schools were well-nigh beyond the reach of young Koreans. Our national language was despised and trampled underfoot. The Japanese imperialist aggressors sought to stamp out our unique national culture and national consciousness and turn our people into "subjects of the Empire."

In spite of this oppression by the Japanese robbers, the Korean people were convinced that they would drive the Japanese aggressors out and attain national independence. The Korean people persistently waged a valiant struggle against Japanese imperialism. The March First Movement of 1919, the June Tenth Independence Movement of 1926, the general strike of the workers in Wonsan in 1929, the peasant riots that lasted from 1930 to 1932 in various places and the fierce anti-Japanese armed struggles waged both within and outside the country from the early 1930's on are a striking demonstration of the fact that our people fought indomitably against Japanese imperialism.

After Japanese imperialism was defeated and Korea liberated, the situation in our country underwent a radical change. Having attained freedom and liberation, the Korean people have a bright future ahead, and have confidently embarked upon the building of an independent and democratic state.

Political parties and social organizations have been formed and are carrying on their activities freely in north Korea today. The Communist Party, the Democratic Party and the Korean Independence Union have begun to function, and various democratic mass organizations—the trade unions, the Women's Union, the Democratic Youth League, the peasants' associations and the Korea-Soviet Cultural Society— have been formed. The trade unions, the peasants' associations and other social organizations have more than 2 million members.

Over 30 different newspapers are being published in north Korea already; textbooks and other kinds of books used in schools of various levels are being printed in our language, and radio programmes are being broadcast in our tongue. The lessons in our schools are also given in Korean, and our Korean language is heard everywhere—in every office and on every street. The art organizations, which were suppressed and trampled upon, have blossomed forth again and are very active.

All this is indicative of the great political enthusiasm of the masses and the ardent patriotism of the Korean people and shows that our national culture is being restored.

All the political parties and social organizations in north Korea have set themselves the common goal of forming a national democratic united front and, on this basis, of building a free, independent and democratic state.

With the liberation of their country, the North Korean people started organizing people's committees, independent and democratic local organs of power. The people's committees undertook, first of all, the task of maintaining social order and stabilizing the people's life.

Many bureaus—such as the Industrial Bureau, Transport Bureau, Communications Bureau, Bureau of Agriculture and Forestry, Trade Bureau, Financial Bureau, Bureau of Education, Public Health Bureau, Judicial Bureau and Security Bureau—were then organized to direct all branches of the national economy and establish economic ties among the various provinces of north Korea.

The bureaus and local people's committees have already achieved considerable success in the work of normalizing the economic life.

However, we cannot say that the work we have performed till now is satisfactory. The work of the bureaus and local people's committees is at present beset with many difficulties and shortcomings.

First, and most important, no central organ of state power has yet been organized in north Korea.

There does not yet exist in north Korea a unitary central organ of state power to orientate the work of the different bureaus and to direct them. This is highly detrimental to the unified, planned development of the political, economic and cultural life in north Korea.

The bureaus function only in their respective fields of economic or cultural life. But the bureaus are closely related to each other in their operations. Life shows in practice that more and more problems crop up which the bureaus cannot solve while acting separately.

The recovery of industry, for example, is the task of the Industrial Bureau, but it is related to the work of all the other bureaus. The Transport Bureau should guarantee transport work in a way conducive to the development of all branches of the national economy. The work of the Financial Bureau is closely connected with the work of various branches of the national economy—industry, agriculture, trade, transport, education, public health, etc. The Bureau of Education will have to train the talents needed in all domains of the national economy.

All this points to the pressing need of a central organ which will head the bureaus, co-ordinating and directing their work. It is the most urgent task to organize a central organ of state power in north Korea today.

We believe that, pending the establishment of a unified government in our country, a Provisional People's Committee of North Korea should serve as such an organ.

The establishment of a central organ of state power is a step in accord with the interests of the masses of the people and fully in conformity with the task of establishing democratic order in Korea. A proposal to set up a central organ of state power—the Provisional People's Committee of North Korea—has been advanced by the leaders of the democratic political parties and social organizations. With the object of organizing the central organ of state power, the leaders of the democratic political parties and social organizations in north Korea have set up an initiative committee.

In order to elect the members of the Provisional People's Committee of North Korea and to consider the important tasks ahead, we have **now called a meeting of representatives of the people's committees of north Korea's six provinces, and of the democratic political parties and social organizations.**

What are the tasks confronting the Provisional People's Committee of North Korea at the present juncture?

First, it is necessary to solidly build up the local organs of state power and thoroughly purge the state power organs of pro-Japanese and anti-democratic elements. This is the most important immediate task of the Provisional People's Committee of North Korea.

To build a new, free, independent and democratic Korea, it is necessary, first of all, to wage an active struggle against the pro-Japanese and the anti-democratic elements, the enemies of the people, and thus wipe out the reactionary forces root and branch. We cannot build a new, democratic Korea as long as the renegades and traitors are allowed to remain in the organs of state power. So, the people's committees in all the provinces, cities and counties and all the democratic political parties and social organizations must thoroughly expose the traitors to the nation and expel them from our ranks.

Second, the land of the Japanese imperialists and the traitors to the nation and landlords of Korea should be confiscated through an agrarian reform and distributed, free of charge, to the peasants who work it, and the forests should be nationalized.

Agriculture is a key branch of our country's national economy. Under Japanese imperialist rule, most of the land was concentrated in the hands of the Japanese and the landlords of Korea, while the absolute majority of the peasants were landless or land-poor. At present the feudal system of tenancy constitutes the economic basis of the reactionary forces. The landlords seek to preserve this system and are opposed to any type of democratic reform.

Unless an agrarian reform is carried out, it will be impossible to rehabilitate and develop agriculture and build an independent, sovereign and democratic state. The agrarian reform will bring the centuries-old dream of our peasantry into reality.

Third, the production enterprises should be rehabilitated and developed.

Only the rehabilitation and development of the production enterprises will enable us to eliminate unemployment; raise people's standard of living; and, at the same time, develop the national economy.

Fourth, railway and water transport should be restored.

Railway and water transport are the arteries of the country. Without them the normal development of the state's economy is inconceivable. The different provinces of north Korea are related economically to each other and we should further develop those relations. Besides the economic relations, the provinces need political and cultural relations as well among them. Yet, our work of transport is out of order at present. We must rehabilitate the dislocated transport at an early date. This will do much to further the reconstruction and development of our industry and trade.

Fifth, the financial-banking system and the goods distribution system should be readjusted.

The rehabilitation and development of the national economy are impossible without the organization of the financial-banking system, development of trade, and a smooth flow of goods between the towns and the countryside and among the different provinces.

We should tap all sources of income, spend funds properly, keep the right amount of currency in circulation and combat the speculators.

Sixth, freedom of activity should be granted to entrepreneurs and traders, and medium- and small-sized enterprises should be encouraged. Only by so doing can we solve the problem of providing consumer goods for the people's life.

Seventh, assistance should be given to the working-class movement, and factory committees should be organized widely in factories and enterprises.

Korea's development into an independent, sovereign, democratic state imperatively demands the active involvement of the broad masses of the people—and the workers first of all—in political life.

The trade unions and factory committees are mass organizations which represent the interests of the workers and, at the same time, draw them into public activities. We will consolidate the trade unions and organize factory committees widely in enterprises and in the field of transport, thus helping to greatly increase the workers' political enthusiasm and further accelerate our economic construction.

Eighth, the educational system should be revamped, in keeping with the democratic development of the country.

Owing to Japanese imperialism's educational system for colonial slavery, large numbers of Koreans have been left in ignorance and darkness, and our children and young people have been subjected to the pernicious influence of reactionary Japanese imperialist thoughts.

We must thoroughly revise the system of education and set up a new, popular democratic one to open up an opportunity of education for the children of the working people and root out the ideological vestiges of Japanese imperialism from the minds of our children and youth.

Ninth, the masses of the people should be educated in democratic ideologies, and the work for their cultural enlightenment should be undertaken on a wide scale. Only then can the people's political awakening and cultural standard be raised and our national culture developed.

What we have achieved in this field up till now is no more than a beginning, and a great deal of work lies ahead of us. This work is also an important one which the Provisional People's Committee of North Korea will have to carry out by all means.

Tenth, the true meaning of the decision of the Moscow Three Foreign Ministers Conference on Korea should be widely explained to the masses of the people.

The reactionary elements are trying to give a wrong interpretation to the decision of the Moscow tripartite ministerial conference, particularly so to the concept of trusteeship. They are endeavouring to block the building of Korea into a genuinely independent and democratic state by giving our people a wrong view of this decision, by ruining the unity of the people and disintegrating the democratic united front.

It is therefore an important task confronting the people's committees at every level to awaken the masses of the people keenly to the true meaning of the decision of the Moscow tripartite ministerial conference on Korea.

Such in general are the immediate tasks lying before the Provisional People's Committee of North Korea.

These huge and complex tasks can hardly be carried out without a central government body, that is, an organ which directs the work of our local people's committees and the different administrative bureaus. So, I believe that representatives of all the administrative bureaus, people's committees at every level, democratic political parties and social organizations present at this meeting will understand very clearly the need for establishing the Provisional People's Committee of North Korea.

I propose that this meeting take up the question of organizing the Provisional People's Committee of North Korea and adopt a relevant and concrete resolution.

TWENTY-POINT PLATFORM

Radio Address
March 23, 1946

Dear fellow countrymen, brothers and sisters,

Allow me to speak on behalf of the Provisional People's Committee of North Korea about the platform of the future provisional government that will be set up.

The U.S.S.R.-U.S. Joint Commission established in accordance with the decision of the Moscow Three Foreign Ministers Conference started its work in Seoul on the 20th of this month.

The U.S.S.R.-U.S. Joint Commission, whose meeting is being followed with expectations by all the people of Korea, must work in the interests of the Korean people and must find a solution to the problem of establishing a unified provisional government which is earnestly demanded by the Korean people.

The provisional government should be a genuine democratic government capable of fulfilling the desire of the entire Korean people.

We hold that the democratic government to be set up by us must without fail put into effect the following platform:

(1) To thoroughly liquidate all the remnants of Japanese imperialist rule from the political and economic life of Korea;

(2) To wage an implacable struggle against reactionary and anti-democratic elements at home and strictly ban the

activities of fascist, anti-democratic political parties, organizations and individuals;

(3) To grant the entire people freedom of speech, the press, assembly and religion. To provide conditions for free activities to democratic political parties, trade unions, peasants' associations and other democratic social organizations;

(4) To see to it that the entire Korean people have the right and duty to form people's committees—the administrative organs responsible for all local affairs—through universal, direct and equal suffrage by secret ballot;

(5) To grant equal rights to all citizens in political and economic life, irrespective of sex, religion or property status;

(6) To assert the inviolability of persons and their residence and protect by law the property of citizens and their private possessions;

(7) To abolish all laws and judicial organs which were in operation during the rule of Japanese imperialism and still retain its aftereffects, elect the people's judicial organs on democratic principles and grant the citizens at large equal legal rights;

(8) To develop industry, agriculture, transport and trade for the enhancement of the people's welfare;

(9) To nationalize big enterprises, transport services, banks, mines and forests;

(10) To allow and encourage free activity in private handicrafts and trade;

(11) To confiscate the land belonging to Japanese, the Japanese state, the traitors, and landlords who continue to rent out their land; abolish the tenant system and distribute among the peasants, free of charge, all the confiscated land, making it their property. To confiscate without compensation all irrigation facilities and place them under state control;

(12) To fix market prices for living necessaries to combat speculators and usurers;

(13) To institute a system of uniform, equitable taxation and introduce a progressive income-tax system;

(14) To introduce an eight-hour working day for factory

and office workers and fix minimum wages for them. To prohibit employment of children under 13 years of age and institute a six-hour working day for children of 13 to 16;

(15) To institute life insurance for factory and office workers and set up an insurance system for workers and enterprises;

(16) To introduce a system of universal compulsory education and widely increase primary, secondary and specialized schools and colleges to be run by the state. To reform the system of public education in line with the democratic state system;

(17) To actively develop national culture, science and the arts, and increase the number of theatres, libraries, radio broadcasting stations and cinema houses;

(18) To set up special schools on a wide scale for training the personnel required in state organs and in all fields of the national economy;

(19) To encourage scientists and artists in their work and give them assistance; and

(20) To increase the number of state-run hospitals, stamp out epidemics and provide free medical care to the poor.

Only when the above-mentioned fundamental requirements are fulfilled, will the Korean people come to enjoy genuine freedom and political rights, will their welfare be promoted and will our country achieve complete independence.

Only a government capable of meeting the aforementioned requirements will become a genuinely democratic government and will enjoy the support of the entire people.

The U.S.S.R.-U.S. Joint Commission should contribute to the founding of a Korean democratic provisional government capable of meeting these demands of the Korean people.

I call upon the entire Korean people and the champions of the freedom and independence of our country to devote all their energies to the building of an independent, sovereign and democratic state.

Long live democratic independence and sovereignty!

Long live the liberated people of Korea!

THE RESULTS OF THE AGRARIAN REFORM AND FUTURE TASKS

Report to the Sixth Enlarged Executive Committee Meeting of the Central Organizing Committee of the Communist Party of North Korea

April 10, 1946

Comrades,

In view of the urgent demands of our social development and the internal and external situation, the Party decided to introduce an agrarian reform in north Korea and directed all its forces to this work.

All Party organizations and members have waged an active struggle to put into effect the Party's decision. As a result, we have carried out the agrarian reform, a great democratic reform, smoothly and victoriously within the appointed time.

Through the agrarian reform, the Party tested the correctness of its policy and made the masses of the people clearly understand that only our Party is the genuine representative of the interests of the people. The entire people, calling for the independence and democratic development of the country, warmly supported our Party's policy.

Relying on the support of the broad masses of the people, the Party carried out this democratic task with daring, overcoming all the desperate manoeuvres and obstructions of the traitors to the people and reactionary elements.

1. HISTORIC SIGNIFICANCE OF THE AGRARIAN REFORM

First, the agrarian reform is the initial step in the implementation of the task of democratization of Korea.

It was the feudal relations that held back the social development in Korea for a long time. Japanese imperialism maintained and strengthened the feudal relations of landownership in the countryside in order to prevent the democratic development of Korea. Owing to harsh feudalistic exploitation and oppression by the landlords, the masses of the peasantry groaned in hunger and poverty.

As a result of the agrarian reform, the feudal system of landownership, the socio-economic basis of the anti-democratic reactionary forces, has been abolished in our countryside once and for all. Before the peasants in north Korea who have been freed from the shackles of feudalism, broad vistas have been opened up for the rapid development of agriculture and the improvement of their life.

Second, the agrarian reform has turned the north Korean countryside from a base of reaction into a base of democracy.

The peasants, who were formerly kept in bondage to the landlords, have become masters of the land and free peasants and, along with the working class, the progressive class in our country, they have become a main force in establishing an independent state, wealthy and strong, unified and democratic.

With the agrarian reform, our Party has embarked upon the great historic undertaking of converting north Korea into a firm democratic base for the reunification of the country. For the building of a unified democratic Korea it is imperative to turn north Korea into a mighty democratic base politically, economically and culturally. This task cannot be accomplished unless the peasants, who comprise the absolute majority of our country's population, are emancipated from the yoke of the landlords and our backward agriculture is rapidly developed.

Our recent agrarian reform will greatly increase the political enthusiasm of the peasants in the struggle to build an independent democratic state that is wealthy and strong, and will accelerate the democratization of north Korea. It will also advance the productive forces of agriculture, improve the livelihood of the peasants and facilitate the rehabilitation of industry. This will prove a tremendous encouragement to the people in south Korea in their struggle for building a unified democratic Korea and further strengthen the democratic forces in south Korea.

The entire Korean people demand a provisional government **of the type of the Provisional People's Committee of North Korea, capable of carrying out such democratic** reforms as the agrarian reform. They consider that the Provisional People's Committee of North Korea, which implemented this reform with determination, should be the nucleus of a unified provisional government of Korea and serve as the model for it.

Third, the agrarian reform has a tremendous international significance.

Since the end of World War II, the liberation struggle of the Asian peoples has been surging forward with tremendous force. The Korean people have carried out a thoroughgoing agrarian reform, the first of its kind in Asia.

Our agrarian reform is therefore not only a great landmark in Korean history but also an event of great significance in the liberation struggle of the peoples of the East. It will greatly inspire the oppressed peoples of the East in their liberation struggle against imperialism and the domestic feudal forces.

2. PROGRESS AND SUCCESS OF THE AGRARIAN REFORM

Following the announcement of the Agrarian Reform Law by the Provisional People's Committee of North Korea, our Party concentrated all its efforts on the successful carrying out of this work. The entire Party, from the centre down to the organs at the lowest level, came to the assistance of the people's committees, and our Party members played the nucleating role among the masses.

The Party strengthened the united front with the democratic political parties and social organizations and roused them to take an active part in this work, while enabling the poor peasants and farm hands to organize the rural committees so that they could play the leading role in carrying out the agrarian reform and become its executors. This policy of our Party proved correct.

In South Pyongan Province, 2,255 rural committees were formed with a membership of 15,785, and nearly 800,000 peasants gave assistance to the rural committees. The number of the rural committees in the six provinces totalled over 11,500 with a combined membership of 90,697.

Thus, the broad masses of the peasants were mobilized and the peasants themselves were made the executors of the agrarian reform, with the result that their political zeal and class awakening increased to a great extent in the course of their actual struggle against the landlords. The formation of the rural committees made up of poor peasants and farm hands was the basic factor in the thorough implementation of the agrarian reform. The broad peasant masses actively participated in the carrying out of the agrarian reform, displaying a high degree of enthusiasm. In the course of the agrarian reform, many activists emerged from among the peasants.

The functionaries and propagandists of all political parties and social organizations explained and publicized the Agrarian Reform Law to the peasant masses, and the entire peasantry were mobilized to investigate the landlords, their lands and other means of production. After the investigation, the distribution of land started, which on the whole was also conducted smoothly.

The peasants know the rural conditions better than those who study the rural affairs at their desks and, therefore, they could correctly survey and distribute the land without their help.

Our Party scrupulously followed its mass line in carrying out the agrarian reform, with the result that it was able to win over vast masses of the people and rally them closely around itself. Through this undertaking, the masses of the people came to regard our Party as the genuine defender of their interests and place boundless trust in it. This is fully proved by the tens of thousands of letters, some written in blood, addressed by peasants to the Party's Central Organizing Committee and the Provisional People's Committee of North Korea, describing how greatly they were moved, and how happy they were, to receive land. Since the agrarian reform, the peasantry have rallied more firmly around our Party and have given warm support to the Party's policies.

In the course of the agrarian reform, our Party recruited the best elements from among the poor peasants and farm hands and thus firmly built up its position in the countryside, improved its composition and further expanded and strengthened its ranks.

Party organizations in North Pyongan Province absorbed 3,272 new recruits into membership and those in North and South Hamgyong Provinces, South Pyongan, Hwanghae and Kangwon Provinces admitted a total of 9,058 new members (one-third of whom are poor peasants) during the recent agrarian reform. All this shows that, through the agrarian reform, the prestige of our Party rose in the eyes of the broad masses of the peasants and it established a firm footing in the rural areas.

Since the agrarian reform, the appearance of our countryside has changed radically. The toiling peasants are masters there now. In every *ri* and *myon* the landlords and rich farmers have been expelled from the organs of the people's power and the toiling peasants, with the poor peasants and farm hands as the core, have taken power firmly into their own hands.

Thus, the agrarian reform has been completed victoriously because our Party members and the broad masses of the peasants, particularly poor peasants and farm hands, have taken an active part in it under the leadership of our Party.

As a result of the agrarian reform, 1,000,325 *chongbo* of land owned by the Japanese imperialists, pro-Japanese elements, traitors to the nation and landlords were confiscated, and 981,390 *chongbo* of it distributed to 724,522 landless and land-poor peasant households.

How was it possible to achieve such a victorious enforcement of the agrarian reform?

First, this reform was an urgent task for meeting the vital demands and centuries-old desire of the peasantry. For a long period, the Korean peasants had suffered from feudal exploitation and were subjected to double or treble exploitation and oppression under Japanese imperialist rule, and they had led a life as miserable as that of serfs, eking out a bare subsistence in the grip of poverty and hunger.

The most cherished desire of the peasantry was to own land and farm it for themselves. But this long-cherished desire of the peasants could not be realized during the rule of the Japanese imperialists, when power was in the hands of those foreign aggressors.

After liberation, the Party, with a view to meeting the long-cherished desire of the peasants for land, inspired them first to the struggle for a three-to-seven system of tenancy, thereby preparing them ideologically for the carrying out of the agrarian reform in the future. The political awareness and enthusiasm of the peasants were enhanced in the course of the struggle for the three-to-seven system. The peasants realized that they had acquired the right to speak up and fight for their own interests, and that they must free themselves from the landlords' exploitation.

Gradually, the demand of the peasantry for land began to rise. Immediately before the agrarian reform, the Party centre alone received more than 30,000 letters from the peasants demanding land. Similar letters are now piled up mountain-high at the Provisional People's Committee of North Korea. Towards the end of February this year, over 300 representatives of the peasants from all parts of north Korea came to the Provisional People's Committee of North Korea to convey the demand of all the peasants for land. On the occasion of the anniversary of the March First Movement this year, over 2 million peasants, carrying sickles and hoes, held demonstrations in various parts of north Korea, demanding land. The Party considered it a fully urgent task to satisfy this vital demand of the peasants for land.

The Party knew that the historic task of the agrarian reform could be carried out successfully only with the active support and participation of the peasants. The Party, therefore, saw to it that the Agrarian Reform Law was discussed at the peasants' meetings. The peasants welcomed the law warmly and fought actively for its enforcement because they fully realized that this law was a precise reflection of their long-cherished desire.

Second, our peasants were politically awakened and prepared to carry out the agrarian reform. After liberation, the peasantry participated in the people's power as genuine master of the state and actively joined in the work of liquidating the pro-Japanese elements and traitors to the nation who stood in the way of the democratic development of Korea. They also safeguarded their class interests by organizing peasants' associations and, through these organizations, grew into a powerful force fully capable of fighting the landlord class. The activities of the social organizations such as the trade unions, the Democratic Youth League and the Women's Union, also played a great part in enhancing the political awakening of the peasantry.

Third, the agrarian reform was carried out on the basis of the formation of a solid democratic united front. Political parties and social organizations in north Korea are not disunited with each other as they are in south Korea but maintain a firm unity of action. All the parties and social organizations in north Korea took part in the agrarian reform as a united, organized force.

In carrying out the agrarian reform, our Party endeavoured to cement the united front with all parties and groupings and all sections and classes and to mobilize their forces to the full. Thus, mobilized to give assistance to the rural committees were not only our Party members, but also the organized masses of more than 3 million people in all—the North Korean Federation of the Peasants' Associations with a membership of over 700,000, the trade unions with over 350,000 members, the Korean Democratic Party, the Korean New Democratic Party, the Women's Union with a membership of over 300,000, the Democratic Youth League with over 500,000 members as well as the Pyongyang Institute, cultural organizations, the Arts Federation, the Teachers' Union, the People's Theatrical Company, etc. This represents a victory for the united front policy which our Party has consistently pursued.

Fourth, the victory of the agrarian reform was assured by a solid alliance between the workers and the peasants. As they were supported by the working class in their battle against the landlords, the peasants grew more confident and showed greater activity.

The North Korean General Federation of Trade Unions selected 1,150 of the finest workers from such trade unions as the miners' union, railway workers' union, metal workers' union and chemical workers' union in Pyongyang and sent them out to all counties in South Pyongan Province to help the peasants. In all the other places, too, the workers actively helped the peasants in the struggle to carry out the agrarian reform. The worker-peasant alliance was thus further strengthened through the enforcement of the agrarian reform. This alliance will prove to be a decisive guarantee of victory in the struggle to build an independent democratic state in the future.

Fifth, the victory of the agrarian reform is a consequence of the positive activities of the rural committees. The rural committees, being the basis of power organization in the rural areas, bore the brunt of the struggle against the landlords, pro-Japanese elements and traitors to the nation.

All this enabled us to achieve a great victory in the historic agrarian reform.

3. DEFECTS REVEALED IN THE COURSE OF THE AGRARIAN REFORM AND THE EXPERIENCE WE HAVE GAINED

Our Party played its leading role creditably in the struggle for carrying out the agrarian reform. The Party crushed the resistance of the reactionary forces and achieved a great victory by enlisting the revolutionary zeal and activity of the peasant masses to the fullest extent on the basis of the mass line and by successfully ensuring the alliance between the working class and the peasantry.

Through the agrarian reform, the strength of the Party increased and its influence and prestige rose greatly among the broad masses.

However, we cannot but admit that some defects were revealed and some errors were committed in the course of the work. We must draw lessons from them.

First, certain organs and Party organizations committed Right and "Left" errors in the course of the agrarian reform.

There were cases in some places in which those with less than five *chongbo* of land were classified as landlords, which led to making more enemies without justification; there were also quite a few instances where people were wantonly listed as pro-Japanese without any principle, thereby causing unwelcome confusion, or regulations were violated out of personal feelings of revenge. Of course, these errors were corrected in good time.

Certain Party organizations committed such errors because their members failed to grasp the essence of the political line and policies of the Party and lacked experience and training in executing the line.

Our Party must, therefore, continue to improve its composition, intensify the inner-Party struggle against petty-bourgeois ideas and strengthen the education of its members in the Party's policies and in Marxism-Leninism.

There were also cases in which some backward peasants sympathized with the landlords and even shielded them by falsely declaring that they were the owners of the land which, in fact, belonged to the landlords. All of this took place because class education in the Party had been insufficient and because propaganda work to inspire the masses with hatred for the landlords had been inadequate.

Hence, the Party should always oppose "Left" as well as Right deviations and educate its members consistently in the ideology of the working class.

Second, the growth of Party ranks was not satisfactory. The South Pyongan and South Hamgyong Provincial Party Committees failed to take measures to get the finest and most progressive elements of the toiling masses into the Party in the course of the agrarian reform.

Party organizations should necessarily draw in finest elements amidst such an acute class struggle and thus organize rural Party cells. But some Party organizations failed to do this properly. We must correct this error, expand the ranks of the Party and strengthen its organizations both organizationally and ideologically to reinforce its positions in the countryside.

One of the main tasks confronting our Party is to unite the masses of the peasants, who have been liberated from the exploitation of the landlords, under the influence of the Party and admit to its membership those poor peasants and farm hands who were active in the struggle for the agrarian reform.

Third, the Party's propaganda work was weak. In particular, propaganda work by the provincial Party committees was unsatisfactory and the organization and role of propaganda squads were below the mark in general. This defect found its most glaring expression in South Pyongan Province. Neither slogans nor posters were put up in some areas of the province. I went to Taedong County a week after the promulgation of the Law, but there was not a poster nor a slogan put up.

The situation is the same in Hwanghae Province. Newspapers carrying the text of the Agrarian Reform Law were not distributed to the peasants, and they did not even know the name of the Party paper. The newspapers lay in piles in the provincial and county Party headquarters. This is indeed a serious matter. It made it impossible for the peasant masses to have a thorough knowledge of the agrarian reform.

Owing to lack of understanding of the Agrarian Reform Law, cadres of North Pyongan Province themselves interpreted it arbitrarily and implemented it in a distorted manner. The Party Committee of Uiju County in North Pyongan Province failed not only to make a profound study of the Agrarian Reform Law but also to study the instructions from the Party centre on its implementation. As a result, it gave no guidance to the people's committees or the rural committees but, instead, formed an absurd "Commission for the Enforcement of Agrarian Reform" within the county Party committee itself and even hung up a door plate bearing this name. This is a concrete expression of improper organizational leadership and propaganda work by the Party.

Owing to such inadequate propaganda work by the Party, the peasants failed to have a full understanding of the political significance of the agrarian reform and engrossed themselves exclusively in the distribution of land. Hence, although land had been distributed to the peasants, some of them did not even know where the land had come from.

This was because the work of preparing and mobilizing the

Party members ideologically was unsatisfactory and the Party functionaries themselves lacked a correct understanding of the Party's policy for the agrarian reform. Party organs and Party organizations at all levels should promptly correct the serious defects in their propaganda activities and intensify their political and propaganda work among the vast masses of the people.

Fourth, we still lack vigilance. Since the agrarian reform the class struggle has become more acute. The landlords are frantically engaged in last-minute manoeuvres and the reactionaries keep up their terrorist activities.

Various plots by the reactionaries and pro-Japanese elements were exposed during the agrarian reform. A landlord held the post of chairman of the Peasants' Union branch in Chasong County, North Pyongan Province and attempted to frustrate the enforcement of the Agrarian Reform Law, and landlords and pro-Japanese elements in Anak County, Hwanghae Province, hid rifles and machine guns underground. Six terrorists were arrested in Pyonggang, Kangwon Province; a Japanese and two Korean traitors to the nation were caught sneaking into Yongpyong with poison.

A counter-revolutionary demonstration against the agrarian reform was held by specialized- and middle-school boys in Hamhung, at the instigation of pro-Japanese elements and landlords. This shows that the South Hamgyong Provincial Party Committee and the Party organizations in Hamhung lacked vigilance.

We must be aware that the plots and sinister machinations of the enemy to wreck our Party and people's power and to weaken the democratic forces of the people are still going on. Our Party organizations, however, are not yet vigilant enough against it. We must rectify this defect without delay.

Fifth, the work of uniting the broad masses in the social organizations was not done well. In the course of the agrarian reform, the prestige of our Party rose greatly among the masses of the people and, accordingly, the social organizations such as the peasants' associations, the Women's Union and the Democratic Youth League which worked in the rural areas under the leadership of the Party, gained the deep confidence of the masses. Nevertheless, these organizations failed to enlarge their ranks in full measure.

Numerous peasant activists who had displayed enthusiasm and activity in the actual struggle for the agrarian reform were not recruited into the social organizations. The peasants' associations put off the expansion of their organizations until after the agrarian reform and the Democratic Youth League, in many cases, merely tailed behind the peasants' associations and did not actively strive to draw the rural youth into its ranks. In future, therefore, Party organizations at all levels should direct deep attention to fortifying the social organizations in the rural districts.

4. OUR TASKS

Comrades, now that the agrarian reform has been completed victoriously, our Party is confronted with the important task of consolidating and following up this victory. The victory of the agrarian reform can only be consolidated and followed up by strengthening the forces of the Party and correctly implementing its policy in the countryside.

What, then, are the immediate tasks of our Party?

First, we should see to it that the peasants, who have become masters of the land, devote themselves to increasing production for their own well-being and for the benefit of the country. If the land is left to lie idle or the harvest falls down after the agrarian reform, it will create conditions favourable to the reactionaries to conduct their pernicious propaganda.

Therefore, our slogan is: "Greet the first spring of liberated Korea with increased production, don't let even an inch of land lie idle!" The Party should make sure that this slogan is thoroughly carried out. It should lead the peasants to do the spring ploughing well and see to it that they are supplied with seeds, farm implements, fertilizers, etc., which are sorely needed. In order to ensure success in the spring ploughing, we should rouse to action the peasants' associations and other social organizations and give full play to the spirit of mutual aid of the peasants.

Party organs and Party organizations at all levels must remember that only by successfully carrying out the first sowing following the agrarian reform, will it be possible to consolidate the victory of the agrarian reform and triumphantly solve all the difficult political and economic problems that lie ahead. Our Party organizations and all the members in the countryside, therefore, should wage a devoted struggle in the forefront of the spring ploughing and sowing campaign under the slogans: "Increase production with might and main!" and "Don't leave your land lying idle!"

Second, the recent agrarian reform has been carried out in a democratic, revolutionary way by means of the rural committees formed with the poor peasants and farm hands in the countryside as their core. The Party has already sown the seeds of revolution in the countryside. We should preserve and nurture these seeds of revolution.

To this end, the Party should amalgamate the rural committees with the peasants' associations and thus reinforce the latter and further elevate their role. In some areas, there once were cases in which landlords and rich farmers wormed their way into the peasants' associations and grabbed the leadership, weakening their role. We should, from now on, select tested activists from among those poor peasants and farm hands who have been on the rural committees, place them in leading positions in the peasants' associations and expel all the reactionaries and thus strengthen the associations organizationally.

In this way, the foothold of our Party in the countryside should be consolidated, the composition of the rural Party organizations be improved and the forces of the Party be enlarged and fortified with the poor peasants and farm hands as their base.

Third, we should intensify the political education of Party members. The recent agrarian reform revealed the very low political level of Party functionaries, not to speak of the rank-and-file members. Some Party workers do not have a good knowledge of the tasks of the Korean revolution at the present stage; many Party members did their work in a bureaucratic manner, instead of thoroughly explaining and bringing home to the masses the policies and line of the Party. In particular, they did not carry on the agrarian reform in close combination with the immediate political tasks—the establishment of a provisional government, the liquidation of the traitors to the nation and reactionaries and other political work—but busied themselves only with the practical work of land distribution.

It is true that the political level of Party members rose markedly during the recent agrarian reform. But, considering the revolutionary tasks confronting us and the increasing political awakening of the masses, the ideological and political level of our Party members is still very low. The Party, therefore, should do all it can to intensify the political education of its cadres and of its entire membership.

In particular, we should fight against Right and "Left" deviations in a proper manner among the cadres and Party members. Our Party members are not yet firmly armed with Marxist-Leninist ideology. We should, therefore, adopt a careful attitude towards those Party members who have committed errors and educate them in all sincerity. We should not lash at them, branding them at random as "Leftists," "Rightists" or "factionalists." Of course, we cannot overlook Right or "Left" deviations. At present, the Right deviations are particularly dangerous for us because not a few people who were under the influence of the landlords and rich farmers have joined the ranks of our Party.

We should always maintain a resolute attitude in waging a principled struggle against all types of deviations from the Party's line and thus thoroughly nip them in the bud. It is not a correct method of work to leave a Party member to himself, without helping him to rectify his defects in good time, and then to drive him out at one blow after his defects have become irreparable. People should be educated with all sincerity to prevent them from committing errors and to make them commit few errors. And those who have committed errors should clearly realize their faults and correct them.

Fourth, we have to strengthen the work of the organs of people's power.

The Party still fails to give satisfactory leadership to the organs of power. In local areas, the Party does not lead and assist the people's committees in their work, but ignores them and does the work in their stead, thereby rendering the people's committees ineffectual. In South Hamgyong and South Pyongan Provinces, the Party organs pushed aside the people's committees and went ahead to do everything themselves, reducing the committees to a secondary role.

This method of work by Party organizations has resulted in paralyzing the creative initiative of the people's power, weakening at the same time the leading role of the Party.

Since our organs of power are set up on the basis of the united front of democratic political parties and social organizations, our Party should collaborate well with friendly parties in the power organs, while playing the central and leading role, and should always carry out all its policies through the people's committees.

In order to strengthen the Party's leadership of the people's power organs, the Party groups within the people's committees should be reinforced and the political education of the Party's membership intensified so that they may have a correct understanding of its leading role in the power organs.

At the same time, we should reinforce the apparatus of the people's committees and assign best workers to them.

In quite a number of local districts the people's committees are still very weak and reactionary elements are entrenched in them. In Kapsan County, South Hamgyong Province, the chairman of the people's committee proposed distributing the land by lottery in an attempt to frustrate the enforcement of the Agrarian Reform Law. The chairman of the Huchang County People's Committee, North Pyongan Province, had been an officially appointed member of the North Pyongan Provincial Council under Japanese imperialist rule and its vice-chairman had been the notorious head of a *myon*. In the early days of liberation, both these men came out against the three-to-seven system of tenancy and the voluntary delivery of farm products. It hardly needs saying that they obstructed the agrarian reform. In no small number of places landlords and corrupt officials are still to be found entrenched in the people's committees.

However, the power organs are not meant to protect the interests of the landlords or reactionaries. The power organs themselves belong to our people. The thing to do is to drive the reactionaries out of them.

We should rid the people's committees of alien elements and complete their staffs with best members of the rural committees. Party organs and Party organizations at all levels should immediately take up the work of reshuffling the people's committees.

Fifth, the activities of the mass organizations should be intensified. During the recent agrarian reform campaign the activities and role of the mass organizations were very great, but these organizations were not sufficiently strengthened and developed organizationally. Particularly unsatisfactory was the work of developing such mass organizations as the Democratic Youth League and the Women's Union. There are not a few counties where Women's Union organizations have not yet been formed. We can no longer tolerate such a state of affairs.

Party organs at all levels and their responsible functionaries should work actively to enrol the masses of rural women and youth in the mass organizations and to rally them around the Party and the people's power in order to mobilize them as soon as possible for the construction of the country.

In connection with the work of social organizations, it should be emphasized that it is important to strengthen the work of the Democratic Youth League in the schools and to work well among the student youths.

Everywhere the reactionaries use the students for their sinister aims. But we would be gravely mistaken if we were to regard all students as reactionary elements. Not all students are scions of the landlords or are reactionaries.

We should not forget that students can play a progressive role in colonial and semi-colonial countries. Our Party organs and Party organizations did not realize this and paid no attention to education and to work among student youths, with the result that not a few students were used by the reactionaries.

We should, therefore, begin by examining and re-educating the teachers in order to improve the educational work radically. Best Democratic Youth League workers should be assigned to all schools as instructors in charge of discipline to get rid of reactionary students and, at the same time, strengthen the work of the Democratic Youth League in the schools. To aid students from poor families, a state stipend system should be introduced in colleges and specialized schools, and the composition of the student body should be improved.

Sixth, our Party should further fortify its footholds in the countryside, consolidating and developing the successes in the agrarian reform. The Party should not only organize its cells in factories and enterprises, but also go deep into the midst of the poor peasants and farm hands in the rural areas and extensively conduct the work of organizing Party cells there. The most important duty facing our Party is to expand and reinforce its positions in order to prepare for the forthcoming battle.

Our Party has not yet taken deep roots among the workers and peasants, the main masses. The rural positions of the Party were widened and fortified considerably in the course of the recent agrarian reform, but that was only the first step.

Therefore, Party organizations and functionaries at all levels should devote all their efforts to the work of strengthening the Party organizationally and expanding its ranks.

Party organizations should thoroughly eradicate such tendencies as keeping the door of the Party wide open in an unprincipled way pretexting to expand the Party ranks, and leaving new members without education and training. They should prevent alien elements such as pro-Japanese elements and landlords from worming their way into the Party and, at the same time, continue to wage an energetic struggle for purging away the factionalists and alien elements in order to assure ideological unanimity and unity of will in the Party.

Last, the wicked propaganda of the landlords and the subversive manoeuvres of the south Korean reactionaries should be completely smashed.

The vile propaganda of the landlords can be generally classified into two categories. One is the falsehood circulated by them concerning a political question, i.e., the question of the establishment of a provisional government. The reactionary landlords are threatening the peasants by saying that Syngman Rhee will come to power and that the peasants will then be deprived of the land again. The other is related to the question of the voluntary deliveries of farm produce. The landlords say that the peasants have received land but their burden will grow heavier than before.

What should be our attitude to such slanders?

We have to carry on vigorous propaganda work to shatter the calumnies of the landlords in the countryside by mobilizing best propaganda forces of all the social organizations. We have to publicize in the most convincing way the fact that Syngman Rhee cannot enjoy the support of the people because he is opposed to democracy, which the entire Korean people unanimously demand, the fact that the peasants from this year on need not pay any farm rent nor the miscellaneous levies exacted from them in the past by the Japanese imperialists and the landlords, but will pay a very reasonable progressive tax according to the crop harvests, and the fact that the organs of people's power will endeavour in every way to improve the livelihood of the peasants.

Not only should we conduct our propaganda work in an

effective way, but we should help the peasants to do the spring ploughing well and should unfold among the broad masses a campaign of volunteer labour service for the building of the country.

At the same time, a resolute struggle has to be waged against the calumnies and the subversive manoeuvres of the south Korean reactionaries.

At present the rural situation in the area north of the 38th parallel presents a striking contrast with that in the area to the south of it. The land problem has already been completely solved in the area above the 38th parallel. But in the area below the 38th parallel the three-to-seven system of tenancy has not even been introduced, let alone the agrarian reform, nor have any ways ever been proposed for the solution of the land problem. The reactionaries south of the 38th parallel are madly slandering the agrarian reform in north Korea, raving, "Just wait and see. You cannot farm without landlords." We should smash up their reactionary propaganda by doing the spring ploughing and sowing properly, raising agricultural production and improving the livelihood of the peasants.

The south Korean reactionaries once clamoured for the abolition of the 38th parallel, shifting the responsibility for its existence onto the Communist Party, but now they dare not utter a single word about its abolition. It seems that they are now very much afraid of the north wind, far from sending the south wind towards us, and are terrified at the democratic reform we have carried out in north Korea and the 20-Point Platform we have announced.

Following the agrarian reform, we announced and are already carrying out in north Korea the 20-Point Platform which will be the foundation of the future political programme of a unified Korean government. Consequently, in north Korea the democratic forces are developing rapidly and the living standard of the people is gradually rising. Scared at this, the south Korean reactionaries engage in all sorts of machinations and send terrorists into north Korea in an attempt to wreck what we have achieved.

Hence, we should not even for a moment slacken vigilance against reaction. The Party's political and organizational work should be strengthened in the countryside, particularly in Hwanghae and Kangwon Provinces, so that the broad masses of the people may sharpen their hatred and their vigilance against the enemy and detect and wipe out spies, wreckers and saboteurs.

Comrades, our Party has victoriously accomplished the agrarian reform, the centuries-old hope of the Korean peasantry, and thereby laid a solid foundation for the democratic development of the country. This great socio-economic reform will be a tremendous force in accelerating the building of an independent and democratic state.

Party organizations at all levels and the entire membership of the Party must devote all their energies to the struggle to consolidate the achievements of the agrarian reform and to successfully accomplish the immediate democratic tasks.

ON THE DRAFT OF THE LABOUR LAW

Speech Delivered at the Eighth Session of the Provisional People's Committee of North Korea

June 20, 1946

Comrades,

The Provisional People's Committee of North Korea has done a great deal of work for the democratization of Korea and has already achieved considerable successes in all spheres of politics, economy and culture under the favourable conditions created by the stationing of the Soviet army. We have triumphantly completed the agrarian reform, which is a great revolutionary event in the history of our country and provides a model for democratic social reform in the East.

The Provisional People's Committee of North Korea makes public now the draft of a democratic labour law which, like the agrarian reform, is of great significance to the life of the Korean people and will greatly inspire the oppressed peoples of the East.

This is a genuinely democratic law aimed at emancipating the factory and office workers of our country from the crushing colonial labour forced upon them in the past, at ensuring the improvement of their working conditions and material life and at opening up an avenue before them to freely build a new happy life. It is an important law which expresses the vital interests of the working class, the main force in founding a new democratic state in our country. Its enforcement is an essential condition for the democratic development of Korea.

As an exclusive colony of the Japanese imperialists, Korea was denied all political rights and suffered from extreme economic disruption and cultural blindness owing to brutal tyranny and plunder such as could scarcely be found elsewhere in the world.

The Korean workers in particular who suffered the most distressing plight, were long forced to do indescribable inhuman toil and to live on the verge of starvation as a result of the Japanese imperialists' rapacious policy of securing high colonial profits. The Japanese imperialists gained fabulous profits by bleeding the Korean workers white; they sought prosperity for capitalist Japan by working the toiling people of Korea like slaves.

Every day Korean workers were forced to toil without respite for many hours and mercilessly exploited. According to watered-down data published by the research bureau of Japan's South Manchuria Railway Company, for instance, in 1937 factories with a nine-hour working day accounted for only 6 per cent of the total while those with a working day of over 12 hours made up 41 per cent of the total. The working day was longer and working conditions were worse for the workers in household industries which accounted for 20 per cent of the industrial output value. In the munitions factories particularly, which grew rapidly in the course of the war of aggression against China and during the Pacific War, the working day usually ranged from 14 to 16 hours. This unrestrained extension of working time brought much higher profits to the Japanese imperialists, but more diseases, hunger and poverty to the Korean workers.

The Japanese imperialists perpetrated double exploitation of the Korean workers by enforcing extreme national discrimination. The Korean workers were insulted and humiliated as an "inferior nation" and were paid far less than the Japanese workers, doing the same work.

The working day of the Korean workers was from one to more than two hours longer than the Japanese workers' as a rule. According to statistics for 1937, the average working day for Korean workers was 13 per cent longer than that for Japanese workers. As for the workers over 16 years of age, the working day for the Koreans was 16 per cent longer than that for the Japanese, and as for juvenile labour applicable to those below 16 years of age, the working day for the Korean children was 25 per cent longer than that for the Japanese.

As for the wage level, while the Japanese male worker averaged 2.03 *won* a day in 1937, the Korean worker was paid 1.03 *won*, namely, only half the pay of the Japanese worker. At the Pusan Rubber Factory, for instance, the Korean workers, men and women, were paid starvation wages—an average of 46 *chon* a day, the minimum being 10 *chon*. There were cases where women workers, in particular, received a daily pay as little as 6 *chon* at the lowest.

At the government-run railway works where treatment was said to be somewhat better by comparison, the maximum monthly wage for the Koreans was 78.30 *won* and the minimum was 15 *won*, the average being 48.28 *won*, as against a maximum of 111 *won*, a minimum of 17.70 *won*, and an average of 72.57 *won* for the Japanese. On an average the Koreans received only a little more than half the wages of the Japanese. This big gap in the average wages indicates that the majority of Koreans received only low wages.

In the schools, too, a Korean teacher with the same qualifications was paid as little as half the salary of his Japanese counterpart and, besides, the Japanese enjoyed a variety of privileges and preferential material treatment.

As these facts show, Korean factory and office workers and people in the field of culture, under colonial discrimination of Japanese imperialism, were forced to do slave labour for the huge profits of the Japanese monopoly capitalists, and they suffered from an unusually long working day, murderous intensification of labour and appalling starvation wages. This was a phenomenon common to all the factories, mines and enterprises governed by the Japanese imperialists' "Factory Law" in Korea, and it explains the wretched conditions of life of the working class in colonial Korea.

All factories, without exception, lacked any labour protection arrangement. The Tongyang Silk Mill in Pyongyang, for instance, sacked a worker without even paying a dismissal allowance immediately after he was caught by a machine and lost his arm. Only after the mill came under the people's ownership following liberation, were measures taken to assure his livelihood. In the railways and certain government-owned plants, such as tobacco factories, there were mutual-aid associations and medical facilities, but they all served as instruments for double or triple exploitation of the workers.

In our country, which was a labour market for Japanese imperialism, the workers suffered all manner of discriminative oppression and barbaric exploitation, and, not only that, countless workers were taken to Japan under various names such as so-called **"voluntary enlistment," "recommendation for jobs"** and **"labour drafting," their number coming to** more than 1,500,000. The Japanese imperialists, far from taking any measure for the protection of the young and middle-aged Koreans whom they dragged off to their country, manhandled them with the lash and exploited them without limit.

In this way, Japanese imperialists bled the Korean workers white, crippling and causing many of them to suffer from diseases. **The so-called "Factory Law"** of Japanese imperialism had no aim other than to shackle the Korean workers to the fetters of colonial slavery and impose poverty and hunger on them.

In such conditions, the Korean workers persistently waged a resolute struggle to defend their class interests and to smash the basis of Japanese imperialism's cruel colonial exploitation in Korea. For instance, only in the period from January to August of 1940, a year of intensified suppression by Japanese imperialism, there were 623 labour disputes, involving 49,000 workers. But owing to repression by Japanese imperialism, the workers' struggle was extremely difficult, and it finally developed into a clandestine movement. The working conditions of our workers became worse and their material conditions more wretched in the closing years of Japanese imperialist rule.

With Japanese imperialism's defeat and our country's liberation the road to a new life was opened up before the Korean people and the Korean working class.

In north Korea today, complete political freedom is assured for the people and democratic tasks are being carried out, one after another.

The Provisional People's Committee of North Korea carried out, first of all, the historic agrarian reform, uprooting the remnants of feudalism which had for centuries checked the socio-economic progress of our country, liquidating the landlord class in the countryside and enabling the peasants to become masters of land and builders of democracy.

With the carrying out of the agrarian reform, the foundations were laid for the speedy rehabilitation and development of the productive forces in our country's agriculture and the first step was taken towards an organic relationship between industry and agriculture and towards their proportionate development. The enforcement of this great and historic reform contributed to the strengthening of the worker-peasant alliance and to the further consolidation of the basis of the democratic united front.

The Provisional People's Committee of North Korea is making tremendous efforts for the speedy reconstruction of industry, the leading branch of the economy in our country. We are carrying on the work of reorganizing Korea's industry, once a tool of the Japanese imperialists in their colonial pillage and policy of aggression, into an independent and peaceful industry to serve the development of our national economy and the improvement of the people's livelihood, and of rehabilitating and readjusting the factories and enterprises left demolished by the Japanese imperialists.

In this connection, it is an important task confronting our organs of people's power to emancipate the workers from the extremely cruel oppression and exploitation to which they were subjected in the past, guarantee them a free life of labour and democratic rights, lead them to take part voluntarily in the building of a democratic state as the leading force of new society, and to bring their enthusiasm and initiative into full play.

Today the workers, freed from the yoke of colonial slavery, take an active part in the reconstruction of our industry, accomplishing great feats of labour; they strive to accelerate the building of a democratic country and to achieve the democratic emancipation of the working class.

But the building of a democratic state has only just begun. Only part of our factories, mines and enterprises have resumed operation, and industrial production and construction as a whole has not yet got into its stride.

In the industrial field, we now have the possibility of liquidating the survivals of the colonial rule of Japanese imperialism, of establishing a democratic system of labour, improving the working conditions of the workers, and raising their standard of living. Yet, the democratic emancipation of the workers has not been fully effected. An eight-hour working day has not yet been enacted, the employment of juvenile labour is widespread, social insurance and labour protection for the workers have yet to be introduced, and the survivals of Japanese imperialism have not been totally abolished in industrial management.

For this reason the Labour Law to be promulgated now by the Provisional People's Committee of North Korea has as its aims the radical improvement of the working conditions of factory and office workers, the enhancement of their material well-being, the elimination of the vestiges of imperialist exploitation in industry and the achievement of the democratic emancipation of the working class.

Conditions are already ripe for realizing the democratic emancipation of factory and office workers. Major factories, mines, enterprises and banks are in the hands of the people; the Provisional People's Committee of North Korea, which represents the genuinely democratic power, has gained considerably in strength, and the worker-peasant alliance under the leadership of the working class has been further consolidated.

It is of great importance to grant full democratic rights in labour and life to the workers, who are the very core of the democratic forces in Korea and who are in charge of the leading sector of the national economy. If the democratic emancipation of factory and office workers and reform of their working life are not effected, if the enthusiasm and creative activity of factory and office workers are not enlisted, the building of our new life will undoubtedly be delayed and impeded.

It is, therefore, an important revolutionary task and a prerequisite for Korea's democratic development to enforce a Labour Law that provides for an eight-hour working day, a proper wage system and social insurance.

As all of you comrades know, the 20-Point Platform of the Provisional People's Committee of North Korea clearly sets forth the task of liquidating the vestiges of Japanese imperialism's colonial exploitation and of introducing a democratic system of labour in Korea. The Labour Law to be promulgated this time will embody in practical life the labour policy of our people's power as specified precisely in the Platform, and will further promote the building of our democratic state by introducing an eight-hour working day, equal pay for equal work, irrespective of age or sex, and social insurance for factory and office workers.

This Labour Law is a democratic law, which fully conforms to the concrete historical conditions in our country.

Our country is now in the stage of the democratic revolution. We are liquidating the remnants of the systems of colonial and feudal exploitation and are encouraging private enterprises to a certain degree.

The economic construction in our country at present is not a socialist one, and yet, it is not, of course, going in the direction of capitalism. We are in the stage of building a democratic state by uniting the patriotic democratic forces from all walks of life on the basis of abolishing the foundations of colonial and feudal exploitation.

For this reason our Labour Law is not identical with that of socialist society and, what is more, it is fundamentally different from the labour law of a bourgeois country which defends capitalist exploitation. This law is a democratic labour law conforming to the actual conditions in Korea. We have to guarantee by law the rights of the wage and salary earners employed in private enterprises, not to mention the rights of workers and office employees who labour as masters in our state organs and state-owned enterprises. Our people's power allows and encourages the business activities of the national capitalists. But it cannot tolerate the unrestrained sweating of the workers by the entrepreneurs. The characteristic of the Labour Law to be promulgated now is that it defends the interests of all factory and office workers and ensures democratic rights for them.

There may be people who, deeming our Labour Law to be a law defending only the interests of the working class, think that it undermines the National Democratic United Front. This is an erroneous idea.

The Labour Law, which defends the interests of factory and office workers, meets and coincides fully with the interests of democratic construction in Korea. To lay excessive emphasis on the interests of the workers and office employees in disregard of the realities of our country, and to ignore the general interests of democratic construction, would contravene the underlying spirit of the enactment of the democratic Labour Law. The proposed Labour Law, however, is enacted with the aim of facilitating the democratic development of Korea as a whole, entirely on the principle of strengthening the national democratic united front. It is our belief that the enactment and enforcement of the democratic Labour Law will not only bring democratic emancipation to the workers, but will also give them opportunities for their active participation in political, economic and cultural life, and further cement the unity and solidarity of all democratic forces with the working class as the core.

During the agrarian reform, too, the working class fought more valiantly than any other class against the traitorous Syngman Rhee clique and the feudal forces. Only by strengthening the central role of the working class can our democratic united front be further consolidated.

Ours is the first democratic labour law not only in the history of Korea but also in the history of the world's colonial and semi-colonial nations.

Agrarian and other reforms have been carried out likewise in the democratic countries in East and Southeast Europe since their liberation, but none of those countries have so far enacted a democratic labour law.

In our own country, too, in south Korea where a U.S. military government has been set up with the support of the traitorous Syngman Rhee clique, the workers, far from having a labour law of this type, are forced to do backbreaking slave labour just as in the days of Japanese imperialist rule, and languish in the living hell of hunger and non-rights. Hundreds of thousands of jobless workers roam the streets, and suffer all manner of persecution and abuse, without even elementary democratic liberties and rights and any security for living.

Besides, there is as yet no democratic labour law, either, in the United States, a self-styled democratic country, where the working class has no democratic rights in the true sense of the word. After the termination of World War II the United States failed to promptly reorganize its munitions industry into a peacetime industry but only reduced the number of workers greatly as compared with the past. In consequence, the streets swarm with unemployed and labour disputes occur one after another.

Our Labour Law to be enacted this time is another striking demonstration of the democratic character of the Provisional People's Committee of North Korea and a graphic illustration of the nature of genuine democracy. It is a perfectly democratic law such as is inconceivable in capitalist countries, and is a progressive labour law fully conforming to the interests of the labouring masses and the entire people. Enforcement of this law will hasten the victory of the democratic revolution in north Korea and, at the same time, provide a guarantee for the accelerated democratization of the whole of Korea and encourage the working class in many countries of the world and the oppressed peoples in the East who are struggling for democratic rights and for their very existence.

We should fully explain and bring home to the masses of the people the progressive content and great significance of our Labour Law, and inspire them to come out as one in the struggle for the thoroughgoing execution of this law.

The lofty feeling of love for the country and the nation is embodied in our Labour Law.

In the past the Japanese imperialists worked the children and youth of Korea day and night, like beasts of burden, paying them the lowest possible wages, and left them ragged, hungry, ignorant and ill, dooming them to fall down or become disabled and wander aimlessly in despair. Furthermore, the Japanese imperialists cruelly sweated and persecuted our Korean women and went so far as to deny them all the elementary rights as mothers.

Nevertheless, the Syngman Rhee clique is bent on retaining in our liberated country the same system of exploitation as in the days of Japanese imperialist rule. They are quislings who, far from loving their nation, betray it. They are trying again to shackle the liberated people of Korea to the fetters of slavery and subject them to humiliation and oppression by retaining the old system under which Koreans exploited Koreans and foreign imperialists oppressed and exploited the Korean people. These acts of theirs are out and out traitorous, criminal actions.

Quite contrary to this, in promulgating the Labour Law now the Provisional People's Committee of North Korea is guided by the aim of liquidating the survivals of heavy forced labour of the colonial type of the past and establishing a new and popular system of labour and, on this basis, of speedily developing our country into a rich and powerful, democratic state, and making it possible for all our men and women workers and the entire nation to live in plenty at an early date.

Who is against such a labour law and seeks to obstruct its enforcement? It is the traitorous Syngman Rhee clique that attempts to turn Korea into a colony of the U.S. imperialists and enslave our nation again. The traitor Syngman Rhee, prompted by an ambition to set up his dictatorship, is working hard to preserve the feudal system and build a foothold for reactionary forces in Korea, and is frantically trying to become the puppet president of the colony whose mission it is to sell out the territory and natural wealth of Korea to foreign countries.

The U.S. military government, in defiance of objections from the American people, supports and encourages the Syngman Rhee gang in its reactionary activities, persecuting and exploiting the workers and labouring people of Korea. This is the customary practice of the imperialists who invade and plunder other nations.

All the Korean people must clearly know that those who are opposed to our Labour Law are, as seen above, the U.S. imperialists anxious to make Korea their colony, and the traitorous, reactionary elements led by the U.S. imperialists' stooge, Syngman Rhee.

All Koreans who love their country and aspire to the democratic independence and sovereignty of the country will, as a matter of course, unanimously support and approve the enforcement of this Labour Law, and will thoroughly expose and smash the traitorous schemes of the Syngman Rhee clique that is opposed to this law.

In conclusion, I should like to stress that it is thanks to the favourable conditions for democratic development created by the Soviet army in north Korea that the Provisional People's Committee of North Korea can guarantee, through the enactment and enforcement of the Labour Law, genuine democratic emancipation and free labour for the workers.

With the defeat of Japanese imperialism and the liberation of our country, our people have become able to build a new life of democracy according to their own will, and freely to form democratic organizations such as the trade unions, the Peasants' Union, the Democratic Youth League, the Democratic Women's Union, thus widely rallying all the patriotic forces. This growth of the patriotic democratic forces has provided the foundation to further strengthen the Provisional People's Committee of North Korea and to successfully carry out the tasks of the democratic revolution.

I am confident that all the political parties and social organizations and the workers, peasants, intellectuals and all other sections of the people will further consolidate the victory of democracy in north Korea by participating as one in perfecting the law through earnest discussion of the draft of the Labour Law which is to be promulgated soon and by guaranteeing its early and thoroughgoing enforcement.

NATIONALIZATION OF MAJOR INDUSTRIES—THE FOUNDATION FOR BUILDING AN INDEPENDENT, SOVEREIGN STATE

Speech Delivered at the Pyongyang City Mass Rally Held in Support of the Law on Nationalization of Industries

August 10, 1946

Dear fellow countrymen,

I would like to convey to you some happy news, news of great significance to the life of the Korean people.

Today the Provisional People's Committee of North Korea has passed and promulgated the law on the confiscation without compensation and the nationalization of all the factories, mines, power plants, railway transport, communications, banks, trade and cultural establishments, etc., which had been owned by the Japanese state, by Japanese corporations and individuals or by Korean traitors to the nation.

This law issued by the Provisional People's Committee of North Korea is of really great historic significance. Under this law, all the factories, mines, power plants, railway transport, communications, banks, trade and cultural establishments, etc., in north Korea which the Japanese imperialists built with the sweat and blood of the Korean people in this land, have become the property of the latter, their sole legal owner. In addition, all the factories and enterprises which had belonged to those who fled with the Japanese, to the pro-Japanese elements and the traitors to the nation have also been confiscated without compensation and passed into the possession of the Korean people.

During their rule over our country the Japanese imperialist robbers did not develop Korea's industries in the interests of the Korean people; they built industrial establishments in our country in order to plunder our country of its rich resources and rake in huge colonial profits by exploiting the labour of our people. Japanese imperialism also made use of quite a number of factories and enterprises in Korea to supply munitions for its aggressive war. By their backbreaking labour the Korean people, up to the eve of the liberation, enriched only the Japanese imperialist colonial marauders, while they themselves suffered from acute hunger and penury.

However, this unfair and humiliating system has now been ended for good. Now the factories, mines, collieries, power plants, railways, banks, etc., have all passed into the hands of the Korean people entirely to secure the prosperity and progress of our country and the betterment of our people's well-being.

There is no doubt that the entire Korean people throughout north and south Korea will warmly approve and support with exultant joy and enthusiasm this law enacted by the Provisional People's Committee of North Korea.

This law enacted by the Provisional People's Committee of North Korea is a new, important step towards the democratization of Korea and the building of an independent, sovereign and democratic country.

In the year since Korea was liberated from the yoke of Japanese imperialism, we have accomplished several democratic tasks in north Korea. The people's committee, the genuine people's power, was set up and strengthened; the agrarian reform whereby the land of the Japanese imperialists and the landlords was confiscated and distributed free to the peasants, and the Labour Law and the Law on Equality of the Sexes were enforced; and measures were taken to establish a system of public education. We have thus laid the foundation for building an independent state of democratic Korea in the future.

One year ago, the heroic Soviet army helped our people to rout the aggressive army of Japanese imperialism and liberate their country. After Korea was liberated, the Soviet army assisted our people in establishing genuine people's power and creating a new, democratic life according to their own will. It has continually given us selfless assistance in the speedy rehabilitation and development of the national economy and culture in north Korea.

Practical life has brought to the Korean people the keen realization that the Soviet people are their closest and truest friends. Our people will forever remember the sincere aid given by the fraternal Soviet people.

The unbreakable bond of friendship between the Korean and Soviet peoples is sealed with the blood shed by the sons and daughters of the great Soviet people in the struggle to defeat the atrocious Japanese imperialist occupants. The Korean people who value this friendship more than anything else will, in firm unity with the Soviet people, surely win fully democratic independence and sovereignty for Korea and achieve happiness for all the people and prosperity for all generations to come.

However, the realities in south Korea under the occupation of the U.S. army are entirely different.

In south Korea today, the people are denied every political freedom and right. The people's committees representing the will of the people have been dissolved by force, and power is entirely in the hands of the U.S. Military Command. The U.S. Military Command declares in words that it seeks "friendship" with the Korean people and wishes Korea early "independence"; but, in fact, it pursues a policy of colonial enslavement in south Korea.

The U.S. military government openly employs as advisers those traitors to the Korean people and those reactionary elements who served as officials of Japanese imperialism before August 15. To this day not any measures have been taken in south Korea to purge the pro-Japanese elements, the traitors to the nation and the reactionary terrorists, and to put an end to the persecution of democratic political parties and social organizations.

With the active support of the U.S. Military Command, American capitalists and domestic reactionaries are resorting to every conceivable scheme to seize the productive facilities and effects formerly owned by the Japanese state or Japanese individuals in south Korea. Particularly, the traitorous Syngman Rhee clique is selling out Korea's industries and natural resources to the U.S. monopoly capitalists at will. It is no secret that a number of American mining corporations have long been casting covetous eyes on the rich mineral resources of Korea. Those corporations have bribed the Syngman Rhee clique with dollars and concluded an "agreement" on the operation of the mining industry in Korea. This shows that, using its lackeys—the Syngman Rhee clique—as its ushers, U.S. monopoly capital is trying hard to monopolize Korea's major industries, convert our country into a U.S. colony and enslave our people again.

The Korean people will never tolerate this, and will fight more staunchly to foil the plot of U.S. imperialism and its running dogs, traitors to the nation, and to achieve the political and economic independence of Korea.

The present law of the Provisional People's Committee of North Korea on the nationalization of major industries formerly owned by the Japanese imperialists and the Korean traitors to the nation constitutes a stern answer and a powerful blow by the Korean people to all the pro-Japanese elements, traitors to the nation, and the reactionaries who are obstructing the building of an independent and democratic state, and to the U.S. imperialists and traitorous Syngman Rhee clique who are attempting to reimpose the yoke of colonial slavery upon the Korean people. The factories, mines, collieries, power plants, railways, communications, banks, etc., which have wholly passed into the hands of the Provisional People's Committee of North Korea under this law, shall never again become the property of any foreign capitalist or private entrepreneur; they will forever remain under ownership by the state whose masters are the people, as the property of the Korean people.

The industrial establishments nationalized now are those important enterprises which can be considered the backbone of Korea's economy. Now they will no longer be run as a means of the imperialists for making profits, as they were before liberation, but will be operated exclusively to make our country prosperous and enhance the well-being of the Korean people. The fact that the key branches of the national economy have thus come into the hands of the Korean people and are geared to the interests of the people is really of tremendous significance to the rapid, planned rehabilitation and development of our country's economy and to the acceleration of the building of an independent, sovereign and democratic state in the future.

The new law enacted by the Provisional People's Committee of North Korea sets new tasks before our people.

We must learn how to manage and run industry better, ensure the prompt return to production of the enterprises still out of operation, and secure the necessary materials and manpower. And a struggle should be waged everywhere to strengthen labour discipline and increase labour productivity.

No longer are we working for the imperialists or exploiters; we are working for our own good, for the welfare of the entire people. The better we work, the more goods our factories and enterprises will produce and supply to the people at cheaper prices. Therefore, all factory and office workers should adopt a new attitude towards labour, actively cherish and thriftily use the property of the state and of the people and endeavour to produce as much as possible and in better quality.

All workers and technicians, and particularly the youth, should make tireless efforts to improve their skills and qualifications and assiduously study the sciences and technology. Only by mastering advanced sciences and technology can we manage our industry and national economy better and develop them rapidly.

Our peasants should strive to increase crop yields, deliver the agricultural tax in kind to the state correctly and punctually, and thereby provide the factory and office workers and urban dwellers with sufficient food.

The pro-Japanese elements, the traitors to the nation and reactionaries will surely manoeuvre to prevent this historic law from being put into effect. These despicable and villainous enemies may destroy our factories and enterprises and even perpetrate acts of terrorism and sabotage.

However, no force can check the onward march of our awakened and united people and no one can reverse the wheel of history rolling fast ahead.

All political parties and social organizations, workers, peasants, intellectuals and all other sections of the people should give unqualified support to the just measure taken by the Provisional People's Committee of North Korea. They should firmly protect the industrial establishments which have become the property of the people against the enemy's plots to destroy them and, at the same time, devote all their energies and enthusiasm to ensure their normal operations and the speedy rehabilitation and development of the national economy. Needless to say, this will bring about improvement in the livelihood of our people and contribute to the cause of building a rich, strong and democratic country.

Of course, this is an arduous and complex task, but we must accomplish it at any cost. The united might of the people, working consciously in their own behalf and for the sake of their country, is fully able to surmount any difficulty and obstacle and will surely win victory.

Let the liberated people of Korea demonstrate to the whole world that they are fully capable of building a free, independent and democratic state and of running it efficiently!

Long live free, democratic Korea!

Long live the Provisional People's Committee of North Korea, our people's government!

Long live the Soviet people, the closest friend and the helper of the Korean people!

Long live Comrade Stalin, the great leader of the Soviet people and a close friend of the Korean people!

FOR THE ESTABLISHMENT OF A UNITED PARTY OF THE WORKING MASSES

Report to the Inaugural Congress of the Workers' Party of North Korea

August 29, 1946

Dear comrade delegates,

The present Congress, called to inaugurate the Workers' Party of North Korea through the merger of the Communist Party of North Korea and the New Democratic Party of Korea, is of great significance in the annals of the independence movement in Korea and in carrying out the tasks of the democratic revolution today.

You comrade delegates have assembled here, not only in the capacity of delegates of the Workers' Party but also as representatives of the entire north Korean people, to discuss state affairs and the momentous problems decisive to the destiny of the fatherland.

We, who have so far been engaged in a great struggle and construction for the country and the people, have convened the present Congress to found a united party of the Korean working masses for the purpose of accomplishing still greater work in future.

The Korean people who are in a complex and acute political situation are following the Inaugural Congress of our Party with the greatest interest and hopes today. We should conduct the present Congress successfully so that we may live up to the great expectations of the Korean people and meet the urgent demands of the popular masses.

1. POLITICAL SITUATION IN KOREA

The situation in our country underwent a radical change after liberation. When the anti-fascist world war was brought to a victorious conclusion thanks to the decisive role played by the Soviet army, the system of barbarous Japanese imperialist rule collapsed in Korea, too, and the way was opened up for building a Korea for the Koreans, for building a new country and a new life in conformity to our people's will and demands.

The revolutionary enthusiasm and creative power of the Korean people liberated from long years of oppression burst forth like an erupting volcano, and this great force has radically changed the appearance of Korean society in the past year.

The democratic reforms carried out in north Korea during this period have put an end to all the colonial and feudal relations that had long retarded the development of our country's economy and culture, and paved the way to unhindered development. The past year was indeed a year of great progress and change that would ordinarily be equal to scores or hundreds of years.

The political readiness of the Korean people has heightened to an unprecedented degree in the course of the bitter struggle with the enemy; Korea today is precisely the people's Korea, a Korea that is governed and built by the people themselves.

North Korea's democratic reforms are also of great significance internationally. Democratic social reforms as thoroughly carried out as those in our north Korea are rarely to be seen in many other countries which have taken the road of creating a new life following World War II. North Korea's democratic reforms are a heartening example to the peoples of many Eastern countries who aspire towards freedom and democracy. Today north Korea is not only the strategic base for democratic development of the whole of Korea, but also plays the role as the cradle of democracy in the East.

The agrarian reform put an end to the feudal relations in landownership, the main cause of the backwardness and stagnation of Korean society, and laid the basis for the democratic development of Korea. In north Korea the tillers have become the owners of land, and landlords and the tenant system have disappeared once and for all.

In north Korea the peasants have come to work their own land, and dispose of their crops for the improvement of their own life and expansion of production after delivering 25 per cent of harvests as agricultural tax in kind to the state. The agricultural tax in kind paid to the state is used not for the enjoyment and enrichment of the exploiters as in the past, but for the development of the national economy as a whole including agriculture and the improvement of the people's living conditions.

The enforcement of the democratic Labour Law has freed factory and office workers from the heavy, forced, colonial-type labour and has ensured them fundamental rights in their labour and life, thus making it possible for the labouring masses to bring their activity and creative initiative into full play.

The nationalization of industries has turned the industrial establishments, the mainstays of Korea's economy, which were owned by the Japanese imperialists and the traitors to the nation, into the property of the people, thereby destroying the basis of imperialist exploitation and laying the economic foundation for the building of an independent, sovereign state. Thus the factories, mines, collieries, railways, communications, banks, etc., formerly used by the imperialists and comprador capitalists to bleed the Korean people white, have now been turned into the people's property dedicated to the prosperity and development of our country and improvement of the welfare of the working masses. These measures taken by the Provisional People's Committee of North Korea clearly express the thoroughgoing and progressive nature of the democratic reforms carried out in our country.

In addition, the Law on Equality of the Sexes emancipated the women in north Korea from thousands of years of humiliation and ill-treatment, and a twofold and threefold oppression, enabling them to enjoy equal rights with men and work actively in all spheres of politics, economy and culture.

As all these facts expressly prove, democratic north Korea today points clearly to the road for the entire Korean people to follow, and the democratization of Korea and her full independence can be achieved only by relying firmly on the democratic base in north Korea.

However, many difficulties lie on the road of the democratic construction of the country, and our struggle is very arduous and complex. This is because the aggressive army of U.S. imperialism is stationed in south Korea, seeking to turn our country into a colony once again, and because a gang of quislings are running wild, who have become its lackeys and are trying to sell out Korea to imperialism as a colony again. Today the U.S. military government monopolizes all powers in south Korea and is doing everything in its frantic effort to suppress the democratic forces and gain a foothold for reaction.

As under Japanese imperialist rule in the past, the people in south Korea are groaning under the savage oppression and tyranny of the domestic and foreign reactionary forces and are stranded in the misery of poverty, deprived of all rights.

The masses of the people are completely denied even the elementary freedoms—freedom of speech, the press, assembly, association, religious belief, and so on. Thus, thousands of patriots are being cruelly tortured in police dungeons and prisons for the "crime" of love for their country, of calling for democracy and the independence of the country. Leaders of the people are shot down in broad daylight by reactionary terrorists, and democratic political parties and social organizations are being wrecked by the terrorism of the traitorous Syngman Rhee gang openly patronized by the U.S. army. The reactionaries shot to death, right in front of a courthouse, one of the middle-school boys who were demanding that the trial in the so-called "forged-note case" be opened to the public.

Patriotic-minded scholars and teachers are dismissed from schools, and schools are being closed down one after another. Patriotic workers in culture and the arts are also placed under surveillance, beaten up and thrown into jail for no reason at all.

Far from carrying out agrarian reform, the land formerly owned by the Japanese is being concentrated in the hands of the Americans and the reactionary profiteers. The south Korean peasants are still groaning under the yoke of the feudal system of high-rents tenancy.

Far from instituting a labour law, workers are slaughtered by planes, tanks and machine guns merely because they have taken part in demonstrations. The situation is such that one has to serve a term of eight years in prison for making a speech appealing for promoting the labour movement. The workers in south Korea are now being driven hard like beasts of burden, subjected to the same cruel colonial oppression and exploitation as in the past.

Far from nationalizing the key industries, the authorities of the U.S. military government declare the industrial establishments formerly owned by Japanese imperialism to be their property; they pay lip service to industrial rehabilitation, but actually they are wrecking even those few factories which are in operation and converting south Korea into a market for U.S. commodities. The traitorous Syngman Rhee clique is guilty of the country-selling, treacherous acts; it has already sold mining and trading concessions in Korea to American capitalists and, moreover, it is now openly selling the country's valuable resources to American big businesses.

Far from granting women equal rights with men, concubinage, licensed and unlicensed prostitution and the *kisaeng* girl system are growing more prevalent, and numerous women suffer unbearable humiliation as playthings for the rich and powerful.

The true worth of a political party or a policy must be assessed not by its words or statements but by the practical activities of that party, or by the concrete facts showing whose interests that policy represents and defends. Over the past year the reactionary "politicians" in south Korea made innumerable speeches and promises and pledges over the mike and from the rostrums. What, however, have they brought to the Korean people in reality? The Syngman Rhee clique, brazen-faced as it is, can no longer conceal its true colours which have now been exposed by the stark facts in all their nakedness in the eyes of the entire Korean people. The traitorous Syngman Rhee clique, instead of introducing democracy, has done nothing else but tyrannizing over south Korea and selling the country to the United States as a colony, in obedience to the orders of its U.S. masters.

Swarms of jobless people roam the streets; hungry people, gourd in hand, crowd the government offices, raising a hue and cry; youths and students fall under rifle fire; schools are closed down; newspapers, magazines and other press organs are closed one after another; patriots are constantly arrested, jailed and murdered. Meanwhile, pro-Japanese elements and traitors to the nation resort to despotism and abuse of power, as if the days of their glory had returned. Precisely this is the true picture of south Korea, a land of lawlessness, lorded over by the U.S. army.

In striking contrast to north Korea, which is advancing in the direction of genuine democracy and national independence, south Korea under the fascist reign of terrorism of the U.S. imperialists and their stooges, the traitorous Syngman Rhee clique, is moving backward along the path of reaction and colonial enslavement. Thus, the southern half of our country is occupied and converted into a colony by the U.S. imperialists, and this very fact presents difficulties to the solution of the Korean question.

The most important task facing the Korean people today is to overcome at an early date the anti-popular and reactionary line pursued in south Korea, to carry out thoroughgoing democratic reforms in south Korea, as was done in north Korea, and thereby build a new, unified, independent and democratic Korea.

2. STRENGTHENING THE NATIONAL DEMOCRATIC UNITED FRONT—AN IMPORTANT GUARANTEE OF VICTORY IN THE REVOLUTION

Consolidation in every way of the National Democratic United Front, which rallies around itself all the patriotic democratic forces of Korea, provides an important guarantee of victory for our revolution.

Democratic reforms in north Korea have from the beginning been carried out through the efforts of the entire people, by the joint endeavours of all democratic political parties and social organizations.

The Communist Party of North Korea, New Democratic Party of Korea, Korean Democratic Party, Chondoist Chongu Party and all the social organizations, acting concertedly at all times under the banner of democracy, have liquidated the pro-Japanese elements of all shades, smashed the intrigues and manoeuvres of the reactionaries and energetically promoted the cause of building a democratic state. The National Democratic United Front of North Korea, which unites all the patriotic democratic forces, was formed and grew in the course of actual struggle to carry out the democratic tasks. It is closely linked with the broad masses of the people; it has already rallied around itself more than 6 millions of the organized masses. This constitutes really a great force, and herein lies the basic factor in our victory.

Reliance on the united strength of all the political parties, social organizations and the people in all walks of life made it fully possible for the Provisional People's Committee of North Korea to successfully accomplish the great democratic reforms in the short period of no more than a half year after its establishment. Every time a democratic task was put forward, all the political parties and social organizations gave it unqualified support by issuing joint statements, sent their workers to different districts and spared neither efforts nor zeal for its victorious accomplishment.

Since the various democratic political parties accord unanimous support to the people's committee and strive jointly for the implementation of its policy, our organs of people's power can accomplish democratic tasks successfully on a broad mass basis. In north Korea, all the political parties, social organizations and the masses of the people in all walks of life are closely rallied around the people's committee, and give unanimous and active support to the policies of the people's power organs. Thus, democratic reforms in north Korea are being and will be accomplished by the united might of the broad masses of the people rallied around the National Democratic United Front.

All our experiences clearly show that the complete independence and sovereignty of Korea and her democratic development can be achieved today only by the strength of the National Democratic United Front embracing all the popular masses without exception—the working class, peasants, handicraftsmen, intellectuals, tradesmen and entrepreneurs.

On the contrary, all the disorder and misery in south Korea under the domination of the U.S. military government can be ascribed mainly to the disunity within our nation. In south Korea, I have been told, there were once more than 200 political parties. Such splitting into parties of three and groups of five and mutual wrangling play right into the hands of the reactionary forces. The enemies of democracy and of our nation want to see more than anything else our working people—the workers, peasants, working intellectuals, etc.—torn apart and fighting and biting each other. For the reactionary forces can exist and achieve their anti-popular ends only by seizing upon this and taking advantage of splits among the democratic forces. Such a divisive policy is an old trick the reactionaries are commonly using all over the world. We must not be taken in or fooled by it. In south Korea, however, people have been tricked by it. The democratic political parties and social organizations in south Korea are disrupted and engage in factional strife, scrambling for power, just as the enemy wishes. Herein lies the principal danger of the situation in south Korea today.

Developments in south Korea over the past year provide us with a striking lesson on how precious the unity of all the patriotic democratic forces is and, particularly, on how urgent and important it is to strengthen the solidarity of the masses of working people.

We should defeat the traitorous reactionary forces and bring the democratic revolution to a victorious conclusion by cementing the united front of all patriotic political parties and social organizations that aspire to freedom, independence and democracy for the country, and by relying on the united strength of all the working people and of the people as a whole.

3. THE MERGER OF THE TWO PARTIES IS INEVITABLE AND MOST APPROPRIATE

Comrade delegates,

The merger of the Communist Party and the New Democratic Party is of really epochal significance in cementing the unity of the democratic forces in our country at present. In particular, the merger of the two Parties means a big progress in closely uniting the broad masses—the workers, peasants and working intellectuals.

In the course of the merger of the Communist Party and the New Democratic Party, diverse opinions were expressed as to what sort of a party the Workers' Party should be and what it should do.

The Programme of our Workers' Party explicitly declares its aims, character and tasks. Our Party is, as is clearly stated at the beginning of the Programme, a party that represents and defends the interests of the Korean working masses, its aim being to build a mighty, prosperous, independent and democratic state. The Workers' Party is the vanguard detachment of the labouring masses of Korea and it is rooted in the broad masses—the workers, peasants and working intellectuals. That is why the Workers' Party ought to become the leading force in the struggle for the independence, sovereignty and democratization of Korea and to play the central role in the National Democratic United Front. Our Party fights to overthrow the pro-Japanese elements, traitors to the nation, landlords and comprador capitalists, to achieve the complete liberation of the country from the yoke of foreign imperialism, and to build an independent, sovereign and democratic state. This is the aim which both the Communist Party and the New Democratic Party have been pursuing.

What, then, is the task of the Workers' Party? The basic task of our Party at the present stage is to carry out anti-imperialist, anti-feudal democratic reforms thoroughly on a nation-wide scale and to establish a Democratic People's Republic by mobilizing the broad masses of the people. Today the programmatic tasks of our Party are: to confiscate the land of the Japanese imperialists and the landlords and distribute it among the peasants; to nationalize the industries, transport, communications, banks, etc., belonging to Japanese imperialism and the comprador capitalists and transform them into the property of the people; to introduce an eight-hour working day and social insurance system for factory and office workers; to grant women equal rights with men; to ensure freedom of speech, the press, assembly, association and religious belief to the people; to institute a democratic system of public education and enforce compulsory education; and to develop science, national culture and arts.

These democratic tasks represent the earnest demands of all sections of the working people throughout Korea. Without introducing democratic reforms, it is impossible to build a fully independent and democratic country, to rescue the working masses from poverty and the absence of all rights, and to develop the economy and culture of our country.

The Communist Party and the New Democratic Party have striven, and are striving, for the materialization of the earnest demands of the labouring masses of Korea. Therefore, it is inevitable that the two Parties, which have similar aims and tasks, should merge into one.

Today our struggle is the struggle not for the old parliamentary democracy of capitalist countries but for a genuine democracy for the new Korea, democracy of the broad popular masses, progressive democracy. The struggle for the rights of the masses of the people in the political, economic and cultural spheres is an arduous, complicated and protracted struggle confronting us. The merger of the Communist Party and the New Democratic Party is urgently needed for the fulfilment of this task.

Disunity of the working masses constitutes the greatest danger in their life-and-death struggle with the enemy. In order to achieve our fighting task victoriously, the working masses should stand together more firmly and forge closer unity. Most decisive of all to the fulfilment of the great democratic tasks facing the Korean people is the formation of a unified general staff of the working masses, the sole militant vanguard of the working people. This problem could only be solved by founding the Workers' Party.

For this reason, the Central Committee of the New Democratic Party proposed the merger of the two Parties, and this met with the full agreement of the Central Committee of the Communist Party. Then at a joint session of the Central Committees of the two Parties it was formally decided to merge the two and develop them into a mass party—the Workers' Party.

The entire people, not to speak of the members of the two Parties, warmly welcomed this historic decision. It was because they were convinced that the merger of the two Parties would greatly contribute to the strengthening of the democratic forces and acceleration of the democratic construction.

Thus, the merger proceeded smoothly in all provinces, cities, counties and *myon* in an atmosphere of very high political enthusiasm of the entire membership of the two Parties and of the entire working masses who supported the merger. So we have today convened the Inaugural Congress of the Workers' Party. This is graphic evidence that the merger of the two Parties is inevitable and most appropriate.

In the course of the merger, however, we discovered wrong tendencies in some Communist Party members. Here are a few examples.

I would like to point out, in the first place, the self-righteous, arrogant attitude of some Communist Party members. They said, "How can we merge with the New Democratic Party?" We should ask them, "When did you become *Poi* and *Shuchi* like that?" This is, above all, an expression of self-importance looking down upon others, an exclusionist tendency of thinking oneself the only one engaged in revolutionary work. This is an error resulting not only from ignorance of our Party's line and policies but from the lack of understanding of even the simple truth that the revolutionary work will be victorious only when all the revolutionary comrades are united and all the masses of the people stand together. To put it strongly, this is a factional tendency, a dangerous one against which we must be most vigilant in establishing a mass political party. If a tendency of this sort is allowed to grow, it may totally ruin our work.

Another grave tendency finds expression in the talk that our Party would be "diluted into the New Democratic Party" or become a "party of the small-propertied classes." This is, on the one hand, an expression of "Leftism" that does not like the merger, but I think rather that we need to sharpen vigilance especially against the Rightist venom contained in this tendency.

We should resolutely combat the tendency that impairs the organizational discipline and ideological unity of the Party, the tendency that seeks to reduce the Party to a club of the labouring masses, a kind of fraternity of the small-propertied classes. The creation of the mass-based Workers' Party which champions the interests of all the working masses and can embrace all progressive elements among the working masses, in no way means that it is permissible to impair the Party's political prestige or weaken the unity and iron discipline in its ranks. The Workers' Party is an organized combat unit and a vanguard detachment of the working masses. We should at all times firmly defend the unity, purity and strict discipline of the Party. If our ranks are lacking in unitary ideology and will and in monolithic discipline, we shall be unable to prevail in the fight against the enemy.

Another thing I would like to point out is the assumption that there will be a "large-scale purge" in the Party. This, too, is a manifestation of passivism disliking the merger and a tendency to distrust the Party.

It is natural for the Party to purge itself of alien elements in order to maintain the purity of its ranks. We should always heighten our vigilance against alien elements, and be thorough in preventing their machinations, and expel them from the Party ranks as soon as they are discovered. Such elements, however, are very few in number, and therefore there can be no "large-scale purge" in our Workers' Party. Any talk about such a "purge" is quite wrong.

4. IMMEDIATE TASKS OF THE PARTY

The basic task of our Party at the present stage is to build up a democratic country, unified and fully independent, at the earliest possible date. For this purpose, we should sweep away all the reactionary pro-Japanese and feudal forces standing in the way of the democratic independence of our country.

We should struggle to further strengthen the Provisional People's Committee of North Korea, the genuine people's power, and transfer all power throughout Korea to the people's committee.

A struggle should be unfolded to further consolidate the gains of the democratic reforms already carried out in north Korea—the agrarian reform, Labour Law, Law on Equality of the Sexes, nationalization of the key industries, institution of a public education system, etc.—and to enforce them throughout the country. For the victorious accomplishment of these fighting tasks, it is important above all to turn our Party into a strong and powerful combat unit.

The broader the united front of the masses of the people and the more complex the tasks confronting us and the sharper the fight with the enemy, the more urgent will be the need for further strengthening our Party, the advanced detachment of the Korean working masses, both organizationally and ideologically.

We should strengthen in every way the community of ideology and will and an iron discipline within the Party ranks, and wage an implacable fight against every tendency incompatible with them.

Many divergent tendencies may appear in our ranks, because the two Parties have just been merged. We, therefore, should arm all members of the Party with one and the same ideology based on our Party's Programme, strengthen their comradely principled unity and enhance their political consciousness.

To fight against all and every factional tendency is of special importance in our Party life today. We should do away completely with the remnants of the accursed factionalism which historically has done great harm to the revolutionary movement in Korea, and thereby build up our Party into a united, powerful, iron detachment.

And our Party should take deep roots in the masses and at all times maintain the bonds of kinship with them. We should in every circumstance defend the interests of the working masses, lend our ear to their views, learn from them and teach them. We should lead and control all the working people's organizations, knit the entire labouring masses closely around our Party and correctly lead them in the building of a new democratic Korea. Whether our Party members deal with this correctly or not is the key to the victory of our Party.

Further, the utmost attention should be devoted to the problem of cadres. If there were no cadres competent to put the Programme and decisions of our Party into effect successfully, the Programme and decisions would, no matter how excellent, only turn out to be dead letters. Cadres decide everything. Yet there are shortcomings in our work of knowing, training and promoting cadres. We quite often hear the expression, "We're hard up for cadres," but we seldom hear any talk about where and how cadres have been trained and how new talents have been promoted. We should do our best to study, know, train and promote cadres.

Last, the Programme of our Party and its policies and decisions should be brought home to the masses of the people. Our Programme, policies and decisions can be materialized in actual life only if the masses of the people grasp them and make them their own. We should see to it that our Party's slogans become the slogans of the masses of the people themselves, and that the people themselves are voluntarily mobilized towards their materialization.

Let us march vigorously ahead for the freedom and democratic independence of our country, closely rallying all the democratic forces around the Workers' Party we are now founding!

Long live the Inaugural Congress of the Workers' Party of North Korea which represents the interests of the working masses!

Long live the National Democratic United Front!

Long live the establishment of a Democratic People's Republic!

ON THE RESULTS OF THE INAUGURAL CONGRESS OF THE WORKERS' PARTY OF NORTH KOREA

Speech Delivered at a Meeting of the Activists of the Party Organization of South Pyongan Province
September 9, 1946

Comrades,

The formation of the Workers' Party of North Korea through the merger of the Communist Party of North Korea and the New Democratic Party of Korea, was achieved triumphantly in the short period of one month through discussions at Party meetings of all levels—general membership meetings of Party cells, conferences of city, county and provincial Party organizations, and the Party Congress—after the decision was taken to amalgamate the two Parties at a Joint Enlarged Meeting of the Central Committees of the Two Parties on July 29.

The triumphant completion of this great work is by no means an accident. This shows that the entire Party membership, unanimously convinced that the formation of the Workers' Party by merging the Communist Party and the New Democratic Party was a historically necessary and most correct measure, took an active part in the fusion of the two Parties with a high degree of political enthusiasm.

What are the reasons that enabled us to successfully complete the merger in a short period of time and what are the merits of this work?

First, the foundation of the Workers' Party representing

the interests of the broad labouring masses through the fusion of the Communist Party and the New Democratic Party was most fitting in view of the present international and internal situation and was a measure fully in conformity to the expectations and demand of the Korean people.

The international situation today is characterized by the fact that, on the one hand, the forces of the people loving peace, freedom and democracy have liquidated the remnants of the fascist forces and are waging a vigorous struggle for world security and social progress and that, on the other, international reaction is raising its head, seeking to drag the world into the horrors of another war.

In this international situation, the Korean people, a component part of the democratic forces of the world, who seized power in their hands in north Korea after liberation, carried out the great democratic reforms and laid the base for the complete independence, sovereignty and democratization of Korea. At present the patriotic and democratic forces rallied around the people's power are growing and gaining strength with every passing day, crushing the remnant forces of Japanese imperialism and all the reactionary forces. In north Korea, where democracy has gained the upper hand, the people enjoy all rights and liberties, and their life is rapidly improving.

In contrast to this, the people in the southern part of Korea have come under a more barbaric rule than in the years of Japanese imperialism and the danger is increasing every hour that the people will meet the fate of colonial slavery again.

Therefore, the Korean people should fight more stubbornly now to eliminate the danger created in south Korea and win complete independence and sovereignty for the country. To this end, it is important above all to unite the broad democratic forces more firmly and, particularly, to secure the monolithic unity of the labouring masses.

For this reason, the foundation of the Workers' Party through the recent merger of the two Parties is most appropriate in the light of the international and internal situation and answers the demands of the whole people.

When the line for merging both Parties was announced, the entire people, not to speak of the members of the two Parties, expressed warm approval for it and the merger proceeded successfully in an atmosphere of extremely heightened enthusiasm on their part.

A major reason that the work of fusing the two Parties has thus come to a victorious conclusion lies, first of all, in the correctness of the line of founding the mass-based Workers' Party.

Second, the victorious results of the recent merger of the Parties have shown that the members of the Workers' Party are politically highly matured and steeled.

Our people, who had no experience of participation in politics under the colonial tyranny of Japanese imperialism for 36 years, grew politically and progressed ideologically in the course of carrying out the democratic reforms after liberation. Thus, our Party members have become able to grasp the present international and internal situation correctly and have been convinced of the correctness of the Party's lines and policies through their practical experience. They have come to know well what the character of Korean society is and what constitutes the major motive power in the democratic revolution today, and to correctly recognize what our tasks are at the present stage of democratization and how to carry them to victory. And it has been proved through the recent merger of both Parties that the trust of the membership in the Party centre and the other leading bodies at various levels was deepened greatly.

All this shows that our Party members made considerable progress politically and ideologically, and this constituted another major factor ensuring success in the recent merger.

Third, our Party has achieved ideological unity and solidarity.

Through all the struggles unfolded in north Korea till now, our Party members have been armed with the Party ideology and united by one and the same purpose and will. The struggle for the ideological unity of the Party has dealt a heavy blow to the impure elements and factionalists lurking in it and cemented the unity and cohesion of the Party ranks. This unity and cohesion is an important guarantee for our Party to ably break down any resistance of the reactionary elements and lead the people on to victory. Eloquent proof of this is the success in the recent Congress of our Party at which 801 delegates representing some 370,000 members correctly accomplished the great task of founding the Workers' Party, united by one mind and one will.

If we had not exposed the factionalists and checked their manoeuvrings beforehand, if we had not firmly secured the unity of ideology and will in the Party, we would not have accomplished the merger of the two Parties so smoothly and successfully.

Fourth, another major factor making for the victorious conclusion of the recent Inaugural Congress of our Party is that its leadership was steadfast and experienced, and organized and directed the work of merging the Parties in a proper manner.

The leadership of our Party consists of seasoned revolutionaries who unfolded underground movements or armed struggles against the rapacious Japanese imperialism during the past 10 to 20 years at home and abroad and who have acquired revolutionary steadfastness and revolutionary theory and accumulated rich experience in the course of the protracted revolutionary struggle. These revolutionaries, working in co-operation, made a scientific analysis of the world situation and the concrete realities of our country and, on this basis, clearly defined the line for the democratic development of Korea and the immediate tasks and confidently organized and mobilized the Party members and the people for victory. So, we were able to achieve great successes in the democratic reforms and democratic construction in the brief period of one year after liberation. Since we had such a strong leadership, we were recently quite able to rally hundreds of thousands of Party members under a single banner and triumphantly found the Workers' Party—the advanced detachment of the labouring masses.

Fifth, the prestige of our Party has been signally enhanced among the masses through the democratic reforms.

Immediately after liberation there were no few instances of impure elements penetrating the Communist Party and impairing its authority and prestige. Following the Third Enlarged Executive Committee Meeting of the **Central Organizing Committee of the Communist Party of North Korea, however,** the impure elements were purged from the Party, and it was united as one with the masses to thoroughly defend their interests and, particularly, played a vanguard role in the struggle to carry out the democratic reforms including the agrarian reform, so that its prestige rose greatly in the eyes of the masses. The masses of the people came out in absolute support of the amalgamation of the Communist Party and the New Democratic Party because they were convinced that when the two Parties were fused into one, it would fight more stoutly and reliably for their interests.

The appearance in this way of a unified party of the labouring masses in north Korea represents a fresh advance of the revolutionary movement and a great victory for the democratic forces in our country. This victory will also exert a powerful and inspiring influence upon the unity of the democratic forces and the merger of the three Parties in south Korea.

While there were merits such as mentioned above, various shortcomings were also revealed in the course of the recent amalgamation of the Parties.

First, I cannot but point out the fact that some Party members fail to have a full understanding of the significance of the formation of the Workers' Party and that there still exist Right and "Left" deviations in our ranks.

Some people think that only Marxists-Leninists can be admitted to the Workers' Party and maintain that the Marxists-Leninists alone can participate in carrying out the democratic tasks at the present stage. This is quite a wrong "Left" deviation.

It is true that the Marxists-Leninists are most advanced and active in fulfilling the democratic revolutionary tasks today and it is natural that those revolutionaries armed with

Marxism-Leninism should become the nuclei of our Party. But it is a great mistake to think that only those who are well versed in Marxism-Leninism can take part in the carrying out of the democratic revolution and join the Workers' Party. It is our view that whoever, even if not yet armed with Marxist-Leninist ideology, displays a high degree of patriotic enthusiasm and activity and plays a vanguard role in the building of a democratic country at present, can join the Workers' Party. And not only the workers but also the peasants and working intellectuals who fight resolutely at the head of the masses, can all be admitted to the Workers' Party.

Others maintain that now that the Workers' Party took shape, Marxism-Leninism should not be the guiding theory of the Party and the Communists should forsake the Marxist-Leninist principles. This is the most dangerous Rightist view.

The democratic revolution of Korea by no means progresses independently of the law of social development indicated by Marxism-Leninism but precisely according to that law.

The Korean Communists do not plan to build communism in our country right now. Our immediate task at the present time is to complete the anti-imperialist, anti-feudal democratic revolution. Today we Communists, in view of the international and internal situation and the character of Korean society, should take the most active part in the struggle to reform society along democratic lines and complete the stage of the democratic revolution at an early date, and should play the foremost role in all work of democratic construction.

Marxism-Leninism is the most scientific and revolutionary theory that illuminates the road of struggle for the people at each stage of social development, at each stage of development of the revolution and, accordingly, it also serves us as the only lodestar in executing the tasks of democratic revolution in Korea today. Therefore, the question can never arise that our Party should not take Marxism-Leninism as its guiding theory because it has become a mass Workers' Party or that the Communists should forsake Marxism-Leninism because they have become members of the Workers' Party.

Only as we Communists become more faithful to the principles of Marxism-Leninism and are closely armed with its ideology and theory, can we successfully fulfil the tasks of the present historical stage which we must inevitably go through in the struggle to attain our ultimate goal.

As pointed out above, the former is a "Left" tendency and the latter is a Right one. We must reject both of these tendencies and follow the correct line required by the Party and by Marxism-Leninism.

Second, the course of building up a powerful mass party through the amalgamation of the two Parties has revealed that there still exists a narrow-minded exclusionist tendency among some comrades. This is due to the lack of a clear understanding of the significance and fundamental purpose of the merger of the two Parties.

The Workers' Party, as a representative and defender of the interests of the broad labouring masses, aims to build a rich and strong, independent democratic state capable of assuring democratic freedom to the labouring masses of Korea and the democratic development of the country. That we have such a mass political party means that we are in a position to lead the broad labouring masses better and unite them more firmly. Only when the broad masses are organized and mobilized, can the victory of democracy and complete independence and sovereignty of Korea be won at the earliest possible date.

We must therefore overcome the hidebound sectarian, parochial viewpoints and all hues of exclusionist tendencies and strive to strengthen and develop our newly-established Workers' Party in every way, and rally the broad masses around our Party. We should subordinate everything to the struggle for democracy and the country's independence.

Third, some acts of weakening the work of the united front have been revealed following the foundation of the Workers' Party. This is also a wrong tendency.

The stronger our Party grows, the more humble it should be towards the friendly parties and the more open-mindedly it should co-operate with them and the closer relations it should maintain with them in the work of democratic construction.

Certain local Party organizations try to boss the show in the work of the organs of the people's power and in other work, adopting the arrogant position that the Workers' Party is almighty. This is a wrong tendency. Today we cannot tolerate acts of weakening or disorganizing the united front.

Last, it is said that there are individuals who claim that the recent merger of the two Parties is temporary and that the Party will certainly be split again some day. This is a groundless slander of the reactionary elements who allege that the recent merger is a trick of the Communists, and to spread such a calumny is a hostile act born from the intrigue to disrupt our Party.

That today our Party unites the broad sections of the workers, peasants and working intellectuals is not a temporary policy but a permanent one and, accordingly, the recent amalgamation of the Parties will be eternal.

We should know that the positions of our working people have changed fundamentally as a result of the introduction of the democratic reforms in north Korea after liberation. Our peasants have already been freed from feudal exploitation once and for all. The living conditions of the peasants are improved, their cultural standard is elevated and their consciousness, too, is undergoing a change. Our peasants took an active part in carrying out the democratic reforms including the agrarian reform, and are displaying high patriotic zeal in the work of democratic construction. The north Korean peasants of today are neither the peasants of the days of Japanese imperialism nor the peasants of the feudal age. Now our peasantry plays a great role in all spheres of politics, economy and culture and, together with the working class, it makes up the main detachment of the patriotic, democratic forces.

The same can be said of the intelligentsia. Formerly, the intellectuals served Japanese imperialism and the propertied classes, but now the absolute majority of the intellectuals in north Korea, except only a handful of elements, are working for the good of the people, particularly for the good of the labouring masses. In the brief period of slightly over one year after liberation, our scientists, technicians, teachers, physicians, writers and artists performed great deeds in democratic construction. They actively participated in carrying out the democratic reforms such as the agrarian reform, the Labour Law, the Law on Equality of the Sexes and the nationalization of industries, and are struggling with devotion to strengthen the people's power, rehabilitate the industries and develop educational and cultural work.

What does this show? This shows that the intellectuals in north Korea have quit their old position where they served the Japanese imperialists and propertied classes, and have changed and are changing into the intellectuals of the people serving their country and people.

Hence, it is reasonable that the staunchest, most conscious and most advanced persons from among not only the workers but also all the labouring masses, that is, the workers, peasants and intellectuals, can all be admitted to our Workers' Party.

As the democratic movement in our country progresses farther and our society develops on to a higher stage in the future, the social and economic positions of our workers, peasants and intellectuals will change further, their level of consciousness, too, will rise higher still, and their interests will be identified more closely with each other. Thus, the unity of the workers, peasants and working intellectuals will be further strengthened and, accordingly, the merger of the two Parties recently effected will become further consolidated.

As is clear from this, the allegation that the merger of the two Parties is temporary or that the Party will be split again in the future has no ground whatsoever. We should clearly understand that it is merely a slander of reactionary elements prompted by their design to wreck the cohesion of our labouring masses and the unity of our Party.

Dwelling upon the results of the work of merging the Parties at this meeting of the activists, I should like to set you some tasks as follows:

First, I put special stress on the need for you to make a profound study of all documents of the recent Inaugural Congress of our Party in connection with practical life and faithfully carry out the tasks set forth at the Congress. A decision which is not carried into effect in practical life, however good it may be, is useless.

Second, the greatest effort should be made to bring home to the entire Party membership the character and aims of the Workers' Party and its Programme and not only to expand the Party quantitatively but also to consolidate it qualitatively.

For this purpose, the propaganda departments of the Party should not concentrate their efforts only on propaganda work designed for the masses at large, but should direct their primary concern to the work of ideological education within the Party to raise the political and ideological level of the membership and increase the fighting efficiency of the Party before anything else. By so doing, every Party member should be made to acquire enough ability to lead the masses and become their core, and to become a pacemaker to the masses capable of uniting, organizing and educating them.

Third, Party members should have a clear understanding of the significance of the National Democratic United Front theoretically and play a vanguard role in the work of expanding and strengthening the united front.

We should always maintain close relations with the friendly parties and social organizations, properly unfold the joint struggle of people from all walks of life in the work of democratic construction, and should never compromise with anything that may impair the united front. Alongside this, in the work of the united front, our Party should by no means lose its identity but should always play the leading part and categorically reject tailist tendencies.

Fourth, all Party members should fight stubbornly to overcome Right or "Left" deviations, execute the Party's line correctly and strengthen the ideological unity in its ranks.

We should energetically wage a principled day-to-day ideological struggle among the Party members in order to expose **and crush all the sectarian and factional** activities and the anti-Party tendency of supporting the Party outwardly while betraying it behind its back and to prevent the penetration of all hues of hostile ideas into the Party.

Fifth, we should greatly heighten revolutionary vigilance, lay bare before the masses the intrigues and subversive activities of reactionary elements and enlist the united strength of the broad masses of the people in waging a mass struggle against those elements.

At present, the desperate manoeuvrings of the U.S. reactionaries and their lackeys, the traitorous Syngman Rhee clique in south Korea become more glaring every day.

In **south Korea the *Haebang Ilbo*, the organ of the Communist Party of South Korea, was closed down long ago, and** last September 5, democratic papers such as the *Choson Inminbo, Hyondae Ilbo,* and *Chungang Sinmun* were also forced out of existence. Evidently, these acts are committed by reactionary elements who, frightened by the victorious foundation of the Workers' Party of North Korea, are seeking to block the formation of a Workers' Party in south Korea and to prevent Korea from attaining independence and sovereignty.

As a matter of fact, the intrigues of the reactionary elements in south Korea are outrageous. According to the reactionary papers *Tonga Ilbo, Taedong Sinmun* and *Hansong Ilbo* of September 6, those elements spread the absurd report that on August 29, National Humiliation Day, more than 5,000 students in Pyongyang raided Soviet Army Headquarters and that over 2,000 students were killed or wounded in a clash with Soviet troops.

Comrades, who have ever killed and wounded Korean people? Who ever were they other than the reactionary elements that spilt the blood of south Korean people as they were going to celebrate the anniversary of the August 15 Liberation, by showering shells and bullets upon them from planes or with guns and rifles? Upset to see that the north Korean people were indignant at the atrocious murder case in Kwangju, those elements concocted such a false report.

We should not relax our vigilance against the reactionary elements even for a moment. These reactionary elements exist not only in south Korea but also in north Korea. We should smash these reactionary forces by relying on the strength of the masses of the people, the united democratic forces, and render the greatest material and moral support to the south Korean people.

Last, I should like to lay the main emphasis on the question of consolidating the people's committee. To consolidate the people's committee by no means implies that Workers' Party members should monopolize its work. We Workers' Party members should uphold the people's committee more actively than anybody else, unite the broad masses around it and should be exemplary in executing all its decisions.

Let us rally all the patriotic, democratic forces and march forward vigorously for the complete independence and sovereignty of the country and fresh victory of democracy, holding high the banner of the Workers' Party of North Korea which has taken the glorious first step through the fusion of the Communist Party with the New Democratic Party.

Long live the Workers' Party of North Korea!

Long live the accelerated struggle for the formation of the Workers' Party of South Korea!

Long live the National Democratic United Front!

Long live the complete independence of democratic Korea!

ON THE ESTABLISHMENT OF THE WORKERS' PARTY OF NORTH KOREA AND THE QUESTION OF FOUNDING THE WORKERS' PARTY OF SOUTH KOREA

September 26, 1946

The foundation of the Workers' Party representing and defending the interests of the labouring masses of Korea through the merger of the Communist Party and the New Democratic Party is the greatest event in the political life of our people at the present time. This great event has aroused profound social interest and focussed the attention of the entire people.

We have triumphantly completed the foundation of a unified Party of the labouring masses in north Korea.

In south Korea, however, the activities of those people who are sincerely striving for the merger of the Parties, are obstructed and the merger has not yet taken place owing to the divisive activities of those who are opposed to the merger and unity. The divisive activities of those who are against the merger are supported by the reactionary Right-wing camp.

As was expected, the reactionary forces have come all out to frustrate the merger of the democratic political parties of the working people. U.S. imperialism and its lackeys smuggled their spies into these parties to rig up the so-called "opposition groups" and cause unprincipled disputes and factional strifes in an attempt to split the democratic forces.

The criminal acts of the factionalists have caused a waste of time which is most precious for the liberation movement and created favourable conditions for the reactionary forces. This is precisely the basic cause of the delay in the merger of the Parties in south Korea.

We cannot on any account overlook the fact that the merger of the Parties is retarded in south Korea nor can we tolerate the double-dealing attitude of the factionalists. For only the unity and cohesion of the democratic forces throughout Korea is the prerequisite to the building of a new, genuinely democratic Korea and constitutes the most important guarantee of the political, economic and cultural development of our country.

We can attain victory only if we have a correct understanding and make a politically right assessment of this matter. For this purpose we must correctly grasp the following questions:

(1) What has happened in north and south Korea in the one year after liberation of the Korean people from the Japanese imperialist yoke of slavery, and what is the difference between them?

(2) Why is it that the merger of the political parties of the working people into a single party, the Workers' Party, and the unity of the entire working people are the most important, inevitable and undelayable task in the political life of our country at the present stage?

What are the tasks of the unified Workers' Party?

(3) What do the opponents of unity want and whither do they try to lead the Korean people?

(4) What, in the final analysis, are the immediate tasks at the present stage?

1

One year has already passed since Korea was liberated from the colonial rule of Japanese imperialism. Great changes have taken place in the political, economic and cultural life in north Korea in this short span of time.

In the past year we have laid a solid foundation for developing Korea along truly democratic lines and building a People's Republic by carrying out the great democratic reforms.

Our people, who took power into their own hands, have come to enjoy democratic rights and liberties never known at any period in the history of our country. This can be seen from the fact that the entire people take an active part in political life, and it is also graphically shown in the social composition of the people's committees.

The composition of the people's committee membership now active in north Korea is as follows:

Workers	5.7%
Peasants	71.8%
Office employees	15.8%
Handicraftsmen	2.1%
Tradesmen	4.6%

The people's committees, incorporating representatives of the broad masses of the people as seen above, strive to guard the interests of the people, maintaining close ties with them. All policies and activities of the people's committees are aimed, first of all, at the democratic development of our country and the enhancement of the well-being of the broad masses of the people.

In carrying out its policies, the people's committee relies on the firm unity and the democratic united front of all the political parties and social organizations. This united front embraces more than 6 million people from all walks of life. This covers nearly all the adult population of north Korea.

Before long the people in north Korea will elect people's committee members in accordance with the democratic Election Law. The forthcoming election will further extend and strengthen our people's power and the democratic forces united around it.

In this manner, the people's committees were set up on the strength of the broad masses of the people, and they have elevated the political zeal of the entire people in north Korea, thereby inducing them to take an active part in the building of a new, democratic Korea.

Already in March this year, the agrarian reform was carried out in the rural areas of north Korea, bringing about a radical change in production relations. The agrarian reform dealt a decisive blow to the landlord class, the most reactionary class in Korea, wiping out its economic base. The peasantry was freed from feudal exploitation and oppression and became the master of land, which had been their centuries-old aspiration. The peasants have not only come to work the land as their own, land which was distributed free by the people's committee, but also have got rid of the system of exorbitant forced delivery of farm produce plus all kinds of exacting taxes and levies extorted from them in the years of Japanese imperialism and have become free to dispose of their farm produce after delivering only 25 per cent of the harvests as tax in kind. As a result, the peasants' zeal for production has risen as never before and our agriculture which had been stagnant for a long time has embarked upon the course of rapid progress.

Last August the Provisional People's Committee of North Korea proclaimed the law on the nationalization of industrial, transport and communications facilities and banks which had been owned by the Japanese imperialists, pro-Japanese elements and traitors to the nation. With this we have brought under national ownership, ownership of the entire people, the backbone of the economy which constitutes the material basis for building a fully independent and democratic state.

In June this year, the Provisional People's Committee of North Korea promulgated the Labour Law freeing factory and office workers from harsh, colonial-type exploitation and introducing the eight-hour working day and a social insurance system. And a law was passed to guarantee the women social rights equal to those of the men for the first time in the history of our country.

Besides, the Provisional People's Committee of North Korea abolished the former system of colonial slave education, established a democratic educational system, and took measures to rapidly rehabilitate and develop the national culture and arts.

Last year boys and girls attended 2,387 primary schools and 91 middle schools, and 126 middle schools have been built anew this year. These figures show that the number of schools has increased by far as against the years of Japanese imperialist rule. Not only that, a university of the people has been built in no more than a year after liberation and now a teachers' training college and a medical college are in process of establishment, whereas there was not a single university in north Korea under Japanese imperialist rule, and 30 various new specialized technical schools are under construction around the major factories. At all schools lessons are given in the Korean language and over 50 types of textbooks have already been prepared and published in our language.

Over 8,000 adult schools were opened last year to eliminate illiteracy among persons beyond school age and provide them with general education. Besides, 83 theatres and cinema houses are in operation, 717 libraries have been set up and more than 30 newspapers are published in north Korea.

The people's committees have done a great deal of work to improve the material and cultural life of the masses of the people and to ensure their political rights. In north Korea the democratic political parties and such social organizations as the trade unions, the Peasants' Union, the Youth League, the Women's Union and the Arts Federation have been organized, with the result that the masses of the people freely participate in political life. The people are assured all political rights and complete freedom of speech, the press, assembly and association.

With the carrying out of the great democratic reforms a radical change took place in the socio-economic basis and the positions of all classes and strata in north Korea.

The enforcement of the Law on Nationalization of Industries has wiped out the foundation of Japanese imperialist colonial rule and deprived the traitors to the nation who had collaborated with Japanese imperialism of their economic footholds. The landlords whose land was confiscated were liquidated as a class once and for all. Thus, all the forces that had oppressed and exploited the Korean people hand in glove with Japanese imperialism, were deprived of their economic footholds and politically liquidated.

Meanwhile, the people's committees protect the property of the national capitalists and encourage the business activities of individual entrepreneurs and traders. They provide all the entrepreneurs and traders who support the democratic reforms and are ready to contribute to the improvement of the people's livelihood with possibilities for having a share in the important economic branches like industry and trade, and assist them in every way. In this manner, we ensure free business activities to entrepreneurs and traders and, at the same time, enlist and utilize all available capital for the development of the national economy.

Our working class that had been subjected to the most barbaric exploitation under Japanese imperialist rule, has now acquired the right to work at the state enterprises which have come under the people's ownership, and works for the people and society. The workers have won all rights and possibilities to take part in the state political life. Our working class constitutes the core of the democratic forces in north Korea, and its organization and its politico-ideological level are quickly rising.

Our peasants have also been freed from the feudal exploitation of the landlords and are able to work freely on the land which has come into their possession. The peasants who have become masters of land are taking an active part in the building of an independent democratic state and their political enthusiasm is running ever higher.

The positions of the intelligentsia have also changed. The absolute majority of our intellectuals have closely united with the entire working people. No longer our intellectuals serve Japanese imperialism and the exploiters as before, but are working with all loyalty for their state, nation and working people. They regard the interests of the state and the people as their own. This means that their views and ideas have changed and that they are resolved to work with all devotion for the country and the people.

All these changes have further strengthened the political unity of the workers, peasants and working intellectuals. Their united strength is the basis of the National Democratic United Front in the struggle for building a new Korea and, at the same time, constituted the unshakable foundation for the merger of the Communist Party and the New Democratic Party into a unified party of the toiling masses.

The establishment of the Workers' Party through the merger of the two Parties is of tremendous historical significance in expanding and strengthening the democratic forces and promoting democratic construction in our country.

A party is the advanced detachment of a class defending its interests and fighting for the realization of its demands and aspirations. The Communist Party as the advanced detachment of the working class has fought in behalf of the interests of the working class. The New Democratic Party was active as a party defending primarily the interests of the peasants and the working intellectuals. Thus, the Communist Party and the New Democratic Party represented the interests of different classes; nevertheless, they fought under a common programme since their inception. This can be explained by the fact that the workers, peasants and working intellectuals are all labouring masses and their interests are identical.

The working class gave active support and assistance in

carrying out the agrarian reform. It is because they were fully aware that agriculture could be developed at a fast tempo only when the feudal tenant system was abolished and the peasants were freed from bondage to the landlords, and that without the development of agriculture neither industry could advance nor the prosperity and development of the country and improvement of the people's welfare could be achieved.

The peasants actively supported the Law on Nationalization of Industries and the Labour Law, for they knew that unless the economic footholds of Japanese colonial rule and the residue of the cruel, colonial-type forced labour were removed, industry could not be developed and this, after all, would also prevent the development of agriculture.

Our intellectuals were also aware that the execution of the democratic reforms was in full accord with their vital interests, and so participated in it with keen interest.

Thus, the common interests of the workers, peasants and working intellectuals determined the common goals and tasks of the Communist Party and the New Democratic Party and furnished the basis for the common struggle of the two Parties for the independence and democratization of the country. That is why the two Parties, actively supporting the people's committee, waged a common struggle for carrying out the democratic reforms including the agrarian reform and nationalization of industries.

Owing to such common features and interests the two Parties have merged into a single party—the Workers' Party.

The greater success the democratic movement gains and the farther our society advances in the future, the closer the unity of the workers, peasants and working intellectuals will become and the stronger the unity and cohesion of the Workers' Party established through the merger of the two Parties will grow. Thus, the foundation of the Workers' Party marks an event of great historical and political significance in strengthening the unity and cohesion of the working people and further developing our country. The Workers' Party as the advanced detachment of the labouring masses of Korea—the workers, peasants and working intellectuals—will lead the entire people to the complete independence and sovereignty of the country and the final victory of democracy.

Our Party, however, is not the one and only Party existing in our country. From this arises the question of mutual relations with other parties and other classes.

Our Party gives active support to the democratic demands of the Chongu Party, and closely co-operates with it in order to advance together in step with it. The Chongu Party, in spite of its religious characteristics, can advance hand in hand with our Party for Korea's independence and democracy.

As for the Democratic Party that represents the interests of part of the intellectuals and the traders and entrepreneurs, our Party will likewise support its democratic programme. For the rapid rehabilitation of the national economy, we encourage the business activities of the national capitalists and actively draw the traders and entrepreneurs into democratic construction.

In this way our Party has waged and is waging a common struggle in unity with all the democratic political parties. We must maintain closer ties with members of the Chongu Party and the Democratic Party and unite with them more firmly under the banner of democracy, thereby steadily expanding and strengthening the National Democratic United Front.

Our Party is now confronted with weighty and complex tasks. To carry out these tasks successfully it is necessary, first of all, to consolidate the successes gained in the merger of the Parties and strengthen and develop our young Party organizationally and ideologically.

We must by all means bring the lines and strategic and tactical policies of the Party home to all its membership and arm the entire Party with the scientific Marxist-Leninist theory and thoroughgoing revolutionary ideas. Thus, we must make each Party member a conscious revolutionary fighter who struggles most courageously for the freedom and happiness of the people, and must turn our Workers' Party into the steel-strong, core detachment of all the patriotic, democratic forces.

2

The actual situation in south Korea is fundamentally different from that in north Korea. There the U.S. military government, having seized all power, oppresses the Korean people, and the introduction of democratic reforms is quite inconceivable.

Some people think that south Korea merely lags behind north Korea. This is an utterly wrong viewpoint implying that south Korea, too, is advancing along the road to democracy, only at a little slower tempo than north Korea. In reality, north Korea is advancing along the road of democratic development, whereas south Korea is moving along an entirely different course.

The indicator by which to tell democracy from pseudo-democracy lies in whether the people can participate in the state administration or not. And the south Korean people are denied the right to participate in government. They have not the slightest elementary democratic rights.

The people's committees set up by the south Korean people immediately after liberation were not recognized and, worse still, they were dissolved and their functionaries were arrested and thrown into jail. The democratic political parties, deprived of the freedom of political activities, are forced to go underground.

It is the Communist Party of all democratic political parties that is waging the most determined struggle for the freedom and independence of the country and happiness of the working people. This is a hard fact admitted by all conscientious people of Korea. And how have the U.S. imperialists and their lackeys who are obstructing the democratic independence and sovereignty of Korea dealt and are dealing with the Communist Party of South Korea? Those villains have arrested, imprisoned and murdered large numbers of the leading cadres and members of the Communist Party and banned its organ *Haebang-ilbo*. To lower the prestige of the Communist Party in the eyes of the masses of the people, the reactionaries have fabricated the so-called forged-note case and staged a farcical trial for it; they have framed the so-called "Right-Left collaboration" plot in an attempt to isolate the Communist Party.

Not only the members of the Communist Party but also those of the People's Party and the New Democratic Party are subjected to suppression and persecution. The reactionaries persecuted Mr. Ryo Un Hyong, the leader of the People's Party, and went so far as to attempt to strangle him in their brigandish violence.

The reactionaries are perpetrating barbarous acts—suspending democratic publications, arresting a large number of members of the democratic political parties, forming terrorist bands to murder patriots in the streets in broad daylight, and so on. The terrorist acts of the reactionaries grow more violent with every passing day and their suppression of the democratic forces becomes still more outrageous.

The persecution of the working class, in particular, has reached extremes. See the massacre in Kwangju of last August 15! With tanks, planes, machine guns and bayonets the Yankees attacked over 1,000 workers of the Hwasun Colliery who were marching towards the city of Kwangju to attend the mass meeting in honour of the anniversary of August 15, killing one and wounding 109 seriously or lightly. What a cruel fact this is! There have taken place tens and hundreds of cases of atrocities of this type committed by the enemy, which are sternly condemned by the whole nation. This is precisely the so-called "democratic order" of the Syngman Rhee clique and this is the "humanitarian assistance" to Korea which the Americans are advertising loudly.

The land problem has not been solved at all in south Korea. The peasants are subjected to merciless exploitation by the landlords and suffer from all kinds of exacting levies and the forced delivery of farm products as in the Japanese imperialist years. The only change, if any, is the transfer to the Korean squires of the land owned by the Japanese landlords and the replacement of the "Oriental Development Company" of Japanese imperialism by the "New Korea Company" of U.S. imperialism.

Far from enforcement of a labour law, the workers are exploited more harshly than ever before and are suffering from unemployment and hunger. The industrial establishments which were owned by Japanese imperialists and the traitors to the nation, far from being nationalized, have rather turned into means for the pro-Japanese stooges and profiteers to line their pockets greedily.

The women, far from emancipation, find themselves in an indescribably wretched plight.

All facts thus irrefutably prove that the goings-on in south Korea are totally different from the developments in north Korea. A firm basis of democracy for the people has been laid in north Korea, whereas the traitorous Syngman Rhee clique with the undisguised backing of the U.S. military government are openly pursuing an anti-popular, anti-democratic policy in south Korea. They are scheming to set up a reactionary ruling machine which, while hanging out the signboard of "democracy," aims, to all intents and purposes, at oppressing the entire Korean people.

In this grave situation, the primary task of our nation and the entire working people is to unite and unite.

Then, what kind of unity do we advocate? Though there are varied arguments about it, the unity we advocate is a unity based on the interests of the toiling masses, namely, the interests of the workers, peasants and working intellectuals. There can be genuine unity only when it is based on this correct principle.

Contrary to this, both the "Right-Left collaboration" pursued by the reactionary clique in south Korea under the manipulation of the U.S. military government and the "unity" with the traitorous Right-wing forces sought after by the Rightist elements in the Left-wing camp are all anti-popular "unity" detrimental to the interests of the labouring masses and the entire people. Such "unity" is a "unity" pandering to the activities of the reactionary groups. We do not need "unity" of this kind.

Genuine democrats must wage an uncompromising struggle against the attempt to forge "unity" of this kind. For such a "unity" will undermine the democratic forces, help the reactionaries and hamper the democratization of Korea.

The factionalists and anti-Party elements who have sneaked into the democratic political parties are noising abroad as if the "unity" they are pleading is for the good of the country and the people; but it is, to all intents and purposes, an act profiting the enemy, which will break up the working masses and help the U.S. imperialists and the traitorous clique.

We call for such unity of the toiling masses as can meet the democratic demands of the workers, peasants and working intellectuals. All democrats must wage a resolute struggle for genuine unity to safeguard the interests of the labouring masses.

The fact that the Communist Party and the New Democratic Party merged and developed into the Workers' Party in north Korea has exerted influence to induce a similar movement for merger in south Korea, too. The initiator of the movement was the leadership of the People's Party; it proposed the merger to the Communist Party and the New Democratic Party on its own initiative. Though more than one month has already passed since the proposal was put forth, the movement has failed to proceed successfully as yet.

The broad segments of the labouring masses in south Korea, aware of the need for unity, are strongly demanding it. Many social organizations in south Korea, for instance, have adopted resolutions calling for the unity of the parties of the working people. The resolutions adopted by the National Council of Trade Unions and the National Confederation of Peasants' Associations point out that the entire memberships of the two organizations unreservedly support the merger. Besides, the joint statement issued by the Central Committee of the Culture and Arts Federation, the National Women's Union, the Co-operative Committee, the Democratic Youth League, etc., stresses that they condemn those who are bent on divisive manoeuvres in opposition to unity and that they give unqualified support to the merger of the three Parties.

The functionaries in the lower bodies of the Communist Party, People's Party and New Democratic Party and all their members, realizing the necessity of merging the three Parties, have actively come out for its early materialization.

The merger movement developing on such a mass scale is of tremendous significance. The movement shows that the merger of the three Parties is the most urgent question at the present stage and represents the unanimous demand of the broad masses. All democrats must duly heed this mass demand.

Meanwhile, a preparatory committee for the merger of the Parties was set up in south Korea, and it has drawn up and made public the draft programme for the merger. This is a democratic programme, a programme that is correct in principle. We give an unreserved approval to this programme.

The question of merger, however, has not yet been solved, and, considering the whole situation, its solution is likely to be much delayed. What is obstructing the accomplishment of this important task?

It is the difficulties created by the hostile activities and subversive plots of the reactionaries supported by the U.S. military government. The reactionaries, manipulated by the U.S. military government, are making every vicious attempt to frustrate the merger. They are brutally persecuting the leaders of the democratic Left-wing political parties and social organizations, and have wantonly suspended or banned progressive publications in south Korea.

Along with this, another main cause of the retarded merger is the factional acts of the anti-Party elements who are manoeuvring within the Parties which are to be amalgamated.

An anti-Party group has appeared within the Central Committee of the Communist Party of South Korea. Six anti-Party elements who belong to the group insist that although they themselves agree to the merger, it should necessarily be approved at a Party Congress. They argue that a merger without the approval of the Party Congress is a violation of the democratic principles of the Party. Upon what grounds do they charge that the democratic principles of the Party are being violated?

In north Korea the merger proceeded in general along the following course. Namely, the question of merger was decided at the Central Committee of the New Democratic Party at first, and then at the Central Committee of the Communist Party. After that, the question was discussed and decided at a Joint Enlarged Meeting of the Central Committees of the Two Parties, and the draft Programme and Rules of the Workers' Party and the Declaration on the merger were submitted to the lower organizations of both Parties for discussion. Following the discussions at the lower organizations of the Parties, the conferences of the provincial, city and county Party organizations elected delegates to the Inaugural Congress of the Workers' Party. Thus, the merger of the two Parties was finally decided at the Inaugural Congress of the Workers' Party attended by the delegates from both Parties.

Do the anti-Party factionalists think that this way of solving the question runs counter to the democratic principles?

If the anti-Party group had had a truly close link with the masses and paid deep attention to their opinions, it would not have committed the grave anti-Party mistake. If the anti-Party group is really conversant with the democratic principles and respects them, why does it not pay heed to the demand of the Party members and the toiling masses who earnestly desire to fuse the Parties quickly without missing the chance and without delay, in the serious situation of reaction prevailing in south Korea? This only proves that the factionalists have got too far out of touch with the masses. Therefore, their anti-Party acts amount, in the final analysis, to opposing the merger itself and helping the reactionaries in their divisive operations, whether by design or not.

These actions of the anti-Party group are doubtlessly attributable to sheer position-seeking. And position-seeking helps the reactionaries and disorganizes the parties of the labouring masses from within. So, the expulsion of the anti-Party elements by the Central Committee of the Communist Party of South Korea is a correct measure. Otherwise, the revolutionary ranks would be torn asunder.

Similar anti-Party elements are found within the People's Party and the New Democratic Party as well. The factionalists in these Parties, like attracting like as fellow factionalists, have gone to the extent of scheming to cook up a separate "Workers' Party."

But no matter how viciously the factionalists might try by means of sophistry, tricks and schemes, the party which they are seeking to organize could not be a militant party for the labouring masses but would only become a party of compromise with the reactionary Rightist elements and traitors.

It is said that the factionalists have even drawn up a programme for "unity" and a programme for organizing the "Workers' Party." But no matter how much they might embellish their programmes, the anti-Party elements cannot conceal the fact that they are helping the reactionaries and only pursuing their dirty ends.

The factionalists have perhaps forgotten that the separatists making up the minority who act in an unprincipled way against the majority will eventually go over to the side of the traitors to the nation and the enemies of the people.

Besides, some members of the democratic parties are standing in the way of the merger because they fail to have a principled, correct understanding of the need for it. For instance, some elements maintain that the present merger is momentary and temporary. What sort of temporariness are they ever talking about? This is quite a wrong view.

A party, whatever party it may be, cannot hope for eternal existence. Because a party is not a party for its own sake, but a weapon necessary for achieving the aims of a certain class.

And it is clear to everybody that the Communist Party, the People's Party and the New Democratic Party are parties of the working people with common aims. What are the aims which the labouring masses of Korea are struggling for today? They aim to establish a unified, democratic provisional government in Korea at an early date, effect thoroughgoing democratic reforms in south Korea, too, as in north Korea, expand and consolidate the democratic victories already gained, and build the rich and strong, fully independent and sovereign democratic state that is required by the Korean people. And even after winning victory in this battle, our working people must all join in a struggle for a better future. This historic cause of the Korean workers, peasants and working intellectuals and their common interests determine the common tasks of the parties of the labouring masses, provide the possibility for and raise the necessity of their merger and unity. This being the case, how can it be said that the merger of the parties of the working people could be momentary and temporary?

And certain people say that unity is impossible because of the difference between the Programmes of the Parties.

If so, does the Programme of the People's Party tally with those of the reactionary Right-wing parties? No. The Programme of the People's Party is poles apart from those of reactionary Right-wing parties and contrasts fundamentally with them. Then, what does it mean that certain elements, shoving aside the question of merging the parties of the labouring masses, insist on the so-called "Right-Left collaboration" and go so far as to hold consultations on it? What could their idea be when they say it is impossible to merge the democratic parties with their programmes in common, while maintaining that it is possible to collaborate with the reactionary political parties whose programmes totally differ from theirs, with nothing in common between them? The intention of those who say so is, in a word, nothing but to desert the democratic Left-wing camp and go over to the anti-popular, anti-democratic, reactionary Right-wing camp.

True, there exist some differences between the programmes of the democratic political parties, but their programmes have more common and coincidental points. These common points provide them with the possibility of waging a joint struggle against the common enemy and uniting into one for accomplishing the same goals. Must we fight and beat the reactionaries by swiftly achieving the unity of the parties of the working people based on common aims and interests? Or else, must we be crushed by the enemy by operating separately and scatteredly? To this question everybody will answer with one voice that the merger of the Parties is the only correct solution.

All democrats, truly mindful of the interests of the labouring masses, must overcome the intrigues and obstructions set up by the reactionary forces, expose and crush the divisive actions of the position-seekers, self-seekers and factional elements, and awake some of their Party members who do not yet have a correct understanding of the merger, thereby completing the work of merging the Parties with concerted efforts in a short span of time.

* * *

United, we stand; divided, we fall.

The independence and sovereignty of Korea on democratic lines can be achieved at an early date only if the labouring masses are united as one and all the democratic forces are knit together.

The establishment of a unified party of the labouring masses is a decisive guarantee for accelerating the expansion and strengthening of the democratic forces and for assuring the triumph of democracy. This has been confirmed by the experience in north Korea where the fusion of the Communist Party and the New Democratic Party has been realized with triumph in a short period of time.

Let us concentrate all efforts on the struggle for the unity of the labouring masses and the foundation of a mass party in south Korea!

Victory belongs to the Korean people who aspire to unity, national independence and democracy. Let us all march forward confidently to victory!

ON THE EVE OF THE HISTORIC DEMOCRATIC ELECTION

Speech Delivered at a Pyongyang City Celebration of the Democratic Election

November 1, 1946

Dear fellow countrymen, brothers and sisters,

The day of election to the people's committees falls on the coming November 3, and it is a day of great significance in the life of our people.

For many ages our people have had no experience in establishing a power according to their own will, nor have they ever had the experience in electing the organ of power with their own hands. In the past the handful of rulers who oppressed the people forged their power by force from above without regard to the people's will, and so it was always an anti-popular and bureaucratic power. But such a dark age is now over.

We have become able to freely elect the people's committees, a genuine people's power, for the first time in the history of our nation. November 3, therefore, is to our people a day of historic significance, a glorious holiday.

On the occasion of this happy, significant election day, I offer warm congratulations to the Pyongyang citizens and to the entire people.

Dear brothers and sisters,

A little over one year has passed since our country was liberated from the Japanese imperialist yoke of colonial rule.

The past year is, though short, a period of great change comparable, in view of the various events that took place in north Korea, to hundreds of years of past history.

The democratic reforms carried out during this period with the active support and enthusiastic participation of the entire people have radically changed the whole face of our society and laid the solid basis for the establishment of a Democratic People's Republic of Korea. As a result of the agrarian reform, the feudal system of exploitation has been abolished in the countryside and the peasants who till the fields have become masters of the land. The industrial establishments owned by the Japanese imperialists and the traitors to the nation having been nationalized, the material basis of colonial dependence has been liquidated. Along with this, a progressive Labour Law beneficial to the workers and office employees, a law on the emancipation of women from social inequalities, a law on the protection of private property, etc., are in force, and the work of abolishing the Japanese imperialist system of slave education and setting up a new, popular educational system is equally well under way.

People from all walks of life have been rallied closely around the people's committees, and the political enthusiasm of the popular masses is running exceptionally high.

That such great changes could be effected in the life of our people in a short span of time is entirely attributable to the fact that the people's committee, a people's power, has thoroughly protected the interests of the people and led the entire people unwaveringly towards the victory of democracy.

From the first day of their liberation from the colonial yoke of Japanese imperialism, our people launched out on the road of founding the people's committees, their power. The immense vitality of the people's committees lies in the fact that this power has close ties with the people and has struck its roots deep among the masses of the people. The people's committees have clearly shown through their practical activities that they are a type of political power best suited to the realities of Korea and capable of realizing the centuries-old dream of the masses of the people in the best way. Our people have been convinced through actual life that the people's committees are precisely their genuine political power. Hence, it is time now to develop the provincial, city and county people's committees in north Korea which have so far been provisional power organs into legally solid organs of power.

The people's committees were established on the initiative of the Korean people in all parts of north and south Korea right after liberation. From this fact alone it can be seen that the people's committees are a type of political power which represents the unanimous aspirations and earnest desire of the Korean people. In north Korea the people's committees have clearly demonstrated their vast superiority and vitality and won high prestige and confidence from the masses of the people.

In sharp contrast to this, however, in south Korea the people's committees have been suppressed and dissolved and it has become impossible to realize the wishes and long-cherished desire of the people.

The south Korean people have been deprived of their power and do not have such liberties and rights as are enjoyed by the people in north Korea. Although in south Korea the people have been liberated from the Japanese imperialist yoke, nothing has ever changed in their position, and it has become utterly unthinkable to carry out such democratic reforms as in north Korea. We deem it highly deplorable.

That the situation has come to this pass is not the people's fault, but is the consequence of the criminal manoeuvres of the reactionary elements against the decision of the Moscow Three Foreign Ministers Conference. Such criminal manoeuvres of the reactionaries have made it impossible for the Korean people till now to set up a unified democratic government for themselves, and keep them split into the north and the south.

No desperate efforts on the part of the enemy, however, will be able to check the Korean people's struggle to establish a unified, independent, sovereign and democratic state. Our country will certainly be reunified, and when reunification is realized, the entire Korean people will be able to enjoy all the benefits of freedom and democracy together.

The people's committees to be elected this time are confronted with the heavy task of expediting our cause of state building further still.

To make our country a rich and strong independent state, the people's committees should further consolidate and develop all the successes already scored in the democratic reforms. First of all, agriculture should be developed rapidly and the peasants' livelihood be improved on the basis of the results of the agrarian reform. Simultaneously with this, the solid economic foundations should be laid for the building of a democratic state and the living standard of the entire people be raised markedly, by rehabilitating and developing industry and transport which are now owned by the people. And private property should be protected and individual business activities be encouraged and developed in industry and trade.

The people's committee should ensure the development of education of the rising generation and the advancement of science, literature and arts, and should do away at an early date with the evil aftermaths of Japanese imperialism in these domains. Particularly, it should train a large number of scientific and technical personnel to fill up the shortage of native cadres which constitutes the biggest obstacle in the way of our advance.

Under the guidance of the people's committee our people should strengthen friendship and solidarity with the peoples of the countries in the international democratic camp headed by the Soviet Union and continue to develop the co-operation with the freedom-loving peoples of all countries of the world in the struggle for preservation and consolidation of world peace.

All these are most important tasks confronting the organ of our people's power at the present stage, and when they are thoroughly carried out, the historic cause of founding a

Democratic People's Republic of Korea, a rich, strong, independent and democratic state, will be accomplished.

We have enough conditions to carry out these tasks successfully. We have the genuine people's power established on the initiative of the people and the might of our awakened people united closely around it. In north Korea our people are masters of the country and all the natural resources have also become their property. If the entire people devote their all to the struggle for the independence and sovereignty of the country and for its prosperity and development, united ever more firmly around the people's committee, they will successfully overcome whatever grave difficulties and certainly win a brilliant victory.

The coming election to the people's committees, therefore, is of really great significance to the political life of our people. The forthcoming election will further reinforce our people's power, thereby consolidating the results of the democratic reforms carried out in north Korea and providing firm guarantee for the establishment of a rich, strong, independent and democratic state.

We should all take part in the election with a high degree of political zeal and elect to the people's committees the finest and most talented and conscientious persons who can serve the country and people faithfully.

There are now elements who spread various kinds of false rumours in an attempt to obstruct a plain sailing of the election to the people's committees. We should sharpen our vigilance against them.

Some are slinging mud at the forthcoming election, alleging that the power elected by the people themselves cannot be a true power and that the people themselves cannot politicize. According to their view, a power can be a real one only when it is framed up by someone from above or forcibly introduced from without by a foreign country. Those who make such allegations usually refer to the old society and say, "Our ancestors, too, lived that way." And what sort of power is it at all, the power framed up from above? It is a power of the rich established without the people's participation, an inequitable power of the minority against the majority. It is a fact well known to all through a long history that such a power pursued the policy of oppressing the people and defending the exploiters. And our people know better than anyone else through their own bitter experience how barbarous and predatory the power framed up forcibly by another country is.

Therefore, those who reject the power elected by the people themselves are, in fact, persons who want to return to the past when the people were subjected to oppression and maltreatment and who attempt to bring our people under the humiliating yoke of colonial slavery again.

And some others demand that the election be put off because it is premature. This is not right, of course.

Though of a provisional nature, the people's committee organized in the past year proved itself, through its policies and work, to be an excellent form of power best suited to the actual conditions of our country, and won high prestige from the broad masses of the people.

Under the guidance of the people's committee our people carried out great democratic reforms and laid the solid foundations for the establishment of an independent and sovereign state. To consolidate and develop the successes of the democratic reforms further still, the people's committee which is provisional in character should be developed into a legally solid one, into a people's committee established through an election. We should, therefore, hold the election on the scheduled day without fail. There is no reason now why we should put it off.

Those who allege the prematurity of the election are persons who do not believe the people's committee to be the people's power, but who undoubtedly demand some other type of power which is not the people's power. They are individuals who consider that the Korean people are not yet capable of self-government and that Korea is still unable to become independent and sovereign; they are the people's enemies bent on frustrating our democratic election.

Yet others insist that no priests and pastors should be elected to the people's committee membership nor should religious believers take part in the election. According to their view, participation in the election constitutes an act of betrayal to the religions. This is sheer nonsense uttered by some of the reactionaries with the sinister intention of inducing the religionists to boycott the forthcoming election.

To be elected to the people's committee membership means enjoying the confidence of the people and entering their service. There should be no such religion as prohibits the believers, priests and pastors from working for their country and people. I think that the believers of any religion, pastors or priests without exception can and ought to work for the people, if they are real patriots. So, a good and patriotic religionist, no matter who he is, can be elected to the people's committees and can elect their members, and can and must take part zealously in their work.

In north Korea the freedom of religion is guaranteed and no religion is suppressed or restricted. All religious persons in north Korea enjoy the full rights and liberties due to a citizen, and they are to take part in the forthcoming election to the people's committees with equal rights. Thus, many pastors and priests have been put up as candidates for people's committee members, and the greater part of the believers are participating in the election work with zeal.

If any of the religious figures try to oppose the participation of the believers, priests and pastors in the forthcoming election under the plea of the religious traditions and doctrines, they must be spies attempting to use religion for their subversive activities, bribed by a foreign country. Those persons try to play upon the good sentiments of the believers and cheat them with the object of conducting subversive activities at the time of election. Certain Protestant pastors, for instance, act in this manner. They are pawns of the enemy who seeks to turn Korea into a colony again. We do not doubt that the believers themselves will lay bare and reject those traitorous pastors who disguise themselves as "friends of believers," but who, in reality, are their enemies and enemies of the entire Korean people.

And still others maintain that women should not be elected as people's committee members and even that they should not be allowed to take part in the election. This is also a wrong idea.

Women account for half of the population. If half of the people do not take part in the election of the organ of power or in its work, such a power can hardly be called a genuine people's power. Women constitute a great force, and large numbers of women are sharing in the work of rehabilitating our country no less creditably than men. In our country women are guaranteed by law completely equal rights with men in all fields. The Law on Equality of the Sexes, therefore, should be fully enforced in the election to the people's committees, too, and only then can the election be a really democratic election.

The election to the people's committees we are going to hold soon is the most progressive and democratic election. This is evident above all from the social composition of the candidates. The candidates jointly put up by our National Democratic United Front for membership of the people's committees comprise representatives of many democratic parties, independent personalities and representatives of people in all walks of life such as workers, peasants, office employees, tradesmen, entrepreneurs, handicraftsmen and men of religion. It is quite unthinkable anywhere, unless it be in a really democratic society where the people have become masters of their own destiny, that workers and peasants elect a large number of their representatives to the power. Many representatives of the intelligentsia are among the candidates, and I think this is also reasonable. Our intellectuals, who serve with all their energies and talents in the building of a rich and strong country and in the creation of a happy life for the people, should as a matter of course play an important role in the people's committees together with the workers and peasants.

The election of people's committee members is an election

wholly based on universal and equal suffrage. All citizens of our country have equal right to be elected and to elect. In no respect, regardless of party affiliation, property status, conditions of residence, religious beliefs and others, discrimination or restriction is put on their right to elect and to be elected.

That the forthcoming election is the most democratic election is also to be seen from the fact that the people themselves **cast secret ballots for the candidates and directly elect the people's committee members. An indirect election is not** necessary at all in electing a genuine people's power, and that form of election is used to deceive the people by the privileged circles who are afraid of them.

The truly popular character of our power and its great tasks place quite heavy duties on the members of the people's committees who are to be elected soon. Our people's committee members should have boundless love for their country and people, devote all their energies and talents to faithfully serve the people and, no matter what difficulties they may encounter, should fight to the end unflinchingly, solely for the interests of the people, surmounting all the difficulties by displaying gallantry and devotion.

The members of the people's committees are statesmen and servants of the people. They should always be principled and fair in executing all kinds of work, properly organize and lead the people, and make day-to-day efforts to raise their own political and intellectual levels. People's committee members should become functionaries who maintain close bonds with the people, carefully listen to their demands and know how to teach the people and also learn from them, and who know always to examine their own work and eliminate its shortcomings. The duties of the people's committee member are heavy but honourable, indeed.

Our constituents should elect such advanced workers to the people's committees, and the elected members should discharge their duties creditably.

And the electors should always check up on the work of the people's committee member they have elected, and if he fails to acquit himself well of his work or goes back on the confidence of the people, should recall him and recommend another person faithful to the people for the people's committee membership in his place.

Dear fellow countrymen, brothers and sisters,

Today our people feel a boundless pride in electing by their own hands the people's committees, the genuine people's power, and greet the election day with hope and confidence.

All the electors should participate without exception in the election to the organ of people's power on the coming November 3 and fulfil their sacred duty to the country. The electors should vote for the fine representatives of people of all classes and strata, for the candidates put up by the National Democratic United Front, for the real patriots who ardently love their country and people and are fighting devotedly to build a rich and strong independent democratic state.

Election day is quite close at hand and the election campaign has reached its height. At such a time there may appear persons who attempt to obstruct our historic election. We should ensure a brilliant victory in the democratic election by thoroughly smashing the manoeuvres of the reactionaries who are bent on frustrating it.

Our people, liberated from the Japanese imperialist yoke of colonial rule, have already achieved a tremendous success in building a new life by their devoted efforts. But this is no more than the first step in building a rich and powerful democratic country, and we are confronted with difficult and heavy tasks. In the future we should establish an independent and sovereign democratic state, rapidly rehabilitate and develop the national economy, promote the material well-being of the entire people and make our national culture bloom and develop.

To carry out all these tasks successfully, our organ of people's power should be further strengthened and the unity and cohesion of the entire people be cemented further still. The forthcoming election to the provincial, city and county people's committees is of very great importance in this respect. The entire people, therefore, should guarantee success in the forthcoming election by their united efforts and concerted action and forge ahead vigorously for a new great victory in the cause of building a democratic country.

Each and every Korean citizen who loves the country and desires happiness for himself and the entire people, should go to the polls and vote for the candidates to the people's committees.

It is my firm belief that you will all zealously take part in the imminent election to the provincial, city and county people's committees and demonstrate the indomitable will of the Korean people to attain the freedom and complete independence of the country, and demonstrate to the whole world that our awakened and united people are capable of self-government and are fully able to build their country into an advanced, independent democratic state.

CLOSING UP THE CONGRESS OF THE PROVINCIAL, CITY AND COUNTY PEOPLE'S COMMITTEES OF NORTH KOREA

Concluding Speech Delivered at a Congress of the Provincial, City and County People's Committees of North Korea

February 20, 1947

Delegates,

At this Congress we have triumphantly accomplished another work which will shine forth forever in our history.

The present Congress has clearly shown that all the delegates present here are true representatives of the people, qualified to stand at the head of the people, bearing the destiny of the nation on their shoulders.

The Congress has vividly demonstrated that our people are firmly united around the people's committee, their own power organ, and that they are fully able to build an independent, sovereign state by their own hands.

The democratic reforms carried out last year and the historic victory in the democratic election of November 3 and then the resolutions adopted by the present Congress have proved that our people earnestly desire a democratic life in all domains of politics, economy and culture and that they have sufficient ability to materialize it for themselves. Now no one can deny the ability of the Korean nation to build an independent and sovereign democratic state. If the reactionary clique of Syngman Rhee, Kim Song Su and the like in Seoul had not disrupted the unity of our nation and if the entire people of north and south Korea had fought united as one in mind and purpose, we would have already established a unified government and achieved the complete independence and sovereignty of the nation after tearing down the 38th parallel.

The Congress has brought us the profound realization that the unity of our people has been further consolidated and that their strength has grown remarkably, and it has convinced us that we can overcome all difficulties and obstacles lying in our way of building the country and achieve a new, greater victory.

Delegates,

We have done a really great work at this Congress. We have sanctioned all our democratic laws in the name of the entire people at the Congress. Thus, all our laws have taken on a perfectly democratic form and the democratic reforms carried out under these laws have been legally approved by the entire people. This is another severe blow at the reactionary clique that attempts to hinder the democratic construction by our people.

The reactionaries have propagated that all the laws including the Agrarian Reform Law were provisional because they were promulgated by the Provisional People's Committee. They have noised abroad that once a reactionary regime is set up, these laws will be repealed and that the democratic reforms effected under these laws will also be invalidated. Last year when the Agrarian Reform Law was proclaimed and the agrarian reform was carried out, the reactionary elements prattled: "Don't be overjoyed that you have got land," and "Don't be grieved that you have lost your land." By this it was meant that though people who received land were glad of it now, they would be deprived of the land in the future, and those who lost their land could take it back. But now this jargon-like wild story of the reactionary clique cannot fool anyone. Our laws are not provisional ones but are permanent laws of the people sanctioned by the entire people. We declare: "Those who have received land, rejoice for all time; the land belongs forever to the peasants who till it."

One of the most important matters decided upon at the present Congress is that a national economic plan has been adopted.

To build an independent democratic state, the basis of an independent economy of one's own nation should be built without fail, and to lay the basis of an independent economy, the national economy should be developed rapidly. Without the basis of an independent economy we can neither achieve independence, nor can we build a state or maintain our existence.

That we have entered upon the road of planned development of our national economy on the basis of the successes achieved in the democratic reforms in one year after liberation, means that we have taken the first step in the great work of laying the economic basis for the building of an independent and sovereign state, and it acquires a tremendous historic importance. We should exert every effort for the successful carrying out of the 1947 Plan for Development of the National Economy.

At the present Congress we have created the People's Assembly, the supreme organ of state power of our people. This is a truly popular form of power required by our people. At the People's Assembly the Deputies elected directly by the people, representing their will, institute all laws which safeguard the interests of the people, and organize the People's Committee, the power organ of the people capable of executing these laws faithfully. After we close this Congress today, the Deputies to the People's Assembly will sit together and reorganize the Provisional People's Committee of North Korea into the People's Committee of North Korea. The People's Committee of North Korea will be the legally established central power organ in north Korea.

In this way our people will fight more vigorously to further consolidate the central power organ of north Korea and win at the earliest possible date the complete independence and sovereignty of our nation under the guidance of the People's Committee of North Korea. Our people will certainly fulfil the

1947 Plan for Development of the National Economy and further consolidate the material basis for a happy life of the people and the building of an independent, sovereign state. The People's Committee of North Korea will guarantee democratic liberties and rights more securely for the people and will wage an unremitting struggle to build a unified independent and sovereign state and to elevate the international position of our country.

With the successes of last year and the victory of the present Congress, we have opened up the road to a yet greater victory in the future. Our nation and country will certainly achieve independence, prosperity and development. For our people have patriotic sentiments unsparingly to devote everything to the building of their state and a strong fighting spirit to break through any difficulties, and are firmly united around the people's power.

Also, we receive fraternal assistance from the great Soviet people. **The Soviet people are giving us material and moral aid so that our nation can build an independent, sovereign state. We are convinced that the Soviet Union, the most advanced and democratic state, will render an active support to our people in their just struggle in future as well and will stand by our people for all time.**

Delegates,

We held the election of November 3 last year with success to consolidate the provincial, city and county people's committees and have now successfully accomplished the work of the Congress of the Provincial, City and County People's Committees of North Korea to strengthen the People's Committee of North Korea, our central power organ, and to create the People's Assembly, the supreme organ of state power. This represents a historic victory of our people in their struggle to build an independent, sovereign state.

Now we have before us the immediate task of successfully conducting the election to the *myon* and *ri* (*dong*) people's committees which constitute the basis of our people's power organ. We should all take an active part in the election to the *myon* and *ri* (*dong*) people's committees and assure the complete triumph of the election. In this way we will legally consolidate the people's committees, the organs of genuine people's power, from the centre down to the lowest terminal units. Victory belongs to us.

Long live the victorious Congress of the Provincial, City and County People's Committees of North Korea!

Long live the People's Assembly, the supreme organ of state power of north Korea!

Long live the People's Committee of North Korea!

Long live the establishment of a unified government of the Korean people!

Long live the independence and sovereignty of the Korean people!

THE WORKERS' PARTY OF NORTH KOREA MARKING THE FIRST ANNIVERSARY OF ITS FOUNDATION

August 28, 1947

1. BRILLIANT ACHIEVEMENTS IN ONE YEAR

We are celebrating the first anniversary of the formation of the Workers' Party of North Korea. In the short period of one year since its inception, the Workers' Party has done a great amount of work which would ordinarily have taken 10-20 years to accomplish.

In a year our Party has rapidly grown into a mass party with a membership of 680,000, whereas it had some 370,000 members at the time of the merger.

The Workers' Party has absorbed into its ranks the best, bravest and most conscious progressive elements who are likely to become vanguards, from among the broad masses of the working people in north Korea. Almost all the true patriots in every factory, farm village and town who are active in state affairs, work in the interests of the people and command their love, have been admitted to the Workers' Party.

Many best workers from among the working class, the class that constitutes the leading force of state building and the core of the working people, have joined the Workers' Party, and they form the nucleating force of the Party. The Workers' Party was organized with progressive elements from among the toiling peasants and working intellectuals with advanced workers as its pivot.

The Party's organizational system has been put in order, with the result that Party organizations at all levels from the Party centre down to the provincial, city, county and *myon* committees and the factory and village cells, are composed of fine Party members, and a large number of competent Party cadres are reared in practical work. The Party has established wide networks of cells in factories, villages and urban residential quarters, and seen to it that every Party member lead a disciplined life at his Party cell.

The Party cell holds regular or extraordinary meetings to discuss pressing Party tasks and strives for their execution. The cell carries on the work of inducing each member to propagate the Party's policies, of ensuring their implementation by giving assignments to the Party members to carry out among the masses, of absorbing non-Party activists into the Party, rallying the masses around it and ensuring the ideological unity of its members.

With the strengthening of the life at the cell, strict discipline has been established in the Party, the entire membership have been united around the Party centre and democratic centralism further consolidated in the Party.

The Party has ensured its ideological unity and concerted action through a resolute struggle against all undesirable tendencies in itself such as the desultory and unorganized liberalistic tendency, tendency of individualist heroism, unprincipled **factional** tendency, and the **sectarian** proclivities, a historical inheritance.

The political and ideological level of the Party members has risen through an energetic struggle against the vestiges of the feudal and colonial ideas which are an evil hangover from the prolonged colonial rule of the Japanese imperialists. By conducting the educational work of arming the entire membership with the Party's political line, the Party has brought them to the profound realization that it was necessary, for the building of a Democratic People's Republic in Korea today, to fight against the pro-Japanese elements, traitors to the nation and remnants of feudalism obstructive to it and unite all the democratic forces without fail.

The Party has formed a national democratic united front with all political parties, social organizations and people of all classes and strata, and established the people's committee, the people's power, by mobilizing the masses of the people from all walks of life. The Party saw to it that all its members took an active part in all democratic reforms carried out by the people's power and that as workers most faithful to the people they brought the democratic reforms to a victorious conclusion in one year by organizing and guiding the people.

Through the practical struggle for the democratic reforms, our Party proved not only theoretically but also in deed that it is a party fighting sincerely in the interests of the people. As a result, our Party has now come to enjoy the deepest confidence of the people, and the Korean people entrust their destiny wholly to our Party which has a bond of kinship with them.

Supported and trusted by the people and rallying the broad masses around itself, our Party has become the nucleating force in the National Democratic United Front of North Korea, and has grown into a powerful, mass political party that plays a leading role in the building of a democratic Korea.

Our Party is mobilizing all its members and the masses of the people to the fulfilment of the 1947 national economic plan aimed at laying the economic basis of an independent, sovereign state for the happiness of the people.

Our Party enlists the resourceful technicians and skilled workers, active workers who are Party members, and the labouring masses, in rapidly rebuilding the factories, enterprises, mines, railways, etc., which the Japanese imperialists demolished when quitting, and it exerts every effort to improve the living standard of the people and develop the national economy.

A large number of progressive educators, cultural workers and intellectuals have joined our Party and are working with devotion to set up and develop educational establishments, theatres, libraries, newspapers and other cultural organizations for the rapid development of national culture and the training of native cadres.

Our Party is rooted deep in the rural areas. Its members in the countryside provide a model for all the peasants in the work of developing agriculture and are active in the drive for an increased output of farm produce.

Many Party members who have earned the love and respect of the masses of the people have been elected people's committee members, and are further strengthening and developing the work of the people's assemblies and the people's committees by taking an active part in it. They are advancing the prestige of the people's committees among the people by faithfully carrying into effect all the laws made by the people and taking an active part in all work of safeguarding the interests of the people.

Those of our Party members who are most faithful in the struggle against all the vicious elements including the pro-Japanese elements and traitors to the nation who infringed upon the interests of the people and sold out the nation, are working in the security organs, fulfilling their mission with credit.

Thus, our Party members are resolutely fighting in all domains for the building of an independent and sovereign democratic state and working with zeal for the overfulfilment of the 1947 Plan for Development of the National Economy in particular. The production results attained in the first half of the year convince us that we will surely win a shining victory in carrying out the plan for the current year.

All this shows that the leading role of our Party and the devoted struggle of its members constitute the surest guarantee of prosperity and honour for our nation.

2. THE CORRECTNESS OF THE POLITICAL LINE OF THE PARTY

The rapid consolidation and development of the Workers' Party and the brilliant victory in democratic construction have not come by chance at all. It is due to the fact that the entire membership have correctly carried out the Party's political line, united firmly around the Central Committee of the Party.

Our Party works out a correct political line suited to the actual conditions in our country and the entire Party strives for its implementation. Our Party has always been with the people, fought together with them, shaped its policies in conformity to their interests and vital needs and enlisted all forces in carrying them out.

The basic political line of our Party was firmly laid down already when the **Central Organizing Committee of the Communist Party of North Korea, the predecessor of our Party, was set up immediately after liberation on August 15, 1945. At that time, our Party set before the entire Korean people the basic duty of fighting for the building of a democratic, people's republic in Korea, and set forth the immediate tasks for its fulfilment as follows:**

1) To rally the broad patriotic, democratic forces by forming a national democratic united front embracing all patriotic and democratic political parties and groups and, on this basis, to work for the establishment of a Democratic People's Republic to ensure our complete national independence and sovereignty;

2) To liquidate thoroughly the remnant forces of Japanese imperialism, the lackeys of international reaction and all other reactionaries, who constitute the biggest obstacle to the building of a democratic country, thereby facilitating the development of our nation along democratic lines;

3) To organize, first of all, people's committees as organs

of genuine people's power in various districts with a view to establishing a unified all-Korea democratic provisional government, and carry out all democratic reforms, restore the factories, enterprises and the national economy as a whole, which were ravaged by the Japanese imperialists, and raise the material and cultural standards of the people, thereby laying the groundwork of an independent democratic state;

4) To further expand and strengthen the Party and energetically push forward the work of the social organizations for organizing and rallying the masses in all walks of life around the Party so as to fulfil all these tasks.

This is the political line set forth by our Party immediately after the August 15 Liberation.

Our Party is the advanced detachment of the working masses of Korea uniting in it the true patriots who fought for the liberation of the Korean nation at home and abroad and the advanced elements who waged an untiring struggle there for the benefit of the toiling masses.

To win victory in the hard struggle against the remnant forces of Japanese imperialism and the feudal forces, accomplices of the former, and against the lackeys of international reaction, and build a completely independent and democratic country by mustering all the democratic forces, it was of prime importance to strengthen our Party and rally the broad masses around it.

Our Party has done a great deal of work to accept into its ranks patriotic fighters and finest, advanced elements from among the toiling masses. We unfolded an extensive organizational work of the Party and the mass organizations during the period from immediately after the August 15 Liberation until before the decision of the Moscow Three Foreign Ministers Conference was announced. As a result, the Party rallied thousands of finest, advanced elements into its ranks and came to have mass organizations embracing hundreds of thousands of members in only a few months.

When the decision on the Korean question was adopted at the Moscow tripartite ministerial conference, our Party immediately started a struggle for its implementation. The decision of this conference marked off a line clearly revealing before the masses the radical confrontation between the progressive and the reactionary forces in Korea. The reactionary elements who were seeking to sell out Korea to the foreign imperialists again and turn it into a colony of imperialism and a feudal society, came out openly in opposition to the decision of the said conference. In contrast, the progressive forces that wanted to develop Korea along democratic lines and build a completely independent and sovereign state without foreign interference, took a resolute stand in support of the decision.

Our Party gave unqualified support to the decision of the Moscow Three Foreign Ministers Conference on the Korean question and fought determinedly against all the reactionary forces that were opposed to it. The Party waged vigorous struggles for the firmer unity of the masses of the people, for the carrying out of the democratic reforms, improvement of the people's living standard and the laying of the political, economic and cultural foundations for the building of a democratic country. Since then, our Party has, through its practical struggle, consolidated its organization, strengthened its unity and solidarity with the broad masses and grown and developed into an ever greater force.

United around our Party, the masses turned out with daring to carry out the democratic reforms proposed by the Party.

On February 8, **1946, our Party called a consultative meeting of representatives of all political parties, social organizations, Administrative Bureaus and all local people's committees and, there, founded the Provisional People's Committee of North Korea and decided on its 11-point immediate tasks as follows:**

1. To make a clean sweep of the pro-Japanese and reactionary elements and appoint competent cadres to the leadership of all organs, thereby strengthening the administrative apparatus in each local district;

2. To readjust the lands and forests confiscated from Japanese aggressors and pro-Japanese reactionary elements in the

shortest possible period of time and make preparations for confiscation of the Korean landlords' lands by appropriate methods, nationalization of the forests, abolition of farm rents and free distribution of land to the peasants;

3. To reorganize production enterprises into ones turning out the necessities of life and promote their development;

4. To completely restore railway transport, communications, and so on;

5. To readjust the system of financial institutions including the banks and establish correct policies for foreign and domestic trade;

6. To promote the development of medium and small enterprises and encourage the creative initiative of the entrepreneurs and traders;

7. To give active assistance to the working-class movement and set up wide organizational networks of factory and mill committees in the factories, mines, collieries, transport establishments, and so on;

8. To reform the educational system along democratic lines, expand primary and secondary schools, prepare for the training of teachers and compile textbooks in our national language;

9. To educate the people in truly democratic ideas and conduct an extensive work of cultural enlightenment among the people from all walks of life in order to dispel the servile spirit implanted by Japanese imperialism in the past;

10. To take appropriate measures at an early date to solve the serious food problem in north Korea;

11. To correctly explain to the whole people the true meaning of the decision of the Moscow Three Foreign Ministers Conference on the Korean question, which is fair and corresponds to the interests of the Korean people.

Our Party fully supported the decision adopted at this consultative meeting concerning the immediate tasks of the people's committee and, considering the decision its practical political line, concentrated the efforts of the entire Party on its implementation.

Our Party gave full support to the Agrarian Reform Law promulgated by the people's committee on March 5, 1946. Regarding the agrarian reform as the most important task to be carried out ahead of all democratic reforms, the Party mobilized all its membership to ensure the victorious accomplishment of the reform.

In the course of the struggle to carry out the agrarian reform, the prestige of the Party rose among the broad masses of the people, and the entire peasantry came to admit that our Party was the only one thoroughly defending their interests.

Thus, large numbers of advanced, finest elements from among the peasant masses were admitted into the ranks of our Party, and it made rapid progress both in quantity and quality.

Our Party mobilized a great number of workers to render active help to the peasants who came out for the agrarian reform, thereby ensuring its smooth progress and further consolidating the worker-peasant alliance.

Giving unconditional support to the 20-Point Platform made public by the Provisional People's Committee of North Korea on March 23, 1946, our Party accepted it as a programme of action for itself and all the social organizations and strove for its implementation.

Our Party played the most advanced role in carrying into effect laws such as the Labour Law promulgated on June 24, 1946, the Law on Agricultural Tax in Kind proclaimed on June 27, the Law on Equality of the Sexes announced on July 30, the Law on the Nationalization of Industries promulgated on August 10 and the democratic Election Law. Through this struggle it has become clearer to everyone that our Party consistently fights for the benefit of the working people, and the confidence of the masses of the people in our Party has increased tremendously.

All the facts show that our Party's political line and all its measures taken in the struggle for the implementation of the line were fully justified. Because our Party has mapped out a correct political line and organized and mobilized the masses of the people for its implementation, we have achieved victory and our Party has been able to develop in a short period of time into a powerful political party enjoying the love of the people.

Our Party will always have the support of the masses of the people and always be victorious in the struggle for carrying out its political line.

3. THE ESTABLISHMENT OF THE WORKERS' PARTY AND THE CORRECTNESS OF THE ORGANIZATIONAL LINE

To strengthen the Party posed itself as the primary task in successfully fulfilling the great historic task of building a completely independent and sovereign state by rallying the democratic forces.

Since its inception, our Party has held fast to the correct organizational line of consolidating its ranks both organizationally and ideologically, ensuring the unity of ideology and will of the Party and achieving its rapid growth. The Party has fought persistently to ensure the purity and unity of its ranks since the Communist Party, the predecessor of the Workers' Party, was founded immediately after liberation.

In the early period of the foundation of the Communist Party there appeared the grave phenomenon that pro-Japanese and alien elements had wormed their way into the Party, infringed upon the interests of the masses and divorced the Party from the masses in violation of the Party's political line.

Local separatists and factionalists attempted to hinder the unity of our Party and tear it up into various factional groups. Many Right and "Left" opportunists sneaked into the Party, and tried to deliberately distort the Party's correct political line and hamper its execution in every way.

The Party, however, adhered to the correct political and organizational lines and waged an uncompromising struggle against all kinds of anti-Party elements. Following the Third Enlarged **Executive Committee Meeting of the Central Organizing Committee of the Communist Party of North** Korea convened on December 17, 1945, our Party launched a decisive struggle against all shades of alien elements that had sneaked into it. The Party undertook the work of screening its members, issued uniform membership cards, expelled the alien and pro-Japanese elements who had crawled into it, dealt a decisive blow at the local separatists with liberalistic and factionalist tendencies running counter to the line of the centre and disobeying the instructions from it and ensured the ideological and organizational unity of the Party.

Through this struggle our Party grew stronger organizationally and ideologically and the Party spirit of its members was enhanced. This guaranteed the decisive role of our Party in the struggle for the triumphant implementation of the democratic reforms.

Our Party correctly executed its organizational line of developing itself into a mass political party on a broader basis at the most suitable stage of development of our country.

Thanks to the democratic reforms carried out in north Korea in one year, a big change took place in the life of the workers, peasants and intellectuals.

The workers, freed from colonial exploitation, have come to work in their own behalf and in the interests of the people and society at the factories and enterprises which have become the property of the people, and are provided with the possibilities of taking an active part in the state political life. As a result, the political level of the working class has risen remarkably.

The peasants, emancipated from the landlords' exploitation and oppression, are enabled to farm freely on the land of their own and actively participate in the work of building a democratic country, displaying political zeal.

The intellectuals, who served the Japanese imperialist exploiters in the past, are now working for the sake of their country and nation and for the benefit of the people and the working people, and their ideas and views have changed and developed fast along new, democratic lines.

All this constituted the solid foundation for strengthening the alliance of the workers, peasants and intellectuals, and also raised the necessity of further solidifying this alliance. The workers, peasants and intellectuals came to the keen realization that their basic interests are in perfect accord and that the strengthening of their alliance is the most important guarantee for further consolidating the National Democratic United Front and for achieving victory in the building of a democratic state.

Thus, the question arose of merging the Parties—the Communist Party which represented the working class and the New Democratic Party which stood for the interests of the peasantry and intelligentsia. The merger of the Communist Party and the New Democratic Party was an urgent demand of the social development in our country and fully accorded with the interests of the toiling masses. The merger of the two Parties, therefore, had warm support from the entire working people, and the merger was successfully completed in only a month.

As a result of the merger of the two Parties, there was a great influx into the Party of advanced elements of the workers, peasants and intellectuals and our Party developed in a short span of time into a mass party uniting in its ranks hundreds of thousands of members.

With this expansion and growth of our Party, the unity of the people based on the alliance of the workers, peasants and intellectuals became firmer still, and the democratic reforms and the movement for building up the country proceeded more triumphantly.

The Party has always fought to strengthen its organization and discipline, while rapidly expanding its ranks. The guidance and inspection of all the provincial Party organizations conducted by the Party Central Committee some time ago have put the organizational system of our Party into definite order down to the lowest terminals. The Party bodies at all levels have turned out a large number of competent cadres capable of skilfully organizing and mobilizing the masses and of directing the democratic construction.

All this proves the correctness of the organizational line of the Party.

4. THE IMMEDIATE TASKS OF OUR PARTY THAT IS GREETING THE FIRST ANNIVERSARY OF ITS FOUNDATION

Our Party has made rapid progress in a short span of time and attained great victories amid very complex circumstances.

But we must on no account become self-complacent. Our Party is not yet tempered as hard as steel in a difficult struggle and lacks in experience.

We should not allow ourselves to be carried away by our victories, but should make every effort to reinforce the Party ranks qualitatively while further consolidating the victories we have already won. We must make a profound study of the rich revolutionary experiences of the advanced parties and of Marxism-Leninism, apply them to suit the situation in Korea, rectify the shortcomings and further the merits in our work.

Thus, our Party should be developed into a powerful party capable of vigorously forging ahead bearing the destiny of the Korean people on its shoulders under whatever difficult circumstances and of surely defeating any enemy.

To this end:

1) The Party organizations must be further consolidated.

The organizational life of Party members must be strengthened further in all Party organizations from the Party committees of all levels down to the cells in towns, factories and farm villages.

The cell is the basic organization which educates the Party members, sees to their ideological training and guides their daily life. Life at the cell is the basis of the political and organizational life of Party members. Without a healthy cell life, the Party spirit of the members cannot be tempered nor can the ideological and political unity be ensured within the Party. It is therefore our prime duty to strengthen the cell life in order to make our Party a mighty one.

Our Party still has some organizations that fail to organize cell life in a sound way. We must put an end to this situation as soon as possible.

Each cell must convene regular or extraordinary meetings in a planned way to discuss Party work, give Party-work assignments to members, verify their execution, conduct criticism for the ideological unity within the Party, and must organize the Party life of the members so that they may propagate all the Party's policies among the masses and strive to carry them out. It is pointless to work perfunctorily without any preparations and plans. The Party organizations at all levels should strive more energetically to strengthen the life of Party cells.

2) The style of Party work must be improved.

The democratic style of work has not yet been established firmly in our Party.

Bureaucratic, formalistic and liberalistic styles of work, survivals of Japanese imperialism, which are still found a great deal in the Party, are highly detrimental to its development and consolidation.

There are tendencies to bluster at the masses instead of organizing and guiding them, and to decry the masses for their backwardness instead of breathing the same air as they and teaching them kindly, and thus become estranged from the masses. Such is precisely bureaucracy.

Formalism refers to the style of work that when dealing with all matters, one does not investigate the truth nor analyses things carefully, but manages things mechanically and perfunctorily instead of organizing work scrupulously and only embellishes the façade void of substance.

It is simply a liberalistic tendency to act as one pleases in an unprincipled manner, disregarding decisions and directions of the organization and to engage in double-dealings, that is, to pretend to be obedient outwardly but counterwork behind the scenes, to express approval for everything at a meeting but act the other way when away from the place.

We should fight resolutely against all these practices.

We should acquire the style of work of going among the masses and rank-and-file Party members to patiently explain to them, study their feelings, and lead them along the path to the goal. Cadres should refrain from ordering the masses about, but personally set examples and become one with them, and should become closest friends of the masses approaching them and teaching and learning from them instead of criticizing or abusing them for their ignorance.

In tackling all matters, you should organize the work scrupulously and carry it out responsibly after gaining a correct idea through a close study of their substance and investigation and examination of the facts. You should establish the style of work of investigating the cause of the mistake when you find any, of analysing its nature, taking measures for its rectification and thoroughly correcting the error. In short, a style of work should be acquired to inquire into the essence and content instead of sticking to the exterior and form in solving all questions.

And the principle of the minority submitting to the majority should be strictly observed. It is the organizational principle of our Party that the Party member obey the decisions of the Party, the individual obey the organization and the minority obey the majority. Liberalism is a harmful tendency which disrupts the unity of the Party and wrecks its united action. We should intensify the struggle against such inimical tendencies as liberalism, individualist heroism, factionalism, parochialism, nepotism, etc., that are still to be found in the Party, and should further consolidate the unity of the Party.

Criticism and self-criticism must be intensified within the Party in order to rectify our shortcomings in good time. Some Party members and cadres only like to blow their own trumpet and love being extolled to the skies, but dislike criticism. This is a wrong attitude. Just criticism and counsel play a great role in correcting the errors of individual Party members and in consolidating the Party organization. We should adopt the sound style of work of promoting principled criticism and accepting comradely criticism with an open mind.

3) Inner-Party education must be intensified if the Party is to be further extended quantitatively and consolidated qualitatively.

Our Party should arm itself firmly with the advanced, revolutionary theory of Marxism-Leninism. Lenin once said: "Without a revolutionary theory there can be no revolutionary movement," and "...**The role of vanguard fighter can be fulfilled only by a party that is guided by the advanced theory.**"

These words must be a guide to our Party's action today, too. Our Party should by all means arm itself with the advanced, revolutionary theory if it really wants to bear the destiny of the Korean people on its shoulders and build a democratic state and a progressive, democratic society that can guarantee a happy life to the people.

We should carry on an extensive educational work to study Marxist-Leninist revolutionary theory and the rich experiences of the Communist Party and people of the Soviet Union and the experiences of the revolutionary movements in various countries of the world and study the history and realities of our country.

We should in this way train each of our Party members into a worker who has a correct knowledge of our Party's policies and is capable of organizing and mobilizing the people, and should make him always be a model and play the leading part in the course of waging the struggle for democracy together with all other political parties and social organizations.

Our Party members should become ardent patriots who love the country and the people. Party members ought to study hard to raise their politico-theoretical level, and make an energetic effort to master techniques so as to be true builders capable of creditably discharging their duties in each field.

Our Party should train large numbers of technicians,

skilled workers, educators, politicians, military personnel, scientists, artists, etc., who are armed with advanced revolutionary ideas and equipped with a high level of techniques and further raise their role in all fields, thus triumphantly fulfilling the great task assigned to our Party by our people of building an independent country.

4) While consolidating the Party, we should further reinforce the mass organizations under its guidance.

Without broad mass organizations around itself our Party would eventually become something like a man with only bones but no flesh. Our Party, therefore, should conduct the work of further consolidating all social organizations, of uniting the broad masses in them, educating the broader masses through those organizations and uniting them closely around the Party. We should make the masses realize that our Party is their advanced detachment and closest friend fighting resolutely for the benefit of the masses of the people, and solidify the unity of the Party and the masses unremittingly.

Our Party should make a constant effort to strengthen the united front with the Democratic Party and the Chongu Party. We should make each Party member understand thoroughly that by acting in close co-operation with those parties at the present stage our Party can win a shining victory in the struggle against the international and internal reactionaries, our common enemies. We should understand that only those Party members who endeavour to strengthen the united front and creditably carry on the work of the united front could be rated as Workers' Party members who really fight for the benefit of our Party and are faithful to our Party's policies. Anyone who disrupts the united front deliberately, should be regarded as a person who creates favourable conditions for the enemy and does great harm to our Party and our people.

5) Our Workers' Party members should be the first to give active support to the people's committee, the people's power, and fight to the best of their ability for the implementation of all its policies, thus proving themselves trustworthy servants of the country and the people.

We should study every decree of the people's committee, explain it to the people and set an example in its observance.

Our Party should fight resolutely against the impure elements still lurking within the people's committees or stealing into them sometimes, and conduct a proper work of propaganda and education in good time for ideological and political unity of the functionaries of the people's committees.

Today, the entire people in north Korea have turned out as one man for the fulfilment of the 1947 plan of the national economy. Our Party members should always be at the head of the masses and lead them to raise their patriotic zeal higher and thus see to the overfulfilment of the national economic plan without fail.

On the occasion of the first anniversary of its founding, our Party should unfold an all-Party campaign to consolidate the results already scored and win a fresh, greater victory, by correctly analysing the brilliant successes achieved over the past year, generalizing the experience and lessons gained in the course of scoring those successes, and by quickly eliminating the errors found in our work.

WHAT SHOULD WE DO AND HOW SHOULD WE WORK THIS YEAR?

Speech Delivered at a Meeting of Activists of the Political Parties and Social Organizations in Kanggye County

January 12, 1948

I extend my warm congratulations to you for your enthusiastic participation in the struggle for carrying out the democratic reforms after liberation and, particularly, for your victorious fulfilment of last year's national economic plan, the first of its kind in the history of our country, and I present my whole-hearted respects to you for your firm determination to score ever greater victories in this year of 1948.

As all of you know, the achievements our people have scored in north Korea are really tremendous. We made a great success especially in economic construction in 1947. Last year we drew up a national economic plan for the first time in order to further consolidate the victories of the democratic reforms and lay the basis for an independent national economy of the country and successfully fulfilled it, and we are making a continued headway for newer victories.

In the short period of slightly over two years after liberation, our people have done what other countries had failed to do in scores of years. The victories of the democratic reforms and the brilliant successes our people have registered in building a new life in north Korea are widely known to the whole world and furnish an inspiring example to the peoples of many Eastern countries. We have thus demonstrated at home and abroad that the Korean nation is a nation who is quite capable of building a politically and economically independent, rich and strong country with a brilliant culture by its own efforts and of advancing proudly shoulder to shoulder with the peoples of all the advanced countries of the world.

This proves that the Korean nation was not dead but remained alive, did not forget its country nor abandoned its history even under the 36-year long tyrannical rule of Japanese imperialism. This also shows that our nation is entirely capable of attaining its independence and sovereignty and will never be overridden by any aggressor if it wages an active struggle with such fine national traits and patriotism.

As you know well, what a cruel rule the Japanese imperialists bore over Korea! They oppressed the Korean people at will and robbed them of everything as they pleased, tried to obliterate the history of our country and exterminate our culture and our language and, to top it all, went so far as to force the Korean people to change their surnames, desecrating our ancestors. And they deprived the Koreans of the opportunities for education and prevented them from learning science and technology. An ordinary nation would probably have perished forever in the face of such persecution and oppression.

The Korean people, however, did not give in, they carefully preserved the history of their country and their national sagacity, loved their culture and did not abandon their language. The Koreans tried hard to lose no opportunity to learn even a thing more and fought through all difficulties for the day of our national regeneration. That is why our people set about building a genuinely independent and democratic state in north Korea without the slightest confusion from the first days of liberation. We use our own language to creditably conduct radio broadcasting and publish newspapers, books and textbooks, and teach Korean history to the younger generation, and even run the institutions of higher learning on our own, training large numbers of native cadres.

As they were driven out of Korea, the Japanese imperialists declared cynically that without them Korea's industry and transport would all be paralyzed. But we soon started operating factories and set trains running. The 17-18 years old stokers who barely shovelled coals under the Japs in the days of Japanese imperialism, have now become engine drivers and are running express trains. Big factories and enterprises such as the Hungnam Fertilizer Factory, Nampo Smeltery, Hwanghae Iron Works, Songjin Steel Works and Supung Hydroelectric Power Station have been rehabilitated and are in normal operation, and all of them fulfilled their plans brilliantly last year.

Needless to say, all this did not come as a gracious gift. These successes have been made possible entirely by the united strength of our liberated people, their lofty patriotic zeal, their indomitable perseverance in overcoming all difficulties, their ability of investigation and creative initiative.

The reactionaries mocked at our plan as an idle dream which would never be realized, and among us, too, there were some who were distrustful of the plan. But our people, displaying a high degree of patriotic zeal and creative activity, have creditably accomplished the things they once chose to. This is really something to boast about. This is the most strongest answer and counterblow to the U.S. imperialists including Hoover and their lackeys who prattled that the Korean people should be placed under an international trusteeship for 25 years because they were incapable of self-government. This has convinced us more deeply, and imbued us with boundless national pride, that the Korean nation is a nation of superb ability, that no aggressor can ever conquer our nation again and our nation is able not only to attain independence but also to build a rich and strong, advanced democratic Korea.

But the U.S. imperialists calculate that they can enslave our nation again because the Korean nation had been a colonial slave fettered to Japanese imperialism for a long time in the past. We must clearly show them what an absurd delusion this is.

The Korean people of today are not the Korean people of the old, feudal era of Li dynasty. The Korean people are a people who waged a tireless, unyielding struggle against foreign aggressors even under Japanese imperialist despotism and, especially after liberation, have become masters of the country and have unshakable faith in the path they are to follow. Moreover, through the victorious democratic reforms and successful economic construction in north Korea, the Korean people have come to possess solid assets for winning the independence and sovereignty of the country and acquired the national sense of dignity that they can solve all their problems for themselves splendidly and a firm confidence in victory. There is no force on earth which can destroy such a nation.

Such national sense of dignity and power is highly precious for the liberation struggle of the people. A nation without it may be ruined, but a nation that has national pride and confidence in victory is invincible.

How is it that we suffered from Japanese imperialist aggression and failed to repulse it by ourselves? It is, first of all, that we lacked a national sense of dignity and power before and our people were weak in awakening and in united strength.

In a little more than two years following liberation, however, the Korean people were awakened and tempered, their strength grew incomparably and our national sense of dignity and power rose higher than ever before. The pride and self-respect of our nation which had been repressed and trampled down under the long Japanese imperialist colonial rule, began to revive and unfurled their wings and soared higher with each passing day in the struggle to create a new life after liberation. This is the most precious thing, which cannot be got for money nor can it be exchanged for any other things. This is a sure guarantee for our nation to grow stronger and our country to prosper and develop further in the future.

Our nation can never again be reduced to a humiliating status as before. Our nation has already got out of that status completely and is waging an indomitable struggle for the independence, sovereignty and prosperity of the country. We are powerful and confident enough to repulse any aggressors and safeguard the honour of the country by the united strength of the whole nation should they turn upon our Korea in an attempt to swallow it up again.

Today ours is a nation that is conscious of its ability and mission, a stout nation now which no force can bring to its knees and override. Particularly, the north Korean people have become masters of the country who handle everything by themselves according to their own decisions, the masters of a new, free and happy life. In north Korea the people have not only become masters of the major industries and the land but also are rapidly developing the economy of the country by managing them ably, and everyone is devoting all his talents and passions to the building of a rich and strong, advanced independent state.

But the situation in south Korea is totally different. The rulers of dependencies who even fail to act as masters of their own countries but work for foreigners have been brought into south Korea by the U.S. imperialists, and are now clamouring that they are going to make our Korea "independent." They are none other than the so-called "U.N. Temporary Commission on Korea." What on earth are they going to do in Korea, those fellows who are unable to run the affairs of their own countries properly and held in bondage to others, while driving their own peoples into a wretched plight?

Today the Korean question can be solved only by the Koreans, and no one but the Korean people has the competence and right to solve it. It is much less possible for such a gang as the "U.N. Temporary Commission on Korea" to solve the Korean question. It is neither the United States nor India or Syria, but only the Korean people themselves that can solve the Korean question. It is precisely the Korean people who should solve the Korean question by themselves, and it is only we who are fully capable of solving it.

Originally, the "U.N. Temporary Commission on Korea" did not come to Korea to solve the Korean question. It has come to Korea simply in the capacity of a minion of the U.S. imperialists who want to colonize Korea. In other words, it has come to help rig up a separate south Korean government designed to further consolidate and perpetuate, in another form, the rule by the U.S. government-general maintained by Hodge now in south Korea.

What is the difference between the Japanese imperialist governor-general and the present governor-general Hodge? The difference, if any, is only that the people's livelihood has become more difficult and suppression is more harsh than under the Japanese governor-general. Indeed, all sorts of evils have increased astoundingly. The number of prisons has increased, the patriots and democrats are persecuted more harshly and savagely than in the years under Japanese imperialism. Forcible deliveries of farm produce have been augmented; in the days of Japanese imperialism there were police, at most, to be present at the places of forcible deliveries of farm produce, but now even terrorists accompany the police to force the deliveries. More factories are closed, unemployment has increased, and the number of children denied schooling opportunities and of students expelled from schools has grown. Traitors to the nation and quislings have increased and so have the profiteers.

So, the people are shivering from fear, hunger and cold, and suffering from lack of rights and poverty. Not content with this, the U.S. imperialists have even brought in the "U.N. Temporary Commission on Korea" with the help of the U.N. for the purpose of carrying out their colonial enslavement policy more rigorously because the military government alone is not strong enough to do that.

However, the south Korean people, not to speak of the people in north Korea, are not taken in by such a thing, and are filled with the resolve to fight against it to the very end. Only the handful of reactionary elements like Syngman Rhee, who are afraid of the judgment of the people, support and welcome the "U.N. Temporary Commission on Korea" under the shameless slogan against the withdrawal of foreign troops. This only calls forth the indignation of the entire Korean people.

The statement of General Shtikov, representative of the U.S.S.R., who suggested that the Soviet and U.S. troops withdraw from Korea simultaneously to open up the way for the Korean nation to decide its destiny by itself, constitutes a just and reasonable proposal which indicates the shortest cut to the independence and sovereignty of the Korean nation today. And why is the reactionary clique dead set against it? The handful of reactionaries are opposed to the withdrawal of foreign troops so as to prolong their days by hanging on the U.S. imperialists, because the moment the U.S. army, their master and patron, pulls out, the game will be up for them. In the meantime, they welcome the "U.N. Temporary Commission on Korea," a tool of U.S. imperialist aggression in Korea, to serve U.S. imperialism as its lackeys by selling out south Korea at least for dollars and subordinating it to U.S. imperialism for good.

But all the manoeuvres of the U.S. imperialists and the "U.N. Temporary Commission on Korea," their tool, all the plots of the domestic reactionaries will fall through in the end. For the Korean people, who have already demonstrated their national superiority and advance along the road of independence and sovereignty with firm confidence, are not fooled by such things but are waging a resolute struggle in a body against the enemy.

Today the liberated people of north Korea are enjoying a happy and worthy life, and our livelihood is becoming more affluent every day. But we cannot forget even for a moment the cruel reality that half of our land of 3,000 *ri* is seized by the U.S. imperialists and that our fellow countrymen and brothers, who are of the same ancestral blood as we are, groan under oppression and suffer from hunger. Under these circumstances it is natural that the north Korean people should feel deep sympathy for the bloody struggle of their south Korean brothers and extend them most enthusiastic encouragement.

We are confident that in the year now beginning, too, the south Korean people will valiantly fight to smash the aggressive machinations of U.S. imperialism and achieve their long-cherished aspirations.

For the complete independence and sovereignty and reunification of the country, the north Korean people should further reinforce the democratic base and score greater successes in economic construction.

What, then, are the specific tasks that should be carried out in north Korea this year? I have already mentioned them in my new year's message, but I should like to stress them again for you.

First of all, it is important to increase production further and raise the people's standard of living higher still. It is true that our national economy has been rehabilitated rapidly and the people's livelihood improved markedly till now. But we cannot, and must not, rest content with it on any account.

What we have done is but the start in the light of the boundless prosperity and development and the abundant, civilized life that are to be achieved in the future in our people's country where the people have taken power and hold the levers of control in the economy. As you all know, the democratic reforms have been brought to a victorious conclusion in north Korea, but this has only provided us with favourable conditions for the future development of our society into one better and nicer to live in. And a big success has been achieved in economic construction in 1947, but this, too, is no more than the first step in the development of the national economy and improvement of the people's life in our country. Some say, "Now that the 20-Point Platform has all been translated into reality in north Korea, it is unnecessary, isn't it?" This is an erroneous view. True, each article of the Platform has been adopted as a law and is being materialized in actual life, but practices running counter to it have not yet been wiped out altogether. We should further consolidate and develop the successes achieved in the implementation of this Platform and wage an unyielding struggle to carry it into effect on a nation-wide scale.

In a word, the victories we have already scored do not signify the completion of social reform and construction, though they are tremendous. They only mean that yet broader vistas have been opened up before us in democratic construction. We should continue to advance with full confidence towards a still brighter future along the road of unlimited development and further develop all our work in terms of quality.

For example, the agrarian reform has already been carried out triumphantly in north Korea. But this does not mean that the agricultural question has all been solved in our country. Our agriculture should be developed further still, and the problems arising in assuring it should be solved in good time. From now on we should improve the methods of farming, increase the number of draught oxen, improve and supply farm implements in larger quantities and undertake irrigation projects on a wider scale. At every opportunity that offers, I emphasize that irrigation projects should be pushed forward energetically so as not to let the rivers flow into the sea uselessly, but to draw their water into the paddyfields, and this is a really urgent task. Our country has rich water resources and an abundance of electric power, and we have also become able to manufacture motors by our own hands. Under these circumstances, if only we make the effort, we will be able to extensively carry out the work of converting dry fields into paddies yielding three times more harvest.

The same applies to the nationalization of industries. The law was promulgated and the major industrial establishments monopolized by the Japanese imperialists have come into the hands of the people, but it does not mean the complete solution of the industrial question. We should increase production rapidly by rehabilitating the dilapidated factories, building new ones and skilfully managing and operating our industries which have come into the people's possession. Only then will the building of a new life by our people be promoted further, our country built into a wealthy and powerful, independent and sovereign democratic state and the entire people lead a happier and more abundant life.

Today the life of the north Korean people is being improved remarkably, indeed. This is beyond all comparison either with the life of the Korean working people in the days of Japanese imperialism or with the miserable life of the south Korean people today. We cannot rest content with this, however.

Our people who have become masters of the country can and should enjoy a more affluent and civilized life. It is our aim to liberate the people and make all of them enjoy a happy and comfortable life, and only when this is attained, it could be said that the revolution has triumphed completely.

And we will earn the support of the people only when we make them well-off. The people always support a government that guarantees freedom and happiness for them and practically sees to the improvement of their life. Only when our democracy secures welfare for the people in reality, will it be proved to be fundamentally different from the "democracy" in the capitalist countries and the entire Korean people will say, "Our democracy is really good!" and will be rallied closely under the banner of our democracy.

We should not talk about democracy only in words, but should embody genuine democracy in deeds. We may say that this is the very point which distinguishes us from the reactionaries. The reactionary clique in south Korea can give nothing to the people, but, on the contrary, they only rob them, while paying lip service to democracy very noisily.

What has the reactionary clique done in a little over two years since liberation during which time we have carried out great undertakings for the people and the country? What else have they done except that they have sold out the country for dollars and made the people tremble with fear, cold and hunger by suppressing, slaughtering and exploiting them? That is why the south Korean people, far from being hoodwinked by them, are more indignant and hate them, and are rising against them.

What we do, however, is quite contrary to what they do. We have brought freedom and happiness to the people not in words but in deeds, and are steadily improving their life. We are zealously carrying out practical work, and are speeding up construction and production. Practice is precisely the best method of publicity and the best politics with us. With us, the most valuable thing is practice, and it is precisely through practice that we will win the people over to our side and gain victory in the revolution.

This year, too, we should increase production, improve the people's livelihood markedly and further strengthen our democratic base through practical struggle.

Our greatest aim is to build the whole of Korea into a rich and strong, independent and sovereign democratic state. And to realize it, the economic basis should be further consolidated and the people's livelihood be stabilized and improved by rapidly developing the national economy in north Korea. The day when our country achieves complete independence and sovereignty can be hastened, only if the south Korean people are shown more clearly how nice life is in north Korea where democracy has triumphed and only if the might of the democratic base is strengthened decisively.

Then, along what lines should we rehabilitate and develop the national economy in order to consolidate the economic basis and improve the people's livelihood in a short space of time?

Some people lay stress exclusively on heavy industry and take up the wrong position that heavy-industrialism should be followed right away. It is important, of course, to rehabilitate and develop heavy industry. Only when heavy industry is developed can the foundations be built for an independent national industry and the material conditions be also created for the improvement of the people's standard of living.

But the present conditions do not permit us to expand heavy industry in a big way at once or devote our efforts only to it. For the time being we should follow the course of turning out and supplying raw and other materials needed for the development of the national economy by rehabilitating and readjusting the existing heavy industry plants. And we should build light industry, which has no foundation whatever, to keep an adequate balance with heavy industry, and energetically push ahead with the development of agriculture. Only by so doing can our people's life be stabilized and improved rapidly and the zeal and creative initiative of the masses of the people be raised higher in economic construction.

As is to be seen from this, it is wrong to neglect the rehabilitation of heavy industry and consolidation of the economic basis of the country, but it would also be wrong not to build light industry for the improvement of the people's life, placing stress on heavy industry alone.

To improve the people's living standard, production should be increased speedily as a whole, daily necessaries turned out in larger quantities and prices reduced systematically. The struggle for increased production should be intensified everywhere—in towns, farm villages, mines and fishing villages. Only when production is boosted and products of good quality are turned out in large quantities, can we use them to further expand production and improve the working people's life and export part of them to foreign countries to buy goods we badly need. In all branches, every factory and every working man should overfulfil their production assignments and increase production further still.

First of all, economic plans should be worked out correctly. Without a correct plan nothing can be done properly, much less can the industries which have come into the people's ownership be developed. Each branch and each enterprise should draw up correct and feasible plans on the basis of carefully investigated and studied data.

A defect of the functionaries here is that they are weak in planning their work and do not know how to prepare the economic plans well. Planlessness is glaringly revealed in the work of the consumers' co-operative in particular. There are no small number of functionaries who know little of the actual conditions in their respective domain and are not versed in their work. Such being the case, they can neither work out a plan properly nor push ahead with their work in a long-sighted way.

In olden times, too, people said that a day's plan should be formed in the morning and a year's plan in the spring. The spring mentioned here means the beginning of the year, of course. Half a month has now passed since we rang in the New Year, and yet this year's plan has not been drawn up correctly. I think this is a serious matter. The plan for 1948 should be worked out correctly on the basis of carefully examining the lessons drawn from, and the merits and shortcomings of work revealed in, the carrying out of the plan for 1947, and even each person, not to speak of each institution and enterprise, should work regularly according to concrete plans.

The economic plans should be interrelated, and should be realistic plans based on a careful calculation of all conditions made from a national standpoint. At the same time, the plans should always be progressive and enterprising. A passive plan confined to maintaining the status quo is of no use to us, it hinders our onward movement.

Take Kanggye County for example. First of all, you have no end of timber resources here, and yet why do you not make a plan to increase the output of timber and use it to turn out larger quantities of various wood products? You may produce, say, vessels and furniture, or writing tables, desks, chairs and blackboards to be used in offices or schools. If you produce such things in large quantities and sell them at reasonable prices, it will be nice because the people's demands will be met; the gains of the enterprises will increase and the workers will get more incomes, and how nice this would be! Nevertheless, the County People's Committee does not give guidance to the state enterprises to make them turn out such products in large quantities nor does it encourage the individual entrepreneurs to do so. Such simple consumer goods may be produced either by the consumers' co-operatives or by individuals who may run a suitable form of enterprise by pooling efforts and funds. It is high time that the individual traders and entrepreneurs conduct trade or run enterprises by honest means, instead of only trying to engage in speculations.

And why do you not make up a plan to further develop stockbreeding and sericulture in this nice area? You can raise as many hogs and sheep and silkworms as you please, to say nothing of cattle. If you do so, it will be nice because more draught animals will be available; it will be nice because a large quantity of highly nutritive non-staple food can be supplied; it will be nice because more raw materials for daily necessaries including hide can be furnished; and it will be nice because plenty of raw materials for silk much needed for the people's life can be obtained. Why not do such a nice thing?

This year each farm household, too, should do farming and sidelines according to clear-cut plans as to what kinds of crops should be planted and how to plant them, what kinds and how much of grains be produced, how many domestic animals be raised and how to raise them, and how many more *pil* of cotton cloth be woven. Each village, too, should draw up detailed plans as to how much more land should be reclaimed into dry field, how the irrigation projects should be undertaken, when and how much fertilizer be procured through barter, how seeds be obtained through mutual help and how draught animals be utilized.

It is necessary for all the *ri*, *myon* and county people's committees, political parties, social organizations and other institutions to shape proper working plans and push ahead with all their work methodically. If all the institutions, enterprises, and individuals from bottom to top draw up correct plans in this manner and overfulfil them by displaying a high degree of patriotic zeal and creative initiative, we will certainly achieve a fresh victory.

There is nothing impossible or unrealizable for us. If we work with full confidence and with energy in this way, the results will be still more remarkable. Let the reactionary clique make noise as they please. Some day stock will be taken of who has done what. Then, the world will be startled once again at the great achievements of our people and the serious crimes of the enemy.

The important task we have to carry out this year is to practise economy while increasing production. No matter how much we may increase production, it will be no use if we keep wasting on the other hand. Particularly, it is of great national importance to practise economy and lead a frugal life in the light of the situation in our country where everything is not yet sufficient. We should thoroughly establish the spirit of practising economy and leading a frugal life everywhere, from the state institutions down to each family.

It is necessary not only to take good care of and protect

state property and wage a resolute struggle against all needless expenditures and wasteful practices, but also to eliminate wastage for useless purposes in private life. From now on, the institutions or organizations should refrain from having banquets frequently, and an end should be put once and for all to the practice of giving feasts on every possible pretext or committing excessive extravagances particularly on mournful or joyous occasions in private homes.

You should also learn how to use state funds effectively. We started construction not long ago, and it can be said that really large-scale construction work will be undertaken from now. Nevertheless, there are still not a few instances of squandering money of the state and the people on useless things in many places. A monument or monumental tower of one kind or another is built with hundreds of thousands of *won*, and then a carousing "ceremony" is held under the name of inaugural ceremony or others. This sort of evil practice should be eliminated as soon as possible, and a system should be established under which all funds are used effectively and economically in the interests of the state and the people.

Some Koreans still have a habit of pretending to know what they do not know and to have what they do not have, and this is a big vice with them. Even homespun cotton clothes and straw sandals are not bad in the present conditions. Yet, even primary-school children think they cannot go to school without Western clothes and rubber shoes on. And there are many public houses everywhere and it is desirable to reduce them to a degree.

We have very ample room for increasing production and improving the working people's livelihood at a faster pace by practising economy. We should use sparingly even a penny and a small amount of materials and turn all that are saved to the building of a rich and powerful country. This is our sacred duty, and this is precisely the idea of national construction. Only when the entire people are armed with this idea and enlist all reserves and potentialities in the cause of national construction, is it possible to further consolidate the democratic base of north

Korea and realize as soon as possible the complete independence and sovereignty and reunification on democratic lines of the country, the long-cherished desire of our nation.

While carrying on economic construction successfully in north Korea, we should fight to realize democracy such as in north Korea on an all-Korea scale by giving an active encouragement to the south Korean people. Only by unfolding a heroic struggle in firm unity can the entire people in north and south Korea beat the U.S. imperialists and the domestic reactionaries and win ultimate victory.

We are now engaged in a work which is of great significance in achieving this cause, and that is precisely the framing of a Provisional Constitution of Korea. All should rise to see to it that the Constitution, which reflects the new, democratic life attained by the north Korean people, be made the Constitution of the entire Korean people and that the building of an independent democratic country where the people are genuine masters be finally achieved.

Victory surely belongs to our people. Today we are provided with every condition for victory. We have the united democratic forces and the genuine people's power. We have a great national pride, burning patriotism and firm faith in victory. We have accumulated a wealth of experience in carrying out the democratic reforms and economic construction and have already trained no small number of cadres. Besides, we have the powerful support and selfless aid of the great Soviet Union. No one can bring such a people to their knees, and neither the U.S. imperialists nor the "U.N. Temporary Commission on Korea," their tool, nor the domestic reactionaries will ever be able to block the way of the Korean people, no matter how desperately they may attempt to. The day will certainly come when the aggressors are driven out of Korea, the reactionary traitorous clique is brought to judgment before the people and Korea is reunified and attains independence and sovereignty.

Let us all unite our strength and march forward vigorously for a fresh victory!

ON THE TASKS OF OUR PARTY ORGANIZATIONS

Speech Delivered at a Conference of the Organization of Sunchon County, South Pyongan Province, of the Workers' Party of North Korea

January 24, 1948

Comrades,

As many comrades have said in their speeches, the Workers' Party of North Korea has turned into a great, strong political party leading our people to freedom and national independence, bearing the destinies of the country and posterity on its shoulders.

It was not long ago that our Party was founded. Only a year and a half has passed particularly since the Communist Party, the predecessor of our Party, and the New Democratic Party were merged to form the Workers' Party of North Korea. In this short span of time, however, our Party has made brilliant achievements for the country and the people and performed great exploits which will shine ever long in history.

Though it is not long since our Party was founded, the struggle waged by the Korean Communists for the restoration of the fatherland and the happiness of the people has a very long history. The Korean Communists are genuine patriots who fought for the honour of the country and the nation, at the cost of blood and lives, under Japanese imperialist rule. In the days when the oppression by the Japanese imperialists was harsh and our nation found itself in an indescribably dire distress, the Korean Communists, weapon in hand, waged an indomitable struggle against Japanese imperialism despite all difficulties and hardships. Our Party is a party that has inherited the revolutionary traditions of those Communists who struggled most devotedly for the country and the people, a glorious party which is heir to the history of the heroic liberation struggle waged by the Korean people. Our Party, therefore, is the most patriotic, most progressive and most powerful party in Korea.

The Workers' Party is the organized vanguard detachment of the Korean working masses, made up of best, advanced elements of the workers, peasants and working intellectuals with the working class, the main force of our nation, as its core. That is why our Party defends the interests of the workers, peasants and working intellectuals and has a bond of kinship with them, and has from the first day of its founding to this date striven for the happiness of the Korean people and a bright future for the country.

Our Party has sprung from the roots of the anti-Japanese national-liberation struggle which imbued the Korean people with hopes and confidence in victory in the darkest days of Japanese imperialist rule, and it is precisely our Party that leads the Korean people along the road of building a new, rich and strong democratic country after liberation, bearing the destinies of the country and the nation on its shoulders. Had it not been for our Party, what would the fate of our country be like today, and who, if not our Party, could have ever pointed to the bright vistas of victory for our nation?

The democratic socio-economic reforms accomplished triumphantly in north Korea were a great work to lay the basis for building a democratic country and served as a beacon light showing the south Korean people the road to follow. Had it not been for our Party, who else could have ever taken the initiative in those great democratic reforms and ensured their triumph in north Korea? Our historic victory in the great cause of transforming society along democratic lines can be attributed solely to the fact that our Party extensively mobilized the patriotic democratic forces, working hand in hand with the friendly parties and drawing firmly on the united front, and always played the leading role in the van of the people from all walks of life.

Our Party has become a party strong and influential enough to rank among the best of the Communist and Workers' Parties in the world in the light of both its exploits in the revolutionary struggle and its high prestige among the masses of the people and its own organized force.

Whereas its membership at the time of the merger was only about 370,000, our Party has now developed into a mass party of over 700,000. Our Party is composed of best sons and daughters of the working people, ready to fight most gallantly and sacrificingly for the country and the people.

In the early days of the Party's foundation, there were no few instances of various shades of alien elements who sneaked into the Party, damaging its prestige in flagrant violation of Party discipline, because some Party organizations did not faithfully abide by the organizational principles and, besides, the factionalists manoeuvred to undermine the unity of the Party. However, as a result of the decisive inner-Party struggle against the alien elements and factionalists, our Party has now grown into a militant, spirited organization, the purity of whose ranks is assured and in which iron discipline is established.

Thus, our Party has, since the merger, grown not only in quantity but in quality as well, and turned into a genuine Marxist-Leninist Party where its organizational principles have been firmly established and ideological unity achieved from the centre down to the lowest units. Today, with the Second Party Congress in the offing, we can say that this is the greatest success we have scored in Party building.

Worthy of particular mention among the successes achieved in Party building is the growth and consolidation of the cells. Previously, many of our Party members did not have a clear understanding of what the cell was, what the cell had to do and what role it had to play. However, from the checkup in the autumn of 1947 on the work of the cells of the Party organizations under all provincial Party committees, from my recent study of the work of the Party cells in the local districts such as Kanggye and Kaechon, and from my analysis of the speeches of many comrades at this meeting today, it is entirely possible to draw a conclusion that the work of our Party cells has improved qualitatively; the political consciousness of the Party members has risen; and their Party life has been strengthened.

Even though our Party has achieved such organizational unity and political and ideological consolidation, we should not rest content in the least nor should we be carried away by victory. More difficult and complex tasks now confront our Party which, carrying the destiny of the country on its shoulders, is leading the Korean people, and the duties devolving on each of us Party members are really great.

Though the successes achieved by our Party and people in building a new life following liberation are tremendous, they represent as yet no more than an initial step in the building of a rich and strong democratic country. The triumph of the democratic reforms in north Korea has only created conditions for the democratic development of our country, and it by no means signifies the complete accomplishment of our cause. We should develop our economy and culture, improve the people's life and reinforce our democratic base further still by steadily advancing along the road of genuine people's democracy on the basis of the victory in the democratic reforms. We should mobilize the united strength of the entire Korean people to introduce democratic reforms also in south Korea, the other half of the country, as in north Korea and achieve the complete independence, sovereignty and reunification of the country.

To reinforce the democratic base in this way and then turn all of Korea into a genuine democratic state of the people is a sacred national task facing us. To carry out this task we should wage a relentless struggle against the internal and external reactionary forces that are seeking to encroach upon the freedom and independence of our nation, and should, first of all, build up our own strength further still.

What is most important in building up our strength? To strengthen in every way the people's power set up by our own hands and rapidly develop the national economy in a planned way to lay the basis for an independent national economy. If only we have a strong people's power and the firm basis of an independent economy, nothing will be impossible for us.

For the first time last year we ran the national economy in a planned way. When the national economic plan for 1947 was announced, a tremendous hue and cry was raised. Our enemy mockingly called it an unattainable dream and even some of our cadres, doubtful of the feasibility of the plan, wavered. But the people in north Korea, particularly our working class and peasantry, boldly set out under the leadership of our Party to carry out the first national economic plan in factories, enterprises and farm and fishing villages. At first, they felt the plan, then tried their hand at its implementation little by little and gradually gained confidence that they were quite capable of carrying it out. Now all the working people turned out as one man in the struggle to overfulfil the plan. As you know, the result was that the 1947 national economic plan was fulfilled ahead of the set time as a whole.

The most valuable gain we made in successfully carrying out the first national economic plan is that our Workers' Party members and the entire working people came to have confidence in the building of the country. Our workers and peasants, who overfulfilled the difficult plan which had seemed beyond their power at first, came to have faith in their own strength and became convinced that they were capable enough of doing anything by their efforts.

In battle, too, it is the rule that an army without confidence in victory is defeated and an army with high morale and firm confidence in victory beats the enemy without fail.

Likewise, the most important thing in the revolutionary struggle or in economic construction is that the masses of the people have confidence in victory, conscious of their own strength. It is, therefore, the principal result of last year's work and the greatest political victory we won in carrying out the first economic plan that our Party members and the entire working people became deeply convinced through practice of the justness of what they were doing and gained a firm confidence that they were fully capable of building an independent and sovereign state for themselves.

Following the road indicated by our Party, our people created the basic conditions for building an independent and sovereign state in 1946 and, on that basis, carried on economic construction to lay the material basis for the prosperity and development of the country in 1947. In this course our people gained confidence in victory, came to have faith in their ability to do anything by their efforts and became deeply convinced that the path traversed by north Korea after liberation was precisely the most right path to be followed by the Korean people. No one can deprive our people of the revolutionary gains they have won in north Korea or shake their firm determination to march farther ahead and their confidence in victory.

Our people have established and run the genuine people's power according to their own will. The state power set up by ourselves is doing its work for the people fairly well. Our people have restored and operated the factories and enterprises destroyed by the Japanese imperialists before quitting. As a result, blast furnaces were put back into operation and began to produce pig iron and the Supung Hydroelectric Power Station, a product of the development of modern technology, went into operation and started supplying electricity to all parts of the country. Our young workers, who served as locomotive stokers in the days of Japanese imperialist rule, have now become engineers and are ably driving locomotives. Our intellectuals started research in various fields of science for the building of the country. Our people have built and are running establishments of higher learning on their own, and set up the security organs and also organized the security forces.

All these things created by our people, though still not free from some shortcomings, have already made a worthy contribution to the cause of building the country. They also show that our nation has as fine a talent as any and is fully capable of building up its country for itself, and they infinitely uplift the national pride and self-confidence of our people.

Our people have taken power into their hands and are administering it and are running factories, mines, railway transport, educational and cultural establishments by themselves. Who can ever deprive our people of their right to do so? Nobody can take it from them, and there is no force in the world capable of doing so. No matter how desperately he may attempt, the enemy can never take away lands from our peasants who are freely cultivating the land distributed by their organs of people's power; factories from our workers who have become masters of the factories and are working with devotion for the prosperity and development of the country and for the enhancement of their own welfare; or schools from our students who are studying assiduously in democratic schools for the construction of an independent national economy and the blossoming of national culture in their country.

If the foreign imperialist burglars and their stooges—traitors to the nation—pounce upon us to rob us of our power, land, factories and schools, our people will fight to the end at any sacrifice and rather choose death than yield to anyone the precious fruits of victory gained over the past two years.

Many things are still in short supply with us. Materials and equipment are short, and so are clothes and footwear, too. We, however, have produced a greater volume of materials and goods in short supply by overcoming all the difficulties and hardships, and thus have created objective conditions to reinforce the economic basis of the country and improve the people's livelihood. Especially, as the result of the successful fulfilment of last year's plan, many factories, enterprises and railway transport facilities have been rehabilitated, and we are in a position to produce various kinds of equipment, materials and consumer goods on a normal basis and ensure transport smoothly beginning this year.

At the same time, our internal force has increased incomparably. In a little more than two years after liberation our Party and people have accumulated a wealth of experience in the building of a new life, and our Party members have acquired the methods and ability to organize and agitate the masses and enlist their force in the implementation of the Party's policies. The elections to the organs of power at various levels held on several occasions and the currency changeover successfully effected at the end of last year clearly showed how cleverly our Party organizes and mobilizes the masses and also how much the masses support and trust our Party. Our Party smoothly carried out such complex work as the changeover of old to new currency in only a week by arousing the entire membership to action and enlisting the conscious enthusiasm of the people. This affords striking evidence of how promptly our Party organizations and organs of people's power can take action in the interests of the masses of the people.

Actual life has already proved the correctness of our Party's lines and policies to the full. Our Party has achieved organizational and ideological unity and has been further tempered and seasoned politically in the struggle for freedom, independence and democratization of the country.

There is therefore no insurmountable difficulty before our Party, and there can be no enemy whom our Party and people cannot beat by fighting in monolithic unity. The people themselves have been convinced through practical experience that if they, united around our Party, march forward along the road indicated by it, they could triumphantly accomplish whatever difficult task.

Our Party will see to the successful fulfilment of the 1948 national economic plan by mobilizing all the patriotic democratic forces, and accomplish without fail the cause of building a unified, independent democratic state by repulsing all the manoeuvres of the enemy.

Comrades, this does not mean, however, that we are free from any shortcomings. Our Party work has shortcomings and drawbacks which must be rectified quickly.

First, the Party members and cadres lack in political training, and Marxist-Leninist ideological education within the Party is still weak.

Our Party is the militant vanguard detachment of the labouring masses of Korea. Our Party should above all equip itself closely with progressive ideology and scientific revolutionary theory in order that, as the vanguard detachment of the working people, it may lead to victory the struggle for the liberation of the Korean nation and social emancipation of the labouring masses.

If the company, battalion, regimental and other superior commanders in an army are ignorant of strategy and tactics, the army cannot win a battle. Likewise, if our Party, the vanguard detachment of the working people, fails to arm itself with the revolutionary theory, it will not be able to correctly guide the struggle of the masses of the people. Especially in the light of the actual conditions, in which we are faced with difficult and complex tasks, we ever more urgently need the theory that indicates our course like a compass and brightly illumines the road ahead like a beacon. Such a theory is undoubtedly Marxist-Leninist theory, the only scientific theory on the revolution in modern society.

Marxism-Leninism is an all-conquering theory which has been tested and whose vitality has been confirmed through the revolutionary practice of the advanced working class in many countries of the world. What our Party must study, study and study is not the Bible nor any religious dogma, but precisely this Marxist-Leninist theory. The entire Party from the cadres in the centre down to the last member must arm themselves with Marxist-Leninist theory and acquire advanced, scientific knowledge. Only by so doing can every cadre and Party member become an able political worker, ideologically steeled and theoretically prepared, and lead the masses confidently along the right path.

Second, one of our Party's shortcomings is that the work of the cells is as yet at a low level. The strengthening of the cells is a question on which the Central Committee of our Party has kept laying stress since its inception.

Our Party cells have grown up markedly as compared with the past. The cells have learned to abide by the organizational principle and discipline of the Party, give assignments to the Party members and sum up their execution, and ensure the fulfilment of the economic plans of the state. Many cells, however, still fail to do their work satisfactorily.

The central problem in the work of the cell is to foster the cell nucleus. The composition of a cell is not simple with regard either to the social origin of its Party members or to their political and ideological level. A cell has Party members who are tempered politically or who suffer from political and ideological backwardness, and Party members who take an active part in the work of the cell or are rather passive in it. We, therefore, must build up the nucleus of each cell with Party activists, steadily expand the ranks of nucleus and make them exert a decisive influence through their example in practice on all Party members so as to enhance the latter's political and ideological consciousness and their awakening from the Party standpoint.

Especially the county and *myon* Party committees must direct profound attention to fostering the cell nucleus. They must select three to four active Party members eligible for the nucleus from every cell, regularly arrange short courses for them, and give them day-to-day help and training. In this way the nucleus in each cell should be guided to play the leading role in improving the work of the cell, in strengthening the Party life of all members and heightening their Party spirit.

Third, in our Party there are still empty talkers who are more ready to talk than to act and only pay lip service to their work. These Party members should be taught to rectify their habit.

Party members must become models and pacemakers in actual work, in economic construction, instead of shouting slogans and only paying lip service to the building of the country in a loud voice. There must be no such persons in our Party as are merely glib of tongue while not knowing how to go about practical work, and as shy away from a toilsome job, loath to take the lead in tackling it.

All our Party members without exception must become able organizers and competent builders. To become an able organizer and builder, each Party member should be well versed in the Party's lines and policies and know how to manage and run the economy.

There should be no idle and leisured persons among our Party members. Our Party is the advanced detachment of the labouring masses, and so it must be seen to that the spirit of industry is displayed in the daily life and work of all its members and that the habit of loving labour prevails throughout the Party. Thus, everybody should be induced to show devotion in all matters, realizing that he will find his life worth living only when he works, and that he is as good as a dead man if he has no work to do.

Our people have a mountain of work to cope with in future in order to rid our country of its backwardness and build it into a rich and strong country. We have to do lots of complex and difficult work—erecting factories, developing agriculture, advancing culture, strengthening the organs of people's power and so on. Our Party members should work with devotion for the country and the people and for the Party from morning till night every day, devoting all their energies and zeal to the historic cause of building a new country. There is no place for leisured and idle persons in our Party.

Now, I should like to dwell on the strengthening of the united front.

The question of strengthening the united front is one of the most important political questions at the present stage of the development of our country. There are a considerable number of members of the friendly parties in Sunchon County alone where you are working.

And the question lies not in whether the members of the friendly parties are few or many or how these parties absorb people into their ranks, but in how our Party maintains close ties with the friendly parties, helps them in their activities and leads their members to expose and drive out in good time the shady elements who have sneaked into their parties and how our Party co-operates with them in achieving the common goal of winning freedom and independence for the country.

To strengthen the united front it is essential to thoroughly realize the importance of the united front and the quintessence of our Party's policy on the united front.

The basic tasks confronting our Party and the Korean people at the present stage are to crush the colonization manoeuvres of the U.S. imperialists, completely liberate the whole of Korea and build a unified Democratic People's Republic. Our Party, therefore, is ready to work hand in hand with any party if it is a democratic party willing to fight for the interests of the country and the nation.

What are the conditions, then, that enable our Party to form a united front with the Democratic Party? The Democratic Party consists of men of the small propertied classes, entrepreneurs, traders, rich farmers, some petty bourgeois and persons of other social strata, and has it as its Programme to oppose the oppression by foreign imperialism and build a rich and strong Korea. Should the wild designs of the U.S. imperialists come into reality and our country be reduced to a colonial market for U.S. monopoly capital, the entrepreneurs, traders and rich farmers who belong to the Democratic Party will also be ruined and go bankrupt, just as under Japanese imperialist rule. Since they are aware of this, the members of the Democratic Party do not want our country to become a colony of a foreign country and its national economy to be ruined, but would like it to become a rich and strong independent country. Besides, they are gradually coming to the realization that not feudal monarchy or U.S.-type democracy but a system of progressive democracy must be established if our country is to achieve independence and become rich and strong, and that, to attain that goal, they must join hands with the Workers' Party and co-operate with the workers, peasants and other sections of the working people. This proves that today our Party and the Democratic Party can form a united front and keep in step with each other in the struggle against the colonial enslavement policy of U.S. imperialism, the common enemy, and for establishing a Democratic People's Republic.

As a matter of course, there are in fact among the Democratic Party members some who commit reactionary acts. Those elements are a handful of reactionaries who have wormed their way into the Democratic Party with the real intention of disrupting it, outwardly pretending to be supporting its Programme.

Those elements who have sneaked into the Democratic Party and are now perpetrating reactionary acts are in general of the following categories:

First, they are the pro-American elements who, influenced by U.S. propaganda in the past, worship the United States and harbour illusions about it. The United States had sent to our country missionaries under the mantle of religion long ago to build churches in many places and disseminate Christianity and ideas of U.S. worship, and made preparations over tens of years to dominate Korea some day. This was an insidious trick of the United States to feign sympathy with the Koreans and establish its influence in Korea under the cloak of religion.

The U.S. missionaries preached to the Koreans, "Whosoever shall smite thee on thy right cheek, turn to him the other also." This implies that the Korean people must not resist but remain submissive even if the United States encroaches upon their freedom. The Korean patriots and people, however, were not fooled by this deceptive preaching of the United States. Our people answered to the U.S. rascals, "If you slap us once, we will return two slaps," and did so in deed.

Yet, some of the pastors and church elders, taken in by such a religious propaganda, are trying to sell out our country for dollars, worshipping the United States like a "God." Precisely some of those reactionary pastors or church elders have crawled into the Democratic Party and are playing nasty tricks.

Second, reactionary acts are often perpetrated by a handful

of speculators and profiteers who have slipped into the Democratic Party. Holding their own interests dearer than the interests of the country and the nation, they have an antipathy to the democratic reforms carried out in north Korea and are none too pleased with the rehabilitation and development of the national economy. For the development of the national economy constitutes a blow to their profiteering acts. This being the case, they set themselves desperately against the progress of our society and the development of the national economy so as to continue with their acts of speculation and profiteering and viciously squeeze the working people.

Thus, within the Democratic Party there are a handful of malicious elements who are operating underhand against the democratic development of the country, but the members of our Party and the Democratic Party, with the exception of those elements, can unite forces with each other and, firmly joining hands, march forward for the common goal of achieving the complete independence and democratic reunification of the country.

Now, let us have a look at the Chongu Party. As for its composition, the Chongu Party consists largely of peasants. We, therefore, can form a united front with it at any time.

Yet, among the Chongu Party members, too, some elements are occasionally found committing reactionary acts. They are reactionary elements and urban loafers who have wormed their way into the Chongu Party in disguise, and are engaged in underhand manoeuvres against the progressive personalities in it while disconcerting its policies in violation of its Programme.

The reactionary elements lurking in the Chongu Party want the peasants to remain in a state of backwardness and ignorance as long as possible in the hope of befooling them and achieving their ends readily. But our Party has made the peasants masters of land through the democratic reform and is leading them along the road to a new, blissful life and continues to awaken them ideologically and to enlighten them culturally. So, these reactionary elements, who are losing their foothold among the peasants with every passing day, indulge in reactionary acts against our Party and people's power, hiding themselves behind the signboard of the Chongu Party.

We should not suspect the friendly parties nor shun them by reason of the fact that a handful of malicious elements who crept into those parties perpetrate reactionary acts, but should trust them and co-operate more closely with them according to their Programmes and policies. This alone will make it possible to correctly implement our Party's united front policy and mobilize all the patriotic democratic forces to build a rich, strong, independent and sovereign state.

All members and organizations at all levels of our Party must further strengthen their unity with the members and organizations of the friendly parties at the lower level and constantly keep close ties with them, conduct the work of democratic education among the members of those parties, raise still higher the ideological consciousness and cultural level of the backward peasants, help the progressive elements in the friendly parties to wipe out the wicked elements lurking in their parties, and unfold a struggle in our Party, too, against the elements who seek to disrupt the united front, thereby strengthening our National Democratic United Front in every way.

We must not lose the identity of our Party in the work of the united front at any time. Our Party members must keep fast to the progressive stand of our Party and exert ideological influence on the friendly parties, and, at the same time, wage an uncompromising struggle against all shades of unjust, anti-popular tendencies. Our Party is the vanguard detachment of the Korean working people, equipped with the advanced theory and possessing the brilliant traditions of the revolutionary struggle for the liberation of the country. Our Party, therefore, is fully able and ought to help the friendly parties with its ideology and theory and its rich experience gained in the struggle for the liberty and independence of the country. We must always be open-minded and modest towards the members of the friendly parties and see to it that they come themselves to our Party members to hold consultations and ask for our help whenever there arises a knotty problem.

The more the rank-and-file unity is strengthened and the closer the mutual ties and co-operation grow between the organizations of our Party and the friendly parties and between their members, the stronger our united front will become, and when things turn out this way, no force will be able to disrupt our united front.

While closely co-operating with all the patriotic democratic parties in this way, our Party must fight to the bitter end against the anti-national, anti-popular traitorous clique. Why is it that we cannot form a united front with the traitorous Syngman Rhee clique? It is because they have turned into stooges of U.S. imperialism and openly betray the interests of the nation. Those who have joined the Syngman Rhee clique are all pro-Japanese elements who were minions of Japanese imperialism in its days and, now that their old master is gone and a new master has come, are acting as henchmen of U.S. imperialism. Patriots and quislings can in no circumstances join hands nor compromise with each other. The henchmen of foreign imperialism must be duly brought to justice by the people.

The Workers' Party of North Korea and the Workers' Party of South Korea know well who our enemy is and with whom we can form a united front. The united front is not to be formed with the enemies but with the friends. We must therefore continue to wage a tenacious struggle against the U.S. imperialists and their stooges by strengthening the united front with the Democratic Party and the Chongu Party that aspire to build a rich, strong, independent and sovereign state and by effecting the general mobilization of the patriotic, democratic forces from all walks of life.

Last, the patriotic spirit of state building, a spirit of loving the country and building it into a rich and strong country more speedily, must be further cultivated in the people. In all factories, mines, collieries, and in all institutions and enterprises there should be established the habit of striving for good care of state property, better use of machines and equipment, economy in labour and materials, reduction of all unproductive expenditures, production of more and better goods and more quick construction with less funds. It is an important task facing our Party organizations to inspire the working people with the patriotic spirit of state building and fight to rid them of the ideological legacy left over from the days of Japanese imperialism, which is manifested in their slipshod ways of working and living.

Our people will before long have their Constitution and their army. We should take due pride in and strictly abide by the Constitution of our country that will lend legal confirmation to the people's power established by our own hands and all the rights and liberties won by our own might, and should actively support and assist our People's Army that will be organized with our beloved sons and daughters.

Through the review of the work of, and elections at, the Party organizations of all levels which are to take place prior to the Second Congress of the Workers' Party of North Korea, we should further strengthen the Party organizationally and ideologically and correctly sum up their precious lessons and rich experience gained in the period under review and thus make them serve as a guide to the development of our Party work in future.

We must further increase the fighting efficiency of our Party, enhance its prestige among the masses and rally them rock-firm around it by electing to the Party's leading bodies and sending to the Party conferences best Party members who are striving with devotion for the sake of the country, the people and the Party, and have been tested and tempered in practical work.

Let us vigorously march forward for a fresh victory, building up our Party ranks ever firmer and leading the broad masses of the people united around the Party!

HOW TO DEVELOP STATE INDUSTRY AND HOW TO MANAGE THE ENTERPRISES?

Talk with the Managers and Technicians of State Enterprises

January 25, 1948

I should like to dwell on how to develop state industry and how to manage the enterprises this year, limiting myself primarily to the questions you have raised.

First of all, we should strive by all means to settle matters on our own which we can cope with by our own efforts.

Through our experience gained in the triumphant fulfilment of the national economic plan for 1947, we have become more firmly confident that it is quite possible for us to develop the national industry independently. Indeed, we need to receive necessary foreign aid in the future, too, but we must have a firm determination to rehabilitate and develop the national economy and build a rich and powerful country by our own efforts, without seeking to rely entirely on others.

This year, the factories should be rehabilitated completely and industrial production be raised to the level of the years of Japanese imperialist rule. And we should not be concerned only in the quantitative growth of production, it is necessary to pay attention to gradually improving its qualitative structure too. We should not send out to foreign countries the raw materials which we extract from the abundant domestic sources, as in the bygone days of Japanese imperialist rule, but should proceed in the direction of processing all of them at home to produce finished goods. The problem of crude petroleum, one of our biggest snags, should be solved through foreign trade, and refined oil should be produced by rehabilitating the Wonsan Oil Refinery within the current year.

The aim of production for the factories that have become the people's property is to fully satisfy the demands of the masses of the people. We should quickly restore and readjust the factories and erect new ones to strengthen the economic foundation of our country and to turn out more goods essential for the improvement of our people's life. At the same time, the goods which our people have in surplus should be exchanged through foreign trade for the goods we need.

The question of deciding on the order of priority in construction work is very important. We have quite a lot to build, for we have taken over a backward and ravaged economy. But all this cannot be built in a day or two. It is, therefore, imperative to build the most urgent ones first. It will not do if we think of only one aspect and lose sight of the whole, or think of today only and forget tomorrow. A strict order of priority should be fixed in construction, and the funds, techniques and labour force should be concentrated on the urgent construction projects, always taking into consideration the prospects of the development of the national economy as a whole and of the country.

And it will not do to try impetuously to build only up-to-date and fine things from the outset. It is a wrong attitude to hasten to do right now what you should do a few years hence. We should combat the tendency to seek after only gorgeous decorations or up-to-date equipment in construction. Economic construction should on all accounts be conducted in keeping with our present conditions, and construction work should be done effectively with less funds and materials, beginning with urgent projects.

Production should be put on a normal basis and the plans fulfilled without fail in the factories and enterprises. To this end, it is undoubtedly important to prepare materials beforehand and organize labour properly, but the most important thing is to check and repair machines and equipment in good time, operate them efficiently and thus prevent accidents in advance. To cause an accident or shorten the life of a machine by overworking it in one's excessive eagerness to fulfil one's norms is tantamount to an act of destroying state property and is seriously detrimental to production.

Now I should like to deal with the ways of securing funds smoothly.

First, measures should be taken to turn over the floating funds of enterprises more quickly. So far, very little attention has been paid to this matter. We should prevent factories and enterprises from receiving too much materials only to keep them idle in storehouses or not selling the produced goods promptly but stockpiling them, and should endeavour to turn over funds for use more quickly and build and produce more with the same amount of funds.

Second, funds should not be allocated to heavy industry alone, but a large amount of funds should be channeled to light industry as well to increase the production of living necessaries sharply. More light industry factories should be built and latent reserves be enlisted to the full everywhere to put out consumer goods in greater quantities. This is not only advantageous to quickly getting back and securing funds but is also essential for meeting in full the needs of the working people's life. According to reports from local districts or to what I have gone out and seen for myself, the requirements of the people in north Korea are now growing rapidly every day. In particular, the peasants who have become masters of land and achieved good results in farming demand lots of textiles and furniture, improved farm implements, building materials to erect new houses, etc. We should satisfy the growing demands of the peasants and thus convince them more firmly of the advantages of the democratic system and, at the same time, should actively absorb funds for economic construction.

Third, gold and other nonferrous metals hidden underground should be extracted in large quantities. If only we have gold and other nonferrous metals, we can purchase any kind of equipment or materials no matter when and where. When could we use gold if we do not mine it in our times when we are building a rich, powerful, independent and sovereign state? This is not the time for us to leave this precious mineral as it is hidden underground.

As technical personnel were originally scarce in our country, it is important to turn to good account the force and talents of technicians at the factories and enterprises. Technicians should not be burdened with cumbersome office work, but should be provided with conditions to study and make new inventions. And the technicians should not be tied down to departments of administration and management, but should be made to work directly at production sites, and they should be given active help to develop techniques there in co-operation with the workers.

Last year our technicians put forward a good many valuable new ideas and made a great contribution to the development of technology. Yet, the creative efforts of the technicians are still insufficient. I hope the technicians will make a still greater spurt in future, and expect them to make a bigger contribution to the industrial development in our country.

It is necessary to properly organize technical study and the pass-on-skill work in all factories and enterprises. The system of technical study has not yet been established and this work is conducted in a very desultory way in factories. This shortcoming should be eliminated, the system of technical education should be established without delay and the technical standards of the personnel and the skill level of the workers be raised systematically.

One of the most important problems in the fulfilment of the national economic plan is to organize labour properly. Nevertheless, this matter is not tackled satisfactorily in the factories and enterprises at present.

At a certain colliery in North Hamgyong Province, they increased only the number of workers haphazardly without endeavouring to raise labour productivity in carrying out the production assignments. In consequence, a tremendous obstacle was offered to lowering the production costs of coal, to say nothing of the work of labour administration of the state. Such a practice should not be overlooked at any factory or enterprise and primary attention should be directed to the rational organization of labour and to increasing labour productivity.

The ratio of office workers to the number of employees of the enterprises is still high. Measures should be taken as soon as possible to decisively simplify office work, curtail the unnecessary staff and divert nonproductive labour to productive work. As regards simplifying the system of cumbrous administrative and statistical reports, I will give a separate instruction in the future.

Even according to preliminary estimates, if the labour force is allocated in a rational way and the organization of labour is improved on a nation-wide scale, production can be increased by some 50 per cent even with a 10-15 per cent cut in the present number of workers at the state enterprises, and the labour force thus released can be diverted to the newly-built factories.

The reduction of production costs requires higher labour productivity and, at the same time, a vigorous struggle against the practice of wasting state property and an energetic economy in all materials and funds. It should be made clearly known to the workers that only by lowering the costs of production will it be possible to increase the gains of the enterprises and supply the working people with cheaper commodities. The costs of production can be lowered and greater successes be achieved in production only if the workers, before anyone else, display creative initiative and all factory employees tap reserves to the full.

Decision No. 104 adopted recently by the People's Committee of North Korea should be executed thoroughly and public welfare service be organized properly from the state point of view. It is one of the most important duties of the manager of an enterprise to look after the life of the workers with meticulous care, supply necessary goods in good time and provide every convenience to them. Only the manager who does this job well can enjoy the deep trust of the workers and ensure the successful fulfilment of production plans by enlisting their enthusiasm and creative initiative. But there should not be committed such act as purchasing commodities from the profiteers with state money on the plea of supplying the workers and office employees with goods which are needful to their life.

It is important to educate the workers, technicians and office employees in the spirit that it is they themselves who are masters of the state and enterprises. At certain places, some workers and managing personnel demand higher wages recklessly, oblivious of the fact that they are themselves masters of the enterprises. It should be brought home to them that this is a wrong idea. In the state enterprise, the machinery and equipment, materials and produced goods and all belong to our people, to the workers. If all the produce is appropriated as income of the workers merely for consumption, it will be impossible to continue and expand production. That is why the workers receive as their wages only part of what they have produced. Here, the expansion of production is also, in the final analysis, for the good of the workers and for the betterment of our people's life in the future. We should therefore make the workers well aware that they should further increase production if they are to get higher wages and that they will be better off all right if only they increase production.

It is wrong only to seek to live above our means avariciously when the conditions of our country are still difficult. When the conditions of the state and enterprises improve, the incomes of the workers, technicians and office employees will naturally rise and their livelihood, too, will improve sharply.

Also, the workers, technicians and office employees should be made to keep a strict vigilance at all times with the realization that we are today building the country amidst a severe fight with the enemy. The enemy is watching for a chance to destroy the people's property and frustrate our economic construction. We should see that order and system be firmly established in the factories and every functionary and worker sharpen vigilance to the utmost in order to shatter the frantic intrigues of the enemy and stoutly defend our enterprises.

In conclusion, I should like to remark that in industrial construction the manager of an enterprise should play a role comparable to that of a regimental commander in the army. You are commanders of the enterprises and bear a heavy responsibility to the state. True, the manager should conduct the enterprise in close co-operation with the Party organization and social organizations in the factory, but you should not forget that the responsibility for the results of production rests with you after all.

I hope you managers of state enterprises will organize and guide all affairs effectively and responsibly and work with the conviction and sense of honour that you are laying the foundation for the eternal prosperity of the country.

ON THE OCCASION OF THE CREATION OF THE KOREAN PEOPLE'S ARMY

Speech Delivered at a Review of the Korean People's Army

February 8, 1948

Comrade officers, noncommissioned officers and men of the Korean People's Army,

Dear fellow countrymen,

Celebrating the second anniversary of the establishment of the People's Committee of North Korea, the genuine people's power, we today proclaim the founding of the Korean People's Army, the first regular armed forces of the people's own in the history of Korea. After liberation, the Korean people, who had been subjected to all sorts of persecution and suppression under the bayonets of the Japanese imperialists, took power into their own hands and set out to create a new, happy life, and now they have their own full-fledged regular army to defend the country and nation.

With the great national pride and joy of the liberated people of Korea, I heartily congratulate the creation of the People's Army.

Now all the people of north and south Korea can take pride before the whole world in having their own modern, regular army to fight for the freedom and honour of the country.

It is for the further promotion of complete independence

and sovereignty of the country on a democratic basis that we have founded the People's Army today.

In slightly over two years after liberation our people have laid the political, economic and cultural foundations for building an independent and sovereign democratic state in north Korea. With the establishment of the people's power and the enforcement of democratic reforms we have brought to realization the age-old, ardent national desire of the broad masses of the people, thus opening up new, broad vistas for developing our society. And last year, we achieved our first great results in laying the foundations of an independent national economy by drawing up a national economic plan and fulfilling it successfully. With the currency changeover, our people have come to possess their own currency and consolidated the foundation of the country's independent finances. And the draft Provisional Constitution of Korea has been drawn up which will legally validate the results of the democratic reforms and democratic construction in north Korea and provide the legal foundations for the Democratic People's Republic of Korea to be set up in the future.

But until now we did not have a regular army of the Korean people to defend all these gains by force of arms.

Any state, if ever an independent and sovereign state, never fails to have its own army. Naturally, no state can be a completely independent and sovereign state without its own army. Our country was occupied by the Japanese imperialists because the Korean people at that time had no army of their own strong enough to defeat the Japanese imperialist aggressor army.

For our country to become a completely independent and sovereign state it is therefore indispensable to have a mighty people's army wholly capable of defending the country and the nation and of repulsing any enemy invasion. It has become a very urgent and vital problem for the Korean people to create their own army, particularly under the serious circumstances whereby our country's reunification, independence and sovereignty have been retarded till now, for more than two years after liberation, as a result of the vicious manoeuvrings by the U.S. imperialists and their lackeys to split our nation and turn our country once again into a colony.

Our people can neither remain mere onlookers at the policy of national division of the U.S. imperialists and their stooges, nor can we wait for any one to give us independence and organize an army for us. The Korean people must build an independent and sovereign democratic state entirely by their own efforts and make all preparations for setting up a unified government by themselves. And they must organize their army on their own, thereby promoting the building of a unified, independent and democratic country.

It is not fortuitous that the task of creating a People's Army has been accomplished in north Korea. This is because only in north Korea, where the people have become masters of the state, has it been possible to create a People's Army whose mission it is to defend the country and the nation. It is inconceivable to found a genuine national army of the Korean people in present-day south Korea which is under U.S. military government and where the pro-Japanese elements and **traitors to the nation have taken "power" and** are training their terrorists.

Our people, who are courageously blazing the path for the whole of Korea to follow by carrying out democratic reforms and successfully building their economy and culture in north Korea, will, through the organization of the Korean People's Army today, further strengthen the might of the democratic base in north Korea and lay a solid foundation for the armed forces of the Democratic People's Republic of Korea to be set up in the not too distant future. The people in south Korea, who are gaining immense courage and hopes from the democratic construction in north Korea, will regard our People's Army founded today as their own army and as their own forces. So, the founding of the People's Army will give mighty encouragement to the fathers and mothers, brothers and sisters in south Korea, now groaning under the oppression of the U.S. military government and the reactionary, traitorous clique, in their struggle for the reunification and independence of the country along democratic lines.

Further, we have created the People's Army to firmly defend the democratic base of north Korea and the fruits of the democratic reforms—the groundwork for the establishment of a unified Democratic People's Republic—from the enemy's encroachment, and to guarantee happiness and security to the people in north Korea.

As is known to all, the U.S. imperialists, the pro-Japanese elements and the traitors to the nation in south Korea, in their attempt to hamper our democratic development and peaceful construction in north Korea, are not only given to slanders and false propaganda. They are also making every attempt to destroy our precious state property and throw the life of the north Korean people into confusion by sending in large numbers of terrorists engaged exclusively in murder, arson and subversion. As a matter of course, these attempts of the enemy are thoroughly exposed and frustrated at every step by the united strength and high revolutionary vigilance of our people. However, the firmer the democratic base of north Korea is strengthened and the greater victories our people win, the more frenzied the U.S. imperialists and the reactionaries in south Korea become and the more viciously the enemies attempt to destroy the fruits of the democratic reforms and economic construction in north Korea.

By founding the People's Army, therefore, we must firmly defend the democratic system established in north Korea and the happy life of our people, and prevent any reactionary forces and subversive elements from spoiling in the slightest degree all the precious results gained by the north Korean people in their struggle for the independence, sovereignty and democratization of the country to this day since liberation.

We must remember that only when we are strong and the democratic forces prevail unchallenged can genuine peace be preserved, freedom be guaranteed for the country and the people, and the enemy cannot attempt any reckless attack on us. Therefore, the strengthening of the democratic forces and the founding of the People's Army in north Korea, far from presenting a threat of fratricidal civil war as is viciously propagandized by the reactionary elements, will on the contrary prevent U.S. imperialism and the reactionaries in south Korea from starting such a civil war.

Comrade officers, noncommissioned officers and men of the Korean People's Army,

Dear fellow countrymen,

The People's Army we have founded today is an army of a new type fundamentally different from that of a capitalist country.

The army of a capitalist country is organized to defend and maintain by arms the system of oppression and exploitation of the working people—the absolute majority of the population—in the interests of a handful of capitalists and landlords and to attack other nations and invade the territories of other countries. We vividly saw such armies in Hitler Germany and militarist Japan, and we see them in all capitalist countries. Particularly, the U.S. army that after the war entered such countries as China and Greece, which are not defeated nations, and interferes in their internal affairs, and enforces military government in south Korea, refusing to withdraw, has become the prototype of the predatory imperialist army of today.

In contrast, the army we have created today is a genuine people's army that is organized with the sons and daughters of the workers, peasants, and other sections of the Korean working people, and fights for the liberation and independence of the Korean nation and for the happiness of the popular masses against the imperialist aggressive forces from abroad and the reactionary forces at home. Therefore, should any enemy attempt to infringe upon our country's freedom and our people's happy life, our People's Armymen will fight to the last drop of their blood to defeat the enemy and defend the country and the people to the bitter end. This is the most important feature of the People's Army we have founded.

Another specific feature of our People's Army is that it

has been formed with the true patriots of Korea as its backbone who devoted everything to the anti-Japanese armed struggle for the liberation of the country and the people in the face of severe Japanese imperialist suppression in the past.

After the Japanese imperialists occupied our country, the patriots with a genuine love for the country and the people took up arms directly in their hands and waged an arduous guerrilla warfare against Japanese imperialism at home and abroad. When the pro-Japanese elements now acting as flunkeys of U.S. imperialism in south Korea were oppressing and exploiting the Korean people in league with Japanese imperialism in the past and went so far as to drive out the dear young men and women of Korea to the battlefields for its aggressive war, the Korean patriots formed anti-Japanese armed units and waged a protracted, bloody struggle against the Japanese imperialist army of aggression which far outnumbered them, thereby stoutly defending the pride and honour of our nation. Our People's Army is created today with these patriotic revolutionaries as its backbone and on the basis of the rich experience accumulated by them during the long-drawn anti-Japanese armed struggle.

Therefore, though our People's Army is founded today as the regular army of democratic Korea, it is, in reality, an army whose historical roots date far back; it is a glorious army inheriting the revolutionary traditions of the anti-Japanese guerrilla warfare, the valuable fighting experience gained and the indomitable patriotic spirit displayed in it. Our army, thus equipped not only with weapons but also with practical combat experience, burning patriotism and noble revolutionary spirit of our revolutionary forerunners, is an iron army that will beat back the invasion of any enemy and will be ever-victorious.

That our people have founded such a superb and glorious People's Army once again demonstrates to the world that the Korean nation is fully capable of building a rich and strong independent country on its own and of raising its country to rank among the advanced states of the world. The fact that we have built such an excellent army by ourselves also shows clearly that we Korean people will not, and cannot, leave our destiny in the hands of the U.S. imperialists and their tool, the "U.N. Temporary Commission on Korea," and will never recognize a "government" or an "army" rigged up by them.

Proclaiming to the world the founding of the Korean People's Army on behalf of the entire people today, I resolutely declare once again that the destiny of the Korean nation should be shaped only by the Korean people themselves, and that the Korean question can by no means be solved by the U.S. imperialists and their aggressive tool, the "U.N. Temporary Commission on Korea."

Comrades and friends,

The founding of the People's Army infuses a great pride in our people and signifies another brilliant victory for them. But, although we have the People's Army, we must not allow ourselves to be content with it or to be carried away by victory. The creation of the People's Army is only the first step towards building up powerful, modern armed forces of the Democratic People's Republic of Korea which must be established in the future. It means that only their skeleton has been built. That is why all the people as well as the military personnel must do everything in their power to further strengthen and develop the People's Army founded today and should ensure that the invincible might of the Korean People's Army can be demonstrated to the world.

The men, noncommissioned officers and officers must, first of all, arm themselves firmly with the spirit of a boundless love for the country and the people and of devoting their all to the struggle for the freedom of the country and the happiness of the people.

Our People's Army should not forget even for a moment that it has been born of the people and serves the people, and that it can be victorious only when it loves the people and enjoys their support and affection. In particular, the People's Army must consistently protect the interests of the entire working people headed by the working class, the main force in building our country. Only when the army is equipped with ardent patriotism and the spirit of serving the working people, can it defend the gains of the democratic reforms in north Korea, reliably safeguard our country and people from the invasion of any enemy and promote complete independence, sovereignty and reunification of our country.

We must vigorously carry on the political and ideological education of the servicemen so that they may emulate the lofty patriotism of their revolutionary forerunners who took part in the anti-Japanese armed struggle, and that all of them may cultivate the spirit of loving, respecting, trusting and uniting with each other and the trait of acting bravely and taking the lead in doing things, and build up an iron discipline in the army.

The men, noncommissioned officers and officers must devote themselves with the greatest zeal to military training and the study of military science. All men and noncommissioned officers must be proficient in handling their weapons and be versed in their military assignments; officers must gain mastery in commanding their units and educating and training their men.

Our People's Army cannot be strengthened merely by the efforts of the men, noncommissioned officers and officers. The active support and assistance of the entire people to the army are required to make our army more efficient and capable of honourably fulfilling the important mission of defending the country and the people. Workers must ensure a timely and sufficient production and supply of good weapons, uniforms and daily necessities to the army; peasants must supply it with provisions. The entire people must love their army, hold dear the men and officers, and exert themselves to turn our People's Army into a mighty and excellent army which we can be proud of before the world.

Dear comrade men, noncommissioned officers and officers,

Dear fellow countrymen,

Through the founding today of an army which is genuinely our own, our people have registered another fresh victory in the history of our nation. The entire Korean people greet today's happy event with boundless emotion and rejoicing, and all our friends the world over extend congratulations on this new victory of the Korean people who are fighting for the freedom and independence of their country.

Let us all march vigorously forward, with an unshakable conviction of victory and ever greater national pride, for the establishment of a Democratic People's Republic of Korea, for a new victory!

Long live the creation of the Korean People's Army, the genuine armed forces of the Korean people!

Long live the establishment of a Democratic People's Republic of Korea!

REPORT TO THE SECOND CONGRESS OF THE WORKERS' PARTY OF NORTH KOREA ON THE WORK OF THE CENTRAL COMMITTEE

March 28, 1948

I. THE INTERNATIONAL SITUATION

Comrades,

One year and a half has passed since the Inaugural Congress of our Party. Short as it is, this period has witnessed tremendous changes in the international and internal situation.

The major events that have taken place in the international situation since the war are: first, a radical change in the alignment of international political forces; second, events occurring in the struggle between the democratic and the reactionary forces in the international arena; third, events occurring in connection with the upsurge of the liberation struggle of the people in colonial and dependent countries.

1. CHANGES IN THE ALIGNMENT OF INTERNATIONAL POLITICAL FORCES AFTER THE WAR

Deep-going changes have taken place in the alignment of international political forces since the end of World War II. The most essential of these changes is that the capitalist system, that is, the reactionary imperialist camp, has become markedly weaker, whereas the international democratic camp headed by the Soviet Union has come into being and has definitely gained in strength.

World War II ended with the rout of fascist Germany and Italy, the most heinous enemies of mankind throughout the world, and with the defeat of imperialist Japan in the East. In particular, the collapse of fascist Germany completely frustrated the plan, conceived by the three countries of the United States, Britain and France before World War II, for using Germany to wear down the might of the Soviet Union and strengthen the imperialist forces of aggression.

On the eve of the war, the U.S.-British-French bloc pursued a vile policy of winking at the aggressive acts of fascist Germany and appeasing her, with an eye to weakening the might of the Soviet Union which was growing and augmenting every day amid the capitalist encirclement. The so-called "Munich" policy, which led to the blackest tragedy in the history of mankind, was a product of this underhand scheme of the tripartite bloc of the United States, Britain and France. As you know, the "Munich" tragedy eventually brought about World War II and left many peoples of the world at the tender mercies of fascist Germany, involving them in the horrors of war.

Nevertheless, World War II ended with the destruction of fascist Germany, and in the course of the war the might of the Soviet Union, far from waning, grew further and the world democratic forces as a whole gained in strength. The victory of the democratic forces headed by the Soviet Union and the defeat of Germany, Italy and Japan in the war brought about radical changes in the alignment of political forces in the international arena. What, then, are these changes?

First, the strength of the imperialist camp as a whole has decreased and the victorious capitalist powers with the exception of the United States all find themselves in a worse position than before. Of the so-called "six great powers," Germany, Italy and Japan were defeated, the national power of France has waned considerably and Britain, too, is gradually surrendering its former positions in many European and Asian countries—West Germany, Austria, Italy, Greece, Turkey, Egypt, Iran, Afghanistan, China, Japan and others—to the United States.

Second, as a result of World War II, the Soviet Union, heading the international democratic forces, has grown into a stronger, invincible power, and a number of countries in East and Southeast Europe have broken away from the imperialist camp to join the democratic camp headed by the Soviet Union.

Third, the national-liberation movement has grown in scope in the colonial and semi-colonial dependent countries, and their peoples have joined the powerful anti-imperialist democratic forces; some colonial peoples, casting off the yoke of the suzerain states, have won national independence.

Last, in many countries of both West Europe and the East which were overridden by the fascist robbers of Germany, Italy and Japan, the democratic movement of the working people led by the Communist Parties is unfolded vigorously on a mass scale.

In short, the balance of world political forces has thus changed rapidly after the war in the direction of the imperialist forces declining in strength and the democratic forces prevailing decisively. This shows that the prewar policy of the U.S.-British-French bloc aimed at isolating the Soviet Union and at instigating fascist Germany to smother the Soviet Union and check the revolutionary movement in Germany and the liberation movements of the peoples of the countries in West Europe and the East, has ended in the very opposite of their intentions.

From these postwar changes in the international arena we can draw the conclusion that the imperialist camp is heading for decline and ruin, whereas the international democratic camp headed by the socialist state Soviet Union is steadily growing in scope and strength as a new great force that no one can suppress.

From these postwar changes in the international situation we can also draw the conclusion that the world is moving not according to the wishes of the Wall Street bosses, but along the course dictated by history, along the course of victory for the people; that the world is moving along the course steered by the people, the creator of history, in the direction they demand.

2. STRUGGLE BETWEEN THE DEMOCRATIC AND THE REACTIONARY FORCES IN THE INTERNATIONAL ARENA

The above-mentioned changes in the balance of world political forces did not come about spontaneously and by chance; they have come about through a bitter struggle between the democratic and the reactionary forces.

As the day when the war ended recedes farther backward, the U.S.-British-French bloc has become more open in its contravention of the commitments made by the Allied Powers during the war against fascist Germany.

As is generally known, the war against the German fascist robbers carried victory and liberation for mankind the world over, entirely by virtue of the decisive part played by the great Soviet people and Soviet army, at the cost of tremendous sacrifices and losses on the part of the Soviet people. And what sort of voice is raised nowadays in those countries which, despite their being members of the so-called Allied Powers, did not take a resolute stand against fascist Germany but only bided their time, even retarding the opening of the Second Front, and in those countries which entertained secret hopes for Germany's victory and went so far as to extend aid to her? A strange voice is being heard more and more loudly. They say: "To us belongs the credit for victory in the war, and so we are entitled to a greater share of rewards and must have a bigger part in settling postwar international issues." It is nobody's secret that the ruling circles of these countries are deliberately complicating the settlement of international issues and are seeking to secure their hegemony in the international arena after the war.

The whole course of the anti-fascist war has shown the groundlessness of their strange argument, providing irrefutable evidence that the war was brought to a victorious conclusion by the Soviet army with the assistance of the freedom-loving peoples who rose in liberation struggle. This notwithstanding, the Wall Street bosses and the reactionary American politicians who act upon their dictation are talking vociferously as if the United States had "saved" Europe, and so, they clamour, they should by right dominate the world.

The U.S. monopoly capitalists, far from sustaining any loss, raked in stupendous profits in the course of the war. In order to obtain huge profits even now when the war is over, they are frantically trying to intensify the exploitation of the working class in their own country, secure more markets abroad, and bring under their control many war-ravaged countries in West Europe and Asia by various means such as threat, blackmail and "aid." They have noisily revived the "claim for world domination" which Hitler had been clamouring for, and have begun spreading an absurd racist theory concerning the superiority of the Anglo-Saxon race.

The U.S. imperialists are resorting to various stratagems such as "A-bomb diplomacy," "dollar diplomacy," the "Truman Doctrine" and the "Marshall Plan" for the purpose of putting into effect their expansionist policy and infringing upon the sovereignty of small and weak nations, and have gone over to a full-scale reactionary offensive for world domination.

Today when the war is over, the U.S. expansionists are stretching out their claws of aggression even to the Western Hemisphere, not to speak of a number of war-ravaged countries in West Europe and the East. The U.S. imperialists are encroaching upon the economies of a number of South American countries and of Canada, and are scheming to dominate the whole of Asia. Most striking evidence of this is the U.S. policy in Japan and China.

The U.S. imperialists seek to subordinate Japan to U.S. monopoly capital and convert her into a forward base for invading many Asian and Pacific countries.

The policy of the United States towards China is a policy aimed at turning her vast territory with a population of 450 million into its colony. This U.S. policy has brought utter economic bankruptcy to China, ravaged her national industry, and has fostered and aggravated the civil war in China in the post-war years. It is clear for all to see what a wicked imperialist policy it is, the U.S. policy of extending civil war in China by abetting the reactionary Kuomintang government of Chiang Kai-shek, and of enslaving the Chinese people. The reactionary Chiang Kai-shek government is kept going only by the military and economic aid of the United States; but for the manoeuvrings of the U.S. imperialists, the Chinese people would have won victory and liberation long ago.

The United States has extended the tentacles of its expansionist policy to a number of countries in the Near East as well. The U.S. monopoly capitalists, who have begun to deprive Britain of her economic footholds in the Near East, covet the oil resources of Saudi Arabia, Egypt and other Arab countries, and are engaging in imperialist interference in such countries as Syria, Lebanon and Iran. The U.S. imperialists are also pursuing an expansionist policy towards Greece and Turkey. Greece has been turned into a base which with the support of imperialism menaces peace in the Balkans; she remains a country totally dependent on U.S. and British imperialism. There, a fierce civil war is continuing to this day, three years after the end of World War II, coupled with open armed intervention by Britain, and the fascist royalists, who have seized power, are terrorizing and butchering the masses of the people.

Thus, everywhere the U.S. imperialists impede the growth of democratic forces, create political confusion, instigate civil wars by aggravating national splits, and repress the national-liberation movements. Worse still, they are attempting to realize their sinister designs by reviving the defeated fascist Germany and militarist Japan.

The U.S. imperialists protect and encourage the reactionary forces in different parts of the world in every way and, under the cloak of the so-called "Marshall Plan," pursue a policy of subordinating West European countries to themselves by taking advantage of the latter's postwar economic difficulties. Furthermore, they are carrying out a vicious policy against the peoples of many East and Southeast European countries which, having broken away from the imperialist camp as a result of World War II, have taken the new path of development along democratic lines.

Such, in brief, is the policy of U.S. imperialism which has emerged as the chieftain of the international reactionary forces after the war.

In opposition to this U.S. foreign policy and the imperialist camp headed by the United States, there has now been formed in the world the international democratic camp, which is growing in scope and strength with each passing day. This powerful democratic camp is headed by the great Soviet Union.

The foreign policy of the Soviet Union led by the great Leninist Communist Party is traditionally a policy of respecting the freedom and independence of the peoples of all countries, actively supporting the liberation movement of small and weak nations and of maintaining world peace and security. Soviet foreign policy is a policy for consolidating the victory and peace won in the bloody struggle against fascism and safeguarding friendship and co-operation among nations. In the complex postwar situation, the Soviet Union has unswervingly followed its just and peace-loving foreign policy and unwaveringly stands at the head of the struggle for the freedom of the peoples, for world peace and security, against the international forces of reaction.

The Soviet Union has concluded treaties of friendship and co-operation with a number of countries in East and Southeast Europe, and pursues the policy of giving aid to these countries to rehabilitate and develop their economy. Soviet aid to those countries is fundamentally different from the so-called "aid" of the imperialists, offered under the "Marshall Plan" and the "Truman Doctrine." It is disinterested aid characterized by genuine respect for the freedom and independence of the peoples of those countries, the aim being to expedite their economic rehabilitation and development.

Already in 1946 the Soviet Union withdrew its troops from the territories of its allies—Norway, Denmark, Iran, China, etc. In spite of vehement objections from the American and British imperialists, the Soviet Union concluded peace treaties with the vanquished countries, such as Italy, Hungary, Romania, Bulgaria and Finland, which were formerly allied with Hitler Germany. The peace treaties with these countries provide an obvious illustration of how the Soviet Union respects the rights, liberties and national independence of their peoples and values peace.

At various international conferences and negotiations in the postwar years, the great Soviet Union has persistently struggled for the freedom and independence of small and weak nations the world over and for world peace and security. The traditional foreign policy of the Soviet Union led by the great Bolshevik Party has been manifested in the stand taken by the Soviet delegates on the postwar German problem, and Greek, Egyptian and Indonesian questions, on the question of opposing the incendiaries of a new war and ensuring world peace and security, on the question of general disarmament and many others discussed in the General Assembly and the Security Council of the United Nations.

The Soviet people have worked out and are successfully implementing their five-year plan for the postwar rehabilitation and development of the national economy. Quite contrary to the state of affairs in the United States which is facing an impending economic crisis with millions of jobless workers thrown out on the streets and prices rising, in the Soviet Union production keeps growing speedily, the people are free from unemployment, rationing has been abolished and prices have been systematically reduced, with the result that the material and cultural life of the working people continues to improve rapidly.

Thus, the Soviet Union has become the powerful bulwark and leading force of the international democratic camp in the struggle against the international reactionary forces. Soviet foreign policy is exposing the reactionary, aggressive policy of U.S. imperialism at every step and is immensely inspiring the peoples and the working people of the world to the just struggle for peace, democracy, freedom and independence.

Further, the new democratic forces of the victorious peoples in many East and Southeast European countries have grown to powerful strength dealing fatal blows to the international reactionary forces. In the East and Southeast European countries such as Poland, Czechoslovakia, Hungary, Romania, Bulgaria and Albania, the newly emerging political forces are successfully eliminating the footholds of reaction in their countries and have launched their countries on the road of democratic reforms and of national regeneration and rehabilitation. The peoples of these countries, who have had the bitterest experience of the horrors of war, are shaping their destinies by themselves and are determined never again to leave their fate to the mercy of the reactionary politicians. Thus, the imperialists have lost their footholds of aggression in these countries. It is not an accident that the U.S. imperialists and their followers, the greedy politicians of the Western bloc, are now slandering and disparaging the democratic countries in East and Southeast Europe.

But realities have conclusively proved the complete baselessness of these slanders of the U.S. imperialists. The postwar situation as a whole clearly shows that things are going well in the lands which are disparaged by the U.S. imperialists, whereas political disorder and darkness reign in the areas which they present in bright colours.

In the West European countries which have been drawn directly into the U.S. imperialists' sphere of influence, powerful democratic forces are also growing now.

The peoples of Britain, France, Italy and a number of other West European countries are becoming more deeply convinced that world peace and security can be ensured and the international reactionary forces can be defeated only when they follow a policy of friendship towards the Soviet Union. Having experienced the shocking horrors of war on account of the bellicose, traitorous reactionary politicians of their countries, they do not want another "Munich" and stand firmly opposed to another war and aggression. Graphic evidence of this is provided by the powerful democratic movement unfolded on an extensive scale in France, Italy, West Germany, etc. The campaign launched in the United States for the formation of a third party on the eve of the presidential election is a tangible indication that voices are raised louder and louder against reaction in that country as well.

The growth of the democratic forces in the capitalist countries is also illustrated by the fact that the Communist Parties, the advanced detachments of the working class, have become stronger than ever. The Communist Parties of France and Italy have now become militant parties enjoying the greatest prestige and deepest confidence among the broad masses of the people. The Communist Parties in a number of West European countries have become powerful political parties leading the revolutionary struggle of the working class and the entire working people; they have become the vanguard of the democratic forces in West Europe.

This growth of the Communist Parties' influence among the masses of the people is attributable, as Comrade Stalin said, to the fact that in many European countries the Communists fought most valiantly and self-sacrificingly against the outrages of the fascist robbers in the grim years of fascist rule and won the deep confidence of the broad masses as fighters for the freedom and liberation of the people.

The great force of the oppressed peoples who have risen in the struggle to achieve national freedom and independence against colonialism forms another component of the international democratic forces. The courageous struggle of the Indonesian and Vietnamese peoples against the imperialists' colonial oppression and plunder, the mounting national-liberation movements in India, Palestine and Madagascar, and the powerful people's liberation movements in China, a semi-colonial dependent country, and Greece are delivering mortal blows to the international forces of reaction. The Chinese People's Liberation Army has already liberated nearly all of Northeast China and wide expanses of other parts of the Chinese territory; in Greece a free Greek Government has been set up in opposition to the fascist royalists.

This is a brief account of the process of the growth of the international democratic forces which are ranged against the reactionary forces of imperialism in the international arena after the war.

From this we can draw the following conclusion in general:

First, class consciousness has been greatly heightened among the peoples of the whole world, who experienced the shocking horrors of war and fought against fascism shedding blood with a view to attaining peace and freedom; their aspirations for a genuinely democratic system and a new life have grown immeasurably.

Second, the masses of the people, having drawn serious lessons from the war, have come to the profound realization that the destinies of their countries should not be entrusted to the anti-popular and reactionary politicians who pursue narrow, covetous ends. The peoples of the world, who experienced war and fascist rule, do not want to live in the same old way again and are shaping their destinies for themselves, waging an active struggle for the establishment of a democratic system against the reactionary forces and the incendiaries of a new war.

Third, those who, heading the international reactionary forces in the postwar years, seek to wreck world peace and security and to enslave the peoples of small and weak countries in Europe and Asia, harping again on "world domination" just as Hitler did and putting forward a new version of racism, will be condemned to suffer the same fate as Hitler and Mussolini.

Fourth, the wilder the U.S. imperialists become in their attempt to dominate the world, the more the international democratic forces opposing it are united and strengthened as an invincible force. Today the world is moving not according to the wishes of the U.S. imperialists but in the direction in which the international democratic forces are advancing, towards a new social system.

II. THE INTERNAL SITUATION

1. THE POLITICAL SITUATION IN KOREA AND THE STRUGGLE FOR THE COUNTRY'S REUNIFICATION

Comrades,

The deep-going changes in the international situation since the war are mirrored most sharply in the political situation in our country. Today the Korean issue is not a question limited to our country alone but constitutes a link in the struggle between democracy and anti-democracy on the international arena.

The political situation in our country from the time immediately after liberation up to the present is characterized by a fierce struggle between the patriotic democratic forces and the traitorous anti-democratic forces. All the domestic political forces have divided mainly into two: all the patriotic personalities and the people of Korea fighting for the freedom and independence of the country have formed a mighty democratic force, while all the traitors and pro-Japanese elements who hold their narrow political gains and their own interests dearer than the interests of the country and the nation, have formed an anti-popular, reactionary force.

But for the reactionary U.S. interference, the struggle between these two forces in our country would have been settled, very easily and without any complications, in line with the demands of the Korean people. For the reactionary forces of Korea formed after liberation with the handful of pro-Japanese elements and traitors to the nation, who were hated and rejected by the entire people, did not have any foothold among the masses of the people and their strength was next to nothing as against the mighty democratic forces of the liberated Korean nation.

Nevertheless, the struggle between these two forces in our country remains unsettled to this day, and the Korean issue becomes more complicated every day. This is because the handful of reactionary forces, comprising the pro-Japanese elements and the traitors to the nation, is under the direct control of U.S. imperialism, the chieftain of international reaction, and is actively protected and supported by it. As a result, the democratic forces in Korea which have grown tremendously in size and strength following liberation have had to fight against the internal reactionary forces on the one hand, and, on the other, against the international forces of reaction headed by U.S. imperialism.

What has caused such a complex situation in our country and has made the settlement of the Korean issue difficult and delicate?

With the defeat of Japanese imperialism and the liberation of Korea, the armies of the Soviet Union and the United States entered our country with the 38th parallel as the demarcation line between them.

In south Korea, too, prior to the landing there of U.S. troops, the pro-Japanese elements and the traitors to the nation remained small and still before the mighty democratic forces; the whole land was seething with the boundless jubilation and patriotic passion of a liberated nation, and our country was advancing along the path of national regeneration and independence in accordance with the people's wishes. But with the landing of U.S. troops in south Korea on September 8, 1945, dark clouds again began gathering over our country.

It is not by chance that today totally different situations have been created in the northern and southern halves of Korea and north and south Korea are proceeding along diametrically opposite courses. To confirm this, I would like to remind you here of the historic statements of the Soviet and U.S. armies addressed to us Korean people on the first days of their arrival in Korea.

On the day of its arrival in our country, the Soviet army, which is led by the great Bolshevik Party that respects and champions the independence and freedom of small and weak nations, declared to the Korean people as follows:

"Korean people!... Korea has become a country of freedom. However, this marks only the first page in Korean history. An abundant, fruitful orchard is the results of man's efforts and vigour. Therefore, the happiness of Korea, too, can only be achieved by the heroic efforts that you Korean people will exert. Remember, Korean people! You have happiness in your own hands. You have attained liberty and liberation. Now everything is up to you. The Soviet army will provide the Korean people with all conditions for the free and creative labour you are bound to embark on. Koreans must make themselves the creators of their own happiness."

This is the very statement the Soviet army made on the first day it entered our territory. How correctly the Soviet army has fulfilled its commitments given in this statement needs no explaining, because it is clearly demonstrated by the realities in north Korea today where the Korean people have taken power into their hands and are building a democratic country entirely in accordance with their will.

But what did the U.S. army proclaim to the Korean people on the very first day it landed in south Korea? I would like to cite a few passages from the proclamation of the U.S. army issued upon its arrival in south Korea:

"...By virtue of the authority vested in me as Commander-in-Chief, United States Army Forces, Pacific, I hereby establish military control over Korea south of 38 degrees north latitude and the inhabitants thereof, and announce the following conditions of the occupation:

"All powers of government over the territory of Korea south of 38 degrees north latitude and the people thereof will be for the present exercised under my authority. Persons will obey my orders and orders issued under my authority. Acts of resistance to the occupying forces or any acts which may disturb public peace and safety will be punished severely.

"For all purposes during the military control, English will be the official language...."

This is what the U.S. army controlled by the Wall Street bosses proclaimed upon its arrival in our land. The wretched conditions of south Korea at present provide glaring evidence that since then everything has turned out just as prescribed in the proclamation, exactly to the letter.

Thus, quite different political situations have been created in the two parts of our country since the arrival of the Soviet and U.S. armies, and our country has been divided into north Korea—a land of democracy, freedom and construction; and south Korea—a land of reaction, massacre and destruction.

The U.S. army set out on a policy of colonial enslavement as soon as it crept into south Korea. In the first place, it adopted two basic policies to attain its goal: politically, it smothered all the democratic initiatives of the liberated people who set themselves against its policy of colonial enslavement, and suppressed all the democratic forces and, at the same time, it rallied and fostered the reactionary forces that were instrumental in the implementation of its aggressive policy aimed at splitting the Korean nation and turning Korea into a U.S. colony; economically, it has pursued a policy of hampering the development of Korea's national industry and economy and subordinating them to the economy of the United States.

From the very first day of its occupation of south Korea the U.S. army has persecuted all patriotic-minded democratic personalities, and set up a U.S. military government after it dissolved the people's committees established immediately after liberation on the initiative of the people. It set out to build up the reactionary forces in south Korea with the traitors it had brought from the United States and China, and with the pro-Japanese elements and traitors to the nation at home.

The U.S. imperialists seek to turn south Korea completely

into their colony and thereby plunder it continuously of its rice, gold, silver, copper, tungsten and all other valuable resources, to dump their surplus goods there, and to bring the whole of Korea fully under their occupation to turn it into their advance base for aggression in the East.

This policy of the U.S. imperialists towards Korea could not but evoke strong resistance from the Korean people. The popular resistance struggles waged in south Korea under U.S. military government were an adequate answer of the people of south Korea to the military rule of the U.S. imperialists and their policy of colonial enslavement.

But in order to carry out their wicked policy of colonial enslavement of Korea, the U.S. imperialists rejected outright the demand of the Soviet side for a simultaneous withdrawal of Soviet and U.S. troops from Korea and for leaving the solution of Korean issue to the Korean people themselves; they unlawfully brought the Korean question to the United Nations and rigged up the so-called "U.N. Temporary Commission on Korea." At the U.N. General Assembly the United States, disregarding the just demands of the delegates of many countries, rejected the participation of the Korean people's representative in the discussion of the Korean question. Thus, the U.N. "resolution" on the Korean question was adopted arbitrarily in the absence of the Korean people's representative, under pressure from the United States and its satellites. This is an insult to, and contempt for, our nation.

Why did the United States reject the participation of the Korean people's representative in the discussions on the Korean issue? It was because the U.S. imperialists were afraid of the voice of the Korean people's representative and of world public opinion. The U.S. imperialists were aware that the truth about south Korea ruled by the U.S. military government would be exposed before the whole world, should the Korean people's representative participate in the U.N. discussions on the Korean question, which they feared most of all. The delegates of Ukraine, Czechoslovakia, Poland and a number of other democratic countries gave unqualified support to the proposal of the Soviet delegation for the withdrawal of foreign troops from Korea and strongly demanded that the solution of the Korean question be left to the Korean people themselves. Nevertheless, the United States, using its voting machine, forced an unlawful "resolution" on the Korean question through the United Nations, in the absence of the Korean representative.

The Korean people have long since been aware of this scheme of the United States. The attitude persisted invariably by the United States from the Moscow Three Foreign Ministers Conference to the two sessions of the U.S.S.R.-U.S. Joint Commission furnishes a graphic illustration of what the U.S. imperialists are driving at today in cooking up the "U.N. Temporary Commission on Korea."

The "mission" of the "U.N. Temporary Commission on Korea" is obvious. It is to justify the U.S. policy for colonizing Korea under the cloak of "elections," to rig up through fraudulent "elections" a "government" to the liking of the U.S. imperialists, which comprises the pro-Japanese elements and traitors to the nation who place their private interests above the national interests and sell out the country and the people to foreign countries, and to tear south Korea away from our country for ever, converting it into a U.S. colony. That is why the entire people and all conscientious patriotic personalities in north and south Korea, irrespective of their political views, religious beliefs or property status, rose against the "U.N. Temporary Commission on Korea" from the beginning. Of late, voices against the "U.N. Temporary Commission on Korea" are raised more and more loudly even in the Right-wing camp.

Those who support the "U.N. Temporary Commission on Korea" and approve of the policy of a national split are none other than the reactionary traitors such as Syngman Rhee and Kim Song Su who clamour that "a government must be established even in Kyongsang Province alone."

Thus, two diametrically opposite lines have appeared in our country. One of them is the democratic line of establishing at the earliest possible date a genuine, unified government of the Korean people and attaining the complete freedom and independence of Korea. The other is the reactionary line of artificially bisecting Korea and converting south Korea into a complete colony by rigging up, in the name of the United Nations, a puppet government serving the United States.

The entire Korean people are resolutely opposed to the reactionary line that runs counter to our national interests, and to the "resolution" of the "Little Assembly of the United Nations" on the Korean question; they will never recognize, under any circumstances or on any conditions, the traitorous, reactionary puppet government to be set up under the patronage of the "U.N. Temporary Commission on Korea."

The Korean people, who were subjected to colonial oppression and experienced a humiliating life of slavery under the long-drawn Japanese imperialist rule, will not allow any imperialists to enslave them again nor will they ever be taken in by such aggressive schemes of Americans. Our people are not the Korean people of the past; they are an awakened, united people who have already carried out great democratic reforms in half the territory of their country, and enjoy genuine democratic rights and liberties and are steadily paving the way to a more radiant future. Our compatriots in south Korea, suffering from hunger and subjected to humiliation and oppression, have also seen the U.S. imperialists in their true colours and have awakened to the real nature of their policy. They are convinced that they will certainly come out victorious, if they put up a resolute struggle in concert with their brothers in north Korea who are creating a new, happy life. No force on earth can subjugate and enslave our people, who have risen in the cause of the country's reunification and independence along democratic lines.

Comrades, in view of the acute situation created in our country and with the object of indicating clearly once more the path to be followed by the Korean people, our Party, together with other democratic political parties and social organizations in north Korea, has worked out the draft of a Provisional Constitution wholly conforming to the demands of the people, and put it before the entire people for discussion. We are now discussing the draft Constitution with the enthusiastic support of all the people in north and south Korea. The draft Constitution we have made public is a historic document which legally confirms and consolidates the gains scored by the north Korean people, after taking power into their hands, in the democratic transformation of society in the two years since liberation, and which shows the whole Korean people the path that their country should follow.

Our Party's stand on the establishment of a unified democratic government remains the same as ever. Our Party holds that a supreme legislative body for all Korea should be elected on the principle of universal, equal and direct suffrage by secret ballot. The supreme legislative body of the people thus elected should adopt a democratic Constitution and form a genuine democratic people's government to lead our people along the road to national prosperity and happiness. The establishment of a unified government on such lines by the Korean people themselves will only be possible when foreign troops are withdrawn.

In order to give effect to this stand of our Party, which is consistent with the demands of the entire Korean people, we must fight to the last against the U.S. imperialists' crafty policy of colonial enslavement by further strengthening unity with all patriotic democratic forces in north and south Korea and with all the conscientious personalities who aspire to freedom and independence for the country.

With this end in view, our Party, together with democratic political parties and social organizations in north Korea, has approached those parties and social organizations in south Korea which are opposed to the establishment of a separate government there, with a proposal to hold a joint conference of representatives of all the democratic parties and social organizations of north and south Korea in Pyongyang on April 14 this year.

At this joint conference we will discuss the situation in the country and adopt a concrete programme and measures to frustrate all the schemes of the reactionary groups to divide our territory, to facilitate the country's reunification and to expedite the establishment of a unified democratic Korean state which will be an equal of all the freedom-loving states of the world.

We firmly believe that this proposal of ours will meet with the full support and approval of all genuinely patriotic political parties and social organizations and of all conscientious patriotic personalities who strive for the glory of the country and the freedom and independence of the nation.

The Workers' Parties of North and South Korea, closely rallying around them all the patriotic democratic forces and all the people both in north and south Korea, will keep up a persistent struggle to shatter the sinister designs of the U.S. imperialists to split our country and make it their colony, and will certainly achieve the reunification and complete independence and sovereignty of the country.

2. ESTABLISHMENT OF THE PEOPLE'S POWER OF A NEW TYPE AND ENFORCEMENT OF DEMOCRATIC REFORMS

Comrades,

Right after liberation our Party put forward the basic political task of establishing a democratic people's republic and thus of developing our country into an independent sovereign state, rich and powerful, which will guarantee welfare, freedom and rights for the people and will be an equal of the democratic countries internationally. To solve this basic task, the Party outlined its immediate tasks as follows:

(1) To rally the broad patriotic, democratic forces by forming a national democratic united front embracing all patriotic and democratic political parties and groups and, on this basis, to work for the establishment of a Democratic People's Republic to ensure our complete national independence and sovereignty;

(2) To liquidate thoroughly the remnant forces of Japanese imperialism, the lackeys of international reaction and all other reactionaries, who constitute the biggest obstacle to the building of a democratic country, thereby facilitating the development of our nation along democratic lines;

(3) To organize, first of all, people's committees as organs of genuine people's power in various districts with a view to establishing a unified all-Korea democratic provisional government, and carry out all democratic reforms, restore the factories, enterprises and the national economy as a whole, which were ravaged by the Japanese imperialists, and raise the material and cultural standards of the people, thereby laying the groundwork of an independent democratic state;

(4) To further expand and strengthen the Party and energetically push forward the work of the social organizations for organizing and rallying the masses in all walks of life around the Party so as to fulfil all these tasks.

As a first step towards the fulfilment of these tasks our Party set out to establish, above all, a new type of people's power organ.

Neither retaining the old state machine of Japanese imperialist rule nor building a state apparatus which would have been only a slightly improved version of it, we had to set up a new type of power organ, fully meeting the demands of the liberated Korean people, most suitable for the democratic development of our country and capable of representing the interests of all sections of the people and, particularly, of the broad labouring masses.

Our Party defined the people's committee established on the initiative of the Korean people, without foreign interference, as precisely such a new-type organ of power. This was because the people's committee is indeed a power established by the people themselves on their own initiative, because it is a power opposed to the enemies of the Korean people—the pro-Japanese elements, traitors to the nation, landlords and comprador capitalists—and representing the interests of the working masses with the working class as the core and those of the entire people, because it is an organ of power which is rooted deep in the broad masses, meets the people's demands most promptly, enjoys their support and maintains the ties of kinship with them, because it is an entirely new, democratic form of power built on the ruins of the repressive state machinery of the vicious Japanese imperialist rule—different from the "parliamentary democratic" form of power of obsolete bourgeois society, and because it is a new type of power that can lead our people to a still more elevated democratic society, free, happy and affluent, in the future.

Only this type of power organ can ensure complete independence and sovereignty to our country, unite the broad masses of the people around itself and give full play to their political zeal and patriotism, mobilizing all their energies for the building of a rich and strong country. That is why our Party has geared the efforts of all its members and of the entire people to the establishment of such a new type of power and to its strengthening and development.

With the establishment and further development of new-type organs of power in the local districts, we were confronted with the task of setting up a central organ competent to give unified leadership to the local people's committees. Only when such a central state apparatus was established was it possible to overcome the lack of system of the organs of people's power and the tendency towards local separatism, and to accomplish more successfully and in a unified way the pressing political and economic tasks confronting the country and the people. Hence, our Party, in conjunction with the democratic political parties and social organizations in north Korea, established the Provisional People's Committee of North Korea in February 1946.

It was no easy task to establish and strengthen the organs of people's power. For the people's power could be established and strengthened only in the course of overcoming all kinds of difficulties—first, a shortage of native cadres competent enough to administer the state and run the power; second, manoeuvrings of the pro-Japanese elements, traitors to the nation and reactionaries to damage the prestige and authority of the people's power organs both from within and from without; third, lack of understanding of the people's power on the part of some Party cadres who were affected with narrow-minded sectarian tendencies, etc.

Our Party, however, resolutely surmounted all these difficulties and schemes of the reactionaries by mobilizing the revolutionary forces of the broad masses of the people, and it further consolidated the organs of people's power from top to bottom through democratic elections held on several occasions. The struggle for the consolidation of the organs of people's power proceeded side by side with the great socio-economic reforms for the democratization of the country.

Our Party embarked on the democratic reforms to put into effect the 11-point immediate tasks facing the Provisional People's Committee of North Korea and the 20-Point Platform which was made public in March 1946 prior to the formation of a provisional government of Korea.

Without smashing the colonial and feudal fetters in all spheres of social life through the democratic reforms, it would have been impossible either to expect the early restoration and development of industry and agriculture, which had been ruined as a result of protracted Japanese imperialist rule, or to improve the material life of the broad masses of the people, who had been driven to extremities of starvation and poverty. Our liberated people demanded the reconstruction of the country not on old but on new lines. They did not want to live again in colonial slavery or feudal bondage. They wanted to work out their destiny by taking the path of a new genuinely democratic life.

Hence our Party and the people's power were faced with heavy tasks that had to be carried out without fail, such as the solution of the land problem which was the centuries-old desire of the peasants, the solution of the problem of industry which was the cornerstone of the national economy, the problem of labour protection which was a vital need to the working class, the problem of ensuring social rights to women and so on. In order to accomplish these tasks our Party, together with the democratic political parties and social organizations, helped the Provisional People's Committee of North Korea to carry out great democratic reforms such as the agrarian reform, nationalization of industries, and enforcement of the Labour Law and the Law on Equality of the Sexes.

First and foremost, our Party devoted all its efforts to the successful accomplishment of the agrarian reform which held the most important place in the democratic reforms. The Party did a great deal of work: in order to ensure the victory of the toiling peasants in the sharp class struggle of the tenant farmers and farm hands against the landlords, it sent to the countryside its best members and workers, the leading detachment in the building of the country; it formed more than 11,500 rural committees with farm hands and poor peasants as their core and ensured the correct execution of the Agrarian Reform Law in the interests of the toiling peasants; and it removed the wicked landlords to other regions in order to smash the resistance of the landlords and eliminate their reactionary influence on the backward sections of the peasantry. At the same time, we sent out able Party propagandists to all parts of the country to explain and bring home to the broad peasant masses the historic significance of the agrarian reform, thus enhancing their class consciousness and exposing and smashing in good time the reactionary false rumours and vile propaganda spread by the landlords and all the other reactionary elements.

In the wake of the agrarian reform, we successfully carried out all the tasks of other democratic reforms—nationalization of industries, enforcement of the Labour Law and the Law on Equality of the Sexes, etc.

The great democratic reforms accomplished in north Korea thanks to the leading role played by our Party and its extensive organizing and mobilizing activities, brought about radical changes in the social, political, economic and cultural life of north Korea in only two years and a half following liberation, meeting the vital needs of the broad masses of the people.

The agrarian reform was, above all, a great revolution that

eliminated the deep-seated source of stagnation, backwardness and poverty in our rural areas and opened up a broad avenue for the development of agriculture and for all-round socio-economic progress of the country.

First, in the countryside it abolished the feudal relations of landownership and made the peasants who tilled the land its owners, thereby freeing the productive forces of agriculture from the old feudal fetters and laying the solid foundation for eliminating the mediaeval backwardness in the methods of farming, culture, customs and in all other spheres in the Korean rural areas;

Second, it satisfied the centuries-old thirst of the Korean peasants for land and emancipated the peasants from feudal oppression and exploitation, with the result that the patriotic political enthusiasm of the peasants and their zeal for production rose to a great height and favourable conditions were created for improving their material and cultural life;

Third, the agrarian reform liquidated the landlord class that had been the main social foothold of reaction, and enabled the toiling peasants—with the assistance of the working class—to become genuine masters of the countryside, thereby decisively strengthening the democratic positions in the rural areas of our country and further consolidating the alliance between the working class and the peasantry;

Fourth, as a result of the agrarian reform, conditions were created to supply industry which is in process of rapid restoration with raw materials and to provide food to the population, thus giving an impetus to the normal development of the national industry of our country and strengthening the economic bond between town and country;

Last, the results of the agrarian reform were of great international significance. North Korea's agrarian reform, the first of its kind in many countries of the East, has given immense inspiration to the peoples and peasants of Eastern countries suffering from colonial and feudal oppression and exploitation and serves as a beacon illumining the path for them to follow.

The Labour Law enabled our working class to show greater activity in its creative endeavours as the main detachment in building the country and improve its material and cultural life rapidly by freeing the workers from appalling colonial working conditions through the introduction of an eight-hour day and social insurance for the first time in the history of our people and the annals of the working-class movement in Korea.

The Law on Equality of the Sexes emancipated from feudal oppression and humiliation the women, who make up half the population of Korea, and provided them with conditions for taking part in the political, economic and cultural life of the country with equal rights with men.

Then, the nationalization of factories, mills, mines, railway transport, communications, banks, etc., which formerly belonged to the Japanese imperialists and comprador capitalists, constituted a democratic reform of great significance in the building of a new society by our people.

First, the nationalization of industries expropriated the foreign monopoly and comprador capital and placed the key branches of the national economy under the direct control of the state, which led to the abolition of the economic foundations of the imperialist exploitation and enslavement in our country and to the creation of basic conditions for using the country's major means of production in the interests of the independent development of the national economy and promotion of the well-being of the entire people;

Second, as a result of the nationalization of industries, conditions were created for the state sector to play the leading role in the national economy and for the economy of the country to develop on a planned basis;

Third, the nationalization of industries freed the working class of our country from exploitation and oppression and turned it into the master of the major factories and enterprises, the master of industry, and this increased its political and labour enthusiasm immeasurably and further enhanced its leading role in the building of the country on democratic lines;

Last, the nationalization of industries in north Korea was

a glorious event which has broken, for the first time, a link of the imperialist chain shackling the peoples and the working classes in many Eastern countries; it has blazed the path for the oppressed peoples of the East to follow in smashing the economic footholds of the colonialist marauders and achieving the independent development of their own national economies.

The victory of the democratic reforms in north Korea has laid the solid political and economic foundations for achieving the complete independence and sovereignty of our country and, under the situation now prevailing in our country, has turned north Korea into a solid base for the democratic development of the country, into a powerful base of the democratic forces to save the country and the nation from falling a prey to the U.S. imperialists' policy of colonial enslavement.

The victory of the democratic reforms in north Korea has demonstrated that our country is advancing vigorously along the path of freedom, independence and democracy towards the establishment of a Democratic People's Republic of Korea, which is the earnest desire of the entire Korean people.

3. OUR PARTY'S ECONOMIC POLICY AND ECONOMIC CONSTRUCTION

The establishment of the people's power and the accomplishment of the democratic reforms mark only the initial step in the building of the country. The point is how our Party, on the basis of the victory of the democratic reforms, will mobilize the entire people to the struggle for restoration and development of the national economy and lead them along the path of building a rich and strong country.

Proceeding from this, our Party and people have embarked on economic construction in order to consolidate the successes gained in the democratic social and economic reforms and, on this basis, to restore and develop the national economy. It was important in this connection to restore and develop the national economy in such a way as not merely to rehabilitate the ruined economy, but to eliminate the baneful aftermath of the protracted Japanese imperialist rule in industry and various other fields and to ensure a predominant position for the state sector.

The fundamentals of our Party's economic policy consisted in ensuring the direct, planned state control of the major industries, railway transport, communications, foreign trade and financial agencies and in the proper co-ordination of the state, co-operative and private sectors of the economy based on the constant strengthening of the leading role of the state sector in the development of the national economy.

The difficulties we encountered in the course of implementing this economic policy of the Party were tremendous.

First, owing to the prolonged Japanese imperialist rule, the economy of our country was generally very backward and its industry suffered from colonial lopsidedness and deformation and, moreover, was severely damaged by the Japanese imperialists.

Second, when we set out on economic construction there was a lack of native technical personnel able to manage the national economy, the working class was very short of skilled workers, and raw and other materials and funds were practically nil.

Third, our economic construction proceeded under conditions of the country's split into north and south, with the domestic and foreign reactionary forces engaging in all kinds of vicious subversive activities against the creation of a new life by the Korean people.

These difficulties and hardships, however, could not block the onward march of the Korean people who were out on the road of building a rich and strong democratic country, nor break their will to lay solid foundations for the national economy. The Party roused the entire people to the struggle for overcoming these grave difficulties; it geared all efforts to the successful fulfilment of the 1947 national economic plan, the first ever made in our country.

At that time our Party, rousing all its membership to action, carried on vigorously among the broad masses of the people a patriotic ideological campaign for national construction and a mass struggle for economy in the use of materials, for good care of machines, strengthening of labour discipline, rise in labour productivity, lowering of production costs and for mastery of technique. Consequently, the 1947 national economic plan as a whole was overfulfilled splendidly in all branches.

When we drew up our first national economic plan and made it public, the waverers and reactionaries disparaged it, calling it a "fantastic" plan and "absolutely infeasible." But the toiling masses headed by our Workers' Party members unfolded a vigorous emulation drive for increased production in the factories, mines and collieries, and farm and fishing villages of north Korea and achieved a great upsurge of labour. As a result, all the false rumours spread by the waverers and reactionaries were shattered to smithereens, and the plan was triumphantly fulfilled.

From the tremendous successes achieved in implementing the economic policy of the Party and in restoring and developing the national economy during the period under review, we can draw the following conclusions:

First, the successes in the democratic reforms and economic construction scored thanks to our Party's leading role, have launched north Korea firmly on the new path of people's democracy.

In 1947, state-owned industry accounted for 80.2 per cent of the total value of industrial output and private industry for 19.8 per cent. In the mining industry, the state sector held 100 per cent. This shows that the state sector held an overwhelming predominance in industry, the leading branch of the national economy. Besides, railway transport, communications, foreign trade, banks, etc., are under state control. All these conditions constitute a sure guarantee for developing the country's economy along the lines of controlling and regulating the private economy through the leading role of the state economy, of managing the national economy in a planned way and of steadily increasing the well-being of the broad masses of the people.

Second, through the practice of economic construction our workers and peasants have become conscious of their own great strength and creative talents and have become confident that they are fully able to overcome any difficulty and accomplish the cause of national construction. The results of the 1947 national economic plan have inspired our Party members and the entire people with the conviction and national pride that the Korean nation, like other nations, is able to build its country splendidly on its own.

Last, it must be mentioned that our Party itself accumulated a good deal of experience and learned lessons in the course of last year's economic construction. In the course of organizing and unfolding a mass struggle for the fulfilment of the first economic plan, our Party was further steeled and grew into a party capable of directing economic construction.

Our Party's great victory in economic construction, however, does not imply that our work is free from any shortcomings. Owing to our failure to give proper leadership to the economy, we have as yet many things left undone which were well within our power.

The first weak point of our Party organizations in economic construction lies in their inadequate knowledge about it and poor experience in the management of enterprises.

The present situation in our country demands not only that our Party should become a party capable of organizing and politically leading the masses, but also that it should become a party of builders able to build the economy and manage enterprises and possessing knowledge of economics and technology. Hence, the momentous tasks confronting our Party are to master the know-how of economic construction, learn the methods of economic management, master production techniques, boldly promote best Party members as cadres to guide the economy, bring the work of Party organizations to penetrate into production, and make all the Party members bear the brunt of the struggle for economic construction.

The second defect of our Party organizations in economic construction is that they are weak in the struggle for the establishment of strict order and discipline in economic management. The result is that in some industrial enterprises labour discipline is slack, labour turnover is excessive, nonproductive expenditure and wastage of materials are found and, worse still, the bad practice of embezzling state property continues.

The tasks of our Party organizations are to build up strict revolutionary order and discipline, establish a new, popular system of management in factories and enterprises, get the workers to settle down, raise their technical and skill levels, considerably increase labour productivity, systematically lower the costs of production and ensure higher gains for every state-owned enterprise. At the same time, Party organizations should conduct an uncompromising struggle against the acts of misappropriating state and social properties, defining them as criminal acts against the people, and tirelessly carry on the work of cultivating among the broad sections of the working people and the functionaries the spirit of cherishing and economizing on state property.

The third major shortcoming is that some of the Party functionaries and leading economic cadres fail to fully understand and correctly carry out the economic policy of the Party for constantly enhancing the leading role of the state sector in the development of the national economy. At present, the state sector holds a very low proportion in such branches as local industry, fisheries and trade, although there is the possibility of further increasing it. In 1947 private business controlled more than 93 per cent of local industry and nearly 85 per cent of the fishing industry, while the private trade accounted for 84.5 per cent of retail commodity turnover and the state and consumers' co-operative trade for 15.5 per cent. This, it may well be said, is traceable to the fact that some leading functionaries in charge of these branches have conducted affairs in an easy-going manner in collaboration with private entrepreneurs, instead of organizing the work from the standpoint of the interests of the state and the people. It is no accident that today valuable goods and fine commodities manufactured by the state-owned industries are not allotted and supplied in an organized way, but a considerable part of them flows into the hands of the profiteers, and that good fishing grounds and fishing boats are used not by the state but by the private interests.

We think that our Party functionaries responsible for the guidance of local industry, fisheries and trade should naturally criticize themselves, on Party principles, at this Congress for the grave errors they have committed. Our Party organizations and functionaries in these fields must correct their errors and conduct their work strictly in accordance with the economic policy of the Party.

In pursuance of the Party's economic policy, the Party organizations at all levels should make sure that the share of the state sector in the national economy grows and its leading role is steadily enhanced so that the country's economy may advance along the path of people's democracy guaranteeing the welfare of the entire people.

For the consolidation of the victory of the democratic reforms, and for the successful restoration and development of the national economy, it is necessary further to strengthen our organs of people's power.

As the history of mankind shows, no class and no people can emerge victorious in the building of a new society and can defend their national independence without a strong political power of their own. Particularly under the conditions in which our country is not yet unified and south Korea is being converted into a colony of the U.S. imperialists, it is necessary to strengthen our organs of people's power in every way in order to achieve the complete independence and sovereignty of the country and expedite national reunification.

Some of our Party members now working in the organs of people's power, however, fail to properly fulfil the important missions entrusted to them by the people, fail to maintain close contacts with the masses of the people, lack the loyalty and enthusiasm to serve them with devotion, and not infrequently commit deviations in implementing the Party's policies.

It is most important for the Party functionaries to acquire the methods and knowledge of administering the state and running the power. To this end, a special education in administrative matters should be given to the Party members and cadres working in the organs of people's power, and the Party should exercise day-to-day control and guidance over it.

The functions of the organs of power at all levels, from top to bottom, should be clearly laid down; the lower bodies should carry out the measures and decisions of the upper bodies in good time and with dispatch; a genuinely popular style of work should be established among the functionaries of organs of people's power, so that they may devote their all to the people and readily respond to the demands and the voice of the masses. Thus, the bonds of kinship between the organs of people's power and the masses of the people should be maintained and the work of the organs of people's power should be rooted deep in the popular masses.

In order to enhance the prestige of the people's power, to consolidate and develop its organs and further improve their work, it is necessary to select boldly from among the people competent cadres who are faithful to the country and the revolution and allocate them to the organs of power, and to establish strict democratic order and stringent state discipline in the work of the people's committees at all levels.

It is an important task for us to further consolidate the people's power and accelerate the restoration and development of the national economy. Successful fulfilment of this task will provide a decisive guarantee for the reunification and independence of the country.

Our Party must energetically enlist the creative power of the masses of the people in the struggle for the overfulfilment of the 1948 national economic plan, which will mark another step forward in the building of the foundation for an independent national economy and in the improvement of the material and cultural life of the people, and it must lead the entire people to the victory of the cause of the country's independence and sovereignty and reunification on a democratic basis.

III. THE PARTY

Comrades,

Our people's great victory and success in the democratic reforms and in economic construction confirm the correctness of our Party's lines and policies, and prove that our Party has grown and developed into a powerful organized force fully equal to the task of building a rich and strong country.

That in the course of the struggle for the country's reunification, independence and democracy our Party has become able to tackle its great mission as it does today is entirely attributable to the fact that it has achieved organizational unity and unity of ideology and will, that the entire Party has rallied around its Central Committee, and that it has solidly united the broad masses around itself. Our Party has now become a reliable mass political party defending the interests of the Korean working masses; it is victoriously fulfilling the great historic task of building a democratic country.

1. THE STRUGGLE FOR THE CONSOLIDATION OF THE PARTY

Immediately after liberation our Party laid down its basic political line: to set up a solid democratic base in north Korea for the complete emancipation of the Korean nation and the building of Korea into an independent and sovereign state, mighty and prosperous, in the future, by thoroughly carrying out the democratic reforms and accelerating democratic construction in north Korea. It was of decisive importance to the building and consolidation of a democratic base in north Korea to develop our Party into a powerful mass party and to rally the broad masses of the people around it.

Hence, our Party deemed it necessary to unite the local Party organizations that had been set up loosely in different parts of north Korea and establish in north Korea a powerful central directing body capable of implementing successfully the Party's political line in conformity with all the favourable conditions and circumstances in north Korea, and formed the Central Organizing Committee of the Communist Party of North Korea on October 10, 1945.

At the time, the need to set up the Central Organizing Committee was abundantly clear to everyone. Nevertheless, some people in the Party came out against the formation of the Central Organizing Committee of the Communist Party of North Korea on the pretext of "supporting the centre": they failed to understand correctly the political situation in Korea, because they were held captive by the old factional habits and the mentality of individualist heroism which they had developed earlier when they bossed the small local groups in the manner of "I am my own Lord" like the frog in the well, without any experience of Party life and ignorant of the fundamentals of discipline which call for submission to the Party organization and the higher Party organs. These people attempted to tear our Party apart into local groups, as of old, and to continue living a musty life of factional grouping, each lording it over his own local sphere of influence.

At that time, in order to conceal their attempts the factionalists and individualist heroists, alleging that "the establishment of the Central Organizing Committee in north Korea would mean splitting the Party," made loud noises as if they were concerned for the preservation of the Party's unity. But the fact was that they themselves refused to submit to the centre and wanted to continue with their activities of individualist heroism and factionalism, bossing the show in their respective districts.

The factionalists were aware that the "Seoul centre," which was exposed to the U.S. imperialist suppression, would not be able to supervise them properly, and hoped to avail themselves of this opportunity to continue their factional activities. That was why they opposed the founding of the Central Organizing Committee of the Communist Party of North Korea which would be fully able to exercise day-to-day leadership and supervision all over them at close quarters. If the "centre" in Seoul had then been in Pyongyang, they certainly would not have raised the slogan "support the centre," but would have opposed the "centre" under some other slogan.

What would have become of the situation in north Korea and the destiny of our country if, as the factionalists insisted, we had not set up the Central Organizing Committee then and, looking only to Seoul, had failed to give unified leadership to the Party organizations scattered in the provinces? Undoubtedly our Party, far from developing into the mass political party as today, would have been manipulated and torn asunder by the factionalists, and thus would have failed to secure the victory of the democratic reforms and to set up in north Korea a solid democratic base for the complete independence and sovereignty of the country.

In the early days of the Central Organizing Committee of the Communist Party of North Korea, many elements who were infected with tendencies to liberalism and individualist heroism and steeped in factionalist ideas made their way into the organizations and leading bodies of the Party at various levels, hampering its unity, fostering a scramble for posts and local separatism and continuing factional activities in the Party. In those Party organizations where such elements ensconced themselves in the leading bodies, the situation worsened to such an extent that many pro-Japanese elements wormed their way into the Party ranks and carried on harmful activities infringing upon the interests of the masses and divorcing the Party from them.

Some factionalists who had sneaked into the leading bodies of the Party opposed the reorganization of the Young Communist League into the Democratic Youth League and made deliberate attempts to foil it, in the hope of confusing the Party's united front policy and preventing the Party from uniting broader sections of the masses around it. Those fellows were utterly ignorant of the united front policy of the Party and did not want to understand it either. That was why they accused us of "steering the Party backwards" and "swaying the Party to the Right." It is needless to say who really sought to steer the Party backwards and sway it to the Right. Had we yielded to their clamorous insistence and failed to reorganize the Young Communist League into the Democratic Youth League, we would obviously have been unable to unite around the Party as today the millions of young people who are playing an important part in our national construction.

In those days, persons who were ignorant of the organizational line of the Party and the elementary standards of Party life and yet pretended to know them, entrenched themselves in the Party's leading bodies and manipulated it at will, instead of appointing people who were capable of putting its organizations in proper order. Consequently, no organizational discipline and organizational system were established within the Party, system and order were absent in all work such as the preparation of the Party's statistics and the keeping of its documents and even the principles laid down in the Party Rules with regard to the admission of new members were not observed.

In no small number of Party organizations, where elements strongly infected with factionalist provincialism held leading posts, fine cadres of working-class origin and other promising and faithful cadres were not promoted while the promotion of cadres was made from considerations of kinship and fellow-provincial ties. The result was that some organs were staffed entirely with persons from Hongwon or from Seoul. All the leading posts thus came to be held by persons without ability and, as a result, good, competent people in the local areas had no opportunity of being promoted. In the work of increasing Party membership, too, the factionalists, instead of admitting to the Party fine, advanced elements from among the working class—the main force in the building of the democratic country—and from among its most reliable ally, the poor peasantry, indiscriminately admitted urban loafers and petty bourgeois, forming Party cells among them where there was no one to rely on.

In order to save our Party from this grave situation, we called the Third Enlarged Executive Committee Meeting of the Central Organizing Committee of the Communist Party of North Korea in December 1945 and took resolute measures for overcoming the wrong organizational, political and ideological tendencies within the Party. The Third Enlarged Executive Committee Meeting brought about a great renovation in Party work and Party life for the first time since the founding of our Party, and this marked the beginning of its development into a truly sound and powerful party.

We allocated new, competent cadres to the Party centre and Party committees at all levels; fought determinedly against those who were infected with provincialism and nepotism and against elements with tendencies to factionalism, local separatism, individualist heroism and liberalism; and worked energetically to set up a well-adjusted system of Party organization from the centre down to the cells, and to ensure the organizational and ideological unity of the Party. Thus, organizational discipline, which permits of no factional activity within the Party and requires unconditional obedience to the decisions and directives of the higher Party organs, began to be established.

Parallel to this, we conducted throughout the Party the work of checking up on the Party ranks, of issuing membership cards and organizationally strengthening the Party organizations. As a result, the pro-Japanese and alien elements lurking in the Party, who were committing acts of infringing upon the interests of the masses and divorcing the Party from the masses, were exposed and expelled from the Party, and great progress was made in preserving the purity of the Party ranks.

Our Party organizations, which had been remaining in suspense like castles in the air, struck roots among the much reliable and unswerving working class and poor peasantry, among whom our Party cells were formed and expanded.

Propaganda for the Party's lines and policies was widely conducted, within and without the Party, through the media of its organ and other publications. And excellent Party members were selected and given systematic education in Party schools. Thus began the mass training of cadres who were to play an important role in Party building. And political education was energetically conducted within the Party in order to acquaint every member with the Party's stand and policies and enable him to know correctly what the duties of the Party member are and how he should lead his organizational life. Members of the Party started working actively to explain its policies to the broad masses and rally them around the Party.

Thus, our Party work and Party life were put on the right track after the Third Enlarged Executive Committee Meeting, and from that time on our Party developed into a powerful party equal to the great task of democratizing the country and capable of skilfully mobilizing the broad masses of the people to carry out democratic reforms and economic construction.

As the Party's organizations were consolidated and it came to enjoy the enthusiastic support of the working masses, we were confronted with the task of developing it into a mass party with broader foundations, in keeping with the social progress and rapid changes in state political life. In other words, there arose the need for a mass-based party representing the common interests of the working class, peasantry and working intelligentsia in order further to consolidate their alliance which had been solidly built up in the course of the democratic reforms and to lead the broad working masses to take a more active part in state political life.

Thus, in August 1946, a congress for the merger of the Communist Party and the New Democratic Party was convened, at which the glorious Workers' Party of North Korea, the leading force in the building of the country, was founded.

As you see, our Party has grown amidst the struggle to consolidate its organization since the time of its predecessor party and, on this basis, it has developed into the powerful mass party of today.

2. THE GROWTH OF PARTY RANKS AND THE WORK OF ORGANIZATIONAL LEADERSHIP

Since the merger, the ranks of our Party have attained rapid numerical growth. Whereas its total membership at the time of the merger was over 366,000, it had grown to more than 708,000, a 1.9-fold increase, by January 1, 1948.

Though the Party ranks grew at such a rapid rate, some Party organizations committed not a few Right and "Left" errors in this course. Some of the Party organizations recruited Party members in the manner of forming an association, thus providing conditions for many alien elements to worm their way into the Party ranks, while some other Party organizations closed their doors on the plea of a strict selection of Party members, to the detriment to our Party's development into a mass party.

For the purpose of overcoming such deviations, immediately after the merger the Party Central Committee issued uniform membership cards to all the members and guided and checked up on the work of increasing the Party membership as a whole. It thus helped the local Party organizations correct their errors in good time, and took measures not only for the quantitative but also for the qualitative growth of the Party, making it possible markedly to improve the composition of the Party. The number of workers in the entire Party membership has grown from over 73,000 at the time of the merger to more than 143,000 now. In the same period the number of poor peasants in the entire membership has increased from over 185,000 to 374,000.

With the rapid growth and strengthening of the Party, the question of establishing its organizational principle and system posed itself more urgently. So, the Central Committee of the Party took measures to firmly build up its leading organs at all levels, from the centre down to the cells, to establish iron discipline in the Party and strengthen the Party life of every member.

In particular, the main effort was directed to the strengthening of the Party cells. The cell is the basic organization of our Party, and its strengthening is essential for the consolidation of the Party as a whole and for increasing its fighting strength. The Party Central Committee has taken important steps to readjust the cells and strengthen life in the cells. As a result, cells in the factories and farm villages have made remarkable progress and it has become an established habit for Party members earnestly to discuss the immediate political and economic tasks at the general meetings of Party cells and to make every effort to implement the directives of the Party centre and Party committees at various levels and the decisions of the cells.

The number of Party cells increased from more than 12,000 at the time of the merger to over 28,000 at the end of 1947, and they were formed in every factory, enterprise, institution and farm village. At the time of the merger there were only 400 odd *myon* Party committees, but now every *myon* has its Party committee.

As a result, our Party today has a powerful, monolithic organizational system which makes it possible to mobilize the entire membership without the slightest confusion at any moment in the event of the country calling for its emergency mobilization.

However, in the building of our Party and in its work of organizational leadership, there are shortcomings which must be rectified without delay.

First, the cell, which is the basic organization of our Party, is not yet sound enough and the work of the Party cell has not attained a high level. The Party cell is the basic organization which gives day-to-day education and training to the Party members, assures the ideological oneness and organizational unity of the Party ranks and translates into practical life the lines and policies of the Party. To strengthen the cells is basic to the strengthening of the whole Party.

This notwithstanding, many Party organizations have so far failed to raise the work of the cells to the required level.

This gives rise to the phenomena that cell meetings are held in a perfunctory way, without plan and adequate preparation, and that cells fail to carry on their work in keeping with the specific realities of the factories, workplaces and farm villages concerned, and to give detailed assignments to each Party member so that no small number of Party members find themselves at a loss what to do. The assignments given are not definite and, moreover, their fulfilment is not verified and summed up; the work of helping the Party members to carry out their Party assignments correctly is almost neglected.

In order to eliminate these shortcomings and strengthen the Party cells, it is necessary that every cell should devote its main efforts to fostering Party nuclei, that it should give assignments properly, that it should always scrupulously lead and check up on the Party life and the activities of the Party members, that it should hold cell meetings in an effective way according to a plan, that it should discuss and decide the direction and plans of work in conformity with the actual situation of the cell, and that it should vigorously carry on the ideological struggle against every negative tendency and actively develop criticism on Party principles within the cell. Thus, all the cells of our Party must be turned into militant, living organizations brimming with vitality.

Second, inadequate verification of how the Party organizations are implementing the policies and decisions of the Party constitutes a serious defect in our Party's work of organizational leadership.

In order to have a correct understanding of the activities of the Party organizations and know their members and cadres, it is necessary meticulously to lead and check up the Party organizations at lower levels and it is most important to organize this work effectively. Properly organized, the work of checking up will serve as a searchlight throwing a revealing light on the activities of Party organizations, a powerful means of exposing and eliminating manifestations of bureaucracy and formalism in Party work. That grave shortcomings persist in the work of some of our Party organizations till now is ascribable, in most cases, to the failure of Party organs to be concrete and scrupulous in leading and checking up on the work of the Party organizations at lower levels.

For an effective work of guidance and checkup on the Party organizations, it is necessary, in the first place, that this work be conducted regularly and systematically, not in sudden jerks, and, in the second place, that responsible cadres personally undertake the checkup work, instead of leaving it to minor functionaries.

Nevertheless, some of our Party organizations fail in the work of regular guidance and checkup on the Party organizations at lower levels and, if they ever conduct any checkup, do so perfunctorily, entrusting it only to minor functionaries. And in many cases, the verification is not conducted with the intention of helping the Party organizations at lower levels in their work and of correcting their defects, but is conducted by summoning the functionaries of subordinate bodies to the higher Party organs in order to scold and shout at them, and in order to draft decisions.

We must make it a rule to check up regularly on how the Party organizations at lower levels carry out the Party's policies and decisions, and must do away with all formalistic attitudes towards verification, thereby decisively elevating the level of the verification work of the Party. It is necessary for this purpose that, from now on, the aims and methods of the verification be explained clearly to the Party members who are sent out to do it. Scolding and penalizing must not be made a substitute for verification, but verification must be conducted in such a way as to go down to the lower Party organizations to give them effective assistance in their work and help them remedy their shortcomings, and as to know, educate and train the functionaries of the Party organizations and Party members.

Third, the improvement of the style of work of functionaries is an important problem that must be solved without fail in the sphere of the Party's organizational leadership.

The bureaucratic, formalistic style of work is still much in evidence in our Party. Some leading Party functionaries persist in the bureaucratic style of work. Instead of going among the masses to breathe the same air with them, mingle with and lead them, they conduct their work in the manner of lording it over the masses, blustering, threatening and browbeating them, and they apply Party penalties and dismiss their subordinates for minor errors or shortcomings in work, instead of assisting them in their work, giving them advice from the Party's standpoint, and patiently educating and training them.

And some of the leading Party functionaries cannot shake off their formalistic style of work. They deal with all affairs mechanically, without serious study and analysis, only send down innumerable decisions and directives without even troubling themselves to know how the matters are dealt with in the lower bodies, gloss over matters and stick to formality. Functionaries of this type seem to believe that everything will be all right if they adopt decisions or directives and send them down, even without organizing actual struggles for winning victory.

Such a bureaucratic and formalistic style of work is the most harmful style of work undermining our Party work and estranging the Party from the masses. We should, therefore, unfold a persistent struggle decisively to eliminate this style of work and build up a genuinely popular style of work in the Party.

We must acquire the work method of explaining matters to the masses, not commanding them, of going deep into the midst of the masses and knowing their feelings, teaching them and learning from them, of making friends and uniting in a body with them and then leading them to the attainment of goal.

We must also acquire the work style of getting down to settle each matter after finding a practical and correct solution for it on the basis of a close analysis of its substance, and seeing the matter through to the end once we have taken it up. In tackling all matters, the stress must not be placed on their superficial appearances and forms, but our main efforts should be directed to delving deep into their essence and bringing about substantial results.

It is a very important part of the Party's organizational leadership to give correct guidance to the mass organizations of the working people.

Our Party's consolidation of its ranks, in the final analysis, has the purpose of victoriously accomplishing the tasks of the revolution by uniting the broad masses around it and mobilizing their strength. The history of the international working-class movement shows no instance of victory by a party that failed to win over the broad masses and was divorced from them. That is why our Party, since its inception, has paid deep attention to uniting the broad masses around itself by drawing them into social organizations of various kinds.

Our Party has organized a number of social organizations such as the trade unions, the Peasants' Union, the Democratic Youth League, the Democratic Women's Union and the Literature and Arts Federation, thereby uniting millions of organized masses around itself. These mass organizations have established their own well-regulated organizational systems, and they have their branches set up in all districts and production units—towns, farm villages, factories, enterprises and institutions. The masses united in them are all under the organizational leadership of both the Party and the social organizations. Our Party, by leading all these social organizations, has mobilized the strength of the broad masses for the democratic reforms and economic construction and has already achieved great results in these tasks.

But there are still not a few shortcomings manifested in the Party's leadership of the mass organizations. Meanwhile, the social organizations have achieved a rapid quantitative growth, but our Party's influence has not penetrated deep into those organizations and their members have not been won over completely as the masses of our Party. There are some people among the members of the social organizations who become detached from our Party's influence and establish contact with religious organizations or come under the influence of other parties which are alien to their class standing.

This is because our Party members working as leading

functionaries or ordinary members in the social organizations have so far failed to deal properly with the work of uniting non-Party masses ideologically and politically around our Party. Our Party members have not yet become one with the non-Party people in those organizations, and have failed clearly to explain to them the community of their class interests.

One of the central tasks facing our Party at present, therefore, is to unite the social organizations still more closely around our Party. To this end, it is necessary to send competent cadres to the social organizations and regularly to educate their leading functionaries, and the functionaries in these organizations must go deep among the masses, breathe the same air with them, pay regard to their interests, solve in good time all the problems of actual life raised by them, and thus become workers enjoying prestige and high popularity among the masses. The leading workers of the social organizations must completely rectify all their wrong style of work—dictating to the masses, refusing to heed their voices and alienating themselves from them.

At the same time, our Party members must not tail in the wake of the masses, but must always maintain the identity and progressive traits of Party members. All Party members in the social organizations must at all times set an example in upholding the Party's stand and in devoting themselves to the good of the country and the people, so that the non-Party people in these organizations may become firmly convinced that our Workers' Party alone is a party thoroughly defending their class interests, that the Workers' Party alone is a party capable of leading the Korean people to freedom, happiness and national prosperity and that the Workers' Party members are indeed their genuine friends.

One of the most evil consequences of the protracted colonial rule of Japanese imperialism is that we are short of native cadres. Our Party, which has embarked on the building of the country, feels an acute insufficiency of cadres in all spheres of politics, economy and culture, which is a serious obstacle to our forward movement.

So, on the one hand, our Party unfolded the work of enlisting new cadres from among the people and educating and training them through practical work and, on the other, began to train cadres for the Party and state organs at permanent educational establishments. During the period under review, we have already trained over 4,000 Party cadres in central and provincial Party schools, and have re-educated numerous cadres in various systems of short courses.

The training of cadres and their correct selection and allocation are of decisive importance in all work, all the more so with us in view of the shortage of cadres and their complex composition.

One of the important principles of our Party's cadres policy is to appoint new cadres who come from among the people and serve the people, constantly educating and training them, and to remould the old cadres who have come of, and who formerly served, the ruling classes, inducing them to serve the country and the people.

To select and allocate a cadre does not mean appointing him to a post and giving him an office to write all kinds of directives in, nor does it mean keeping a lot of people constantly on the move by transferring them from one post to another without any purpose at all. By proper selection and allocation of cadres we mean, as Comrade Stalin said, valuing and respecting the cadres as the most precious treasures of the Party and the state; we mean studying cadres thoroughly to get a full and close knowledge of their political level and practical abilities, their merits and demerits; we mean educating cadres, training them in the course of practical work and making persevering efforts to raise their level of ideological consciousness and practical ability; we mean promoting promising young cadres boldly and in good time; we mean allocating them to the right posts where they can bring their talents and abilities into the fullest play.

Yet, we still have many defects in implementing the Party's cadres policy. There are not a few serious defects—work with cadres, and particularly that of drawing in, educating and remoulding the old cadres, is not up to the mark; too much hesitation is shown in promoting young cadres; and cadres are selected not according to their fidelity to the Party, the country and the people and to their practical abilities, but according to personal considerations, ties of friendship or, worse still, to factional connections. Such wrong tendencies of ignoring Party principles in personnel management can, in the end, provide opportunities for alien elements to worm their way into our state institutions, and lead to unfaithful and incompetent persons holding important posts and neglecting state affairs or making a mess of the work.

Party organizations at all levels, therefore, must not tolerate the slightest manifestations of lack of Party principles and political vigilance in the selection and allocation of cadres, but must fight uncompromisingly against such practices. Party organizations must pay primary attention to the correct implementation of the Party's cadres policy, and thus successfully assure the work of discovering able, new cadres from among the working class and other sections of the working people and boldly appointing them, of teaching inexperienced young cadres with patience and giving them political training through practical work, and re-educating the old cadres in the progressive ideas of new society. For the thoroughgoing implementation of the Party's cadres policy, it is necessary to further improve the work of the Party's personnel departments and to replenish them with new, competent cadres tested in work.

3. THE PARTY'S WORK OF PROPAGANDA AND IDEOLOGICAL EDUCATION

In view of our Party's development into a mass party and the rapid growth of its ranks following the merger of the Parties, there has arisen a still greater need for extensive Party propaganda work and for strengthened educational work to equip the Party members and cadres with Marxist-Leninist ideology.

The Party's propaganda work and work of Marxist-Leninist

education are powerful weapons for strengthening our Party organizationally and for ensuring its unity based on singleness of thought and will. If the Party's propaganda and ideological work are not done well, this will inevitably give rise to errors and deviations and hamper the correct implementation of the Party's lines and policies, even if the purity of the Party ranks is preserved, its organizational principles are established and cadres are allocated correctly. If the Party's propaganda and ideological work become slack, the cadres and Party members will lose faith in the justice and victory of our cause and become blind executors of instructions from above, without any clear political conviction of their own. In these conditions, one obviously cannot expect creative initiative of the cadres nor voluntary enthusiasm of Party members, and there can obviously be no vigorous progress in Party work. On the contrary, if the Party's propaganda work and work of Marxist-Leninist ideological education are successfully conducted, there will surely be innovations in Party work and the cause of national construction will be promoted victoriously.

This explains why our Party ever since the merger of the two Parties has paid the most profound attention to the improvement and strengthening of its work of propaganda and ideological education, and great successes have already been achieved in it.

At present our Party has at its disposal the Party press and many other media of propaganda as well as extensive networks of Party education. Since the merger, the Party Central Committee has published materials for Party study, propaganda materials and a great many books on Marxism-Leninism. The Propaganda and Agitation Department of the Party Central Committee alone has published nearly 3,000,000 copies of books by now. Our Party publishes its central organ *Rodong Sinmun*, and the theoretical magazine *Kulloja*, while provincial Party committees also have their own papers.

Nevertheless, there are many shortcomings in our Party's propaganda and educational work, too. Some Party organizations carry on this work in a very perfunctory manner and do not pay due attention to propagating the Party's policies and raising the ideological and theoretical level of its members.

The lecturers of the provincial Party committees fail to speak on current political affairs and on Marxist-Leninist theory on a high level and with full preparation; they are frequently assigned to tasks not associated with the Party's propaganda work. The Party's libraries have been set up at the provincial, city and county Party committees in accordance with a decision of the Party Central Committee, but they are not utilized well for the Party's propaganda and educational work and more often than not their doors are kept closed. These facts show that the leading functionaries of the Party actually do not concentrate on explaining and bringing the Party's policies home to its members and the masses and on equipping them with Marxist-Leninist ideology, but only talk about the need for doing so. This impedes the progress of our Party's ideological work.

It is therefore an urgent task for the Party organizations at all levels to improve and strengthen the Party's work of propaganda and ideological education work at the earliest possible date.

By markedly improving the quality of the Party's organ and the other Party publications, making better use of all the propaganda media and running the Party's education networks more effectively, we must decisively strengthen the work of propagating our Party's stand and policies among the masses of the people and of equipping the cadres and entire Party membership with the ideas of all-conquering Marxism-Leninism. At the same time, it is necessary to improve the work of the central and provincial Party schools, the permanent establishments of Party education, and to extend their terms of study, so as to train larger numbers of competent Party cadres who are qualified both politically and ideologically. And the role of the lecture sections and the lecturers of the provincial, city and county Party committees must be enhanced, the lecturers must be provided with conditions for raising their theoretical level, and the work of the Party's libraries must be improved.

Always mindful that bourgeois ideas alien to our Party and to the working people will assert themselves wherever ideological work is slackened, we must wage a determined ideological struggle in all fields against the infiltration of reactionary ideologies of all hues. The tendencies of slighting the propaganda and ideological work of the Party or neglecting the studies of Marxist-Leninist theory must be criticized severely from the standpoint of Party principles.

One of the most important problems in the Party's ideological work is to enhance the class consciousness of the working class and other sections of the labouring people and to sharpen their political vigilance against class enemies by giving them a correct understanding of the past and present situation and social and class relations in our country.

Which classes and which social strata, then, are against our Party's policies today?

First, it is the pro-Japanese elements, pro-American elements and traitors to the nation whom U.S. imperialism has bought over with dollars. Why? Because our Party is fighting thoroughly to expose their political ambitions and their anti-popular nature and smash their schemes for selling out the country and the nation;

Second, it is the reactionary landlords and the handful of evil entrepreneurs and profiteers that are opposed to our Party's policies. Why? Because our Party has confiscated the landlords' land, and deprived the evil entrepreneurs and profiteers, through the democratic reforms and development of the national economy, of their foothold for exploiting the people and extorting excessive profits;

Third, some wicked church elders and pastors who have been bought over by the U.S. imperialists are against us. We have proclaimed freedom of religious belief and permitted religions. Nevertheless, why do they set themselves against us? Because our Party has carried out the democratic reforms and has rapidly heightened the political and ideological consciousness and cultural level of the people and, as a result, the wicked church elders and pastors find it increasingly difficult to deceive the masses of the people under the cloak of religion.

We must not forget even for a moment that the greater our victories, the fiercer will be the death struggles of all the traitorous reactionary cliques.

In order to smash all sorts of frantic schemes by the reactionaries and guarantee victory in the fierce class struggle, we must strengthen the Party's propaganda and ideological education in every way, firmly equip the entire Party with Marxist-Leninist ideology, greatly heighten the class consciousness and conscious enthusiasm of the masses of the people.

Comrades,

Such, in general, is the path our Party has traversed over the past one year and a half.

There have been victories and successes with us and also there have been defects and errors. The Party Central Committee laid bare and corrected in good time the shortcomings of our Party organizations and the errors committed by some leading Party functionaries, set forth a correct policy and line of struggle for each period, and carried them out thoroughly.

As a result, our Party has made great achievements for the country and the people during the period under review.

In view of the complex situation prevailing in our country, our Party has strengthened the people's power, consolidated the victories won in the democratic reforms, and accelerated the rehabilitation and development of the national economy in north Korea, thereby turning it into a steel-strong bulwark for the reunification, independence and democratic development of the country. This is a great victory scored by our Party and the democratic forces of Korea since liberation, and it is a most severe blow to U.S. imperialism which is seeking to colonize Korea again.

Our great achievements in the period under review have inspired our Party and people with the firm conviction and confidence of victory. The path our Party has traversed has clearly shown that there was nothing impossible for it to perform once it chose to, that there was no insurmountable difficulty for the Party and people when they worked in a body. Our Party members and the entire people, therefore, have now acquired the unshakable conviction that they can attain victory by defeating any enemy who might infringe upon the freedom and independence of the country and by surmounting any difficulties lying in the way of their advance.

The path our Party has travelled and the realities in north Korea have completely belied the imperialists' slander: "Being an inferior nation, the Korean people are incapable of governing the state, and they cannot have a powerful political party." We are now legitimately proud that the Korean nation, ranking among the advanced nations of the whole world, is creditably administering its country and has a great political party capable of shaping the destinies of the country and the people.

Our Party and people have thus won a great victory. But we have not yet set up a unified Democratic People's Republic, the earnest desire of the entire Korean people. The U.S. imperialists are pursuing an aggressive policy designed to split our country and our nation and to turn Korea into a colony; they are engaged in sinister plots against our Party and the Korean people. Our Party and our people, however, will never tolerate their crafty schemes.

Today our Party is entrusted with a great historic mission by the country and the people. Along with the democratic forces throughout Korea and with the entire Korean people, our Party will wage an unyielding struggle to attain without fail the complete independence and sovereignty of the country and lead the country and our nation to victory and happiness.

On behalf of the Central Committee of our Party, I call upon all the Party organizations and members to further strengthen the Party both organizationally and ideologically in order to consolidate and carry forward the brilliant victories it has won in a year and a half since its founding, guarantee the freedom and independence of the country and safeguard the honour of our nation.

On behalf of the Central Committee of our Party, I call upon all the Party organizations and members to strengthen the National Democratic United Front more than ever, to continuously maintain a tense, mobilized attitude, and to rouse the entire Party and people vigorously to the building of a rich and strong country and to the struggle for the overfulfilment of the 1948 national economic plan.

On behalf of the Central Committee of our Party, I call upon all the organizations and members of the Party to sharpen their revolutionary vigilance to the utmost against the sinister manoeuvres of the enemy, firmly to unite the broad masses of the people around our Party and our people's power and to mobilize the strength of the entire Party and all the people to the struggle for the country's reunification and to the nationwide struggle against the U.S. imperialists' policy for splitting our nation, by drawing on the valuable experience and lessons gained in past struggles.

On behalf of the Central Committee of our Party and the Party Congress, I send warm militant greetings and brotherly encouragement to the Workers' Party of South Korea and our heroic compatriots in south Korea who, for the sake of the country and the people, are waging a fierce and bloody struggle against the reactionaries.

EVERY EFFORT FOR THE CONSOLIDATION OF THE DEMOCRATIC BASE AND THE REUNIFICATION AND INDEPENDENCE OF THE COUNTRY

Concluding Speech Delivered at the Second Congress of the Workers' Party of North Korea

March 29, 1948

Comrades,

At the Congress many comrades spoke enthusiastically in support of the line and all the policies set forth by the Party Central Committee. I think the work done by the Central Committee of our Party in the period under review was appraised fully in the speeches of many comrades.

In general, it has been once again clearly confirmed at the Congress that our Party has grown into a powerful party enjoying undisputed authority and confidence among the masses of the people and has triumphantly accomplished the tasks of the democratic revolution and achieved tremendous successes in economic and cultural construction in north Korea by enlisting the great creative energies of the entire people. This is a brilliant victory attributable to the fact that the political line of the Central Committee of our Party has been correct and the entire Party membership and all the people, upholding the Party's line, have waged a heroic struggle for its implementation.

Our Party has endeavoured to fulfil the internationalist

duties devolving on our people as a member of the world democratic camp and has turned the situation of Korea, a link in the chain of world-wide struggles between democracy and anti-democracy, decisively in favour of democracy. Our Party has turned the northern half of the country not only into the democratic base of the Korean revolution but also into an Eastern outpost of the world democratic camp, and is defending it stoutly.

Our people, no longer an oppressed colonial nation but a liberated nation, have taken their destinies firmly into their own hands and are fighting gallantly against the U.S. imperialist policy of colonial enslavement and displaying to the whole world the brilliant successes achieved in the building of a new life.

The social organizations such as the trade unions, Women's Union and Democratic Youth League have launched into the international arena, and delegates of our country have already participated in international conferences many times, where they have given wide publicity to the achievements of our nation.

From the first days of the Party's foundation, the Party Central Committee called upon the entire membership and people to struggle for the establishment of a Democratic People's Republic, and has organized and mobilized all forces to lay the political and economic base in north Korea for the building of a unified, independent and democratic country.

Forming a firm united front with the democratic parties and social organizations that truly love the country and isolating the reactionary forces, the Party is exposing and crushing the aggressive policy of the U.S. imperialists at every step. The National Democratic United Front of North Korea has united under itself more than 6 millions of organized masses, and our Party always plays the central role in it. It is an important guarantee of our victory to correctly carry out the Party's united front policy and thereby unite and mobilize the patriotic democratic forces of all walks of life to a joint whole-nation struggle against U.S. imperialism and its stooges.

The democratic base built in north Korea by our Party is now playing the decisive part in the liberation struggle of the Korean people.

The new, free and happy life materialized in north Korea as a result of the people assuming power and carrying out the democratic reforms gives boundless encouragement to the people in south Korea who are deprived of their rights and suffer from poverty, and graphically shows to all the Korean people that the path followed by north Korea is right. With the rapid restoration and development of the national economy in north Korea, the material basis for complete independence and sovereignty of the country and prosperity of the nation is consolidated further still.

In order to legally consolidate the successes achieved in the carrying out of the democratic reforms and the building of a new life and to clearly indicate the path for the entire Korean people to follow, we have worked out the draft of the Provisional Constitution of the Democratic People's Republic of Korea and referred it to the entire people for discussion. To safeguard the gains of the revolution won by our people and defend the interests and peaceful labour of the people, our Party has built up the people's security organs solidly and founded the People's Army.

All these achievements in the revolutionary struggle and economic construction would be quite inconceivable apart from our Party's leading role. Our Party has built up its ranks as the vanguard fighting detachment of the Korean revolution and firmly united around itself the millions, and thus has continuously led the Korean people towards victory.

The Party Central Committee has paid deep attention, above all, to eliminating the ideological virus of factionalism and local separatism and to ensuring the organizational and ideological unity of the Party.

The Party has accepted into its ranks a large number of best advanced elements from among the workers, peasants and working intellectuals, expelled vacillating petty bourgeois and good-for-nothings and established strict organizational discipline in the Party. We have built up the Party organs of all levels, from the centre down, with able cadres by training an army of new cadres and appointing many activists of working people origin.

In the period under review our Party has done a really great amount of work and the achievements of our people are tremendous. We, however, have taken only the initial steps in the cause of achieving the complete liberation of our nation and building a unified, rich and strong country. Our Party and people still have many difficulties ahead of them and are confronted with many important tasks.

First of all, the most urgent task is to frustrate the intrigues of the U.S. imperialists to split our country and hold a reactionary separate election in south Korea. We should mobilize the strength of the entire Party and all the people to the struggle for the attainment by our people themselves of the independence and sovereignty and democratic reunification of the country, free from foreign interference, after making the foreign troops withdraw simultaneously from north and south Korea as proposed by the Soviet Union.

In order to reject and crush up the colonial enslavement policy of the U.S. imperialists, the democratic base set up in north Korea should be strengthened decisively. We can build a unified, independent and sovereign state of the Korean nation by our own hands only when the people's power is further consolidated, the democratic forces are rallied still firmer around our Party and the national economy is rapidly developed in north Korea.

What is important here is to raise the level of Party ideological consciousness and political and practical qualifications of the leading functionaries of the power organs at all levels from bureau directors down to *ri* people's committee chairmen, so that they carry out their Party assignments exactly without fail. The work of educating the high-ranking cadres should not be neglected on the ground that they hold high positions, but their Party education should be strengthened so much the more as they hold high positions.

Every cadre from bureau directors down to workers in the lowest organs should know how to administer the power and how to execute the Party's policies properly. It can be said that things beneficial to the landlords, capitalists and profiteers were done in the field of economic construction because bureau directors did not know how to administer the power and how to execute the Party's policies. The education of functionaries of the organs of state power should be intensified so that they fulfil their assigned tasks satisfactorily.

We should concentrate our efforts on the battle for the fulfilment of the current national economic plan for 1948. Important tasks of the current year's national economic plan are to develop light industry and, particularly, local industry to turn out large quantities of essential goods for the people and advance agriculture rapidly to secure food for the population and provide raw materials to industry, while promoting the rehabilitation of heavy industry. The power organs at all levels should not talk only about economic construction in words, but should, in practice, carry out the work of boosting production, lowering prices and raising the living standards of the people.

What we felt most keenly in the course of carrying out the national economic plan last year was the need to heighten the functionaries' level of economic and technical knowledge. All our Party members should without exception acquire a concrete knowledge of economic construction and techniques and become well versed in their respective domain of work. This alone makes it possible for our Party to ensure the rapid rehabilitation and development of the national economy and further expedite a happy and bountiful future for the Korean people.

We should pay great attention to the development of national culture as well as to economic construction. The building of a rich, strong, independent and sovereign state can be hastened only if the cultural standard of the people is raised, native cadres are brought up and national culture developed. All should strive to overfulfil the assignments of the national economic plan in the branches of education, culture and public health.

Of importance in this connection is that our Party should conduct its work properly with the intellectuals including the teachers, writers, artists and physicians. There are many people among our intellectuals who still have survivals of old ideologies of Japanese imperialism, know little about the peculiarities of the history and culture of their own country, and are poorly informed of the direction in which the progressive peoples of the world are advancing. We should strengthen the work with the teachers, writers, artists and physicians and arm them adequately with lofty ideas of patriotism and scientific Marxist-Leninist world outlook, thus inducing them to devote all their wisdom and zeal to the development of national culture and the cause of building the country.

It is an urgent task for us to wage a vigorous struggle against the reactionary thoughts in all fields. Our country is now divided in two, north and south, and the U.S. imperialists and domestic reactionaries are frantically spreading decadent and pernicious reactionary thoughts in the area south of the 38th parallel. Those fellows resort to every possible means to dampen the patriotic enthusiasm and revolutionary consciousness of the Korean people and are at pains to propagate the reactionary thoughts even to north Korea. We should wage an intensified struggle to prevent those hostile thoughts from exerting influence on our Party and people and should smash up the wicked attempt of the enemy to reduce our people once again into bondage to foreign imperialism and landlords and comprador capitalists.

We should not forget that the overthrown landlords and comprador capitalists are still nurturing the wild dreams of restoring the old system, and that their thoughts can exert influence on some backward sections of our people. As a comrade said in regard to factionalist thinking, the thoughts of the expropriated landlords, too, will disappear only after they die. We should understand this clearly and make constant efforts to eliminate the influence of all reactionary thoughts.

Mention should also be made of the need to heighten vigilance against the profiteers, wicked church elders and pastors.

None of the workers, peasants and office employees suffered loss in the currency changeover effected in December last year. Only the profiteers sustained losses and so they are grumbling about it. Moreover, their discontent is growing further still as our state industry and state and consumers' co-operative trade are developing every day.

And among the reactionary church elders and pastors there are few who did not own land and none who did not eat the bread of idleness, and so they are also discontented with us. Particularly, the U.S. scoundrels have desperately attempted for 40 years to spread their ideological influence in the land of Korea through the means of religion and worked hard to train and protect reactionary church elders and pastors as the social foothold for their aggression against Korea. In this connection there is a tendency among the Christians towards unconditional worship of America, and the reactionary pastors dislike our Party which enlightens and politically awakens the people, and come out against its policies because it becomes more difficult to attain their ends if our people get awakened.

We should not allow ourselves to feel at rest and relax because the democratic reforms have come off victorious and our Party's line and policies are being carried into effect with success in north Korea, but should maintain still greater vigilance against the landlords, profiteers, reactionary church elders and pastors and thoroughly prevent the infiltration of all hues of reactionary ideologies by explaining and making known our policies and ideas widely to the Party members and the masses of the people.

Special attention should be directed particularly at preserving the purity of our Party ranks. Although we have already driven out the pro-Japanese elements who sneaked into the Party, we should in future, too, continue to fight resolutely to keep alien elements of hostile class and exploiter origins from slipping in and spreading the influence of reactionary ideologies within our Party.

Lastly, I should like to mention the question of factions in the Party. Though this question has been much talked about yesterday and today, I am going to say a few more words.

At present there is no big faction in our Party. It would be proper to say that there only remain factional elements, who impede the development of the Party.

In the past no small number of Korean Communists operated in isolation in various areas including Hongwon and Seoul and, working underground in small groups owing to the harsh repression by the Japs, acted each as his own Lord as if his theory had been the best and he had been the "leader." It was impossible to pool their strength, build up a unified revolutionary Party and establish normal relations with the Communists of other countries, because each of them acted as the "leader." They formed factions such as the M-L group, the Tuesday group, the Seoul group, the Com-group, etc., each comprising a few persons, and were engrossed only in a scramble for power, each insisting on the superiority of his own group. This shows that at the time the Party had no mass foundation.

The situation, however, is utterly different now. Today our Party already stands on a solid mass foundation and its ranks are composed of finest, advanced elements of the workers, peasants and working intellectuals fighting in good faith and with devotion for the country and the revolution and for the happiness of the people. So, there can be no faction, and there actually is not and there will not be in the future, too.

Factional elements, however, are still lurking in the Party and continue underhand mischiefs in this or that corner.

In the first place, they pretend allegiance outwardly and perpetrate antagonistic acts behind the scenes. This is what is called double-dealing, and O Gi Sop has done a great deal of mischief of this kind. Although he cannot voice objection when sitting face to face, he whispers and calumniates the Party behind the scenes. When the Young Communist League was reorganized into the Democratic Youth League, for instance, we explained many times that if the Young Communist League was left alone, there was a fear that a large number of youths might be taken away by other parties and religious organizations, and so it had to be reorganized into a mass organization, the Democratic Youth League. And O Gi Sop, too, agreed to it in the end. Nevertheless, he made a speech quite in reverse to it at Haeju. Also, Chong Dal Hon said when he went down to South Hamgyong Province that it was decided to retain the Young Communist League organization in that province alone.

Further, the factional elements draw people to their side for the sake of kinship, schoolfellowship or for fellow provincial ties and in consideration of these people having belonged to the same faction or served time in the same prison in the past, and make sly mischiefs by inviting and treating them to a drink at their homes. These are all dangerous factional courses. We have already set up Party schools and turn out thousands of leading cadres of the Party every year, and when would they be able to form factions by such an amateurish method? This is a foolish mischief.

Now that it is impossible for him to make a big faction, it seems O Gi Sop is seeking to form a small one at least. When transferred from the Propaganda Bureau to the Labour Bureau, he took along with him so many people whom he trusted. This is just the same practice as was followed by such warlords of China as Wu Pei-fou, Chang Tso-lin and Han Fu-chu. But no matter how craftily he may make mischief like this, the Party sees clearly through it as the "devil-finding mirror" penetrates the "ghost."

All these tendencies can be regarded as deriving from individual careerism. By the nature of things, at the bottom of factionalism lies the wrong idea of individual careerism. This is an anti-Party idea implying that one does not truly love his country and nation and is not willing to fight with full devotion for the Party and the revolution, but, quite on the contrary, looks only after his own interests and seeks to give prominence only to himself. The treatise of O Gi Sop on the trade unions, too, is a product of individual careerist idea. If he wanted to publish a theoretical treatise on questions like that, he ought to have submitted it to the Political Committee for advice at least. O Gi Sop, however, plagiarized a treatise written by Lenin in the period of NEP and published it under his own name. It is clear to all that what was applicable to Russia at the time cannot fit in squarely with Korea today. Yet, O Gi Sop pretends to know while he knows nothing, and makes no scruple to do anything to make himself conspicuous.

O Gi Sop, Chong Dal Hon and Choe Yong Dal did not criticize themselves well but made empty speeches at the meeting. O Gi Sop bites at others by saying, "Why do you torment me only without criticizing people like Comrade Mu Jong?" This attitude is also wrong. Anyone is liable to commit errors in work, and so it is important to seriously reflect on his errors and try not to repeat similar mistakes.

When we were going to institute the Organizing Committee, O Gi Sop had no objection at first, supposing that he would head it, but when another person became the head, he began opposing it. Chong Dal Hon said that he had turned against those who had come from abroad and supported the "centre" in Seoul. In reality, however, he objected to the establishment of the Organizing Committee because he could not form a "centre" consisting of people from South Hamgyong Province. But at the time I left them as they were in charge of important duties from the standpoint that it did not matter who should hold the posts if only they performed their work properly.

In the first few months after the establishment of the Organizing Committee, too, the alien and speculative elements who had sneaked into the Party perpetrated subversive activities and the factionalists kept making mischiefs, and not a few responsible cadres were turning their eyes only towards Seoul, and so the Party could not perform its functions satisfactorily. We, therefore, called the Third Enlarged Executive Committee Meeting of the Organizing Committee and took resolute organizational steps.

The errors committed by O Gi Sop since the foundation of the Party are very grave and his acts deserve expulsion from the Party. But if only he repents thoroughly of his errors and makes a resolve never to repeat similar acts, I think we can deal with him leniently, at least in consideration of the fact that he fought against Japanese imperialism once before.

The defect of Choe Yong Dal is that he has no class awakening at all and does not respect the Party. And he often perpetrated the act of making friends with pro-Japanese elements, had an antipathy to expelling them and is brazen-faced enough to propose at the People's Assembly that a scoundrel who had been a member of the "Concordia Association" be elected judge of the Supreme Court. The self-criticism he has made today has no content at all. As a matter of course, vigilance should be heightened against individuals like him. If there exists the slightest vacillation or arises ideological disunity within our Party, the reactionaries will immediately try to trade on it.

To conclude, we should wage a determined struggle to ensure iron discipline in the Party and the unity of the Korean communist movement and should bind the factionalists hand and foot so as to prevent them from making mischiefs freely. Anyone, whether a bureau director or no matter what post he holds, should be duly criticized and severely criticize himself whenever he has done harm to the Party and the revolution in word or in deed, however trifling it may be.

Another thing I want to refer to is the question of guidance of the social organizations. Not a few organizations of our Party now fail to exert adequate Party influence on the members of the social organizations and overlook the phenomenon that those members join parties alien to their own classes. To take an example, it is a serious fact that poor peasants in the remote mountain regions are joining the Chongu Party, although they have no ground whatever to join another party from the class point of view. This is proof that our Party organizations are weak in their work with the masses and the political activities of our Party members among the masses fall short of the mark. It is necessary above all to reinforce the ranks of cadres in the social organizations. Politically-tempered, competent cadres should be dispatched to the social organizations instead of sending those cadres who have been punished in the Party for having committed errors of this or that kind.

Comrades,

This time we have held a Congress of tremendous importance in the history of our Party and our people. The resolutions adopted at the Party Congress will make a great contribution to further strengthening our Party and leading the Korean people to a new, great victory in future.

I am convinced that the Party organizations at all levels and the comrades who have attended this Congress as delegates and the entire Party membership will splendidly fulfil the historical mission devolving on our Party in the struggle for the reunification and independence of the country and the prosperity of the nation by upholding the resolutions of the Party and vigorously striving for their implementation together with the masses of the people.

THE POLITICAL PROGRAMME OF THE GOVERNMENT OF THE DEMOCRATIC PEOPLE'S REPUBLIC OF KOREA

Political Programme Announced at the First Session of the Supreme People's Assembly of the Democratic People's Republic of Korea

September 10, 1948

Deputies to the Supreme People's Assembly,

Our nation, liberated from the Japanese imperialist yoke of colonial rule, waited impatiently for the earliest possible establishment of a unified democratic central government in our country and for the building of an independent state capable of holding its own as a full-fledged member of the world democratic camp.

But the traitors to the nation in south Korea under the manipulation of the U.S. imperialists have sabotaged the decision of the Moscow Three Foreign Ministers Conference on the Korean question and turned south Korea into a land of lawlessness where the reactionary elements are on the rampage. Cruelly suppressing all the democratic, patriotic forces in conspiracy with the U.S. imperialists, those traitors established a separate puppet government at last and are crying for the prolonged stationing of U.S. troops. The U.S. imperialists and their lackeys are desperately seeking to perpetuate the division of our nation, keep our territory partitioned in two forever and turn south Korea into a complete U.S. colony.

Under these circumstances, the Government of the Democratic People's Republic of Korea, a unified central government of Korea set up by the general wishes of the people in north and south Korea, will strive to carry out the following tasks with the object of achieving the complete reunification of the country and building a rich and strong, independent and sovereign democratic state:

First, the Government of the Republic will unite the entire Korean people firmly around itself and mobilize them to the struggle for the reunification of the country and will make every effort to carry into effect the proposal of the Soviet Government on the simultaneous withdrawal of the Soviet and U.S. armies which is the prerequisite for territorial integrity and national reunification.

Second, the Government of the Republic will take all necessary measures to clear the political, economic and cultural life in our country of the evil effects of Japanese imperialist rule and will punish by the laws of the Republic the pro-Japanese elements and traitors to the nation who betrayed the interests of the Korean people and actively collaborated with the Japanese imperialists.

The Government will wage a resolute struggle against the remnants of the servile spirit left over by the Japanese imperialists and against the traitors to the nation who manoeuvre to sell out our country again as a colony of foreign imperialism, and will thoroughly expose and crush all the attempts of the enemies to demolish the democratic system established in north Korea and the results of the economic and cultural construction.

Third, the Government of the Democratic People's Republic of Korea will declare null and void all the laws made by the Japanese imperialists in the past and all the anti-democratic, anti-popular ordinances of the puppet government.

The Government of the Republic will further consolidate and develop the democratic reforms such as the agrarian reform, nationalization of industries, the Labour Law and the Law on Equality of the Sexes enforced in north Korea and will strive for their introduction on an all-Korea scale.

Fourth, the Government of the Republic, with a view to

building Korea into a rich, strong, independent and democratic state, will rid our economy of its colonial dependence, oppose the economic enslavement policy of the foreign imperialists, and build an independent national economy capable of steadily improving the well-being of the Korean people and assuring independence and prosperity for our country.

The Government will work out a unified national economic plan so as to make a rational use of all the resources of the country in the interests of the people and will actively develop the national economy and culture according to that plan.

For the successful carrying out of this task, the Government will take the following measures:

(1) The metallurgical industry, machine-building industry, chemical industry, ship-building industry, light industry, fishing industry, etc., will be actively developed in order to abolish the colonial distortion of industry, lay the basis of an independent national economy and meet in full the country's needs for manufactured goods, and the railway, motor and shipping transport services will be developed to satisfactorily ensure transportation.

The Government of the Republic will see that the factories now in operation work to full capacity, rehabilitate all the factories not yet restored and build a number of new factories.

With the object of rapidly expanding the production of consumer goods for the people, the Government will actively develop the textile, leather, shoe-making and other light industrial branches, and, especially, will give generous assistance to the co-operative enterprises and encourage the creative initiative of the private enterprises in this field.

(2) While consolidating the results of the agrarian reform carried out in north Korea, the Government of the Republic will on this basis vigorously develop farm production and stockbreeding.

In developing agriculture the Government will encourage in every way the creative initiative of the peasants, render them every possible state assistance such as supplying an adequate amount of fertilizer and farm implements and taking measures for the improvement of the methods of farming, and will give active guidance to their farming.

The arable land and the sown area will be extended to increase grain output. Especially for the purpose of extending the paddies and increasing rice yields, the Government will vigorously carry on irrigation projects with state funds and, on the other hand, will encourage and help the farmers in their voluntary irrigation works.

The Government will enlarge the area sown to cotton and develop sericulture in order to meet the demands of the people for textiles, and will also develop forestry to satisfy the requirements of the national economy for timber.

(3) To supply the people with sufficient necessaries of life, the Government will pursue a policy of ensuring commodity circulation smoothly between town and country and of reducing prices systematically.

The state and the consumers' co-operative trade will be developed rapidly by setting up state and consumers' co-operative stores widely in towns and farm villages, and private trade, too, will be encouraged to supply the people with necessaries.

The Government will actively expand exports by tapping the resources of the country to the full and steadily increasing production and, at the same time, import machinery, equipment and other goods essential for the economic development of the country and the people's life.

Fifth, the Government will direct great efforts to the development of education, culture and public health services. In the domain of education the school networks will be largely extended to enrol the children now out of school to the greatest possible extent and raise the rate of admission into the junior and senior middle schools, and will introduce compulsory primary education in 1950.

It is impossible to build an independent state without able native cadres to work in all domains of politics, economy and culture. It is, therefore, one of the most important tasks confronting the Government of the Republic to train in a big way native cadres who are needed in all fields of state building.

To train large numbers of able native technical cadres wanted in all fields of the national economy, the Government will build more specialized technical schools and colleges and take steps to perfect all the facilities of the institutions of higher education and improve the contents and methods of instruction.

At the same time, on-the-job education networks and short technical training courses will be set up at the enterprises and institutions to disseminate techniques among factory and office workers, and many production technique schools will be opened to train skilled workers. Also, more schools and middle schools for adults will be established to conduct adult education on a wide scale, so that illiteracy will be wiped out from among the working people and their cultural standard heightened.

With a view to raising the people's level of political consciousness and their technical and cultural standards, newspapers, magazines and books will be published in large quantities and the activities of libraries, cinema houses, theatres and clubs will be promoted briskly.

So as to strengthen and develop health services for the people, hospitals and clinics will be set up widely in the enterprises and farm villages, production of medicaments and medical appliances will be increased and a large number of medical workers trained.

Sixth, the Government of the Republic will consolidate and develop the organs of people's power at all levels in every way. The people's committee, which is a new type of popular government founded according to the free will of the people following the August 15 Liberation, has become a genuine people's power enjoying the undivided support of the Korean people.

The Government will further strengthen the local people's committees, the political basis of the Democratic People's Republic of Korea, in the area of north Korea where they have already been organized, and struggle for their restoration in the area of south Korea where they were organized but have been dissolved by the reactionary forces.

Seventh, in the foreign policy the Government of the Republic will endeavour for our country to establish friendly relations, as an equal member of the world democratic camp, with various freedom-loving countries that respect the liberty and independence of our nation and approach us on an equal footing.

The revival of Japanese imperialism is a menace to the independence of our nation and so the imperialist countries that are attempting to revive Japan as an imperialist aggressive state will all be considered enemies of our nation.

The Government of the Republic will strongly demand the implementation of the decision of the Potsdam Conference on liquidating the forces of Japanese militarism and democratizing Japan.

Eighth, the Government will strengthen the People's Army in every respect to defend the territory of the country against the foreign forces of aggression and safeguard the achievements of the democratic reforms already scored in north Korea.

IDEOLOGICAL EDUCATION OF THE YOUTH IS THE BASIC TASK OF THE DEMOCRATIC YOUTH LEAGUE ORGANIZATIONS

Speech Delivered at the Third Congress of the Democratic Youth League of North Korea
November 13, 1948

Dear comrades,

I warmly congratulate all the democratic youths and the delegates present at this Congress who have performed great feats in the struggle for building an independent and democratic state after liberation.

And I join you in sending congratulations and encouragement to the entire patriotic youth in south Korea who are continuously waging a heroic struggle for the freedom and independence of the country against the reactionary forces at home and abroad.

I also extend warm congratulations to the Young Communists of the Soviet Union and other democratic youth all over the world who are fighting for world peace and the democratic rights and liberties of the youth.

Dear comrade delegates,

The Third Congress of the Democratic Youth League of North Korea is convened at a momentous time when our people have achieved a historic victory in their struggle for freedom and independence. Some time ago the Democratic People's Republic of Korea was founded, which the entire Korean people had been impatiently looking forward to, and now our country has established diplomatic and economic relations with the Soviet Union and democratic states of the world such as Poland, Czechoslovakia, Romania and the People's Republic of Mongolia, and entered the international arena as an independent state capable of holding its own.

The selfless struggle of our democratic youth went a long way towards this great victory won by our people. Since its foundation up till the present Congress, the Democratic Youth League of North Korea has waged a heroic struggle for the reunification and independence of the country and its democratization, for the building of an independent national economy and the efflorescence and development of national culture, and has achieved immense successes. In the course of this struggle the Democratic Youth League has further grown and strengthened organizationally and ideologically and has been tempered and seasoned.

In scoring these brilliant successes, you have performed great feats for the country and the people and laid a solid basis for winning a yet greater victory in the future.

I will not go into details of the successes you have achieved. I should like to take this opportunity of briefing you on what you should do for the future of the country and the people and what to do to perform still greater feats.

Comrades,

The achievements and successes we have scored for the sake of the country and the people till now, no matter how great, are only a flower bud which is yet to come out gaily and brilliantly, only the initial step in the work we have to carry out. We are confronted with more difficult and complex tasks yet.

Today we are living in an era of great prosperity in the history of our country and nation; we are entrusted with the honourable task of paving the way to the eternal prosperity of our country and a happier future of our people. The future destinies of our country and nation depend on our struggle. We are immensely happy that we are born in this age and take part in such a glorious struggle.

To enjoy this honour and happiness to the full, however, we have to successfully discharge our historical mission, bravely surmounting all difficulties.

If we, who are in the most stern period in the history of our nation, fail to work out the destinies of the country and nation in the right way, we shall bring about great misfortunes not only for our own generation but also for our posterity and commit a crime indelible for all time. If we carve out the destinies of the country and nation correctly at this solemn juncture, we shall provide happiness to all generations to come and our exploits will shine forever in the history of the country.

Comrades,

We have now entered a new stage in the struggle for the reunification and independence of the country and its democratization.

According to the general will of the people in north and south Korea, the Supreme People's Assembly of Korea has been elected as our highest organ of state power, the Democratic People's Republic of Korea proclaimed and the central government of the Republic set up. The Soviet Government, which always respects the liberties and rights of the peoples of other countries, has decided, at the request of the Supreme People's Assembly of Korea, to withdraw its troops from our country by the end of this year. The Soviet troops are now returning to their country.

Today when a lawful central government enjoying the support of the entire Korean people has been set up in our country and the Soviet troops are withdrawing from our territory, there can be no conditions and excuses whatsoever for only the U.S. troops to remain in south Korea. If the U.S. troops do not withdraw from south Korea but continue to stay there, it reveals more clearly that the U.S. imperialists are manoeuvring to meddle in our internal affairs and to realize their aggressive designs on Korea. The Korean people will never tolerate such U.S. policy of aggression.

The U.S. imperialists say in their propaganda that they are "worried" about a "civil war" and "disorder," as if they were concerned for the Koreans. But the fact that the absolute majority of the north and south Korean people took part in the general elections of August 25 and established their central government, has positively proved that there will be no disorder or confusion even when the foreign troops withdraw from our land.

If the Americans were really "worried" about a "civil war" and "disorder," they should quit our territory at the earliest possible date. It is known to the peoples all over the world that a state of disorder and confusion has now been created precisely in south Korea under the domination of the U.S. imperialists. Of late, extreme confusion and disorder prevail in south Korea, and a large-scale mutiny broke out in the puppet army, too. This testifies to the fact that so long as the U.S. troops are stationed in south Korea and the pro-Japanese elements and traitors to the nation lord it over there, disorder and confusion are inevitable. The responsibility for the grave situation created in south Korea rests entirely with the presence of U.S. troops there and the reactionary rule of the pro-Japanese elements and traitors to the nation.

The situation in our country is complex still now, and we have an enormous amount of work in hand. The foundation of the Republic and the establishment of the central government are no more than the initial victory in the struggle for the complete independence and sovereignty of our country and its territorial integrity.

We cannot forget even for a moment the fact that the reactionary puppet government in south Korea made up of pro-Japanese elements and traitors to the nation is selling out the country and the people to the foreign aggressors and driving the people in south Korea into a dire distress. It should be borne in mind that the conditions of our struggle for the reunification and independence of the country will become more difficult and complex after the withdrawal of the Soviet troops from our country.

In this situation the Democratic Youth League should unite the entire youth firmly in its ranks and fight more vigorously for the reunification and independence of the country.

Comrades, the basic tasks confronting the Democratic Youth

League of North Korea are, first, to firmly equip the youth politically and ideologically.

To equip the youth politically and ideologically means educating them in the spirit of loving the country and the people and arming them with scientifically-motivated advanced thoughts and theory.

The young people are the future masters of our country. It can be said that the future of any nation depends largely on how its youth are educated, trained and equipped. The education of the young people, therefore, posed one of the most important problems for all nations in all ages.

The protracted Japanese imperialist rule exercised evil effects upon the development of our youth. To work our youth at will as their servants, the Japanese imperialists implanted servile spirit in them and prevented their ideological and cultural development.

But we are now living in a new society, and our young people have a happy future and broad vistas of development opened up before them. We are now provided with all conditions for educating and bringing up our young people, who were denied the opportunity of education and were humiliated in the past, into learned and cultured men of a new type.

To rear our youth into fully qualified masters of the new era, we should, first of all, eradicate the survivals of Japanese imperialism from their minds and educate them in the spirit of love for the country and the people. We should thoroughly convince the youth that they should fight not for any privileged class but for their country and people, exerting all their talents and energies.

To this end, we should arm the youth with advanced thoughts and theory, namely, Marxism-Leninism. We should bring the youth to know the laws of development of human society, to study and assimilate the valuable fighting experiences of the world people and the best things in the treasure house of world civilization, and should see that they study the past and present of our country and the history of our people's struggle.

Second, the Democratic Youth League should educate the youth through labour and construction, through the struggle with difficulties.

The publication of many scientific books for the youth and their school education alone are not enough to arm them with advanced scientific theories. Books and schools only give knowledge to the youth and provide them with conditions for shaping the progressive world outlook. If the knowledge of the youth obtained from books and at school is to become a powerful weapon in transforming both nature and society, it should be linked with actual life and they should be tempered in the practical struggle for the country and the people. Only when the youth are educated through labour and the practical struggle, therefore, will they be able to valiantly march forward while successfully overcoming whatever difficulty and storm they might encounter in the struggle for the country and the people.

The organizations of the League should induce the young people to play the role of a shock brigade in economic construction and educate them to become a model for the working people through their devotion and creative initiative.

Our young people should love labour, think it the greatest honour to work and consider it a shame to loaf and live idle. No matter what kind of labour we may engage in, it is all an honourable job to build our country and carve out our destinies for ourselves. It is only in the course of labour that we can become true builders of a new society and qualified persons. The organizations of the League should wage an unyielding struggle against the degenerate and backward idea of hating to work and seeking to live at the expense of others' labour, which remains in the minds of some young people.

Third, it is important to educate our youth in the spirit of hating the enemy and fighting against him without compromise.

The U.S. imperialists who are now occupying the southern half of our country resort to every conceivable intrigue and machination to turn our country into a colony.

They are trying madly to rearm Japanese imperialism, the sworn enemy of our nation, and even to draw it into the struggle against our people. It is by no means an accident that the pro-Japanese elements and traitors to the nation installed in the south Korean puppet government are seeking to conclude the so-called "ROK-Japan agreements."

We should widely acquaint the youth with how the Japanese imperialists exploited and oppressed our nation and what cruel atrocities they perpetrated to exterminate it, and should bring the youth to heighten vigilance against the manoeuvrings they are carrying on today to invade our country again in league with other aggressive forces.

We should educate the youth in the spirit of defending the state and fighting with all devotion for the sake of the country and the nation so that our nation may not suffer again its painful history of colonial slavery.

We have enemies not only external but also internal. Those who lived in opulence by squeezing the people—the landlords expropriated from their land, pro-Japanese elements, traitors to the nation, etc.—are plotting to overthrow our people's power and wreck our democratic construction if only an opportunity arises, in conspiracy with the external aggressive forces. We should therefore see to it that the youth maintain a close vigilance against the enemy, and should educate them to discern the enemy, detect, expose and crush him.

Self-complacence and indolence are most harmful to us. We should always remember that we are waging an acute struggle against a heinous enemy.

Over the three years since liberation, we have kept advancing in triumph and achieved great successes in democratic construction. So, some comrades, carried away by the victory, think, "Everything is plain sailing," and reckon as if our enemies have all been wiped out and everything would proceed of its own accord without a hitch once an entry is made of it in a decision.

This is a very dangerous tendency. Such indolence and self-complacence blind the people in the struggle against the enemy and paralyze their enmity and vigilance against the foe.

There is no ground to become self-conceited on account of the Democratic Youth League having grown into a powerful mass organization with a membership of over 1,300,000. The history of all countries and all ages provides us with many instances where a powerful army which brags of its invincibility is taken unawares and perishes as it, carried away by a victory, makes light of its enemy and neglects preparations for action.

It is very dangerous to be caught unawares. When one fails to be in constant readiness and is taken by surprise, he loses his head and is thrown into confusion, and may be defeated before he can employ his force properly. It is therefore important to heighten vigilance against the enemy at all times, maintain oneself in readiness to crush any attack of the enemy, keep a sharp watch on every movement of the enemy and foil his intrigues and manoeuvres in advance.

We should educate the youth to repudiate depravity and indolence, constantly maintain a tense posture, frustrate all sinister machinations of the enemies within and without, and thoroughly defend the interests of their country and people.

Fourth, what is important in ideological education is to equip the youth with the internationalist spirit.

Genuine patriotism is inseparable from the internationalist spirit. We should educate the youth in the spirit of loving their country, of treasuring its revolutionary traditions and waging a devoted struggle to liberate the country and the people from the aggressors and exploiters and, at the same time, in the spirit of respecting the freedom and equality of other nations and strengthening friendship and solidarity with the freedom-loving peoples throughout the world in the struggle against the international reactionary forces that oppress and exploit the peoples of other countries.

We should bring home thoroughly to the youth the fact that friendship and close co-operation with the freedom-loving peoples of the world, particularly with the peoples of the Soviet Union and other countries of the democratic camp, constitute an important guarantee of victory in our people's struggle for the freedom and independence of the country and its democratic development.

Fifth, an important task confronting the organizations of the League today is to make all the youth master advanced sciences and techniques.

Liberated from the protracted Japanese imperialist colonial rule, our people with their ravaged economy and backward culture and techniques have embarked on the road of building a new country. It is of prime importance to master sciences and techniques in order to rapidly develop the economy and culture, which suffer from backwardness, and to build a new, rich and strong country.

Without techniques we can neither build our industry nor rehabilitate and develop the economy speedily. Without sciences and techniques we can neither administer the state nor run the factories.

It is the most important and sacred task facing our youth at present to study sciences and techniques. All should study and study tirelessly to equip themselves with advanced sciences and techniques.

With regard to the need of mastery of science by the youth, Comrade Stalin said: "In order to build, we must have knowledge, mastery of science. And knowledge entails study. We must study perseveringly and patiently....

"Before us stands a fortress. That fortress is called science, with its numerous branches of knowledge. We must capture that fortress at all costs. It is our youth who must capture that fortress, if they want to be builders of the new life, if they want to be real successors of the old guard."

Our youth should capture the fortress of science by all means in order to do away with ignorance left over from the past, accomplish their tasks creditably as real masters of the state and build a prosperous country.

Our fast developing metallurgical, electrical, chemical, mining and textile industries, railway transport and so on call for an ever-increasing number of technical cadres and skilled workers, and specialists equipped with advanced sciences.

The Democratic Youth League organizations should carry

on the pass-on-technique work extensively among the working youth under such slogans as "Let us learn techniques!" and "Let us become skilled workers versed in the machines entrusted to us!" We should organize the youth to march on to master the techniques and knowledge of all branches and capture the fortress of science.

Comrades,

Last, I should like to say a few words about how the Democratic Youth League members should take part in economic and cultural construction.

As you know, our people should carry out the difficult task of rebuilding their economically, technically and culturally backward country into a rich, powerful and civilized one, while waging a fierce struggle against the enemies at home and abroad. Unflagging efforts of the entire people, particularly a heroic struggle of the youth who constitute an important force in the building of the country, are required to overcome all difficulties lying before us and execute the task of national reconstruction set forth in the Political Programme of the Government of the Republic.

Next year we will set out on the fulfilment of a two-year national economic plan which will be of great significance in the democratic building of our country. For the successful carrying out of the two-year national economic plan, we should fulfil and overfulfil the national economic plan for 1948 in the first place. All members of the League should become model workers and fulfil their assigned tasks in their respective fields, no matter in which field of the national economy they may be working.

Young workers at factories should become expert in the operation of the machines in their charge, become proficient in their jobs, economize on materials, steadily raise labour productivity and become standard-bearers of the movement for new ideas and inventions.

Young workers at collieries and mines should master advanced coal cutting and mining methods, make innovations in mining coal and ores, and produce still larger quantities of coal and various kinds of ores for the prosperity and development of the country.

Young workers in the field of transport should learn advanced techniques in railway and marine transports and become able engineers, assistant engineers, locomotive drivers and skippers, thus leading the van in the struggle for the development of transport.

The young people working in the rural areas should take the lead in acquiring the knowledge of agricultural science, in introducing advanced methods of farming in agriculture and developing culture in the countryside, and should make every effort to supply more provisions and raw materials to the country and the people. The Democratic Youth League members should strive devotedly for widely disseminating scientific knowledge among the peasants, for briskly carrying on the work of cultural enlightenment at the democratic publicity halls and clubs, and for quickly eliminating the cultural backwardness of our rural areas.

The organizations of the League should be actively mobilized in the preparatory work for the introduction of universal compulsory primary education in 1950. To introduce universal compulsory primary education, the construction and expansion of schools should be carried out in a nation-wide movement throughout north Korea in 1949. As a matter of course, the Democratic Youth League members should stand in the forefront of this movement.

As you see, Democratic Youth League members are confronted with weighty tasks in the struggle for the reunification and independence of the country and its democratic construction. The Government of the Republic and the entire people entertain great expectations of the young people. I am convinced that our Democratic Youth League members, deeply conscious of the honourable tasks assigned to them, will courageously surmount difficulties and obstacles by displaying patriotic devotion and heroism in all fields and thus will certainly win brilliant victories and creditably live up to the profound expectations of the state and the people.

EVERY EFFORT FOR VICTORY IN THE WAR

Radio Address to the Entire Korean People
June 26, 1950

Dear fellow countrymen,
Dear brothers and sisters,
Officers, noncommissioned officers and men of our People's Army,
Guerrillas operating in the southern half of the Republic,

On behalf of the Government of the Democratic People's Republic of Korea, I appeal to you as follows:

On June 25, the army of the puppet government of the traitor Syngman Rhee started an all-out offensive against the areas of the northern half of the Republic all along the 38th parallel. The valiant garrisons of the Republic, fighting fierce battles to counter the enemy's invasion, frustrated the advance of the Syngman Rhee army.

The Government of the Democratic People's Republic of Korea, having discussed the prevailing situation, ordered our People's Army to start a decisive counteroffensive action and wipe out the enemy's armed forces. On the orders of the Government of the Republic, the People's Army drove back the enemy from areas north of the 38th parallel and has advanced 10-15 kilometres south. It has liberated a number of towns including Ongjin, Yonan, Kaesong and Paechon, and many villages.

The traitorous Syngman Rhee clique has launched a fratricidal civil war against the people, although the entire patriotic people of our country have made every effort to reunify the country by peaceful means.

It is universal knowledge that the Syngman Rhee clique that is dead set against the country's peaceful reunification, had long since prepared for civil war. It frantically expanded armaments and desperately endeavoured to prepare the rear by bleeding the people in south Korea white. Through unheard-of terrorist despotism, it outlawed all democratic political parties and social organizations in south Korea, arrested, imprisoned and slaughtered patriotic, progressive personalities, and ruthlessly suppressed the slightest manifestations of discontent against Syngman Rhee's reactionary regime. Hundreds of thousands of our people's best sons and daughters who fought for the country's independence, freedom and democracy have been imprisoned and slaughtered by the enemy.

To cover up their design of launching a civil war, the Syngman Rhee clique incessantly provoked clashes on the 38th parallel to keep our people in a state of constant unrest, and sought to shift the responsibility for the provocative clashes on to the Democratic People's Republic of Korea. In the course of preparing for the so-called "expedition to the north," the Syngman Rhee clique, on the instructions of the U.S. imperialists, did not even hesitate to enter upon the road of collusion with the Japanese militarists, the sworn enemy of the Korean people.

The traitorous Syngman Rhee clique has sold off the southern half of our country as a colony and a military strategic base to the U.S. imperialists and placed its economy under the control of U.S. monopoly capitalists.

The U.S. imperialists have seized the arteries of the economy and completely dislocated the national economy in the southern half. The U.S. imperialists are plundering rice, tungsten, graphite and many other natural resources vitally needed in our country. Middle and small entrepreneurs and traders in south Korea, under the pressure of U.S. capital, find themselves doomed to bankruptcy. In the southern half of our country, the majority of factories and mills have been closed down, the number of unemployed people has reached several millions, peasants have not yet been given land and agriculture keeps declining year by year. The people in south Korea are in a wretched plight, and are on the verge of starvation.

Dear fellow countrymen,

The Government of the Democratic People's Republic of Korea, together with all the patriotic, democratic political parties, social organizations and the entire people of our country, has done all it could to avoid a fratricidal civil war and horrors of bloodshed and to reunify our country by peaceful means. As early as April 1948 the Joint Conference of Representatives of Political Parties and Social Organizations of North and South Korea made the first attempt to reunify our country in a peaceful way.

The traitorous Syngman Rhee clique, however, frustrated this attempt and, on instructions from the U.S. imperialists and their tool of aggression, the so-called "U.N. Commission on Korea," staged separate elections in south Korea on May 10, 1948 and stepped up preparations for an armed attack on the northern half of our country.

In June last year, 72 patriotic political parties and social organizations in north and south Korea affiliated with the Democratic Front for the Reunification of the Fatherland proposed reunifying our country peacefully by means of holding general elections with a view to attaining the peaceful reunification and complete independence of the country. The entire Korean people enthusiastically supported the proposal, but the traitorous Syngman Rhee clique rejected it, too.

The Democratic Front for the Reunification of the Fatherland, reflecting the will of the entire people, again made a proposal on June 7, 1950 to expedite the peaceful reunification of the country. But the traitorous Syngman Rhee gang also prevented this proposal of the D.F.R.F. for promoting the peaceful reunification of the country from being carried out, threatening to label anyone favouring it as a traitor.

On June 19, 1950, the Presidium of the Supreme People's Assembly of the Democratic People's Republic of Korea, expressing its unshakable will for the reunification, independence and democratic development of the country in accordance with the wishes of the democratic political parties and social organizations, advanced a proposal for achieving the peaceful reunification of the country by means of uniting into a single all-Korea legislative body the Supreme People's Assembly of the Democratic People's Republic of Korea and the south Korean "National Assembly."

The traitorous Syngman Rhee clique responded to the unanimous desire of the entire Korean people for the country's peaceful reunification and our just, sincere proposal by launching a civil war.

What objective does this traitorous clique intend to achieve in the fratricidal civil war which it has ignited?

Through the fratricidal war the traitorous Syngman Rhee clique seeks to extend the anti-popular, reactionary ruling system in the southern half to the northern half of the Republic and rob our people of the achievements they have made in the democratic reforms.

The reactionary Syngman Rhee band tries to take the land away from the peasants, who have become its masters as a result of the agrarian reform effected in the northern half of the Republic on the principle of confiscation without compensation and of free distribution, to return it to the landlords, and deprive the people in the northern half of all democratic liberties and rights they have won. The traitorous Syngman Rhee clique seeks to turn our country into a colony of U.S. imperialism and make the entire Korean people slaves of U.S. imperialism.

Dear brothers and sisters,

A great danger has befallen our country and people.

In this war against the Syngman Rhee gang the Korean people must defend with their lives the Democratic People's Republic of Korea and its Constitution; wipe out the traitorous puppet regime in the southern half and liberate the southern half of our country from the reactionary rule of the traitorous Syngman Rhee clique; restore in the southern half the people's committees, the genuine people's power, and accomplish the cause of the country's reunification under the banner of the Democratic People's Republic of Korea.

The war we are fighting against the civil war started by the traitorous Syngman Rhee clique is a just one for the country's reunification, independence, freedom and democracy.

The entire Korean people, if they do not want to become slaves of foreign imperialists again, must rise as one in the national-salvation struggle to overthrow and smash the traitorous Syngman Rhee "regime" and its army. We must win ultimate victory at all costs.

All the Korean people must always watch sharply and heighten vigilance at every movement of the U.S. imperialists who stand behind the traitorous Syngman Rhee clique.

Our People's Army must display gallantry and devotion in the just struggle to defend with their lives the gains of the democratic reforms in the northern half of the Republic, to liberate the compatriots in the southern half from reactionary rule and reunify the country under the banner of the People's Republic.

The officers, noncommissioned officers and men of our People's Army have come from among the people. The People's Army, made up of best sons and daughters of our people, is the genuine armed forces of the Korean people. The People's Armymen have been educated and trained in the spirit of loving the country and the people, are equipped with highly efficient modern weapons, and are armed with the lofty patriotic spirit of fighting in the interests of the country and the people at the sacrifice of their lives. All the People's Army officers and men must fight to the last drop of their blood for the country and the people.

The people in the northern half of the Republic must reorganize all their work on a war footing and muster up all their strength to achieve victory in the war in order to wipe out the enemy in a short space of time. All-people assistance to the People's Army must be organized; the People's Army must be continuously reinforced and replenished; all necessities and munitions must be transported quickly to the front; and affectionate, kindly care must be given to the wounded.

In order to ensure victory at the front, the rear of the People's Army should be consolidated as an impregnable fortress.

In the rear, an implacable struggle must be waged against deserters and rumour-mongers and work must be promptly organized to detect and wipe out spies and subversive elements. The enemy, crafty and sinister, will make every effort to spread misleading rumours. People must not be fooled by such pernicious rumours spread by the enemy, and the organs of state power of the Republic must mercilessly dispose of traitors who aid the enemy.

Workers, technicians and office employees in the northern half of the Republic should defend the factories, mills, transport and communications establishments against enemy encroachment, faithfully carry out production plans and all their assignments, and promptly meet the needs of the front.

The peasants in the northern half of the Republic should turn out more farm produce and supply enough food to the People's Army, and give it every assistance to ensure victory in the war.

Men and women guerrillas in the southern half of the Republic must wage guerrilla warfare more fiercely and more bravely and set up or extend the liberated areas by enlisting broad masses of the people in the guerrilla detachments. The guerrillas should attack and wipe out enemies behind their line, raid their headquarters, cut off and destroy railways, roads, bridges, telegraph and telephone lines, etc., cut communications between the enemy's front and rear by every possible means, and everywhere finish off traitors, restore the people's committees, the organs of people's power, and actively co-operate in the operations of the People's Army.

Compatriots in the southern half of the Republic should not obey the puppet Syngman Rhee government's orders and instructions but sabotage their execution, and throw the organization of the enemy's rear into confusion.

Workers in the southern half must organize strikes and raise riots everywhere; they must defend factories, mills, mines, railways and their other workplaces against destruction by the fleeing enemy, and give active aid to the People's Army to ensure victory in the war.

Peasants in the southern half should not give food to the enemy; they should take good care of the current year's crops, take an active part in the guerrilla movement and spare nothing in giving all forms of co-operation and assistance to the People's Army.

Middle and small entrepreneurs and traders in the southern half should co-operate in the struggle to extricate our country's national economy from subordination to U.S. monopoly capital by opposing the Syngman Rhee "regime" and assisting the People's Army.

Cultural workers and intellectuals in the southern half must actively co-operate in the war against the traitorous Syngman Rhee clique to achieve the country's reunification and freedom and to secure conditions for the development of national culture. They should thoroughly expose the crimes of the traitorous Syngman Rhee gang among the masses of the people and fully play the role of agitators in organizing mass revolts.

Officers and men of the "National Defence Army" of the puppet south Korean government,

Your enemy is none other than the traitorous Syngman Rhee clique. In the interests of the country and the people, you should lose no chance to turn your guns upon the traitorous Syngman Rhee clique.

You should come over to the side of the People's Army and the guerrillas, and join in the all-people struggle for the country's reunification and freedom. You must take an honourable place in the ranks of fighters for the country's freedom and independence by coming out against the enemy of our people.

Dear compatriots, brothers and sisters,

I call upon the entire Korean people to unite more closely around the Government of the Democratic People's Republic of Korea in order quickly to destroy and wipe out the armed forces and the police system of the traitorous Syngman Rhee clique.

The history of mankind shows that a people who rises in the struggle for freedom and independence in defiance of death is always victorious. Ours is a just struggle. Victory will surely be on our people's side. I am confident that our just struggle for the sake of the country and the people will certainly be triumphant.

The time has come to reunify our country. Let us march forward valiantly with firm confidence in victory!

Direct all efforts to assisting our People's Army and the front!

Direct all efforts to defeating and wiping out the enemy!

Long live the Korean people who have risen in the just war of the entire people!

Long live the Democratic People's Republic of Korea!

Let us march forward for victory!

LET US RESOLUTELY REPEL THE U.S. IMPERIALISTS' ARMED INVASION

Radio Address to the Entire Korean People
July 8, 1950

Dear fellow countrymen,
Dear brothers and sisters,
Valiant officers, noncommissioned officers and men of our People's Army,
Guerrillas operating in the southern half,

The U.S. imperialists have launched an armed invasion against our country and our people.

The U.S. air force is barbarously bombing the towns and villages of our country and massacring our peaceful people. U.S. naval fleets have unlawfully intruded into our territorial waters and are bombarding the coastal towns and villages, and its army troops, defiling our territory with their bloodstained paws, have opened a front in the areas not yet liberated in the southern part of our country and are resorting to every brutal violence in an attempt to check the southward advance of the People's Army.

Why are the U.S. imperialists hurling their troops into the territory of our country? Why are these rapacious bloodsuckers invading the sacred territory of our country?

The Korean people have never encroached upon an inch of the territory of the United States of America, nor have they ever infringed upon its sovereignty in the slightest degree. Our people have never committed any hostile act against the American people, nor have they ever done any harm to the life and property of the peaceful inhabitants of the United States of America. Why then do the U.S. imperialists send their troops into our territory, perpetrate military interference in the internal affairs of our country, slaughter our people wantonly and soak the beautiful land of our country with blood?

It is that the U.S. imperialists, in a wild dream to dominate the world, aim to turn our country into their permanent colony and enslave our people. To achieve this aim, the U.S. imperialists installed Syngman Rhee, the sworn enemy of the Korean people, as ruler in the southern half of our country and rigged up the south Korean puppet government. Also for this purpose, they have stubbornly hindered the peaceful reunification of the country, the ardent desire of the Korean people, by every possible means—terrorism, massacre, intimidation, fraud and so forth—and instigated their lackeys, the traitorous Syngman Rhee clique, to unleash a fratricidal civil war in our country and then immediately launched out into open armed invasion.

The U.S. imperialists do not recognize the legitimate rights of the Korean people to freedom and independence, they do not regard our people as human beings. The U.S. robbers think that the Korean people are only destined to be colonial slaves to fill the moneybags of the Wall Street warmongers.

The U.S. imperialist aggressors have turned our peaceful towns and villages into their military training grounds and are making targets of our boys and girls, women and old folk in their air strafings and bombings. Pyongyang, Nampo, Haeju, Wonsan, Hamhung and many other cities north of the 38th parallel, and villages in their suburbs, have already undergone repeated, barbarous air raids. In the area south of the 38th parallel, the liberated cities—Seoul, Chunchon, Kaesong, Uijongbu, Chumunjin, Kangnung and others—and numerous villages are subjected to incessant vicious bombings by the U.S. air force. The U.S. imperialist bandits strafe from the air village women who are bent on transplanting rice in paddyfields and shower bombs on innocent children.

The U.S. imperialists are attempting to cover up their

armed invasion of our country with the so-called "resolution" of the U.N. Security Council on the Korean question. And this "resolution" of the Security Council was "adopted" in violation of the United Nations Charter without the participation of the Korean representative and without the participation of either the delegate of the Soviet Union or China.

Despite their false propaganda, the true colours of the U.S. imperialists who are perpetrating armed invasion against our country have been exposed in full to all honest-minded people of the world. The fraudulent statement of the U.S. imperialists who clamour that the U.S. troops are only performing the functions of police in Korea on behalf of the United Nations, can deceive no one.

The United Nations Organization was not established so that the U.S. imperialists under the U.N. flag might bomb the towns and villages of our country and slaughter our people who aspire to liberty and independence. While showering bombs on the Korean people, the U.S. imperialists claim that they are doing so for the sake of peace, but there is no one who will take their ravings for truth.

Such lies and fraudulence were once the infamous stock-in-trade of the Hitler fascists and Japanese imperialists. It is known to the world that Hitler said, "Whenever I speak of peace, I think of war." The Japanese imperialists covered up their aggressive acts in the Far East with the hypocritical statement that they were for peace in Asia. The "imperial edict" issued by the Japanese Emperor on August 29, 1910, stated that Japan was annexing Korea "in order to preserve a lasting peace in the East," as though Korea had posed a threat to peace in the East.

The U.S. imperialists, who are today making desperate attempts to deprive our country of its independence and turn Korea into their colony, have the effrontery to try to justify their armed intervention in the internal affairs of our country and their barbarous bombings of our peaceful inhabitants with the false statement that they are intended for peace, just as the Hitler fascists and Japanese imperialists did.

But no amount of falsehoods and deception can cover up or

justify the bestial atrocities the U.S. aggressors are perpetrating in Korea in gross violation of all the norms of international law and the United Nations Charter.

However massive an armed force they may mobilize in their desperate attempt to invade our country, the U.S. imperialists will never be able to break the indomitable fighting spirit and patriotic stamina of our people who have risen as one for the reunification and independence of their country. The Korean people, united rock-firm around the Workers' Party of Korea, will defy death fighting against U.S. imperialist aggression and will safeguard the freedom and honour of their country to the end.

Still young and inexperienced in battle as it is, our People's Army, by displaying valour and patriotic devotion, has already achieved great combat results in a few days' time.

The People's Army units that liberated the capital city of Seoul have crossed the Han-gang River in the teeth of savage bombing by the U.S. air force and broken through the enemy positions on its southern bank. And pursuing the stampeding enemy troops, they have completely liberated our country's industrial districts such as the towns of Yongdungpo, Pupyong and Inchon and their environs. The brave soldiers of our People's Army have now liberated Suwon, which the enemy called his second base, and are continuing their southward advance.

Those People's Army units which were fighting in the Chunchon and Hongchon areas have liberated many towns such as Wonju, Hoengsong, Ryoju, Chechon and nearby villages and, in their continued advance southward, have freed Chungju.

Our young air force is disorganizing the battle order of the enemy forces and valiantly attacking U.S. planes. In fierce air battles Korea's gallant war birds have downed or damaged scores of enemy fighters and bombers including B-29s, the so-called "flying fortresses," thereby successfully covering the advance of our ground force.

The tankmen, the pride of our army, have broken through

the defence positions of the enemy and gave him no breathing space by making decisive attacks on the enemy, and thus put him to disorderly flight. The tank unit, in pursuit of the enemy, was the first to storm into Seoul, our country's capital, and has now won the honourable title of "Seoul Tank Division."

Our infantrymen and artillerymen are advancing continuously, demonstrating perseverance on the march and dealing a heavy blow at the enemy force and combat material by exhibiting resolution and bravery in attack.

The young naval forces of the Republic have also demonstrated valour in fulfilling their combat missions. The meritorious feat our torpedo-boat unit performed in sinking a U.S. cruiser by valiantly attacking the overpowering enemy will brilliantly go down in the history of our fleets.

In their engagements with the ground forces of the U.S. armed invaders the People's Army units inflicted on them their first serious defeat.

The results we have achieved at the war front show that the might of our people, who have risen in the struggle for the independence and freedom of the country, is inexhaustible, and that the heroic People's Army can and will surely drive the U.S. imperialist aggressors from the land of our country.

Our People's Army is provided with all necessary conditions for completely smashing the enemy.

Our army is equipped with modern military technique.

Our army is not fighting for dollars or for subjugating other nations, as are the U.S. mercenaries, but for the country's independence and the people's freedom. The lofty patriotic spirit of fighting with all devotion for the country and the people is the inexhaustible source of courage and valour of our People's Army soldiers.

The forces of the U.S. aggressors are fighting on foreign soil, whereas our People's Army is fighting on the territory of its own country amid the love and support of the entire people. The U.S. imperialist robbers are hated by all our people and are meeting with retaliation from the people at every step on account of the brutalities they are committing.

The U.S. armed intervention in our country has evoked the Korean people's utmost indignation and hostility against the U.S. imperialist colonial plunderers and their running dogs, the Syngman Rhee clique. Our brave youths are pouring into the ranks of the People's Army like a flood to volunteer for the front, and their number has exceeded 500,000. Volunteer units and combined units are being formed across the country with the patriotic people who have risen to rout the armed invaders in good time no matter in what part of the country they may show up and to defend every inch of the fatherland with their blood.

In response to the heroic advance of the People's Army, the intrepid guerrillas are extending their areas of operation in North Kyongsang, South Kyongsang and South Cholla Provinces and, with the active support of the people, are unfolding vigorous struggles against the U.S. armed invaders and the traitorous Syngman Rhee band.

In the areas liberated by the People's Army, the people from all walks of life are enthusiastically welcoming the valorous men and officers of the People's Army who have rescued them from the rule of police terror by the traitorous Syngman Rhee clique. The liberated people are striving to restore the people's committees dissolved by the reactionaries and to carry into effect the Constitution of the Democratic People's Republic of Korea which guarantees liberties and rights for the people. The peasants have started carrying out the agrarian reform, their centuries-old desire, in accordance with the decree of the Presidium of the Supreme People's Assembly of the Democratic People's Republic of Korea. All land which belonged to the U.S. imperialists and the Syngman Rhee puppet government and to Korean landlords and the traitors to the nation is being confiscated and turned over without compensation to the ownership of the peasants.

The debacle of the puppet Syngman Rhee's army and the reactionary state machine has fully revealed the inner corruption of the puppet Syngman Rhee's regime forced upon the people in south Korea at U.S. imperialist bayonet-point, and has shown that that regime had no support from the Korean people.

The victory of the People's Army and the unanimous love and assistance of the people for its men and officers prove the superiority of the state and social system of the Democratic People's Republic of Korea and the firm unity of the people, and show that all the Korean people fervently support the policy of the Government of the Republic for repulsing the armed invasion of the U.S. imperialists and safeguarding the country's reunification and national independence. Our victory has been achieved because the people in the northern half of the Republic have risen as one to defend with their lives the people's democratic system established in the northern half and it is clear proof that the people in the southern half support the Democratic People's Republic of Korea and ardently desire that democratic reforms, which are guarantees of the political, economic and cultural development of the country and the improvement of the people's well-being, are carried out in south Korea, too.

As the Syngman Rhee clique, the faithful minion of U.S. imperialism who has been carrying out U.S. policies in south Korea, has been defeated, the U.S. bandits have become more undisguised in their armed invasion against the Korean people. Had it not been for the direct armed intervention of the U.S. imperialists, the fratricidal civil war ignited by their underlings would have ended, our country would have already been reunified and the people in the southern half completely liberated from the rule of police terror by U.S. imperialism and the Syngman Rhee clique.

The U.S. imperialist armed invasion of Korea is arousing the indignation of the peoples the world over. In many countries of the world including the Soviet Union, China, France, Britain, Germany, Australia, Italy, Pakistan, and Japan, and even in the United States itself, popular movements are unfolded against U.S. imperialist aggression in our country under the slogan "Hands Off Korea!" The just cause of our people for the freedom and independence of the country is receiving warm support and encouragement from the freedom-loving peoples of the whole world.

Dear fellow countrymen, brothers and sisters,

The U.S. imperialists, the vicious enemy of the Korean people, have extended their bloodstained claws to our land in order to subjugate our beloved country by force of arms. The entire people must unite as one and counter U.S. imperialist armed intervention with decisive blows.

The U.S. imperialists will certainly realize how great and inexhaustible the united might of the Korean people is and how strong their indomitable fighting will and aspirations for their country's freedom and independence are.

Under no circumstances can our people become colonial slaves again.

We will never forgive the crimes committed by the U.S. imperialists on the soil of our country, we will never pardon them for barbarously bombing our peaceful towns and villages and slaughtering our parents, brothers and sisters and innocent children. The brute U.S. imperialist aggressors who have soaked the land of our country with the blood of the people, will be cursed forever, for all ages to come, not only by us but also by our posterity.

All Koreans who hold dear the honour of the country and destiny of the nation, whoever they may be, should come out as one man in the sacred war for the liberation of the country against the aggression by the U.S. imperialists.

The names of the patriotic fighters who have accomplished heroic feats in the battle against foreign armed invaders for their country's freedom and independence will shine forever in the history of the country.

All patriots of our country,

Dear brothers and sisters,

The work of winning freedom and independence for the country is the work of the Korean people themselves. The entire people should strengthen in every way the work of assisting our People's Army that continues its southward advance, routing and wiping out the enemy by displaying courage and patriotic devotion in the fierce battles against the armed invaders of U.S. imperialism.

Let us mobilize all forces and resources for victory in the war and for aiding the People's Army, produce more food, fabrics, coal, steel, etc., and practice the utmost economy in their consumption in order quickly to rout the U.S. imperialist aggressors and the Syngman Rhee clique.

Let us further strengthen labour discipline, make great labour achievements and rapidly rehabilitate the industrial enterprises damaged in bombings to increase wartime production, and build up our rear into an impregnable fortress by heightening vigilance sharply.

Heroic men and women guerrillas,

People in the areas not yet liberated,

Wage the guerrilla struggle against the U.S. imperialist marauders and their flunkeys in an all-people movement. Guerrillas, attack the enemy more daringly, more bravely and more ruthlessly. Destroy roads, railways, bridges and communication lines. Disrupt the troop movement of the aggressors and their transportation of weapons and war supplies; raid and destroy the enemy's armories and ammunition depots and wipe out his effectives that come your way. Let fire start from under the very feet of the heinous enemy who is encroaching upon the sacred soil of our country.

Your heroic struggle in the enemy's rear will further speed up the advance of the People's Army and move up still nearer the day of great victory in the Fatherland Liberation War.

Valiant men, noncommissioned officers and officers of the People's Army,

The entire Korean people are following with profound affection and pride your great feats performed in the fight for the country and the people.

Annihilate the vicious aggressors more mercilessly and determinedly. Clear our land of the U.S. imperialist aggressors and their lackeys.

Officers of the People's Army,

Deftly apply the commanding art of modern warfare.

Conduct mobile operations of your units boldly, and surround and wipe out the enemy. Turn the excellent techniques of our army to full account.

Infantrymen, tankmen, artillerymen, fliers, navymen of the People's Army,

You have already demonstrated valour and devotion in the battles to rout the Syngman Rhee puppet troops. More bravely and thoroughly crush the aggressive forces of U.S. imperialism that have invaded our land. Use your arms proficiently to shower straight shots on the enemy.

You should not forget for a moment that you are carrying out a sacred duty for your country and your people. Render heroic service, all of you, in this sacred war for the liberation of the fatherland, emulating the noble patriotic spirit of our ancestors such as Generals Ulji Mun Dok and Kang Gam Chan and Admiral Li Sun Sin who valiantly safeguarded our country against foreign aggressors.

Let us march forward to drive out the U.S. imperialists to the last man from the soil of our country where generation after generation of our ancestors lie buried and where our dear younger generation is growing up. Let us carry our righteous liberation struggle to a victorious conclusion so that the glorious flag of the Democratic People's Republic of Korea will wave high over Pusan, Mokpo and Mt. Hanna-san on Cheju-do Island.

Forward on to victory!

Long live the freedom and independence of Korea!

ON SOME QUESTIONS OF OUR LITERATURE AND ART

Talk with Writers and Artists

June 30, 1951

Writers and artists,

Our writers and artists are entrusted with very important tasks today when the Korean people are fighting a sacred war of liberation against the U.S. imperialist aggressors in defence of the freedom and independence of the country. Our writers and artists, as engineers of the human soul, should vividly represent in their works the lofty patriotism and staunch fighting spirit of our people and their unshakable conviction of final victory, and should see that their works serve our fighting people as a powerful weapon and as a great inspiration spurring them on towards ultimate victory.

Since liberation there has been rapid progress in our literature and art and the writers and artists have scored brilliant achievements.

But we must not rest content with the achievements of the past, and must remember that there are many shortcomings in the activities of our writers and artists. Our writers and artists have failed to represent the noble ideas and sentiments of the people and their life and work on a high artistic plane. Their creative activities have lost touch with life and are lagging behind our rapidly advancing reality. Our writers and artists have failed to give a vivid portrayal, on a high level of presentation and artistry, of men engaged in the creation of a new life, and to produce many excellent works of literature and art that can be made textbooks of life. Our writers and artists still fail to depict with skill the creative labour and heroic struggle of our people; they fail to give a good representation of the criticism and hatred of things old and of the love and longing for the new.

Many works of literature and art have been produced by our writers and artists during the Fatherland Liberation War, but, in terms of ideological content or artistic quality, it cannot be said that they are worthy of our heroic people.

Availing myself of this small gathering today, I would like to tell you writers and artists about some important problems of our literature and art.

Our writers and artists must show the lofty patriotism of our people in their works. Patriotism stems only from a good knowledge of the past of one's country and of the fine traditions, culture and customs of one's nation. Patriotism is not an abstract concept, but is a boundless love for the land, history and culture of one's country. It is manifested also in the attachment to one's native place and its people, affection for one's parents, wife and children. Patriotism lives in concrete forms and finds concrete expression in human feelings.

The writers and artists should therefore give a concrete, profound presentation of the lofty patriotism of our people through the thoughts, feelings and life of men living in reality, instead of marshalling abstract and dry slogans in their works. Only then will the patriotism represented in the works acquire the concreteness and truthfulness as it has in reality.

Never before in their history have the Korean people displayed such lofty patriotism as today. At the front and in the rear, in town and country, our people are displaying a patriotic devotion unimaginable in the past.

This shows that our people are deeply concerned about the fate of their country and that they are fully conscious of their historical mission. This also shows that our people, emerging from their narrow national limits, have become profoundly aware of their position and stand from the viewpoint of world history.

The Korean people of today are different from what they were under Japanese imperialist rule, or from what they were in the feudal era of Li dynasty.

Literary and art works must mirror this great change in our nation's history.

Lofty patriotism and national pride are alien from narrow nationalist or chauvinist sentiments, and they find a genuine expression only when these remnants of outdated ideologies are totally eliminated. It goes without saying, therefore, that our patriotism must be combined with the thoroughly internationalist spirit that allows of no vestige of nationalism and chauvinism.

Further, the writers and artists must portray in their works the heroism and fortitude of our People's Army. Though young, our People's Army has accumulated incomparably rich combat experience for its age. In the course of the First Offensive our army learned how to carry on offensive action to defeat the enemy, and during the strategic retreat it learned how to regroup its ranks in the face of a strong enemy and how to prepare its combat force for a fresh offensive. Our army has thus grown and strengthened into a full-fledged modern army.

The heroism of the People's Army is found in its mass heroism, not in the heroism of a few individual soldiers. The innumerable instances of heroism and gallantry displayed by our men and officers in battles are graphic evidence that they are fully conscious of their sacred duty to the country and the people and that they are fulfilling it splendidly.

Writers and artists must portray our numerous heroes who have sprung forth from among the people. And there are people who take pains to seek out a novelty or a legendary man in order, they claim, to portray heroes. With such an attitude in creative work, it is impossible to depict our heroes truthfully. Our heroes are yesterday's workers, peasants, office employees and students, and their sons. Depict their rich sentiments and human traits, their lofty ideas and convictions and their unaffected, simple behaviours as they are, and you will have the images of the heroes of our Republic today.

In this respect, too, you must not proceed from an abstract concept but from concrete reality. Remember that abstraction means death in art.

It is to be regretted that among our writers there are people who, not acquainted with the features of a hero and without a detailed study of him, try to portray him after hearing his brief personal history. This is not only a debasement of the hero himself but shows an intolerable disdain for our readers.

Our writers must always remember that their works go into the hands of the people. The writers must bear in mind that people read literary works not for killing time, instead of taking a nap, but for acquiring a deeper understanding of life, learning from the lofty spirit of ordinary people who devotedly serve the country and the people, and for gaining confidence in the happy future of mankind.

Our works of literature and art must not only represent the struggle of heroes at the front but also the struggle of our people who fought heroically in the rear and in enemy-occupied areas.

The writers and artists must produce literary and artistic works which will help our People's Army men and the entire people fortify their confidence in victory. One's conviction of victory becomes real and acquires great force only when one is well aware of one's own strength and conditions and makes a correct calculation of the enemy's strength and situation. The writers and artists, while portraying the indestructible superiority of our social system, the inexhaustible strength of our people, their unity and lofty ideological preparedness and so on, should also give a clear picture of the enemy's fatal weak points and his situation. It is important here to describe on a high artistic plane that the war we are waging now is a just war and a war for the freedom and independence of the country and the happiness of all generations to come.

Also, our writers and artists should arouse a burning hatred for the enemy through their works. Here a question arises as to how to depict the enemy. Our writers paint the U.S. imperialist aggressors as sly. That is right, of course. It must be remembered, however, that not only are the U.S. imperialists sly, they are also the most heinous and abominable barbarians of modern times. The U.S. imperialists have shown their true colours in all their ugliness in Korea.

The U.S. robbers have reduced our towns and villages to ashes and are slaughtering our people en masse. The American missionaries who once behaved themselves as "apostles of God" in Korea are now bringing pregnant women together by scores and shooting them all at once with carbines, and are running over children with tanks. The "gentlemen of Wall Street" who used to boast arrogantly of the "Goddess of Liberty" to the world, now carry Korean girls stripped naked in cars and tanks, perpetrating all kinds of outrages and atrocities against them which surpass all human imagination.

The barbarities of the U.S. imperialists in Korea will incur the indignation and curse of the world people for all ages as the most heinous crime against humanity and a deadly insult to posterity. We must thoroughly expose the crimes of the U.S. scoundrels before the people of the whole world, and must educate our people in the spirit of hostility against them.

The writers and artists should also expose in their works the detestable features of the traitorous Syngman Rhee clique, along with the barbarities of U.S. imperialists.

But mere reproduction of the enemy's atrocities does not in itself mean realistic art, nor do works of this sort always invoke hostility against the enemy. It is to be regretted that naturalistic technique still finds glaring expression in the works of our writers and artists. Without thoroughly rectifying such a tendency, it is impossible to develop our literature and art in a wholesome direction.

The writers and artists should know that the genuine creator of great art is always the people. No excellent work of art fails to command the people's love, and if a work of art does not enjoy the people's understanding and appreciation, it cannot be an excellent one. Our writers and artists must delve deeply into the life of the people, study popular literature, oral literature, folk songs, etc., and make extensive use of them in their creative activities. But all folk songs are not good, and all pieces of oral literature are not worthy of use.

Here a question arises as to what and how we should inherit. From the literature and art of the past we must take over and develop those things that are genuinely of the people and cast aside whatever is unscientific and vulgar.

There are people who think that inheriting national culture means singing all the folk songs of the past in their original tunes, but that is wrong. Such a tendency runs counter to the basic line for the development of our national culture. It is necessary to preserve the fine features peculiar to our nation in all spheres of folk song, music, dance, etc., and, at the same time, create new rhythms, new melodies and new rhythmic forms demanded by the new life, and learn to put new content in the rich, varied artistic forms possessed by our people.

While taking over and developing our literary and art heritage, we should study that which is excellent and progressive in the literature and art of the Soviet Union, China and other People's Democracies, thereby enriching our national culture still further.

Our literature and art have given an unsatisfactory picture of the Soviet Union as the bulwark of world peace and of the Soviet people as an eternal friend of our people; an incomplete portrayal of the Chinese People's Volunteers who are valiantly fighting shoulder to shoulder with the Korean People's Army; a poor representation of the peoples of the People's Democracies who are giving our people internationalist support and encouragement.

Our Korean writers and artists must produce many works of high artistic quality on these subjects, so that they strike terrors into the aggressors and war-incendiaries and provide songs of warm friendship to the peace-loving people the world over.

There should be lively criticism and self-criticism in the creative activities of our writers and artists. Works having either a formalistic trend or cosmopolitan elements also have appeared in our literature and art after liberation. And the work of literary and art criticism still remains backward.

For the further development of creative work, stagnation and backwardness must be overcome in the sphere of criticism. It goes without saying that the sound development of literature and art cannot be expected without criticism. Needless to say, however, criticism should not proceed along the lines of "Let's smash up," but should be constructive in every sense.

Among some critics there is still found the tendency of seeking to "knock down" the authors and their works, instead of giving them advice and assistance and indicating them the right course of creative work. This sort of criticism is not the literary criticism we are calling for.

Criticism by the critics should be thoroughgoing and sharp and, at the same time, should be permeated with the spirit of comradely mutual co-operation aimed at jointly correcting defects with the authors, achieving still greater results and mutually contributing to the treasure house of our culture. Committing errors in creative work is nothing to be feared. Authors may commit errors and their works may reveal defects. What is to be feared most is that the defects are not corrected, that they are connived at.

Not only should the unity of authors and critics be strengthened, but also that of all the creative teams in the literary and art world. An implacable struggle must be fought against any and every sectarian act and tendency that impedes the implementation of the Party's policy on literature and art and weakens the unity of the literary and art world.

Dear writers and artists,

You have the glorious task of introducing to the whole world the heroic struggle of our people and acquainting posterity with it through your creative activities. Our people more than ever are showing a keener interest in your work.

The art demanded by a heroic people must naturally be a heroic one, and the art demanded by a people who has entered the world arena must naturally rise to the world level.

The people expect you to work heart and soul to create such literature and art.

You are glorious soldiers on the literary and art front. How can a writer who is not an ardent patriot create patriotic works and how can an artist with no love for the people create art for the people?

Great writers and artists of the world were great patriots and great champions of the people's happiness. So, they have the love and respect of all peoples down through the ages and are the pride of mankind.

Today the Korean people are valiantly marching forward to ultimate victory in the Fatherland Liberation War, overcoming all difficulties and ordeals. I firmly believe that you writers and artists, best sons and daughters of our heroic people, will emerge on the world scene with great works of art and will make our glorious era shine through all generations to come.

ON SOME DEFECTS IN THE ORGANIZATIONAL WORK OF PARTY ORGANIZATIONS

Report to the Fourth Plenary Meeting of the Central Committee of the Workers' Party of Korea

November 1, 1951

After liberation the Korean people, under the leadership of our Party, established the people's government and carried out democratic reforms in the northern half of the country and are now striving to accomplish the national-liberation revolution throughout the country.

In the struggle for the freedom and happiness of the Korean people and the reunification and independence of the country, our Party has grown and strengthened rapidly and has become the leading and guiding force of the entire Korean people. The Korean people consider our Party's policies as their own and know that the policies of our Party alone accord with their interests. The unity of our Party and people has been further consolidated particularly in the course of the fierce struggle against the armed invasion of the U.S. imperialists.

Basing itself on the theory of Marxism-Leninism, our Party has organized and mobilized our people to the sacred struggle to defeat the internal and external enemies and win freedom and independence for the nation, overcoming all difficulties. The policies and slogans of our Party have become a great force inspiring and encouraging the workers, peasants and all other labouring masses to victory.

Under the leadership of our Party, the Korean people have fought bravely against the U.S. imperialist armed invaders and their stooges for 17 long months and are displaying their inexhaustible might. Through the war, our Party has further strengthened its ties with the broad masses of the people and accumulated a wealth of valuable experience in the struggle.

It is because our Party has always been faithful to Marxism-Leninism and has remained true to the interests of the working people to the last that it has won the deep confidence of the masses of the people and achieved enormous successes in its activities, successfully surmounting the hard trials of the war.

Marxism-Leninism teaches that close bonds between the Party and the popular masses are the decisive condition for victory in revolution. In his work *What Is To Be Done*? Lenin called upon the revolutionary Social-Democrats to "go among all classes of the population, dispatch units of their army in all directions." Comrade Stalin said that the wellspring of the great strength of the Bolshevik Party lies in its close bonds with the masses of the people just as the unbreakable strength of Antaeus, a hero in Greek mythology, was derived from his bond with the earth, his mother.

Our Party has always tirelessly endeavoured for firm unity with the broad labouring masses with the working class as the core, and drawn its inexhaustible strength and courage from it.

For the further organizational strengthening of its ranks, our Party has in recent months conducted the re-registration and organizational rearrangement of Party members in the areas liberated from the enemy's temporary occupation. We have basically restored the Party organizations in a short period of time. This represents a great victory for us. This means that our Party has the active support of the toiling masses in the struggle for the freedom and independence of the country and has gained the possibility of exercising greater influence on the masses in the future.

But some of the Party organizations and leading functionaries fail to carry through the Party's line correctly in the work of readjusting the organizational matters. Some of the leading functionaries and organizations of our Party commit the grave error of straying from its line without taking into account the historical conditions of the country's development and the specific circumstances prevailing, because they fail to direct due attention to the organizational and political work of the Party and lack in scrupulous study of inner-Party work, occupying themselves simply with the shock campaigns conducted in each period.

The defects revealed recently in the work of some of the Party organizations can be divided into two categories. One of them is the deviations manifested in dealing with the organizational matters and the other is the wrong tendencies found in their work with the Democratic Front for the Reunification of the Fatherland and the affiliated political parties.

1. ON THE PARTY'S ORGANIZATIONAL WORK

The organizational principles of our Party are a powerful weapon for carrying into effect the Party's Programme and tactics. Without steel-strong organization and without good organizational work it is impossible to successfully fulfil all the tasks confronting the Party. We have therefore always emphasized that the organizational work has a great significance.

Our Party is the vanguard of the labouring people with the working class as the core and a new-type, revolutionary Marxist-Leninist Party. It takes theoretical guidance in its activities from Marxist-Leninist theory and learns constantly from the experience of struggle of the Communist Party of the Soviet Union and the other brother parties. At the same time, our Party has a series of peculiarities in its development due to the historical conditions and specific realities of our country.

Our Party always proceeds from the Marxist-Leninist principles and the specific realities of our country in determining its organizational principles and political line. The organizations of the Party at all levels, therefore, should conduct its organizational and political work in such a way as to firmly build themselves up, strengthen their bonds with the masses, develop the Party into a mass party, temper the Party spirit of the members and steadily raise the level of their leadership, and this invariably on the basis of our Party's line.

Some Party organizations, however, fail to have a full understanding of the mass character of our Party and do not reckon with the fact that the history of our Party is short and the political level of its members is low. Not allowing for the facts that many ideological survivals of Japanese imperialism are still left in the minds of the masses, that our struggle is going on under very complex circumstances, with the country divided into the north and the south, and so on, and regarding the Party members as spotless Marxists-Leninists, they demand of them what is above their level.

We should absorb the advanced patriotic elements from among the people of all sections and classes into the Party ranks and expand and strengthen the Party on a mass basis with the working class as the core, consistently preserving the ideology of the working class and its leading role.

Today the enemies are engaged in malicious tricks to disrupt our Party, the chief motive force in state building and the militant core in the Fatherland Liberation War, isolate it from the masses and sap its fighting power. Under these conditions, it is very important to improve and strengthen our Party's organizational work in conformity to its mass character.

But some Party organizations have carried on the Party's organizational work in a mechanical way without taking into account the prevailing conditions, with the result that many defects are revealed.

(1) SHORTCOMINGS REVEALED IN THE WORK OF INCREASING THE PARTY MEMBERSHIP

Many organizations and leading functionaries of the Party fail to conduct the work of increasing its membership satisfactorily owing to their lack of correct understanding of the mass character of our Party and the present situation. Some Party organizations have developed a closed-doorist tendency to refuse admission of advanced patriotic elements to the Party by putting up various unjustifiable conditions.

Quite a number of organizations and leading functionaries of the Party have a wrong tendency towards not absorbing widely into our Party those toiling peasants who are fighting at the front and in the rear with all their patriotic devotion, for fear of a drop in the proportion of workers, clinging only to the prewar rate of its growth without consideration for the present situation when owing to the barbarous bombings of the enemy factories have been destroyed and the number of workers has dwindled sharply.

Despite the fact that the work of increasing the membership of our Party should be stepped up among the labouring peasants in such an area as Chagang Province where production enterprises are not many, the provincial Party organization has admitted to the Party in the first half of the current year an insignificant number of peasants accounting for no more than 0.8 per cent of the province's Peasant Union members with no party affiliation who are aged 20 or above. And the Pakchon County Party Committee of North Pyongan Province mechanically places a limit, so that not more than 17 peasants should be accepted into the Party on an average a month, although there are a good many people qualified for membership.

Though no small number of active peasants, who displayed patriotic devotion both in the work of increasing production and giving aid to the front and in the struggle against the reactionaries, and many families of those servicemen who have fought well in the war and of those murdered by the enemy, wanted to join our Party, the Kangso County Party organization in South Pyongan Province did not accept them. And the cells (sub-cells) accounting for 77 per cent of the Party organizations in that county including those in Kusan and Sori *myon* totally neglected the work of increasing the membership in the first half of this year.

Some of the Party organizations in the Ministry of Transport did not pay due attention to the work of increasing the Party membership and, therefore, did not admit even a single person to the Party in the first half of the year though there were thousands of employees of worker and poor peasant origins. Today in the People's Army there are a great number of servicemen who are displaying patriotic devotion and heroism in the fight against the enemy. Nevertheless, they are not given active education to be admitted regularly into the Party. The position is that the work of increasing the membership is discontinued when there is no battle, for some Party organizations absorb armymen into the Party only on the basis of their momentary combat results.

The enterprises in the fields of industry and transport where the workers are concentrated, are important sources for the growth of our Party. This notwithstanding, the Party organizations did not conduct their work with the workers well, with the result that the work of increasing the Party membership made little progress in the first half of the current year. Shortcomings of this sort are revealed in no small measure in some Party organizations of collieries in Hwanghae Province and of the timber industry in Chagang Province as well.

The primary Party organizations at some collieries of North Hamgyong Province do not regularly conduct the education of those qualified for membership and, moreover, fail to accept into the Party ranks many middle-aged workers who exhibit patriotic devotion in the struggle for increased wartime production, under the pretext that they are old and ignorant.

If steadfast persons qualified for membership are admitted

to the Party and then given good political education and organizational training, their political level can be raised speedily. Some Party organizations, however, have the tendency to reject candidates for membership on account of trifling matters or vote down their admission to the Party for lack of education simply because they have answered political questions somewhat unsatisfactorily at the Party meetings which discussed the question of their admission.

The Hyesan County Party Committee of South Hamgyong Province rejected 212 applications for admission in the first half of 1951, of which those rejected for lack of education held 77.4 per cent.

Some Party organizations in the People's Army mechanically have not accepted into the Party those servicemen of worker and peasant origins who displayed patriotic devotion and bravery in battle, for the reason that they could not learn by heart the Programme and Rules of the Party or their political and theoretical levels are low.

The Nampo city Party organization in South Pyongan Province, though there are over 100 working people including working women under the Haesin-ri primary Party organization, pays no attention to them from the Party point of view, branding them as untrustworthy persons on the ground that they stood sentry for two or three days unavoidably on the threat of the enemy during his temporary occupation. And although the workers who have been transferred in an organized way work with zeal at production enterprises and apply for membership in our Party, the leading functionaries of the primary Party organizations do not accept their applications on the ground that their length of service at the present factories is short, without taking into account the period of their service at the previous workplaces. There was even a case where the decision of a Party sub-cell in the field of civil engineering and construction on the admission of a model worker into the Party was turned down for the reason that the period of his service was 15 days short of the required number of days.

Those persons whose social backgrounds coincide with the

basic composition of our Party and who faithfully perform their duties, enthusiastically implement the policies of the Party and the Government and also are active in the life of the working people's organizations after seceding from other parties they once joined, can be admitted to our Party. But many Party organizations mechanically refuse to accept into the Party those who once joined other parties.

(2) DEFECTS REVEALED IN THE QUESTION OF PENALTIES

Through the work of registering the membership of the Party and readjusting its ranks, the Party ranks have been cleared of the hostile and subversive elements who had sneaked into our Party, and it has grown stronger.

But in dealing with the organizational matters, some Party organizations have committed the grave error of trying to settle all matters by means of meting out Party penalties at random, instead of waging an ideological struggle and conducting the educational work better in order to strengthen the organizational discipline of the Party members. This erroneous method cannot strengthen the discipline of the Party but, on the contrary, leads to the weakening of it.

Not a few Party members were expelled from the Party or given Party penalties because they buried their Party membership cards in the ground or left them with other persons during the retreat in order to prevent the enemy from depriving them of the cards. Of course, the membership card is a very precious thing for the Party member, since it is a paper certifying him to be an honourable Workers' Party member, and each member should keep it properly. It is also true that if a Party card falls into the hands of the enemy, he may utilize it to the detriment of our Party. But it is very wrong to expel a member from the Party or issue a penalty against him thoughtlessly for the mere reason that he parted with his Party card, without taking into account the very critical situation he found himself in under the wartime circumstances and his level. The fact that the Party members punished on account of their membership cards are 80-85 per cent of all punished members, clearly shows how mechanically Party penalties have been applied.

Some Party organizations ignore even the principles and procedures concerning Party penalties provided for in the Rules. The Party organization of the Pongung factory in Hamhung reduced the Party members who had committed errors to candidate membership and, still not content with it, imposed on them additional penalties such as reprimand or serious warning.

The Unsan County Party organization in North Pyongan Province had failed to give persistent education to those members who were not faithful in Party life or lacked in activity at ordinary times, and then, when the registration work began, took the measure of expelling all of them from the Party ranks. As a result, 80 per cent of the entire Party members expelled were ousted for unwarranted reasons, which the Provincial Party Committee found out and rectified. There was a similar tendency in the Ryongchon County Party organization too.

The Party members already punished were fighting devotedly for the Party and the country at the front and in the rear. Nevertheless, Party organizations at various levels did not remit the penalties applied to them. So, the Organizational Committee of the Party Central Committee adopted on September 1 this year a decision on quickly remitting the penalties imposed on those Party members and issued strict instructions to the Party organizations at all levels. But some Party organizations still do not actively promote the work of cancelling the penalties. Some provincial Party organizations not only fail to give correct guidance to the lower Party organizations in this work, but also do not solve in good time the questions raised and show no readiness to boldly correct the registration work that has proceeded in a wrong way. By September 15 the Hwanghae provincial Party organization gave ratifications to only 16.2 per cent of the decisions of city and county Party organizations on the expulsion of some persons from the Party or their demotion to candidate membership.

(3) SHORTCOMINGS REVEALED IN THE WORK OF FOSTERING THE CORE MEMBERS OF THE PARTY CELL

The ties of the Party with the masses should be further strengthened in order to lead the great Fatherland Liberation War to victory. We should energetically carry out all work among the masses and properly organize and mobilize the entire Party membership and the broad masses to displaying activity and initiative.

It is the leading workers of the primary Party organizations and chairmen and core Party members of the cells who play the leading role in bringing our Party's policies home to the masses and arousing them to action.

And yet, those comrades who have not undergone enough Party training and have little experience in Party work are now working as cadres in the primary Party organizations, since many core members of our Party are fighting at the front and some of the active Party members were murdered by the enemy during the temporary retreat. They are not good at the Party organizational work and the work of educating and mobilizing the masses. One of the most important tasks in rehabilitating and readjusting our Party is, therefore, to train the chairmen and members of the primary Party committees, and chairmen and core members of the cells.

This spring the Political Committee of the Party Central Committee stressed time and again the need of raising the level of practical ability of the core members of the cells and cadres of the primary Party organizations, of helping them in their actual work and giving them political education and training. But the Party organizations at all levels, while mobilizing the cell cadres and core Party members to shock campaigns alone and only scolding them for their unsatisfactory work every day, scarcely conduct the work of helping and training them. Some functionaries think that those who shout at the masses and run about busily to mobilize them by force are core Party members. This is quite wrong. Today there are many instances where the policies of our Party are not well communicated to the masses, Party work is conducted in a mechanical and formalistic way and the masses are mobilized not by explanation and persuasion but by order and coercion. The chief reason is that core Party members competent to work with the masses have not been reared.

(4) DEFECTS REVEALED IN CONNECTION WITH THE ALLOCATION OF CADRES

Proper appointment and allocation of cadres are the most important problem in the organizational work of our Party. Many Party organizations still do not pay due attention to the systematic training and proper appointment of cadres. The rearing of reserve cadres is not up to the mark and urgent gaps are stopped by means of picking up cadres from this or that place at random, instead of selecting and allocating them in a planned way by studying and knowing the cadres in different branches.

As a result of transferring cadres frequently, instead of selecting and allocating them in a planned way according to their qualifications and retaining them for a considerable period, they cannot give play to their abilities in their work. The instructors of the Manpo County Party Committee of Chagang Province cannot remain working at their posts longer than four months on an average, and the Koksan County Party Committee of Hwanghae Province replaced the vice-chairman of the Koksan Mine's primary Party committee four times in six months. Cadres, therefore, cannot settle down to their work and have no time to study their work and delve deep into it and, accordingly, their professional level is very low.

2. ON THE WORK OF OUR PARTY ORGANIZATIONS IN RELATION TO THE DEMOCRATIC FRONT FOR THE REUNIFICATION OF THE FATHERLAND

We are now fighting against the U.S. imperialists and their stooge, the traitorous Syngman Rhee clique. The U.S. imperialists and the traitorous Syngman Rhee clique are the sworn enemy of the entire Korean people. We must unite all forces to crush the heinous enemy.

In the present situation it is imperative more than ever to rally all the patriotic forces longing for the freedom and independence of the country. That is why our Party should further expand and strengthen the Democratic Front for the Reunification of the Fatherland which embraces the broad patriotic forces of all sections and classes. The question of strengthening the D.F.R.F. is one of the fundamental questions and represents one of the basic lines of our Party in the struggle for ensuring the reunification and independence of the country and its democratic development.

For the strengthening of the D.F.R.F. it is essential to further improve our relations with all the political parties and social organizations in it and educate every member of these parties and organizations in the spirit of loyalty to the country and the people. If our Party organizations fail to have a deep understanding of the significance of the D.F.R.F. and to give correct guidance to it, we cannot strengthen the D.F.R.F. nor achieve victory in the struggle for the reunification of the country.

This notwithstanding, there has appeared among some Party functionaries a tendency to entertaining wrong views on the D.F.R.F. after the start of the Fatherland Liberation War, especially after the temporary retreat.

1. Some of our Party functionaries think the D.F.R.F. un-

necessary. Saying that the happenings during the temporary retreat of the People's Army have already clearly shown who is our enemy and who our friend, they reject all those who committed this or that kind of errors, and try to label them as our enemies. This is a grave mistake.

We cannot regard as our enemies all those who had joined reactionary organizations or committed this or that sort of crimes during the retreat. Of those involved in the reactionary organizations, a handful of wicked prime movers were reactionary elements, but the absolute majority were people who followed the enemy under compulsion. It is a big mistake to regard them as our enemies, branding them as reactionary elements all alike.

As regards those who had joined reactionary organizations, we should concretely analyse the causes of their involvement in the reactionary organizations and take into account their level of consciousness. The Korean people had no opportunity of learning advanced ideas for a long time under Japanese imperialist rule and began receiving democratic education for the first time after liberation. The entire masses could not be equipped with progressive ideas in so short a period as 5-6 years following liberation. Therefore, as for those who were compelled to join the reactionary organizations or to commit slight errors under compulsion by the enemy, we should not reject but educate them perseveringly and win them over to our side without fail.

Of course, our Party accepts into its ranks only the most advanced elements from among the masses. Our Party, even though it is a mass party, cannot admit all who, at best, hope for or sympathize with the democratic reunification and independence of the country.

But we, instead of leaving the progressive individuals and broad masses outside the Party as they are, should embrace them in some organization, give them political and ideological education and mobilize them to the struggle against the aggressors.

The D.F.R.F. comprises people in all walks of life aspiring to the freedom and independence of the fatherland, irrespective of their professions, sexes, religious beliefs and party affiliations. The D.F.R.F. is an important organization indispensable for making our Party's policies known to the broader masses and mobilizing all patriotic forces to the struggle against the aggressors. We should continue striving to expand and strengthen the D.F.R.F.

2. Some comrades think that such friendly parties as the Chongu Party and the Democratic Party are reactionary and that it is unnecessary for us to join hands with them. This is a wrong view. To wage the anti-imperialist struggle successfully, we should firmly join hands and co-operate with the democratic political parties and help them perseveringly to follow the right course.

We should learn to work with the friendly parties, adhering steadfastly to the principles of Marxism-Leninism. It will not do to stigmatize all friendly parties as reactionary on the ground that there exist some reactionary elements among their members. During the enemy's temporary occupation, reactionary elements appeared in no small measure in the friendly parties. But it did not derive from the policies of the friendly parties.

We should not regard the friendly parties as politically on a level with our Party. Our Party is guided by Marxism-Leninism, has the brilliant revolutionary traditions of the struggle for the freedom and independence of the country, is organized with the most progressive elements of the Korean working people and performs the leading role in state building. It will not do to label the friendly parties as reactionary or unnecessary parties because they fail to play the same role on the same political level as our Party.

The friendly parties are democratic in their aims and policies and, accordingly, are fully qualified to form a united front with our Party in the struggle against foreign aggressors for achieving the reunification and independence of the country. We should not judge the friendly parties by the deeds of reactionaries within them but see their basic line and policies.

3. Some of our functionaries have a tendency to meddle in the internal affairs of the friendly parties allegedly for strengthening the work with them. The Yonghung and Tanchon County Party organizations interfere in the friendly parties' arrangements for meetings and go so far as to instruct their own subordinate Party organizations to ensure that the meetings of the friendly parties are attended by large numbers of members of those parties. Our Party organizations' assistance to the friendly parties consists in getting their members to take an active part in all state affairs, helping in their political education in every way and aiding those parties to clean away by themselves the reactionary elements lurking within. In this way it should be seen to that the friendly parties maintain their identity and display activity in the great task of wiping out the enemy of our people.

3. THE CAUSES OF SHORTCOMINGS REVEALED IN PARTY WORK

It is necessary to make a correct analysis of the causes of the defects revealed in all work in order to know them thoroughly and rectify them. Wherein lie the causes of the shortcomings manifested in handling the Party's organizational matters and in the work of the Party organizations in relation to the D.F.R.F.?

1. Some organizations and cadres of the Party are oblivious of the fact that the close ties with the masses are the wellspring of the great strength of our Party. This is the most dangerous phenomenon sapping the strength of our Party.

Our Party represents, and fights for, the interests of the labouring masses of Korea. To defend the interests of the masses, it is essential to strengthen our bonds with the masses at all times and lend an ear to their voices.

We can learn living experience from the masses, educate

and mobilize them to a struggle only if we strengthen our bonds with them. Without close ties with the masses our Party cannot become a mass party guiding the millions led by the working class.

We should discover things new among the masses, make a deep study of all phenomena and take measures in good time. The primary cause of the drawbacks in our Party work today lies in the fact that some of our Party organizations are detached from the masses.

2. Some organizations and cadres of the Party fail to play a vanguard role in carrying out their assigned tasks.

For our development from a lower stage onto a higher, we must courageously do away with all the shortcomings revealed in our work and make an uninterrupted advance towards a new, higher goal. Some Party functionaries, however, are very lukewarm in remedying their defects, and drag at the tail of the masses. If our Party merely recorded what the masses experienced and thought, followed in the wake of their spontaneous movement and, swayed only by the momentary and partial interests of the masses, failed to firmly guard more vital interests, it could not lead the struggle of the masses purposefully nor become a party truly defending their interests.

We should always look farther ahead into the future than the masses, set an example to them and lead them forward.

If one is to become a model for the masses, one should on no account conceal but boldly expose one's shortcomings, analyse in detail the causes, conditions and circumstances of the shortcomings and take measures for their correction. Only a party of this type can unite with the masses and lead them.

Some of our functionaries, however, are not well aware of this truth. This is one of the causes of the shortcomings in our work today.

3. Criticism and self-criticism are conducted inadequately among some of our Party organizations and cadres and, in many cases, in a wrong way.

Criticism should be conducted not for criticism's sake, but constructive criticism should be offered for the development of work. Criticism for eliminating faults and educating cadres is a constructive criticism. Sharp criticism should be offered against bureaucracy, flattery, liberalistic acts based on arbitrariness, senseless obstinacy, petty bourgeois self-conceit and tendencies towards localism and nepotism marked by mutual connivance. All these things should be rectified through timely criticism, for they impede our advance. Each Party member should be modest and always be uncompromising in matters of principle. A vigorous struggle should be waged against those who suppress criticism or dislike constructive criticism. And a resolute struggle should be put up against the tendency to make no effort to correct one's errors while admitting them when criticized.

Criticism and self-criticism of our errors and shortcomings are a great driving force that advances our work. Those who fear criticism and obstruct it are cowards and not entitled to the respect of the masses. Because criticism and self-criticism are dull now, there are not a few instances of fully corrigible shortcomings and mistakes being aggravated till at last they go so far as to grow into grave political errors.

4. Some organizations and cadres of the Party, engrossed entirely in the shock campaigns in hand, pay little attention to inner-Party work. For the successful fulfilment of all the tasks facing the Party organizations, it is necessary, first of all, to improve and strengthen the Party's organizational and political education work.

As Comrade Stalin pointed out, if we, underestimating or oblivious of political matters, put stress only on economic campaigns and are tempted by economic results alone, all work could be driven into a blind alley. We must combine political work with economic work without fail and constantly direct deep attention to inner-Party work.

Of course, we cannot lay emphasis only on one of those work. The organizations and functionaries of our Party must not back down from economic guidance. The organizations and functionaries of the Party, however, should not take upon themselves the work of economic and administrative bodies but guide and help the functionaries of these bodies to do their work well, and should continue to strengthen these bodies. In order to raise the level of Party leadership of economic and administrative work it is essential to strengthen inner-Party work. Without the consolidation of the Party itself it cannot conduct political work actively among the masses and give its guidance to the economic and administrative work.

The strengthening of inner-Party work means elevating the level of the Party's organizational and ideological work.

In the Party's organizational work it is very important to strengthen Party leadership. Some organizations and cadres of the Party have not yet done away with the armchair method of guidance. We have pressing need of living guidance enabling us to maintain normal relations with the lower Party organs, know cadres, lend an ear to the voices of the masses, learn from their experiences, give them correct guidance and assistance in good time and rectify their errors and faults. Today the overwhelming majority of the chairmen of primary Party organizations are newly selected people with no experience in Party work, and so the provincial, city (district), county Party committees and political organs should endeavour to give them kind and concrete living guidance.

Some Party organizations and cadres think as if everything is all right if only a good resolution is adopted. This is wrong. The resolution records no more than what we have resolved to do. There is a considerable distance between the resolve and practice. A concrete and planned organizational work is needed to carry our resolve into effect. Without such organizational work and systematic verification of its execution, the resolution, however good it may be, will remain only a dead letter.

Whether our Party work can be pushed ahead briskly or not depends also on the political and ideological standards of the Party members. Political education, therefore, is a most important work for each Party organization and cadre. But many Party organizations conduct this work in a perfunctory manner.

Besides, there are not a few shortcomings in inner-Party work. Every organization and functionary of the Party should direct greater attention to inner-Party work to strengthen the Party.

5. Some of the organizations and cadres of our Party fail to thoroughly analyse all negative and positive facts revealed in Party work and draw appropriate political conclusions.

Records and statistics of Party work are not arranged in correct order and no analysis is made of them. Party statistics prepared by Party organizations at various levels serve only as data to be submitted to the upper organizations and very few organizations and cadres of the Party make a scrupulous analysis of those statistics and draw political conclusions therefrom to improve their work.

In Party work accurate statistics serve as a true mirror of inner-Party life. But statistics themselves cannot point the direction to be taken for the improvement of our work. The point is to analyse statistics scrupulously, draw a definite political conclusion therefrom and take relevant measures for the improvement of work.

When analysing the statistics of the growth of the Party membership, for instance, attention should indeed be paid to its numerical aspect, too. But it is necessary to conduct organizational and educational work in conformity to the goal of consolidating the Party qualitatively, taking into account the qualitative aspect—how many more people with what degrees of knowledge and political levels we now have.

The theoretical level of Party cadres with regard to Party work can be raised only through practice, namely, actual Party work. We can acquire a living theory by systematizing and generalizing the experience gained in our work. If Party cadres really want to raise their theoretical level as regards Party work, they should analyse abundant data on Party work, synthesize and systematize the experience and lessons obtained from it, and apply them again to their future work. They should thus endeavour to elevate their theoretical level steadily in the course of work.

4. OUR TASKS

The following tasks are raised to eliminate the shortcomings in Party work quickly and further strengthen and develop the work of Party organizations:

1. In view of the present conditions in our country it is the most important task for us to expand and strengthen our Party into a mass party. The leading functionaries of the Party organizations at all levels and the entire Party membership should be brought to have a clear understanding of our Party's organizational line of expanding and strengthening the Party in keeping with its mass character and the specific features of its development.

We must develop our Party into a still larger mass party by thoroughly repudiating the closed-doorist tendency of going only by the proportion of workers and refusing to admit advanced toiling peasants to the Party for fear of a drop in the proportion of workers in the composition of the Party membership, or rejecting those people at factories and in the People's Army who are qualified for membership, on the unwarranted conditions and pretexts that their training is insufficient, their level is low, or that their length of service is short.

This, however, in no way means that haphazard admission to the Party without screening and verification of the candidates for membership is permissible. We must strictly follow the procedure of individual handling of those who join the Party. We must prevent the spies and agents provocateurs of the U.S. imperialists and the traitorous Syngman Rhee clique and other shady elements from worming their way into the ranks of our Party. The door of the Party should always be kept closely shut to those scamps.

We should accept into the Party advanced elements who support our Party's policy in the struggle for freedom and independence and display enthusiasm for its implementation.

2. A struggle should be waged thoroughly in all Party organizations, from the centre down to the cells, against the tendency towards penalty-first policy which has been manifested in the work of readjusting the Party ranks.

According to the decision of the Organizational Committee of the Party Central Committee dated September 1, 1951, unjustified penalties applied to Party members must be cancelled, penalties which were too severe be corrected and those members who have been displaying enthusiasm in their work after being penalized must be acquitted of their penalties quickly. And the level of the political consciousness of the Party members should be further raised, so that they observe discipline in the Party voluntarily.

3. The Party Central Committee and the Party organizations at all levels should pay great attention to the work of fostering the core of the Party cells, and the chairmen and members of the primary Party committees and the cell chairmen and core members should have a correct grasp of all the decisions and instructions of our Party, become a model for the Party members and the masses and lead them in the struggle for their implementation.

To foster the core of the cells is the most important measure for reinforcing the ranks of our Party and strengthening the bonds between the Party and the masses. Only by so doing can our Party overcome all difficulties and win a brilliant victory in the Fatherland Liberation War.

In order to train the core of the cells, the cadres of the Party centre and provincial Party organizations should go down to the primary Party organizations and help the members of primary Party and cell committees and active Party members in their practical work and lead them to elevate their political and theoretical standard and work level.

4. The Party organizations at all levels should direct profound attention to educating and training the cadres in practical work. The chairmen of the Party committees at all levels should

personally assume the responsibility for the task of training more than two cadres of vice-chairman class. There should be no frequent transfer of cadres, but they should instead be retained in one place for a long period, and should be promoted in due time on the basis of ascertaining their progress in practical work.

5. The Party organizations at all levels should raise the level of ideological consciousness of the entire Party membership. Special attention should be devoted to educating the Party members in Marxist-Leninist theory and, particularly, the education of newly-enlisted Party members should be intensified and they should be tempered ideologically. The education of new members should not be conducted through the Party education networks alone; it should be conducted through mass cultural activities and by means of discussing problems of theoretical and educational significance at Party meetings, and it may also be conducted by assigning the task to qualified comrades. Thus the entire Party membership should be firmly armed with the advanced theory of Marxism-Leninism and our Party be further strengthened organizationally and ideologically.

6. We should strengthen the work of the Democratic Front for the Reunification of the Fatherland. Our Party, as it plays the leading role in the D.F.R.F., should endeavour more actively to strengthen this work.

For improving and strengthening the work of the D.F.R.F., the tendency to lay accent only on formalistic shock campaigns should be eliminated and democratic personalities from different sections and classes should be educated in a planned way to promote their ideological progress and constantly encouraged to take an active part in state affairs.

Our Party should give day-to-day assistance to various organs of the D.F.R.F. in matters ranging from the drafting of work plans to the concrete organizational work for their execution.

For the strengthening of the work of the D.F.R.F., attention should be paid especially to the following points:

a) All the forces of the political parties and social organizations should be enlisted in the struggle against the U.S. imperialist aggressors and their stooge the Syngman Rhee clique, the counter-revolutionary elements lurking in various political parties and social organizations and in all social strata should be ferreted out and liquidated, and people of all walks of life be led to further heighten hatred against the enemy.

b) The present situation in our country should be correctly publicized and explained, so that the entire people give fuller play to their patriotism and further strengthen their conviction of victory and that all patriotic forces be mobilized to the fulfilment of the political and economic tasks set forth by the state.

c) Great efforts should be exerted to strengthen the unity of all the political parties and social organizations under the D.F.R.F. and to further expand the united front.

d) In order to properly push forward the work of the D.F.R.F., the Party members should be taught the method of work with the friendly parties, and much effort should be exerted to strengthen not only the unity of the upper strata but also the unity of the lower strata between the members of our Party and the friendly parties. The rank and file of all political parties and social organizations now affiliated with the united front are our allies who can go along with us to the last, since the absolute majority of them belong to the labouring masses. We should always approach the rank and file of all political parties and social organizations and give them democratic education, so that they become champions who, joining hands with us, fight for the reunification and independence of the country and the freedom and happiness of the people.

The united front of the lower strata should be further strengthened to make it possible to bring pressure from the progressive rank and file to bear upon some waverers remaining in the upper strata and check their vacillation and to isolate some undesirable elements of the upper strata from the masses.

To strengthen the unity of the lower strata it is necessary to bring our Party's influence to bear upon the members of the friendly parties through frequent mutual contacts. The tendency of operating separately detached from each other should be eliminated, activities in the clubhouses and democratic publicity halls, round-table talks, reading sessions, etc., should be conducted jointly, and all political, economic and cultural shock campaigns should also be carried on in common to exert ideological influence upon the members of the friendly parties.

7. An unremitting struggle should be waged against the bureaucratic style of work still found in our Party. The entire Party should struggle against all bureaucratic, formalistic styles of work—which consist in unsparingly calling down comrades who are politically at a low level and weak in practical ability instead of giving them education and assistance; in making compromises, swayed by flattery and personal considerations, instead of criticizing and rectifying the errors committed by comrades; stifling up the creative proposals made by the subordinates without heeding them; sticking jealously to one's own subjective views to make a mess of work; trying to mobilize the masses by orders and compulsion instead of by explanation and persuasion; mechanically introducing foreign things and forcing people down below to accept them when those things are totally out of place, in disregard of the national peculiarities of our country, and so on.

At this Plenary Meeting we should sincerely discuss the above-mentioned problems, boldly disclose the shortcomings in our work, take measures to correct them and arouse the whole Party to action to bring about a remarkable progress in Party work in the future.

ON THE IMPROVEMENT OF THE PARTY'S ORGANIZATIONAL WORK

Concluding Speech Delivered at the Fourth Plenary Meeting of the Central Committee of the Workers' Party of Korea
November 2, 1951

Comrades,

We have achieved great successes at the present meeting. If we do not rectify our shortcomings in time, they may prove a great hindrance to the development of our Party. Many good suggestions have been advanced at this meeting for the elimination of our shortcomings. These good suggestions will be greatly conducive to the development of our work in future.

Although measures for improvement of our work were already set out in detail in the report, I would like to make further remarks on several questions.

1. ON THE WORK OF INCREASING THE MEMBERSHIP OF THE PARTY

First, in the work of increasing the Party membership some of our Party organizations committed the error of closed-doorism. This was already pointed out clearly in the report.

However, many comrades still fail to understand this and express doubt and concern, asking: "If a great number of toiling peasants are admitted into the Party, what will become of its composition? Won't our Party become a party of the peasants?" This is a needless apprehension.

Our Party is a party with the working class as its core, a party guided by the ideology of the working class. Therefore, petty-bourgeois ideology cannot be the ideological foundation of our Party, and our Party cannot become a party of the peasants simply because peasants make up a large part of it.

Our Party can never be anything but a Marxist-Leninist Party. Even if it absorbs large numbers of toiling peasants into its ranks, our Party will invariably be guided by the ideology of the working class. Therefore, it can never become a party of the peasants or a party of the small-propertied classes.

Even if the proportion of workers in the Party decreases to some extent at the present stage, the nature of our Party cannot alter in the least nor is there anything for us to worry about as long as Marxism-Leninism, the ideology of the working class, remains its guiding ideology and the organizational principle of Party building is strictly based on the principles of the Marxist-Leninist Party.

We will recruit best elements of the toiling peasantry into the Party, arm them with the ideology of the working class and continue to strengthen and develop our Party into a mass political party with the working class as its core.

Second, an analysis of the Korean working class reveals that its composition is complex owing to the peculiar conditions of our country's development. The absolute majority of our workers are peasants of yesterday.

Immediately after the August 15 Liberation, the northern half had no more than 300,000 workers. With the development of the national economy after liberation, the number grew to nearly 600,000. This means that in the five years after liberation the number of workers increased by more than 300,000. All of these people had been engaged in farming in the countryside before they became workers. So our working class is young.

The workers, of course, belong to the working class. But not all of them have working-class consciousness. Much less can we say that the peasants of yesterday, who have recently left the countryside and started working in industry, are all equipped with working-class consciousness, even though they are workers today. Therefore, there is little difference between the admission into the Party and education in Marxism-Leninism of those workers who were peasants up until yesterday and are now working in factories and the admission into the Party and education of those toiling peasants who may develop into workers in the future.

Our peasants are not the peasants of the past. The people's power having been set up and democratic reforms such as the agrarian reform and nationalization of industries having been carried out following the August 15 Liberation, our peasants are heading for socialism, not taking the path of capitalism. This makes it possible for us to absorb large numbers of toiling peasants into the Party ranks and educate them in Marxism-Leninism.

Third, at the time of the merger of the two Parties, we elucidated the mass character of our Party by defining it as the vanguard of the working masses representing the interests of the broad sections of the working people headed by the working class. Already at that time we clearly analysed the reasons why our Party should be a Workers' Party.

Why have we made our Party a Workers' Party instead of continuing to develop it as a Communist Party? Because, owing to the peculiarities of the development of our country at the present stage, it is necessary to rally the broad masses closely around our Party in the struggle for the reunification and independence of the country.

To see the ratios of the population in our country, the peasants hold nearly 80 per cent. Such being the socio-economic structure of our country, what will become of our Party if labouring peasants are not admitted into the Party for fear of a drop in the proportion of workers? If we accept only the workers and the small number of Communists, how can our Party grow into a mass party and fulfil its leading role among the masses satisfactorily?

Since the socio-economic structure does not change overnight, the proportion of peasants will increase in our Party for many years to come. This is nothing to worry about.

The peculiarity of our country's socio-economic structure and the present situation created by the predatory colonial policy of U.S. imperialism bring forward the tasks of rallying the broad masses around our Party, of further expanding and reinforcing its ranks and of developing it into a mass party. It is therefore correct at the present stage to absorb large numbers of advanced elements of the working people into our Party, not going by the proportion of workers alone.

It runs counter to the line of our Party to keep its doors actually closed on various unjustifiable pretexts. Along with the workers, we should admit into our Party without hesitation advanced elements from among the peasants and working intellectuals, and thus continuously develop it into a mass political party.

As pointed out in the report, however, to open the door of the Party does not mean admitting to the Party everyone who comes along. As a comrade said yesterday, landlords, pastors, profiteers, or urban loafers should not be admitted to our Party. We should strictly guard against reactionary-minded, impure elements and spies sneaking into our Party ranks.

2. ON THE QUESTION OF PENALTIES

It was clearly pointed out in the report and in the speeches of many comrades that owing to the tendency of penalty-first policy, many Party members had been punished wrongfully in the manner of a shock campaign. This is a serious defect and error in our Party work.

I consider that the errors committed recently in the matter

of penalties must be rectified according to the following principles:

Unwarranted penalties must be cancelled and unfair penalties, i.e., those which were too severe, must be corrected. Those comrades who have been working enthusiastically since they were punished must have their penalties remitted.

Many of our Party workers do not understand the significance of penalties. The aim of Party penalties is to educate Party members and prevent them from repeating errors. Therefore, the application of Party penalties must not be considered in the same light as the trial of criminals in a court. The penalties stipulated in the Party Rules are educational in their purpose. It is quite unnecessary to impose penalties on those who are convinced of their mistakes without being punished.

However, it has become a fashion now among some of our functionaries to mete out penalties. They apply penalties because others do so, just as the old saying goes: "People cry because others are crying." Some comrades boast of the many penalties they have meted out, saying: "Well, you say you have meted out so many penalties, but I have imposed some more than you." These comrades have punished people indiscriminately for having buried, soiled or burned Party membership cards during the enemy occupation, without taking account of the circumstances at the time and without consideration of the pain and anguish of those punished. This is wrong.

We must make it clearly known to the Party members that the sole aim of penalties lies in education.

Some county Party committee chairmen said in their speeches that they did not want to apply penalties, but did so in fear of the higher organs. This shows that the provincial Party organizations suffer from bureaucracy. Party organizations apply penalties without knowing why, merely out of fear of the higher organs, and this is a very dangerous practice. By coercion no question can be solved. It is necessary to lead our members to observe Party discipline consciously. When penalties are applied, too, it must be with the aim of educating members to observe Party discipline voluntarily.

3. FOR THE CONSOLIDATION OF THE DEMOCRATIC FRONT FOR THE REUNIFICATION OF THE FATHERLAND

The need of strengthening the Democratic Front for the Reunification of the Fatherland was dealt with in detail in the report and has been expounded at full length in many documents of the Party Central Committee. So, I think it unnecessary to speak about it again. It is required to study more profoundly the previous documents and reports on this subject.

The aim of our struggle at the present stage is to accomplish the whole nation's task of opposing the armed invaders from 16 countries headed by the U.S. imperialist marauders and their lackeys, the traitorous Syngman Rhee clique, and of achieving the reunification and independence of the country. To carry out this national task, we should join hands and unite with whoever opposes the U.S. imperialist plunderers and their stooges and desires the country's reunification and independence, no matter what party or group he may belong to. We must mobilize all forces, big and small, irrespective of political views, religious beliefs or property status, to the struggle against the U.S. imperialists and their running dogs.

Since we are fighting a life-and-death battle against the U.S. imperialist aggressors and their lackeys, it is most harmful to disperse our forces. We must join hands with, and give leadership to, all political parties, social organizations and individuals who oppose the U.S. imperialists and their henchmen, no matter whether they be the Chongu Party, the Democratic Party, the Toiling People's Party, the People's Republican Party, people of the propertied classes or religious believers.

Our Party members must not interfere in the internal affairs of friendly parties or hamper their development; they must conduct themselves modestly with people from these parties. We must encourage them to take an active part in the state affairs together with us, influence them with progressive ideas and with advanced experience, and in cases where bad elements who have sneaked into the friendly parties seek to alienate these parties from our Party, we must help their members eliminate these undesirable elements through their own inner-Party struggles. There is no secret in our Party's policies. We must at all times explain the policies of our Party and of the state to the members of the friendly parties, inspire them with confidence in victory, and see to it that they stand with us in the struggle for the accomplishment of the great cause of the country's reunification.

Some of our comrades are insolent and immodest towards the members of the friendly parties. It is wrong to make our companions aggrieved without reason.

Of course, this does not mean that unprincipled compromise is permissible. We must always keep firmly to our principled stand, exert a favourable influence on members of the friendly parties and unite with them. When some of them do not clearly understand our policies, we must earnestly persuade them to know; when they do not do their work well, we must help and encourage them to do their work properly; we must educate them patiently so that they may understand us well and cooperate with us.

The united front is aimed wholly at ensuring the successful carrying out of the revolutionary tasks that confront us. Therefore, we must not meddle in the work of the friendly parties, but for the sake of better work, we should give advice to each other. It is not a principled attitude to leave them to follow a wrong path. When members of the friendly parties carry out government policies incorrectly while working with us in government or economic bodies, we must help them to execute them correctly. We should encourage and lead the members of the friendly parties to implement government policies in all fields together with us, no matter whether the scope of the work involved is wide or limited.

In our relations with the friendly parties, we must always

display activity. We should not wait for them to follow us, but take them by the hand and give them kind advice and constant explanation to follow the right path. Our work in this respect is not up to the mark, and our functionaries are not skilled at it. The Party Central Committee has emphasized this more than once, but many of our Party organs and organizations still fail to do so.

What is important in the work of the united front is to strengthen unity not only with the upper circles of the friendly parties but with their rank and file. By making closer contact with the upper circles of those parties, we shall have a favourable condition for strengthening the united front with their rank and file. At the same time, by strengthening the united front with their rank and file we can further consolidate the united front with their upper circles, and exert our Party's influence upon those working people who make up the absolute majority of the masses under the influence of these parties.

To strengthen the united front with the rank and file of the friendly parties, we should have many contacts with their members, inspire them with patriotism and firm confidence in victory and make them understand the justice of our struggle. We must give them a clear understanding that their class position is the same as ours; we must influence them so that they will always follow our Party hand in hand with our Party members even if the upper circles waver. We must induce them to isolate reactionary elements within their parties.

It was because unity with the rank and file was not strong enough that some vicious elements within the friendly parties killed our people during the temporary retreat of the People's Army. If the united front with the rank and file of the friendly parties had been strong, their members who had shared in the distribution of land and were of the same class position with us would not have perpetrated criminal acts against the people at the instigation of the reactionary elements.

If we attempt to take vengeance upon certain members of the friendly parties because they were with reactionary organizations for a time and killed our Party members or their families, it will only gladden the U.S. imperialists. The U.S. imperialists are trying, by breeding discord among our people and causing them to kill each other, to sap our strength and attain their sinister aggressive ends without shedding their own blood.

Many of our Party members still do not have a correct idea of the importance of the united front, nor do they understand fully that to strengthen the united front is the basic line of the Party.

Many comrades think that things will go well if they only shout the slogan: "Let us strengthen the united front!" The united front can be maintained only by working closely with the friendly parties and keeping close ties with their members.

Some comrades think that the united front at the lower level is something that concerns only the Party rank and file. This is wrong. There are no superior or inferior members in our Party. Though their assignments are different, all are equal as Party members. In accordance with the united front policy, every Party member, regardless of his position, must keep close ties with the rank and file of the friendly parties, have talks with them and exert the influence of our Party on them, thus inducing them to follow us. If our Party members strengthen their work with members of the Chongu Party, maintain intimate relations with them and imbue them with progressive ideas, the question of unity with the rank and file in the countryside will be solved.

The united front can never be formed through coercive measures. Coercion will give rise only to antipathy. By influencing the members of the friendly parties through education and persuasion, we must make them sincerely support us and be determined to stand by us to the last.

In future, the Central Committee and all the provincial committees of the Party should further strengthen the work of bringing all its members to have a correct understanding of the united front policy.

4. ON THE QUESTION OF CADRES

I think that many comrades have spoken correctly about this question. The Party Central Committee, too, has many shortcomings in cadre work. The education and training of cadres have been conducted without a plan. Despite the general shortage of cadres, they are largely concentrated in certain branches, while other branches are very short of cadres. And when we want to select cadres, we find that no reserves have been trained.

The Personnel Department is busy filling vacancies. It fails to do satisfactorily the work of training cadres according to plan and allocating the right cadre to the right post with due consideration for the opinions of people down below.

Personnel management is dealt with almost exclusively by the Personnel Department of the Party Central Committee. There is no need for this. Such work as drawing up general plans for the training of cadres, supervising their allocation and promotion, and selecting cadres of the categories that are subject to approval by the Political Committee or Organizational Committee, must be undertaken directly by the Personnel Department. However, it is advisable that cadres of other categories be dealt with by each branch concerned. This will not only shorten the time needed for endorsement of matters relating to cadres, but also enable all departments to study their work more profoundly and give constant attention to cadre training. The regulations governing personnel management must be re-examined and appropriately modified.

5. ON THE INTELLECTUAL CADRES

It was revealed in the speeches that some comrades did not yet have a correct knowledge of the cadres of intelligentsia. This is very regrettable. This question was clarified a long time ago. But, since even some of the provincial leading functionaries do not yet have a correct understanding of the question, I should like to emphasize the point once again.

More wrong views are held against the intellectuals who studied in the past, under Japanese imperialist rule, than against the new intellectuals who have been reared in the six years since liberation. I gave a clear explanation on this problem already at the time of the merger of the two Parties.

Our intellectuals served in economic and cultural institutions of Japanese imperialism before. But since liberation they have been serving the country and the people. By keeping contact with the workers and peasants, they are learning the thinking, fortitude and staunchness of the working people, and are gradually being transformed into intellectuals of a new type.

They have been remoulded noticeably in the six years, and have displayed devotion and initiative in the course of democratic construction. The overwhelming majority of them have fought courageously for the country during the war. Many of them went down as far as the Rakdong-gang River area to fight the enemy and, during the temporary retreat, they withdrew following our Party, overcoming all difficulties. What else do we have to demand of these intellectuals, and what ground is there to distrust them? We should promote them boldly, without suspecting them, inspire them to render active service to the country and the people, and remould them thoroughly into people's intellectuals.

There is nothing wrong in the intellectuals having acquired technique and knowledge in the past. They are now passing on their knowledge to our workers and peasants; they played a big role in rehabilitating and building factories and enterprises after liberation.

The services rendered by the intellectuals are great. They are not to blame for their parents having been landlords or capitalists. If they stand by their parents and set themselves against our social system, that is another question. But what is wrong with them when they are struggling against the stand of their parents and faithfully serving the Party and the people? We should not reject their patriotic zeal but inspire them to display greater activity.

Some intellectuals think: "We are people of the transition period and will be replaced by new intellectuals some day." They are wrong. Whoever does not make progress will be replaced. Whatever is old and stagnant is sure to be replaced by the new. This is the law of development of things. But if the intellectuals advance continuously in the direction that conforms to the requirements of the new society, who will reject and replace them? We expect the old intellectuals to make steady progress, and we will continue to help them advance.

We should explain to the old intellectuals our Party's line in regard to them and prevent them from wavering ideologically or feeling uneasy, promote them boldly and inspire them to take pride in their active service for the country and the people. And we should strive to provide them with conditions for continuous progress and for displaying their abilities to the full.

6. ON THE STYLE OF WORK

There are serious shortcomings in our functionaries' style of work. These shortcomings are more in evidence in the government bodies at higher levels.

There is a tendency to be indifferent to subordinates and

think everything is settled once papers have been sent down to the lower organs. There are also such cases as demanding the chairmen of *ri* people's committees or Party cells to submit many superfluous documents and statistics, the preparation of which prevents them from attending to their duties. When reports and statistics worked out at great pains by the functionaries at the *ri* level are submitted to the higher organs, the ministers or bureau chiefs do not even look well through them but tuck them away in drawers. I think decisive measures must be taken to reduce complex statistics and reports.

The struggle to eliminate the bureaucratic style of work must be waged continuously. There must be no such unjust practices as mobilizing only the people for voluntary labour service, while cadres hold themselves aloof from it. It is advisable that the cadres work with the people and conduct educational work during breaks in the work, explaining and propagandizing the Party's policies to them.

Only by sharing the sweets and bitters with the people will the cadres be able to hear their opinions and take measures in time to meet their demands. We should not command the masses, but should explain to them, persuade and educate them.

After this meeting all provincial Party committees must convene meetings of Party activists to discuss and immediately rectify the shortcomings in our work.

All the provincial Party committee chairmen should personally go down to the cells, have talks with Party members, hear their opinions, and then carefully study their own work and make sincere efforts decisively to improve the work of our Party which carries the destiny of the country on its shoulders.

THE TASKS AND ROLE OF THE LOCAL ORGANS OF POWER AT THE PRESENT STAGE

Speech Delivered at a Joint Meeting of the People's Committee Chairmen and Leading Party Functionaries of Provinces, Cities and Counties

February 1, 1952

Comrades,

Many comrades referred, in their speeches, to the practical activities of local organs of power in wartime. As revealed in the speeches, there are a lot of shortcomings in the work of our local organs of power. Therefore, I deem it necessary to emphasize once again the fundamental problems concerning the tasks and role of local organs of power at the present stage.

1. THE CHARACTER OF THE PEOPLE'S POWER AND ITS BASIC TASK AT THE PRESENT STAGE

Comrades,

The Government of the Republic—our central organ of state power—and the people's committees at all levels—the local organs of power—are genuine people's power organs of a new type.

After our country was liberated from the yoke of Japanese imperialist colonial rule, our people came to have their own government for the first time. This government is a government organized with the representatives elected by the broad sections of the people including the workers, peasants, working intellectuals and petty bourgeoisie—the absolute majority of the Korean people.

The characteristic features of this power organ lie in the fact that it is a government which was organized by the hands of the people themselves, and which champions the interests of the people and fights for their freedom and welfare. This power organ maintains close ties with the people, relies upon them in its work and enjoys the support of the masses of the people. The organ of people's power is an organ of power that performs its work with the participation of the broad popular masses in it, rooted deep among the masses of the people.

Our people's power exercises dictatorship over the landlords, comprador capitalists, pro-Japanese and pro-U.S. elements and traitors to the nation who are stooges of imperialism and implant its influence, and exercises democracy as far as the people are concerned.

Under the leadership of the Workers' Party of Korea, the vanguard of the working masses, our people's power sets it as its basic task at the present stage to rally around itself the working class and all other sections of the people, and all the patriotic democratic forces under the Democratic Front for the Reunification of the Fatherland and thereby wage a nation-wide struggle against the reactionary Syngman Rheeites representing the traitors to the nation, pro-Japanese and pro-U.S. elements, comprador capitalists and landlords and foreign aggressors, the heinous enemies of the Korean people, and to strive for the complete independence of Korea and the democratic development of the country, for the building of an independent national economy and the improvement of the people's living standard.

As you all know, the seizure of power by the working class is but the beginning of the proletarian revolution. Comrade

Stalin said that following the seizure of power by the working class it was necessary to carry out the following three major tasks that confront the dictatorship of the proletariat:

"a) to break the resistance of the landlords and capitalists who have been overthrown and expropriated by the revolution, to liquidate every attempt on their part to restore the power of capital;

"b) to organize construction in such a way as to rally all the working people around the proletariat, and to carry on this work along the lines of preparing for the elimination, the abolition of classes;

"c) to arm the revolution, to organize the army of the revolution for the struggle against foreign enemies, for the struggle against imperialism."

Our Party and people's power have been and are guided by these principles laid down by Comrade Stalin.

Since they took power into their hands the Korean people have steadily fought to shatter the attempt of the foes of the people—pro-Japanese and pro-U.S. elements, traitors to the nation, comprador capitalists and landlords—to restore their power. Our people's power, under the leadership of the Party, has prepared the political and economic forces to secure the reunification, independence and democratic development of the country by carrying out the democratic reforms and pushing ahead with the economic and cultural construction in the northern half; and it organized and has striven to strengthen its people's army capable of crushing foreign aggressors and the armed forces of internal reactionaries.

But under the conditions in which the territory is divided and the nation split in two, we could not gear all the country's resources and the strength of the entire people to the work of democratic construction. Moreover, due to the surprise armed invasion launched by the enemy on June 25, 1950, peaceful construction in our country was suspended and our people entered the Fatherland Liberation War to safeguard the independence and freedom of the country.

As mentioned above, notwithstanding the complex situation

in our country after liberation and the very short period of our peaceful construction, we have built in this period the powerful democratic base in the northern half and accumulated the political, economic and military forces to consolidate and safeguard it.

Already since the days of the Provisional People's Committee of North Korea the Korean people, under the leadership of the Workers' Party of Korea, carried out the democratic reforms of historic significance such as the agrarian reform, the nationalization of industries, the enforcement of the Labour Law and the Law on Equality of the Sexes and performed tremendous work to consolidate the democratic system. The people's power carried out the work of economic and cultural construction such as rehabilitating and developing the national economy and national culture rapidly, improving the material and cultural life of the masses of the people and training large numbers of native cadres needed for different branches, reared our People's Army into an army capable of fighting as well as it does today and educated the people in progressive ideas.

Had it not been for these preparations, we could not have thwarted the enemy's advance and gone over to counterattack to drive him down to the Rakdong-gang River area, nor could we fight against the armed invaders of American and British imperialism for a long time as at present.

All these achievements are the great victory won by the entire Korean people under the leadership of the Workers' Party of Korea, and the outcome of the strenuous struggle waged by our people's power. These achievements show that the new form of power organ the Korean people set up by their own hands is an excellent form of government fitting to the actual conditions of our country.

2. THE FATHERLAND LIBERATION WAR AND THE PEOPLE'S POWER

Our people's power demonstrated its advantages not only in the period of peaceful construction but also during the war. The Fatherland Liberation War has proved that this power is the only power that can defend the independence and freedom of our country from the encroachment of foreign aggressors and lead the Korean people to welfare.

The Korean people could reorganize all work in the country on a war footing and mobilize everything for victory at the front without confusion when the U.S. imperialists launched a surprise attack, because they had further strengthened their state power and reinforced the People's Army. As a result, the Korean people under the leadership of the Party and the Government could attain the victory of today in the 19 months of battle against longer odds.

In the war the Korean people inflicted a heavy blow upon the enemy and convinced him that he would never be able to subjugate the Korean people.

The enemy reckoned that he could conquer our country and our people at a stroke with his tanks, aircraft and superior military techniques. The Korean people of today, however, are not the Korean people of the days of the feudal Li dynasty, nor are they a people who live under such corrupt rule as at that time. The Korean people today are a people led by the Workers' Party of Korea armed with the Marxist-Leninist ideology, a people who have seized power in their hands, a liberated people who are ready to fight to the last drop of their blood for the freedom and independence of their country.

The war waged by the Korean people against the U.S. imperialist plunderers today is not only a Fatherland Liberation War to defend the independence and freedom of our country from imperialist aggression but also a war to safeguard peace and security throughout the world. The heroic struggle of our people against the armed invasion of the U.S. imperialists and their lackeys has become the banner of liberation movement for the colonial and oppressed nations in the East. That is why all the progressive peoples of the world support the just struggle of our people and the public opinion and attention of the whole world have been focussed on the Korean war.

Our people's power has withstood severe trials and grown stronger in the course of the war.

The Korean people infinitely love this new type of power which is their own power. Because they are convinced that only this power is a genuine power of the Korean people, that only this power can safeguard the independence and freedom of our country against imperialist invasion and carry the Fatherland Liberation War to victory, and that only this power can ensure a happy life for our people and lead our country along the road of democracy and socialism after winning victory in the war.

Our most important task at present is to annihilate the enemies, defend the independence and freedom of our country and safeguard the Democratic People's Republic of Korea. The U.S. imperialists have not yet given up their wild design to turn the whole of Korea into a colony and are attempting to extend the war. The enemies are rearming Japanese imperialism, the inveterate enemy of our people, and are manoeuvring to conquer Asia and ignite another world war, using our country as a springboard for aggression. Our victory in the Fatherland Liberation War, therefore, will be a victory not only for the Korean people but for the peoples of Asia and the whole world who aspire to peace.

We are winning victory and will be surely emerge victorious from this sacred war.

Some people ask, "How can we defeat the mighty U.S. imperialists?" Some functionaries of *ri* people's committees in Kaepung, Yonbaek and Ongjin, areas which were once under the rule of the traitorous Syngman Rheeites, say: "The Government of the Republic is a genuine government for the Korean people and the people's power is a genuine power for the Korean people. The policies pursued by the Government of the Republic are policies truly for the Korean people. You are right both in word and in deed. But once the Yankees come, we will all be killed as we are engaged in the work of the *ri* people's committee." They say, "How can Korea win the battle with America? Korea was no match for Japan, and how can she win the battle with America which is bigger and stronger than Japan?"

We can win, however. The 19 months of war furnishes ample proof of this. The Yankees have made every desperate effort but failed to conquer the Korean people.

If we fight alone, in isolation, that will be another question, of course. Ours is an era when the banners of socialist and democratic countries are fluttering from the Elbe to the Pacific.

We are not fighting single-handed. The Chinese People's Volunteers sent by the Chinese people are fighting side by side with us. Standing on our side are the people of the People's Democracies headed by the Soviet Union, the strongest in the world, and the freedom-loving peoples throughout the world, and the colonial and oppressed peoples in the East support us. So, we are mightier than the enemy.

Also, from the strategic viewpoint, the Korean People's Army and the Chinese People's Volunteers are fighting in its own land and at the approach to their territory, and they are fighting without being separated from their solid rear. But the U.S. imperialist aggressor troops are fighting thousands of miles away from their rear. So we have by far greater advantages in this respect, too.

Let us see the morale of the soldiers. The U.S. soldiers were sent to the Korean front for money and the troops of Britain and other countries were brought against their will. As they wage an unjust, aggressive war, they have no justifiable objective in the war. As days go by, they come to realize on whose account and for whom they die a worthless death on the Korean front. That is why their morale is declining day by day.

But quite contrary is the case of our People's Army and the

Chinese People's Volunteers. They are fighting a death-defying battle because they know that they are waging a just war for the independence and freedom of their countries, for the peoples and for the revolution.

What, then, are we lacking as compared with the enemy? In the military aspect our technical preparations are poorer than the enemy's. Technique, however, is not inbred. Even one who is not acquainted with it can acquire it. Our military technique develops and improves every day. Time works in our favour. As time passes, our army will be equipped better technically and grow into a stronger army, and will eventually achieve the ultimate victory.

In order to win victory we must muster up all the internal forces better, perform all work more properly and further consolidate the people's committees, our people's power organs.

What should our organs of people's power do in order that we can win a long-drawn-out fight against the enemy?

The organs of people's power should further enhance their role, mobilize all forces for victory in the war by maintaining closer ties with the people and rallying them around the power more firmly, and heighten their political consciousness so that they may display activity in all work.

3. THE TASKS AHEAD FOR THE CONSOLIDATION OF THE PEOPLE'S POWER

In order to strengthen the people's power the following tasks should be performed:

First, a struggle must be waged against the ideological residues of Japanese imperialism and the remnants of obsolete feudalistic ideas, and against the bureaucratic style of work which is their manifestation.

The ideological residues of Japanese imperialism do tremendous harm to our work in every respect. Of course, it is impossible to solve the question of rooting out these old ideological remnants in a short span of time. A persistent struggle must be waged for a long time.

To combat the ideological vestiges of Japanese imperialism, we should further intensify political education among the masses and energetically conduct the work of patiently explaining and bringing government policies home to the broad masses of the people.

Why are the ideological survivals of Japanese imperialism revealed much with us, above all in running the government?

The Korean people have had no government of their own and, accordingly, had no experience in running the government because they were in colonial bondage to Japanese imperialism for nearly half a century. If there are any who have ever served in power organs, they are a handful of pro-Japanese elements and only a few elders who had participated in the feudal government of the Li dynasty before.

What the absolute majority of our functionaries saw and heard were things Japanese. The Japanese imperialists ruled the Korean people by bureaucratic, police methods. Consequently, even those who did not serve with Japanese imperialism's ruling organs were naturally affected by its ideology, let alone those who did.

Some of the functionaries in the people's power organs have not yet got rid of the ideological survivals of Japanese imperialism. Oblivious of the fact that they are the people's representatives elected from among the people, they behave themselves like officials of Japanese imperialist days and dictate to the people. These functionaries do not realize that those who work in the organs of people's power are by no means bureaucrats but servants of the people. Though they have come from among the people and have been elected by the people, they forget it once they are elected. They spoke the language of the worker or the peasant and were modest until yesterday, but after their election as representatives of the people they start using niminy-piminy words and behave themselves in a bureaucratic and arrogant manner. In other words, they become not cadres of the people's power in the service of the people but bureaucrats.

In some villages, the people till the lands of *myon* or *ri* people's committee chairman, raise money for him on the occasion of his birthday or other feasts, and are saddled with various financial burdens, besides taxes, under this or that pretext. And a certain county people's committee chairman in Hwanghae Province had a cow slaughtered to give a banquet in celebration of his decoration with an order, and then made the people pay for the cow. All these facts show that some of our functionaries are turning into bureaucrats.

Many of our functionaries act in the fashion of Japanese imperialist officials when collecting taxes and, what is worse, they commit such a preposterous act as to make state purchases on credit. Even when collecting the tax in kind some functionaries do it in the way of forced delivery practised in the Japanese imperialist days and do not hesitate to ransack rice-bins or clothes-boxes of the people.

What is the difference between such acts and those of *myon* chiefs, county heads and policemen under Japanese imperialist rule? There is no difference. If there is any, one is the people's committee chairman and the other is the Japanese imperialist official, but their bureaucratic acts are the same.

Without getting rid of such bureaucratic acts on the part of the functionaries of the people's power organ we cannot strengthen the bonds with the people, and no decision or law, however good, can produce effect. We must know that we are not bureaucrats but servants of the people elected by them.

Besides excessive acts of bureaucracy, we should combat the bureaucratic work style which finds expression in all work in this or that way.

Instead of paying heed to the voices of the people, meeting their demands and using the method of explanation and persuasion in conducting their work, some of our cadres issue orders and commands to the people and bring pressure to bear upon them so that they divorce themselves from the people.

These bureaucrats do not bother to know what the masses

want but assert that anything they do is right, nor do they trouble themselves to heed the advice of others and the voices of the masses. This kind of persons, when going down to local areas, do not give ear to the voices of the people but listen only to flatterers and take consolation from their false reports, and subject their subordinates to abusive language if ever they advance any opinion, thus giving them no opportunity to tell the superiors of their opinions on work. Therefore, the lower units report to the higher organs only what is good, and try to conceal what is bad as best they can for fear of it coming to the knowledge of the superior organs or other people.

Such practice is manifested because the superiors hold down the subordinates for no reason, do not carefully study what sorts of troubles and hardships confront the lower units and smooth out the difficulties for them, nor help them to achieve success in their work by providing them with conditions for work.

For example, though autumn ploughing is not completed, the *ri* reports to the *myon* that it has been completed 100 per cent, so does the *myon* to the county and the county to the province. The provincial people's committee chairman also reports the same to the centre though he knows this fact.

Let us have a look into the question of tax in kind. Complaints are made against the unreasonable assessment of tax in kind in some localities. What is the reason?

The unwarrantable assessment of tax in kind is due to the mishandling of things already at the time of spring sowing. The area not sown to crops is reported as sown, while the higher authorities assess the tax in kind on the basis of such reports without investigating into the real state of affairs.

The county people's committee chairman does not collect the tax in kind according to a correct assessment, but even when crop yields are poor, he reads the face of his superior and, if the superior seems to be in a good mood, he puts in a word—impossible; and if he is out of humour, he says without hesitation that it is possible. The upshot is that too heavy a burden of taxation is imposed on the peasants in the way of uniform allotment. So, the tax in kind is not collected correctly in different localities—too much in some cases and too little in the other.

In certain local districts, when collecting the tax in kind, they do not take into account the actual conditions but press the peasants for delivery within the set time and are strict only about the rate of collection. Consequently, unripe grains are gathered in, which does tremendous harm both to the peasants and the state. There is another case where the peasants are urged to deliver rice even by purchasing it in order to fill up their quotas although floods have rendered it totally impossible to collect the tax in kind from them. All these practices show the serious bureaucratic style of work on the part of our functionaries.

If we do not rectify this bureaucratic method of work, we will inevitably divorce ourselves from the people and may spoil our just cause. We may thus foster discontent among the peasants and estrange ourselves from them even though we have given them land and instituted the excellent system of tax in kind.

Despite these serious defects in the work of the functionaries of government organs, our people trust our Party and Government. Though the tax in kind is assessed incorrectly in a way of allotment, the peasants deliver it to the state as required without complaint, saying, "War must need lots of rice." If we continue to follow this bureaucratic method of work just because the peasants do not complain, it will do much harm to our work and discredit the people's power in the eyes of the broad masses of the people.

Bureaucracy has been revealed in the cloth production drive too. This drive is a splendid patriotic movement to satisfy the demands of the army and relieve the war victims. But the bureaucrats are spoiling this patriotic movement.

The centre fixed a three-month term for the production of fabrics but, in order to perform the feat of completing it before the deadline, the province shortened the term fixed by the centre by 20 days, the county by another 20 days, the *myon* again by 20 days and the *ri* by yet another 20 days. In the end, only ten days were left out of the set term of 90 days for the people, the actual producers. The people make every effort but can never fulfil their assignments in ten days. But they are dunned so hard that some peasants cannot but put out the fabrics kept for the marriage of their daughters or sons and those peasants who have not got them buy them in the market at high prices for delivery. So, it is natural that the people should harbour grievances.

This is just an act of shirking one's responsibility no matter what will become of the masses, an act of establishing one's fame at the expense of the masses. The cloth production drive is a good campaign, but it produced a harmful effect in the long run as it was conducted in a bureaucratic way.

Discontent is fostered among the peasants in this way since some functionaries of power organs do their work in a bureaucratic manner. When the peasants become discontented, however, some functionaries say, "Why, the peasants grumble because they are backward. We needn't care about it." This is wrong. This is an act of spoiling our work. We should carefully study and analyse the people's demands and public opinion and take measures.

And when they conduct a work, the bureaucrats do not enlist the subordinates and activists widely in it, but take it upon themselves and try to carry it out at their discretion, thereby making a mess of the work. We should combat such bureaucratic style of doing work arbitrarily. Many of our power organs often adopt decisions conflicting with local conditions, because they take no heed of the opinion of the lower units and fail to know well how matters stand with them, and even if they adopt good decisions, they do not bring into full play the creative initiative of the masses of the people in their implementation but execute them in a bureaucratic way, with the result that the work goes amiss.

Take autumn ploughing for instance. Of course, autumn ploughing is a good thing, and must be done to increase the harvest. But though it is a good thing, the peasants just scatter earth over the fields perfunctorily and report to the higher authorities that they have finished the ploughing, because you simply urge the peasants to do it without taking account of their interests. It is all an outcome of the bureaucratic style of work on the part of the functionaries of our power organs who are ignorant of how matters really stand at the lower levels, do not give ear to the views of the people but do their jobs in a formalistic way, eager only to distinguish themselves.

Ideological survivals of Japanese imperialism which linger in our minds find expression also in the fact that some of our functionaries do not work as one with the masses but behave themselves like bureaucrats or nobles. Cadres do not take part at all in such voluntary labour service as road repair work but only mobilize the people. Such functionaries, too, were ordinary people until yesterday, but now that they have either been elected or appointed people's committee chairman or interior service sub-station head, they think their dignity would be compromised if they work together with the people. What a shameful and deplorable thing! What is wrong if you work with the people, breathe the same air as they do and give explanations to them at a time of hardship? Nothing is more honourable than working with the people. Nevertheless, some of our functionaries lose sight of the people once they come to hold the post of "head." We should fight against such goings-on.

The functionaries of the organs of people's power should become genuine workers for the people, who rely on the people in work, pay regard to their interests, persuade and educate them instead of dictating to them, always learn from them and serve them in all sincerity.

That we should expose and rectify the shortcomings in the work of the power organs and eliminate the ideological remnants of Japanese imperialism and the bureaucratic style of work still found in some of the functionaries does not in any way mean that taxes should not be collected or that procurement work should not be carried out. It does not mean either that we should not combat the petty bourgeois ideas of the peasants.

Among the peasantry there are both progressive peasants

and backward ones who look only after their own well-being without caring about the interests of the state. We should do all we can to support the toiling peasants and, at the same time, fight with the backward greedy peasants who seek to get a good living only for themselves by taking advantage of the hardships of others.

We should shape correct policies and execute them properly for the benefit of the country and the people. We should collect taxes exactly as assessed by the state, and ought to carry out the necessary procurement work. There should never be the practice of procuring things on credit.

We should combat the backward ideas of some peasants who falsify their accounts of crop yields and are reluctant to deliver choice grains for the tax in kind and to pay taxes to the state in time and are engaged in speculation trading on the difficult wartime conditions. We should intensify ideological education and Party political work among the broad masses of the people on the one hand and should, on the other, strengthen the wartime state discipline and apply the revolutionary laws to such practices as shirking tax payment, cheating the state and indulging in speculation.

Second, we should ensure victory in the Fatherland Liberation War by increasing production and practising economy.

The war is going on, and the enemy would not quit our soil soon. We should fight on till the enemy desists from his aggressive acts.

Our factories should ensure smooth production and produce more in spite of the difficult wartime conditions. They should, in this way, turn out war supplies and daily necessaries in larger quantities so as to meet the demands of the front and the rear.

The peasants should increase the production of grain. More grain and raw materials should be turned out by cropping all the lands without leaving even an inch uncultivated, and stockbreeding should be developed further so as to meet the demand for meat and solve the problem of draft animals as well.

We should devote all our efforts to the struggle for increased production to satisfy the demands of the front and stabilize the people's livelihood.

We should endeavour to turn out for ourselves everything needed in the war, which can be produced in our country. It is wrong to look simply to foreign aid instead of producing what can be produced by our own efforts.

We should so organize work as to keep up production day and night. The production plan for 1952 is by no means an easy one. However, if the plan could not be fulfilled under the wartime circumstances, it would be a serious crime against the country and the people, and a disgrace to ourselves before the men and officers of our People's Army and the Volunteers who are fighting on the front at the cost of their blood. We should try every possible means and method in our power to fulfil and overfulfil the production plan for this year.

Even in conditions of continued war, we should make more investments in production by practising economy in every way, stabilize the people's life by properly adjusting commodity prices and secure victory in the war by supplying the front and the rear with more war supplies and products.

To this end, the broad masses of the people should be brought to display greater activity and creative initiative and roused to the wartime drives for increased production and economization.

The people's committees at all levels are confronted today with the following economic tasks:

1. Proper guidance should be given in agriculture and the patriotic zeal of the peasants be further enhanced so that they tide over difficulties and obstacles by virtue of mutual co-operation and self-reliance and do all they can to overfulfil the 1952 plan for an increased production of grain.

2. Guidance should be given so that the workers, handicraftsmen and members of co-operatives may turn out war supplies and daily necessaries in larger quantities and the livelihood of the people should be stabilized through proper organization of the work of commodity circulation.

3. In order to ensure the livelihood of the workers and

office employees, measures should be taken to meet the needs of their livelihood in kind, casting aside the tendency of merely raising their wages.

To this end, an extensive movement should be launched to draw the dependents of the factory and office workers into production by organizing side lines and producers' co-operatives.

4. We should stringently economize in food and materials and distribute them properly in order to wage a prolonged war.

It should be seen to that many people are enlisted in production by cutting down the staff to the minimum and reducing the non-productive labour force. We have now very much non-productive manpower. Although factories and enterprises have been ravaged and production has decreased, the productive and non-productive labour forces have increased by nearly 70,000 men as against the prewar years, even not counting the army and the interior service organs. This means that our functionaries have not simplified the clerical institutions but extended them wantonly during the war, augmenting the non-productive labour as against the peacetime. This sort of thing is impermissible in wartime conditions. The Cabinet, therefore, should simplify the apparatuses of the administrative offices of the state and divert the surplus work force to the rural areas for agricultural production.

We should exercise strict control over irregularities in rationing and ensure the correct rationing of food and other supplies. To this end, the food administration organs and the goods distribution agencies should be assigned people who are politically dependable and well versed in calculation and statistics.

Strict control should be exercised over the consumption of materials and food. A mass struggle should be unfolded against squandering and pilfering state materials.

5. Financial discipline should be tightened.

The movement for strengthening financial discipline was conducted for some time after the meeting of activists of the Pyongyang city Party organization. However, it has now subsided again as if everything had been settled. This movement is not yet extensive enough among the entire people, among all our Party members and among the cadres, functionaries of the state organs and servicemen. The movement for strengthening the financial discipline should be conducted as a whole-Party, all-people movement.

State revenue has dropped sharply as against peacetime, since we have been barred from peaceful construction for 19 months now. Under the conditions in which many factories have been demolished and transport obstructed due to the bombings and barbarities of the enemy, the production and revenue have dwindled, while expenditures and consumption have greatly increased.

Nevertheless, some people do not take into account such grave circumstances but behave selfishly to preserve the same living conditions as in peacetime. Government functionaries, unable to endure hardships and ideologically corrupt, often commit irregularities and violate financial discipline: they conduct trade hand in glove with profiteers, pilfer and sell off state goods, use state property to give banquets for the purpose of winning the favour of their superiors or to buy and present gifts to individuals, squander state property in purchasing unnecessary office supplies and equipment, and so on. We should fight relentlessly against such dishonest acts of pilfering and squandering state property.

Some people's committees, when asked to strengthen the state financial discipline, impose a considerable amount of financial burdens, besides taxes, upon the people under the pretext of economizing on state property. This is a more serious practice.

The tightening of financial discipline means precisely the strengthening of Party spirit. Those who strive to spare even a penny in the difficult wartime conditions are men of strong Party spirit who fight sincerely for the Party, the state and the people.

It should be borne in mind that the struggle against violations of financial discipline and squandering of state property is a struggle to get rid of the ideological remnants of Japanese imperialism and the influence of capitalism. Without liquidating the survivals of the old Japanese imperialist ideas and strengthening the financial discipline, it is impossible either to win victory in the war or build a wealthy and powerful, independent and democratic state.

Therefore, we should see that the entire Party is mobilized to wage a relentless struggle against negative practices of all shades such as embezzlement, pilfering, squandering and selfishness which have been left over by Japanese imperialist rule, and to further strengthen the financial discipline of the state.

Third, the functionaries of the people's power organs should properly organize and lead the administrative work.

1. To give correct guidance to the work of the people's power organs, it is necessary, above anything else, to organize all work in a planned way and enhance the sense of responsibility of the leading functionaries.

The functionaries of our Party and government bodies should deal with all work with a high sense of responsibility, and draw up a correct plan for its execution after a deep study and detailed analysis of it.

After the plan has been mapped out, organizational work is also necessary to put it into effect.

Then, it is essential to organize a checkup on the implementation of the plan after it has been worked out and organizational work conducted for its execution. The checkup should be carried out not merely for checkup's sake but to help correct shortcomings. It should be conducted by the responsible functionaries personally and not by the subordinates.

You must learn to take stock of any work after or in the course of carrying it out. You should thus turn to good account in your future activities the experience you have gained in taking stock of the work.

Along with this, all work should be guided not in a general, monotonous way but in an analytic, concrete way.

2. In their activities the city and county people's committees should put stress on the *ri* people's committees.

The *ri* people's committee is the power organ at the lowest level which works in direct contact with the people. That the city and the county people's committees should lay the main emphasis on the work of the *ri* people's committee means, therefore, that priority in their work should be given to the rural areas and factories. The masses are not in the offices of the city and county people's committees but in the rural areas and at the factories. The work of a people's committee divorced from the masses will produce no results but will turn into a bureaucratic affair.

The work level of our *ri* people's committees today is very low. The functionaries of the city, county, *myon* people's committees, therefore, should go down to the *ri* people's committees, directly render them practical assistance and teach them how to organize work and how to get in touch with the masses and induce the masses to take part in the activities of the *ri* people's committees. Also, they should explain government decisions and ordinances to the *ri* people's committee cadres so that they have a correct understanding of them and put them into effect correctly.

You should know that if the work of the *ri* people's committee goes off well, all work will shape out well and, if not, it will go amiss.

3. You should not conduct work arbitrarily but do it collectively. You should not take all work upon yourselves and make a mess of it but give assignments to many people and organize and encourage them to display creative initiative in their respective work. Only then can you achieve success.

This, however, does not mean at all that the people's committee chairman should sit idle warming his chair after he has given out assignments to his subordinates. You are mistaken if you think, "I'm a big shot, so I needn't work" or "This sort of matter concerns only the rank and file, and the chairman needn't care about it." You should combat such a backward idea. Some comrades say that they can work as chairman, but not as department chief. Then, what is the chairman? No one has ever become a chairman because he was born under a lucky star. He has been elected chairman so that he may do more and better work, organize and direct work.

Many of our people's committee chairmen today have no clear idea of how matters stand at the lower levels. Once they become "heads," they try to put on airs, to start with. When asked about something, they reply that it is not they but the section chiefs who know about it. A people's committee chairman of this sort would have to be always accompanied by section chiefs. "Heads" are appointed not for cutting a wide swath but for doing work.

In order to organize and direct any work you should have, above all, a good knowledge of it, and when you do not know it, you should not feel ashamed to learn but study it hard.

You should become functionaries who know how to organize work scrupulously, how to direct it in a concrete way and how to mobilize the masses in the course of carrying it out, and should set an example to people in every action.

4. You should know how to allocate and appoint cadres properly.

An end should be put to such practice as to appoint cadres without carefully studying them and to transfer them right and left. You should know that to study the cadres constantly and train them well is precisely the work of strengthening the people's committee.

5. Efforts should be made to elevate the political and theoretical standards of the people's committee functionaries at all levels.

Each political worker should become a fighter who has a correct understanding of the Party's political line and the government policies, bring them home to the masses and strive devotedly for the Party and the people. The political workers should equip themselves closely with the Marxist-Leninist world outlook in order to have an unshakable faith in the justness of our cause and its victory and organize and direct work with foresight.

You should successfully carry out all these tasks, and thereby enhance the functions and role of our people's power organs and mobilize the strength of the entire people for victory in the war.

THE ORGANIZATIONAL AND IDEOLOGICAL CONSOLIDATION OF THE PARTY IS THE BASIS OF OUR VICTORY

Report Delivered at the Fifth Plenary Meeting of the Central Committee of the Workers' Party of Korea

December 15, 1952

1

Comrades,

One year has already passed since the Fourth Plenary Meeting of the Party Central Committee. The past year is radiant with the great successes which the Korean people achieved in their righteous struggle against the U.S. imperialist armed invaders and their lackeys—the traitorous Syngman Rhee clique.

This period has witnessed many changes in the international arena and internal life. In international life, the might of the socialist and democratic camp headed by the Soviet Union has grown further and, in contrast, the general crisis of the world capitalist system has become more serious.

Encouraged by the decisions of the 19th Congress of the Communist Party of the Soviet Union and the wise leadership of Comrade Stalin, the Soviet people have embarked upon the implementation of the magnificent programme for the building of communism. The Soviet Union, while carrying into effect the plan for the building of communism, pursues the policy of peace and friendship among nations.

Comrade Stalin's work *Economic Problems of Socialism in the U.S.S.R.* has made a new contribution to the treasure house of Marxism-Leninism. This work has provided a powerful weapon to the peoples fighting for the building of a new life, and enriched our knowledge of the laws of development of capitalism and the contradictions between capitalist states. Comrade Stalin further developed the Marxist-Leninist theory concerning the objective laws of development of modern society and made it clear, by reviewing the course of World War II and all the events that ensued, that world capitalism entered on the second phase of its general crisis.

Many countries in Europe and Asia broke away from the capitalist system and formed People's Democracies, with the result that there came into being the world socialist system headed by the Soviet Union. This strengthened the forces of peace and democracy to a great extent, and markedly weakened the reactionary forces of war and imperialism headed by the U.S. imperialists.

Having taken the path of socialism, the People's Democracies, together with the Soviet Union, achieved great successes in building a new life in the past year. The working masses of those countries have become convinced through their own experience that only the road of socialism can bring steady economic advancement to each country. They have come to the realization that socialism changes the once oppressed and exploited labouring masses into full masters of their own destinies, into conscious creators of history.

The results of the economic development in the People's Democracies show that the economic blockade policy of the U.S. imperialists against the socialist and democratic camp has come to grief. Such blockade only backfired to its proponents. As for the socialist and democratic camp, the countries of this camp, in answer to the blockade of the imperialists, formed their own world socialist market in opposition to the world capitalist market by achieving greater solidarity and strengthening economic co-operation among themselves.

With the world capitalist market dwindling, the struggle has become more acute between the imperialist states for goods markets and raw materials sources. Today, U.S. imperialism, the most aggressive and brutal, not only plunders the peoples of the underdeveloped countries but also is trying frantically to put the economies of other capitalist countries under its control. So, contradictions between the United States and Britain, between the United States and France or various other European countries are growing sharper with every passing day, and the struggle is fierce also between West Germany and France, between Britain and Japan, and between other capitalist countries.

The cracks in the aggressive Atlantic military bloc whipped up by the U.S. imperialists are widening more and more owing to the contradictions between the United States and Britain, between the United States and France or other member states of the bloc. Despite the fact that the United States is resorting to all possible means in the hope of covering up the serious differences among the member states of the bloc, the governments of other member states are voicing their discontent more frequently at the undisguised highhandedness of the United States under the pressure from the masses of the people and due to economic difficulties.

In an attempt to find a way out of this crisis of the capitalist system, the U.S. imperialists entered on the road of preparing for a new world war. To that end, they are carrying on a hysterical armament race and are militarizing the economies of their dependent countries, inciting war psychosis, stepping up propaganda against the Soviet Union, the People's Republic of China and other People's Democracies, and are rampant to ignite war wherever possible. The armed invasion of our country by the United States, too, is a product of the policy of aggression and war ignition long pursued by the U.S. imperialists.

Since they launched out on the invasion against the Democratic People's Republic of Korea, the U.S. imperialists have more openly revealed their true colours as aggressors in the eyes of the peoples the world over. The armed invaders headed by the U.S. imperialists have destroyed peaceful towns and villages in our country at random and slaughtered innocent people, aged and children, thereby evoking hatred and indignation not only from our people but from all the peace-loving, honest-minded peoples of the world. Thus, the voices of hundreds of millions of people throughout the world are growing louder every day demanding an end to U.S. imperialism's aggression of Korea and protesting against the use of chemical and bacteriological weapons by the U.S. savages.

To justify their policy of war and plunder, the U.S. imperialists and the scholars in their pay advertise the reactionary theory of overpopulation and are singing the praises of atomic and bacteriological weapons designed for mass destruction of human beings. The American Malthusian Pendell published a book with the title of *Population on the Loose* in 1951, in which he openly prated that some 700 million people, or about one third of the world population, must be cut from the globe.

Our Korea has become an experimental ground for the U.S. gangsters to practise their techniques of murder and put into reality their man-hating ideas. Why the U.S. generals have delayed the ceasefire talks for one and a half years and sought to break them off by all means is nobody's secret.

On September 4, 1952, Eisenhower, who has recently been elected U.S. President, stated, "Today our initiative, illusions and productive system are all gathered into the war and prospect of the war. Our economy is a war economy and our prosperity is a war prosperity." This clearly shows what a shameless and deceptive empty talk the U.S. propaganda on the "love of peace" is.

As is universally known, the war has brought fabulous profits to U.S. billionaires. They have earned a stupendous amount of dollars at the expense of blood and sufferings of the Korean people. The insatiable U.S. big businesses make every attempt to expand the Korean war on all accounts and turn it into a war of aggression against the People's Republic of China and the Soviet Union. They are trying to break off the cease-fire talks, turning down our reasonable proposals unconditionally.

As all of you know, the Soviet delegation put forward a new proposal on the Korean question at the Seventh Session of the U.N. General Assembly. The proposal suggested that the military actions be stopped at once and the work of repatriation of all war prisoners be handed over to the Commission for Peaceful Settlement of the Korean Question in accordance with the draft Armistice Agreement already agreed upon by both warring sides. Nevertheless, this time too, the U.S. imperialists used their voting machine in the United Nations to vote down this reasonable proposal aimed at the cessation of war in Korea.

The U.S.-British interventionists have been carrying on the war of aggression for over two and a half years now in their efforts to conquer our freedom-loving people by force of arms. During this period the armed invaders lost hundreds of thousands of men and officers and a vast amount of weapons and war materiel. Thus, all their attempts to conquer the Korean people and strangle the Democratic People's Republic of Korea ended each time in an ignominious failure.

In their fresh attempt to strangle our young Republic by all means, the U.S. generals are now hatching a sinister intrigue to replace their troops with Japanese and Chiang Kai-shek's mercenaries. But there is no doubt that this intrigue, too, will fall through and end in disgrace for its organizers.

Our people, who are in the third year of the war, are receiving wholehearted aid from the Soviet Union, the People's Republic of China, Poland, Czechoslovakia, Romania, Bulgaria, Hungary, the German Democratic Republic, the People's Republic of Mongolia and many other countries, and friendship and solidarity between our Republic and those countries have been further consolidated. The fraternal peoples of the socialist and democratic camp are using all possible means to assist our people in their hard struggle against the U.S. aggressors. The aid given to the fighting people of Korea by the peoples of the fraternal countries is a tangible expression of the true internationalist friendship between the peoples of the socialist and democratic camp.

With the tremendous assistance from the peoples of the fraternal countries and the unanimous support from the peace-loving peoples throughout the world, the Korean people will rout the aggressors and certainly emerge victorious from their just war of liberation for the freedom and independence of the country.

All the events in international life inspire us Korean people with firm confidence in the final victory and indicate that the day is drawing nearer when the U.S. imperialist aggressors and the Syngman Rhee clique will be expelled and wiped out for good from the soil of our country.

2

The situation on the front in the past year is characterized by the fact that both sides, standing face to face fast in the vicinity of the 38th parallel, kept on with fierce offensive and defensive battles.

Our valorous People's Army and Chinese People's Volunteers, while further strengthening the defenses, successfully beat back the enemy's local attacks by active defense and inflicted a tremendous loss of manpower and military materiel on the enemy.

The units of the People's Army and the Volunteers have become more tempered and accumulated rich experience in the course of the protracted defensive battles, and achieved great successes in strengthening themselves qualitatively and technically as well.

Making use of the spare time between battles, we saw to it that the commanding officers of the People's Army summed up their experience, and conducted the work of re-educating them to master advanced military theory and military art. And a movement for creating model companies was unfolded on an extensive scale in the units and each unit was made to concentrate its main efforts on reinforcing the technically weak points. Supply work for the units on the front has been greatly improved and the armament and transport capacity of the units have also been strengthened considerably. Thus, the People's Army units have grown further in quantity and quality. Now our People's Army is doing its utmost to train itself into a powerful army, modernized and regularized further still.

Upholding the slogan, "Everything for victory in the war!" the entire people in the rear have waged a sustained, persistent struggle for the consolidation of the rear and firmly defended the freedom and independence of the country.

The road our Party has traversed leading the people along amid the fierce flames of war was by no means a royal road. It was beset with countless grave difficulties and obstacles. But our Party, successfully overcoming all the difficulties and obstacles, has always emerged victorious from the fierce struggle against the enemies within and without.

We demonstrated to the whole world the solidity and indestructible vitality of our social system in the past course of war. Under the guidance of our Party, our people, full of ardent love for their country and an unshakable determination to safeguard the people's democratic system with their blood, fought at the risk of their lives to drive out the U.S. imperialist aggression army from the soil of their country as soon as possible, displaying unrivalled heroism and an indomitable fighting spirit. The great feats performed by the brave soldiers of our People's Army in the battle line and by the working people in the rear will shine forever in the history of our country.

Our people have achieved considerable successes in all fields of the national economy between the Fourth and the Fifth Plenary Meeting of the Party Central Committee. Thus, we could continue to turn out and supply weapons and all kinds of war materiel to the units of the heroic People's Army, and could stabilize the livelihood of the people in the rear to a certain degree.

In the past year all branches of industry, transport and agriculture of the Republic showed an uninterrupted growth. In 1952 the total output value of state and co-operative industrial organizations increased by 19 per cent as against 1951, the output value of the co-operative industrial organizations scoring an 18 per cent increase.

Thanks to the growth of production registered by the state light industrial factories and the co-operatives and to the aid from the Soviet Union, the People's Republic of China and other People's Democracies, the retail commodity turnover of the state and co-operative trading organizations increased to 232 per cent in 1952 compared with 1951.

In 1952 our Party and Government took a series of financial and economic measures to secure the stabilization of currency and eliminated deficits from the state budget. The currency stabilization played a big role in improving the planned management of the wartime economy and in stabilizing the livelihood of the labouring masses.

Our transport workers have been ensuring swift goods transport in the teeth of the enemy's frantic bombings by promptly restoring damaged bridges and roads and repairing locomotives and cars. In 1952 the railway freight turnover increased to 113 per cent as against 1951 and the number of rolling stock also grew remarkably.

Our peasants have unfolded a titanic struggle to supply more food to the People's Army and the working people. Though irrigation facilities were destroyed, supply of electric power and chemical fertilizer stopped and labour and animal power ran short owing to the barbarities of the U.S. imperialists, the peasants, undaunted by the enemy's bombings and strafings, finished before the set time all work from spring ploughing to sowing, rice transplanting and harvesting this year, and scored a big success in increasing the production of grain. In 1952 the total grain output increased to 113 per cent as compared with 1951, and the population of livestock has also been increasing steadily.

These successes attained in all branches of the national economy this year provide favourable conditions for the rehabilitation and development of industry and agriculture in the future.

Next year the total output value of our state and co-operative industrial organizations will rise to 123 per cent as against this year; railway freight turnover, to 118 per cent; total grain output, to 105 per cent; and the cattle population will increase by 14 per cent. And the retail commodity turnover of the state and co-operative trading organizations will rise to 117 per cent compared with this year. We have no doubt that these difficult tasks will be successfully fulfilled next year.

The successes achieved in industry and agriculture have enabled the Party and the Government to take a series of measures to improve the material conditions of the working people.

At the instance of our Party Central Committee, the Government of the Republic has exempted the poor peasants from the tax in kind and repayment of the grain loaned out by the state, and increased the food rations to the families of workers, technicians and office employees in order to better the livelihood of the working masses. Steps have been taken to supply winter clothes and shoes to the workers, office employees and college and specialized-school students and provide the working people with dwellings, and, according to the special decision of the Government, free medical care for the working people has been introduced. All these measures have stabilized the living conditions of the workers, office employees and toiling peasants considerably and inspired them to the struggle against the U.S. imperialist aggressors.

As the result of the successful implementation of the line of the Party and the Government on continuing with educational work even under the grim war conditions, most of the children of school age now go to school regularly and all institutions of higher learning of the Republic which had been closed for a time have been reopened to train native cadres.

We are highly proud that the Academy of Sciences, which is the highest sanctuary of science in our country and whose mission it is to organize and direct all scientific research work in a unified way, has been established amid the flames of war. A considerable success has been achieved in literature and art, too, in this period. Many fine works have been created that truthfully depict the life and heroic features of the Korean people fighting against the U.S. imperialist aggressors on the front and in the rear, and they encourage the people to more valiant struggles and patriotic feats.

Our public health establishments, too, are successfully carrying out their assigned tasks. Our health workers promptly and successfully got rid of the serious consequences of the germ weapons used by the U.S. imperialist aggressors.

In the northern half of the Republic where the people are masters of the government and economy, industry and agriculture have been restored in spite of harsh wartime conditions to firmly ensure supplies to the front and the livelihood of the people in the rear, but the situation is quite different in south Korea which is under the rule of the U.S. imperialists and their lackeys, the Syngman Rhee clique.

The U.S. imperialists who rave about "democratic freedom" have set up a ruling system of fascist police terrorism in south Korea and cruelly suppress even the slightest discontent of the people.

Even when "electing" the so-called "legislative organ," the U.S. imperialists and the traitor Syngman Rhee arrested and jailed all of their opponents by force of the military and police and herded the people to the "polls" by threats and blackmail. As a result, the posts in the state organs have been occupied entirely by traitors to the Korean people, who sell out the independence of the country and the interests of the nation.

Owing to the colonial predatory policy of the U.S. imperialists and the country-selling policy of the traitorous Syngman

Rhee clique, the national economy of south Korea is going headlong towards bankruptcy and its people are in the wretched plight of poverty and starvation.

The so-called "agrarian reform" introduced by the Syngman Rhee puppet government in 1951 has further precipitated the bankruptcy of the peasants. They extorted 65-80 per cent of the harvests from the peasants under the name of "land acquisition tax" and levied 265 kinds of exacting taxes upon them. In South Cholla Province alone 10,000 million *won* was collected under the item of the "operational secret service funds."

Such harsh exploitation and plunder of the peasants forced them to quit farm villages and go wandering to towns, and caused agricultural production to drop rapidly. Consequently, grain yields in the southern half known as the granary of Korea have decreased sharply to bring food shortage to over one million tons this year alone.

Industry has also been dislocated in south Korea. The national industry is not supplied with the necessary equipment, raw and other materials, and finds it hardly possible to compete with the floods of U.S. or Japanese goods. In consequence, many factories and enterprises have been closed one after another.

The production of daily necessaries has gone next to nothing in south Korea. Even according to the watered-down data officially released by the traitorous Syngman Rhee clique, in 1952 the textile industry which was said to be the most developed branch in south Korea declined sharply, by 63 per cent, as against the prewar years and the food industry dwindled by 70 per cent.

The bankruptcy of the national industry and the decline of agriculture cause a constant swelling of the unemployed. At present the full-time unemployed number 1,000,000 in south Korea, and the semi-unemployed and war sufferers numbering 14 million are left without any protection, of whom 5 million are living in misery in special camps. Even the starvation wages paid to the employed workers were so sharply reduced after the outbreak of war that they find themselves in such a plight as hardly possible to scrape along. As of September this year, the wage index in south Korea fell by 33.3 per cent compared with June, 1950 and the price index rose 15 times during the same period. Today the number of suicides is increasing markedly all over south Korea owing to living hardships.

In defiance of outrageous police terrorism, the south Korean people support our Republic wholeheartedly and are fighting valiantly against the U.S. imperialist policy of aggression and the treacherous country-selling policy of the Syngman Rhee clique, which have spelled disaster and distress for them. Gaining in scope and strength every day are the activities of the "League of the Anti-Imperialist, National Salvation Struggle" to expose and condemn the barbarities of the U.S. imperialist aggressors and their lackeys and arouse the people to the just struggle, and the guerrilla struggle of the people in the southern half who have risen in arms for the freedom and independence of the country.

All the patriotic people in the northern and the southern half are united firmly around our Party and the Government of the Republic and are heroically fighting to defend the country's freedom and honour against U.S. imperialist aggression.

All the changes in the military, political and economic life at home vividly show that the Korean people will surely win the final victory in their righteous struggle against the aggressors for the country's freedom and independence.

Comrades, we attained great successes in all fields of the national economy including industry and agriculture in 1952, but we still have grave shortcomings.

Many ministries and bureaus fail to turn out goods whose production is fully possible even under the present conditions of war. In the past year these ministries and bureaus, sticking only to the state plans, did not so much as think of producing goods not listed in the plans. If the ministries and bureaus had displayed initiative and activity, a large quantity of varied products could have been turned out in excess of the state plans. No doubt, the State Planning Commission is also responsible for this, for it had failed to make a correct calculation of the production capacities of enterprises under the ministries and bureaus.

I should like to make a few remarks on the activities of each economic establishment.

The Ministry of Heavy Industry not only failed to carry out the production of war supplies stipulated in the state plan satisfactorily, but totally fails to produce certain kinds of munitions and turns out a very little quantity of daily necessities to meet the people's demands. Iron produced by the state flows into the private enterprises, with which individuals make household articles and various kinds of daily necessities and sell them in the market at speculative prices. But nothing of the sort can be seen at our state trading organizations and the consumers' co-operative stores.

The Ministry of Chemical and Building Materials Industries is very sluggish in the work of preparing for the production of cement, hydrochloric acid, nitric acid, fertilizer and other materials urgently needed by the state. The leading functionaries of the Ministry of Chemical and Building Materials Industries say that the work does not go well because it is not long since its establishment. But half a year has already passed since the Ministry was set up. If the functionaries of that organ simply had shown zeal to work actively in keeping with the wartime circumstances, their work would have already been put on the right track.

The Ministry of Light Industry fails in the production of enough cotton fabrics, silk goods, rubber shoes, paper, etc., that are essential for the people's life, and has fulfilled no more than 60 per cent of its plan. Nevertheless, the leading functionaries of the Ministry of Light Industry, too, are working in an easy-going manner without combating to eliminate the shortcomings of the enterprises under their Ministry. At the local textile mills not only much cotton is wasted, but also no small quantity of raw materials is stolen, and production costs are rising and rejects are increasing. Nevertheless, no one would bear the responsibility for this fact.

In particular, the functionaries in every ministry and bureau do not take good care of the machines and equipment imported from foreign countries and direct little concern to their effective use. Consequently, many machines, rusty, damaged and out of order, fail to operate as they should.

A major defect of the Ministry of Railways is that many cars are running empty. Eighty per cent of the cars are run empty back and forth, while there is no end of goods lying about waiting for transportation. It cannot be regarded as an accident that mountains of salt lying in the western areas are not carried properly to the eastern areas.

The Ministry of Agriculture has not yet restored the prewar level in the area of cultivated land. At present as much as 70,000 *chongbo* of land are lying out of crop. This is quite an intolerable thing. Yet, some of the leading functionaries of the Agricultural Ministry harbour the fallacious idea of reducing the land under cultivation pleading the difficult wartime conditions as their excuse, and have gone so far as to back the suggestion of the local people's committee functionaries to leave the land idle.

In agriculture, the poor yields of quite a few crops such as wheat, barley, soy beans and vegetables, are also attributable to the fact that the direction and activity of the functionaries of the Ministry of Agriculture are insufficient and advanced methods of farming have not been widely propagated. Also, this Ministry has not taken measures to increase the gains of the state agro-stock farms. Particularly, the functionaries of the Agricultural Ministry and the local organs of power have not taken exhaustive measures to improve and stabilize the life of the ultra-small peasants.

The Ministry of Finance still falls below the mark in exercising its function of ensuring the strict observance of financial budgetary discipline and inspecting and controlling the work of the financial and credit establishments. As the Financial Ministry failed to conduct the work of inspection and control satisfactorily, the Peasant Bank committed the grave error of lending 60 per cent of its funds to institutions, oblivious of its basic duty to provide loans to the peasants. Taking advantage of this misconduct of business affairs by the Peasant Bank, the usurers bound up the poor peasants in the fetters of debts everywhere. Thus, the Government of the Republic was compelled to take measures to settle the debts of poor peasants appropriately by adopting a Cabinet decision.

The Ministry of Public Health does not take good care of the medicines imported or received as relief goods from foreign countries. As a result, while local hospitals are short of medicines, they are spoilt in the drug warehouse of the Ministry of Public Health. Not only that, tens of million *won's* worth of medicines are stolen from it. And hospitals, too, are poorly managed.

The Ministry of Education has not taken measures to reorganize the educational system and manage the schools well to suit the difficult wartime conditions. Many orphanages are poorly managed and the children are in bad health.

The producers' co-operatives are still turning out goods of low quality and goods not demanded by the people, either. Without paying due attention to this, the central organization of the producers' co-operatives and the organs of people's power have left the work of the co-operatives to follow its own course.

The common shortcomings in the work of all ministries and bureaus are that they lack plan and collective consultation, there is not established a strict system of statistics, calculation and reports, selection and allocation of personnel and their training are unsatisfactory, there is no strong demand for and strict verification of the fulfilment of decisions and instructions.

The Party organizations of all levels and the state and economic institutions should do away with such defects as early as possible and mobilize all efforts and creative initiatives for the successful fulfilment of the national economic plan for 1953.

3

Comrades,

Our Party is fighting in the van of the Korean people, holding high the banner of national independence and sovereignty, against the U.S. imperialists and their running dogs, the traitorous Syngman Rhee clique. The future destiny of the Korean people is wholly dependent upon the issue of this struggle.

This struggle, on the one hand, is an anti-imperialist, national-liberation revolution, the task of which is to defend the freedom and independence of the country against the foreign imperialist aggressors and, on the other, is a democratic revolution of the entire people, the task of which is to throw out the traitorous Syngman Rhee clique, a band of traitors to the nation, landlords and comprador capitalists who are allies and running dogs of the U.S. imperialists in our country, and to safeguard the Republic and integrate the territory under its banner. The enemies of the Korean people are the U.S. imperialist aggressors and the traitorous Syngman Rhee clique, a gang of their minions —pro-Japanese and pro-U.S. elements, traitors to the nation, landlords, comprador capitalists. So, the task of our revolution at the present stage is to destroy the two enemies, internal and external, safeguard the freedom and independence of the country, and realize its reunification under the banner of the Republic.

These two tasks of our revolution are interrelated. For unless the foreign imperialist forces are driven out of the territory of our country, neither the task of national liberation can be achieved nor can the people be freed from the oppression and exploitation of the pro-Japanese elements, traitors to the nation, landlords and comprador capitalists who are under the patronage of the imperialists. We must concentrate all our efforts on crushing and wiping out the U.S. imperialist armed invaders and their stooge—the traitorous Syngman Rhee clique.

The struggle of the Korean people against the U.S. imperialist armed invaders is a struggle for complete liberation and independence of our country and, at the same time, a struggle for world peace and security, and a struggle which serves as the banner of national-liberation movement for the peoples of colonial and dependent countries. For U.S. imperialism is today the chieftain of the international reactionaries and new world war incendiaries, and is playing the role of the international gendarme against the emancipation of the working people and national independence.

The Workers' Party of Korea bears the destiny of the country and the people on its shoulders as the vanguard of the Korean people fighting heroically against the U.S. imperialist armed invaders, and has the sacred internationalist duty to contribute to the common cause of the peoples for peace and progress. Our Party should creditably perform the honourable mission entrusted to it by waging a more resolute struggle, holding high the banner of Marxism-Leninism.

To win ultimate victory in the struggle against the U.S. imperialist aggressors and their stooge—the traitorous Syngman Rhee clique—in defence of the independence of the country and the people's democratic system, we must further consolidate our Party organizationally and ideologically, and unite all the patriotic and democratic forces of the country closely around it.

As you all know, the Fourth Plenary Meeting of the Party Central Committee held in November last year was a meeting of great significance in correcting the "Left" errors found in the Party's organizational work and in consolidating its ranks. Following the Fourth Plenary Meeting of the Party Central Committee, our Party's organizational work has improved markedly and its ranks have grown rapidly in scope and strength.

First, the closed-doorist tendency committed by many Party organizations in the work of increasing the Party membership was rectified, with the result that by October this year hundreds of thousands of best comrades were admitted to our Party from among the servicemen, workers, toiling peasants and working intellectuals who had displayed patriotic zeal and devotion at the front and in the rear. Our Party has today grown and strengthened into a mass political party uniting in its ranks over one million members, a mighty party with 48,933 primary organizations. In our country there is no farm village, work-place or army unit without an organization of our Party or outside its influence. This means that our Party's prestige has risen higher than ever among the broad masses of the people and shows that they are giving active support to its lines and policies.

Here is a table of analysis of the growth of our Party membership in respect of its composition.

COMPOSITION OF THE PARTY MEMBERSHIP

(in percentages)

	July 1, 1950	November 1, 1952
Workers	21.2	22.2
Poor peasants	54.7	57.4
Middle peasants	7.5	3.9
Office workers	11.4	12.5
Students	1.0	1.4
Rich farmers	0.3	0.1
Tradesmen, entrepreneurs, handicraftsmen, men of liberal professions and others	3.9	2.5

As you see, the composition of our Party has improved further as compared with the time when the war broke out. In this period the proportion of workers increased by one per cent, poor peasants by 2.7 per cent, and office workers by 1.1 per cent respectively. In contrast, middle peasants decreased by 3.6 per cent, rich farmers by 0.2 per cent, tradesmen, entrepreneurs, handicraftsmen, men of liberal professions and others by 1.4 per cent respectively.

Second, the Party organizations rectified their error of penalty-first policy committed in the registration of the Party members.

In the course of registering the Party members, our Party organizations committed the error of meting out unwarranted penalties to many members at random. This entailed very serious consequences in which the Party organizations were weakened and Party members' zeal and creative initiative were paralyzed.

The Fourth Plenary Meeting of the Party Central Committee, therefore, decided to cancel, rectify or remove the penalties mechanically meted out by the Party bodies and organizations at various levels. As the result of the execution of the decision, by the end of October this year 29.8 per cent of the cases of expulsion from the Party were cancelled, 62.1 per cent of the cases of demotion from full membership to candidate membership corrected, 69.2 per cent of the penalized Party members were rehabilitated. This clearly shows what a grave error our Party organizations committed while registering the Party members and what a serious damage it would have caused to the strengthening and development of our Party if this error had not been corrected in good time.

Because this error committed by the Party organizations was rectified in good time, the activity of the Party members has increased in Party life and Party work and their conscious discipline has been strengthened. Thus, our Party has become more united and cohesive organizationally and ideologically.

Third, since the Fourth Plenary Meeting of the Party Central Committee, the role of the Party organizations has been enhanced, the Party members have come to take an active part in Party work, criticism and self-criticism become lively within the Party, and inner-Party democracy has been brought into fuller play.

The bureaucratic and formalistic styles of work found in many Party bodies and Party workers began to be rectified and the bonds between the Party and the masses of the people have been further strengthened.

What is noteworthy after the Fourth Plenary Meeting of the Party Central Committee is that undesirable facts in the work of the Party and state organs which were overlooked and concealed before are detected and laid bare. This means that the work of the Party organizations has been strengthened, and the zeal and creative initiative of the Party members elevated.

In this way, after the Fourth Plenary Meeting of the Party Central Committee, the organs, organizations and leading workers of the Party have rectified in the main the "Left" errors they committed in the course of executing its organizational line, and further expanded and strengthened our Party. Today our Party has become the more reliable force of leadership and guidance for the fighting people of Korea.

Comrades, the rapid growth of the Party ranks following the Fourth Plenary Meeting of the Party Central Committee has resulted in a certain degree of discrepancy between the quantitative and the qualitative growth of the Party. During the war our Party ranks absorbed nearly 450,000 new members, the absolute majority of them are green both in the political level and experience in work, and about half of all the recruits barely manage to write and read the Korean letters. These circumstances make it imperative to consolidate the Party qualitatively and, in particular, to strengthen the Party's political education of the members recently admitted.

It is necessary to raise the level of the Party's organizational work and decisively strengthen its work of ideological education in order to consolidate the Party ranks.

4

The organizational work holds a very important place in Party work. Our Party's organizational work has shown a considerable improvement since the Fourth Plenary Meeting, but its level is still low. The Party's organizational work falls short of the level of the Party's political duties and fails to ensure the prompt and correct execution of its decisions.

What, then, are the shortcomings in our Party's organizational work and what should we do to rectify them?

1. There are not a few instances where some Party organizations bent themselves only to the quantitative aspect of the growth of Party membership and took no heed of its qualitative aspect, and carried on the work of increasing the membership in a manner of a shock campaign in violation of the procedure of individual admission to membership, with the result that they afforded opportunities for chance and hostile elements to sneak into the Party ranks. These instances were found in the Party organizations of some mountain regions and coastal areas of South Hamgyong Province.

There is even an instance where the enemy bribed cadres at the *ri* level and used them in anti-popular activities of sabotage in a place where the revolutionary vigilance of the Party organizations was relaxed. This is a very dangerous thing. We must draw a lesson from this fact for our future work.

Some Party organizations in North Hamgyong Province dealt with the matter of admitting people to the Party haphazardly, so that nearly 70 per cent of those whose application for membership was turned down at the county Party committees were politically untrustworthy. This means that the primary Party organizations conducted their work without revolutionary vigilance in constant violation of the repeated instructions of the Party Central Committee to observe the procedure of individual admission in the work of increasing the Party membership.

We will continue to increase the membership in future, but should exercise rigid control to prevent spies, agents provocateurs and timeservers sneaking into the Party ranks. At the same time, we must concentrate our efforts on the endeavour to heighten the class consciousness and the ideological and theoretical standard of the Party members and temper them politically for the qualitative strengthening of the Party. If we fail to give political education to the recruits who joined the Party during the war and to temper them through their Party life and practical work, it will be impossible for our Party to play the role of the vanguard detachment of the working people and increase its fighting capacities.

2. The role of the Party bodies as organs of political leadership and the role of the Party functionaries as political leaders should be enhanced higher.

Many of our Party's leading bodies are now conducting their organizational work in an administrative way, failing to bring Party leadership closer to the lower units.

Many Party organs still now take upon themselves the functions that properly belong to government bodies. This is a practice most inimical to our work. When Party organs take upon themselves the work belonging to the government bodies, the Party organizations will not only become unable to fulfil their own role, but will paralyze the sense of responsibility and creative initiative of the government bodies, and, in the end, will undermine the work of Party organs themselves as well as the work of the government bodies.

In certain localities, for example, the Party organs took into their hands the work of government bodies so excessively that things have come to such a pass as to make the latter impotent to manage independently, without the approval of the Party organs, even the matter of mobilizing just a few oxcarts to assure transport of supplies to the war front. This is quite a dangerous thing. We must see to it that the authority and role of the people's power are enhanced and the government bodies display autonomy and initiative.

The mission of Party organs consists in giving political leadership to the government bodies in their work of executing economic tasks, not taking the work into their hands, and in organizing the work by proper deployment of Party forces to make each Party member play the vanguard role in carrying out the economic tasks.

And the leadership of our Party and government bodies and of their functionaries is still on a very low level. It can be said that a wide gap exists between their work position and their qualifications. Yet, many leading workers do not endeavour to raise their political and practical levels, do not try to learn the professional knowledge and technique of their branches of work and analyse and sum up their work, do not properly employ the method of collective leadership in work.

It is one of the important tasks confronting our Party today to raise the political level and practical ability of the leading functionaries of the Party and state organs. We must direct profound attention to this matter.

We fail to give sufficient living guidance to the local Party organizations, and higher Party bodies are working unsatisfactorily to give concrete and scrupulous assistance to their lower organizations in the execution of the Party's policies. There still remain a harmful armchair, bureaucratic style of work and formalism in many ways in the work of some Party organs. This has encouraged self-conceit, ostentation and flattery among some functionaries in Party work and, furthermore, individualist heroism, a typical feature of bureaucracy, has even given rise to the practice of attempting to replace the Party centre's line with so-called "one's own line."

We can see such examples in the work of the South Hamgyong Provincial Party Committee. The South Hamgyong Provincial Party Committee, on the "initiative" of Comrade Pak Yong who suffered from individualist heroism, sent down to the lower units an appeal drafted under his own name instead of spreading among the people the appeal of the National Peasant Congress sent by the Party Central Committee, and displayed an original "initiative" to unfold a "movement for doubling production" instead of waging a struggle for increased production as told to. Thus, they left untilled a considerable area of farmland and hanged on only to a limited area to conduct the "movement for doubling production," the upshot being that the yields dropped by half instead of increasing double. Also, they did not provide fertilizer to the poor peasants, but supplied it exclusively to the "participants in the movement for doubling production" so that only these could increase production, with the result that the livelihood of the poor peasants has gone from bad to worse. Moreover, they organized ox-sharing teams in favour of the rich farmers, thus "providing" conditions by authority of the Party for the rich farmers to exploit the poor peasants.

We should fight resolutely against such a tendency of individualist heroism. All Party organs should conduct their work of leadership strictly in accordance with the line of the Party centre.

3. Another shortcoming in the organizational work of many Party organs and organizations is that checkup on the execution of decisions and selection and allocation of personnel are not satisfactory.

The aim of Party work lies not in adoption of decisions but in correct execution of the adopted decisions and fulfilment of revolutionary tasks. It cannot be attained without a strict checkup on the execution of decisions. Checkup on the execution of decisions, therefore, is one of the basic forms of our Party's organizational work.

Checkup should not be checkup for its own sake. It must be combined closely with the organizational work for the implementation of decisions. Those who undertake the work of checkup should not confine themselves to finding faults with work, but help the Party organizations to rectify them promptly. Checkup should be conducted without fail in a planned way, with definite aims, and organized with qualified responsible cadres, and it must be seen to that the causes of the manifested defects are brought to light and the way to correct them is clearly indicated.

As Comrade Stalin said, what is of importance in checkup is, first, that fulfilment be checked up systematically and not spasmodically; second, that the work of checking up be entrusted not to second-rate people, but to really dignified, experienced and competent people with sufficient authority; third, that it be confined not to recording events, but be intended to render concrete guidance and assistance on the spot so that the revealed defects can be corrected quickly.

But success cannot be fully assured in work only by checkup.

Selection and allocation of cadres are of great importance in ensuring the implementation of the Party's decisions. Cadres constitute the decisive force of Party and state leadership, and the fate of all work depends upon them.

After a correct political line and policies are laid down, there must be personnel who accept them wholeheartedly, defend them firmly and know how to carry them into practice. Without proper selection and allocation of competent cadres faithful to the Party, whatever excellent line and decisions will remain scraps of paper.

For proper allocation of cadres, it is necessary to carefully study the merits and shortcomings of each of them and know in what kind of work he can put out his ability and talents to the full.

Once a cadre has been placed, it is essential to educate him patiently, give assistance to enable him to deal independently with everything, check up his work and rectify its shortcomings, and uncork bottlenecks in his work in good time. This must be a rule with all upper leading bodies.

With the development of our country, demands for personnel are growing further still and the problem of educating and training cadres and raising their practical qualifications presents itself as a more urgent task. Our work is far from satisfactory in this respect.

A major shortcoming in personnel management is the frequent transfer of cadres. This causes enormous harm both to the activities of our Party organizations, institutions and enterprises and to the progress of cadres themselves.

We must exert all our efforts to rectify all the shortcomings in personnel management, firmly build up the ranks of cadres and train and cultivate them in a revolutionary way.

4. The Party spirit of the Party members should be heightened and an unyielding struggle waged against the liberalistic tendency and the survivals of factionalism.

The heightening of Party spirit means for each member of

the Workers' Party to be boundlessly loyal to the Party and active in its work, to regard the interests of the revolution and of the Party as his life and soul and subordinate his personal interests to them, defend the interests and principles of the Party any time, anywhere and in whatever conditions, fight uncompromisingly against all hues of anti-Party, counter-revolutionary ideas, lead his organizational life in the Party conscientiously and observe its discipline strictly and always to strengthen the bonds between the Party and the masses. Only such a Party member can be a Party member who has Party spirit and whose Party spirit is strong. Such is the criterion for appraising the Party spirit of each of our members and his Party attitude. As the great Lenin said, we must see to it that Party spirit is expressed not in word but in practical work.

Though young, our Party has achieved considerable successes in tempering the Party spirit of its members and the absolute majority of our Party members are all loyal to the Party. Particularly in the Fatherland Liberation War, they are fighting with readiness even to lay down their lives and give the last drop of their blood for the Party, for the revolution. Tens of thousands of our Party members have already sacrificed themselves for the sake of the country and the people.

But cases are found in which some of the Party members lack Party spirit and are politically corrupt. Once promoted to responsible positions at the state and government bodies or Party organs, these elements more often than not become blind with material privilege, estrange themselves from the masses by carelessly infringing upon their interests, lose sight of Party work and revolutionary tasks and only seek after their personal selfish interests, thus committing serious crimes before the Party and the state. Particularly, there are elements among some leading functionaries of the Party who, at a time when the country and the people are going through difficulties, do not faithfully carry out the tasks assigned to them by the Party but only make unprincipled complaints against the Party, go so far as to grumble for this and that among the discontented elements who flock together, make abusive remarks behind the scenes instead of advancing their opinions to the Party organizations or speaking at meetings or in the presence of the men concerned, do not submit to the Party's decisions and to the interests of the revolution but think their own opinions to be the best, ignore the Party's organizational discipline on the pretext of allocation of cadres, and recklessly give themselves to mere wordplay. There are also found self-protectionists who are little concerned about their duties, assume an air of indifference even when they see something wrong, and are eager only to take care of themselves while passing their days with a betwixt-and-between attitude; there also exist elements who care only for high positions, have not the least sense of responsibility for their work, only put on airs for their past revolutionary career, and do not care to take on minor jobs in spite of their inability to tackle big tasks. Phenomena are also observed that people are drawn in without principle only because they are relatives, old boys, friends, or because they come from the same native places, localities, south Korea or north Korea, and that even when they commit errors, they are overlooked.

All these are very harmful, liberalistic tendencies. Such liberalists are men lacking Party spirit who, swayed by the egotistic ideas peculiar to the petty bourgeoisie, do not subordinate their personal interests to the interests of the revolution. We must fight with determination against these liberalistic tendencies.

And survivals of factionalism are still found within our Party, though it is said to be free from factions. These survivals of factionalism can possibly hinder the unity and solidarity of our Party.

The survivals of factionalism find expression in persisting in the old habit of unprincipled factional strife, in mustering elements with a parochial tendency, those discontented with their positions and those penalized by the Party, and bringing Party members of relatively impure social origins over to one's side by agitating them with groundless remarks, "The Party does, or does not, trust you."

The vestiges of factionalism are also manifested in the fact that one displays a keen interest when it comes to the appointment and allocation of cadres while remaining rather callous to other matters, tries to indiscriminately appoint to high offices people who are intimate with him or who had belonged to his group before, in disregard of their level of ideological consciousness, social origins or abilities, and even attempts zealously to appoint renegades of the revolution to high posts. Consequently, those whose past political career is not clean and those who have not been given high offices on account of their social origins, hang on those factionalists in the hope of securing a good position in the Party or government organs by some chance under their patronage, instead of endeavouring to win the confidence of the Party by enhancing their Party spirit and devoting themselves to the Party and the revolution through the practical struggle. Those who have not discarded the survivals of factionalism take advantage of this and engross themselves in bringing these people over to them.

The remnants of factionalism are also manifested in keeping dark the unsavoury facts in one another's past "revolutionary career" and in logrolling and shielding one another in order to obtain a good position in the Party or government organs, and in driving in a wedge between cadres by taking advantage of their differences or discord in the hope of making hay out of it.

Another expression of the survivals of factionalism is the practice of supporting the Party line and the Party centre outwardly but opposing them behind the scenes, agreeing to everything by word but thinking otherwise inside, pretending to be faithful in the presence of the men concerned, but playing underhand tricks behind the backs. We must unfold a resolute struggle against such double-dealers.

If such behaviour of the factionalists be overlooked, it could grow into a factional action. Today we can no longer leave such elements to go unchecked. These elements had better make a clean breast of it before the Party and stop their un-Party activities. All our Party members must further raise their revolutionary vigilance and Party spirit and keep a sharp watch on the movements of such elements, preventing the factionalists from moving even an inch in our Party. Particularly now, when we are waging a fierce war against the U.S. imperialist armed invaders, we cannot tolerate such factional activities in the slightest degree.

As is shown by the experience of all revolutionary parties, the factional elements, if left alone, will eventually turn into agents to the enemy. This we must bear deep in mind.

And some of the Party members have a tendency to believe in individuals and depend on them instead of relying on the lines and organizations of the Party. This may in the long run play into the hands of individualist heroists.

In order to overcome all these wrong tendencies, it is necessary to persistently temper the Party spirit of the members, intensify the Party's organizational discipline and strictly observe the principle of democratic centralism in Party life. Only when the Party is united as one and acts with iron discipline on the principle that the Party member submits to the Party organization, the minority submits to the majority, the lower Party organization to its higher body and the entire Party to the Central Committee, can we lead the people to victory in the protracted, complex, hard revolutionary struggle.

A major attribute of Party spirit is fidelity to principle which is expressed in resolutely defending the interests of the Party and the revolution, and intransigency towards defects in work and all hues of un-Party or hostile tendencies. Therefore, when we evaluate the work of each leading functionary of the Party and state organs, and of each military cadre, we place importance on whether or not he is possessed of such a fidelity to principle as a revolutionary, intransigency towards defects, a high degree of Party consciousness and revolutionary vigilance.

5. We have the sharp, tested weapon of criticism and self-criticism in the struggle to temper Party spirit. Wielding this weapon, we must sweep away all tendencies that run counter

to Party spirit, expose and rectify defects and errors in work and thus improve our work constantly.

Comrade Stalin said: "Should we fail to recognize or to bring out into the open, in all frankness and honesty, as behoves Bolsheviks, the shortcomings and mistakes in our work, we will be barring ourselves the road to progress. But we want to advance. And precisely because we want to advance, we must pose to ourselves, as one of the most important tasks, the task of honest and revolutionary self-criticism. Otherwise there will be no advance. Otherwise there is no development."

Criticism and self-criticism is inadequate as yet in our Party. It is not that there is nothing to criticize but, so it seems to me, that some comrades in leading posts do not like criticism and self-criticism, and the Party organizations do not pay due attention to this work, either.

Our Party has never classified, and cannot classify, its members into junior members and senior members, the latter being "immune" to the Party Rules or Party obligations and enjoying some sort of "privileges." Party discipline is equally binding on all members; no one is allowed to violate it, no matter what his position may be. If any leading functionary or military cadre does not endeavour to raise his political level but leads a dissolute life or neglects his duties to the Party, such a leading functionary must be severely criticized by its members at Party meetings. Such criticism will make him aware of his error, help him rectify it and preserve his dignity as a Party member.

Principled and open-minded criticism and self-criticism are the motive power for our Party's development. We have people, however, among some Party functionaries, cadres in particular, who think as if their "prestige" will suffer when they make self-criticism, and try to evade it by all means. Only self-conceited and incorrigible bureaucrats can think that way. By frankly admitting their errors and making up their minds to correct them, those functionaries will rather boost their prestige than lowering it.

And the self-criticism we require is not confession which

amounts to empty wordplay. What is of importance in self-criticism is not that one merely admits his errors and shortcomings in word but that one corrects the exposed errors and shortcomings promptly and improves one's work actively.

To recognize the validity of criticism only in words is in reality to evade criticism and conceal and camouflage one's errors and shortcomings. By criticism and self-criticism we mean criticism which is always conscientious, bold and practical, words corresponding to deeds. To encourage such criticism every Party organization and every leading worker should create an atmosphere conducive to the development of criticism and self-criticism and fight resolutely against those who hinder criticism and self-criticism.

Criticism must be concrete; it is advisable that criticism show the clear way of correcting the shortcomings, not confining itself to pointing them out. Only then will criticism be more effective.

Criticism and self-criticism is of great significance in preventing each Party member from becoming self-conceited and arrogant and from lapsing into a bureaucratic style of work, and in keeping him from relaxing his revolutionary vigilance. If criticism and self-criticism is combined with the creative activity of the broad labouring masses, it will prove a great force to promote the political, economic and cultural development of our country.

Our Party should educate its members and cadres in the spirit of criticism and self-criticism and see to it that every member cultivates the habit of critically checking and summing up his work of the day every evening for himself, not limiting himself to making criticism at meetings only.

A specific feature of the revolutionary Marxist-Leninist Party is that it is uncompromising towards shortcomings and errors, and educates its members and cadres in the spirit of criticism and self-criticism to make them habituated to open and principled criticism and frank and honest self-criticism. This constitutes an important requisite for strengthening our Party and making it a vigorous and militant party.

6. It is posed as a more urgent question than ever to intensify the activities of the primary Party organization, the basic unit of our Party, and to raise the vanguard role of the Party members. Many of our Party organs, however, are far from satisfactory in their guidance of the cells.

It is important in strengthening a Party cell to foster the cell nucleus and properly select the chairman of the cell before anything else. Since many Party organs had failed to pay deep attention to the selection of cell chairmen, as many as 79 cell chairmen were read out of the Party in the first half of this year alone, some of the expelled having been found to be spies bribed by the enemy. Also, no small number of cell chairmen were released from office because their working ability and political level were too low. Meanwhile, Party organs frequently change cell chairmen, thus allowing them no time to acquire experience and skill in work. The Pyongyang city Party organization, for instance, changed 37.3 per cent of the total number of cell chairmen in the first half of this year. Such a practice must by all means be rectified in future.

Implementation of all our Party's policies depends upon the work of the Party cells that make the policies known to the masses and directly carry them into effect. Unless the cells are consolidated, our Party cannot be strengthened nor can the revolutionary tasks be performed successfully.

To consolidate a Party cell, it is necessary to foster the nucleus fully capable of building up the cell. The question of fostering the nucleus has been emphasized time and again for many years now, but it has not yet come to a satisfactory solution.

We are now making preparations for a reform in the administrative division to bring the guidance of the higher organs closer to the lower units and more quickly carry into effect the policies of the Party and the state. The preparations for the reform of the administrative division are going on in the direction of dividing the county into smaller units, abolishing the *myon* and reinforcing the *ri*. Our Party, therefore, is now confronted with the task of training a great multitude of cadres for the Party and government bodies at the *ri* level. We must lose no time in taking measures to train cadres of the *ri* level through various short-course systems, provincial Party schools and cadre training schools under the provincial people's committee.

Fostering of the cell nucleus alone is not sufficient for the strengthening of the cells. To strengthen the cells, we must give full scope to inner-Party democracy and give Party assignments properly to make all members take an active part in Party work, and must raise the political and ideological level of Party meetings to make them serve as schools to educate the Party members.

The enemy is making every attempt to disturb our rear and is madly trying to stretch his crooked tentacles to the corners where the activities of our Party cells are dull. The recent information from various localities shows the fact that the enemy bribed cadres at the *ri* level in those places and used them for their sabotaging activities. This is a very dangerous thing.

Party organs of all levels, therefore, must pay close attention to the proper selection and training of cell chairmen, fostering of cell nuclei and consolidation of primary Party organizations.

7. A matter of importance in the organizational work of our Party is to maintain close bonds between the Party and the masses. The wellsprings of our Party's strength are traceable to its bonds of kinship with the broad masses of the people. The strengthening of the bonds is essential for the further development of our Party as an invincible revolutionary party.

The work of strengthening the bonds between the Party and the masses has improved markedly since the Fourth Plenary Meeting of the Party Central Committee. However, we have not yet eliminated the bureaucratic work style in our work with the masses of the people.

Bureaucracy is a method of work manifested in dealing with matters apart from the masses, without heeding their creative opinions, in drawing up plans on the desk with doors closed, imposing decisions and orders on people down below, and only blustering at the masses. Such a method of work is bound to evoke dissatisfaction among the masses, estrange the Party from them and do enormous harm to Party and state work.

We must do away with this kind of work style, lend an ear to the voice of the masses, thoroughly defend their interests and work faithfully as their servants under any circumstances, persuade, educate and lead them to accept the Party's slogans wholeheartedly and to rise consciously to perform the tasks set by the Party. Every Party organization and member should work precisely in this way and deal with the masses in this style. We must always bear in mind the principle, "Teach the masses while learning from them."

Any of the slogans put up by the Party expresses the interests and cherished desire of the people, and so is sure to enjoy support from the popular masses and bring out their inexhaustible creative power. We must understand this clearly and, instead of domineering over the masses, should discuss everything with them and awaken them politically and lead them to devote all their energies and zeal to the final victory of the revolution.

The basic method to acquaint the masses of the people with the Party's lines and policies is persuasion and education. The Party should always explain its policies to the labouring masses and convince them of the correctness of its policies. This is indispensable to induce the working masses to fight devotedly for the implementation of our Party's policies. There should be no one who says: "Why should we waste time in giving explanation when war is going on!" The more difficult our wartime situation is, the more persistently the Party should persuade and educate the popular masses to arouse their conscious enthusiasm and the deeper roots it should sink among the masses to unite with them as one and crush the enemy.

5

Comrades,

To strengthen our Party it is not enough to improve the organizational work alone; it is needed to strengthen the ideological work, too. The ideological work always figures large in our Party work, and especially today it acquires vital importance. Because we are now carrying on an unprecedentedly severe war against the U.S. imperialist aggressors and our Party ranks have new recruits accounting for more than 40 per cent of the total membership.

As the great Lenin said, small production engenders capitalism and bourgeoisie daily, hourly, spontaneously, and on a mass scale. In our country where small production holds big proportions, bourgeois ideas breed at all times.

Meanwhile, we should take into consideration without fail the specific situation created in our country owing to U.S. imperialist aggression. Already in the period of peaceful construction, the U.S. imperialists and Syngman Rhee puppet clique incessantly sent spies and saboteurs into the northern half of the Republic with the aim of wrecking our people's democratic system. After they unleashed the war, the U.S. rogues further extended the scope of their despicable and dirty sabotaging activities. The spies of the U.S. imperialists and the traitorous Syngman Rhee clique are attempting to employ in their subversive activities some unsound elements who waver in the face of wartime difficulties. The U.S. imperialists and traitorous Syngman Rhee clique have mobilized all their propaganda media to imbue reactionary ideas in those elements. Under the circumstances where we are fighting a severe war with the enemy, the influence of the hostile bourgeois ideology cannot but penetrate even into our Party. Therefore, we should strengthen the ideological work without fail, and the entire Party should concentrate attention on this work.

What is fundamental in ideological work is to arm the working people of our country with the revolutionary Marxist-Leninist ideology.

The Korean people have undergone revolutionary training and largely got rid of the remnants of bourgeois ideology and of bourgeois habits during the protracted national-liberation struggle against Japanese imperialism and in the course of building a new life after liberation. Especially, in the course of the just war of liberation to beat back the armed invasion of U.S. imperialism and to defend the liberty and independence of the country, the national awakening and class consciousness of our people have been enhanced to a high degree. The Korean people have fought valiantly without yielding to any severe trials, displaying lofty patriotism and boundless loyalty to the Party and the revolution. This has been an important factor in frustrating the aggressive plan of the U.S. imperialists to occupy our country and conquer our people.

The communist ideology is gaining ground and getting the upper hand in many countries of the world. The communist ideology was born as the ideology of the proletariat, the most advanced class, that represents the fundamental demands of the development of modern society.

The triumphant advance of the revolutionary Marxist-Leninist ideology has sent the moribund capitalism beastly desperate. The imperialists are using every means to instill their corrupt ideas into the masses of the people and paralyze their revolutionary consciousness.

The vicious enemy calls himself a "champion" of liberty and democracy. He employs every possible means to hoodwink the people, dull the consciousness of the masses and foster mean habits among them. Particularly, the imperialists are bent on infusing youths with corrupt ideas.

The U.S. imperialists are now trying to contaminate the masses of the people and armymen with mediaeval man-hating ideas so as to create the possibility of easily unleashing a new world war. In the course of the war the Korean people have fully experienced, and are experiencing, such mediaeval-type barbarities of the U.S. imperialists. The barbaric bombings by the U.S. imperialists on our towns and villages and their brutal slaughter of women and children are a direct expression of the man-hating ideas.

Never before has the imperialist ideological "offensive" against democracy and socialism assumed so malicious a nature as today. Without waging an uncompromising struggle against the reactionary and putrid bourgeois ideas and intensifying education in revolutionary Marxism-Leninism, therefore, we cannot defend our people against the ideological invasion of imperialism and emerge victorious in the arduous revolutionary struggle.

We have many shortcomings in the domain of ideological work.

Our ideological work is conducted as yet in a formalistic way and fails to go deep among the Party members and the masses of the people.

The propaganda and agitation work has failed to produce the desired effect, because in many cases it has been conducted pointlessly, without aim, detached from the questions of our country's specific realities. The leading functionaries who hold responsible positions in Party and government bodies seldom take part in the propaganda and agitation work.

The operation of the Party political schools and study circles is also qualitatively at a low level and the work of proper allocation and reorientation of teachers and instructors is far from satisfactory. Many leading cadres of Party and state organs are little concerned about elevating their own ideological and theoretical level, and the studies of those Party members who are in independent study groups are left almost without control.

The work of putting out the writings of Marx, Engels, Lenin and Stalin is not yet satisfactory and our periodical publications—magazines and newspapers—leave very much to be desired as to their ideological contents.

The work with writers, poets, composers, artists and actors, too, is inadequate and no upsurge has been brought about in literary and artistic creation to suit the era of heroic resistance of our people for freedom and liberation. As a result, we now have very few good literary works, songs, paintings, plays, films, etc.

Such shortcomings with our ideological work can never be tolerated any longer.

The enemy is trying to capitalize on the survivals of old ideas in the minds of our people, particularly, the mentality of colonial slaves left over by the Japanese plunderers. The U.S. imperialists attempt to take advantage of all our shortcomings in ideological work, however minor they may be, in order to sap the united power and patriotic fighting spirit of our people. So, we should rectify all the shortcomings as soon as possible and develop the ideological work onto a level commensurate with the revolutionary tasks required by the present situation.

We should do away with the practice of underrating the ideological work, fight decisively against the liberalistic tendency to overlook ideological errors, and exert every possible effort to heighten the class consciousness and revolutionary awareness of the working people by arming them with Marxist-Leninist ideology.

The significance of Marxist-Leninist theory lies in the fact that it indicates definite aims of struggle and the way to attain them to the Party members and the working people and increases their revolutionary will and confidence in victory. The routineers who have no knowledge of theory and pay no heed to raising their theoretical level, cannot have confidence in their work.

Lenin taught us that without a revolutionary theory there could be no revolutionary practice and that a revolutionary party would be able to play its role as the advanced detachment of the working class only when it was equipped with the Marxist theory. Comrade Stalin said that if it intends to lead the people to victory in the revolution without going astray and suffering big losses, the Party should master the Marxist-

Leninist theory and use it as a compass and that a party without theory would be as good as one who gropes in the dark.

We should intensify the work of ideological education in the Party to give our Party members a clear perspective of the revolution and to train them into Marxists-Leninists capable of correctly analysing all events from the class point of view and carrying out their revolutionary tasks with precision.

By the intensification of education in Marxism-Leninism it is not meant to make the Party members read aimlessly whatever works of Marx, Engels, Lenin and Stalin they can lay hands on and learn by heart the individual propositions contained in them. It is meant to see that they acquire the Marxist-Leninist ideological viewpoint and method and become able to apply them to suit the actual situation in our country, and that they learn to analyse the military, political and economic situation in our country on the basis of Marxism-Leninism and correctly grasp not only its present but also forecast its future.

But there is very much as yet to be desired in our work of studying Marxism-Leninism in combination with the concrete practice of our revolution. We have very few theoretical writings or articles which give a Marxist-Leninist analysis to the problems of our country. This is a serious shortcoming of our ideological and theoretical work that must be rectified without fail.

In our universities and colleges, Party schools and Party educational system, the studies of Marxism-Leninism and of the fraternal parties' advanced experience should be oriented to the rectification of those shortcomings. Newspaper and magazine offices and other publishing establishments should widely carry or publish articles, books and various educational materials concerning the creative application of Marxist-Leninist theory in our country.

Meanwhile, in our ideological work there still partly remains the practice of casting away the precious heritages of the culture created by our ancestors, instead of endeavouring to inherit and develop them from the Marxist-Leninist standpoint. The extreme case is that there is even the wrong practice, in regard to the old tales and songs, too, of regarding all foreign ones as nice and all our own things as unworthy of note.

We must be aware that we can properly assimilate the advanced culture of other countries only on the basis of inheriting and developing the precious cultural heritages of our nation.

The Party organs at all levels should radically improve the work of the Party political schools and study networks, pay deeper attention to the selection of teachers and lecturers and take measures to elevate their theoretical level. To this end, the winter classes, above all, for the Party study instructors and core elements of the cells, should be ensured on a high qualitative level and theoretically qualified Party cadres should conduct lectures at those classes.

We should further develop socialist culture and art and bring all our propaganda and agitation media including the radio and publications to serve the purpose of elevating the politico-ideological level of Party members and heightening the political awakening of the workers, peasants and intellectuals.

We should vigorously conduct the work of oral propaganda and agitation and ensure that the leading functionaries personally take part in it in order to raise its quality. We should bring the policies of the Party and the Government of the Republic home to the masses and run the democratic publicity halls, the bases of mass political work in the rural areas, in an effective way.

Guidance over all the organs and organizations concerned with ideological work should be radically improved and great attention should be directed especially to the work of the General Federation of Literature and Arts. It is necessary to thoroughly crush the narrow-minded parochial and sectarian tendency now expressed in the grouping of southerners, northerners and what not within the General Federation of Literature and Arts. Thus, all men of culture without exception should be made to devote all their strength and talents to the victory of the Fatherland Liberation War with the lofty idea of serving the Party and the revolution.

All Party organs and organizations should not take upon themselves the administrative functions that properly belong to the government bodies, but should concentrate their efforts on the work of ideological education in the Party and mass political work so as to firmly build up the Party ranks and rally the masses around the Party.

If their politico-ideological level is raised, the Party members will naturally do their work better and the Party will be fortified, and the work of the government bodies, too, will be improved as a matter of course, not to mention Party work. Only when the education in Marxism-Leninism and mass political work are strengthened, will the iron unity of thought and purpose be assured in the Party and will its members and the masses of the people display a high degree of political zeal and creative initiative.

Our Party should mobilize all forces of the ideological front for the great cause of defending the country's freedom and honour against the aggression of the U.S. imperialists, the most ferocious enemy of the Korean people, and their lackeys.

We are confronted with the historic task of attaining the independence of the country and national reunification under the banner of democracy. Only the improvement and strengthening of the Party's ideological work can bring successful solution to this glorious task of the Korean revolution.

Comrades,

Today, victory in the liberation war of the Korean people, a war which is decisive of the fate of the country, entirely depends on the united power of our Party and its guiding role.

In order to defeat and wipe out the U.S. imperialist armed invaders and their stooges and win the freedom, reunification and independence of the country, we should further consolidate our Party before everything.

What does it mean to consolidate our Party?

It means that our Party should be equipped with Marxism-Leninism, the all-conquering revolutionary theory that indicates the way to the overthrow of capitalism and emancipation of the working people.

Consolidation of the Party means that iron discipline should be established in the Party, the unity of its ranks defended, the slightest factionalist tendency not tolerated, and that the Party be firmly protected from the infiltration of bourgeois ideas and tempered politically and ideologically.

Strengthening of the Party also means educating the Party members in the spirit of serving the Party, the country and the people with all loyalty, of devoting themselves to the cause of emancipation of the labouring masses, remaining faithful to the principle of proletarian internationalism, hating the class enemies, sharpening revolutionary vigilance and of waging an uncompromising struggle against the slightest expression of bourgeois ideas.

Consolidation of the Party means strengthening the bonds between the Party and the masses of the people, fighting stoutly against the bureaucratic and formalistic style of work that divorces the Party from the masses and establishing the revolutionary style of work in the Party.

Consolidation of the Party means permitting no conservatism, stagnation and indolence within the Party and cultivating in its members an indomitable fighting spirit to win victory through a selfless struggle by overcoming all difficulties and lively creative traits.

Today the situation is turning in favour of the Korean people who have risen in the just Fatherland Liberation War against the imperialist armed invaders and their lackeys. Our Party, the organizer and inspirer of all victories for the Korean people, confidently leads the entire people to victory in the war by rallying them rock-firm around itself.

Let us exert every effort to further consolidate our Party organizationally and ideologically for the ultimate victory in the Fatherland Liberation War, for the freedom and bright future of the Korean people!

Let us all march forward valiantly for the victory of our just cause!

EVERYTHING FOR THE POSTWAR REHABILITATION AND DEVELOPMENT OF THE NATIONAL ECONOMY

Report Delivered at the Sixth Plenary Meeting of the Central Committee of the Workers' Party of Korea

August 5, 1953

Comrades,

The present Sixth Plenary Meeting of the Central Committee of our Party is convened under the new situation created in our country following the signing of the Armistice Agreement.

The heroic struggle waged by the Korean people for three years in defence of the country's freedom and independence against the U.S. imperialist armed invaders ended in victory for us. The U.S. imperialist aggressors suffered an ignominious defeat in their military adventure to turn our country into their colony and enslave the Korean people. The enemy was compelled to sign the Armistice Agreement owing to his irretrievable military, political and moral defeat in the Korean war, and thanks to the tenacious and patient efforts of the Korean and Chinese peoples to restore peace in Korea and to the public opinion and pressure of the peace-loving peoples of the world. Thus, the Korean people won a glorious victory in their Fatherland Liberation War.

In this sacred war our Workers' Party members fought courageously in the forefront of the entire Korean people.

Our Workers' Party played the role of the pivot and organizer in the People's Army, and performed a great function in strengthening it. Members of the Workers' Party in the People's Army always bore the brunt of battles in any offensive or defensive, any mountain or field operation, courageously waging hand-to-hand fights. Our Party members constituted the backbone and acted as models in the People's Army.

Our Workers' Party members in the rear surmounted all hardships and difficulties in the face of barbarous enemy bombing under difficult wartime conditions; they restored and developed factories and mines, ensured railway transport, and steadily increased production in farming and fishing villages. Our Workers' Party members, in factories built underground, kept up munitions production for the front; assured the transport of war supplies satisfactorily by running trains and trucks even on dark nights and in defiance of the enemy's bombings; continued fishing in face of frenzied enemy warships; and ploughed and sowed with camouflaged oxen.

During the enemy's occupation, our Party members did not yield to the enemy at all, but fought and were victorious in guerrilla warfare, holding high the banner of the Republic to the end. In the enemy's POW camps, too, despite all sorts of persecutions and barbarous massacre by the enemy, our Party members never gave in but defended to the last their honour as Workers' Party members as well as the banner of our Republic.

Who but members of our Workers' Party could have ever organized so heroic a struggle at the front and in the rear? There is no doubt that if the members of the Workers' Party had not heroically fought at the head of all the popular masses, we would have failed to win, and would have been doomed to colonial slavery to the U.S. imperialists.

Today the Workers' Party of Korea, through its devoted, heroic struggle, has proved itself a reliable vanguard to which the Korean people can entrust their destiny and future without hesitation; it represents the wisdom and glory of the Korean people. Thus, our Party, in the struggle for safeguarding the country's freedom and independence and for a happier and more resplendent future of the people, has been strengthened and developed into a revolutionary party armed with all-conquering Marxist-Leninist theory. In the Fatherland Liberation War, our Party, as a member of the "shock force" of the international working-class movement, made a tremendous contribution to the consolidation of the camp of democracy and socialism and to the safeguarding of world peace.

I feel a boundless pride at the fact that I, as a member of so glorious a party as the Workers' Party of Korea, share this great honour with you.

On behalf of the Sixth Plenary Meeting of the Party Central Committee, I extend warm thanks to all the functionaries and Party members in the People's Army, factories, urban communities, farming and fishing villages, on the railways, in interior service organs, self-defence corps, garrison troops, Party and state organs, cultural institutions, and social organizations.

Also, in the name of the Sixth Plenary Meeting of the Party Central Committee, I express warm gratitude to the members of all the democratic political parties and people of all walks of life who, shoulder to shoulder with our Party members, fought actively for the freedom and independence of the country against the U.S. imperialist armed invaders.

And I extend warm gratitude and congratulations to the men and officers of the Chinese People's Volunteers who aided us in our struggle for the freedom and independence of our country at the cost of their blood.

I express warm gratitude to the peoples of the great Soviet Union, China and other People's Democracies, as well as to their Communist and Workers' Parties, for the continuous and unselfish aid they gave us during the period of peaceful construction and especially during the war.

I extend profound thanks to good-minded people all over the world for rendering active support and encouragement to the sacred cause of us Korean people.

1. ON THE ARMISTICE AND THE QUESTION OF THE COUNTRY'S REUNIFICATION

Comrades,

The armistice signifies a great victory for us. Though the armistice did not bring complete peace to Korea, the conclusion of the Armistice Agreement marked an initial step towards the peaceful settlement of the Korean issue, a first exemplary contribution to the relaxation of international tension. By concluding the Armistice Agreement, we have come to open up the possibilities for the peaceful settlement of the question of our country's reunification.

It is wrong to think, as some comrades do, that war might soon break out again and that peaceful construction could not be undertaken because the armistice does not mean a complete peace. It is likewise a wrong tendency to be indolent, lax and self-contented, thinking that an end has been put to war and complete peace is ensured in our country. The point is to consolidate the victory embodied in the armistice, which we have won at enormous sacrifices by going through the tribulations and calamities of war, and to struggle unremittingly for a lasting peace in Korea and the peaceful reunification of the country.

The first and foremost task confronting us in connection with the conclusion of the Armistice Agreement is to struggle persistently for a complete peaceful settlement of the question of our country at the forthcoming political conference. The basic aim of the political conference is to get all the troops of the United States and its satellite countries to withdraw from south Korea and to enable the Korean people to settle the Korean issue by themselves, and to prevent foreigners from interfering in the internal affairs of our country. We have advocated with all consistency the peaceful settlement of the Korean issue

—the peaceful reunification of the country. It is quite evident that if the U.S. imperialists had not interfered and if the Korean question had been solved in accordance with our line and claims, our country would have long ago been reunified, and our country and people would have been freed from all the sufferings and disasters resulting from the country's division. Our task is to carry our just line and claims into effect and to do everything for their realization.

The Korean nation is one and Korea belongs to the Koreans. The Korean question must naturally be settled by the Korean people themselves. The Korean people absolutely do not want to remain split. No aggressive force can break the desire and will of the Korean people for the reunification of their country.

The forthcoming political conference should naturally reflect and defend the just claims, desire, will and fundamental interests of the Korean people. Therefore, our people will under no circumstances tolerate and thoroughly reject any attempt or plot of the imperialist interventionists contrary to them.

With the political conference approaching, the U.S. imperialists are already making a fuss behind the scenes. Notwithstanding the signing of the Armistice Agreement in which it was stipulated that the chief aim of the political conference is to discuss the question of withdrawal of foreign troops from Korea, the notorious warmonger Dulles, U.S. Secretary of State, concluded the so-called "ROK-U.S. Mutual Defence Pact" with the traitor Syngman Rhee. This pact is aimed at stationing aggressive forces of the United States in south Korea indefinitely and, whenever necessary, unleashing another criminal war of aggression in Korea, in violation of the Armistice Agreement. The "ROK-U.S. Mutual Defence Pact" is an aggressive pact which allows U.S. imperialism to obstruct the peaceful reunification of our country and interfere in our domestic affairs. It is a glaringly country-selling pact under which the Syngman Rhee clique sell the southern half of our country to the U.S. bandits. To conclude such a pact at a time when the political conference is in the offing is an act hindering a reasonable solution of the Korean question at the political conference. It can be easily foreseen that they will seek to throw the political conference into confusion, resorting to all sorts of intrigues, obstructive tactics and provocations at the conference, too, just as they did during the truce talks.

We, however, must by all means fulfil the just claims and demands of the Korean people by relying on the powerful support and encouragement of the peace-loving peoples all over the world, and by the unanimous will and struggle of the Korean people, just as we did in the course of the truce talks. Thus, the political conference should certainly be brought to the expected results and our country reunified peacefully without fail. To attain this goal, we must wage an unremitting struggle.

All our Party members and people should not relax their keyed-up attitude and, without slacking off in the least, should increase their revolutionary vigilance to a high degree, keep a close watch on every movement of the enemy, and be ready at all times to see through the enemy's vicious designs and frustrate them in advance.

All the Party members and the entire people should rally still more firmly around the Party Central Committee and the Government and do their utmost to increase the might of the country in every way. We have ample conditions and possibilities triumphantly to carry out this task which confronts our nation, our state and our Party.

Today, following the armistice, the situation in south Korea has been plunged into hopeless chaos. Antagonisms and contradictions are being further aggravated within the enemy camp, and the life of the people becomes more and more wretched. Growing and gaining in scope among the masses of the people are hatred and rebellious trends against the U.S. imperialist aggressors and the traitorous Syngman Rhee's reactionary rule which is maintained by their bayonets. The enemy's military, political and economic crises are becoming more grave. This will no doubt provide a favourable condition for the Korean people in their struggle for the peaceful reunification of the country.

The task is to arouse to the struggle for the peaceful reunification of the country all the democratic, patriotic forces of popular masses throughout the country, rallying them around our Party and Government, and to make it possible to settle the Korean question by us Koreans by repudiating the colonial occupation policy of the U.S. imperialist aggressors and the traitorous rule of their lackeys and by compelling the U.S. forces of aggression to withdraw.

2. ON THE POSTWAR REHABILITATION AND DEVELOPMENT OF THE NATIONAL ECONOMY

Comrades,

With the signing of the Armistice Agreement, our country and people passed from a state of war into a period of peaceful rehabilitation and construction.

Our Party and the Government of the Republic are confronted with the important tasks of restoring and developing the war-ravaged national economy and of stabilizing and improving the people's deteriorated livelihood.

Most important of all for the accomplishment of the reunification and independence of our country is to further strengthen the people's democratic system established in the northern half of the Republic and consolidate still more the democratic base politically, economically and militarily, by rallying the patriotic forces of the popular masses. This alone will assure us national reunification and the accomplishment of the people's democratic revolution in our country. Our Party and the entire people, therefore, should devote all their energies to postwar rehabilitation and construction aimed at consolidating the democratic base, taking full advantage of the peaceful duration of the armistice.

The basic direction for the rehabilitation and development

of the national economy of our country should be mapped out on the basis of taking full account of the experience of the war and of a correct analysis of the historical conditions of our country's economic development in the past and of our present situation.

The havoc wrought by the war upon our national economy is beyond description. Therefore, an overall, simultaneous rehabilitation and construction of every branch of the national economy is quite impossible. This makes it necessary for us to undertake the postwar rehabilitation and construction of the national economy basically in three stages.

The first stage will be one of preparations for overall rehabilitation and construction of the national economy ranging from six months to one year when preparations and adjustments should be made for the rehabilitation and construction of the ruined national economy as a whole.

In the second stage a three-year plan should be carried out for the rehabilitation and development of the national economy to regain prewar levels in all its branches.

In the third stage, a five-year plan should be drawn up and carried out to lay the foundations for industrialization so that the first stage of the industrialization of our country be completed.

In postwar economic construction we must follow the line of giving priority to the rehabilitation and development of heavy industry simultaneously with development of light industry and agriculture. This alone will enable us to consolidate the economic foundations of our country and improve the people's life in a short period of time.

(1) BASIC DIRECTION FOR THE REHABILITATION AND DEVELOPMENT OF INDUSTRY

The basic direction for the postwar rehabilitation and development of industry is to give priority to the restoration and expansion of heavy industry and to rapidly restore and develop light industry for the stabilization of the people's livelihood with a view to eliminating the shortcomings of industry revealed during the war and its colonial one-sidedness, an evil aftermath of prolonged colonial rule by Japanese imperialism, and to laying the foundations for the future industrialization of our country.

In the rehabilitation and building of industry we should pay serious attention to the redistribution of our country's industry. Out of sheer necessity the Japanese imperialists built a deformed, colonial-type industry in our country in the closing years of their colonial rule. In doing this, they were in no way motivated by any concern for the future development of our country and the good of the Korean people. They built industrial establishments in places convenient and easy to ship materials from Korea to their own country, entirely for the purpose of colonial plunder. This is apparent above all in the fact that they set up all major plants on the east and west coasts of our country. As a result, these plants, far removed from the production centres of raw materials, posed tremendous difficulties and troubles in transportation and, in particular, they all suffered serious damage from the enemy's naval bombardment during the war.

In the rehabilitation and construction of industry, therefore, we should not follow the course of mechanically restoring the destroyed factories on their former sites, but should redistribute industry. Of course, no small number of factories ought to be restored just where they were before for the sake of speedy reconstruction and economy. But new plants and mills, especially machine-building plants, should be located in new places. We should set up factories in places easy of access where raw materials and products can be transported readily.

And in the rehabilitation and construction of industry, the order of priority should be properly fixed; important factories and enterprises should be rebuilt first. If we fail to determine correctly which should be given preference in the rehabilitation and construction of industry this will retard the rehabilitation and development of the national economy as a whole and may lead to the waste of a vast amount of funds, materials and labour or to their remaining idle. We must, therefore, start with the building of basic industrial establishments which can facilitate the overall rehabilitation and development of the national economy.

In the iron and steel industry, we should rapidly reconstruct, to begin with, the Hwanghae and the Kim Chaek Iron Works and the Songjin and the Kangson Steel Plant on their original sites, and thus start production of pig iron, steel and rolled steel in 1954 and bring their output up to the prewar level by 1956. Thus, we should produce as much steel, iron pipes, rails and other rolled steel as are needed to satisfy domestic demands.

Development of the machine-building industry constitutes the basic condition for the future industrialization of our country and is of great importance for national defence. So, we have to pay particular attention to developing this industry, importing many machine tools from foreign countries on the one hand and, on the other, producing them at home on our own. Along with this, measures should be taken that machine tools may be concentrated and used in machine-building enterprises.

In the machine-building industry the main accent should be placed on producing a great number of lathes and motors, on turning out such machines as are needed to newly set up and develop other factories and transport equipment, automobile parts, mining and farm machines and machines required for the ship-building industry. The Huichon Machine Plant and the automobile parts factory should be put into commission in 1954. Work should be started without delay to build the Rakwon and Pukjung Machine Factories, an electromotor repair plant, a tool factory, a pumping equipment factory, all of which should be put into full operation in 1955.

In the light of the fact that our country is seabound on three sides, the ship-building industry acquires special importance both in strengthening defence capacities and improving the people's livelihood. In the postwar rehabilitation and development of the national economy, therefore, the Party and the state should direct serious attention to the ship-building industry: shipyards should be built immediately in Nampo and in North Hamgyong Province, so as to build patrol boats, fishing boats and river transport ships of up to 100-odd tons, to start with. In this way, we should build large numbers of fishing vessels and thus fully develop the fishing industry and restore and readjust river transport.

Our Party should devote serious attention in the postwar period to the exploitation of abundant mineral resources. Owing to the war, a large number of mines were abandoned and flooded. Within the next year or two we should see to it that all mines can basically go into operation, and that mining operations should be mechanized to increase labour productivity and production. Various minerals should be extracted on a large scale so that not only the country's requirements are satisfied but also some 200-300 million rubles' worth of export is assured in foreign trade.

The Kapsan Copper Mine and the Songchon Lead Mine should be rapidly developed; the Munchon and Nampo Smelteries should be rehabilitated to start production in 1954. At the same time, we should organize prospecting on an extensive scale so as to develop new mines in the future.

The power industry is of great importance for the overall rehabilitation and development of the national economy. During the postwar Three-Year Plan, all existing power stations should be rehabilitated and generators corresponding to their capacities should be completely installed, thereby bringing the generating capacity up to a maximum of 1.4-1.5 million kw.

Electrical appliances factories should be erected to produce electrical appliances for civilian use at home.

In the chemical industry, an ammonium sulphate plant and an ammonium nitrate plant should be restored or newly built in Hungnam. Thus, it should be made possible to supply agriculture with much chemical fertilizer in the next 2-3 years.

We should restore and build the Korea-Soviet Oil Company and the Aoji Synthetic Oil Plant.

Experimental work should be undertaken for the production of synthetic rubber and chemical fibres; measures should be taken for the rapid rehabilitation of the Chongjin Staple Fibre Factory.

In carrying out the vast postwar rehabilitation work, the need for building materials is great. All Party members and the entire people should be made to strive for the rapid development of the building-materials industry, by being brought to realize the fact that the building-materials industry is of special great importance for rebuilding ravaged towns, villages, factories, mills, mines, railways, highways, bridges, schools, hospitals, theatres and cinema houses.

The Ministry of the Building Materials Industry should produce building materials in large quantities, relying chiefly on the big plants; other ministries and bureaus, too, should organize the production of building materials, and locally obtainable building materials particularly should be extensively tapped and brought into use throughout the country. Depending on local conditions, private funds should be drawn into use extensively to organize producers' co-operatives for turning out simple kinds of building materials; individuals also should be allowed to run small enterprises to produce building materials.

The Ministry of the Building Materials Industry should set up brick and roofing-tile yards in Pyongyang, Hamhung, Chongjin, Kanggye, Uiju, Wonsan, Kaechon, Haeju, Sariwon and other places to turn out annually 500 million bricks from 1954, of which 300 million should be produced by state-owned brick yards and 200 million by local industry, and 40 million roofing tiles.

In cement production, all cement factories which had been in operation before the war should be rehabilitated to produce annually 200,000-300,000 tons of cement from 1954; by 1956 the output of cement should exceed the prewar level.

Factories should be built attached to the smelteries, iron works and railways in order to make cement with powdered slag. Immediate measures should be taken to make bricks and prefabricated parts from slag; slate yards should be rebuilt in Chongjin and Sunghori.

The Nampo Glass Factory should be speedily restored so as to start producing sheet glass in the first half of 1954. Factories for making cement sewer pipes should go up in the near future to ensure their mass production.

A new factory should be built to begin the production of cast iron pipes in 1955 so as to ensure water supply and sewerage works.

The ceramic industry should be developed on a large scale so as to turn out sanitary porcelain needed in new construction as well as ceramic articles of daily use; masonry should be developed so that marble and granite in which our country abounds can be put to great use.

We should extensively set up or expand building instruments plants to fully meet the requirements of postwar rehabilitation work for those instruments.

In order to stabilize the people's life and satisfy their requirements for necessaries, our Party should pay deep attention to the development of light industry. First of all, both the Pyongyang and Kusong Textile Mills should be expanded to turn out 60-70 million metres of cotton fabrics annually; silk yarn should be produced in quantities by processing silkworm cocoons procured in the countryside.

For the development of the food industry, foodstuffs factories for producing soy, bean paste, bean oil, milk products, canned goods, liquors, tobacco, etc., should be restored or newly built.

And the rubber footwear factories which existed before should be restored and a new rubber factory should be built to ensure the production of rubber goods and footwear in large quantities; leather shoes also have to be produced in abundance.

In order to meet the domestic needs for paper, the Kilju and Sinuiju Pulp Factories should be rapidly rehabilitated so as to ensure an annual output of 40,000 tons of pulp, and a new kraft paper factory should be built.

Every provincial people's committee should work for the development of local industry to produce and supply large quantities of daily necessaries for the people.

The fishing industry occupies an important place in the

national economy of our country. In view of the fact that livestock breeding is underdeveloped, it is especially important to supply sea foods to the People's Army and the entire working people. Therefore, we should immediately begin catching fish on an extensive scale. To this end, we should organize state fisheries and fishermen's co-operatives widely and the state should take measures for boosting their catches.

Most important of all for the development of the fishing industry is to ensure the supply of fishing equipment. The State Planning Commission, the Ministry of Heavy Industry, the Ministry of Light Industry and the Bureau of the Fishing Industry should start building fishing boats and manufacturing fishing nets on a wide scale to bring the production up to the prewar level by 1955. In order to prevent fish from spoiling or rotting, plans should be drawn up to build refrigeration plants and tanks, drying facilities and canneries.

We should carry on fish breeding on a big scale in all reservoirs and actively protect fishes so as to enrich the fish resources of our country. Our country has all the necessary conditions for this. The question is that our functionaries should not concern themselves only with immediate tasks, but organize work in a prospective manner, looking forward into the future.

(2) DIRECTION FOR THE REHABILITATION OF TRANSPORT AND COMMUNICATIONS

For the rapid development of the national economy in the postwar period, the railways must be rehabilitated before anything else.

In railway transport, all the major trunk lines in the northern half of the Republic should be restored within 20 to 30 days so that trains can be operated; railway transport should be brought to normal throughout the northern half of the Republic by the end of 1953. Thus, it should be made possible to transport 12-15 million tons of freight in 1954, and 15-18 million tons in 1955 to exceed the prewar level.

In railway reconstruction, medium and small railway bridges should be restored to their prewar state; the big, important railway bridges over the Rivers Taedong-gang, Chongchon-gang, Amnok-gang and Songchon-gang should be restored for temporary use, and they should be rebuilt and readjusted for permanent use after the country's economic foundations have been strengthened.

The Yangdok-Chonsong and Kaego-Koin sections, where there are steep gradients, must be electrified.

Proceeding from the experiences gained in the war, we must lay a new railway line between Yangdok and Koksan in the future, and the Palwon-Kujang and Kujang-Tokchon lines now under construction should be completed by the first quarter of 1954.

The damaged railway lines for exclusive use in factory compounds should be restored quickly so that they may be used in rebuilding the factories; work should be started now on station yards to restore them in the shape of temporary buildings by the end of 1954, and in some areas the station yards should be rehabilitated completely by incorporating their construction in the Three-Year Plan. Meanwhile, the railway communication networks should be put in perfect order by the end of 1953.

For the speedy repair of damaged rolling stock, new rolling stock repair shops should be built so that they can be put into commission at the end of 1954, and they should be expanded to make it possible to produce domestic freight and passenger cars beginning with 1957.

We must see to it that the Hongui railway line is opened to traffic at an early date.

During the war, particularly great strides were made in motor transport. But meanwhile, we overused motorcars in many cases to meet urgent wartime needs, and failed to exercise strict control over their use. As a result, the life of thousands of motorcars was greatly shortened.

With the beginning of peaceful construction, we can no longer tolerate such shortcomings in motor transport. Motor transport should be placed under centralized control, and the long distance runs which were allowed during the war must be strictly forbidden; the operation of motorcars should be limited, as a rule, to the areas where no railway service is available, or to short runs.

To prolong the life of motorcars and repair damaged ones we must rehabilitate or newly construct repair shops, while setting up garages in various places.

Motor freight turnover should be upwards of 5 million tons during 1954-55; regular bus service should be organized in and between urban communities for the convenience of the passengers.

For smooth motor transport, highways should be restored and renovated in the next one or two years.

The most important question in marine transport following the armistice is to rehabilitate and construct ports and wharves for foreign trade. We must first of all rehabilitate and put in order the wharves in the ports of Nampo, Chongjin and Hungnam in the near future.

We must salvage and repair sunken vessels, and organize work to repair civilian boats and naval vessels.

With a view to developing river transport we should take a long-sighted view and take measures to open regular freight and passenger boat services between Pyongyang and Chaeryong, Pyongyang and Nampo, and Manpo and Supung.

As to air transport, the Korea-Soviet Aviation Company should immediately start operation and regular passenger service should be opened on the Pyongyang-Hamhung-Chongjin-Aoji and Pyongyang-Sinuiju-Shenyang routes.

Tasks for the normalization of communications in the Republic are as follows:

Before the end of the third quarter of 1953, the telegraph and telephone grids linking the centre with provincial seats, cities and counties, should be restored; in Pyongyang and other major cities telephone wires should be replaced by underground cables in accordance with city construction planning; in the Pyongyang area automatic telephones and switchboards should be installed; and wireless network must needs be formed to link the provincial seats with the capital.

To develop the broadcasting service which plays an important role in propagating the policies of our Party and Government and in enlightening and educating the people, the equipment of the existing radio stations should be further improved; a 150 kw. medium-wave transmitter should be installed in Pyongyang by 1954; the five kw. medium-wave transmitter in Chongjin should be replaced in 1953 by a ten kw. one, and a new broadcasting station of over two kw. capacity should be set up in Kaesong. By the end of 1954, through-wire broadcasting should be organized in every provincial seat and industrial district, and by 1956 the through-wire broadcasting network should cover every *ri* and big village.

The construction of a communication equipment and apparatus factory, to be commissioned towards the end of 1954, should be included in the Three-Year Plan and the existing dry battery factory should be expanded to produce wireless and telephone sets, switchboards, loud-speakers and dry batteries so as to satisfy the requirements of the population and the People's Army for them.

Work should be started in 1954 to restore and build, according to yearly plans, post offices in the provincial seats, cities and counties; some post offices should be housed in temporary buildings. The Ministry of Communications itself should reduce superfluous personnel and allocate more people to mail delivery in local areas, in order to make it possible to directly organize door-to-door delivery in keeping with the extension of the *ri*'s size.

(3) BASIC DIRECTION FOR THE REHABILITATION AND DEVELOPMENT OF AGRICULTURE

Comrades,

Our agriculture suffered enormous damage during the three years of severe war against the U.S. and British armed invaders. There is a serious shortage of farm labour; the number of domestic animals has dropped drastically; many reservoirs and irrigation facilities have been destroyed by the enemy's bombing; many peasant families are short of food and seed grain.

As all of you know, during the war when nearly all our industrial facilities were ravaged, the Party and the state directed all their attention to rural work. Of course, this policy of our Party proved correct.

But we have not yet settled the rural question, which must be solved on all accounts. First of all, there is the problem of the ultra-small peasants and slash-and-burn peasants who are land-hungry and whose lands are poor.

We have ultra-small peasants accounting for 30-40 per cent of all peasant households. From the time of Japanese imperialist rule until now, they have lived in poverty.

To improve their livelihood, the Party and the Government have loaned food and seed grain to them, exempted them from the tax in kind, and given them various other benefits. Nevertheless, because their land is insufficient and poor, the problem of the ultra-small peasants remains unsolved to this day. Therefore, our primary task in the postwar rehabilitation and development of agriculture is to solve the problem of the ultra-small peasants.

The improvement of the living conditions of these peasants requires careful, proper measures by the state. In the first place, they should be induced to make good use of their land and some of them should be moved to areas where soil is fertile and land sufficient, while sideline co-operatives should be organized on a wide scale to improve their livelihood.

At the same time, as industry develops, part of the ultra-small peasants and slash-and-burn peasants should be drawn into industries, while others should be widely taken on by state livestock farms.

To speedily rehabilitate devastated agriculture and further advance its productive forces in the future, we should gradually co-operativize individual peasant farming. Beginning with 1954, agricultural co-operatives should be organized in an experimental way in some areas on the basis of preserving private ownership of land and production implements.

We should direct great efforts in the postwar period to the development of state farms and agricultural co-operatives and provide measures for the gradual mechanization of our agriculture in the future.

Individual peasant farming will be maintained in our country for some time to come. We must further increase the farm production of the peasants by widely popularizing new methods of farming in individual peasant economy, by taking steps for the state to supply the peasants with sufficient new production implements and supplying enough irrigation water, good strains of seed and fertilizer.

It is of exceptional importance for the rehabilitation and development of agriculture to ameliorate soil and obtain new lands.

First of all, irrigation work should be undertaken on an extensive scale so that the fields, which are low-yielding, are turned into paddies which give high yields. We should include in the Three-Year Plan the Pyongnam Irrigation Project which was begun already before the war, and should start full-scale work on it from 1955.

Our country is very short of arable land. It is therefore very important for the development of agriculture in our country to expand the cultivated area by obtaining new land. To obtain new land, we must recover the farm lands devastated in the war, washed away by flood or taken up by unnecessary road building. In the mountain areas of Chagang, North Pyongan, North and South Hamgyong Provinces, etc., all the land should be converted into farmland or pasture, except that which can be developed into forests in the future, and surveys should be made of the tidelands on the west coast.

For the purpose of securing raw materials for our advancing industry, we must encourage individual peasants to cultivate industrial crops and, at the same time, must set up state industrial-crop farms.

In order to promote the work of seed improvement, the state should organize the work of seed collection everywhere on a wide scale, and the experimental farms should be restored and expanded.

Animal husbandry occupies a very important place in the rehabilitation and development of agriculture. It supplies the working people and the People's Army with meat and, at the same time, furnishes necessary raw materials to industry.

Though the animal husbandry of our country had many shortcomings, it made steady progress even under difficult wartime conditions. The hundreds of thousand head of cattle and sheep sent by the fraternal Mongolian people provide the foundation for the state stock farms of our country.

In the postwar period, we should develop our animal husbandry along the following three lines:

First, state-run animal husbandry should be developed. It should be developed in places where there are breweries and distilleries, oil factories and rice mills, as well as in the mountain areas of North and South Hamgyong and Chagang Provinces, etc. It is important in state-run animal husbandry to make rational use of labour and utilize natural fodder on a big scale in order to increase the proceeds.

Second, measures should be taken by the state to organize combined agricultural and stockbreeding co-operatives for the collective breeding of livestock by the peasants in the mountain areas and by the ultra-small peasants with small and poor land. At first, these agro-stock co-operatives should be organized in an exemplary way in many places with ultra-small peasants and then, drawing on the acquired experience, they should be formed in all mountain areas of the country.

Third, stockbreeding should be encouraged and an all-people movement should be launched for abolishing peasant households that do not keep domestic animals, so that by 1956 the number of livestock kept by the individual peasants attains the prewar level in all regions. To this end, the state should undertake the task of supplying many breeding animals, while inducing the peasants to be interested in the development of animal husbandry by allowing them freely to dispose of the domestic animals they keep.

To prevent epizootics and perishing which constitute the greatest menace to the development of animal husbandry, the training of veterinaries should be stepped up, various veterinary facilities be kept in good shape, production of veterinary medicine developed, and measures should be taken to prevent epizootics.

Courses in practical matters for managers and responsible personnel in charge of livestock farms should be organized according to plan in order to bring about improvement in the management of state stock farms and ultra-small peasants' agro-stock co-operatives; special attention should be paid to the work of training cadres for the development of animal husbandry, so as to prevent state stock farms from causing losses to the state as at present; at the same time books on animal husbandry should be published in large numbers to widely popularize breeding techniques.

(4) DIRECTION FOR THE DEVELOPMENT OF FORESTRY

The war played havoc with our country's forestry. Yet, the needs for timber are increasing as never before in the postwar rehabilitation and construction of the national economy. This places before us the task of unfolding an all-people movement for extensive afforestation to make up for the damage our forests sustained during the war.

In afforestation work it is necessary to select suitable land for it and good species of saplings and give correct guidance in tree nursery work so that sufficient saplings are prepared. Seed collection and tree planting should be conducted in a nation-wide drive; the ideological work of educating the broad masses of the people and the forestry workers in the spirit of preserving the forests with good care should be conducted so as to strictly prohibit reckless deforestation and tree stealing; and stringent measures should be taken to prevent forest fires.

Lumbering should be conducted strictly according to the regulations with scrupulous regard to the future prospects of forest resources. There should be no waste but effective use should be made of timber. At the same time, every ministry and bureau should practise maximum economy in timber and the State Planning Commission must exercise strict control over its use. And the pulp mills must have their own forest areas and plant them with trees, thus securing their own pulp wood.

To turn out timber urgently needed for the rehabilitation of the national economy, forestry stations should be further strengthened; the Paekdu-san forest railway should be rapidly rebuilt to ensure the smooth transportation of timber.

To organize the development of forest resources with a long-sighted view, the State Planning Commission should include the training of forestry workers and survey of forest resources in the postwar Three-Year Plan.

(5) DIRECTION FOR THE REHABILITATION AND RECONSTRUCTION OF TOWNS AND COUNTRYSIDE

In rebuilding cities, townships and factory districts destroyed in the bombings by the U.S. imperialist barbarians, we must reject the outmoded way of town building prevalent before in the days of Japanese imperialist rule, which was uncivilized and catered to the selfish ends of the privileged classes. We must build cities and townships in such a way as to suit the convenience of the working people's life and a modern, cultured life. In urban construction, therefore, hygienic conditions for the people should be the first consideration; and in thickly populated major towns and factory districts attention should be paid to the building of waterworks, sewerage, and recreation grounds, ensuring of enough sunlight and good lighting, and heating systems. The building of cultural and welfare facilities such as schools, cultural institutions, cinema houses, theatres, hospitals, bath-houses and, especially, of safety facilities should be envisaged to provide conveniences for the life of the working people.

In urban construction, the necessary area of the city and its centre should be rightly laid out on the basis of a correct estimate of the rate of population growth, and the main traffic network and thoroughfares should be properly planned. We should do away with all planless, disorderly practices in construction, and see to it that all construction projects are placed under strict state control. We should strictly define the order of priority in construction and start with the most urgent and necessary projects.

The present organizational system of the Ministry of Urban Construction is inadequate to guide the rehabilitation and construction of towns and factory districts. So, the Cabinet has reorganized the Ministry of Urban Construction into the Ministry of City Management whose principal duty is confined solely to city management, and newly set up the State Construction Commission under the Cabinet to organize and guide all construction work. The State Construction Commission should guide the drawing up of necessary designs for the construction of towns and factory districts, organize construction work, exercise control over the construction trusts and urban construction commissions and check up on all state construction work. To guarantee success in construction work, all building technicians and skilled builders in the country should be concentrated under the Construction Commission, and the construction trusts in the cities should be reinforced.

In building towns and factory districts, priority should be given to factories, schools, hospitals, etc., with second place going to institutions and dwellings. For this purpose, the Construction Commission should work out standard designs for basic buildings and temporary ones (for five-ten years' use), which should be sent to the construction agencies and made known to the entire people. When the city limits have to be extended in the course of urban construction, it must also be done according to the order of priority. Erecting temporary structures in city centres should be strictly forbidden; they should be built outside the city centres.

To speed up the rehabilitation and construction of towns and ensure smooth progress in construction in the future, we must see to it that state and public treatment of architects is improved, help the architects and building technicians to understand correctly the direction for the postwar rehabilitation and construction of the national economy, and strive to get them to show greater enthusiasm and creative initiative. In order to successfully cope with the vast postwar construction, we have to take immediate measures to send architects abroad to study, set up research institutions, and expand and consolidate training centres and schools for building technicians and skilled builders. In view of the labour shortage, measures should be taken for the mechanization of building work so as to reduce the time required in construction.

(6) BASIC DIRECTION FOR EDUCATIONAL WORK

In order to fulfil successfully the basic tasks of postwar rehabilitation and development of the national economy and turn our country into an industrial country in the future, the entire Party and the whole state should direct their attention to the training of a huge army of native cadres by improving higher and technical education.

In the sphere of higher education, all the institutions of higher learning which existed before the war should be completely restored, and an Institute of National Economy should be newly established to raise the government functionaries' level of leadership and to train reserve cadres. The Institute will have such faculties as planned economy, finance and banking, co-operative economy and foreign trade; its students should be chosen primarily from among the excellent functionaries working in the institutions and model factory workers, and be trained as a reserve of cadres.

A college of construction should be newly set up to train building technicians and leading personnel for construction work who are in great demand in postwar rehabilitation and construction. To develop livestock breeding, a new veterinary and stockbreeding institute should be established.

In higher education emphasis should be put on the training of technical personnel essential for the development of the national economy; upwards of 70 per cent of the total number of students should major in engineering and natural science; evening and correspondence courses of the colleges should be established on an extensive scale.

In the domain of technical education the practice of organizing work without any plan, as is now the case, should be remedied, the level of the specialized technical schools should be raised, necessary textbooks quickly compiled for them, and their facilities expanded.

In the sphere of general education the number of schools and school children should regain the prewar level by 1956. To that end, we must rebuild 3,960 primary schools and bring the number of primary school children to 1,500,000; all the junior and senior middle schools which existed before the war should be restored, and their enrolment, too, should be brought up to the prewar level.

With a view to raising the qualifications of teachers and re-educating them, we should improve the work of the normal schools, teachers' training colleges and normal colleges, and set up short-term training courses attached to them.

The Party and the state should direct attention to the writing and compilation of textbooks. To step up the publication of textbooks, we should expand the printing house under the Ministry of Education and the state combined printing plant; each institution of higher learning should have its own printing facilities of a simple type and mimeographing facilities in order to ensure the printing of those college textbooks, the demand for which is not great.

In building and rehabilitating schools, the state will bear the costs for institutions of higher learning, specialized schools, and senior middle schools in some industrial districts. And establishments of general education should be built through a movement of the people as a whole. To fill up the shortage of teachers we have to look up ex-teachers who are now working scatteredly in various other organs, and assign them to the educational field.

(7) DIRECTION FOR THE REHABILITATION AND CONSTRUCTION OF CULTURAL AND PROPAGANDA ESTABLISHMENTS

To fulfil successfully the political, economic and cultural tasks which confront our Party and Government after the war, we have to restore and readjust the war-ravaged cultural and propaganda establishments, and improve their work. Thus we should further step up the work of cultural and propaganda establishments in factories, rural areas and in fishing villages, restore and put in order the clubs at places of work and the village democratic publicity halls, regularly furnishing them with material and equipment for cultural use, propaganda material, publications and so on, and organize the work of re-educating those in charge of the clubs and halls.

In order to widely popularize movies, a powerful means of mass propaganda, we should regularly operate mobile movie teams in the countryside and envisage in the Three-Year Plan the construction of cinema houses in the county seats and factory districts.

As for film production, arrangements should be made to start producing documentaries at once; the national economic plan should provide for the capital construction necessary for the production of feature films at home from 1954.

The Three-Year Plan must provide for the building of art and drama theatres in Pyongyang, the democratic capital, and in the provincial seats; record and gramophone factories should be built to start production in 1955.

We should expand the State Publishing House to put out

books in large quantities, and reorganize part of the apparatus of the Ministry of Culture and Propaganda to direct and control all the publishing agencies and printing shops in the country and assure the supply of necessary materials for them.

To improve the work of libraries, the national economic plan should provide for the restoration and expansion of the State Library in the capital and for the building of libraries in the provincial seats and other major towns. We have to erect revolutionary and historical museums so as to widely publicize the historical relics of our country and the heroic feats of the Korean people in their struggles both during the war and in the period of peaceful construction, and promote the work of preserving historical relics and restoring and rearranging the war-devastated places of historical interest.

To train artists whose number is short at present and to develop Korea's national art, art schools should be set up attached to the State Art Theatre and State Theatre. On this basis, an art institute should be established in the future.

(8) BASIC DIRECTION FOR PUBLIC HEALTH SERVICE

Our Party should pay attention to the growth of population in order to make up for the loss of human lives in the war.

Measures should be taken to improve conditions for the protection of mothers and care of children; medical assistance to those who were wounded in enemy bombing and in battle during the war and the upbringing of orphans, should be regarded as an important task of the state and the public, and great attention should be directed to it.

It must be stipulated in the Three-Year Plan that destroyed hospitals and clinics shall be reconstructed, and that a central general hospital and a municipal hospital be established in Pyongyang, a provincial hospital in each provincial seat, and people's hospitals in factories and townships.

The technical qualifications of doctors should be improved

and, at the same time, the work of medical colleges and medical schools be strengthened. Prevention of epidemics and dissemination, through the medium of various newspapers and magazines and radio, of knowledge of public health and sanitation should be promoted.

Medicine production should be organized by widely collecting medicinal materials abundant in our country. The construction of a pharmaceutical factory should be included in the Three-Year Plan.

A mass movement for developing physical strength should be launched everywhere—at schools, factories and villages; sports organizations should be rapidly restored; many stadiums and swimming pools should be built.

3. SOME PROBLEMS FOR THE SUCCESSFUL CARRYING OUT OF THE REHABILITATION OF THE NATIONAL ECONOMY

Comrades,

As I have said above, we are confronted with enormous and difficult tasks in the postwar rehabilitation and development of the national economy.

The great significance of the postwar rehabilitation and development of the national economy in the future development of our country and the improvement of the people's livelihood must be thoroughly brought home to all Party members and all the people so that they rise as one in this work. The best use must be made of the truce period to mobilize without a moment's delay all the forces of the Party and the people in the rehabilitation and construction of the national economy.

Even though the task of postwar rehabilitation of the national economy is difficult, we must carry out this honourable task without fail; we have every condition and possibility for its fulfilment.

First, we have the valuable experience of rebuilding, during the five years after the August 15 Liberation, the national economy which had been wrecked and destroyed by the Japanese imperialists. We have a priceless experience acquired in the struggle to build underground munitions factories and meet the needs of the front during the severe three-year Fatherland Liberation War waged against the U.S. imperialist aggressors. Also, we have political workers, economic personnel, technicians, skilled workers, and workers steeled in the severe and difficult war.

Second, we are rich in resources. All kinds of resources—ferrous and nonferrous metals, coal, lumber, etc.—needed in the rehabilitation and development of our national economy are inexhaustible. The thing is to use this wealth of resources to turn out, through our labour, necessaries of life for our people and products which can be of use in laying the foundations of the state economy, and to convert them into the vital, material force of our national economy.

Third, in the struggle for the rehabilitation and development of the national economy in the postwar years, too, we shall receive reliable support and assistance from the international democratic camp. The peoples of the great Soviet Union, China and many other brotherly countries have promised to render us as much aid as possible to satisfy the requirements of our people for the rehabilitation and development of the national economy.

The Soviet Government has notified us that it has decided to give our people one thousand million rubles of aid for the rehabilitation and construction of the national economy of our country.

The Governments of many countries such as Poland, Czechoslovakia and Hungary have also decided to give us aid for the rehabilitation and development of the national economy of our country. Mass movements are already unfolded by the peoples of these fraternal countries to assist the Korean people in the rehabilitation and construction of the national economy.

The aforementioned conditions, plus all the other favourable conditions we have, constitute a sure guarantee of our victory in the struggle for the postwar rehabilitation and development of the national economy, too.

The question depends upon whether or not we do our job well as masters of the state and how well and how rapidly we transform all these possibilities into reality. First of all, we must have faith in our own strength—the strength of our Party, our power and our people. With this inexhaustible strength we shall triumph in the struggle for the postwar rehabilitation and development of the national economy, too, just as we emerged victorious from the severe war against the enemy.

What, then, are the problems to which we should direct attention in connection with the postwar rehabilitation and development of the national economy?

(1) CONCERNING THE EXPLOITATION OF INNER RESOURCES

All the inner resources of our country must be exploited to the maximum and utilized effectively and rationally for the rehabilitation and development of the national economy. The trouble lies not in the lack or shortage of materials and underground resources, but in the fact that some of the responsible economic personnel refuse to recognize and utilize the inner resources of our country, and do not exploit them. As in the saying, "Nose clogged, short of wind," some workers, while raising the cry of "shortage of materials," think little of how to tap and utilize inner resources for meeting the shortage. People of this sort are probably waiting for timber, iron and other raw materials to come to their offices and ask them to be used effectively. Our task is to explore, mobilize and utilize our inner resources quickly. At the same time, extensive surveying and prospecting of inner resources should be conducted. This work, of course, cannot be done if it is entrusted only to a certain specific branch. The entire Party must devote attention to this work, and large numbers of scientific workers, scholars and specialists must be drawn into it.

On the other hand, old materials, tools, and equipment which were scattered about during the war, must be quickly collected and put to rational use. Special attention must be paid to the production of building materials. We must mass-produce bricks, cement, timber, and structural steel which are greatly needed in postwar rehabilitation. We may import machinery from foreign countries, but how can we import such things as timber, bricks and cement in large quantities? If we organize their production capably at an early date, we can produce at home as much as we need. We must strive to produce by ourselves all the materials that can be turned out at home.

We should also step up the production of all kinds of exportable goods which can bring us foreign currency and thus obtain a large amount of foreign currency with which we should import more machinery and equipment and build more new factories.

The whole Party and the entire people must direct their attention to the exploration and utilization of our inner resources.

(2) ON SECURING LABOUR POWER AND USING IT RATIONALLY

A large number of skilled hands and workers—the main detachment of our industry—joined the People's Army and went to the front during the Fatherland Liberation War; they still are standing honourably at the outposts for the defence of the country. In addition, the loss of lives in the war is inevitably having its effect on our labour front. At present our labour power falls short of the enormous demands of the postwar rehabilitation and development of the national economy. Can we solve the problem of labour power? Of course, we can. And the solution of this problem requires the most careful and detailed plans and organizational measures.

To solve the problem of labour power needed in the postwar rehabilitation and development of the national economy, it is first necessary to make rational use of manpower and stop wasting it. During the war, with a view to protecting the lives of people from the barbarous bombing of the enemy, we evacuated urban dwellers and allocated them to new factories and farms set up in the remote mountain areas. In many cases, attention was given to allocating an excessive number of workers and settling them down in disregard of the financial loss involved in their management. This measure was necessary and correct in the prevailing conditions at that time. However, today when we have set about the overall postwar rehabilitation and development of the national economy, there must be a radical change in this state of affairs. Workers should be shifted from those production units which have surplus manpower or are of secondary importance to important factories and key branches of production according to priority. For example, many of new farms and livestock farms established during the war still have tens of thousands of surplus workers; in some livestock farms the work hands remain as they were allocated there, whose number is many times larger than the number of the animals. If the thousands of scattered orchards and small enterprises now in existence are readjusted and amalgamated, much manpower can be curtailed.

Second, non-productive labour power should be cut and the apparatus simplified. Under the dispersed work conditions of wartime, various administrative offices took on much non-productive labour of little importance. For example, in peace time, one dining-room will suffice for the needs of one institution, but in wartime it had three or four dining-rooms. Consequently, many more general-service workers, accountants, dining-hall managers, storekeepers, cooks and odd-job men, etc., had to be employed. As in the old saying, "The more pots, the more waste," this resulted in a tremendous waste of labour power, to say nothing of materials. This is but one familiar instance. We have still quite a number of superfluous apparatus and departments. Waste of labour is virtually a common practice. The question is to save much manpower by means of amalgamating and readjusting, in conformity with the postwar circumstances of today, what had to be dispersed during the war.

The tasks facing our Party members and state functionaries are boldly to simplify the administrative offices, mobilizing and shifting all the unnecessary, non-productive labour power to the rehabilitation of factories and to production, and to make rational and effective use of labour power, eliminating its waste.

Third, we must replenish and extend our labour front by extensively enlisting woman labour. It was indisputably demonstrated in the course of the Fatherland Liberation War that the strength of our heroic Korean women is inexhaustible. On the labour front, too, they are working as well as men and performing great exploits. Many women should be enlisted in light industry, where jobs are suitable to their physique and abilities. Women should be employed extensively in office work in institutions of trade, communications, health service, culture, education, etc. Various conveniences must be provided for them in their work. In this way man labour should be replaced by woman labour in many offices and thus men should be transferred to production enterprises.

Fourth, work processes should be mechanized to save labour and raise labour productivity. Needless to say, what we mean is not mechanization in the sense of advanced technique. A high level of mechanization is a problem which we should solve gradually in step with the development of industry and progress of technology. What we mean by mechanization under present conditions is primarily that technicians and workers make their operations simple, easy and efficient through original ideas and devices. Not long ago, at the Nampo Smeltery we saw a worker carrying no more than two shovelfuls of earth on his back and dumping it in a place barely twenty or thirty paces away. If a wheelbarrow were employed in such a work, the job could be done easily and efficiently. If the primitive work methods commonly used at the places of work such as the Cholsan Mine were mechanized in this way, the labour of thousands of men could be easily saved and work could be done speedily and efficiently. We must show special concern for the mechanization of work processes and rational organization of labour.

Fifth, along with the question of rational utilization of labour power, setting correct work norms poses a very serious question before us. The current work norms which were set in 1947-48 are now outdated and out of keeping with actual conditions. Because by now the level of ideological consciousness of the working people, particularly workers, has risen immensely, their technical level has gone up, and work methods have improved. The situation has changed, the working people have changed, and techniques, too, have improved, but our economic personnel are marking time, adhering as ever to the work norms fixed seven or eight years ago.

The work norms set in the past are irrational and low in many respects. This can be judged easily from the following instance: Last winter we mobilized the men of a People's Army regiment for lumbering. Its servicemen did 1,000 per cent as much work as the work norm now in force. This is indeed a puzzling miracle. What does this situation reveal to us? There is no secret or puzzle here. This hard fact shows that past work norms are now outdated, inconsistent with reality and quite unreasonable in many respects. Taking into account all the changed conditions, we should carefully re-examine old work norms and set new, correct ones to suit actual conditions.

In setting new work norms, we must wage a relentless struggle against departmentalism, fame seeking, selfishness, and all other backward notions and attitudes. Here, too, things old and backward stand in the way of our progress.

Sixth, as many slash-and-burn peasants as possible should be made to join industry according to their wishes.

Since liberation we have carried out various measures to improve those peasants' living conditions. Nevertheless, this problem still remains unsolved.

We have arrived at the conclusion that it is impossible to improve the life of the slash-and-burn peasants as long as their original working and living conditions are left unchanged. But the functionaries in the Ministry of Agriculture and the people's committees at all levels are doing such a harmful and irresponsible work as to fell trees at random in state forests to keep enlarging burns under the pretext of obtaining more sown area, in violation of the policy of the Party and the Government and of state regulations. Such a practice can no longer be tolerated, and must be corrected immediately.

The Ministry of Agriculture and the organs concerned should carry on adequate explanation among the slash-and-burn peasants to induce the majority of them to voluntarily join industry, and should take concrete, organizational steps for the rest to take jobs on farms, livestock farms or in the fisheries. This, too, will enable us to secure no small labour force for the postwar rehabilitation and development of the national economy.

Seventh, we should extensively conduct the work of patriotic labour service of the popular masses in rehabilitating the national economy.

During wartime, the people solved many problems and made a great contribution to our victory by participating extensively in patriotic labour service for victory in the war.

We must develop a mass labour service campaign, calling on the masses of the people to display patriotic devotion in rehabilitating the war-ravaged production enterprises, educational and cultural establishments of our country, too.

In the rehabilitation of the national economy, there are many cases when tremendous labour power is required at a time. For example, in building factories, schools or hospitals, the foundation work requires enormous labour power at a stretch. In a brickyard, a small labour force can fully ensure production after it is completely equipped, but in the course of its construction, especially at the beginning, huge labour power is needed. Such a huge temporary demand for labour should be met by the patriotic labour service of the masses of the people.

Therefore, we should mobilize patriotic labour service on a wide scale in a movement of the Party and the people as a whole. We must arouse and organize all the members of the Party and social organizations and the entire people to participate voluntarily in patriotic labour service, regarding it as their sacred duty and high honour.

All that has been stated above shows that we have enough resources and potentialities to meet labour shortage in the post-war rehabilitation and construction of the national economy.

We should see that deep attention be directed by the Party to such work as exploration of labour reserves, rational utilization and adjustment of labour power, elimination of its waste, and strict control over the fluidity of labour, and should solve these matters without fail.

(3) ON THE PROBLEM OF TECHNIQUE

Neglect of technique will lead to many errors and failures in economic construction, and will make it difficult to build factories, enterprises, schools, cultural establishments and hospitals. The situation in our country where technicians are short, makes it imperative to allocate and use them in a rational way. Technicians should not be concentrated in a certain branch; their allocation should be adjusted so that they may be used in a proper way in all branches of industrial construction. Adequate consideration must be given to them so that they can give full play to their technique and skill.

Further. Technical personnel must be allocated to branches in their own lines. Thus, they must be provided with every condition for putting their technique to full use and for displaying creative initiative in their work. Party organizations, government bodies and economic agencies at all levels should look up and register dispersed technicians, and transfer those technical personnel who serve in non-technical establishments to industrial construction. The Party must give serious attention to this work and conduct work with technicians systematically and persistently to give every possible aid in their practical activities.

At the same time, in order to solve the problem of technique, the re-education of technicians must be strengthened and the training of technical personnel carried out on an extensive scale. To raise the technical level of our technical personnel to that of technicians of the advanced countries, instruction and education at specialized technical schools, technical colleges, engineering colleges, and universities must be improved, and correspondence and evening courses in technical colleges and various technical training courses must be organized and operated effectively. An end should be put as soon as possible to all the existing formalistic, disorderly, irresponsible practices and attitudes in this work and education should be made substantial and practical.

Another important matter in the solution of the problem of technique is that of receiving technical aid from the fraternal countries. We have invited a large number of technicians from the Soviet Union for postwar rehabilitation. Our task in this connection is to learn technique from them sincerely and quickly. It would be very wrong merely to look up to and rely on them without learning technique from them. Technicians of the Soviet Union, an advanced country, have come to our country not only to help us solve our urgent technical problems but also to pass on their technique to us. Our management workers and technical personnel must learn from them and raise their technical standards in the course of living and working with them. This is the right attitude which will meet both the expectations of the technicians from this fraternal country and our own demands. Our technical personnel must strive to study the necessary advanced technique at the earliest possible date and thus become trustworthy technical cadres capable of tackling all technical problems independently. This is one of the most important tasks facing the management workers and technical personnel at present.

(4) FOR SECURING FUNDS NEEDED IN THE REHABILITATION AND CONSTRUCTION OF INDUSTRY

It is clear to all that the rehabilitation and construction of the national economy are impossible without funds. We are confronted with the important task of securing necessary funds for restoring and building factories and enterprises. Thanks to our correct financial and monetary policy, even during the war annual revenue was not less than in prewar years, and this year, too, it has surpassed last year's. In order to provide funds smoothly for production and construction, we must further increase the revenue in the future.

To secure necessary funds for the rehabilitation and construction of the national economy, we should first wage a resolute struggle against the practice of wastage and stealing. Some people pay little attention to wasting small things. The old saying has it: "Many a pickle makes a mickle." We should not waste even small things, but utilize and economize on all things. At a garment factory under the General Logistics Bureau, for example, an enormous amount of manpower and materials will be saved in producing, say, 1,000,000 uniforms if one less button hole is made per uniform. Even a small thing like this, when amassed, will amount to much.

In sawmills, wood chips—waste from sawing—can be used to make match sticks, chessmen, and the like. Nevertheless, they are cast aside. This is a great waste. In the timber industry and at the State Planning Commission work is done in a planless, irresponsible manner, which results in immense waste. For example, allocations are made in such a way that timber needed in Sinuiju is brought from North Hamgyong Province, and logs required in North Hamgyong Province, from Manpo. This not only inflicts an enormous financial loss on the country, but causes disorder in work. Many a kindred instance can be found in our daily life; we often come across such cases. We must acquire the habit of effectively utilizing and economizing on even trifling, insignificant things. Without this, we cannot manage the country's economy well.

Second, work must be done properly in the sphere of light industry. To produce consumer goods necessary for the people's life on a large scale and market them, is of great importance both in stabilizing the people's life and in increasing state revenue to secure necessary funds. Nevertheless, things are not going well in this respect. First of all, the commodities turned out by light and local industries are of poor quality and appearance, not to mention their meagre variety for the time being. Why is it that the daily necessities manufactured by light industry are of such a poor and inferior quality? We can no longer tolerate the lag in this sphere. We deem it necessary to call to this the attention of the responsible functionaries in this field from the Party viewpoint.

Special attention must be devoted to producing daily necessities in large quantities by tapping all potentials and local resources. This will constitute an important source for ensuring necessary funds for the rehabilitation and construction of the national economy.

Third, necessary funds for the rehabilitation and construction of the national economy should be obtained from trade. In every respect, our state trade enjoys favourable conditions. Nevertheless, state trade is partly lagging behind private trade owing to irresponsibility and unfaithfulness on the part of trade workers. Individual tradesmen went by bicycle, by cart or on foot, to places 40 or 50 *ri* away, sometimes as far as several hundred *ri*, to purchase goods for sale. In selling the commodities, too, they arranged them neat and tidy, though small in volume, and carried on trade in a businesslike manner. In contrast, state and consumers' co-operative stores make little effort to tap the sources of commodities. And in selling goods allocated by the state, too, the personnel set them out in a disorderly manner, and wait for customers amid dust and mould. It is therefore natural that the state stores are not popular with the consumers.

Thus, the workers in state trade and consumers' co-operatives prefer to sit idle, and to do the work assigned to them by the state in an easy-going manner, without using their heads. Can it be said that this is the right attitude to answer to the Party and the state for one's work? That commodities have thus far been sold in state and consumers' co-operative stores is, in fact, not because the state trade personnel have done their job well, but because prices at state stores are cheaper than the market prices.

When distributing commodities to local areas, too, the state trade workers are doing their work in an irresponsible and bureaucratic manner. Namely, in allocating commodities to all parts of the country, they send them at will without taking into consideration each area's demands, purchasing power and all other conditions. Therefore, commodities which are short in some districts are piled up mountain-high and left to decay in others. This is a common practice in the networks of stores under the Ministry of Commerce and in the networks of consumers' co-operative stores. Such practices cannot be ascribed to their lack of skill or inability, but are a shortcoming resulting from their ideological malady. Party organizations at all levels should pay special attention to radically remedying this harmful ideological disease of the trade workers.

Thus, we must make every possible effort not only to ensure the smooth supply of commodities required by the working people but also to secure funds for the state, by expanding and developing the circulation of commodities between town and country.

And we must launch an extensive savings campaign in order to tap and use the money in the hands of the people for postwar rehabilitation.

Fourth, the question of earning foreign currency and using it economically is of great significance for increasing capital investment in the rehabilitation and construction of factories and enterprises. To expand the volume of exports by exploring and developing the resources needed by the fraternal countries in order to obtain foreign currency, and to import, in return, the machinery and raw materials we need, is a national task of tremendous significance for the development of our national economy. The Party should direct special attention to this work.

Parallel with the procurement of foreign currency, a vigorous campaign for using it economically should be waged. To start with, we should economize on gasoline. If only we save half the gasoline we are now importing, we can purchase so much more machinery.

It is of great significance to economize on imported raw and other materials which are needed in the factories and enterprises. A certain factory, where production is carried on mainly with precious imported raw and other materials, applies to the state for 10-20 per cent more imported materials than its plan calls for, with the estimated rejects taken into account in advance. At the present time, the amount of rejects is in fact greater than estimated. It is quite easy to see what a great loss this causes to the country and how badly it affects the finances of those factories and enterprises.

Ideological work should be conducted among the management personnel and workers in factories and enterprises with regard to obtaining and saving foreign currency, and Party organizations at various levels must devote deep attention to this work.

(5) ON DRAWING UP CORRECT NATIONAL ECONOMIC PLANS

The most important work which we must do before anything else in starting postwar rehabilitation and construction is the mapping out of correct plans for the rehabilitation and development of the national economy. Without a correct plan which takes close account of actual conditions and is consistent with the objective requirements of social development in our country, it is impossible for us to take even a single step forward.

In working out the state plans it is the most important question to have accurate statistics. It is esssential to have accurate statistics for the country as a whole, for each ministry, and for each factory and enterprise under the ministries. It is no more than an empty talk to speak of working out a plan without detailed and accurate statistics of equipment, raw and other materials, funds and labour power. If, in restoring and constructing our huge, complex national economy and building and operating numerous factories and enterprises, we are to work not blindly but in a far-sighted manner on the basis of scientifically substantiated plans, without counting on luck or accident, we ought to have accurate statistics on our national economy.

The work of our economic institutions and their personnel, however, is very backward in this respect. A formalistic, bureaucratic style of work manifests itself very often in our economic institutions. Such a situation today presents a great obstacle to our collection of accurate, detailed statistics. We must quickly correct this intolerable style of work on the part of the economic institutions and their personnel and raise this work to a level commensurate with the demands of the Party and the state.

Further, in charting state plans, special attention should be given to finding the main link in the whole chain of the national economy. Rehabilitation and construction work should be started first of all in the key branches and enterprises of our national economy, so that when the main link is shored up all the others may follow it. It is necessary to locate the main link correctly, and it is important to concentrate all our efforts on this main link.

Under our present conditions, the diffusion and equal allocation of materials, labour force and funds will impede progress in work and eventually bring about waste of time and energy. This, of course, does not mean that the other branches may be neglected. It goes without saying that we must start work for rehabilitation and development of the national economy as a whole. But we must carry out our construction work according to the order of priority and the relative importance of the projects in an orderly manner. The state plans must be worked out so that our materials, labour power and funds may be utilized in a rational and flexible way.

(6) FOR RAISING THE STANDARD OF LEADERSHIP OF FUNCTIONARIES IN THE PARTY, GOVERNMENT AND ECONOMIC ORGANS

The Party Rules stipulates that every Party member should constantly raise his political and cultural level and become master of his own work and technique.

Leading personnel of our Party and state organs and Party members have made big strides in fulfilling their duties. But their work is still not done qualitatively and is far below the standard demanded by the Party.

The huge and complicated work of the postwar rehabilitation and development of the national economy makes it all the more imperative for our personnel to master knowledge of economics. If we fail to acquire it, we shall not be able to guide economic construction and advance our work even a single step forward.

Nevertheless, some of our responsible cadres are not well versed in their work; they do their work with little knowledge of the branch they work in. Wherever they go, such cadres take with them their proxies, vice-chairmen, section chiefs and chief engineers whom they ask to submit reports and dispose of affairs. They seem to think that their duties are to hold their posts, fix seals and stand on their dignity.

If responsible cadres wish to discharge their duties properly with a sense of responsibility, they ought to have a full understanding of their work and to be well versed in it. Otherwise, how can they be called responsible cadres of our Republic?

Some other responsible cadres pretend to know what they do not know; they are arrogant and only bent on preserving their dignity. Such cadres are not those our society needs. None of us had experience in state administration; the absolute majority of the leading functionaries of the state organs are of worker or peasant origin and are newly-appointed cadres. When one does not know, it is no shame to acknowledge ignorance.

The trouble is that some pretend to know or do not want to learn what they do not know. It behoves anyone who is ignorant to learn, he must learn from those who know.

It is not very easy for us to invent a new principle and technique. But it is not so difficult to learn the scientific and technological achievements made already in the Soviet Union and other advanced countries, and apply and use them effectively in our construction work.

We must learn continuously from the experience of the Soviet Union and other fraternal countries. The road of learning is open to us; we are provided with every condition to do so. We must learn open-mindedly, modestly and humbly, from Soviet scholars, specialists and technicians.

Since liberation we have trained large numbers of intellectuals and technicians. They can also be good teachers to our leading personnel as well as good helpers to us.

The work of translating and publishing Soviet books on technology should be conducted more extensively. This is an important step to help our leading personnel in their study, an important means of disseminating advanced science and technology among the cadres and the working people.

To raise the functionaries' standard of leadership, the system of collective consultation must be strengthened. The consultative bodies should serve as bodies not only for adopting measures collectively to conduct affairs, but also for people to learn from each other. We must strive to advance faster. To this end, we, through consultation, should sum up the experience in work and pool collective wisdom while discarding what is old and adopting what is new for progress in work. By running their councils properly, all the ministries and central organs should raise their level of leadership and improve their guidance of subordinate organs.

Immediately after liberation, there appeared among the people the watchword, "Ignorance means ruin." This was an outcry of the Korean people who had been thirsting for knowledge, and an appeal frankly expressing their burning zeal for learning.

Now, as ever, we are in need of advanced science and advanced technology. The question whether or not we acquire a good mastery of advanced science and technology is not only the key to success in the rehabilitation and development of our national economy, but one of decisive factors affecting the destiny of our nation. The task is to raise our responsible workers' standard of leadership on the basis of advanced science and technology.

Our Party will certainly achieve the expected results in this work, too.

4. ON STRENGTHENING IDEOLOGICAL WORK AMONG THE WORKING CLASS

Comrades,

In the wartime conditions when our industrial establishments were demolished by the barbarous bombing of the U.S. imperialists, our Party concentrated its attention on the rural question. This, of course, was a correct line. Had we not concentrated our attention on the rural policy when the countryside was ruined and there was an acute dearth of labour power and draught animals, we could not have supplied enough provisions for the front and the rear and stabilized the people's livelihood.

In the postwar period, too, our Party will hold to its correct policy on the rural question, and strive continuously for the rapid rehabilitation and development of agriculture and improvement of the peasants' life.

At the same time, in its future activities our Party should not put one-sided emphasis on the rural question as in wartime, but devote no less attention to the rehabilitation and development of industry. This means that our Party should direct its attention to industry and strengthen work among the working class—the leading class in our country.

Viewed from a historical standpoint, the working class of our country is young. The colonial industry which had developed to a certain extent, though in a deformed way, in the closing years of Japanese imperialist colonial rule, demanded cheap labour from our country's labour market. The source of such labour power consisted mainly of the poor peasantry in the rural areas who had been deprived of their land owing to the colonial land expropriation policy of the Japanese imperialists, and of the petty bourgeoisie who had gone bankrupt because of pressure from Japanese imperialist capital. Accordingly, the absolute majority of the workers of our country were formerly small commodity producers, and are even now linked directly or indirectly with small commodity production through their families and relatives. So, even though they themselves have ceased to be private owners of the means of production or independent commodity producers, petty-bourgeois mentality inevitably remains in their minds to a great extent, and continues to affect them.

On the other hand, the Japanese imperialists refused to initiate our Korean workers in technology or to train them to become skilled workers. As a result, in the years of Japanese imperialist rule, the absolute majority of our Korean workers were "casual labourers" without any technique or skill. The Japanese imperialists did not impart to the Korean workers even the minimum knowledge indispensable to industrial workers in modern capitalist society, keeping them in a benighted and ignorant state. Moreover, in the years of Japanese imperialist rule our workers toiled under wretched conditions beyond description. They usually worked 12 to 13 hours a day and their wages were so low that they could scarcely stave off starvation, far from supporting their families and giving schooling to their children. As a result, the Korean working class had neither the time nor the economic possibility to raise their cultural standard and their technical and skill level. In general, their cultural and technical standards were very low.

However, since the liberation of our country great changes have taken place in the class structure of our society and new social relations have emerged. The position of the working class of our country has radically changed and they have become masters of the state.

During the five years of peaceful construction after liberation, the workers' material and cultural standards went up and their class consciousness rose. Particularly, in the course of the three-year war, the political consciousness of our working class was elevated immensely. But among factory workers at present there are no small number of workers who are not yet armed with working-class consciousness, lack discipline and organization and fail to understand correctly their class stand that they are now masters of the state.

The reasons are:

First, with the outbreak of the Fatherland Liberation War large numbers of workers joined the People's Army and went to the front, and hosts of peasants and war-bankrupt petty bourgeois were newly drawn into industry to take their places. Thus, a big change has taken place in the ratio between the old and new workers. Now new hands comprise the majority of workers in our industry. For example, only 4 per cent of all the workers in heavy industry have over ten years' record and more than half have less than one year's labour experience. This has inevitably given cause to various backward ideas and habits of life that persist among the workers today.

Second, small commodity production still accounts for a very large proportion of the national economy in the northern half of the Republic. Such a state of affairs cannot help exerting an influence on the consciousness of the working people, especially the workers; it impedes the enhancement of the class consciousness and revolutionary spirit of the workers.

Third, the ideological remnants left over from the years of Japanese imperialist rule still persist in the minds of our people, and the U.S. imperialist aggressors are now ceaselessly spreading reactionary ideology among our people by every conceivable means and method. This also hinders our workers from strengthening their organization and discipline and arming themselves firmly with working-class ideology.

Hence our task to eliminate all the outmoded customs and consciousness of the working masses and to arm them thoroughly with new working-class ideology. To this end, we must take measures to train the core of the working class, heighten its political and cultural level, raise its skill and technique and improve its living conditions.

Party organizations, trade union and Democratic Youth League organizations at all levels must strive to strengthen political, ideological and mass cultural work among the workers, better the work of factory clubs and libraries, vigorously carry on various forms of technical education and the work of passing on technique and improve the workers' living conditions and their way of life.

No great successes can be scored in the postwar rehabilitation and development of the national economy, unless the level of consciousness and cultural and technical level of the working class are raised.

5. CONCERNING THE WORK IN THE NEWLY-LIBERATED AREAS

The work in the newly-liberated areas is of tremendous importance.

The newly-liberated areas—Kaesong, Kaepung, Panmun, Namyonbaek, and Ongjin—embrace a population of several hundred thousand. The people living in these areas groaned under long years of Japanese imperialist rule, and after the August 15 Liberation were subjected to oppression and exploitation under the fascist police rule of the U.S. aggressors and the Syngman Rhee puppet regime. They were greatly misled by the enemy's reactionary anti-communist propaganda. During the war the fleeing enemies drove many people to the south by force. In Kaesong, for instance, about 60-70 per cent of the entire population were taken away. In the Namyonbaek,

Ongjin and Kaepung areas, too, the absolute majority of the young and middle-aged men were dragged away by the enemy.

Some of our comrades, not taking into consideration such peculiarities of these areas, are ready to deprive the inhabitants of their citizenship and even confiscate their property, all without distinction, on the ground that they are the family members of those who have gone over to the south.

In view of the specific conditions in the newly-liberated areas, our Party and Government must take special measures concerning these areas.

It is necessary to make a sharp distinction in dealing with those who were forcibly taken away by the enemy and those who served the U.S. imperialists as their henchmen for a long time. To the families of those who have gone to the south, forced and deceived by the enemy, citizenship must be guaranteed according to the Constitution and their livelihood stabilized. Political education must be conducted well among them and thus they must be helped to live and participate in state affairs, free from anxiety. In this way we should see to it that even those who have gone to the south come back to their native places with a sense of security and live happily with their families.

In the newly-liberated areas, therefore, we will: first, unconditionally return to the owners all the property which some local functionaries have confiscated from the families of those who were forcibly driven by the enemy to the south;

Second, take all necessary measures to ensure the living conditions of the people in these areas—speeding up the rehabilitation and readjustment of local industries, handicrafts, mines, salt fields, farmland, etc., and drawing those people actively into production activities;

Third, set up networks of schools and cultural institutions on a wide scale in the liberated areas and thus vigorously conduct political and ideological education among the students and people; and take measures to train many promising people in the newly-liberated areas into cadres to work in local Party and state organs.

Comrades,

There is no doubt that our Party will also win victory in the peaceful construction for strengthening the democratic base of the northern half of the Republic, just as it, leading the entire people, organized and mobilized them for victory in the severe Fatherland Liberation War against the invasion of the U.S. imperialists.

The Party members, functionaries of the Party and state organs, and patriotic people, rallying more closely around the Party Central Committee and the Government of the Republic, should all march forward vigorously, holding aloft the slogan: "Everything for the postwar rehabilitation and development of the national economy to strengthen the democratic base!"

ON THE IMMEDIATE TASKS OF THE WORKERS IN THE FIELD OF TRANSPORT

Speech Delivered at a Conference of Model Workers in the Field of Transport

May 11, 1954

Comrades,

The Korean people have won a historic victory in the Fatherland Liberation War. The transport workers played a really great part in winning this victory.

During the war, the transport workers waged a valiant struggle, displaying noble patriotic spirit; many heroes and model workers emerged from among them.

Under the difficult circumstances of war, the transport workers not only carried munitions to the front without a moment's interruption but also successfully carried out the national economic assignments in transportation. Even in the teeth of severe bombings by enemy planes, our trains kept on running between the front and the rear, whistling loudly. The whistles of locomotives driven by our brave engine drivers in defiance of bombing and darkness immensely stirred the people and encouraged them to victory. The shrill of the first whistle sounded immediately after the armistice filled the people with a sense of pride and honour as victors, and roused them to the grand struggle for the postwar rehabilitation and construction of the national economy.

The heroic struggle of the transport workers will go down forever in the history of the Korean people's struggle for the freedom and independence of their country.

If our transport workers had not fought so valiantly, our People's Army, however heroic, could not have won victory in the war.

I should like to tell an anecdote about how much the whistles of the locomotives running in defiance of bombing and darkness during the war touched the heartstrings of our people and inspired them with confidence in victory.

A leading functionary of the Party Central Committee, on an official trip to local areas during the war, happened to stop for a night at a village in the Hamhung area together with a People's Army soldier. That night the old host lay awake until the small hours, unable to bring himself to sleep. Just then, the shrill whistle of a locomotive engine came from afar, as usual, intermingled with the sound of bombing by enemy planes. At that moment the old man asked, "You hear that whistle, young men?" The People's Army soldier assented, but he found nothing strange in the whistle, for it was quite familiar to him. But the old man said, "When we don't hear the whistle we don't feel like eating or sleeping, and we feel quite despondent. But when only that whistle sounds we feel relieved, thinking that our sons at the front are going to be supplied with ammunition and food; then we can sleep and also we can go to work with hundreds of times more spirit." Only after hearing the whistle, I was told, did the old man fall asleep that night.

What does this tell us? It tells us how closely our railway transport linked the front with our people in the rear who had sent their sons and daughters to the battlefield in the just war, it tells us what great expectations the people placed in the transport workers, and how much the heroic struggle of the railway workers inspired the people with faith in victory.

Our workers in railway and motor transport fought perseveringly going through fire and water for victory in the war, and were steeled in overcoming difficulties and hardships. The Workers' Party of Korea and the Government of the Republic pay high tribute to the noble patriotic spirit and indomitable fighting will you displayed and the great feats you performed during the three-year long Fatherland Liberation War.

On behalf of the Central Committee of the Workers' Party of Korea and the Government of the Republic, I extend warm thanks and congratulations to the railway, motor and water transport workers, to the officers and men of the railway detachments of the Chinese People's Volunteers, and to the valorous officers and men of our railway restoration units.

Just as the transport workers rendered great services during the Fatherland Liberation War, so their role is also great in the struggle for postwar rehabilitation and construction. I should like to speak about the tasks lying ahead of the transport workers.

First, the successes and experiences gained during the Fatherland Liberation War should be correctly summed up, so that they serve as lessons for future work.

The victory we achieved in the war consists not only in the defence of our country's democratic base but also in the fact that our people, our army, our cadres, and our Party and government organs accumulated valuable experience. If we draw on this experience properly, we can wage the struggle for the peaceful reunification of the country more effectively and carry out socialist construction more successfully as well in future.

It would be a great mistake to neglect the experience acquired in the three years of war. It is a precious experience gained at the cost of blood and sweat under a rain of shells and amidst powder-smoke. We must not rest content merely with adorning a page of history with the experience, but must treasure and study it systematically for proper application to our future activities.

We should not forget even for a moment that there remains a danger of imperialist aggression against our country as long as it is not reunified and the U.S. army occupies the southern half of our country and Japan, and unless Japan is democratized. If we do not heighten vigilance and draw on the lessons of the war, the peaceful reunification of the country cannot be achieved. We must always be ready and keep ourselves in battle condition so as to be fully capable of crushing any surprise attack on the part of the enemy. This is necessary not for waging a war but for safeguarding peace and accomplishing the peaceful reunification of the country and socialist construction in the northern half of the Republic.

What is important in summing up the experiences of the war is to have a clear idea of how we, fighting back the enemy's attack, advanced down to the Rakdong-gang River area, and what was lacking and what our shortcomings were at that time. In particular, the bitter experience of the period of retreat in October 1950 should be correctly reviewed. To my knowledge, work was also misled in the railways during the retreat, which caused much confusion and heavy losses.

When the People's Army, in closely co-ordinated operations with the Chinese People's Volunteers, resumed the offensive and liberated the northern half of the Republic, and entered a state of confrontation with the enemy, the enemy heavily bombed our railway junctions—Kaechon, Sinanju, Pyongyang, Yangdok, etc.—every day. Yet, the heroic servicemen of railway restoration units and railway transport workers of Korea and China repaired the enemy-bombed spots in no time so that trains could pass without delay; when the enemy bombed again, they repaired again to ensure wartime transportation. We must properly review and turn to account all these experiences which were gained at the cost of our blood.

In this connection, it is essential that we bear in mind the following points. The thing is to create ample reserves of manpower and materials for the future of the country and against any contingencies. If the People's Army had had sufficient reserves at its disposal, there would have been no retreat in October 1950. The railways also had little reserves when they followed our People's Army that went down to the Rakdong-gang River.

In the People's Army today, it is set as an important task to train our army into a cadre army. Following this example, the railways should also train reserve cadres in a big way and strive to raise the qualifications of all workers to the level of cadres in the future. Besides, there must be factories in reserve for repairing freight cars, and a reserve of locomotive engines, cars, coal, materials, etc., should also be kept. All preparations should thus be made for successfully beating back any surprise attack, no matter when the enemy may launch it.

The data on the feats and good experiences of the numerous combatants who fought valiantly in the war should be collected and arranged in a systematic way and made widely known to the people. It is particularly important to widely popularize, in book form, the heroic feats performed by the transport workers during the war.

The engine driver who took the floor just before has related many good experiences. They will all serve as highly precious lessons to the present and the coming generations. This time, activists from the transport field have assembled here and exchanged the experiences they acquired in their devoted struggle for ensuring wartime transportation, and this not just to make conference minutes and file them away in a desk drawer, but to correctly review and widely popularize the experiences and chart out appropriate measures to advance our work to a higher stage.

Second, the rehabilitation and construction of railways should be pushed forward successfully.

As is generally known, thanks to the great efforts of our railway transport workers and the sincere aid of the Chinese railway transport workers, our railways were, on the whole, put into operating condition only a few days after the armistice. But it cannot be said that normalcy has yet been restored in the railways, nor are the tracks in proper shape. So the railway workers should strive to keep the tracks in good repair and especially to fix the bridges and detour lines well to guarantee a higher running speed for the trains.

And a broad campaign for protecting the railways must be launched. The railway workers and entire people should take part in this campaign. Railways may be compared to the blood vessels of the human body. The people should therefore be educated to care for the railways as for their own bodies and guard them vigilantly.

The important task ahead now is to restore the locomotive engines, passenger coaches and freight cars and put them in good order. If they are insufficient in number, it is evident that no smooth operation of the railways could be expected, however excellent the tracks may be. Should the railways fail to meet the enormous transportation needs of postwar national economic rehabilitation and construction, due to a shortage of locomotives, passenger coaches and freight cars, that would be a big disgrace for the railway workers. All difficulties should be overcome to restore and fix up the locomotive engines and cars quickly, and efforts should be made to restore the rolling stock repair works at the earliest possible date.

We should step up capital construction in every way. Station buildings and locomotive depots are insufficient as yet, and the dwelling houses for the workers are short. Nevertheless, the capital construction plan for the first quarter of the year was carried out at only 39 per cent in the field of railway transport. People in this field ought rather to have complained about setting them small state targets for capital construction. And yet it is much to be regretted that they have failed to fulfil even the assignments given them.

In capital construction, it is most urgent of all to restore or newly build dwellings for workers, station buildings, locomotive depots, and so on. It could in no way be profitable to be "sparing" in using the funds allocated for capital construction; it would be profitable to make effective use of them quickly. We should overfulfil on all accounts the capital construction plans by days, weeks, months and quarters, both in quantity and quality.

Third, the plans for railway freight transport should be fulfilled exactly in terms of quality.

Our railway workers are often concerned about carrying out the plans for freight transport only in terms of aggregate volume, without directing profound attention to their fulfilment by items. Even though the plans for the aggregate volume of carriage are fulfilled in the railways, the implementation of plans at enterprises and the all-round rehabilitation and development of the national economy will be greatly deterred when items essential to the national economy are not transported as planned. If the railways do not carry goods urgently needed by the state, but convey goods of secondary importance, this will mean a waste of coal, materials and labour. Hence, from the beginning the state should draw up the freight carriage plans strictly by items of goods and send them down, and the railway workers, instead of carrying any kind of freight haphazardly in an effort to fulfil the plans, must strive to fulfil the transport plans exactly by items of goods.

The most important thing in railway freight transport is to reduce the turnaround time of freight cars. We should prevent unnecessary congestion of freight cars in one place. Suppose there is an enterprise which needs two or three freight cars a day. The railways fail to regularly assign cars for the enterprise, and then allocate scores of cars at one time; when the consignor fails to load all of the cars in time, the railway authorities complain and make a fuss about it, demanding charges for the delay. Such an outmoded method of work should not be tolerated any longer.

Freight cars should be operated as accurately as the hands of a clock. Transport should necessarily be organized in a rational way, so that freight cars do not run empty and the time of holdups en route is reduced to the minimum.

You should display activity and creative initiative in mechanizing the loading and unloading operations, and strive to make full use of the loading capacity of the freight cars. Only by raising the utilization rate of the rolling stock and saving labour power in this way can the cost of freight carriage be lowered and profitability be assured in railway transport.

To reduce the cost of transportation, coal must also be economized. Today, the need of the national economy for fuel is sharply increasing, while the production of coal fails to keep up with this need. We are importing a large amount of coal from foreign countries every year, and it is planned this year to import 200,000 tons of coal for the railways alone. Saving of coal in the railways, therefore, is of great importance for the state.

Nonetheless, coal is now being used more wastefully in the railways than during the war. This is tantamount to a great crime committed against the state. Such a grave fault has resulted from the fact that the railway workers, carried away by victory, are working in an easy-going manner.

The railway workers should launch a mass struggle for saving coal, and endeavour to carry more freight with less consumption of coal. If you save just a few kilogrammes of coal per kilometre of run by each locomotive, it will mean saving a huge amount of coal for the state. The previous norm of consumption needs re-examination.

And domestic coal ought to be used primarily and foreign coal less. Nevertheless, there is a noticeable tendency to use much foreign coal, while domestic coal is used less. This is a wrong practice. If, instead of importing 200,000 tons of coal, the money were spent to purchase other kinds of goods, what great benefit it would bring to our national economy and to the people's livelihood! The claim that domestic coal is unfit for use should be dropped; we must proceed to use as little imported coal as possible.

Further. Freight should be prevented from being damaged in the course of loading and unloading. It is a serious matter that the aid materials from the peoples of the Soviet Union, the People's Republic of China, and other fraternal countries are being stolen or damaged in transit. And yet, some railway workers adopt an attitude of indifference to this and do not even compile statistics of it. Travelling along the railway, I saw in many places valuable imported equipment and materials scattered in a disorderly and damaged state.

The railway workers should handle all kinds of freight with care so that it will not be stolen, spoilt or damaged en route, and should wage a resolute ideological struggle against the tendency to carelessness in handling freight.

Fourth, the tasks set forth by the March Plenary Meeting of the Central Committee of our Party to enhance production culture in the enterprises should also be thoroughly implemented in the field of railway transport.

Though there are many aspects worthy of praise for their good work, the railways are lagging considerably behind in the matter of production culture; locomotives, passenger cars, freight wagons, etc., are not kept neat and tidy. It is to be regretted that passenger cars are untidy and the inside appointments of the cars are partially out of order due to negligence on the part of our railway workers.

Today we are not living in isolation. The visits of foreign guests to our country, which performed heroic feats in the war against the U.S. imperialists, are becoming more frequent from day to day.

If you fail to keep the inside of the cars clean and to manage the railways in a cultured way, foreign guests will not be able to get a correct idea of our country's level of culture, and may say that the Koreans are brave but are not yet civilized. Thus, you may stain the honour of us intelligent Korean people because of your failure to elevate production culture in the railways.

How could it be that we Koreans, who have won the fight against the U.S. imperialist aggressors, are unable to win the battle against such an uncivilized practice? We are fully capable of elevating production culture, and we must do so without fail. Production culture should be enhanced quickly in the field of transport, always keeping the locomotive engines, passenger cars and motor vehicles clean, to begin with. To this end, the employees should be educated to heighten their cultural standard, and transport as a whole be improved.

Fifth, as is always emphasized, the most important thing in the railways is the prevention of operation accidents.

As a comrade from the Paegam-Musan line said in his speech, many accidents occurred on that line in the past. I still remember the serious accident which occurred in the Unjon-Koup section.

If the railway workers allow accidents to occur repeatedly in this way, the prestige of the railways will be lowered and people will not want to travel by train. Nevertheless, some railway workers, even when they give rise to an accident, do not take it seriously. To cause an accident in peace time, like today, is a very serious matter.

The main reason for railway accidents lies in the personnel's failure to observe the railway rules and discipline and in their low level of technique and skill. Many new workers have entered the field of railway transport. They are not yet well acquainted with the rules and do not observe discipline strictly.

Moreover, in the course of the war our workers formed a valorous and indomitable character, while on the other hand they acquired undesirable habits as well. There still remains the practice of running the train carelessly against the rules, which was inevitable under the wartime conditions, and some personnel have a tendency to become insolent and work at ease on the ground that they have got proficient in their work to a certain degree. All this gives rise to accidents.

Indeed, the imperfection of semaphores, safety devices and other equipment is partly responsible for the accidents. But, as a locomotive engineer said just before in his speech, even in case a locomotive took a wrong track when pulling into a station, it could be prevented from crashing into another if the engineer watched ahead carefully and made an emergency stop. This is a good experience.

The railway workers are like armymen. Just as the army should follow the rules and drill regulations scrupulously in order to win victory, so you should strictly observe the railway rules and regulations in order that accidents may be avoided and transport properly assured. Everyone must act according to the demands of the rules and regulations, and should launch an uncompromising fight against their violation.

If an airman, for example, flies his plane below the normal altitude in violation of the rules pertaining to the altitude for diving, in order to make a show of his dexterity, it cannot be positively appreciated, no matter how skilled he may be. Because if such violation of the rules is considered correct, airplane accidents will become frequent and there will be the risk of increased casualties. No one, therefore, has the right to go against the demands of the rules and regulations which have been laid down on a scientific basis, even when one has long experience in his work.

Our railways have good rules, which are precisely the law for the railways. Violation of the rules is precisely the violation of the law.

Three years have already passed since the railways were put on a military footing and you wore uniforms. However, the high standard of military discipline called for by the Party and the Government has not yet been established.

If accidents are to be prevented in the railways and successful transport be ensured, every worker is required to observe the rules and strictly obey the orders of the superiors and, at the same time, strengthen the internal, operational and administrative systems.

And personnel in the service of the railways must learn techniques without exception. Though originating new technique is difficult, it is easy to learn the technical achievements of the Soviet Union, China and other advanced countries. We must always learn good experiences from the Soviet Union and other brother countries. We must do our utmost to arm ourselves with new advanced techniques.

Sixth, I should like to make a few remarks on motor transport.

The workers in the field of motor transport played a big role in the Fatherland Liberation War. During the war, the qualifications of the automobile drivers were improved and they were deeply loved by the people. When the railways were out of normal operation, motor vehicles took the place of railways. No small number of heroes and many model workers emerged from among the automobile drivers.

In carrying out the postwar national economic plans, the role of motor transport is also important. However, the motor transport workers have grown somewhat slack after the war, whereas they rendered great services through their struggle during the war. Now that the war has stopped, enemy planes are no more in the sky and motor cars are free to run in broad daylight, there ought to be no accidents. But they occur rather more often than during the war. As a driver pointed out in his speech just before, it is very important to build up discipline in the field of motor transport.

Motor transport workers should launch a broad campaign for making major repairs as few and far between as possible and for running long distances without accidents. To this end, motor repair and service stations should be set up in all places, thereby strengthening the work of repairing and tending motor vehicles in good time.

Another important point in the field of motor transport is to maintain the vehicles well and, at the same time, economize on the consumption of gasoline. Motor vehicles and gasoline are all imports. Motor transport workers, therefore, should launch a widespread campaign for maximum economy on foreign currency by taking good care of and properly maintaining their vehicles and saving every possible drop of gasoline.

Seventh, I want to remark on water transport.

An important question in our water transport today is to make proper use of rivers. River transport which can substitute for motor transport should be developed actively by utilizing the Rivers Chaeryong-gang, Taedong-gang, Amnok-gang, Tuman-gang, etc.

River transport service still falls far short of our requirements. Suffice it to cite the case of the Kangnam Ceramic Factory. This factory is easily accessible by boat. Nevertheless, no boat service can be operated because the lock on the river has been left unrepaired, and bricks have to be carried by trucks.

At the same time, ships should be repaired and put in good shape; renovation of wharves including those of Hungnam and Nampo should be promoted; as many vessels sunken in the sea as possible should be salvaged and restored.

Eighth, patriotism based on the spirit of proletarian internationalism should be promoted continuously among the transport workers.

No doubt the transport workers displayed patriotic devotion admirably in the Fatherland Liberation War. But we cannot rest satisfied with this. We should endeavour to give greater scope to their patriotism.

What we mean by patriotism is boundless love of our country, undivided loyalty to the Party and the Government of the Republic, and devotion of all our energies and ardour to upholding our social system which has brought freedom and happiness to the people. Patriotism should manifest itself in safeguarding the gains of our revolution against encroachment by enemies of all shades and in protecting the property of the state and the people, and, particularly, in taking good care of machines, saving materials and overfulfilling one's quotas of work at production enterprises.

Such patriotism presupposes the strengthening of internationalist friendship and unity with the peoples of the great Soviet Union, the People's Republic of China and other fraternal countries. Only when based firmly upon proletarian internationalism can our patriotism become genuine socialist patriotism.

All the victories of the Korean people were and will be, in the future too, possible only under the banner of proletarian internationalism. This has been proved by the whole history of the Korean people's struggle for liberation and, in particular, was borne out more graphically by the experience of the recent Fatherland Liberation War.

After liberation, our railway transport received a great deal of sincere assistance from the peoples of the fraternal countries. When our country was liberated from the yoke of Japanese imperialist rule, there were few cadres in the field of railway transport. For example, most of the locomotive crew had to be selected and allocated from among those who had worked as stokers in the days of Japanese imperialist rule; there was scarcely anyone who had experience as an engine driver. The Soviet Union sent a railway regiment to our country to help restore the ravaged transport facilities and render all-round assistance in the training of engine drivers. Such assistance motivated by the spirit of proletarian internationalism enabled us to achieve success in peaceful construction and to win victory in the Fatherland Liberation War waged against the armed invasion of the U.S. imperialists and their satellite states.

Our transport workers, holding high the banner of proletarian internationalism, should cement friendship and unity with the peoples of the Soviet Union, the People's Republic of China and other fraternal countries, and display patriotic devotion in implementing the decisions of the Party and the Government with national pride and a high sense of honour as masters of the country.

Comrades,

Our dauntless transport workers, who have turned out in the grand struggle for postwar rehabilitation and construction, should restore and fix up at the earliest possible date the war-ravaged railways, bridges, locomotive depots, factories, docks, and other important facilities, economize in labour power, take care of materials, and strengthen discipline so as to carry out the state plan assignments for the field of transport, not only in terms of quantity but also of quality, and keep up a tense and mobilized stance at all times, thereby living up to the expectations of the Party, the Government and the people. If we fail to maintain a tense and mobilized stance, the peaceful reunification of the country cannot be achieved.

I am firmly convinced that following the path shown by the Workers' Party of Korea, you will fulfil the plan for the postwar rehabilitation and development of the national economy ahead of schedule and discharge your honourable duties with success in the struggle for facilitating the peaceful reunification of our country.

ON OUR PARTY'S POLICY FOR THE FURTHER DEVELOPMENT OF AGRICULTURE

Concluding Speech Delivered at a Plenary Meeting of the Central Committee of the Workers' Party of Korea

November 3, 1954

Comrades,

Very great significance attaches to the problem of developing agriculture which has been discussed at the present plenary meeting.

It is most important to solve the problem of food, clothing and housing for the people in the postwar rehabilitation and construction of the national economy. In order to rapidly stabilize and improve the people's life, which was extremely deteriorated in the war, to further strengthen our country's economic foundations and thus expedite the reunification of the country, the problem of food, clothing and housing should be solved before anything else for the entire people. This is impossible without the development of agriculture.

Agriculture not only meets the people's need for food but supplies the necessary raw materials for industry. Hence, without swift progress in agriculture, it is impossible to solve the questions of industrial restoration and construction and improvement of the people's livelihood.

Since the prewar period of peaceful construction, our Party has regarded the problem of agriculture as one of the cardinal problems in our country's economic construction. We, therefore, effected the historic agrarian reform and took every possible state measure for the development of agriculture. A series of measures taken by the Party and the state for building irrigation facilities, improving seeds, securing draught animals and so forth, greatly contributed to agricultural development.

After the war was started by the armed invasion of the U.S. imperialists and the traitorous Syngman Rhee clique, our Party directed its greatest efforts to rural work so as to meet the demands of the front and stabilize the life of the people in the rear. Under wartime conditions when most of the factories were destroyed, the Party assigned all its best forces to the countryside. The wartime rural policy of our Party not only made it possible to guarantee supplies to the front and to stabilize the people's life in the rear, but was an important factor making for our victory in the bitter three-year war.

Because our Party directed its efforts to rural work during the war, we have been able to attain no small success in grain production this year, the first year after the war, although North Hamgyong Province was hit totally by a natural calamity and South Hamgyong and Kangwon Provinces also suffered considerable damage. As for stockbreeding, our state agro-stock farms never once produced as much as several hundred tons of meat before the war. But this year 6,000 tons of meat have already been produced in the state agro-stock farms because our Party set up a large number of new state agro-stock farms and strengthened and developed their work during the war in order to develop stockbreeding which holds an important place in agriculture.

As mentioned above, we have done a great deal of work for the development of agriculture in the postwar period as well as in wartime.

1. ON IMPROVING THE GUIDANCE OF AGRICULTURE

We have scored great success in the struggle to develop agriculture during the past years. Needless to say, this is ascribable to the correctness of our Party's rural policy in the prewar period, during the war and in the postwar period, and to the devoted struggle of the entire Party to put the policy into practice.

But we cannot rest content with what we have already achieved.

The rehabilitation and development of industry is proceeding apace in our country now. First of all, take heavy industry for instance. We do not confine ourselves to rehabilitating the previously existing factories; we are newly building factories such as our country never had before, especially many machine plants to eliminate the colonial one-sidedness in our country's industry. The machine plants we are now planning to build alone number as many as 20 to 30. Construction of the Huichon Machine Plant, begun in 1951 following a decision of the Political Committee of the Party Central Committee, is to be completed by the winter of this year. Beginning next year the plant will turn out lathes, drilling machines and other machine tools. The Pukjung Machine Plant, too, will produce as many as 300 marine engines beginning next year. Among other branches of heavy industry, the machine-building industry will thus develop rapidly. We are now working to lay the basis for the future socialist industrialization of our country.

Along with heavy industry, light industry will also make rapid progress in the future in our country. In prewar days the light industry of our country was insignificant. In the postwar period our Party has followed a policy of rapidly rehabilitating and developing light industry to improve the people's standard of living. As a result, a new textile mill with 60,000-70,000 spindles and later on 100,000 spindles will be built in the near future, with an annual production capacity of 40-80 million metres of fabric. We must make great efforts to develop the textile industry so that at least 75 million metres of cotton fabric, 15 million metres of silk fabric and 10 to 15 million metres of rayon can be manufactured beginning 1957. In addition, canneries, meat-processing factories and many other light industry plants will be built.

The number of factory and office workers has also increased with the growth of industry, and will go up further in the future. Factory and office workers already number 810,000 this year and in the not too distant future their number will exceed one million.

Cities are also developing rapidly in our country. For instance, the population of Pyongyang, which was some 70,000 to 80,000 during the war, is now already 400,000.

Swift progress in industry, the increase in the number of factory and office workers and the development of cities necessitate rapid advance in agriculture. Our present rate of agricultural development cannot keep pace with that of industry. We need more food and meat and more industrial raw materials. In the near future we must boost annual grain output to at least 2.9-3 million tons and output of meat to 100,000-200,000 tons. We must also turn out more industrial crops. Only then will our living standards improve in some degree.

At present we are still short of food and meat, and fabrics too. Even if we produce 20,000 tons of meat next year, little will be left after supplying the People's Army. This amount is still very small to supply all the people. In the Three-Year Plan period we must raise meat production greatly. Two hundred thousand tons of meat are needed to ensure a sufficient supply to the people.

We are now short of meat but, on the other hand, our country has inexhaustible marine resources. If large quantities of fish are caught by reinforcing the work of the state fisheries and fishermen's co-operatives and organizing agro-fishing co-operatives extensively, the shortage of meat can be covered. We must see to it that the annual fish catch reaches upwards of 700,000 tons by the end of the Three-Year Plan period. The people's standard of living can be raised to a very high level when we catch 700,000 tons of fish and produce 200,000 tons of meat annually.

Can we possibly carry out all these tasks? Of course, we can. We have every condition for carrying out these tasks. The point is whether our Party guides the work of the rural economy properly or not. In his report Comrade Vice-Premier dwelt on concrete problems. We must make a profound study of the report and the resolution, and give proper guidance in the work of agriculture.

It is most important to correct the wrong attitude assumed in the past towards the work of agriculture. In our previous guidance of agriculture, we of course drew up plans every year and sent them down to the lower levels. But in many cases organizational work in production—introducing advanced farming methods, improving soil, planting the right crop on the right soil, timely sowing and so on—was left to chance. The outmoded farming methods used by the peasants from olden times have been left alone as they were. Even when a leading functionary gave guidance, the way he did it was to make a tour in a car and ask the peasants: "Can you manage farming well this year or not?" And when assured they could manage it well, he would make a note of it in his memo and leave. My conversations with chairmen of county Party committees and county people's committees and with many of the functionaries working in the countryside reveal that they do not know much about agriculture.

We should not leave the work of the rural economy to take its own course, but should take positive measures to guide it. Had we worked a bit harder and guided the peasants more actively this year, we could have achieved greater results. If we simply introduce advanced farming methods and work the land now under cultivation properly, we can gather a good harvest without expanding the crop area.

Out of our total area under cultivation the dry fields are roughly 1.5 million *chongbo*; if we increase per-*chongbo* yield from the present 700 kilogrammes to 1.5-2 tons, then we shall be able to gather 2,250,000-3,000,000 tons of farm produce from these fields. If we gather one ton more from each *chongbo* of paddyfields, we shall have over 400,000 tons more of rice.

In order to do this we must first of all improve our methods of work. When asked about the reason for poor crops, some people tend to complain of poor land, saying: "It's because of the land," "The land is sterile." We should not complain of poor land but improve and transform it.

Careful study of the experience of those peasants who raise rich crops shows that the secret of a rich harvest is no more than liberal fertilizing, proper seed selection and diligent crop tending. They have no special secret for a rich harvest. These methods are not so difficult. Therefore, if we organize the work well and give proper guidance, we can increase harvest to any extent. If we simply apply plenty of fertilizer, select good seeds, go in for opportune planting of the right crop on the right soil and timely weed, we can reap a rich harvest. This method is not difficult to learn or pass on to others. There is no big secret for increasing farm production.

Not a few functionaries of our Party and government bodies, however, are indifferent to this.

Take North Hamgyong Province, for instance. In July this year we visited North Hamgyong Province. Finding the crops in bad condition, we said to the responsible persons of the province: "Your method of farming is wrong." To this, the answer was: "No, you don't know, Comrade Premier! The crops may look bad now, but soon there will be a sudden turn for the better." So we said, "Even if that's so, the turn must be gradual. And we do not understand what you mean by the sudden turn. You probably are going to apply magic to us. But it seems your method is wrong after all."

The leading personnel in North Hamgyong Province took no measures for overcoming frost damage. In the past, North Hamgyong Province suffered from frost damage, not for a year or two but consecutively. Yet, members of our Workers' Party in the province have failed to make scientific study to bring the matter to light. Since this region is in the cold zone, it has a short crop season. In this area, therefore, measures should have been taken for early maturity of crops by planting early-ripening or hardy crops, or by growing seedlings in hothouses at least. Even in a region as cold as Siberia, farming is done and high yields are obtained. Why, then, is it impossible to farm successfully in North Hamgyong Province?

We must learn to give proper guidance in work and gain the mastery of nature. It is wrong to just sit around and deplore one's lot, making no effort to conquer nature. All Party members in North Hamgyong Province must study why they suffer from such frost damage every year. If seeds are bad, you should improve them so that they may resist the cold, and if you have not been planting the right crop on the right soil, you should do so. Frost damage cannot be prevented just by raising smoke to keep the crops from the frost. We must guide the peasants on the basis of scientific study and knowledge.

Cases of half-hearted guidance in rural work have also occurred in other places. In North Hamgyong, South Hamgyong, Chagang and South Pyongan Provinces there is a common practice such as abandoning cultivated lands, alleging that they are slash-and-burn plots. There are some peasants who till their reclaimed land for only three years and then reclaim other land so that they may be exempt from agricultural tax in kind. Our functionaries fail to see this, and allow good lands to be abandoned. If land is poor and unsuitable for cultivation, it is advisable to use it as fodder fields to grow grass for livestock.

The same applies to the question of introducing advanced farming methods. If you just make a tour in a car and talk to peasants instead of taking measures for energetically disseminating advanced farming methods through active publicity and explanation, that will not do.

This is not the proper way to guide agricultural affairs. The entire Party must pay greater attention to guiding work in the rural areas. Rural work is the most important job of the county Party committees, county people's committees, provincial Party committees and provincial people's committees in farming regions. Our Party functionaries working in the countryside must therefore make a profound study of the rural economy and give active guidance to the peasants.

2. ON THE ECONOMIC STRUCTURE IN THE NORTHERN HALF OF THE REPUBLIC AND THE SOCIALIST TRANSFORMATION OF THE COUNTRYSIDE

I shall now pass to the question of the socialist transformation of the countryside in our country, that is, agricultural co-operativization.

First of all, I feel it necessary to make an analysis of the economic structure in the northern half of the Republic. As everyone knows, the economy in the northern half of our country consists of three sectors:

First, the socialist state economy;

Second, the co-operative economy, which is of a socialist or semi-socialist character;

Third, the private economy, which comprises the capitalist and small commodity economies.

What, then, is the situation of these three sectors in industry and agriculture?

First of all, the socialist state economy holds unchallenged sway in industry. This is the result of the nationalization of key industries in the northern half after our country's liberation from the yoke of Japanese imperialist colonial rule. The economic laws of socialism operate in the industry of our country, because the state economy rules supreme in it. Accordingly, we are building industry not in accordance with the economic laws of capitalism, but in conformity with the economic laws of socialism.

The private economy makes up a very small proportion of industry in our country. State-owned industry accounts for about 90 per cent of total industrial output. Of the remaining 10 per cent, co-operative economy represents 7-8 per cent and private economy only 2-3 per cent. Before the war, the proportion held by private economy was larger than now. But because private enterprises suffered great losses during the war, private entrepreneurs find themselves in a very difficult situation. Our country now has only a small number of private enterprises and they are rice mills, blacksmith shops, small-scale rubber factories, and the like at the best. Moreover, the existing private enterprises in the northern half of the Republic, far from exerting any influence on state and co-operative industries, are being influenced by them and rely on them. This is because our means of transport, banks, factories and other major means of production have been nationalized and there is the people's power based on the firm worker-peasant alliance led by the working class.

What, then, is the situation of these three economic sectors in agriculture?

The great bulk of agriculture is in private hands. In agriculture the small commodity economy is overwhelmingly predominant, and a large part of the individual peasants follow very backward farming methods.

Besides the private economy, there is also the co-operative economy in agriculture. We have started organizing agricultural co-operatives for the first time this year on an experimental basis. They are now developing swiftly and 21.5 per cent of all peasant households have already joined the co-operatives.

Besides agricultural co-operatives, there are socialist economies in our countryside. They are state agro-stock farms, and the farm-machine and the draught-animal hire station, consumers' co-operatives, peasant banks, rural side-line producers' co-operatives, fishermen's co-operatives, and irrigation facilities held in the hands of the state, which serve as bases for the socialist transformation of the countryside. All these are of a socialist or a semi-socialist form. Socialist state-run industry exerts a great influence on the rural areas and socialist elements are now growing in our countryside from day to day.

This, in general, is the economic structure of our country.

Our task is to expand and consolidate the socialist sector in industry and agriculture further still, step by step.

As all of you know, our country, still divided into north and south, has not yet been reunified. In the northern half under the leadership of our Party and the people's power, the economy is developing daily and the people's ideological consciousness is being heightened. But the southern half has been reduced to a U.S. imperialist colony and plunged into poverty and economic ruin. Thus, in our divided country one half is following the road to development and prosperity while the other is on the road to decline and ruin. We must struggle more tenaciously for our country's reunification and independence.

The most important thing in the struggle for reunification is to consolidate our revolutionary democratic base to make it impregnable. The consolidation of our rural positions is a matter of utmost importance in strengthening the democratic base, because the countryside accounts for a great proportion of the population in our country.

What, then, is to be done to strengthen the rural positions? We must develop the socialist sector in the rural areas and transform our countryside step by step along socialist lines.

As mentioned above, at present individual farming predominates in the rural areas of our country. What would happen if we left it alone? Some of the peasants would become rich farmers while many others might not improve their livelihood radically despite all the assistance given by the Party and the Government.

Ultra-small peasants, who now represent 30-40 per cent of our peasantry, have received enormous benefits from the state since the agrarian reform. But because they were doing individual farming on poor land, using backward farming methods and implements, their economy could hardly be improved. Of course, for the purpose of solving the problem of the ultra-small peasants, we moved them down to the plains where there are vast tracts of fertile land, and took various other measures. Their problem, however, cannot be solved thoroughly by this method. We must solve the question of ultra-small peasants once and for all, in the shortest possible time. Only then will the worker-peasant alliance be further consolidated. The only way to the final solution of this problem lies through co-operativization in the countryside.

We also cannot close our eyes to the fact that rich farmers are constantly emerging in the countryside. Of course, we successfully carried out the agrarian reform. Since then there has been no serious trouble, but it is a fact that rich farmers are gradually coming forth in the countryside. Though they benefited from the agrarian reform, those who are growing into rich farmers, as their farming gradually takes on a capitalist character, are liable to be influenced by south Korean reactionary circles. An analysis of those who collaborated with the reactionaries during our temporary retreat shows that some of them had benefited by the agrarian reform and some had even worked as farm hands for the landlords. The reason is that as they were becoming rich farmers after the agrarian reform in our countryside, they were all influenced by the reactionary circles of south Korea and by the U.S. imperialists. Inasmuch as rich farmers are emerging in the countryside and reactionary influence is affecting them, the class struggle goes on in the rural areas at any rate, even though it has not yet come out into the open, and it may gradually grow sharper in the future.

For this reason, we should further consolidate the worker-peasant alliance, improve the livelihood of the labouring peasants, restrict the rich peasant economy, and gradually transform the countryside along socialist lines so that agriculture may also be governed by the economic laws of socialism.

Some people question the wisdom of reorganizing the countryside along socialist lines in the northern half when reunification has not yet been achieved. They have forgotten that the matter of our reunification depends on the strengthening of the democratic base in the northern half. To fortify the democratic base in the northern half, it is required not only to develop industry, but also to strengthen our rural positions.

In order to strengthen the rural positions at present we must gradually lead our countryside onto the path of socialist co-operativization. There is no other alternative. This is the first reason why our countryside should be co-operativized.

Second, agricultural co-operativization is also needed for us to manage not only industry, but agriculture in a planned way, and to ensure proportionate development of industry and agriculture.

In the industry of our country, where the state sector holds unchallenged sway, a planned economy has been introduced. But in agriculture where private economy predominates, no planned economy can be introduced. At present, we work out plans for agriculture and send them down to the lower bodies, but, in fact, this cannot be called a planned economy. The present plan for agriculture is no more than a kind of target for ensuring production at a certain level.

Such conditions not only make it impossible to develop agriculture rapidly, but also may impede the advance of industry. For the planned development of industry, the complete planning of agriculture is also necessary. Without this, agriculture cannot keep pace with the rate of development of industry. Without this, the aforementioned grain, industrial raw materials and meat cannot be secured.

In order to develop agriculture in a planned way, we must reorganize agriculture on co-operative lines. Only then can we further develop our agriculture.

Third, we must also co-operativize agriculture in order to solve the question of labour and draught animals which are short in the countryside. Three years of war brought about an acute dearth of labour in the rural areas. Because many young and middle-aged men joined the army, the greater part of the rural labour force is now made up of women and old people. Farm villages are now short of draught animals, too. Consequently, even those who own fertile land cannot farm well owing to the lack of labour, while those who lack draught animals also cannot farm well, however hard they try, and those with poor land cannot even produce enough to feed themselves, no matter how hard they work. It was for this reason that the peasants thought out and voluntarily organized co-operatives in order to overcome these difficulties during the war. This was how the first co-operatives were organized in our country.

All this shows that co-operativization is a movement which is completely law-governed and reflects the objective requirements of social development, for it has evolved from the matured conditions at the present stage of development of our country. We must take the road of agricultural co-operativization in order to further develop our agriculture and radically solve the peasant problem.

As was proved by the experience of the Soviet Union, agricultural co-operativization makes it possible to develop agriculture in a planned way, introduce advanced farming methods and agro-technology, mechanize agriculture, develop farm production and thereby ensure an abundant life for the people.

We began to organize agricultural co-operatives on an experimental basis this year. Some comrades think we have organized them on an experimental basis because we are afraid of making mistakes. But that is not the case. We have done so not because we are afraid but because we aim to manage better by accumulating experience. One year's experience has proved more clearly that the co-operativization of agriculture is the only correct path for us to follow.

Here is an example. This year we visited the Chunghwa Agricultural Co-operative three times. In spring, some peasants received us with heads lowered; in summer when farming was picking up, their faces were beaming with joy; and in autumn they were so full of joy that their faces were all smiles.

An old man said: "I've been farming since the closing period of the Li dynasty, then under Japanese rule, and in the era of our Republic, and I have never seen as fine crops as this year's." In fact, as this old man said, the crops in this district are really fine this year thanks to the organization of the co-operative.

Where a co-operative has been formed and crops have been grown well, the worker-peasant alliance has been consolidated and the work of the united front also proceeds successfully.

We have proved in practice that agriculture can also be developed in a planned way if we organize co-operatives. We did not give agricultural co-operatives any plan this year. But they worked out plans on their own and farmed in a planned way on the principle of planting the right crop on the right soil. Beginning next year we will be able to farm even better. Next year the state should set plans to the co-operatives. We must include in the plan the distribution of crop area and the introduction of advanced farming methods, not to speak of production targets, and ensure that the plan is carried out as a matter of duty. Though the organization of co-operatives and distribution of income should be carried out on the principle of voluntariness on the part of the peasantry, things like the introduction of advanced farming methods cannot be left entirely to the free will of the peasants. Such a task should be carried out with some resolution.

Further, the experience gained in the organization and management of co-operatives has covinced us even more firmly that we can thoroughly solve the question of the ultra-small peasants who suffer from barren land and shortages of labour and draught animals. This year we have been able to save 20-30 per cent of labour power in the agricultural co-operatives even though mechanization of agriculture has not yet been effected. So, it is probable that more than 50 per cent of labour power can be saved by introducing semi-mechanization alone in the future. We can further increase production and develop side-line occupations on a large scale by making proper use of the labour thus released. Then the incomes of the peasants will further increase.

We have thus come to the conclusion from the past year's experience in the organization of agricultural co-operatives that agricultural co-operativization is necessary to strengthen the worker-peasant alliance and consolidate our rural positions, that it is necessary in order to ensure proportionate development of industry and agriculture by introducing a planned economy in agriculture, and also to fundamentally solve the problem of our country's ultra-small peasants.

Now, I should like to pass on to the forms of our agricultural co-operatives. At present there are three forms, all of which are good and necessary.

The first form, which is called the mutual-aid team, is necessary for the peasants to get the taste of co-operativization. We are going to transform the countryside along socialist lines step by step, not at one stroke and in a short time. Therefore, individual farming will remain in the countryside for a certain period. Hence this first form is needed in leading the individual peasants along the road of co-operativization.

The second form is that of pooling land and jointly managing the economy, and getting shares according to the land contributed and the amount of work done. This is a transitional form. The first form may be called the bud of socialism, and the second, a semi-socialist form.

The third form is of a socialist type. Here all the land and implements of production are placed under common ownership and distribution is made only in accordance with the amount of work done, and only small kitchen gardens, some chickens and hogs are allowed as an individual side line. This is the highest form of agricultural co-operative in our country.

But some comrades consider that in organizing co-operatives they must go step by step from the first form to the second and then to the third. It is wrong to think that they must advance thus like pupils in school who are promoted from the first grade to the second and from the second to the third.

The question lies in the degree of preparedness and the level of consciousness of the peasants. We should not force peasants who demand a higher form to take a lower form, nor can we impose a higher form from the beginning on peasants who are ready only for a lower form.

In the Soviet Union, too, there were different forms of co-operatives when the agricultural co-operative movement was developed. The first was the association for joint cultivation of land (TOZ), which is equivalent to the second form in our country, and the present kolkhoz is similar to our third form.

The principle we must abide by in agricultural co-operativization is to organize co-operatives always in accordance with the voluntariness of the peasants. It is absolutely impermissible to organize a co-operative by forcibly drawing the peasants into it simply because it is a good thing.

This by no means implies, however, that the co-operative movement may be left to take its own course. In organizing co-operatives, we must not permit the tendency to leave things to chance. Our Party must carry on propaganda vigorously among the peasants, educate and persuade them so that co-operatives may be organized and make progress.

Another principle we must abide by is to organize agricultural co-operatives not all at once in a spurt, but gradually in accordance with the degree of preparedness of the peasants. For the co-operativization of agriculture cannot be completed at once in accordance with the wishful thinking of some leading functionaries. It depends on the level of the peasants' consciousness, on the level of the development of our industry and various other conditions.

And it is not advisable at present to organize co-operatives of too large a size. In his speech, a certain comrade said that as many as 500 households are united in a co-operative. This is too large. I consider it appropriate to incorporate at first some 15 or 20 households and then, as conditions mature, increase the number gradually to some 30, 50 and 70. Unless we have cadres and unless conditions are ripe for mechanization, it is impossible to run large-scale co-operatives in a proper way. Therefore, it might be well not to organize oversize co-operatives at the beginning.

To proceed. We should not direct our efforts only to organizing new agricultural co-operatives, but should give proper guidance to the existing co-operatives to consolidate and develop them.

We must, first of all, properly select and appoint the chairmen and other leading personnel of co-operatives and train them. Also, we must give full scope to democracy in the co-operatives and raise the ideological and political level of their members so as to keep malicious elements from worming their way into the co-operatives to carry on exploitation and subversive activities. In this way, we must see to it that every co-operative member has the opportunity to express his views freely and thus prevent any "extraordinary fellow" from placing the co-operative under his thumb.

Class education among agricultural co-operative members should be further strengthened. It must be brought home to them that the agricultural co-operative, as a socialist economic form, is the only correct system, absolutely necessary to put an end to the system of exploitation of man by man and to eliminate the capitalist elements in the countryside, and especially that payment is made here according to the amount of work done on socialist principles.

It is also important to strengthen labour discipline and order in the co-operatives. Only then will loafers disappear. At present it is the most important problem to increase the returns of the co-operatives by organizing labour rationally and managing them according to well worked-out plans.

In the future the relations between agricultural and consumers' co-operatives should be strengthened and the contract system should also be introduced between them.

In order to strengthen the co-operatives and raise the ideological and political level of their members, it is necessary, above all, to strengthen the Party organizations in the co-operatives. Otherwise, it will be impossible either to consolidate the economic foundation of the co-operatives or to remould the outdated ideological consciousness of their members.

To reorganize our countryside gradually along socialist lines, we not only need to promote the co-operative movement actively, but also should ensure the steady growth of other socialist elements in the rural areas.

The state-owned farm-machine hire station and draught-animal hire station play a big role in the countryside. They are organizations to help the working peasants and combat their exploitation by rich farmers. Some simple-minded functionaries in the rural areas regard those stations as organizations for making money or undertaking transportation. That is a wrong view. Those stations serve as important bases for transforming the countryside along socialist lines. Besides, socialist elements such as state agro-stock farms, state irrigation services, consumers' co-operatives and peasant banks render much help to the co-operativization of agriculture. We must continue to strengthen and develop these socialist elements.

We must do everything in our power to lead the peasant masses along the socialist path. But we cannot lead them along that path by force or in a rush. I want to emphasize again that the co-operative movement should be unfolded gradually but actively, always on the principle of voluntariness of the peasants.

The socialist transformation of the countryside will not hinder the country's reunification, as some comrades are thinking, but will favour it. If we properly organize and guide the work and transform the countryside along socialist lines, our labouring peasants will enjoy a more bountiful life; their level of ideological consciousness will rise further; the influence of the rich farmers and other capitalist elements in our countryside will gradually disappear. Accordingly, the alliance between the workers and the toiling peasants will grow stronger and our rural positions will be further consolidated. Then the peasants in south Korea will follow us in the hope of living a life as prosperous as the peasants in the northern half. It is apparent that all this will further promote the cause of our country's reunification.

3. ON THE COUNTRY'S PEACEFUL REUNIFICATION

The recent session of the Supreme People's Assembly advanced proposals and issued an appeal for the peaceful reunification of the country. Some of our comrades, however, have an incorrect idea about this.

Some people say that the country's reunification cannot be achieved because of the presence of the American bandits in south Korea. Their ideas on the country's reunification are so stupefied that they do not even want to put up the slogan of reunification. Some comrades, I was told, even think that north and south Korea can coexist on the ground that the socialist and capitalist systems can coexist. A certain teacher has gone so far as to give a lecture to this effect at school.

The theory of coexistence of the capitalist and socialist systems is quite correct and it is possible. But the idea that north and south Korea can coexist separately in our single country, is very dangerous, and it is a harmful view which hinders our cause of reunification. People who have such an idea think that the responsibility for the revolution in south Korea rests only upon the south Korean people, and we, the people in north Korea, are not responsible for liberating south Korea. This is nothing but an attempt to justify the division of the country and perpetuate it. Such a tendency must be thoroughly eliminated. While our people are unanimously demanding the reunification of the country, how can our Party which represents the people discard even the slogan of reunification and advocate the "theory of coexistence of the north and the south"?

The country's reunification is the basic revolutionary task of our Party at the present stage. Therefore, when it issues an appeal and advances proposals for reunification, this is not just a formality. Our Party sincerely desires the country's reunification and struggles for it with might and main. The question of the country's reunification is a matter to be taken up not only by the Foreign Ministry, the propaganda organs or by the press; it is a task which the entire people must accomplish through united action.

Without achieving the cause of the country's reunification, our Party cannot say that it has fulfilled its tasks. "The country's reunification is impossible. The proposals for it are a formality. The north and the south can coexist"—such a way of thinking only tends to paralyze the zeal of the entire Korean people in their struggle for the country's reunification, and it is tantamount to abandoning south Korea. It is all for the purpose of hastening the country's reunification that we are consolidating the democratic base and strengthening the Party and the people's power. We must have a correct idea and a clear perspective as regards the reunification of the country, and fight with all our might to attain it.

Exploiting the aspiration of our people for reunification, the enemy continuously blows his trumpet to the stale tune of "march north and reunify." Then, if our Party gave up even the slogan of reunification and retreated, what would happen? Eventually our Party would forfeit the people's confidence, and the cause of the country's reunification, the unanimous desire of the Korean people, would not be realized.

Needless to say, it is not easy to achieve the peaceful reunification of the country in a short time. Because if it were only the Syngman Rhee clique which stood in the way of the country's peaceful reunification, it would not mean much, but they are backed by the U.S. imperialists who persist in their aggressive schemes towards Korea. Of course, the strength of U.S. imperialism cannot be underrated. But though it is strong now, it is doomed to perish eventually according to the laws of historical development. The thing is that we should struggle to hasten the downfall of imperialism and defeat it. Then, whatever support the U.S. imperialists may give to the Syngman Rhee clique, it can never hinder us from realizing the cause of the country's reunification. The reunification of our country will be achieved without fail.

In the past, even when Japanese imperialism ate up Korea, occupied half of China and then made inroads into the Pacific areas, we Korean revolutionaries never gave up the slogan of Korea's independence, but holding it still higher, resolutely waged the anti-Japanese national-liberation struggle. And at last the desire of the Korean patriots came true. Our country was liberated from the yoke of Japanese imperialism.

We should not forget the lessons of history. As a consequence of World War I, tsarist Russia fell and the socialist revolution triumphed in this land. World War II led to the ruin of such imperialist states as Germany, Italy and Japan, and to the emergence of a number of People's Democracies in Europe and, in the East, to the triumph of revolution in China and establishment of a powerful people's democratic system in the northern half of our country.

Imperialism still remains in the world. But, as history has proved, the collapse of imperialism is inevitable.

The contradictions between the capitalist countries are now becoming more acute. We should not overlook the sharpening of the contradictions between U.S. imperialism and its subordinate capitalist countries, Japan, for instance. One of the weak points of the imperialists is these inevitable contradictions between them. These contradictions will create very favourable conditions in the future for the reunification and independence of our country.

No matter how strong the U.S. imperialists may be, they will have no alternative but to get out of south Korea in the end when they are further isolated from their own people, have lost the support of their colonies and dependent countries and the south Korean people rise against them. Whether the south Korean people will rise against the U.S. imperialists or not, depends upon our organizational work to rouse the people in the southern half to action. When the south Korean people rally firmly around our Party and rise up, we can certainly drive the U.S. imperialists out of Korea.

We have had bitter experience in this respect. In the early

days of the war, when we counterattacked and drove the enemy into the narrow strip along the Rakdong-gang River, if we had organized properly the people in the southern half, if not all but at least some section of them, to rise up in strikes and carry on resistance movements, the enemy would have had no alternative but to pull out. But we failed to do so. We should draw a lesson from this experience.

Though the peaceful reunification of our country is an arduous task, whose achievement requires a protracted struggle, it is not beyond our power. We can reunify our country, and this we must do by all means. If we do not endeavour and do not struggle for reunification merely because it is difficult, the question of the country's reunification will forever remain unsettled. The solution of this question also depends upon our Party's strenuous fight for it.

For the reunification of the country we are required to do our work well in two ways: we must work tirelessly to exert our Party's influence upon the people in south Korea and arouse them to a struggle against the U.S. imperialists and the traitorous Syngman Rhee clique on the one hand, and, on the other, we must further fortify the democratic base in the northern half into an impregnable bastion.

If we are to properly inspire the growing revolutionary forces in south Korea and to grasp the revolutionary situation in time to turn it to account actively and solve the revolutionary tasks, our own strength must be great; and this requires the consolidation of our democratic base. Therefore, when our country was liberated we already laid down the line of building the democratic base in the northern half and of strengthening and developing it.

Strengthening the democratic base is a decisive guarantee of the country's reunification. The slogan calling for the strengthening of the democratic base should remain in force until our country is reunified. It is necessary to further strengthen the democratic base. We need a strong Party and government, and solid economic power. Only when we have them can we correctly appraise the revolutionary forces and revolutionary situation and take the initiative in settling matters. Hence, the strengthening of the democratic base and the country's reunification are revolutionary tasks which are closely interrelated.

In order to strengthen the democratic base in the northern half, it is necessary to further consolidate our Party and government bodies. We should strengthen our Party's political and ideological unity, and turn it into a more reliable force leading the people. We must further strengthen our people's power and enhance its functions in every way. It is also important to reinforce the social organizations. In short, we must further strengthen the Party and government bodies and the social organizations, further expand and intensify the work of the united front, and thereby rally all the patriotic democratic forces more firmly around our Party and the Government of the Republic.

Also, we must consolidate our democratic base economically. We must rapidly improve the people's living standard so as to turn our northern half into a great land of bliss. In order to improve the people's life, it is necessary to carry out economic construction successfully. We must grow crops well, erect fine factories, build up towns beautifully, and construct many houses. To this end, we have to industrialize and develop our country into a rich and strong one. First of all, the Three-Year Plan must be fulfilled and overfulfilled, and then, later on, a five-year plan must be carried out.

In this way, when we carry out economic construction well and improve the people's life, thus turning the northern half into a great land of bliss, no force on earth will be able to suppress the revolutionary spirit of the people in south Korea who, longing for the northern half, will rise against the reactionary regime in south Korea, and we will be able to easily solve the problem of the livelihood of the south Korean people after the country is reunified.

Then, we must strengthen the People's Army in every way. Without strengthening the People's Army we cannot conduct economic construction nor preserve our Party and Government.

Only by strengthening the People's Army can we defend the revolutionary gains and repel foreign aggression.

If we strengthen the Party and the Government, consolidate our economic foundation and strengthen the People's Army in this manner, the democratic base will be further fortified and our strength will become greater still.

Peaceful reunification will not be achieved just by shouting slogans; it will come only when our strength is great. While fighting actively for the peaceful reunification of the country, we must also take an active part in the world peace movement. For the more the peace forces grow and the peace movement is stepped up on an international scale, the more favourable it will be for the cause of our country's reunification.

We shall surely be able to solve the question of the country's reunification when our democratic camp is more fortified, when the democratic base in the northern half is further strengthened and the revolutionary tide runs high in the southern half.

Therefore, we must thoroughly do away with the tendency to entertain doubts about peaceful reunification, and to waver; we must do everything in our power to carry out the basic task of our revolution, the reunification and independence of our country.

EVERY EFFORT FOR THE COUNTRY'S REUNIFICATION AND INDEPENDENCE AND FOR SOCIALIST CONSTRUCTION IN THE NORTHERN HALF OF THE REPUBLIC

Theses on the Character and Tasks of Our Revolution

April 1955

1. CHARACTER OF THE REVOLUTION IN OUR COUNTRY AT THE PRESENT STAGE

After their liberation from the shackles of the protracted colonial rule of Japanese imperialism, the Korean people came to enjoy genuine freedom and began shaping a new history for the independence and prosperity of their country.

However, the U.S. army, from the very first days of its landing in the southern half of our country, revived the Japanese imperialist ruling machine, whipped up the landlords, comprador capitalists, pro-Japanese and pro-American elements, and traitors to the nation—heinous enemies of the Korean people—suppressed the people's committees formed spontaneously by the people soon after liberation as well as the patriotic democratic forces, and followed a colonial policy, opposing the building of a unified, independent state by the Korean people. As a result, the Korean revolution has taken on a complex, arduous and protracted character.

In view of the situation obtaining in our country, our Party, taking advantage of the favourable conditions created by the great Soviet army, set out to build up a powerful, revolutionary democratic base in the northern half of the Republic to serve as the basis for the country's reunification.

The fundamental question of every revolution is the question of power. After liberation, the working class in the northern half under the leadership of our Party formed a broad united front with all social sections opposing imperialism and feudalism, on the basis of a solid alliance with the toiling peasants, and set up people's power.

People's power, which was formed by the people themselves, defined it as its basic tasks to oppose foreign forces of aggression, to exercise dictatorship over the pro-Japanese and pro-American elements, the traitors to the nation, the landlords and comprador capitalists, the heinous enemies of the Korean people, and steadily to consolidate the democratic system designed for the freedom and welfare of the people, while rallying around itself patriotic democratic forces from all walks of life with the working class, the most advanced class, as its leading force; and it led the entire people to strive for the fulfilment of these tasks.

Guided by our Party and supported by all social sections and classes, the people's power liquidated the remnant forces of Japanese imperialism and carried out the historic agrarian reform, confiscating the land of the landlord class that had helped the imperialists implant their influence, and distributing it among the broad sections of the peasantry without payment; it confiscated industries, railway transport, communications, banks, etc., formerly owned by the Japanese imperialists, pro-Japanese elements and traitors to the nation, and turned them into the property of the entire people; enacted the Labour Law, the Law on Equality of the Sexes, the Law on Agricultural Tax in Kind, etc.; effected the democratization of judicial bodies and educational institutions; promoted the development of a progressive national culture and art; and founded the people's armed forces.

As a result, all the tasks of the anti-imperialist and anti-feudal democratic revolution were fulfilled in the northern half and its people gradually entered the period of transition to socialism.

But the struggle of the people in the northern half for the gradual transition to socialism was obstructed by the three-year war unleashed by the U.S. imperialists and the Syngman Rhee clique, and, thus, the struggle required a long time.

The war was the most severe trial for our people and the democratic system they had established.

The victory of the democratic revolution in the northern half and the achievements of its people in economic construction constituted the great force that made it possible to repulse the armed invasion of the U.S. imperialists and their lackey, the traitorous Syngman Rhee clique, and to safeguard the democratic base of the northern half, the fountainhead of the revolution in our country.

To this day, however, when the 10th anniversary of the liberation is in sight, our country has not yet been reunified, the territory and nation remain divided in two and the southern half has been turned into a colony of the U.S. imperialists.

The U.S. imperialist aggressors still remain in south Korea and, implacably set against the peaceful reunification of our country, they are constantly creating tension in Korea, reinforcing Syngman Rhee's puppet army, and, meanwhile, are uttering the "march north and reunify" prattle.

Under the "ROK-U.S. Agreement on Military and Economic Assistance" concocted recently by the U.S. imperialists and the traitorous Syngman Rhee clique, the U.S. imperialists are more openly pursuing their policy of colonial plunder.

The traitorous Syngman Rhee gang is selling out the "properties under custody" to foreign capitalists, comprador capitalists and profiteers, and guarantees free investment of foreign capital in south Korea by its "Constitution."

In the southern half today, industry is almost at a standstill, and the workers are subjected to appalling slave labour and unemployment. The countryside has been devastated and the exploitation by the landlords is further intensified. Prices are skyrocketing; the people are denied even the faintest semblance of freedom and are distressed by hunger and poverty.

The situation prevailing in the southern half, along with the territorial division of the country and the splitting of the nation, brings the entire people in the southern half immeasurable misery and suffering, and hinders the normal social development of our unitary country.

Hence, the basic tasks of our revolution at the present stage are to overthrow the aggressive forces of U.S. imperialism and their ushers and allies—the landlords, comprador capitalists, pro-Japanese and pro-American elements and traitors to the nation in the southern half—and to free the people there from imperialist and feudal oppression and exploitation, thereby achieving the country's reunification along democratic lines and attaining complete national independence.

In the southern half, the motive force of the revolution is the working class and its most reliable ally, the peasantry, and the broad sections of the small-propertied classes opposed to U.S. imperialism and the feudal forces. And even national capitalists can join in the anti-imperialist, anti-feudal struggle in no small number.

The enemies of the revolution are the aggressive forces of U.S. imperialism, and the landlords, comprador capitalists, pro-Japanese and pro-American elements and traitors to the nation in the southern half who usher in and are allied with those forces.

Were it not for the interference by the United States, the chieftain of world reaction, the Korean people would long ago have beaten the domestic reactionary forces and triumphantly fulfilled the tasks of the anti-imperialist and anti-feudal democratic revolution throughout Korea.

We cannot carry out the tasks of the revolution without driving the U.S. imperialists out of our country, and without liquidating their running dogs, the Syngman Rhee clique.

Our revolution is, therefore, to carry out the task of anti-imperialist national liberation on the one hand and, on the other, the anti-feudal task of liberating the broad sections of the peasantry in the southern half who are still oppressed and exploited by the landlords.

In the conditions prevailing in the southern half today, particularly under circumstances in which it has been turned into a U.S. imperialist colony, our revolution will be carried out through a nation-wide struggle of an arduous, protracted nature.

We have to rally all the revolutionary forces and launch a strenuous struggle to drive out the aggressive forces of U.S. imperialism, crush the traitorous Syngman Rhee gang who is under its thumb, and win victory in the revolution.

Today, the might of the camp of peace, democracy and socialism headed by the Soviet Union is growing every day and its internationalist solidarity is gaining in scope and strength as an invincible one, whereas the imperialist camp is becoming ever weaker owing to its internal contradictions and mutual conflicts. The question depends on how we strengthen, organize and mobilize our forces to be more faithful to the banner of internationalism and to hasten the downfall of imperialism.

We must further strengthen our Party, people's power and social organizations; unite more firmly around our Party all the patriotic, democratic forces of the people in the northern and the southern half and rouse them to a nation-wide revolutionary struggle against the U.S. imperialists and the Syngman Rhee gang; we must further consolidate the democratic base of the northern half, the fountainhead of our revolution, politically, economically and militarily, and turn it not only into a force powerful enough to defend the northern half of the Republic against aggression by imperialism and its running dogs but also into a decisive force for attaining the reunification and independence of our country. For this purpose, we must further advance the revolution and thoroughly carry out the tasks of building the foundations of socialism in the northern half.

Gradual transition to socialism is an inevitable demand of the social and economic development in the northern half.

To strengthen the democratic base, it is necessary to develop the productive forces of industry and agriculture rapidly and further raise the material and cultural standards of the people. The small commodity and capitalist economies that still remain in our country hinder the growth of the productive forces, and, in particular, the individual peasant economy predominant in the countryside is a big obstacle to the speedy rehabilitation and future development of agriculture. Without transforming the peasant economy and individual trade and industry along socialist lines, it is impossible to ensure the development of the productive forces, radically improve the people's livelihood and further cement the unity and solidarity of all the people based on the worker-peasant alliance led by the working class.

The state and co-operative economies, which are predominant in the national economy in the northern half, are exerting a decisive influence on the small commodity economy based on private ownership and the capitalist economy which makes up a small proportion, leading them inevitably to the road of socialist transformation.

Thus, the social and economic conditions in the northern half of the Republic at the present stage make the building of socialism there an inevitable requirement of social development.

Socialist construction in the northern half will be a great inspiration to the people in the southern half, especially to the workers, peasants and the broad sections of small-propertied classes, and conducive to the formation of a united front even with some of the national capitalists in the southern half.

The successes gained in socialist construction in the northern half will not only be a decisive force in achieving the reunification of the country, but also a strong material guarantee for speedily rehabilitating and developing the economy in the southern half and ensuring socialist construction on a nationwide scale after the country is reunified.

2. TASKS OF CONSOLIDATING THE REVOLUTIONARY DEMOCRATIC BASE AND BUILDING SOCIALISM IN THE NORTHERN HALF

(1) ECONOMIC FORMS AND CLASS RELATIONS IN THE NORTHERN HALF OF THE REPUBLIC

The socio-economic formation of the northern half underwent a radical change as a result of the democratic reforms effected after liberation. At the present stage, the socio-economic forms in the northern half can be classified into three main categories:

First, the socialist economic form;

Second, the small commodity economic form;

Third, the capitalist economic form.

The socialist economic form is composed of state and co-operative economies. Today, the socialist economic form constitutes the leading force in the northern half and, particularly, it holds an overwhelming proportion in industry. At present, the state economy represents some 90 per cent of total industrial production in our country and the co-operative economy 7-8 per cent.

Human relations in the socialist economic form are characterized by the comradely co-operation and assistance among the working people who are freed from exploitation. They do not work for the enrichment of the exploiters as in the past, but engage in free, honourable labour for themselves, for the prosperity and progress of their country, and get their share according to the quality and quantity of labour expended. The economic laws of socialism operate and production grows according to plan here, serving the purpose of satisfying the ever-increasing material and cultural needs of the working people.

The small commodity economic form is composed of the individual peasant economy which still accounts for an overwhelming proportion of the rural economy, and of the urban handicraft economy. At the present stage of the transition period, the majority of the population of our country is embraced in the small commodity economic form.

Small commodity production is based on private ownership of the means of production and individual labour. The petty bourgeoisie can be remoulded along socialist lines although they waver between the two paths—socialism and capitalism—because of their dual nature. In particular, the petty bourgeoisie in our country received benefits directly from the agrarian reform and other democratic reforms, and are remoulding themselves voluntarily into socialist working people (either as workers or co-operative members) with the rapid growth of the socialist economic form in the national economy, realizing by experience the superiority of the people's democratic system and the correctness of our Party and Government policies.

The capitalist economic form is made up of individual capitalist trade and industry in towns and the rich farmer economy in the countryside. It is the form of exploitation still remaining in the northern half of the Republic. In this economic form the economic laws of capitalism operate in a limited range.

In the national economy of the northern half, the capitalist economic form holds an extremely small proportion compared with the socialist economic form. Particularly in the field of industry the whole of private ownership accounts for no more than 2-3 per cent of industrial production, and even this consists mostly of small-scale enterprises limited to such secondary branches as rice cleaning, cotton-willowing, etc. As the socialist economic form grows and develops in the national economy in the northern half, the capitalist economic form is being gradually transformed along socialist lines.

Because the small commodity economic form still remains in the rural districts in the northern half at present, class differentiation of the peasantry is taking place more or less and rich farmers are emerging and growing. They employ hired labour either seasonally or permanently, and exploit the poor peasants by manipulating the grain market and by the methods of covertly lending money and various goods at usurious rates and exacting heavy charges for the use of farm implements and draught animals, etc.

But the economic foothold of the rich farmers is extremely weak in the northern half of the Republic, for the agrarian reform was carried out under the slogan, "Land to the tillers!" Particularly, with co-operatives rapidly growing in the rural areas, the objects of exploitation by the rich farmers are disappearing. These circumstances will bring them to join the agricultural co-operatives voluntarily and to be remoulded gradually into working peasants. Yet this cannot be realized smoothly without class struggle in the countryside, but will be accompanied by the fight against certain resistance on the part of the enemy.

Such are the fundamental features of the economic structure of a transitional character and the objective laws of social and economic development in the northern half of the Republic. This determines the policy of our Party for socialist construction in the northern half.

(2) TASKS OF OUR PARTY FOR LAYING THE FOUNDATIONS OF SOCIALISM IN THE NORTHERN HALF

The basic task of our Party at the present stage of the period of transition to socialism is to lay the foundations of socialism on the basis of the achievements gained in the struggle for the postwar rehabilitation and development of the national economy, further consolidating the worker-peasant alliance.

We should further expand and strengthen the predominant position of the socialist economic form in all spheres of the national economy by gradually transforming the small commodity and capitalist economic forms along socialist lines, and should further develop the productive forces to lay the material and technical foundations of socialism.

To this end, it is necessary to eliminate the colonial one-sidedness and technical backwardness of industry and build the foundation for socialist industrialization. The building of the foundation of socialist industrialization means the completion of the first stage of industrialization in our country.

The keystone of socialist industrialization lies in the priority development of heavy industry. Only with the establishment of a powerful heavy industry is it possible to ensure the development of all industries, transport and agriculture, and the victory of the socialist system.

After liberation, the backwardness and deformation of our heavy industry, a legacy of Japanese imperialist colonial rule, hampered the development of the economy as a whole in our country and greatly obstructed a proportionate development of heavy industry, light industry and agriculture in particular.

If we do not set up a powerful heavy industry in our country in the future, we shall not be able to shore up light industry which was originally very backward, nor provide the countryside with modern farm machinery, nor ensure radical improvement in the people's livelihood. Only with the establishment of a powerful heavy industry, can the independence of the economy and the independent progress of the country be ensured.

In the rural economy, the individual peasant farming should be converted into a socialist collective farming by gradually enlisting the peasants in agricultural co-operatives on the voluntary principle. Unless the rural economy is developed along the line of socialist collectivization, agriculture cannot catch up with the fast developing industry, cannot supply it with raw materials and labour reserves, and so will hamper industrial development in the long run, and, accordingly, will obstruct the overall socio-economic development in the northern half. At the same time, unless the rural economy is transformed into a socialist collective economy, it will be impossible to rapidly improve the standard of life of the peasants, eliminate rich farmers and other exploiting elements that are reviving in the countryside, and consolidate our Party's rural positions.

Handicrafts and small individual trade should be gradually transformed along socialist lines through the co-operative economy.

The capitalist elements still remaining in town and country will have to be restricted and utilized, and remoulded, step by step, on socialist lines.

And not only should the production bond between industry and agriculture be strengthened, but their economic ties should also be further expanded and strengthened through the market.

Along with this, the masses of the people should be educated in socialist ideology, and new technical and cultural workers trained in large numbers from among them.

In order to carry out these tasks after the war, our Party marked off three main stages in the rehabilitation and construction of the severely war-ravaged national economy, and has been waging a struggle for carrying out those tasks successfully.

For postwar rehabilitation and development of the national economy, our Party set the following stages: the stage of six months to one year preparatory to overall restoration and construction; the stage of carrying out a three-year plan designed to rehabilitate completely all branches of the national economy from war damage and attain the prewar level of industrial and agricultural production; and the stage of implementing a five-year plan which will lay the basis for socialist industrialization.

Our Party set it as the basic line of postwar economic construction to ensure the priority growth of heavy industry simultaneously with development of light industry and agriculture.

During the Three-Year Plan, in the field of industry we are following the policy of concentrating our efforts on those branches of heavy industry closely associated with the improvement of the people's standard of living and laying emphasis on the restoration of destroyed factories and mills and, at the same time, rebuilding them on the basis of new technology and building some new ones. And it was decided that the destroyed factories should not be mechanically restored on original sites; some factories should be restored in their former locales for the sake of speedy rehabilitation and economy but factories and mills to be built anew should be distributed in consideration of their organic connection with our country's sources of raw materials, transportation facilities and existing industrial establishments.

In 1956, the last year of the Three-Year Plan, the total value of industrial output will grow 1.5 times that of the prewar year 1949, with output of the means of production increasing 1.3 times and consumer goods 2 times. To ensure this growth of industrial production, funds amounting to 37,360 million *won* are to be invested in industry in the three years.

During the Three-Year Plan, not only will the old factories and enterprises be restored, but also many new machine plants will be built and light industry will also be rehabilitated and developed rapidly in the northern half of the Republic.

By 1956, a new textile mill equipped with 60,000-100,000 spindles with an annual production capacity of 40,000,000-80,000,000 metres of fabrics will be built, as well as canneries, meat-packing factories and many other light industry plants.

The Three-Year National Economic Plan envisages enormous state support for the rapid rehabilitation and development of the rural economy and its socialist transformation. During the Three-Year Plan 5,575 million *won* will be invested in the rural economy, of which 2,225 million *won* will go into irrigation projects.

The speedy development of agriculture will supply the population with more food and provide more raw materials to light industry. In 1956, total grain output will surpass the level of the prewar year 1949 by 19 per cent, with total rice output increasing by 30 per cent.

The rapid rehabilitation and development of industry and agriculture during the Three-Year Plan will meet the population's increasing demand for the necessaries of life and create the indispensable conditions for abolishing the rationing of food and manufactured goods and switching over to free trade.

In the sphere of education and culture, conditions will be created for introducing the system of universal compulsory primary schooling and the number of university and college students will reach 22,500 in the period of the Three-Year Plan. National culture and arts will be further developed; theatres, cinema houses and clubs with a total seating capacity of 134,000 will be restored or newly built.

By 1956, the last year of the Three-Year Plan, the national economy which was destroyed by the war will be rehabilitated in the main and, thus, in the northern half the postwar rehabilitation period will come to an end. Industry and agriculture restored in this period will become the solid base for completely refashioning our country's economy into the socialist economy in the future.

The central task of the First Five-Year Plan for Development of the National Economy, which will be worked out on this basis in future, is to build the foundations of socialism in our country.

In the field of heavy industry, the iron works not yet fully restored in the Three-Year Plan period will, first of all, be completely rehabilitated during the Five-Year Plan so as to produce approximately 1,000,000 tons of pig iron annually, and the machine-building industry will be further developed to produce 2,000 machine tools annually.

It is envisaged that in 1961, the last year of the Five-Year Plan, the total generating capacity will be 1,850,000 kw. and the output of coal 8,500,000-9,000,000 tons.

Our chemical industry will supply the state with more than 400,000 tons of fertilizer.

In the period of the Five-Year Plan, the mineral resources of our country will be tapped in larger quantities to help towards building the foundations of socialism, and they will become the main source of foreign currency.

During the Five-Year Plan the necessaries of life will be turned out in quantities for the betterment of the people's welfare.

In the field of light industry, chief attention will be paid in the Five-Year Plan period to the production of textiles and processed foodstuffs which are the main necessaries of the people's life. In 1961, the output of different kinds of fabric will be 150 million metres, or about 15 metres per head of the population in the northern half of the Republic, and vegetable and meat processing factories and flour mills will be built in the vicinity of major cities.

In the field of agriculture, 3,500,000 tons of grain, 150,000 tons of meat, 150,000 tons of sugar beet, 50,000 tons of cotton, 80,000 tons of fruit and 30,000 tons of cocoons will be produced annually during the Five-Year Plan. Thus the question of food will be solved in the northern half and the requirements of light industry for raw materials will be more fully satisfied.

During the Five-Year Plan, agriculture will be co-operativized as a whole in the northern half of the Republic, thereby eliminating the roots of exploitation and poverty in the countryside and completing the socialist transformation of the rural economy.

To carry out this tremendous plan, we need hosts of cadres who are politically seasoned and have a mastery of advanced science and technology. In 1961, the last year of the Five-Year Plan, we must have over 130,000 highly qualified engineers and assistant engineers.

To lay the foundations of socialism in the northern half is a huge and difficult job. But led by the Workers' Party of Korea, the Korean people will be able to carry out this great task successfully.

Under the leadership of our Party, the political and moral unity of the broad masses of the people is taking shape and developing on the basis of the worker-peasant alliance with the working class as its core, and socialist construction in the northern half enjoys the active support of the millions of working people.

We have precious experience, accumulated during the five years of prewar peaceful construction and in the struggle for the postwar rehabilitation and construction of the national economy, and one million Party members and a heroic people, tried and seasoned in the bitter three-year war.

Our country also abounds in natural resources necessary for socialist construction.

We not only can draw on the advanced experience of the Soviet Union, the People's Republic of China and the People's Democracies, but also receive enormous economic and technical assistance from them.

All these are favourable subjective and objective conditions for socialist construction in the northern half of our country.

But there are obstacles and difficulties in our socialist construction, too.

Industry of our country has a very short history, and it was completely destroyed in the war. Our abundant resources have not yet been fully developed and there is an acute shortage of cadres in industry.

The cultural standard of our people is still low, and survivals of outdated thinking have not been obliterated from the minds of people.

Our socialist construction is going on under conditions in which the northern half, an industrial zone, is artificially separated from the southern half, an agricultural zone, and U.S. imperialism, the chieftain of international reaction, still occupies the southern half, making frantic efforts to disrupt construction in the northern half.

Surmounting all these obstacles and difficulties, we should and can successfully carry out the task of building the foundations of socialism.

The Workers' Party of Korea is the organizer and inspirer of all the victories of the Korean people. The organizational and ideological consolidation of our Party is the guarantee for our victory in the struggle for the reunification and independence of the country and for socialist construction in the northern half of the Republic.

To further consolidate the Party organizationally and ideologically, it is imperative to ensure steel-strong unity and solidarity of its ranks, strengthen Party discipline and further promote inner-Party democracy. The promotion of inner-Party democracy can be ensured only if the work of the Party committees is improved and the collective leadership of the Party strengthened. Every Party member and leading cadre should observe the principle of collective Party leadership, and resolutely combat any and every tendency towards individualist heroism and liberalism which runs counter to it.

All Party members should arm themselves more firmly with Marxist-Leninist theory, systematically study the history of our Party and its decisions and earnestly study and assimilate the experience gained in the building of socialism by the Communist Party of the Soviet Union and other Communist and Workers' Parties of the fraternal countries, tirelessly learn theories on economic construction and knowledge of science and technology and elevate their practical abilities and cultural standards.

To carry the Party's lines and policies into effect, we have to further strengthen our state power based on the worker-peasant alliance under working-class leadership.

The U.S. imperialists who occupy the southern half of the Republic and their minions, the domestic reactionary forces, are trying to use all conceivable means to oppose the reunification and independence of the country and to frustrate the building of the foundations of socialism in the northern half.

Only by strengthening the organs of state power is it possible to rally the masses of the people more firmly around the Party and the Government, thoroughly suppress the resistance of the enemies of the revolution, and more successfully carry out the cause of socialist construction. The strengthening of the dictatorship over counter-revolutionaries, spies, wreckers and saboteurs and the promotion of democracy among the masses of the people are important conditions for successfully carrying out socialist construction.

One of the most important tasks our Party must fulfil is to further strengthen our people's armed forces.

Only by further strengthening our People's Army is it possible for us to defend firmly the precious achievements our people won by their sweat and blood and our democratic base from the enemy's encroachment and to ensure the successful carrying out of socialist construction. Therefore, our Party should do everything in its power to train the People's Army into a steel-strong cadre army and intensify the support of the entire people to it.

Our Party's lines and policies for the country's reunification and independence, and for socialist construction in the northern half of the Republic, illumine the path for the entire Korean people to follow.

Under the leadership of our Party, the Korean people have always won victories in their arduous struggle, overcoming all difficulties and trials. No force on earth can prevent our people, united rock-firm around the Party, from marching forward towards a bright future along the path indicated by the Party.

The Korean people, led by our Party and holding aloft the banner of Marxism-Leninism and proletarian internationalism, will surely win victory in their just struggle for the reunification and independence of the country and for socialism by strengthening their solidarity with the peoples of the camp of peace, democracy and socialism headed by the Soviet Union, and by further augmenting their own revolutionary forces.

ON FURTHER INTENSIFYING THE CLASS EDUCATION OF THE PARTY MEMBERS

Report Delivered at a Plenary Meeting of the Central Committee of the Workers' Party of Korea
April 1, 1955

1. THE CHARACTER OF OUR REVOLUTION AND THE BASIC TASKS OF OUR PARTY AT THE PRESENT STAGE

Comrades,

Nearly ten years have already elapsed since our country was liberated from the yoke of Japanese imperialist colonial rule.

From the time when the Soviet army stationed its troops in north Korea and the aggressive forces of U.S. imperialism occupied south Korea, north and south Korea followed two opposite paths—democracy and anti-democracy. And although the Soviet army withdrew from the northern half of the Republic, the U.S. troops remained occupying the southern half. In such conditions our country's revolution took on a complex character. Consequently, the fighting tasks of our Party were defined in accordance with the different situations in north and south Korea.

In the northern half of the Republic, a genuine people's power was established, which represents and safeguards the interests of the working class and of all the masses of the working people; the agrarian reform, nationalization of industries and other democratic reforms were effected; and the political unity and solidarity of all the working people were strengthened on the basis of the worker-peasant alliance led by the working class.

Thus, the tasks of the anti-imperialist, anti-feudal democratic revolution were completely carried out in the northern half of the Republic, which, as a result, was transformed from a colonial, semi-feudal society into a new society of People's Democracy, and gradually entered the period of transition to socialism. Carrying out the tasks of the transition period under the leadership of our Party, the people in the northern half strengthened and developed the democratic base, the fountainhead of our revolution, politically, economically and militarily.

This constituted the great strength with which the Korean people won a historic victory and defended our revolutionary gains from the enemy's encroachment in the three-year long Fatherland Liberation War against the U.S. imperialists and their running dogs, the traitorous Syngman Rhee clique.

However, up to this day when the tenth anniversary of the liberation is close at hand, the U.S. imperialists continue to occupy south Korea and our territory and nation remain divided, with the southern half completely reduced to a colony of U.S. imperialism and its military base for unleashing a new war.

The splitting of the country brings great suffering and misery not only to the people of south Korea oppressed by the U.S. imperialists and the Syngman Rhee clique, but to the entire Korean people; it constitutes the main obstacle to building our country into a rich and strong state, unified and independent.

The Korean people, therefore, are still faced with the tasks of the anti-imperialist, anti-feudal democratic revolution: to wipe out the aggressive forces of U.S. imperialism and the landlords, comprador capitalists, pro-Japanese and pro-American elements and traitors to the nation in the southern half who usher in those forces and are allied with them, and to free the people in the southern half from imperialist and feudal oppression and exploitation, thereby attaining the democratic reunification of the country and complete national independence.

Under conditions in which U.S. imperialism, the ringleader of world imperialism, is occupying the southern half of our country and south Korea has turned into its colony, we shall have to unfold an arduous and protracted nation-wide struggle for the country's reunification.

The motive forces of our revolution are the working class, the most advanced class in Korea, and the peasantry, its most reliable ally, and broad strata of the small propertied classes who are opposed to the forces of imperialism and feudalism; not a few national capitalists might also join in the anti-imperialist and anti-feudal struggle.

Our Party should rally all the patriotic, democratic forces in north and south Korea around itself and the Government of the Republic to isolate the reactionary forces from the broad masses of the people and should arouse the popular masses to a decisive struggle in support of the people's democratic system established in the northern half of the Republic against the U.S. imperialists and the traitorous Syngman Rhee clique. And we should further strengthen and develop the democratic base of the northern half of the Republic, the fountainhead of our revolution, politically, economically and militarily, and thereby convert it into a decisive force for winning the reunification and independence of our country.

To strengthen the democratic base, our Party should further consolidate and develop the socialist economic sector that has become predominant in the northern half of the Republic as a result of the victory of the people's democratic revolution and the successes scored in democratic construction, and should further cement the alliance between the workers and peasants, thereby building socialism, step by step, in the northern half.

Only by building socialism in the northern half will it be possible to further strengthen the democratic base and promote the reunification and independence of the country. Even after reunification, the socialist force in the northern half will serve as the leading force in rehabilitating and developing the ruined economy of the southern half and building socialism on a nation-wide scale in the future.

To carry out the tasks of socialist construction successfully in the northern half, we must bring into play the creative enthusiasm of the entire working people rallied around the Party, and heighten their revolutionary consciousness.

Socialist construction in the northern half is attended by a sharp class struggle in all spheres, and this sets us the task of further intensifying class education among our Party members.

2. THE NECESSITY OF INTENSIFYING CLASS EDUCATION IN THE PARTY AT THE PRESENT STAGE

Comrades,

Our revolutionary struggle against U.S. imperialism and the traitorous Syngman Rhee clique is the struggle of the whole nation for the reunification of the country and complete national independence and, at the same time, it is a sharp class struggle for the social emancipation of the working class and all the toiling masses in our country.

To effectively carry out the protracted struggle against the U.S. imperialist aggressors for the complete reunification and independence of the country and to successfully build the foundations of socialism in the northern half, we must arm all our Party members with the revolutionary ideology of Marxism-Leninism and raise their class consciousness, thereby training them into out-and-out revolutionary fighters leading the working masses in the struggle. We cannot build a new society successfully without arming the Party members and working masses with the progressive ideology of Marxism-Leninism and without eliminating from people's minds the ideological survivals of capitalism left over from the old society.

We shall be victors in the protracted struggle only when our Party members are armed with revolutionary optimism and conviction that socialism will win and capitalism and imperialism will inevitably fall, only when they are trained to be revolutionary fighters who can scientifically analyse all the objective phenomena of society.

Through the new political, economic and cultural life created in the northern half of our country after its liberation from the shackles of Japanese imperialist rule, and through the education in Marxist-Leninist ideology conducted by our Party, new, progressive ideological consciousness and moral traits have been formed and developed among our people. These new, progressive ideological consciousness and moral traits have been important factors in all the victories we have hitherto scored.

Definite successes have been achieved in the ideological education conducted so far by our Party, but it also has a number of defects and shortcomings.

The internal and external circumstances faced by our Party today, and especially the task of laying the foundations of socialism in the northern half of the Republic, confront us with the necessity of giving Marxist-Leninist education in the Party a more concrete content and purpose.

First, we are building socialism in circumstances in which we have long been standing face to face with the enemy, capitalist elements still remain internally, and the enemy is not only persisting in his attempt at armed invasion, but also infiltrates rotten capitalist ideas by every fraudulence and underhand means and is plotting various acts of subversion and sabotage in alliance with the reactionary elements lurking in the northern half.

The historical process of the transition from capitalism to socialism entails sharp class struggles. As Stalin said, moribund classes have never voluntarily quitted the scene of history; history still knows no case where the dying bourgeoisie did not make last-ditch attempts to continue its existence.

The landlord class, comprador capitalists, pro-Japanese

elements, traitors to the nation and other reactionary elements, who were liquidated in the northern half of the Republic as a result of the democratic reforms, have not yet given up the wild dream of restoring their old positions, nor have they abandoned their true colours as exploiters.

And the survivals of the thinking, customs and traditions of the old society, which had been implanted over a long period, have not yet been completely eliminated from the minds of the masses of our people.

All these are obstacles to socialist construction, and inevitably exert a negative influence in all fields of politics, economy and culture, overtly or covertly, consciously or unconsciously.

What is more, the U.S. imperialists and the traitorous Syngman Rhee clique are resorting to all kinds of manoeuvres to spoil the achievements of socialist construction in the northern half, as the political and economic footholds of the enemy have been basically eliminated and our patriotic, democratic forces have been further united in the northern half, the revolutionary awakening of the people in the southern half has grown gradually and the enemy has been isolated still further. In a desperate attempt to hinder socialist construction in the northern half of the Republic, they incessantly dispatch secret agents, wreckers and saboteurs to spy out our state and military secrets and organize espionage and sabotaging activities in factories, mills, railways and farm villages and resort to all conceivable means such as murder and arson.

In his subversive activities, the enemy attempts to utilize the wavering elements who are not steadfast ideologically and those with an unclean record. The exposure and punishment of the Pak Hon Yong-Li Sung Yop gang, the hireling spies of U.S. imperialism, and of other wreckers and saboteurs is an instance which reveals the despicable and sinister hostile activities of U.S. imperialism and the Syngman Rhee clique against the northern half of the Republic.

The U.S. imperialists and the puppet Syngman Rhee clique are spreading all kinds of falsehoods and slanders, resorting to all their media and methods of propaganda. These facts mean that, under the conditions in which the reactionary elements in the northern half of our country have not yet been completely eliminated, the enemy's influence may be exerted on some backward elements in our ranks.

Only by intensifying class education in the Party and among the entire people can we prevent our people from being contaminated with reactionary ideas, and carry out socialist construction successfully in the northern half of the Republic.

Second, due to the peculiarities of the development of our country in the past, class awakening is insufficient among the workers and peasants who make up the main mass of our Party.

From the first days of its formation as a class, the working class of Korea has fought in the van of the anti-Japanese, national-liberation movement, and emerged as the glorious leader in the anti-Japanese, national-liberation struggle inspired by the victory of the great October Socialist Revolution and the successes of socialist construction in the Soviet Union. Especially since the August 15 Liberation, the Korean working class has been and is carrying out with credit its tasks in all fields of Party and state building, as the leading class, as the core detachment.

However, the Korean working class is still young; it has not yet been tried and seasoned in large-scale revolutionary movements. The ranks of the working class in our country started to grow rapidly following the August 15 Liberation and have been expanded on a mass scale especially in the postwar rehabilitation period, with the majority coming from the peasantry and urban petty bourgeoisie.

This situation has allowed various kinds of backward ideological consciousness to infiltrate the ranks of our working class. It is by no means an accident that indolence, dissoluteness and lack of discipline are now found among some workers, and that they do not behave in a way as befitting masters of the state.

In the ranks of the peasantry, too, there has been a considerable ideological change.

Throughout the whole period of Japanese imperialist rule, the majority of the Korean peasants groaned under the whip of colonial plunderers and feudal landlords; they led as miserable a life as that of the workers, subjected to double and triple plunder by the Japanese imperialists and the landlords and capitalists. Therefore, the Korean peasants, encouraged by the struggle of the working class, waged their struggles against the Japanese imperialists and the landlords. It was in these circumstances that the Korean peasantry greeted the August 15 Liberation. After liberation, through the agrarian reform carried out by the people's power, they were freed from the age-old feudal exploitation and given land without compensation. Broad segments of the peasants, therefore, played a progressive role in the democratic reforms and in the great undertaking of democratic construction, giving positive support to the policies of the Workers' Party of Korea and the Government of the Republic and taking an active part in the people's power; and they markedly improved their own living conditions.

But with their living conditions improving some of our peasants have already forgotten the misery of their life in the past when they were exploited, oppressed and maltreated in every way by the Japanese imperialist colonial rulers and the landlords. Among the peasants one can often find such manifestations as slackening their vigilance and hatred against their class enemies and as placing their own personal interests above those of the state.

Our intelligentsia, too, fails in class consciousness. Of course, in the days of Japanese imperialist domination, a considerable number of intellectuals joined the revolutionary ranks against Japanese imperialism under the influence of the working-class movement. They have greatly heightened their Marxist-Leninist ideological consciousness since liberation, in the course of serving the country and the people, and especially in the course of democratic reforms, democratic construction and the Fatherland Liberation War.

Some intellectuals, however, have not yet completely got

rid of their old bourgeois habits formed in the past while serving in the Japanese imperialists' economic and cultural institutions, and particularly of their liberal tendencies and their habit of dissoluteness and dissipation. They are not sensitive to what is new, and cannot keep up with newly developing realities. Moreover, some of our intellectuals who have lost sight of their duty to serve the country and the people, fail to work in a manner as befitting masters and have not yet completely discarded the servile mentality fostered in the days of Japanese imperialist rule.

Third, in the period of the national-liberation struggle against Japanese imperialism in the past, our working people did not have a revolutionary party, their own vanguard.

In our revolutionary movement in the past, there were factionalists, such as of the M-L group, the Tuesday group, the North Wind association, the Com-group and other groups, who over a long period had committed criminal acts of disrupting the working-class movement and exerted harmful effects upon it. Because there was no party, our working people could not receive Marxist-Leninist education or be trained through organized revolutionary struggles.

In an attempt to numb the revolutionary consciousness of the Korean working masses, the Japanese imperialists cruelly suppressed the spread of advanced ideas and, in particular, resorted to every sort of malignant false propaganda, slander and vilification against the revolutionary ideology and theory of Marxism-Leninism. Moreover, the dissemination of "Marxist literature" intentionally distorted by the Japanese imperialists had a harmful ideological effect on the intelligentsia of our country. The poison of such reactionary propaganda by the Japanese imperialists has not yet been thoroughly removed from the minds of the masses of our people, and some backward Party members, too, have not yet completely freed themselves from its influence.

Historically, these facts constitute the main reason why Marxist-Leninist ideology and theory were not disseminated thoroughly among the working masses of our country.

Fourth, we must realize that our Party has a short history and its qualitative composition is still at a low level.

Our Party is young, with only about ten years of history. As conditions after the August 15 Liberation were comparatively favourable to our struggle, many progressive elements from among the working class, toiling peasantry and working intellectuals joined the ranks of our Party.

Our Party members were tried and tested during the five years of peaceful construction and especially during the three years of bitter war. But many of fine Party members were killed in the war, and nearly 50 per cent of total Party membership are new recruits admitted since then. And approximately 60 per cent of the total membership are of peasant origin.

A large part of the Party members have direct or indirect connections with the small commodity economy. Petty-bourgeois ideological consciousness thus stemming from the connections with the small commodity economy inevitably exerts a negative influence on our revolutionary work and on our ideological front.

Owing to these circumstances, the bulk of our Party members today have not been tempered in practical work, and are not fully prepared ideologically and theoretically.

Fifth, ideological and political education within the Party to heighten the class consciousness of its cadres and rank and file has in many cases been conducted perfunctorily in the past.

Marxism-Leninism teaches that the development of people's consciousness lags behind that of economic conditions. The economic conditions of the workers and peasants have been conspicuously changed under the people's democratic system established in the northern half, but they still lag behind in their ideological consciousness and have not yet thoroughly rid themselves of their old feudal and bourgeois ideological remnants and conventions.

In not a few cases, however, our Party's ideological work has been conducted without any profound consideration of the actual situation, and it fails to correspond fully with the political, economic and military tasks of the present stage.

Many Party organizations do not yet regard the class education of the Party rank and file as the first and foremost task, because they fail to clearly grasp Lenin's words that the weakening of the influence of socialist ideology means precisely the strengthening of the influence of bourgeois ideology.

In many cases, our Party organizations have failed to explain fully to each member that the ultimate goal of our Party, a Marxist-Leninist Party of a new type, is not only to reunify the country but also to build a socialist society throughout the country, and then a communist society, and they have paid little attention to educating and training Party members in the lofty socialist ideology which is opposed to the exploitation of man by man.

On the pretext of reckoning with the Party's policy concerning the united front, many of our Party organizations did not fully explain to Party members the tasks confronting the Party in each period and at each stage and the class character of events at home and abroad, and conducted educational work designed to promote their class awakening very inadequately.

These organizations have failed to acquaint all their members thoroughly with the fact that the democratic reforms carried out in the northern half of the Republic in the past were accompanied by an acute class struggle, that the Fatherland Liberation War against the U.S. imperialists and the Syngman Rhee clique was the manifestation of a fierce class struggle, that the socialist construction which is in progress in the northern half of the Republic at the present stage is also attended by class struggle, and that all our activities for the accomplishment of the Party's tasks, without exception, reflect specific aspects of the class struggle.

The result is that many Party members do not have a clear idea of what path we have followed and what path we should take, nor do they thoroughly understand what the building of the basis of socialism in our country demands of them or what tasks they should perform for the Party and the state.

The conditions peculiar to the development of our country and the inadequacy of the class education conducted by our

Party in the past years have given rise to a number of negative manifestations in thinking and in action among some Party members and cadres, manifestations which are detrimental to the interests of our revolution.

First, one of them finds expression in the fact that some of our Party members lack a correct understanding of the character and fundamental tasks of our country's revolution, the prospects of its development and the methods for carrying it out.

We can see that some Party members lack conviction concerning the cause of reunification and independence of our country and, in particular, have a vague idea of the prospects of our country's revolution. There is no doubt, of course, that our struggle has assumed a protracted, complex and arduous character due to the occupation of the southern half of our country by the U.S. imperialists, the ringleader of world imperialism. But we Marxists must not forget even for a moment that imperialism is doomed, and that the hastening of its fall depends on our struggle.

The U.S. imperialists and the Syngman Rhee clique can still swagger around in the southern half of our country because the entire Korean people are not yet fully united. If we Korean people unite as one, there can be no enemy we cannot fight and defeat.

Nevertheless, because of their low level of revolutionary consciousness, some Party members lack firm confidence in our final victory, are indifferent towards the policy of our Party for the attainment of the reunification and independence of the country and do not take an active part in the struggle for its implementation.

Second, some of our Party members attach more weight to their personal interests than to the interests of the revolution, the Party and the people.

When they joined the Party, they solemnly swore that they accepted its Programme and Rules, would go through thick and thin to perform their duties as decided or instructed by the Party and would fight for its interests at the cost of their lives, but, in deed, they place their personal interests above the interests of the Party and the revolution and, worse still, they pursue their personal interests even at the cost of the Party and the revolution.

Such a practice has been manifested openly during the recent grain procurement work. This work, which was conducted in accordance with the decisions of the Party and the Government, was an important task designed to increase direct benefits to the peasants and to facilitate the postwar rehabilitation and construction of the national economy. Nevertheless, some rural Party members not only failed to respond actively to the Party's call, but even resorted to such intolerable non-Party, non-class practices as pursuing only their personal interests and besmirching the honour of a Party member for a few bags of rice.

Third, because of their feeble class consciousness, some Party members do not wage a principled struggle against exploitative practices, have not rid themselves of the obsolete bourgeois viewpoint towards labour, and take a dishonest attitude towards state and social property.

Such Party members do not regard the violation of labour discipline and failure to fulfil the state plans as shameful or criminal, but unscrupulously perpetrate acts of embezzling and squandering state and social property and of flagrantly violating financial regulations of the state, or fail to wage an intense struggle against such practices.

Besides, some rural Party members have gone so far as to secretly employ hired labour or practise usury, though such cases are few in number. And some fuctionaries of state organs, because of their low level of class consciousness, grant business licences without principle on the pretext that this will provide tax revenue, and thus revive the bankrupt middle and small entrepreneurs in the towns and, in the long run, help the growth of the exploiting elements.

Fourth, some of the Party members and responsible cadres do not faithfully serve the interests of the revolution and the Party, nor do they courageously struggle to uphold principle in their work. On the contrary, blinded simply by a desire for fame, careerism and avarice, they persist in such bureaucratic work methods as glossing over facts and flattering their superiors while blustering at their subordinates.

Thus, undermining the bond with the masses which is the source of our Party's strength, they injure the Party's prestige and weaken its might. They are afraid of criticism and self-criticism, especially of justified criticism from below, and suppress it, thereby doing great harm to the work of the Party and the state.

This found glaring expression during the recent grain procurement work. Many leading cadres, instead of deeply imbuing the masses with the political significance of the grain procurement work and endeavouring to assure its success on the basis of detailed investigation and preparation, carried out the Party's policy by force and coercion in the style of the Japanese imperialist bureaucrats and officials. This provoked complaints and discontent among the peasant masses and resulted in the alienation of the masses from the Party.

Fifth, among some of the Party members there are still to be found the evil factional practices which tend to undermine the unity of the Party and to split it; they are steeped in the factional poison.

The factionalists consort with their old coteries and engage in factional activities, trying to establish their influence. Outwardly they pretend to support the Party, but behind the scenes they speak ill of it; they do not take part in Party work enthusiastically, but resort to all sorts of manoeuvres to climb up to high posts in the Party or in the state organs, sowing dissension among the cadres and attempting to wreck its unity. And there are others who whip together discontented elements within the Party, shield one another among people of the same local origin, ventilate complaints and discontent among themselves and indulge in nepotism. The aggravation of such acts will finally lead to the destruction of the Party and to the betrayal of the class interests.

Sixth, lack of class consciousness on the part of some Party members and cadres is observable in the fact that they, carried away by successes, become indolent and slack and do not sharpen their vigilance against the enemy.

Some Party members whose political consciousness is low and whose class stand is not firm, misunderstand the lenient policy of our Party and extend their "generosity" even to hostile elements with whom we can never compromise. Instead of exposing and smashing the espionage, sabotage and subversive activities of various hostile elements in good time, they connive at these activities and reconcile themselves to the hostile elements or reveal Party and state secrets to them. Owing to their political ignorance and lack of vigilance, such Party members do not realize that they are playing into the hands of the enemy, that they are helping the enemy and doing tremendous harm to the class interests of the workers and peasants and to the interests of the revolution.

All these facts mentioned above confront us with the urgent task of intensifying Marxist-Leninist education in our Party and further enhancing the revolutionary consciousness of its entire membership.

3. THE BASIC ORIENTATION OF CLASS EDUCATION IN THE PARTY AND THE MEASURES FOR CONDUCTING IT

The Party organs and organizations at all levels should devote special attention to conducting class education in the Party for the attainment of the country's reunification and independence and the successful building of the basis of socialism in the northern half of the Republic—the Party's fundamental tasks at the present stage.

The basic orientation of class education in the Party should be as follows:

First, we should study the theory and principles of Marxism-Leninism by linking them with the specific realities of our country, and should conduct the class education of Party members in combination with the vigorous actual life of our country and through practical struggle.

We must in no case permit such tendencies as mechanically introducing and instilling into the minds of Party members the fighting experience of the parties of other countries, without studying it in relation to the actual situation in Korea.

On no account do we study Marxism-Leninism and the fighting experience of the parties of other countries just for the sake of knowledge itself. We study Marxist theory, viewpoints and methods and the experience of the fraternal parties in their revolutionary struggles in order to analyse accurately the problems of the revolution and political and economic questions in our own country and to have a guide to action in our own struggle.

However, many of our Party members do not critically assimilate the battle experience of the parties of other countries; they swallow it whole. They know how to copy foreign things intact, but not how to apply them properly to the actual conditions of our country. Thus their knowledge fails to benefit our practical work, and they commit dogmatic errors by applying foreign things mechanically to the realities of our country.

The political education of our Party members should not be confined to learning Marxist-Leninist theory and advanced experience merely for the sake of knowing them; instead, the emphasis should be laid on learning how to apply them properly to the actual conditions of our country and, on that basis, how to analyse the situation in our country, and not only to see the present but also to forecast the future.

In order to elevate the class consciousness of Party members through the practical life and struggles in our country, it is most important to get the entire Party membership to acquire a correct understanding of the objective laws of social development in our country, and, in particular, to enable them to analyse scientifically the economic forms and social and economic conditions of the various classes and their mutual relations at each stage of social development.

The great Lenin taught that the essential condition for cultivating revolutionary activity among the workers is to make them realize clearly the economic character and socio-political features of each class. We must give all Party members a clear understanding of the reactionary nature of our hostile classes, by teaching them which classes oppressed and exploited the Korean people in our country in the past and are doing so at present, why these classes betray the country and the people and how craftily they deceive the workers and peasants. We must also give the Party members a correct understanding of the problems concerning the main motive force and its allies in the revolution by teaching them who is capable of fighting in the most revolutionary way for the country's freedom and independence, which classes and strata can join hands with us, and this on what grounds.

Only if we make clear the relations between friends and enemies in the revolution can our Party members know how to co-operate with their allies, how to win even the not very trustworthy allies and wavering elements over to their side so as to isolate the enemy, and how to take advantage of all possibilities and forms of struggle in order to attain the victory of the revolution. Only if they are able to tell friend from foe can they clearly understand our Party's line and policies which are based on a scientific analysis of the concrete situation and of the positions of different classes in our country, and display their revolutionary activity in putting them into effect.

Second, we should educate our Party members in the all-conquering ideology of Marxism-Leninism, so that they establish a dialectical materialist outlook with regard to both nature and society and are convinced of the final victory of our revolution.

To this end, we should instill into all Party members a clear idea of the general laws governing the development of nature and society and, especially, arm them with the scientific knowledge about the essence of class struggle under capitalism, about the inevitable fall of capitalism and imperialism and the certain victory of socialism and communism.

As a result of World War I, the socialist revolution won victory in the Soviet Union, and as a result of World War II, the People's Republic of China and the other People's Democracies broke with the capitalist system. Thus world capitalism is daily moving towards ruin and breakdown. Should the imperialists unleash another world war, then the total collapse of the world capitalist system will be unavoidable.

We should educate Party members to maintain a high sense of honour and pride in taking part in the struggle to overthrow imperialism and attain the victory of the world socialist revolution, and we should foster in them revolutionary optimism based on a firm belief in the emancipation of the oppressed working people and the inevitable victory of socialism and communism and on awareness of the righteousness of their cause.

We Korean people are not isolated in our struggle against U.S. imperialism. The Soviet people and progressive mankind throughout the world are all opposed to the aggressive acts of U.S. imperialism and in Asia, particularly, the 600 million people of China stand side by side with us on the battle front against U.S. imperialism.

We should give every Party member a full understanding of the fact that this internationalist solidarity serves as an important guarantee for the victory of our revolution, and arm him with the idea of proletarian internationalism and the lofty spirit of patriotism.

We can win final victory only by uniting firmly with the peoples of the Soviet Union and all other fraternal countries, by tirelessly striving for the unity of the entire people against the U.S. imperialists and by struggling to build up our revolutionary forces.

Third, we must bring up and train all Party members to be indomitable revolutionary fighters and ardent political workers, who, as the vanguard of the working masses of our country, will always be ready to sacrifice even their lives in the interests of the Party and the revolution, not only in the present stage but until the attainment of the final goal of our revolution.

All Party organizations should educate and train each

member of the Party to preserve clean his glorious title as a Workers' Party member, to subordinate his own wishes and actions to those of the Party, to take it as his duty to implement Party decisions and directives and observe state laws, to maintain consistency of deeds with words and of practice with theory and to adhere strictly to Party, as well as revolutionary, discipline and order which are uniform and obligatory for all.

All Party organizations should guide each Party member and cadre to be faithful in Party life, to extensively develop criticism within the Party, particularly criticism from below, to rectify in good time all types of shortcomings and mistakes that run counter to the interests of the Party, and to wage a stubborn struggle against flatterers and deceivers who are not frank with the Party, conceal the truth and are fond of ostentatious show.

All Party organizations should make each Party member realize clearly that labour is a matter of the highest honour and an essential of human life, and see that each member in his daily life is guided by the collectivist spirit of protecting social property as the apple of his eye and valuing the interests of the Party, the state and society above his personal interests. It is necessary to let all the Party members and working people display their devotion and creative activity in all domains of socialist construction, correct wrong attitudes towards labour through practical struggle, and fight actively for the elimination of all exploiting practices in town and country.

Party organizations should educate the broad Party rank and file to discern class enemies, to struggle resolutely against political blindness and all varieties of indolence and laxity, to watch out sharply for the enemy's manoeuvres of subversion and sabotage, detect and expose them in good time, and take the lead in the anti-espionage struggle of the people as a whole.

Fourth, in conformity with the above-mentioned basic orientation for class education in the Party, a fundamental change should be made in the methods of political education and study within the Party.

Our Party organizations have so far failed to get rid of such formalistic methods of political education as passing on and cramming the teaching material into the heads of Party members in the manner of reading a talmudic service, according to one and the same study programme, without concretely taking into account the knowledge and political and theoretical level of individual Party members.

In Party study emphasis has been laid merely on memorizing or citing unnecessary dates, phrases and theses, while making little effort to grasp essential ideas or political content. As a result, Party study has failed to provide a living knowledge which can be of help in practical life, nor has it been helpful in elevating their class consciousness.

Furthermore, some propaganda workers in charge of Party education fail to give their explanations in plain and simple language understandable to the masses, but reel off difficult terms and theses which they themselves do not fully understand. In many cases, our press carries poor and extremely tedious propaganda articles and comments under headings which all sound more or less the same, the result being that they cannot interest the readers, but are more apt to confuse the Party rank and file in grasping the key points.

We must overcome this sort of dogmatism and formalism in Party education and see to it that our Party's lines and policies are brought home in time to the Party rank and file and carried into practice successfully.

For this purpose, the educational systems at all levels and the teaching materials should be so revised as to intensify class education; especially the study of Marxist-Leninist theory should be promoted among the leading cadres of the Party and the state; close attention should be paid to the selection, allocation and training of propaganda and educational workers who are always in contact with the Party rank and file, and their political and theoretical level should be raised. And our Party press should be improved decisively both in form and content so that the masses at large can understand them easily and find them interesting.

At the same time, Party organizations must improve their

guidance of class education within the Party. All provincial, city and county Party committees and primary Party organizations should eradicate any wrong tendency towards underestimating the Party's ideological work; they should regard the Marxist-Leninist education of the cadres and the Party mass as the most important task of Party organizations and should give systematic day-to-day guidance in it.

A number of our Party organizations and leading cadres still do not understand that they can ensure the fulfilment of the economic tasks confronting the Party bodies by inspiring, organizing and mobilizing the masses to carry out these tasks through the Party's ideological and political work, and they fail to link the Party's political work with economic work in a proper manner. In such Party organizations the significance of ideological work has been underrated; ideological work is given a secondary place and relegated to the background in their day-to-day activities.

Those Party workers who are oblivious of the importance of the Party's ideological and political work and neglect to guide it, have become petty routineers in that they either take the administrative work into their own hands or tail behind it, that they do little to keep up daily contact with the masses, addicting themselves only to shock campaigns, are out of touch with actual conditions in the lower units and fail to see important problems of Party policy. As a result, they are blind to original experience in work, cannot foresee coming events, and thus fail to prevent shortcomings in advance.

Party organizations should conduct propaganda work purposefully, its primary content being the basic line of the Party and problems concerning its immediate policies and the organizational and ideological consolidation of its ranks.

From now on, Party organizations and Party bodies at all levels should discuss the content and methods of Party educational work at their meetings and conduct the work of guiding and checking up on the fulfilment of decisions of those meetings in a systematic way, thereby giving timely currency to good experience while eliminating the lack of class stand and of ideological content and all kinds of formalism and talmudism in the work of Party education.

The Party Central Committee is convinced that Party organizations at all levels, by further intensifying education in Marxism-Leninism, will educate and train the entire membership into iron-willed revolutionary fighters that no force can subdue, and that they will lead the entire people in north and south Korea still more successfully in the struggle for the country's reunification and independence, under the leadership of the Central Committee of the Party, holding aloft the immortal banner of Marxism-Leninism.

ON ELIMINATING BUREAUCRACY

Report Delivered at a Plenary Meeting of the Central Committee of the Workers' Party of Korea

April 1, 1955

Comrades,

The cardinal task of our Party at the present stage is to drive the aggressive forces of U.S. imperialism out of south Korea and overthrow the traitorous Syngman Rhee clique and bring about our country's reunification along democratic lines and its complete independence, by mobilizing the broad masses of the people.

Proceeding from this cardinal task, our Party is today waging a struggle to further strengthen—politically, economically and militarily—the democratic base which constitutes the real guarantee for the country's reunification, by organizing and mobilizing the entire people in building socialism in the northern half.

This heavy task confronting our Party makes it more imperative than ever to enhance the Party's role as organizer and leader, strengthen its fighting capacity, further strengthen its bond with the masses and improve and strengthen the leadership by Party and state organs in the rehabilitation and construction of the national economy. An especially important question facing our Party in this struggle is that of the methods of Party leadership and the cadres' style of work.

When the Party's line and policies are correct and proper

measures are adopted for their implementation, success in work depends on what methods the functionaries employ in actual work, on how they organize and mobilize the masses to do the work.

If the functionaries of our Party and government bodies use the wrong work style and methods and fail to enlist the broad masses in carrying out Party decisions, our Party's correct political and organizational measures will all come to nothing. Therefore, the question of improving the methods of Party leadership and the style of work of the cadres is one of the most important questions facing us.

Since the first day of its founding, our Party has consistently fought against the wrong style of work in the Party and for the establishment of correct methods of leadership by its functionaries. This question was dealt with, particularly, in the February Speech made during the war and at a number of plenary meetings of the Central Committee, and a struggle has been waged to eliminate bureaucracy.

But the struggle has not been a day-to-day and systematic one; it has been waged primarily in the manner of a shock campaign. As a result, the cadres' incorrect style of work has not as yet been rectified. Harmful and anti-popular style of work finds expression in various forms within the Party and government bodies, high and low. This is a big obstacle both to successfully carrying out the Party's policies and to strengthening our Party's ties with the masses.

What, then, is the main shortcoming to be found in the work style of some functionaries today? It is bureaucracy.

Bureaucracy is an anti-popular method of government adopted by the ruling classes to oppress the overwhelming majority of the popular masses under the feudal and capitalist systems. That is why it is a harmful style of work which can never be tolerated under our people's democratic system in which the people themselves exercise power.

Bureaucracy literally means bureaucratic action. It is a factor divorcing the Party from the masses. Therefore, bureaucratic action is utterly impermissible in the revolutionary work of our Party. Revolutionary work is for the good of the working masses; it is the work of relying on the working masses, of defending their interests and of fighting to bring them liberty and happiness by crushing all the unjust systems that oppress them. How can such revolutionary work be compatible with bureaucracy, an anti-popular method of rule which goes against the masses and is divorced from them, defending the interests of the handful that make up the ruling classes? Revolutionary work is for the people and bureaucracy is against the people. Therefore, bureaucracy is absolutely impermissible in revolutionary work.

Why, then, do some of our Party workers continue to commit bureaucratic errors? It is because they still do not know that the basis of our Party's policies is to fight for the interests of the revolutionary masses.

Since our Party fights for the interests of the masses, the Party spirit of each member should be manifested in organizing and performing all kinds of work from the mass viewpoint. And yet some Party members lack this revolutionary mass viewpoint, and often hurt revolutionary work through their bureaucratic actions, detrimental to the interests of the masses, by which they divorce themselves from the masses.

Today, quite a few functionaries are oblivious of the fact that our people's power and Party organs are bodies that serve the interests of the revolutionary masses and serve the people; they identify the people's power and Party organs with the government offices of the days of the Li dynasty or of Japanese imperialist rule, and regard their work in these organs not as service to the people but as holding a post in a government office. This gives rise to various wrong tendencies: army officers act like old-time commanding officers, interior servicemen act like old-time policemen, and state functionaries assume the airs of old-time officials, while Party workers show off the Party's authority. Persons of this sort in our Party and government bodies have failed to become genuine servants of the people; they have degraded themselves to bureaucrats.

Bureaucracy is a manifestation of the survivals of rotten

and outmoded ideas left over from the old feudal system of the Li dynasty and from the Japanese imperialist regime. Our revolutionary work is not only alien to bureaucracy but irreconcilable with it. Nonetheless, a number of Party members practise bureaucratic acts which are alien to and in no way compatible with revolutionary work, despite the fact that when joining the Party, they vowed to devote their lives and property entirely to the struggle for the sake of the Party and the revolution.

In what main forms, then, does bureaucracy manifest itself in the various activities of our Party and government bodies? It appears in different forms. It shows up quite often notably in the leadership work of people in the superior bodies, that is, in higher positions. Their bureaucratic style of work finds expression mainly in a slipshod manner of work, which is incompatible with the Party viewpoint: they just stand on their dignity because they are superiors; they do not study their work closely, are half-hearted in their work and do not carry out their duties in all responsibility to the Party and the state.

Once promoted to higher posts, some functionaries consider themselves to be special beings and, becoming self-conceited, do not bother to raise their political and theoretical level and practical qualifications, but work in a hit-or-miss way. These people do not study, they do things in a haphazard manner and just stand on their dignity, considering it their natural right to hold the positions they currently occupy.

Some people do not study or analyse their work carefully; nor do they take any measures to solve problems correctly by listening to other comrades and investigating matters at the lower levels. Instead, they do their job in a formalistic way or just skimp it, sticking to their own subjective views. In the long run, such formalistic and slipshod manner of work leads to confusion and trouble in the execution of work at the lower levels, preconditioning the functionaries down below to deviate from revolutionary work methods and divorce themselves from the masses.

Still other functionaries, blinded by a desire for fame and

rank, stop at nothing to rise to high positions; they concern themselves only with winning the favour of their superiors, without any regard to the fate of the masses. For the sake of their own fame and careers, these people talk as if they had done what they have not done, and as if they are able to do what they are incapable of doing, and they habitually make false reports. They flatter their superiors and hold down their subordinates; they are careless in all matters and do not try to organize their work properly. Those who are ready to flatter their superiors believe that once they have succeeded in currying favour with some influential figures by flattery, they will be able to preserve their positions and fame and to live under the wing of those influential persons forever. Those who flatter and those who accept such flattery are, in the last analysis, all alike as two peas in a pod. Such a tendency to flattery and hanging on to others instead of working, might have been tolerated under the old social systems, but it can never be tolerated under our social system today.

Our Party is the vanguard organization of the working masses, armed with advanced theory and knowledge of the laws of class struggle. Our Party is a Marxist-Leninist Party which leads the working class and the whole working people to the accomplishment of the great cause of our revolution and has this as its fundamental task. Our Party can fulfil its revolutionary task only by breathing the same air as the masses, by safeguarding their interests, rallying them around the Party and the Government and organizing and mobilizing them to take part consciously in the revolutionary struggle.

However, some of our Party functionaries deviate from this basic Party method of work, and employ the extremely harmful method of dictation and command in their work; they behave themselves recklessly without regard for the interests of the masses. This not infrequently leads to the masses becoming alienated from the Party and the Government.

Instead of carrying out their Party assignments, some foolish Party functionaries wield Party authority as a substitute for Party work. These functionaries do not trouble themselves to check whether the Party's policies are being correctly executed or not, to organize work for their correct execution and rectify errors in good time, but only sit around and bluster. So their subordinates regard them not as real leading workers but as fearful beings, and, naturally, feel it unnecessary to visit them. Misusing the Party authority, they then bark at these subordinates for lack of Party spirit simply because the latter keep away from the Party organs. Only when the Party functionaries direct work properly can the prestige of the Party be upheld and only in this way can Party members willingly visit Party organs. When the Party organs are occupied by those workers who do not give any effective leadership to work, their prestige can never be enhanced and nobody will ever visit them.

Certain Party functionaries, thinking that instructions issued in the name of government organs are ineffective, issue Party directives at random on administrative and business matters. A Party directive deserves the name only when it orients the work of government bodies, only when it has a mobilizing effect and is analytical. A directive can never gain authority merely by putting the name of a Party organ to it instead of some other organ.

When organizing Party work, and especially when carrying out a checkup, some Party functionaries do not educate the Party members, nor criticize and correct their mistakes or render them practical assistance in their work, but do their work by a kind of detective or police method, threaten and intimidate the Party members and punish them indiscriminately. Thus they not uncommonly frighten the Party members undergoing a checkup and make them fear the Party's checkups and regard them as a nuisance. As a result, many Party members tell lies during the checkups, and Party organs are unable to grasp the actual conditions at the lower levels.

Some of our Party members not infrequently show such tendencies as to follow blindly whatever instructions their superiors may issue, no matter whether these are correct or not and whether or not they conform with the Party's policies and decisions, without considering the specific conditions of their own work and without closely studying the decisions of the Party and government bodies. These persons, who have lost independence as revolutionaries and are swayed by a servile mentality, do not feel a sense of responsibility for the work of the Party and the state.

Some people, taking advantage of their positions, suppress others' criticism and prevent them from speaking out against the errors found in their own writings, works or activities. Such an action does the most serious harm to our Party's advance.

Some people are very fond of showing off. They pretend to know what they do not know; they pretend to be men of great character when they are paltry fellows; they are not concerned with the work of the state and the Party, but are keenly alive only to their own personal affairs; they claim for themselves the credit that belongs to others; they are half-hearted in their work or at meetings, and are simply avid when it comes to a feast, just being on the lookout for it.

When someone advances original ideas on a matter, some people who, although they have been utterly unconcerned with the matter and have not studied it, claim to know all about it and ignore the good ideas, instead of paying regard to them and putting them into practice.

Some people are just greedy for higher positions, while having neither practical ability nor enthusiasm for their own work.

All these practices are manifestations of bureaucracy which our Party cannot tolerate. What evil consequences does such a wrong style of work bring us?

It leads to the distortion of our Party's policies and the paralysis of its fighting capacity, causes serious obstruction to the implementation of its correct lines and tends to block its forward movement.

Bureaucracy lowers the prestige of the Party and government bodies, divorces our Party from the masses of the people and thus leads to the prevention of the Party from fulfilling its honourable revolutionary tasks.

We cannot tolerate such things any longer. We must wage a tireless struggle to uproot the bureaucratic style of work. We should correctly understand the source of bureaucracy and endeavour to wipe it out, and thus improve the work of Party and government bodies and strengthen the ties that link the Party and government organs with the people, thereby rallying the masses of the people still more firmly around the Party.

What is the source of bureaucracy?

As you all know, the public, or state, sector holds dominating sway in the national economy of our country, and the worker-peasant alliance led by the working class is the decisive social force in all the life of the state. So the social source of bureaucracy has been basically eliminated. Bureaucracy springs from the influence of capitalist elements which still remain in the economic system of our country and from the remnants of the old ideological consciousness left over from Japanese imperialist rule; its ideological source lies in selfishness, careerism, the servile mentality typical of hirelings, etc. No small number of our functionaries who, not yet free from the survivals of these feudal and bourgeois ideologies, do not really know that the interests of the revolution and the Party stand above their own; they do not understand that the revolution is a struggle of the masses and this struggle is aimed solely at the emancipation and welfare of the masses of the people, and that the Party can carry out the revolution only by relying on the masses of the people.

Further, a large portion of our Party cadres is made up of young Party members who have little revolutionary experience and have not yet acquired the ability and methods of correct revolutionary leadership of the masses. Therefore, some of them, despite their subjective loyalty to the revolution, are often careless in the conduct of their work and fail to show regard for the masses, thereby causing harm to the work of the Party and the state.

This is partly due to past shortcomings in our Party's policy on cadre work. We did not originally have many veteran revolutionary cadres with experience of long revolutionary struggle. The good features of the veteran revolutionary cadres are that they devoted their all to the struggle in the past, solely for the sake of the revolution and the people, overcoming all difficulties through a long period of time, that they have boundless loyalty to the revolution and unshaken fidelity to principle, and that they possess modest and simple moral traits as befitting revolutionary workers. But even these few revolutionary cadres have not been properly placed and no attention has been paid to them under the pretext that they are "old and incompetent."

It is a good thing that many Party organs appoint new cadres. But these organs have been so unprincipled in cadre management as to appoint cadres without careful study and, after their placement, just leave them alone without giving them any education, claiming that they are good because they are of worker origin. In selecting cadres, their ideological and political qualifications have been ignored and only the practical side has been taken into account, with the result that the ranks of cadres consist of inexperienced persons with no knowledge whatsoever of revolutionary work. This has eventually given rise to such phenomena as being irresponsible towards Party and state work and encroaching upon the interests of the masses.

As a result of unprincipled appointment of cadres, a number of tried and tested persons who displayed heroism during the recent Fatherland Liberation War have been ignored, and these revolutionary cadres have been excluded from the composition of some provincial, city or county Party committees. Thus, the local Party committees are for the most part composed of people who are politically immature.

This is one of the reasons why bureaucracy has not been eliminated, and has instead been nurtured in Party and government bodies.

Another major reason for the failure to thoroughly eliminate bureaucracy is that our Party has not fought resolutely against this wrong style of work and neglected the work of cultivating in our cadres the revolutionary work style and noble qualities as befitting revolutionaries and of acquainting them with scientific, Marxist-Leninist methods of leadership.

Our leading functionaries in the centre have worked inadequately to check up on the activities of local functionaries and give them leadership and assistance on the basis of correctly anticipating possible shortcomings that might appear in the course of implementing the Party's policies. As a result, local functionaries have been left to continue with wrong methods of work instead of rectifying them.

Besides, quite a few of our Party functionaries engage only in administrative campaigns, side by side with the administrative personnel, and take administrative work into their own hands, failing to understand that the Party work in the people's power organs and social organizations is aimed at ensuring the successful implementation of their work by explaining to the functionaries of those organizations the political aim of their work and inducing them to take part in it willingly. Hence the Party's failure to rid our functionaries of bureaucracy in their work.

Comrades,

These are the main reasons why our personnel suffer from bureaucracy.

We should have a clear idea of the sources of bureaucracy and wage a serious ideological struggle for their elimination and should at the same time take practical measures to root bureaucracy out.

First, a correct method of leadership should be established.

The important thing regarding the method of leadership is to combine general guidance with individual guidance in work.

What I mean by general guidance is the Party's general call and guidance designed to make the masses understand its political aim in a given work and to achieve that aim. Without such general call and guidance, all our work would become aimless and go astray and it would be impossible for the Party to give unified guidance in work.

Our work, however, does not end in general guidance. It can be accomplished successfully only when general guidance is coupled with individual guidance. Individual guidance implies that in carrying out a given task a profound study be made of its specific conditions and of the level of consciousness of the masses and their trends and, on this basis, concrete, practical measures most appropriate to the specific conditions be taken. If a functionary puts emphasis only on general guidance and ignores individual guidance, his work will end in mere wordplay and no result will be produced.

In implementing Party decisions and directives, it is only by combining general guidance with individual guidance that we can discover forms of struggle suited to the specific conditions and acceptable to the masses, and carry them into effect in the proper order of priority with a clear idea of the main direction of the work.

There is no doubt that if in the recent grain procurement work our leading functionaries had correctly put into practice the Party's political aim and general principles in regard to the work (i.e., given general guidance) and had roused the peasantry to activity through concrete measures suitable to the actual conditions of each locality (i.e., given individual guidance), there would have been no grave shortcomings and the procurement work would have been brought to a more satisfactory conclusion.

The genuine method of Party leadership is to correctly combine general with individual guidance, and thus put the Party's policies in line with the actual life and struggle of the masses of the people, provide them with conditions for displaying creative initiative, and then generalize once more the experience gained by the masses in their struggle.

Further, the most important question regarding the method of leadership is to use the method of persuasion and explanation in mobilizing the masses to the performance of all work. In leading the masses, the method of persuasion rouses them to unending activity and creative initiative, strengthens the ties between the Party and the masses and makes it possible to fulfil the tasks in hand promptly by relying on the consciousness of the masses.

Thus, we should correctly combine general with individual guidance, and link the guidance by cadres closely with the needs of the masses, thereby eliminating the bureaucratic method of guidance and establishing the correct method, the scientific, Marxist method, of leadership.

Second, the class education of our personnel should be intensified.

Style of work is, generally speaking, a comprehensive expression of the thoughts and methods of functionaries in the course of work. If you rely on revolutionary Marxist-Leninist theory and methods, then a really revolutionary, Party style of work will result, and if you rely on bourgeois ideology and non-Marxist methods, then bureaucracy, formalism and various other anti-popular style of work will come forth.

Therefore, style of work is not merely a question of the working ability of personnel or their character, but has to do with their world outlook or ideological consciousness. One of the main causes of the wrong style of work found among a considerable number of our functionaries is that they have not acquired an adequate understanding of revolutionary Marxist-Leninist theory and do not stand firmly on revolutionary principles and the working-class position.

By strengthening the class education of Party members, we should cultivate in them the noble qualities of being boundlessly loyal to the revolution, of defending the interests of the Party, the state and the popular masses, and of waging a resolute struggle for their sake. We should help Party members to grasp the ideology and methods of Marxism-Leninism so that they can put an end to their bureaucratic style of work, which is a survival of obsolete ideology, and acquire a genuinely popular style of work.

Unwavering fidelity to principle in work is an essential trait for our personnel. They should acquire the qualities of making no compromise with the slightest deviation in the implementation of the Party's lines and policies and of always considering everything from the angle of the revolution and the interests of the Party and the people.

Thus, Party and state functionaries should be boundlessly faithful and honest to the Party and the state, and attain a working level high enough always to perform their assigned tasks with credit as highly qualified revolutionary cadres.

Third, collective leadership should be strengthened in our work.

Collective leadership prevents subjective, arbitrary decisions by any one individual and ensures the right solution for the matter in hand through broad consultation and collective wisdom in the performance of all Party and state work.

The overwhelming majority of bureaucrats are subjectivists held captive by prejudice. This is self-evident. If we always give ear to the opinions of the masses and the majority in our routine practical work and in mass political work, we shall not commit bureaucratic errors. So, the strengthening of collective leadership makes it possible to do away with bureaucracy, the noxious style of work still found among some of our personnel. We must see to it that our functionaries adhere strictly to the principle of collective leadership in all the work of the Party and the state, and thereby establish the work style of heeding the opinions of the masses and the majority at all times and of conducting their work on this basis.

We should, at the same time, promote inner-Party democracy and intensify criticism and self-criticism so as to ensure actual conditions in which the Party rank and file can boldly advance their creative views.

One of the most important questions in regard to collective leadership is to heighten the role of the leading bodies of the Party and the state at all levels. However, some of our functionaries confine their committee work solely to the drafting and passing of resolutions, neglecting to promote the creative initiative of committee members. This has nothing in common with the principle of collective leadership; it is an expression of the bureaucracy mentioned above.

One of the measures for enhancing the role of committees at all levels in the Party and government organs is to improve their composition. Often, the committees at all levels do their work in a formalistic way and fail to play their role as leading bodies. One of the main reasons for this is that the committees are composed of people lacking in political training and in experience in the revolutionary struggle. From now on, the Party should see to it that the leading Party bodies and the state organs at all levels be composed of veteran revolutionary cadres and of people who are well-grounded politically and skilled in practical matters.

We should thus enhance the role of the committees and further promote collective leadership, thereby raising the level of work of the Party and government bodies and, at the same time, getting rid of the wrong style of work and bureaucracy.

Fourth, intensified guidance should be given to the functionaries in Party and government organs.

As I have mentioned above, many of our functionaries are still immature both from the political and professional points of view. Therefore, it is an important task for our Party to teach them correct methods of work by further strengthening education and guidance designed to raise their political, theoretical level and practical qualifications. Particularly, we have to strengthen guidance and control over the responsible local functionaries so as to promptly rectify their distortions of Party and state policies and their wrong behaviour toward the popular masses. Only in this way can we eliminate the bureaucratic methods of work found among some of the responsible local functionaries, markedly elevate the level of guidance by the local Party and government bodies and maintain close ties between the Party and the masses.

Comrades,

The question of rooting out the wrong style of work and of everyone acquiring a new, popular work style cannot of course be solved in a few days. But it must be solved by all means. We should develop a persistent and stubborn struggle for the elimination of bureaucracy by further strengthening the guidance and checkups on our functionaries and by promoting criticism and self-criticism. Each Party member should display all his enthusiasm and activity in the struggle against bureaucracy, bearing deep in mind that this struggle is an important prerequisite for ensuring the successful fulfilment of our revolutionary tasks.

I am convinced that through the successful struggle for acquiring a new style of work all our Party members will further enhance the leading role of our Party among the masses of the people and fulfil with credit the glorious revolutionary tasks which confront our Party.

ON SOME QUESTIONS OF PARTY AND STATE WORK IN THE PRESENT STAGE OF THE SOCIALIST REVOLUTION

Concluding Speech Delivered at a Plenary Meeting of the Central Committee of the Workers' Party of Korea

April 4, 1955

Comrades,

This April Plenary Meeting of our Party Central Committee has discussed very important questions.

We have discussed the most important questions facing our Party at the present stage—the questions of intensifying class education, of improving the style of work in our Party, exercising economy and strengthening financial discipline in order to further accelerate economic construction in our country.

All the speakers at this Plenary Meeting of the Party Central Committee have unanimously approved and supported the questions of the Party's policy put forward by the Political Committee of the Party Central Committee. And, I think, the questions raised have been satisfactorily thrashed out.

What I should like to emphasize in this concluding speech are the following points:

During the three-day discussion on the questions raised at this Plenary Meeting of the Party Central Committee, we have noted many defects. Since various defects have been criticized at the meeting, some people may think that there are many good-for-nothing people in our Party, that our functionaries are all liars and our work is going entirely amiss.

Needless to say, our Party has quite a few defects which require immediate rectification. But it would be a gross mistake to think that everything our Party has done so far is wrong.

Our Party has performed many heroic feats in its work and has done great things in the years gone by for the fatherland and the people, for the prosperity and development of our country.

There were numerous heroic Party members who fought to the last drop of their blood for the Party and the country, blocking the loopholes of enemy pillboxes with their own breasts during the Fatherland Liberation War. And there were also tens of thousands of heroic Party members who never yielded—though captured by the enemy while fighting bravely in the enemy's rear during our temporary retreat—and upheld their honour as Party members at the cost of their lives, shouting, "Long live the Democratic People's Republic of Korea and the Workers' Party of Korea!" in their last breath.

During the temporary retreat in the Fatherland Liberation War, many military and political cadres of our Party, and Party functionaries who had been sent to the southern half for political work, retreated in an organized way across mountains and rivers following our Party and Government, leading their troops out of the enemy encirclement; and many of our writers, professors and actors, in the face of heavy enemy bombing, broke through the enemy encirclement and followed our Party and the Government of the Republic, travelling thousands of *ri* on foot. Such heroic deeds are rarely to be found in the war history of any other country.

These facts prove that to this day our Party has educated all its members properly and united them firmly, and that they are ready to fight to the end, laying down their lives for the country and the people.

Our Party has now become a powerful and reliable party that is surrounded by the love and confidence of the entire

Korean people and is fully capable of shaping their destinies. Through its historic struggle over the past ten years, our Party has won the active support of the broad working masses; it has trained many political workers, military cadres, young scientists and economic personnel, writers and artists.

These successes are by no means accidental. Our Party has achieved them in its arduous struggle over the past ten years. They serve as a guarantee for the future prosperity and development of our country, and signify that there have been created ample conditions to lead our people to happiness and freedom.

As is to be seen from this, the achievements scored by our Party in the past are great and the feats of our Party members —who fought for the Party and the country at the cost of their blood—are really tremendous.

Why, then, should we today speak so much about the shortcomings in spite of such great successes achieved by our Party?

The reason is that our Party intends to do its work better in the future, to lead our country faster along the road to happiness and to achieve the reunification and independence of the country as early as possible; and that it wants its members not to mark time but advance farther. With this in view, we always boldly expose every shortcoming within the Party and correct it. Only by doing so will our Party be able to advance and develop further.

It is simply wrong to take our Party's admission of its own shortcomings for inertness and impotence as is alleged by certain anti-Party elements or factional elements. Our Party knows no pessimism; it only has a bright future and revolutionary optimism.

Our Party not only fought well against the enemy in the recent Fatherland Liberation War, but has also achieved great success in postwar rehabilitation and construction of the national economy. The rapid rehabilitation and construction of factories, enterprises, mines and railways in Pyongyang and all other parts of the northern half of the Republic after the truce were possible simply under the leadership of our Party. This also proves that our Party will be fully able to surmount any difficulty and obstacle and build the basis of socialism in the northern half in the future.

1. ON FURTHER INTENSIFYING CLASS EDUCATION IN THE PARTY

This is not the first time the question of intensifying class education in the Party has been raised by us. It would be wrong for any of our comrades to think that formerly our propaganda work was wholly misconducted, that it was an error to avoid using the word socialism in the past, and that we are raising the question of class education in the Party for the first time today.

Our Party sets forth appropriate political and economic tasks in given periods on the basis of its assessment of all the objective conditions and internal forces of our country. If the Party does not take into full consideration the level of our people's preparedness and the objective conditions but acts subjectively as it pleases, then it will eventually commit Right or "Left" errors.

If we had talked noisily about building socialism in Korea immediately after liberation, who would have approved of it? People would not have come near us. For the Japanese imperialists had conducted malignant propaganda, even alleging that socialism meant sharing the same bed and eating from the same pot. If we had hung out a slogan of socialism at that time without taking all this into account, the people would have feared us and would not have come near us.

However, today when we point at the agricultural co-operatives organized in the countryside and say to the peasants that through them lies the way to socialism, they are pleased and ask us why, then, we did not build socialism earlier.

In fact already before the war we proceeded to carry out the tasks of the period of transition to socialism in the northern half after fulfilling the tasks of the democratic revolution, and conducted socialist education to suit it. Yet, we could not launch full-scale socialist construction under the circumstances prevailing at that time.

Our Party, taking into account all the mature conditions today, is more definitely and more resolutely raising the questions of building socialism in the northern half and of intensifying class education in the Party.

Such instance can be seen in our Party Programme as well. It did not specify our ultimate goal. When we adopted the Party Programme in 1946, it was necessary and proper not to specify it in the light of all the conditions prevailing in our country.

But now it has become necessary for our Party to stipulate in its Programme not only the task of bringing about the reunification and independence of the country, but also the Party's ultimate goal of leading our country to socialism and communism in the future. Therefore, the Party Programme we adopted in 1946 was not wrong; it was correct to word it in the way we did in view of the then prevailing conditions.

Today, however, the level of preparedness of our Party members, and the level of social development, and the objective conditions in which the U.S. imperialists have been occupying south Korea for a long time, place new fighting tasks before our Party. Unless we intensify class education within the Party under these circumstances, we cannot win the protracted, arduous struggle. Proceeding from these varied objective conditions, we are raising the question of intensifying class education today.

However, it would mean committing a "Left" error if an attempt is made to build socialism in a day or to wipe out all the capitalist elements in a single day just because we raise this question.

We must imbue our Party members and people with socialist consciousness, gradually eliminate the capitalist elements in the northern half of the Republic, further increase our strength, and thus make ideological and material preparations for achieving the reunification and independence of the country and building socialism throughout Korea in the future. This is why we are now raising the question more seriously and more urgently than ever before of intensifying class education in the Party.

Now I should like to pass to the question of the method of education.

In Party education, we must emphasize the following two points:

First, in the study of Marxism-Leninism, Party members must learn to apply it to the realities, and not swallow it whole. In former days the old-fashioned private schools forced the pupils to learn characters by rote. Those who were educated in this manner could only read the characters in a fixed order, but could not read them in other combinations. Today we should not study Marxism in this way.

It serves no purpose to learn Marxist theory by rote. We should grasp the content and essence of that theory and learn how to apply it to suit our actual life. This is the main thing that must be remedied in our Party's educational work.

We have translated many Marxist books or written them ourselves. Our situation today is different from that in 1946. In her speech Comrade Minister of Culture and Propaganda said that the Marxist-Leninist classics did not sell well. Since our Party members read such classics mechanically, they have no interest in them, nor do they feel any urgent need for them.

If they want to rely on Marxist-Leninist literature for the correct orientation when they meet with difficult problems in the course of work or when they wish to develop their work creatively, they will naturally be interested in their study and feel a keen need for Marxist-Leninist classics. Only when they reach such a level, will those books sell well.

Second, it is important to learn many of our own things in Party study. Some comrades are not willing to learn well about their own things and regard them as alien to Marxism. We should know that things of our own constitute living Marxism creatively applied to Korean reality.

Many of our people do not know our own history. It is therefore very important to learn it. In art, too, our own things should be developed.

Needless to say, we must learn to tell good from bad among our own things and cast off the bad. Some insist that we should even learn what is useless among our own things, just as we have to know things that are ours well. This is quite wrong. We should discard the bad and learn only what is good from among our own things.

What is important in learning and studying many of our own things is to correctly link them with Marxism. Some of our young cadres, however, know the general theory of Marxism well, but do not know our history, whereas those who are well-read in old books lack sufficient knowledge of Marxist theory. You should not call yourself a genuine historian simply because you know many things about ancient times. Only when we have a correct knowledge of Marxism and are versed in the history of our country can we correctly analyse history at each stage in a Marxist way, that is, can we make a correct analysis as to which quarter is our enemy and which quarter for the revolution, and as to the balance of forces between ourselves and the enemy at each stage of social development in our country. We should thus learn to analyse history in a Marxist way.

In my opinion, it must be the main point in intensifying class education in the Party to learn about our own things and study Marxism not in a talmudic but in a creative way like this in Party study.

Another important question is to train all Party functionaries and members to be political workers, economic executives, and staunch revolutionary fighters.

If we now have hundreds of persons who have mastered Marxism and are able to correctly analyse the prospects of our country's development and all other questions, they will be a very great force for us. But we should realize that we have not yet reached that level.

Some of our functionaries are haughty just because they received a great deal of education in the past, while some give up studies saying that they had no opportunity to study formerly and are too ignorant to catch up with others. Both of these tendencies are wrong. Even those who had no college education before may be wiser than those who attended college in the past, if they acquire Marxism correctly today.

We should not become complacent but should always study and study with modesty.

2. ON FACTIONAL ELEMENTS IN THE PARTY

Whenever the question of factionalism is referred to in a report, some open their eyes wide and ask who are the factionalists. They wonder whether factionalists still remain in our Party despite the tenacious and tireless struggle waged in the past for the unity and solidarity of the Party, and demand that the factionalists be purged.

But our vigilance against the activities of factionalists in the Party should not be heightened in this way only. In other words, we should not wage a struggle in such a manner as to heighten vigilance only when a Party meeting warns against the factionalists, and slacken it otherwise. For the Party's unity and solidarity, we should always be vigilant against the factionalists who may split it.

I will now speak once more of the question of factionalism inside our Party and its sources.

In our country there existed conditions from previous times for the birth of factional elements. But today there are no factions in our Party, though there are individual elements who are engaged in factional activities.

Then what is at the root of the formation of factions and of the activities of factionalists in our country?

First, it is the fact that after the Communist Party of Korea founded in the 1920's was disorganized owing to the strife between various factions, the working class had had no vanguard until our country was liberated from the colonial rule of Japanese imperialism.

If the Communist Party of Korea organized in 1925 had not been destroyed owing to the manoeuvres of factionalists and saboteurs but had continued in existence, our Party would have greeted the August 15 Liberation as a party with its own organizational system and its leading core would have been formed solidly from the first days of the liberation.

The disorganization of the Communist Party in the 1920's resulted, among other things, from its failure to root itself deeply in the broad working masses. The Communist Party of Korea at that time only had an upper structure and failed to organize its cells in factories and rural districts. In other words, it had failed to become a mass political party. In addition, there were no genuine Marxists in the Party who correctly grasped Marxist-Leninist theory. The Communists of those days had an imperfect mastery of Marxist-Leninist theory and were not steadfast in ideology or class stand. On top of this, the Japanese imperialists had smuggled their agents into the Party to undermine it.

As can be seen, its "leaders" being not well-versed in Marxism and the Party lacking deep roots among the masses, it fell asunder in the end. At that time, there appeared in the working-class movement of our country various factions—the M-L group, the Tuesday group, the North Wind association, etc. They did not struggle for communism, but were only engrossed, under the signboard of communism, in factional strife for hegemony in the Party, which unavoidably resulted in its destruction in the end.

Those factionalists should regard it as a grave crime that they destroyed the Party and did great harm to the working-class and revolutionary movements in our country by their factional strife. On the contrary, they think they have done much for the revolution, and are even now attempting to secure high posts in our Party.

In our Party, there are now persons who formerly belonged to or even were "leaders" of the M-L group, the Tuesday group, the North Wind association, the Com-group and various other factions. We do not mean to arraign them or kick them out of the Party for their previous participation in factions. We only expect them to drop the bad factional habit of the past and become good Party members. Now, they have only to fully realize their errors and continue to behave sincerely, desisting from repeating their evil tricks, in the interests of the revolution and the preservation of the Party's unity and solidarity. But if they carry on such activities even now, we will never tolerate them.

And no small number of people who once participated in factional strife often talk about the "unity of the Party" and say, "I'm for the Party," and so on. They behave with propriety at times, but, on many occasions, having not entirely given up their old habits, these old factionalists get together for sly tricks, whenever the chance presents itself. Some of those who were "leaders" in factional conflicts in the past are still filled with individualist heroism and try to seize any and every opportunity to form factions again. Instead of tirelessly working for the revolution, they continue their sly tricks to muster around them old factionalists and those who had been under their influence, for the purpose of occupying high positions. This is exactly what Pak Hon Yong did in the past.

The factionalists play sly tricks just like rats. As all of you know well, a rat plays the mischief, sneaking all about the house when people are asleep, but disappears somewhere the moment they shout at it. And as long as the rat is running about and gnawing only at useless bundles, we can tolerate it, but we get very upset when it starts gnawing at a good chest of drawers. If we do not catch the rat in good time, it multiplies, makes holes here and there and may possibly ruin the house in the end.

Likewise, though there are no factions in our Party now, if we are not on the alert and vigilant against those elements engrossed in factional activities, they may form a group by rallying their coteries in previous factional strife or other unsound elements and, what is more, may attempt to undermine the Party. Therefore, we must always guard against a factional tendency so as to prevent them from doing such tricks.

Second, the revolutionaries in our Party today are composed of those from the Soviet Union, China, the southern half of our country and various other places, and those who carried on struggles at home. Factionalists often try to use this for their factional purposes.

Among those who came from the southern half are persons who profess themselves to be representatives of the people from there. As soon as they rise to high positions, they behave as if they have found jobs and afforded a living to the people from the southern half and as if they decide their destinies, aiming to use them as cat's-paws in their personal manoeuvres. Li Sung Yop once enticed some comrades from the southern half in this way.

Of the people from the Soviet Union, we can take Ho Ga I as an example. He behaved as if he were the representative of those who returned home from the Soviet Union.

As for the people from China, we can take Pak Il U as a typical example. He considers himself a figure representing those from China and stealthily schemes to gather around him comrades whose class consciousness is weak, alleging that "Comrades from China are not promoted to be cadres" or that "People from the Soviet Union do not agree with those from China in their way of life."

There is a saying: "In ten years even mountains and rivers will change." Has there not been any change in the ideological consciousness or way of life of the Party members during the ten years since liberation? Needless to say, there has been change and even new moral traits have been formed. Moreover, since people have breathed, worked and received education in one and the same place for ten years now, there can be no excuse for them to talk about difference in their ways of life and styles of work, no matter where they may have returned from. Yet, these elements indulge in talking about this sort of thing, because they have ulterior motives.

Pak Il U thinks nobody knows about his underhand tricks. But this is a gross miscalculation. In fact, nearly all comrades from China, adhering to Party principles, regard him not as a figure representing people back from China but, on the contrary, expose him as an anti-Party element.

For instance, Comrade Kim Chang Dok is a man with strong Party spirit. Since Comrade Kim Chang Dok was from China, Pak Il U tried to entice him to his side. But this comrade fought resolutely against Pak Il U's iniquitous action, stating that he had returned home from China trusting the Party, the country and the people, not Pak Il U.

Pak Il U and his ilk always look for unsound grumblers and malcontents and try to pull them over to their side in an attempt to carry out their plots. Pak Il U exploited the discontent and grumbling of Pang Ho San. After he was criticized by the Party for his blunders in battle during the closing phase of the war, Pang Ho San began to vilify the policies of the Party and the Government behind the scenes. Pak Il U capitalized on this opportunity to win him over.

As described above, these people prattle: "People from the Soviet Union are different from those from China," "Those who have returned from China are not appointed to high positions," "The Party does not trust you because you once took part in factional activities." In the last analysis, they say this because they have some ulterior motives.

We never tolerate such actions on the part of people suffering from individualist heroism. We cannot permit them to behave in an unorganized manner within the Party, posing as some sort of representative figures. Because this kind of actions can disrupt the Party organization.

Let us take a person like Kang Mun Sok, for example. Having become a member of the Presidium of the Party Central Committee, he styled himself a figure representative of the southern half of the country; he called in people from the southern half and said, "What difficulties do you have?" "I will solve things for you." Thus he has performed an unorganized action alien to a Party worker. When a man who is from the southern half approaches you with a request, you should not try to solve the matter for him personally, but educate him properly to have it solved through channels of organization.

Those who came from the Soviet Union, China or from the southern half, no matter who they may be, must all bear in mind that they are now members of the Workers' Party of Korea. The selection and allocation of cadres should not be decided according to the subjective view of any individual, but always on Party principles. Those who lack Party spirit, who have no enthusiasm to work for the Party and the revolution and think themselves outstanding figures, are of no use to our Party, whether they returned from the Soviet Union, China or even from Heaven. You should understand this clearly.

Our Party members should work by relying on the Party and the organization, have a strong Party spirit and constantly improve themselves. To rely on an individual and try to settle one's own problems through his help or by means of currying favour with him, is against the principled stand of a Party member, and this will in the end be exploited by the individualist heroes.

All the cadres and members of our Party must sharpen their vigilance against the activities of the factionalists.

Now I should like to touch upon the ideological survivals of localism. We can take, for example, O Gi Sop who tried to form a group with people from the Hongwon region in South Hamgyong Province. It cannot be said, indeed, that all the factional activities in the years of Japanese imperialist rule were wrong. But what result did the factional activities in those years bring about? The lack of a united party and the lack of unified leadership from the centre to lower units, based on the principle of democratic centralism, allowed O Gi Sop to act as the biggest figure in the region, and the local people in their ignorance believed him to be the greatest person in the world. O Gi Sop attempted to utilize this to extend his influence.

That was already ten years ago and his attempt was foiled at that time. Though, of course, there are no local separatists today, their ideological survivals still persist.

During the past ten years, our Party has been educated and steeled in the revolutionary ideas of Marxism-Leninism and has grown into a mass political party rooted deep among the masses. Hence, today our Party cannot be identified with the one in the 1920's.

However, we must not leave alone people who are captivated by bourgeois ideas and individualist heroism to play sly tricks in the Party. We must always be vigilant against them. Whenever we find people engaged in factional tricks in the Party, we should give them a Party warning, demand their immediate rectification and keep them under control to prevent them from repeating such acts, and we should educate them according to the relative seriousness of their actions. Those whose misdeeds are serious should be exposed before the masses without delay so that they can be placed under mass control. Only by doing this can we save those under their influence, and prevent others from being badly influenced by them.

And it is necessary to intensify the activities of the Control Commission of our Party. The Party Control Commission should always keep under strict control and supervision the factional elements who undermine Party unity, and it should launch an implacable struggle against any and every unorganized act. In this way, we should always preserve the purity of our Party ranks and sweep away bad elements. Just as we have to get rid of rats when they, not content with sneaking about, start making holes, so we must make a clean sweep of the bad elements who pay no heed to our warnings.

Experience shows that sly tricksters in the Party will grow rampant if they are left alone. As for Pak Hon Yong and the like, we might have detected them still earlier, if we had been more critical in the Central Committee meeting at the time of the merger of the Workers' Parties of North and South Korea. This clique claimed that "The fellows from the south are all good" and appointed them to influential positions and played sly tricks. And eventually they attempted to subvert our Government in collusion with the U.S. rogues and sell out our country.

We must draw a lesson from past experience and always sharpen our vigilance against factional activities. We should bear in mind particularly that when the individualist heroes and factional elements are rendered unable to carry on their activities within the Party, they will degenerate into spies and saboteurs and do all sorts of despicable things.

The unity and solidarity of our Party is the source of its strength. Therefore, each Party member should always fight for the preservation of Party unity as for the apple of his eye, and remain vigilant against any factional elements and individualist heroes to prevent them from weakening our Party ranks.

3. ON INTENSIFYING ECONOMIZATION AND FINANCIAL CONTROL

An overall analysis of the extravagant practices existing in our state and economic institutions reveals that the greater part of them (about 70 per cent) results from the inability of our functionaries in these institutions to run factories and enterprises. Indeed, there are cases of impure elements worming themselves into state and economic institutions and intentionally embezzling state property. But the losses caused in such cases are not much bigger than the economic losses resulting from mismanagement. Waste in our state finances is due, in most cases, to the mismanagement of enterprises by our personnel and to the lack of order in state organs and enterprises.

What is important, therefore, in intensifying economization and financial control and stepping up the struggle against misappropriation and waste is as follows:

First, leading functionaries in our state and economic institutions should improve their ability to manage and operate enterprises.

Under the present conditions in our country, efficient management of enterprises is, in fact, a difficult matter. Historically our country was short of native cadres. At the close of the Li dynasty there were no native cadres to manage industry, because capitalism had not developed. The situation remained the same after our country was turned into a colony of Japanese imperialism. In running factories and enterprises, the Japanese imperialists occupied all the posts of manager, chief engineer and engineer while Koreans served under them. There were very few skilled workers among the Koreans, and the majority of Korean workers did unskilled labour. Take the railways, for example. When Korea was liberated, we had only a few Korean locomotive engineers. The Japs had almost exclusively held even the post of locomotive engineer and assigned Koreans only to the job of stoker.

Because we were so cruelly exploited by the Japanese imperialists during their nearly 40 years of rule, immediately after liberation we had very few cadres even of propertied-class origin, not to mention those of working-class origin. Right after liberation, there were in the northern half of the Republic only a few score technicians with a college education. It was under these circumstances that we took over the factories and enterprises the Japs had dilapidated when quitting. Despite such difficulties, we have been running factories and enterprises up to now, and this is a big success. But we must not rest content with this.

We have now quite a few big factories. There are iron works, steel plants, chemical factories, power stations, and many other big factories which can serve as the foundations for socialist industrialization. They are very large in scale. With our lack of experience and shortage of native cadres, it is quite difficult to run these factories and enterprises.

For Communists armed with Marxism-Leninism, however, there is no fortress that cannot be conquered. If only we are firmly determined and organize work properly, we can certainly run these large factories. What is more, we have assistance from the great Soviet Union, China and the other People's Democracies.

As you know, when we set about establishing a university

for the first time in 1946, there was much discussion about whether we could do it or not. We were not even able to compile textbooks at that time. Thus, our country had practically no native cadres.

For the past ten years, however, we have trained large numbers of native cadres by persistent efforts. As a result, we now have hosts of our own college graduates plus those who have returned from study in the Soviet Union, and many intellectuals and scholars who came from the southern half in support of our system.

After liberation we set out on tremendous economic construction without enough native cadres and, therefore, we had to replenish the ranks of our cadres with workers, peasants and working intellectuals who had had no experience in running factories and enterprises on their own. This means that our cadres have not yet attained a level high enough to run industry.

Our functionaries commit errors in the course of economic construction not because they are all bad but because they lack sufficient knowledge and ability needed for managing industry. So, it is of prime importance for cadres to acquire the knowledge and ability for industrial management.

Nevertheless, some of our functionaries quite often pretend to know economics, despite the fact that they do not know it, that, for instance, they do not know what makes up production costs. Pretending to knowledge while not knowing is a grave malady with us. When we do not know, we should not pretend to know but learn with an open mind. It is by no means a shame to learn.

Some managers think they are "born" managers. And they only behave arrogantly and idle away their time indifferently every day instead of striving to learn. This is a very wrong tendency. If we are to remove shortcomings in the management of enterprises, all cadres must acquire sufficient knowledge to operate industry and must manage enterprises efficiently.

Second, strict discipline and order should be established in state and economic institutions in order to intensify economization, financial control and the struggle against misappropriation and waste.

We have just laws and regulations enacted by the state. The thing is that our functionaries execute these laws and regulations correctly and do not violate them.

In the army, even a sentry is posted in accordance with the garrison regulations. How, then, can we run a big factory or enterprise without observing regulations? There must be discipline and order on all accounts.

If regulations are observed and discipline and order are firmly established in the enterprises, impure elements will not be able to commit theft and nothing will be stolen. You should not be bent only on catching thieves, but should concentrate your attention on the establishment of strict order and discipline in factories and their faithful observance. Experience shows that where there is no order and discipline, theft, embezzlement and waste cannot be prevented, and, further, even such dishonest practices take place as making false reports to higher organs that production plans have been fulfilled, in spite of the fact that the plans have not been carried out. That is why the establishment of discipline and order is of the utmost importance in the management of factories and enterprises.

Third, to intensify economization and financial discipline, stress should be placed not on throwing embezzlers and squanderers into a house of correction but on unfolding a confession campaign. But we should not forgive those who have pilfered state funds on many occasions. While laying emphasis on the confession campaign, we should follow the line of punishing by law those embezzlers and squanderers whose crimes are very serious.

And after the confession campaign, it is important to prevent them from committing crimes again. By stepping up educational work within the Party so that the functionaries in our state and economic institutions can manage enterprises efficiently and firmly establish discipline and order, we should intensify economization and financial control.

4. ON IMPROVING THE STYLE OF PARTY WORK

What I should like to emphasize now is the question of improving the style of Party work.

What is important in improving the style of Party work is, first, to see that correct assistance is rendered from the higher organs to the lower levels, ranging from the Party Central Committee down to *ri* Party committees. Nothing can be settled if we do work in a peremptory manner, giving no help and education to those in lower units, only heaping abuse on them for their poor conduct of work.

To render correct assistance to the lower levels, the Department of Organizational Leadership and all other departments of the Party Central Committee should, first of all, give day-to-day education to those at the lower levels; they should summon provincial Party committee workers and hear their reports to see how they are doing their work and what their ideological viewpoints are and, at the same time, should take measures to rectify their mistakes when they have misconducted their work.

And the responsible personnel should not give guidance in such a way as making tours by car and hurling abuse, but must personally go down to the lower levels and stay there for a long period to assist their functionaries in their actual work.

Practical and systematic checkup on the fulfilment of work is an essential condition for improving the style of work in the Party. But when such a checkup is made in a formal, bureaucratic manner, it will be fruitless. As yet, no small number of our Party functionaries conduct checkups to flaunt their authority and not to assist the lower units in their work and assure the correct implementation of Party and state decisions. Many functionaries still conduct checkups in the manner of a policeman or a detective and give guidance to the lower levels in a bureaucratic manner. As a result, those at the lower levels become afraid of checkups and are cowed when they undergo checkups. After conducting checkups in a police fashion, such functionaries just scold the personnel at the lower level without discrimination for failures in work, with the result that the latter acquire the bad habit of trying to evade checkups and hide their defects and making false reports to the higher organs.

And some functionaries, when they go down to the lower units to conduct checkups, pay no attention to any merits, but simply pick flaws, exaggerate and make a big noise about trivial things, unnecessarily finding fault with people. Such checkups bring no good to our work at all. Our functionaries should learn to go down to the lower units and assist them in work, solve knotty problems through consultation and help them rectify their shortcomings if they have any. Only in this way can we replace the old style of work, still to be found among ourselves, with a new, popular style of work.

You cannot expect any success in work if you send down Party decisions and various directives and only go about shouting at people to carry them out willy-nilly.

The bureaucratic style of work is still largely to be observed in our Party. Our Party has repeatedly laid stress on eliminating bureaucracy and has also waged a struggle against it, but this harmful style of work still persists to a considerable extent.

We should unfold a decisive struggle to do away with the bureaucratic style of work completely. In the struggle against bureaucracy, too, emphasis should be placed on assistance from higher to lower. All Party, state and economic bodies should work in such a way that the higher levels render assistance to the lower levels. This alone will inspire personnel at the lower levels to display activity and creative initiative in their work.

If each cell of our Party leads a healthy, active and militant life, further strengthens its ties with the masses and works vigorously to bring the creative initiative of the masses into play in the struggle for carrying out the Party's policies, a still bigger stride will be made in our work.

Second, it is important to strengthen the work of educating the cadres and members in our Party in the spirit of overcoming difficulties.

As we well know, the great October Socialist Revolution in Russia, the people's democratic revolution in China and the revolution in any other countries have all emerged victorious only through an arduous struggle. If a revolution could be carried out easily without a hard struggle, the world revolution would have already triumphed.

Our country is now carrying out the revolutionary movement under very favourable conditions.

We underwent many difficulties during the three years of the severe Fatherland Liberation War, but we fought with the active support of the Soviet Union, the People's Republic of China and the other People's Democracies. Even in wartime we fought without knowing hunger. Even during the difficult period of the war, we never reduced factory and office workers' food rations, and nobody was in rags in wartime.

In fact, we are now providing factory and office workers with much more textiles than we did before the war. This means that we have so far been engaged in the revolutionary struggle without meeting with great difficulties. For this reason, if we do not educate the functionaries in the spirit of overcoming difficulties, they may be unable to persevere in surmounting hardships but instead succumb to them when they encounter any in the future.

In anticipation of forthcoming great events, we should increase state accumulation and educate Party members and cadres in the spirit of overcoming difficulties. It is also important, I think, to let the Party members clearly see the broad vistas lying ahead of our country and cultivate them in revolutionary optimism.

5. ON THE SUCCESSFUL FULFILMENT OF THE CURRENT NATIONAL ECONOMIC PLAN

This is the most difficult year in the carrying out of the Three-Year National Economic Plan, and the fulfilment of this year's plan is of great significance. We must fulfil it under any circumstances.

If we fail to carry out this year's plan because of hardships, we shall remain as ever in a difficult position. Only by surmounting all hardships and building factories will we be able to solve the problems of food and clothing satisfactorily.

Therefore, to improve the people's living standard as quickly as possible and make our country rich, we must carry out the Three-Year National Economic Plan with success, overcoming difficulties, organizing the work well and turning every possibility to good account.

If we are to improve the people's standard of living, we must have various plants such as textile, foodstuff, daily necessities and machine-building factories. To expect good results while sitting idle without building factories, would be like the Christians praying to "God" for a blessed life. Our freedom and happiness cannot come from Heaven. They must be won by our own efforts and struggle.

What is most important in fulfilling this year's national economic plan is to see that all the personnel of the Party and state organs and economic agencies assist each other in close mutual contact and fight unyieldingly with a higher sense of responsibility towards the work assigned them by the Party and the state.

When you cannot fulfil your plan, you should honestly say so, and should not make false reports. Whenever you encounter difficult problems in carrying out the plan, you should inform your superiors in good time and take steps to break through the difficulties; everyone should fight for the fulfilment of the plan in a manner befitting a revolutionary. It is wrong to waver in the face of trivial difficulties, and it is also wrong to make a false report out of a desire to win fame despite a failure in the fulfilment of the plan.

I should now like to speak about this year's agricultural production plan. In short, it seems to me that the plan has not been correctly made. The reasons for this are, on the one hand, incorrect reports from below and, on the other, incorrect calculations at the higher level. As a result, the agricultural production plan was set too high to suit actual conditions. It is by no means an accident that the plan itself has been worked out incorrectly in this way.

Some say grain output last year was 2,800,000 tons, and others say 2,700,000 tons.

Now let us once calculate last year's actual grain output. According to statistics, we produced 2,790,000 tons of grain in 1949. As for the grain situation at that time, there was much grain on the market, quantities of grain were used as raw materials for industry and as much as 100,000 tons were exported, and yet the peasants lived in abundance. Rice price was 170-180 *won* per *sodu* at that time. In every village the peasants' living standard improved. Peasants built houses and bought furniture. And they met nearly all their food requirements by themselves without receiving grain loans from the state. Thus, with the output of 2,790,000 tons of grain, the life of the peasants was improved and even grain was exported, while the state stored up 50,000 tons of rice in reserve every year.

And last year's plan was to produce 3,000,000 tons. It was first reported that 2,900,000 tons were produced, but, finally, they said 2,800,000 tons were turned out. This means that we produced more grain than before the war. Why, then, do we feel a shortage of food?

Last year, no grain was exported, but, on the contrary, 220,000 tons were imported from the Soviet Union and China. What is more, our population decreased during the war.

Where on earth, then, has all the 2,800,000 tons of grain

gone? After all, the only explanation is that last year's grain output was inaccurately computed.

It appears that last year we turned out only about 2,300,000 tons of grain, minus the losses caused by the flood in North and South Hamgyong Provinces. Convincing proof of this is provided by our food situation today.

This notwithstanding, some of our provincial people's committee chairmen and leading agricultural personnel have no intention of drawing a lesson from their past work. Even this year they claimed that 4,100,000 tons of grain could be produced. The report to the Political Committee of the Party Central Committee says that it is planned to turn out 3,600,000 tons this year. The Political Committee did not agree with it and cut the grain production target sharply.

This was because we took into consideration the following points:

First, the land under cultivation shrank greatly as compared with the prewar period. Our cultivated land diminished because land was left idle as a result of the shortage of labour, was laid waste in wartime, or was cut out for road construction, and for other reasons. Therefore, the assertion that we can harvest more grain than in prewar times is at variance with the reality;

Second, the countryside has less labour force than in the prewar period. At present, the greater part of the labour force in our countryside is made up of old people and women. In conditions where overall mechanization has not been realized, how can we compare the countryside of today with the prewar countryside which had many young people? After all, women are different from men in labour, because they have to take care of children and do kitchen work;

Third, fertilizer, too, runs short as against the prewar period. At present, we supply only 50,000 tons of chemical fertilizers to the rural areas, whereas we used to supply 180,000-220,000 tons before the war. It is said that compost is being applied in large quantities, but there is much falsity here.

This being the case, how is it possible to produce more

grain than before the war? No analysis provides grounds for claiming larger output.

In 1952, I asked Comrade Minister of Agriculture how it was possible to turn out so much grain. He told me that more grain was produced by the method of planting close in small clusters. I believe we could not produce so much grain even if we introduced the "method of planting close in big clusters," let alone the method of planting close in small clusters.

We should work out an accurate plan for agricultural production this year. Let there be no such thing as forcing the lower units to do what is simply beyond their power and thus making them submit false reports, for the sake of winning fame, saying that they have done what they have failed to do. I think it necessary for the chairmen of the provincial, city and county people's committees and the Ministry of Agriculture and the State Planning Commission to re-examine the plan for this year's agricultural production. It is good to examine and rectify defects.

To draw up a correct plan of agricultural production may also exert a great influence on the development of agricultural co-operatives which are now being organized in the countryside. Therefore, the chairmen of the provincial, city and county people's committees should personally go down to the agricultural co-operatives and pay special attention to helping them map out accurate plans for agricultural production. In this, they should help them work out production plans correctly by basing themselves not on the target figures which were previously sent down, but on actual harvests and the new figures to be assigned later.

And the assessment of actual harvests should be made, as much as possible, in consideration of the opinions of the inhabitants of the locality concerned and based on the analysis of harvests before, during and after the war. Then, on this basis, the tax in kind should be imposed.

This year, in each locality per-*chongbo* yields should be assessed accurately after weighing the actual harvests at agricultural co-operatives. The cultivated area should also be correctly estimated. Its underestimation causes a loss to the state, whereas overestimation brings heavy burdens on the peasants.

If you deal with all matters from the viewpoint of the revolution, nothing will go wrong.

Now I should like to say a few words about forestry.

Forestry is one of the most important links in the rehabilitation and construction of our country's national economy.

Today our country is engaged in large-scale construction. The scale of our restoration and construction work is very big; we are carrying out not only new construction but also rehabilitation, and we are rehabilitating roads, bridges and reservoirs, while building houses. Particularly, the Anju irrigation project is a large one which envisages excavation of hundreds of kilometres of waterways including tributary channels. There is an acute dearth of building materials needed for such a huge construction project.

For the reconstruction of factories, railways and bridges, etc., destroyed in the war, the question of building materials, above all, acquires vital importance. For this reason, we must give much help to cement production and the timber industry. Our Party should mobilize manpower for them and educate the personnel in these fields to surmount hardships, and provide conditions for their work.

Party organizations, in particular, should mobilize raftsmen now in the rural areas and send them back to the timber industry. In the countryside raftsmen are not allowed to leave on the grounds that the land will be left idle should they go away. They say land is left out of crop due to labour shortage in the rural areas, while the cities have great difficulties in assigning jobs to discharged armymen and those who have been released from work as a result of the simplification of the state apparatus. These phenomena all arise from the failure of our functionaries to organize their work well. We should know how to organize work properly.

In carrying out the vast plan for the postwar rehabilitation and development of the national economy, our personnel should not work in an irresponsible manner, or doze off. Leading functionaries of our Party, state and economic bodies should devote all their talents and creative energies to the fulfilment of the state plan. Only in this way can we build a new society in our era.

By successfully carrying out the Three-Year Plan for Postwar Rehabilitation and Development of the National Economy, we must further consolidate the democratic base of the northern half of the Republic, which is the firm guarantee for the reunification and independence of the country, politically, economically and militarily.

Comrades,

This April Plenary Meeting of the Party Central Committee is of great historic significance for the progress of our Party.

I am convinced that just as they boldly eliminated the defects noted at the Third, Fourth and Fifth Plenary Meetings of the Party Central Committee, so will our Party members rectify as soon as possible the shortcomings pointed out at this April Plenary Meeting of the Party Central Committee, and correctly accept and carry out the Party's policies set forth at this meeting, so that they march more vigorously forward in the future for the attainment of the reunification and independence of the country and of the cause of socialist construction in the northern half of the Republic, firmly rallying around the Central Committee of our Party.

ON ELIMINATING DOGMATISM AND FORMALISM AND ESTABLISHING JUCHE IN IDEOLOGICAL WORK

Speech to Party Propagandists and Agitators

December 28, 1955

Today I want to address a few remarks to you on the shortcomings in our Party's ideological work and on how to eliminate them in the future.

As you learned at yesterday's session, there have been serious ideological errors on the literary front. It is obvious, then, that our propaganda work also cannot have been faultless.

It is to be regretted that our propaganda work suffers in many respects from dogmatism and formalism.

The principal shortcomings in ideological work are the failure to delve deeply into all matters and the lack of *Juche*. It may not be proper to say *Juche* is lacking, but, in fact, it has not yet been firmly established. This is a serious matter. We must thoroughly rectify this shortcoming. Unless this problem is solved, we cannot hope for good results in ideological work.

Why does our ideological work suffer from dogmatism and formalism? And why do our propagandists and agitators fail to go deeply into matters, only embellishing the façade, and why do they merely copy and memorize foreign things, instead of working creatively? This offers us food for serious reflection.

What is *Juche* in our Party's ideological work? What are we doing? We are not engaged in any other country's revolution, but precisely in the Korean revolution. This, the Korean revolution, constitutes *Juche* in the ideological work of our Party. Therefore, all ideological work must be subordinated to the interests of the Korean revolution. When we study the history of the Communist Party of the Soviet Union, the history of the Chinese revolution, or the universal truth of Marxism-Leninism, it is all for the purpose of correctly carrying out our own revolution.

By saying that the ideological work of our Party lacks in *Juche*, I do not mean, of course, that we have not made the revolution or that our revolutionary work was undertaken by passers-by. Nonetheless, *Juche* has not been firmly established in ideological work, which leads to dogmatic and formalistic errors and does much harm to our revolutionary cause.

To make revolution in Korea we must know Korean history and geography and know the customs of the Korean people. Only then is it possible to educate our people in a way that suits them and to inspire in them an ardent love for their native place and their motherland.

It is of paramount importance to study, and widely publicize among the working people, the history of our country and of our people's struggle, before anything else.

This is not the first time we have raised this question. As far back as the autumn of 1945, that is, immediately after liberation, we emphasized the need to study the history of our nation's struggle and to inherit its fine traditions. Only when our people are educated in the history of their own struggle and its traditions, can their national pride be stimulated and the broad masses be aroused to the revolutionary struggle.

Yet, many of our functionaries are ignorant of our country's history, and so do not strive to discover and carry forward its fine traditions. Unless this is corrected, it will lead, in the long run, to the negation of Korean history.

The mistakes made recently by Pak Chang Ok and his kind, too, may be attributed to their negation of the history of the

Korean literary movement. They closed their eyes to the struggle of the fine writers of the "KAPF"—Koréen (Coréen) Artiste Prolétarienne Fédération—and to the splendid works of progressive scholars and writers of our country. We told them to make a profound study of excellent cultural heritages and give them wide publicity, but they did not do so.

Today, ten years after liberation, we have all the conditions for collecting material on our literary legacy and turning it to full use. Nevertheless, the propaganda workers remain wholly indifferent to this.

At the Fifth Plenary Meeting of the Party Central Committee it was decided to actively publicize the history of our people's struggle and valuable cultural heritages, but workers in the field of propaganda failed to do so. They did so much as forbid the newspapers to carry articles on the anti-Japanese struggle of the Korean people.

The Kwangju Student Incident, for example, was a mass struggle in which tens of thousands of Korean youths and students rose against Japanese imperialism; it played a big part in inspiring the anti-Japanese spirit in broad sections of the Korean youth. As a matter of course, propaganda workers should have publicized this movement widely and educated youth and students in the brave fighting spirit displayed by their forerunners. They have failed to do so. Instead, Syngman Rhee has been making propaganda of this movement in his favour. This has created a false impression that the Communists disregard national traditions. What a dangerous thing! It will be impossible for us to win over the south Korean youth if we go on working in this way.

So far propaganda work in this respect has all been dropped and laid aside, though no one has ever given instructions to. Newspapers do not write about it, nor is any meeting held to commemorate it. Things like the Kwangju Student Incident ought to be taken up by the Democratic Youth League. The Kwangju Student Incident is an excellent example of the struggle of the youth and students of our country against imperialism.

The same must be said of the June Tenth Independence Movement. This was another mass struggle in which the Korean people rose against Japanese imperialism. It is true that the struggle was greatly hampered by the factionalists who had slipped into it. Considering that even after liberation, the Pak Hon Yong-Li Sung Yop spy clique crept into our ranks and wrought mischief, it goes without saying that in those days the factionalists could carry on subversive activities more easily. But, even so, was the struggle itself wrong? No, it was not. Although the struggle ended in failure because of a few bad elements who had wormed their way into the leadership of the organization, we cannot deny its revolutionary character; we should learn a lesson from that failure.

No publicity has been given even to the March First Movement. If you work in this way, you cannot expect to lead along the right path the progressive people who have a national conscientiousness. The lack of leadership by a Communist Party was the principal cause of the failure of the March First Movement. But who can ever deny the fact that the March First Movement was a nation-wide resistance movement against Japanese imperialism? We ought to explain to the people the historic significance of this movement and educate them by its lessons.

Many past revolutionary movements ended in failure in our country because of the scoundrels who managed to install themselves in the leadership of those movements, but there can be no denying the struggles waged by the people on those occasions. The popular masses always fought well with courage. Pak Chang Ok may have denied this arbitrarily. But no true Marxist-Leninist dare deny the people's exploits in their struggles.

When I asked Pak Chang Ok and his followers why they rejected the "KAPF," they answered that they did so because some renegades were involved in it. Then, did they mean to say that the "KAPF," in which prominent proletarian writers of our country worked as its very core, was an organization of no importance? We must highly value the fighting achievements of the "KAPF."

What assets do we have for carrying on the revolution if the history of our people's struggle is denied? If we cast aside all these things, it would mean that our people did nothing. There are many things to be proud of in our country's peasant movements of the past. In recent years, however, no articles dealing with them have appeared in our newspapers.

In schools, too, there is a tendency to neglect lectures on Korean history. During the war the curricula of the Central Party School allotted 160 hours a year to the study of world history, but very few hours were given to Korean history. This is how things were done in the Party school, and so it is quite natural that our functionaries are ignorant of their own country's history.

In our propaganda and agitation work, there are numerous examples of extolling only foreign things, while slighting our own.

Once I visited a People's Army vacation home, where a picture of the Siberian steppe was hung. That landscape probably pleases the Russians. But the Korean people prefer the beautiful scenery of our own country. There are beautiful mountains such as Mts. Kumgang-san and Myohyang-san in our country; there are clear streams, the blue sea with its rolling waves and the fields with ripening crops. If we are to inspire in our People's Armymen a love for their native place and their country, we must show them many pictures of such landscapes of our country.

One day this summer when I dropped in at a local democratic publicity hall, I saw diagrams of the Soviet Union's Five-Year Plan shown there, but not a single diagram illustrating the Three-Year Plan of our country. Moreover, there were pictures of huge factories in foreign countries, but there was not a single one of the factories we were rehabilitating or building. They do not even put up any diagrams and pictures of our economic construction, let alone study the history of our country.

I noticed in a primary school that all the portraits hanging on the walls were of foreigners such as Mayakovsky, Pushkin, etc., and there were none of Koreans. If children are educated in this way, how can they be expected to have national pride?

Here is a ridiculous example. Even in attaching a table of contents to a booklet, foreign ways are aped and it is put in the back. We should learn, as a matter of course, from the good experience of socialist construction, but what on earth is the need of putting the table of contents in the back of a booklet in foreign style? This does not suit the taste of Koreans. As a matter of course, we should put it in the front of a book, shouldn't we?

In compiling schoolbooks, too, materials are not taken from our literary works but from foreign ones. All this is due to the lack of *Juche*.

The lack of *Juche* in propaganda work has done much harm to Party work.

For the same reason, many comrades do not respect our revolutionaries. At present more than 100 comrades who took part in revolutionary struggles in the past are attending the Central Party School; until recently they had been buried in obscurity.

We sent many revolutionaries to the Ministry of the Interior, but many of them were dismissed on the ground that they were incompetent. At the Central Party School, I once met a comrade who had formerly taken part in revolutionary activities; he had been left in his post as chief of a county interior service station for eight years. This is quite an improper attitude towards revolutionaries.

Today our functionaries have become so insolent that they show no respect for their seniors. They have been allowed to fall into such a habit, whereas Communists naturally have a higher moral sense than any other people, and hold their revolutionary seniors in high esteem.

In our People's Army a vigorous struggle has been waged to uphold the revolutionary traditions and, as a result, most of the people who had taken part in revolutionary activities have become either regimental or divisional commanders.

If we had not organized the People's Army with old revolutionary cadres as its core, what would have been the outcome of the last war? It would have been impossible for us to defeat the enemy and win a great victory under such difficult conditions.

During our retreat certain foreigners predicted that most of our army units, trapped by enemy encirclement, would not be able to get back. But we were firmly convinced that all of them would manage to come back. In fact, they all did return, with the exception of the dead. The foreigners were greatly impressed at this and said there were few armies like ours in the world. How did this come about? The explanation is that our army cadres were comrades who in the past had taken part in guerrilla warfare or in local revolutionary movements. That is precisely why our army is strong.

Ten years have passed now since our Party was founded. Therefore, the Party members should naturally be educated in the history of our Party. If our functionaries are not educated in the revolutionary history of our country, they will be unable to carry forward our fine revolutionary traditions, nor will they be able to realize which direction to take in the struggle, or show enthusiasm and creative initiative in their revolutionary activities.

We should study our own things in earnest and be versed in them. Otherwise, we shall be unable to solve creatively in keeping with our actual conditions the new problems that confront us one after another in practice.

As a matter of fact, the form of our government should also be fitted to the specific conditions of our country. Does our people's power have exactly the same form as in other socialist countries? No, it does not. They are alike in that they are based on Marxist-Leninist principles, but their forms are different. No doubt, our platform, too, is in keeping with the realities of our country. Our 20-Point Platform is the development of the Programme of the Association for the Restoration of the Fatherland. As you all know, the Association for the Restoration of the Fatherland existed before our country was liberated.

Our functionaries often commit errors due to lack of a clear understanding of these matters.

Some people even think it strange that the agricultural co-operative movement is progressing rapidly in our country. There is nothing strange about this. In the past, the economic foundation of the Korean peasantry was very weak. Under Japanese imperialism, the peasant movement developed and the revolutionary spirit of the peasantry ran very high. What is more, the peasants were tempered politically through the democratic construction after liberation and during the bitter war. So, it is natural that the agricultural co-operative movement should be making rapid progress in our country today.

Pak Yong Bin, on returning from the Soviet Union, said that since the Soviet Union was following the line of easing international tension, we should also drop our slogan against U.S. imperialism. Such an assertion has nothing to do with revolutionary initiative. It would dull our people's revolutionary vigilance. The U.S. imperialists scorched our land, slaughtered our innocent people en masse, and are still occupying the southern half of our country. They are our sworn enemy, aren't they?

It is utterly ridiculous to think that our people's struggle against the U.S. imperialists conflicts with the efforts of the Soviet people to ease international tension. Our people's condemnation and struggle against the aggressive policy of the U.S. imperialists towards Korea are not contradictory, but conducive to the struggle of the people of the world for lessening international tension and for defending peace. At the same time, the struggle of the peace-loving people the world over, including the Soviet people, to ease tension creates more favourable conditions for the anti-imperialist struggle of our people.

Pak Chang Ok was ideologically linked to the reactionary bourgeois writer Li Tae Jun in that he did not study the history of our country and our realities. Besides the remnants of bourgeois ideology in his mind, he had the conceited idea that he knew everything without even studying the realities of our country. Consequently, things went wrong. The harm he did to our ideological work is very serious.

After liberation he and his ilk said that Li Gwang Su was a talented man, and that, therefore, it would be advisable to give him prominence. But I pointed out it would be wrong to do so. Li Gwang Su wrote a novel, *The Wife of a Revolutionary,* in which he insulted the revolutionaries discharged from prison. Li Gwang Su was a villain who used to rave that the Korean people and the Japanese imperialists came of "one and the same ancestry and roots." Therefore, I told them that it was totally unthinkable to give prominence to such a man, and never allowed them to do so.

Some comrades working in the Propaganda Department of the Party tried to copy mechanically from the Soviet Union in all their work. This was also because they had no intention to study our realities and lacked the true Marxist-Leninist spirit of educating the people in our own merits and in the traditions of our revolution. Many comrades swallow Marxism-Leninism whole, instead of digesting and assimilating it. It is therefore self-evident that they are unable to display revolutionary initiative.

Propaganda workers have so far failed to take proper measures for a systematic study of our country's history and our national culture. It has been ten years since liberation. And yet, we have failed to tackle the matter energetically; we have conducted it only in a hit-or-miss way. We had few cadres before, but now we have scholars, funds and materials, and have sufficient conditions for conducting it. This is quite possible if only you make a good study and organize the work. Every effort should be made to unearth our national legacies and carry them forward. True, we should be active in learning from what is progressive internationally. But we should develop fine things of our own while introducing advanced culture. Otherwise, our people will lose faith in their own ability and become a spineless people who only try to copy from others.

Hearing us say that it is necessary to establish *Juche*, some comrades might take it simply and form a wrong idea that we need not learn from foreign countries. That would be quite wrong. We must learn from the good experiences of socialist countries.

The important thing is to know what we are learning for. The aim we pursue in learning is to turn the advanced experience of the Soviet Union and other socialist countries to good account in our Korean revolution.

During the war, Ho Ga I, Kim Jae Uk and Pak Il U once quarrelled stupidly among themselves over the problem of how to carry on political work in the army. Those from the Soviet Union insisted upon the Soviet method and those from China stuck to the Chinese method. So they quarrelled, some advocating the Soviet fashion and others the Chinese way. That was sheer nonsense.

It does not matter whether you use the right hand or the left, whether you use a spoon or chopsticks at the table. No matter how you eat, it is all the same insofar as food is put into your mouth, isn't it? What is the need of being particular about "fashion" in wartime? When we carry on political work to strengthen our People's Army and win battles, any method will do so long as our aim is achieved. Yet Ho Ga I and Pak Il U squabbled about such a trifle. This only weakens discipline within the Party. At that time the Party centre maintained that we should learn all the good things from both the Soviet Union and China and, on this basis, work out a method of political work suitable to the actual conditions of our country.

It is important in our work to grasp revolutionary truth, Marxist-Leninist truth, and apply it correctly to the actual conditions of our country. There can be no set principle that we must follow the Soviet pattern. Some advocate the Soviet way and others the Chinese, but is it not high time to work out our own?

The point is that we should not mechanically copy forms

and methods of the Soviet Union, but should learn from its experience in struggle and Marxist-Leninist truth. So, while learning from the experience of the Soviet Union, we must put stress not on the forms but on learning the essence of its experience.

In learning from the experience of the Soviet Union there is a marked tendency just to model after the external forms. Once *Pravda* puts out a headline "A Day in Our Country," our *Rodong Sinmun* carries the same title: "A Day in Our Country." What is the use of copying even this sort of thing? The same is true of clothing. When there are very graceful Korean costumes for our women, what is the use of discarding them and putting on dresses which are unbecoming to them? There is no need to do this. I suggested to the Women's Union functionaries to see that our women dress in Korean costumes as far as possible.

Just copying the forms used by others instead of learning Marxist-Leninist truth brings us no good, only harm.

Both in revolutionary struggle and in construction work, we should firmly adhere to Marxist-Leninist principles, applying them in a creative manner to suit the specific conditions of our country and our national characteristics.

If we mechanically apply foreign experience, disregarding the history of our country and the traditions of our people and without taking account of our own realities and level of preparedness of our people, dogmatic errors will result and much harm will be done to the revolutionary cause. To do so is not fidelity to Marxism-Leninism nor to internationalism; it runs counter to them.

Marxism-Leninism is not a dogma, it is a guide to action and a creative theory. So, Marxism-Leninism can display its indestructible vitality only when it is applied creatively to suit the specific conditions of each country. The same applies to the experience of the fraternal parties. It will prove valuable to us only when we make a study of it, grasp its essence and properly apply it to our realities. Instead, if we just gulp it down and spoil our work, it will not only harm our work but also lead to discrediting the valuable experience of the fraternal parties.

In connection with the problem of establishing *Juche* I think it necessary to touch on internationalism and patriotism.

Internationalism and patriotism are inseparably linked with each other. You must know that the love of Korean Communists for their country does not go against the internationalism of the working class but conforms fully with it. To love Korea is just as good as to love the Soviet Union and the socialist camp and, likewise, to love the Soviet Union and the socialist camp means precisely loving Korea. They constitute a complete whole. For the great cause of the working class has no frontiers and our revolutionary cause is a part of the international revolutionary cause of the working class throughout the world. The one supreme goal of the working class of all countries is to build a communist society. The difference, if any, lies only in the fact that certain countries do this earlier and others later.

It would be wrong to advocate patriotism alone and neglect internationalist solidarity. For the victory of the Korean revolution and for the great cause of the international working class, we should strengthen solidarity with the Soviet people and with the peoples of all the socialist countries. This is our sacred internationalist duty. The Soviet people, on their part, are doing all they can to consolidate solidarity not only with the countries of the socialist camp but also with the working class of the whole world, both for communist construction in their country and for the victory of world revolution.

Thus, patriotism and internationalism are inseparable. He who does not love his own country cannot be loyal to internationalism, and he who is unfaithful to internationalism cannot be faithful to his own country and people. A true patriot is precisely an internationalist and vice versa.

If we cast aside all that is good in our country and only copy and memorize foreign things in ideological work, it will certainly bring losses to our revolution, and thereby prevent us also from properly carrying out our internationalist obligations to the international revolutionary cause.

In the report to the Second Party Congress, I quoted the

following passage from the statement of the Commander of the Soviet army published on the first day of its entry into our country: "Korean people!... You have happiness in your own hands.... Koreans must make themselves the creators of their own happiness." This statement is perfectly correct, and if we fail to act accordingly, we may lose broad segments of the masses.

The formalism of our propaganda workers also finds expression in exaggerating things in propaganda work. For example, such bombastic expressions as "all have risen," "all have been mobilized," etc., have long been in fashion in speeches and articles.

We advised Pak Chang Ok more than once against it. Pak Chang Ok made mistakes because he could not break away from this "all" type of bombast he had created. Later, he took a fancy to the superlative of the Chinese ideograph "great," and abused the adjective "great." I do not know whether this practice was due to his ignorance of Chinese ideographs or to his erroneous ideological viewpoint.

When propaganda work is conducted with such exaggeration without any substance to it, it will lead people to be carried away by victory and to become easy-going. This bad practice is also responsible for the false reports handed in by junior officials.

The use of an adjective may seem a simple matter, but when wrongly used it may cause our work to fail. In future, such a practice should be discontinued thoroughly.

Now, I should like to refer to a few other immediate problems in ideological work.

The Party Central Committee has issued written material on the character and tasks of our revolution to help study the documents of its April Plenary Meeting. So, I will not make any further comment on this.

I would just like to stress once more the prospects of the revolution in our country. Our revolution has two prospects. One is the peaceful reunification of our country, and the other is its reunification under the conditions in which the forces of imperialism are sharply weakened by a big war.

We, of course, have been striving with all our might to bring about the first prospect.

Our struggle for the peaceful reunification of our country boils down to two points—to carry on construction successfully in the northern half and to conduct effective political work towards the southern half. If we fortify the democratic base by promoting socialist construction in the northern half and arouse the people in the southern half to the liberation struggle through effective political work directed to the southern half, the peaceful reunification of our country can be realized.

Political work towards the southern half means strengthening the influence of the northern half on the people in the southern half and inducing its broad popular masses to support us. To this end, socialist construction in the northern half should be carried on successfully. The living standard of the people should be raised and the economic foundation strengthened in the northern half through successful economic construction, and the entire people should be rallied around our Party. Then, no matter how desperately Syngman Rhee may try, he will never be able to dampen the fighting spirit of the people in the southern half who are constantly inspired by the socialist construction in the northern half.

A man who came over from the southern half some time ago said: "Syngman Rhee says in his propaganda that the northern half has a population of only 3 million and there is nothing left in Pyongyang but heaps of ashes. But I have seen here that the bridge over the River Taedong-gang has been restored to its former state and Pyongyang is being built into a much more beautiful city than before. Syngman Rhee has told a whopping lie." This is what will happen when we carry on construction successfully.

In 1948 when a joint conference of political parties and social organizations from north and south Korea was held, we did not have much to our credit in construction in the northern half. But all the Right-wing personalities of south Korea came to us with the exception of Syngman Rhee and Kim Song Su. The joint conference was of very great significance. Many of those who came to the northern half at that time remained here.

This is what Kim Gu said: "I have found north Korea to my liking. I have seen many Communists both in Shanghai and in south Korea (if he met any, they must have been those of the Tuesday group or the M-L group), but north Korean Communists are different. I thought before that Communists were narrow-minded and wicked people, but as I have found here this time, you are broad-minded and generous people with whom I can fully co-operate. I will co-operate with you by all means. I am old now, and have no ambition for power. If I do not go back to south Korea, Syngman Rhee will certainly clamour that I have been detained. And it is my desire to go back and give publicity to the fine things I have seen here. So I must go back at any rate. Do not think that I am going to collaborate with the Yankees. When I return here later, please give me an apple orchard, as I want to live in peace in the countryside for the rest of my life." Kim Gyu Sik, too, spoke in the same vein. After that, Kim Gu fought against the Yankees.

As you all know, Kim Gu was a nationalist. From the beginning he was against both imperialism and communism, and came to us with the intention of negotiating with Communists. In view of the fact that even Kim Gu who had regarded communism as an inveterate enemy changed his view of our endeavours to build up the country, it is quite easy to imagine what the workers, peasants, and the public figures with a national conscience in south Korea will think once they come and see the northern half.

Before liberation, the mere words that in the Soviet Union the working class held power and was building socialism made us yearn boundlessly for the Soviet Union where we had never been. How then can the people in the southern half possibly help yearning for the socialist construction of our people in the northern half who are of the same ethnical stock with them?

That is why successful construction in the northern half is more important than anything else.

As can be seen from the above, when the people in the

southern half are roused to action against U.S. imperialism and the Syngman Rhee regime by successful socialist construction in the northern half and through effective political work directed towards the southern half, the peaceful reunification of our country can be materialized.

This is the internal factor making it possible to achieve peaceful reunification.

The external factor conducive to the country's peaceful reunification should likewise be taken into consideration. If we succeed in maintaining peace for a five to ten years period, China, with her more than 600 million population, will grow incomparably in might, not to mention the Soviet Union, and the power of the whole socialist camp will be further strengthened.

Parallel with the growth of the might of the socialist camp, the national-liberation movement of the peoples in the colonial and dependent countries has been ever more intensified, and many countries have achieved national independence. The peoples of India, Indonesia, Burma and other independent states in Asia and the peoples of the Arab countries are fighting for peace against imperialist aggression.

All this is a telling blow to imperialism, especially U.S. imperialism. When the forces of peace, democracy and socialism grow stronger, the U.S. imperialists will finally be compelled to withdraw from Korea.

Of course, the struggle for the country's peaceful reunification is an arduous and protracted one. But when we grow stronger and the forces of peace, democracy and socialism are further strengthened internationally, we will be able to achieve peaceful reunification. This is one prospect of the development of the revolution in Korea and of the country's reunification.

The problem of the country's reunification might also be solved not by peaceful means but by war. If the imperialists were to unleash a war on a world-wide scale, we would have no alternative but to fight, and then it would be quite possible for us to fight and defeat the U.S. imperialists in Korea by our own strength. Although it would be somewhat hard for us to fight against U.S. imperialism single-handed, we should be able to defeat it rather easily when it is compelled to disperse its forces all over the world. In that case, we shall sweep the forces of U.S. imperialism from Korea and achieve the reunification of the country. This is the other prospect of the development of the Korean revolution and the reunification of the country.

We, however, do not want this prospect. We desire the first prospect, that is, reunification by peaceful means, and we are struggling for its realization.

No matter what the prospects of the country's reunification may be, it is more important than anything else to strengthen our Party and steel the Party spirit of its members.

In case negotiations start between the north and the south, and then the barriers between them are torn down and we come to work among south Koreans, will it not be necessary for our Party to be strong? Only when our Party is strong, can it take advantage of such a favourable situation.

The proportion of our Party membership to the population is now one to ten, the membership being one million out of a population of 10 million. Indeed, this is not a small proportion. But, when compared with the total population of Korea, 30 million, one million is by no means large.

In south Korea the growth of the Party's force cannot help but be seriously limited, because the underground movement is conducted there in extremely difficult circumstances.

After reunification, it will be difficult to carry on our work with a small number of Party members, although the number will grow in south Korea, too. What is wrong with our training a large number of Party members in the northern half from now on and assigning them evenly to work in the north and south after reunification? There is nothing wrong in this. Yet, at the time of the Fourth Plenary Meeting of the Party Central Committee Ho Ga I insisted that the Party close its doors in spite of the fact that it had a membership of no more than 600,000. Then the Party criticized his view and has since continued to increase its membership.

The point now is to give a good education to our one million Party members. Among our members there can sometimes be found those who even lag behind the non-Party masses. But even so, these people must not be expelled from the Party. They must be kept in the Party and educated; if they were expelled, our Party's strength might be weakened. This is all the more so since ours is not the only party.

It is our invariable organizational line to train the nuclei of the cells constantly while building up a mass party. By the nuclei we mean those Party members who are aware of communist truth and are capable of holding to the road of revolution without vacillating. It is difficult to arm the one million Party members overnight with an equal degree of communist consciousness. We must follow the line of training the nuclei first and then gradually raising the level of consciousness of all Party members.

Our line is to educate Party members with the help of core members. So, since the Fourth Plenary Meeting the Party has put special emphasis on the question of training the core members of the cells. It will be all the more gratifying if their number increases from five today to ten tomorrow and thus all Party members become core elements, and even if not all but only 50 per cent of the Party membership does so, it will be a good thing.

In the development of our Party into a mass political party, the merging of the Communist Party and the New Democratic Party was of great significance. As a result of our correct organizational line and energetic struggle to win over the broad working masses, our Party has now developed into a mass political party embracing one million members. This success has by no means been easy to gain, but has been achieved through extremely hard struggles.

We demand and fight for democratic rights and liberties in south Korea—freedom of speech, the press, assembly and association—which are prerequisites for the peaceful reunification of the country. We aim at securing conditions for our own free activities in the southern half while allowing political parties of south Korea to conduct political activities freely in the northern half.

When a situation is thus created for free political struggle in the north and the south, whoever wins over more of the masses will win the day. Therefore, it is of the greatest importance to strengthen our Party and the Party spirit of its members.

In order to steel the Party spirit of our members, we should have all of them make a constant and deep study of the documents of the Fourth and Fifth Plenary Meetings of the Party Central Committee.

Our comrades must direct more efforts to the organizational and propaganda work of the Party, instead of being engrossed only in economic campaigns. Party cells must be built up well and Party members educated through the nuclei of the cells. It is particularly necessary to temper the Party spirit of those members who hold leading posts—ministers, vice-ministers and bureau directors. Vigorous educational measures should be taken to fortify the Party spirit of the entire membership.

Our Party's composition is very complex. All sorts of people have joined our Party—those who once belonged to the Tuesday group and the M-L group, those who were affiliated with the Toiling People's Party after liberation, and others. Many were under the influence of the factional elements in the past. These people are to be found both among responsible cadres in the central organs and among the members of the Party Central Committee.

Not all of these people are worthless. Education will make them all useful. But their education must not be conducted through a short-term campaign. Long, persistent education and criticism are needed.

A determined struggle must be fought to arm every Party member firmly with our Party's ideology and eliminate all remnants of bourgeois ideology persisting in the minds of Party members and working people. The Party spirit of our members should be tempered thoroughly, until their shortcomings and ideological maladies are completely remedied.

We were too late in criticizing Pak Chang Ok and Ki Sok

Bok. If they had been criticized at the time of the Fifth Plenary Meeting of the Party Central Committee, things would not have gone so far. Therefore, it is especially important to remould the ideas of those leading cadres who have been influenced by Ho Ga I or Pak Il U and help them establish the Party's ideological system. This work must be undertaken by the Department of Organizational Leadership and the Propaganda and Agitation Department of the Party.

What is important in the education of Party members is to make them, especially the cadres, establish a mass viewpoint. Because this is lacking, bureaucracy continues to manifest itself. This is a grave shortcoming in our Party work.

In order to achieve our lofty aims of reunifying the country and building socialism and communism, we must win over the masses. We must clearly know what great losses bureaucracy can cause to the revolution.

Listening to the voices of the masses and championing their interests is an entirely different matter from basing one's work on misleading opinions current in the streets. The latter has nothing in common with the revolutionary mass viewpoint. By the masses we mean the main masses we are relying on—the workers and the peasants, and our allies who support and follow us. We should listen to them and defend their interests. Everyone, whether a Party worker, an administrative official or a functionary in a social organization, must work consistently in the interests of the revolution and the masses.

How was it possible for the anti-Japanese guerrillas to hold out for a long time? Why was it that the Japs failed to destroy us although they had a formidable armed force? Because the guerrillas had the correct mass viewpoint and the support of the masses. When guerrillas were wounded and entered a village, the peasants took care of them as though they were their own sons; they would manage to get rice, which they could hardly afford themselves, and boil it for them. Even the peasants living inside the earthen walls of the concentrated villages set up by the Japs, managed to send food to them outside the walls.

The masses supported and protected us in this way, because we had always defended their interests and fought for them at the risk of our own lives. All Party members have to learn from the attitude of the guerrillas towards the masses.

In the days of Japanese imperialist rule everything was imposed upon us by force—compulsory military service, compulsory labour draft, compulsory delivery of farm produce, etc. We are resolutely opposed to such practices.

A party divorced from the masses is like a fish out of water. With whom can the party carry out the revolution if not with the masses? Such a party will not only be unable to win in the revolution, but also will eventually find its very existence endangered.

It is solely for the purpose of protecting the interests of the masses that the party puts forward its programme and seizes state power. Therefore, would it not be against the aims of the party and the revolution to encroach on the interests of the masses?

Our laws and decisions are indisputably excellent. But all this will come to nothing if, in the course of putting them into effect, our functionaries impinge on the interests of the masses. You must bear this in mind and further strengthen educational work among Party members so that they can liquidate bureaucracy and acquire a correct mass viewpoint. If at least 50 per cent of all Party members acquire a correct mass viewpoint, it will mean a great change for our Party.

At present quite a few Party members are not firmly equipped with a correct mass viewpoint. The situation is especially worse among the cadres. Whether a Party member has a correct mass viewpoint or not also depends on his Party spirit. So, tempering Party spirit is also of decisive importance in this respect.

Further, it is important to cultivate faith and optimism regarding the prospects of the revolution in the minds of the Party members. Without firm faith in the final victory of our cause and without optimism regarding the future of the revolution, under any and all circumstances, it would be impossible to overcome the difficulties one inevitably encounters in the course of the revolutionary struggle.

In order to make our Party members indomitable fighters who are always optimistic about the future of the revolution, it is necessary to intensify their Marxist-Leninist education. Without a clear understanding of the laws of social development and the inevitability of the triumph of socialism and communism, one can neither have faith in victory nor have the high-toned spirit and combativeness to withstand any difficulty.

Let me take an example of vacillation and defection in the ranks of the revolutionaries that was caused by a lack of knowledge of the laws of social development and of a clear understanding of the trend of developments in a complex situation.

When the defeat of Japanese imperialism was near in sight, some people in the guerrilla detachments lost faith and deserted. This was partly because of certain formalistic defects in our propaganda work at that time. In those days propaganda about the Soviet Union was of special importance, and it was propagandized in the guerrilla army that "A big clash will certainly occur some day between the Soviet Union and the imperialist states, because fundamental contradictions exist between them. Then, Japanese imperialism will perish and our country will be able to achieve independence." That was wrong. Though it was right to propagandize about the contradictions between the socialist state and the imperialist countries, the truth about the developments was not explained. As a result, when in 1941 a treaty of neutrality was concluded between the Soviet Union and Japan and a non-aggression pact between the Soviet Union and Hitler Germany was signed, some elements in the ranks of the guerrillas lost hope for the future and faltered. These waverers deserted our ranks, saying that after 10 years with the guerrillas, they had a dark future, uncertain whether they would have to spend there another 10 or 20 years. So we explained the revolutionary situation and the truth of revolution fully to the guerrillas. After that, there were no more deserters.

There is no doubt that sooner or later we shall see a great revolutionary event. That event, as I have already said, may either occur peacefully or non-peacefully. Whatever form the event may take, we must always be prepared to meet it.

In order to meet this great revolutionary event, the Party spirit of the Party members should be steeled; they should be educated to have a correct mass viewpoint and to have faith in victory and optimism regarding the future of the revolution.

Another important thing is to struggle properly against all sorts of anti-Party tendencies. If we had not had the experience of fighting the *Minsaengdan* in Chientao before, we would not have been able to give appropriate leadership to the struggle against the counter-revolutionaries in Korea after liberation, especially during the war.

The Japs organized a counter-revolutionary espionage organization called *Minsaengdan* and smuggled it into the revolutionary districts in Kando. Then they resorted to the vile trick of alienating the Koreans from the Chinese and inciting strife among the Koreans. For some time those in the revolutionary camp fell victim to the enemy's crafty scheme, going the length of killing one another. As a result, many people lost their lives without any justification.

This experience proved very useful when we dealt with the case of the Pak Hon Yong clique. We adhered strictly to the principle of drawing a sharp distinction between spies and non-spies. We emphasized this many times in the Political Committee. There was a danger that we might possibly play into the hands of the Yankees and ruin many persons.

Of course, there must be a relentless struggle. Otherwise, some spies may escape punishment. But the struggle must always be carried on as an ideological struggle.

Those who were influenced by Pak Hon Yong cannot all be his ilk or spies. But his ideological influence still remains in the minds of these people. We must fight against this.

The experience acquired in the course of the struggle against the Pak Hon Yong clique and in the counter-espionage campaigns should be made fully known to the Party members so that they may wage a rigorous struggle against espionage agents and correctly distinguish the spies from others. If you do not do so and suspect everybody, in the end you will find yourselves suspicious of your own shadow.

The enemy always plots to make people distrust one another and set them at odds with each other to disintegrate our ranks from within. You must learn to discern clearly and to combat such plots and slanders by the counter-revolutionaries. Party members should be educated in such a way that they can distinguish spies, waverers, nepotists, parochialists and factionalists.

Such a struggle can be conducted properly only when the cadres and all the members of the Party are on a high level. Without attaining a high level of Marxist-Leninist knowledge, Party members cannot properly carry out such a difficult duty. In order to enable them to fight skillfully against the counter-revolutionaries, it is necessary to intensify their Marxist-Leninist education and, at the same time, to acquaint them extensively with the experience of the fight against the counter-revolutionaries.

Further, the work of propaganda and agitation should be stepped up among the broad masses. Education of the masses of the people in socialist ideology should be the main content of the work of propaganda and agitation. What is most important in this connection is to give the workers and peasants, especially the workers, a clear understanding that they are masters of power. When they have such intense consciousness, the workers will do everything as masters—take good care of their places of work, machines and equipment, work hard, maintain good discipline, and effectively combat counter-revolutionaries.

The same is true of the peasants. If they realize that the working class is not only their ally but also their leader, and that they too are masters of power, the peasants will work their land well, take good care of their implements and willingly pay the tax in kind.

Everyone will show enthusiasm when he realizes that he is

master. When we were engaged in revolutionary activities in the past, who could ever have got us to do so for money? We fought without sleep, forgetting hunger, because we had realized that by making a revolution we could not only improve our own lot but also save our country. The workers will likewise throw all their energy and zeal into their work when they become clearly aware that their labour is for their own happiness and for the prosperity of society.

Long, persistent education is needed to get all the working people to have such consciousness. We must patiently educate the masses and unite them around our Party still more closely.

In conclusion, I should like to make a few remarks about our newspapers. Our papers still fail to discharge their duties fully.

The central task of *Rodong Sinmun,* our Party organ, is to educate the Party members through day-to-day explanation of the Party's lines and policies and their fighting tasks; the central task of *Minju Choson* is to mobilize the masses to implement the policies of the state by explaining to them and giving them a full understanding of the laws and regulations of the people's power and the policies of the state. The organs of the General Federation of Trade Unions, the Democratic Youth League, and other organizations should likewise be edited in accordance with their respective characteristics and tasks.

Our newspapers have no specific features to distinguish one from another. This is a big failing. Whether this is because they are all furnished with material by the Korean Central News Agency or because some of them are limited in space, I do not know.

Here, too, much formalism and dogmatism are noted. I think it necessary for you to look into this matter seriously.

I have so far touched upon some problems arising in the ideological work of our Party. I hope you will take account of them, eliminate the shortcomings hitherto revealed and strive to raise our Party's ideological work to a higher level.

FOR INNOVATION IN CONSTRUCTION WORK

Speech Delivered at a National Conference of Architects and Builders

January 30, 1956

1

Comrades,

The National Conference of Architects and Builders, which has been in session for several days now, is of tremendous significance in the development of construction work. The reason is, above all, that this conference can make a contribution to innovating our construction work with new methods. This is exactly what I want to emphasize to you at this conference.

And why is it necessary for us now to innovate construction work by new, advanced methods?

First, because the volume of our construction will not remain at the present level, but will increase continuously in keeping with the development of the national economy, and everything we are now building is different in quality from what it was in the past.

As you know, we have been carrying on the rehabilitation and construction of the war-ravaged national economy during three postwar years. In these three years we have done a tremendous amount of work. Indeed, the achievements have been indescribably great. The blast and open-hearth furnaces of the major factories such as the Hwanghae Iron Works, Kim Chaek Iron Works and Songjin Steel Plant have been restored and are turning out pig iron and steel; scores of machine factories including Machine Plant No. 11, Pukjung and Rakwon Machine Plants have been rehabilitated and constructed and put into operation; the Hungnam Fertilizer Factory has also been rehabilitated in part and is now capable of turning out over 100,000 tons of chemical fertilizer. Many light industry factories such as the Pyongyang and Kusong Textile Mills have been newly built and are producing necessaries of life for the people. In Pyongyang and other major cities a considerable number of working people's dwellings and cultural and educational establishments have been erected. The railways have also been restored to ensure transport service. Quite a few irrigation works, including the Pyongnam irrigation project, are under way in various localities for the development of agriculture.

Needless to say, these great achievements have not been attained without difficulty. They have been registered because our workers, technicians, office employees, leading functionaries of the Party and the state and the entire people have unreservedly thrown into action all their talents and enthusiasm, courageously overcoming all difficulties and hardships. They serve as a basis for us to undertake construction today on a larger scale and in a modern way.

This success, however, is only an initial step when viewed in the light of what we are going to do in the future.

What our ancestors had built in our country over thousands of years was reduced to ashes in the barbarous destruction wrought by the enemy during the past three-year war. We should not only restore them completely in a short space of time but also build more, and build in a more attractive and grand way. In view of these tasks the successes achieved in our work are only initial ones.

By now we have restored and built quite a few factories and enterprises, but only partly; as yet we cannot regard them as completed. In order to completely restore and build those factories and wind up the construction of those now projected, we still have a lot of work to do.

In the metallurgical field, for example, the blast furnace of the Kim Chaek Iron Works has been rehabilitated, but its by-products shop, coke oven, etc., are yet to be rebuilt; the revolving furnace of the Chongjin Steel Plant is also in need of rehabilitation, which is partially envisaged in the plan for this year.

What is most urgent for us now is to produce more pig iron and rolled steel. But at the Hwanghae Iron Works, too, only a few rolling shops and open-hearth furnaces are in operation and the blast furnaces have not yet been restored. The Kangson Steel Plant also needs further expansion.

In the power industry, the Supung Hydroelectric Power Station has been partly rehabilitated, but its full-scale repair work has not yet been started. Besides, the Changjin-gang and Pujon-gang Hydroelectric Power Stations have likewise been only partly rebuilt, with preparations for their overall rehabilitation now under way.

In the chemical industry, too, a lot of work lies ahead for full rehabilitation of the Hungnam Fertilizer Factory, the Pongung Chemical Plant, dyestuff and pharmaceutical factories, and so on.

The same applies to the engineering industry. The Pukjung and Rakwon Machine Plants should be further expanded, and Machine Plant No. 3 and the Pyongchon-ri Integrated Works should also be constructed. In the future, the Tokchon Automobile Repair Works should also be built completely into a plant with its assembly shop.

As can be seen, our tasks in the field of heavy industry alone are tremendous.

In light industry, too, many things have to be done in order to further increase the production of the essentials of life. Dye factories should be built, cotton textile mills and silk mills expanded continuously and daily necessaries factories newly erected.

As for urban construction, work has just been started in

Pyongyang and Hamhung, while the rehabilitation of other major cities is in the preparatory stage. A considerable number of houses for working people, clubhouses, theatres, hospitals, creches, bathhouses and public dining rooms have been built, but they are still far from meeting the requirements of our working people.

Thus, we have done a great deal of work in the past period, and yet this is just the beginning, in view of our future tasks. That is why we have no right whatever to become complacent, nor do we have any grounds to become arrogant. We must not be elated by our initial successes, but must build more from now on.

It is impossible to fully ensure such a huge amount of construction by the methods now used. We should innovate our work with new methods. This is precisely the question which has been discussed by many comrades for several days.

And we should do our construction work at a high level of quality for the future. Until now we have carried on only the work of rebuilding destroyed factories, and the number of factories newly erected is as yet small. Construction of new factories is about to begin. As for the housing question, most of the dwellings built hitherto are for temporary or semi-permanent use. From now on, however, modern, three- to four-storey blocks of flats should be built in urban communities. This means that our construction should undergo a qualitative change. It also implies that since we are engaged in the building of socialism, all the facilities should be well suited to the needs of the working people—the builders of socialism.

It is therefore imperative that we introduce new methods in construction.

Another necessity of employing new methods in construction arises from the labour situation. We need to take new organizational measures to economize labour power. This is an important matter. Never before in the history of our country has the question of economizing labour power been raised as so important a matter as today.

When the Japanese imperialists were ruling our country,

the national industry could not develop and, owing to their colonial rule, swarms of unemployed were roaming the towns and villages. Under the circumstances, the Japanese imperialists did not feel a labour shortage in building their colonial industry in Korea, and could get as much labour power as they wanted at a bargain. Therefore, the Japanese imperialists did not need to modernize production facilities in Korea; they worked us Koreans like slaves, by very barbaric methods of exploitation. In those days the Japanese did not feel it necessary to introduce mechanization in production and construction, nor were they capable of doing so.

During the five years of peaceful construction following the August 15 Liberation, we just rehabilitated the factories destroyed by the Japanese imperialists, and did not build many new ones. At that time, as the war had caused little damage to the factories, cultural establishments and dwelling houses, the need for construction was not so great as today and, accordingly, the question of labour power did not come to the fore. It could be said that labour power was sufficient to keep abreast of the building tempo at that time.

However, we lost no small number of workers in the war and, moreover, since we are merely in a state of ceasefire at present, with a lasting peace not yet achieved, and the U.S. imperialists and their stooges, the traitorous Syngman Rhee clique, are all out to unleash a new war, we are obliged continuously to assign the necessary number of young and middle-aged men to national defence. Under these circumstances, as we endeavour to rapidly rebuild the war-ravaged national economy, we inevitably come to feel the shortage of labour power. We must deeply realize how important the question of labour power is today.

Especially this year, the question of labour power has become still more serious. For a certain period following the armistice, labour power was concentrated mainly in rehabilitating and building factories, but the demand for labour power is further increasing today when many factories have already been rehabilitated partly or completely and have started production, while, at the same time, rehabilitation and construction are being carried on. In other words, up until recently the major emphasis in labour distribution was put on rehabilitation and construction, but at present, with production going on along with construction, a huge amount of labour power has to be allocated to production as well as to restoration and construction.

Thus, a great deal of labour power is required by the rapidly developing national economy and the steadily expanding scale of construction. But our sources of labour are extremely limited.

Let us take a look at the situation in the rural areas which ought to supply labour power to the growing industries. The rural areas, which have to meet the needs of the state for food, find themselves very short of labour power, let alone supplying labour to industry.

That is why the Party and the Government are increasing investments in agriculture and, while paying close attention to the socialist transformation of agriculture, have started to allocate discharged soldiers and a considerable number of other work hands to the countryside since last year. These are important measures for ensuring the proportionate development of industry and agriculture in our country.

But this does not mean a thorough solution to the question of labour power in the rural areas today. It will take considerable time to solve the question of labour power in the countryside. This problem will be solved only when socialist co-operativization has gained further in scope and organization of labour has been further improved in the rural areas, and mechanization—though of an initial character, in other words, small-scale mechanization—is widely introduced in agriculture.

As you see, the countryside is not in a position to supply the labour power needed for industrial construction. The only way out of this lies in economizing labour power by rational organization of work and mechanization, and particularly in economizing labour in the field of construction, and diverting the released manpower to rapidly expanding production and to new construction. Otherwise, the speed of production and construction cannot be increased, nor can the development of the national economy be guaranteed.

Mechanization in construction is essential not only to ensure modern construction and make up for the labour shortage but to ease the hard toil of workers and improve and impart culture to their working conditions. We can no longer confine ourselves to hard manual labour. We must free ourselves from it as soon as possible. This is precisely the path to socialism.

Can we cope with this problem? Certainly, we can, and we must. The Party and the Government have already pointed out the importance of this problem in detail, and at the present conference many comrades have put forward widely divergent views to solve it.

2

In connection with this problem, I would like to remind you of the question I posed to you already at the Conference of Builders in March 1954. At that time, we called for introduction of advanced experience in construction—standardization and specification of designs, industrialization of the production of building materials and mechanization of construction, etc.—basic to achieving a faster tempo and better quality in construction.

The Sixth Plenary Meeting of the Central Committee of the Workers' Party of Korea, in its resolution, set forth the mechanization of construction as an important task.

However, we have so far failed either to learn such advanced methods in full or to introduce them. It is true that, as a call to learn was issued at that time, some did learn and some others did not. So let us admit that it was not actively carried out.

But nowadays we must not just shout the slogan of learning, we must energetically learn and act with energy too. Active introduction of the advanced experience in construction accumulated by brother countries is the way to economize and make a rational use of labour power, the way to cope successfully with the increasing volume of construction, further step up its tempo and raise its quality. Can we do so? Of course, we can. Some organizations have already introduced the standardization of designs, industrialization of the production of building materials and mechanization of construction partially and in rudimentary form, though not perfectly.

You have said in your speeches that it is convenient to erect buildings according to standard designs; that in multi-storied buildings it is expedient to use staircases, trusses and beams made by industrial methods according to standard designs, and to produce and put to use large quantities of door frames of the same size; you have also said that it is good to bring scattered wood-working shops together and lay tiles by assembly-line methods. Such experiences demonstrate that we are fully able to standardize designs, industrialize the production of building materials and mechanize construction.

And we are now fully capable of applying advanced building methods not only because we have gained experience but also because material conditions for it have been created to a certain degree. In 1953 or 1954, it was impossible for us to use advanced methods in construction, however hard we might have tried. We were then very short of bricks, cement and steel reinforcements, and were seriously lacking in machines, too. But we now have machine plants, and bricks, steel reinforcements and cement are being turned out.

Besides, we are receiving aid from the Soviet Union, China and other fraternal countries, and learning advanced building methods at first hand in the course of building many factories and cities with their technical assistance.

What, then, should we do, if we are to effectively introduce advanced building methods—standardization and specification of designs, industrialization of the production of building materials and mechanization of construction?

(1) ON STANDARDIZATION AND SPECIFICATION OF DESIGNS

Why are standardization and specification of designs necessary?

The standardization and specification of designs make construction work easier, save you labour power and make it possible to industrialize the production of building materials. In former times, for example, the carpenter had to measure the door frames for every house and fit the doors into them. But today when designs have been standardized and specified, the only job is to produce doors of the same size in large quantities and fit them. This makes it possible to raise the quality of buildings, to increase the speed of construction and to do a lot of work with a smaller number of skilled workers.

Except for individual factories and special buildings, the standardization and specification of designs can be applied equally in the construction of many buildings, above all, dwellings, public buildings, clubhouses, schools, clinics, hospitals, theatres, and facilities of a sort attached to factories. This is now done in the Soviet Union and other socialist countries, too.

We should introduce these methods actively. In our country where designers are scarce and persons with rich experience in construction are few in number, the standardization and specification of designs become all the more essential. This acquires particular importance in the light of the tremendous construction we have undertaken. How can we draw up a design for each building when we are short of designers? It is impossible.

We, therefore, should consider the standardization and specification of designs to be the law in construction. Otherwise, we can neither increase the tempo nor raise the quality of construction in our country.

And only by standardization and specification of designs will it be possible to reduce building costs and build more with limited funds.

We should therefore begin by standardizing designs in order to industrialize construction.

Further, the designs should by all means be socialist in content. Advanced architectonics requires the designs to be national in form and socialist in content.

What do we mean by socialist content in architecture? In short, it means showing concern for the people. This means that all buildings should meet the requirements of the working people.

We are now engaged in socialist construction in the northern half of the Republic. All the dwellings and public buildings we are now constructing will be used by the builders of socialism. Then, how can we furnish the working people with buildings which are void of socialist content?

But many of our designers fail to embody socialist realism in their designs. Some of our construction workers still pay only lip service to socialist realism in construction, and they are not in fact making designs in accordance with socialist realism in architectural art. In many buildings we find the stoves do not burn well in winter, sunlight is ill admitted and ventilation is poor, causing considerable inconveniences in the life of the working people.

Such things can be explained by the fact that some of our designers do not stand pat on the ideological viewpoint of the working class. In other words, this stems from the fact that some of the designing workers, captivated by the old bourgeois ideological viewpoint, have not rid themselves of the non-class attitude that they could do things perfunctorily for the workers. A relentless struggle should be waged against such ideas.

Another serious thing is that bourgeois formalism finds expression in architecture. Buildings which are ostentatious but of little utility are something like the folk saying: A wild apricot is showy but does not taste good. This is bourgeois formalism. A vigorous struggle should also be waged against this kind of tendency.

We are socialistic and not capitalistic builders. We need socialist buildings which are good-looking, useful, cosy and durable. All our builders, as befitting builders of socialism armed with socialist ideology, should carry out construction in a way congenial to the requirements of the working people. So, the designing of dwellings should not be done carelessly as it is now, but should always be performed in such a way as to provide convenience to the life of the working people, agree with the customs and sentiments of the Koreans and ensure good lighting, good ventilation and good heating. In this way, we must see to it that all the working people live in houses which are convenient, safe and provided with good sanitary conditions.

Some functionaries seem to be inclined even to think that such buildings are too good for our working people. This is very wrong.

The same is the case with the public buildings. I went and saw many of the public buildings we erected, and found them very poorly furnished. The public buildings we build ought to be ones that will not only satisfy the working people, but also have educational value, capable of remoulding the working people on socialist lines.

But some of our public buildings look like garages, and quite a few of them just have huge porticoes and are entirely lacking in utility. Carrying out their work in this way, certain people think it easy and not much of a job to build a theatre or a clubhouse. It is clear that such buildings cannot meet the convenience of the working people, let alone having any educational value for them.

Another important question in construction is to build many service establishments such as public dining rooms, laundries and creches so as to enlist women in socialist construction. It is of tremendous importance to create conditions for everybody to live in a way worthy of a socialist builder, remould his consciousness along socialist lines and render service to socialist construction.

Things are still not going well in the building of factories, too. Our factories are schools for the working people, and great living quarters for them where they, and their descendants, will spend their lives in creative labour. Our builders, however, as yet pay little attention to this. To be workers' living quarters, factories should have good lighting, good ventilation and be provided with sanitary facilities and safety devices. But some of our factories are lacking in these conditions.

Yet another important question is to combat wastage in designing. In capitalist architectural art, much material and money is used wastefully for the sake of extravagant exterior appearance. We cannot adopt that way in construction. Our designs should be against formalism and proceed from the standpoint of economy. Only in this way can we build more and better and provide good living conditions for the working people.

In the planning of urban construction, too, emphasis should be put on ensuring convenience for the broad sections of the working people.

(2) ON INDUSTRIALIZING THE PRODUCTION OF BUILDING MATERIALS

The industrialization of the production of building materials poses itself as an important question in construction. To undertake construction by new methods according to standard designs, the production of building materials should also be industrialized.

In view of our present conditions, we should start with simple things rather than big ones in industrializing the production of building materials. Let us start with doors and door frames, aside from other things. And production of staircases, beams, inter-floor slabs, and trusses, too, can be industrialized by using reinforced concrete. This, at least, is the industrialization of production of building materials.

In their speeches many comrades have referred to the industrialization of the production of building materials and to the question of installing machines in building-materials factories. What they have said is good, indeed.

But, first of all, we should bring the scattered factory equipment together and gradually replace handicraft methods with industrial methods, instead of trying to install big machines all at once.

Only by industrializing the production of building materials, is it possible to supply construction sites with large quantities of building materials and guarantee the quality of buildings. We have tried this ourselves, too. Several enterprises in Pyongyang have tried it in a simple, small way and the results are all good.

We must build many reinforced concrete plants. As a matter of fact, there is nothing to be wondered at in such reinforced concrete plants. We can and must do all such things in the future.

But under the present conditions, it is important to start with small things rather than big ones. If we produce building materials in a concentrated way even by small-scale methods and use them in construction work, instead of placing our hope on the construction of reinforced concrete plants alone, we can economize enormous amounts of labour power, speed up the tempo and improve the quality of construction. This is important. Even if we cannot carry out all of our construction by prefab methods, we should industrialize part of it at least.

Construction will be started this year of a reinforced concrete plant with a production capacity of 50,000 tons in Hamhung and another with a production capacity of 45,000 tons in Pyongyang. However, we should not just wait for them, but should first set up reinforced concrete workshops everywhere by widely applying even the small-scale methods which are now used by the construction trusts under the Ministry of Transport or the Ministry of Construction.

In the manufacture of wooden furniture, too, it is necessary to bring carpenters together, not dispersing them.

My recent conversations with many comrades show that we can industrialize the work of collecting and selecting gravel, and mechanize its transportation. The problem is that we do not tackle it. Much labour can be saved if specialized trusts are organized to collect gravel and sand, instead of doing it separately as now. Yet, even such a simple method has not been adopted. We must put an end to such non-creative practices in our work.

Also important in the production of building materials is the question of using cement widely as a building material in the future. At present we are not so rich in cement, but plenty of it will be produced in the future. Cement will be more abundant with us than timber and iron, because limestone is found everywhere in our country and more cement factories can be set up. It is, therefore, important to substitute timber and iron by cement in construction. Sleepers, electric poles, mineprops and girders of railway bridges can be made of cement. We have to proceed in this direction in the future.

Even in a country like the Soviet Union which is rich in timber and steel reinforcements, steel and timber are economized to the utmost and reinforced concrete is used in their place. Why should we not do the same when we are neither rich in timber nor in steel? We must do so without fail. The building-materials factories should advance boldly towards mass production of reinforced concrete parts.

Building materials decide the fate of construction. Because we fail to produce sufficient building materials today, we cannot carry out construction as we should, and at some construction sites there are cases where work is discontinued due to the shortage of building materials. We are short of timber, steel and bricks. It is therefore necessary to further mechanize the building-materials industry to mass-produce building materials.

Our building-materials industry is still lagging. So far we have paid little attention to the building-materials industry and made small investments in it. Some comrades thought the production of building materials was a very easy job, and considered that bricks could be produced without any trouble merely by setting up kilns and putting moulded pieces of clay in them. But that, too, requires technical skill and art. Last year, we became aware of this defect and began to pay attention to it. We have made larger investments in this field beginning this year.

It is also important to mechanize transportation in the building-materials industry. I have mentioned this question many times, but no action has been taken as yet.

We can take, as an example, the process of transporting bricks from the Kangnam Ceramic Factory to construction sites in Pyongyang. If we make iron baskets for carrying bricks and install cranes at the piers, we can put the bricks coming out of the kilns in them and carry them by handcart to the piers, to be loaded on boats by cranes, and upon arrival in Pyongyang by boat, the bricks can be delivered to construction sites with very little labour power and in a simple way, if cranes unload them from the boats directly onto trucks for transportation. But at present we carry bricks coming out of kilns on our own backs, load them onto trucks and unload them at the piers, where we again carry them on our backs to load on boats. Upon arrival in Pyongyang, they are unloaded again on our backs and loaded onto trucks for the second time, to be delivered to construction sites, where bricklayers, too, carry them on their backs.

Large numbers of bricks are damaged in the course of such repeated loadings and unloadings. This is a backward method of work our ancestors used hundreds of years ago. How can we, who are building a socialist society, do work today in this way?

Our country can produce as many small-size cranes as we want, which are needed in mechanizing the transportation of bricks. The Party Central Committee already raised this question long ago. We asked the Kangnam Ceramic Factory, first of all, to effect mechanization. When asked to make iron baskets for conveying bricks, the factory made a trial basket, and it was dragged around the courtyard of the Cabinet building. But we have heard no more of it of late.

Things being done in this way, not only is labour wasted in construction and production, but also an enormous amount of labour power is used wastefully in the transportation of building materials. Therefore, the workers in the building-materials industry should without fail introduce mechanization in the transportation of building materials.

In his speech yesterday, the manager of the Ryongsong Machine Plant said that machines could be supplied only after his plant had received bricks and cement first. It seems to me, however, that machine plants should first produce and supply good machines to the building-materials industry. Then, they will be able to get large quantities of building materials at an early date.

We have to pay more attention to the building-materials industry and make greater efforts to industrialize the production of building materials.

Now, it is very important to tap local materials widely and use them in construction. According to the speeches of many comrades, there are no few cases of the wrong practice of not properly utilizing local materials, of often retransporting materials, and so on. In view of the scale of our construction it is extremely important to mobilize local materials and use them widely.

Some comrades insist recklessly on building only brick houses. This is wrong. Other comrades say that the adobe houses are temporary ones and only brick houses are permanent. The interpretation of the terminology may differ, but, in my opinion, a permanent house means a house of long durability and a temporary house, short. And adobe houses could be so built as to be no less durable than brick houses. Yet, many believe that permanent houses must be built with bricks, and are thinking of building only brick houses even in farm villages and mining areas.

Another good example of failing to make use of local materials was cited by a comrade in his speech yesterday. According to him, in Ryonggang bricks are brought from other places for the foundation work of buildings, while good stones dug out there are carried and thrown away. What reason can there be to say that bricks are better for laying the foundation of buildings and what grounds can there be to argue that stones are worse than bricks? There can be no such grounds. In laying the foundations of buildings, the stones dug out on the spot would be better than the bricks brought from far away. Nobody would do such a thing except bureaucrats who sit at their desk and carry out state business in a perfunctory manner.

Last year when I visited Machine Plant No. 99, I saw quite a lot of good granite around it, which we can hardly obtain in urban areas even if we try to. In a country where building stones are scanty, granite has to be brought even from thousands of miles away for important construction projects. Nevertheless, this factory threw away all the stones dug out in large quantities while building the plant and was planning to build dwellings with bricks to be brought from Pyongyang.

I asked the manager of the factory which was more advantageous and less expensive, brick or stone. In reply, the manager said that it was advantageous to the factory to use bricks, while it seemed it was profitable to the state to use stones. Then, is the factory an organization independent of the state? All our factories are enterprises belonging to the state. Therefore, a factory manager should not separate his factory from the state in making any economic calculation, but should always think of it in relation to the state and proceed from the standpoint of the state.

When they say it is advantageous to the factory to use bricks, they have no other reason than that it is easier to use bricks than to use stones in building houses. So, I asked if it was not true that bricks were bought with money and stones could be obtained for nothing. Only then did the manager honestly admit that using stones was more profitable. As can be seen, they are not concerned about utilizing local materials.

Even at a mine located in such a mountainous area as Koksan, people are anxious to build only brick houses. If they do so, the cost of dwellings will be very high. Why can they not build stone or adobe houses in such places?

In the area of Kanggye, too, there are people who are eager to bring bricks from Pyongyang and build only brick houses.

Thus, they only ask for bricks in disregard of state interests and without using local materials.

Comrades, what is wrong with turning out adobe locally? Why should adobe houses with stone foundations be worse than brick houses?

We must consider it an important task to make wide use of local materials. Otherwise, it will be impossible to unfold a broad mass campaign for construction, and it will likewise be impossible to accelerate the speed of construction. An extensive movement should be developed to erect public buildings, schools and public health and cultural establishments in county seats by utilizing such local materials as adobe and stones, and the people should be taught such methods.

We have decided to undertake construction projects costing approximately 600 million *won* this year through a broad mass movement, in addition to the construction to be carried out with materials supplied by the state. The utilization of local materials, namely, adobe and stones, is scheduled in such projects. This is the only way that the county seats can be built and villages and workers' settlements be got up rapidly.

At present the state encourages not only individual peasants but also factory and office workers to build many dwellings by making available to them state loans and supplying them with some materials. Only in this way is it possible to build many houses and expedite our construction.

(3) ON THE MECHANIZATION OF CONSTRUCTION

This, too, is not a question that has been raised for the first time today. Everybody will say mechanization is good and there are none who will say it is bad. Yet, little attention has been paid to it.

Even though we are not in a position to introduce large-scale mechanization now, we are capable of effecting partial and small-scale mechanization, and we must start with that. To carry things on wheelbarrows instead of on the human back is also a sort of mechanization, because the wheelbarrow is more advanced and efficient than the human back.

If full-scale mechanization is impossible, it is imperative to introduce partial mechanization at least and to carry out mechanization in construction and production by switching over from manual labour to small-scale mechanization, comprehensive mechanization, and then to automation, by the method of gradually going over from the simple to the complex, and from the imperfect to the perfect. Only by so doing can labour be saved and cultural standards and productivity of labour be raised.

For this purpose, it is important, above all, to utilize the existing machines rationally. Statistics show that the number of machines we now possess is not small. Compared with prewar times, the number of machines in our possession has increased considerably. After the war, we received a large number of building machines from the Soviet Union and other fraternal countries. In the first place, they should be properly distributed so that the right persons may use them, and their operation rate should be raised, not allowing them to stand idle.

According to the report, most of the building machines are operated for one shift, and they are not worked full time at that. Why can we not work in two or three shifts a day under the present conditions in which we are short of building machines? This is a question connected with the thinking of the workers in this field. Everyone must strive to make rational use of the existing machines.

Further. To get the most out of existing machines, we must put the repair shops in proper order and supply spare parts in good time. Work is often suspended because spare parts are not supplied and machines not repaired on time.

Besides, no system has been established for making the necessary checkups on machines. When machines get out of order, they are neglected and left abandoned for weeks. This is a serious crime against the state and the people. It is important to handle the machines with care, supply spare parts in good time, and systematically carry out the work of repairing and checking machines.

Another important thing is to manufacture large quantities

of small building machines. Experience shows that all factories which have lathes or other metal-cutting machines can make small building machines.

Some of our functionaries, however, have the wrong tendency to refuse to make such small machines and instead try to make only big ones, the production of which is difficult. For instance, the Bureau of Irrigation Administration has produced big pumps. I advised the bureau chief to stop producing pumps, suggesting that it would be preferable to make many wheelbarrows needed for irrigation works. This is because big pumps are being produced in highly skilled, specialized machine plants, and, moreover, the ones turned out in those plants are qualitatively superior. If it takes 10 man-days to make a big pump at a specialized factory, it would be hard to make one even in 100 man-days under the Bureau of Irrigation Administration. Therefore, the need to manufacture machinery should not lead every building organization to jump recklessly at anything. It is advisable for them to start producing a great deal of simple machines, the production of which is within their power and which they need.

We must start with the production of simple wheelbarrows and then proceed to the production of winches, mixers, small-size cranes and all the other things we can make, which will make it possible to mechanize construction work. The enterprises under the Bureau of the Engineering Industry and the First Bureau should be given higher production quotas for building machines. The State Planning Commission should organize this.

We have to push ahead energetically with the mechanization of construction work in this way. We have no other way. Some people suggest that we drop this because we are busy. Those who insist on this are passive elements who want to give up socialist construction. We must not compromise with such elements. However busy we may be, we must do what we have to do. Otherwise, it is impossible to raise the living standard of the people, improve the appearance of our towns, and build the foundation of socialism. Of course, many difficulties lie before us. But such difficulties can be overcome.

Parallel with mechanization in construction, labour should be organized rationally and an active struggle be waged against all sorts of waste of labour power. In order to organize labour rationally, defects in the organizational system should be eliminated, first of all. Now, some workers in the field of construction have contracted the "construction trust disease." People in Chongjin seem to be suffering seriously from this malady. So, they should be given a remedy for the "construction trust disease."

We must merge the scattered construction trusts and amalgamate the needlessly dispersed gravel-collecting yards in a rational way. It would also be good to merge, in a proper manner, the small construction stations owned respectively by various organs. If enterprises are thus merged in a rational way, wastage of labour power can also be eliminated. We should fight the tendency towards departmentalism in construction work.

Likewise, steps should be taken to settle cadres down in the field of construction, to heighten the technical and skill levels of building workers, and prevent labour turnover. In particular, it is important to establish the work carry-over system in the construction of buildings. The work carry-over system is necessary also to settle the workers down and to raise their technical and skill levels.

Measures should be taken to enable the workers to acquire various skills and enlist even their dependent family members actively in production. When incidental labour power is widely used even in agricultural co-operatives, why should it not be used in construction enterprises? In the sphere of construction, too, we should extensively introduce the man-day piece-work system and utilize incidental labour power in a large measure.

Through all these measures, 20,000-25,000 men's labour power should be saved this year in the field of construction alone. Is this possible? Yes, it is. According to the results of investigations conducted in each branch, rational organization of labour alone, without mechanization, can save 20,000 men's labour power, and if small-scale mechanization is partially introduced, up to 25,000 men's labour can be saved quite easily. Tremendous reserves exist for saving labour power now in the field of construction.

In order to encourage the saving of labour power, extra wages corresponding to the amount of labour saved should be given to the workers as a bonus. We mean that if a quota of work to be done by 100 men is performed by 80 men, the money equivalent to the wages of 20 men should be given to the 80 men as bonus. This is not only beneficial to the workers themselves, but very profitable to the state as well.

In conclusion, I should like to make a few more remarks. First, the question of economizing on materials. The Party has appealed for this on a number of occasions. Materials fall short of the ever-expanding scale of construction. Therefore, the control of materials should be tightened and an extensive movement launched for economizing them.

We must make it a rule to use everything to the full, be it a nail, a piece of brick, or a handful of cement. Many factories such as lumber mills, iron works, steel plants and machine factories should set up subsidiary workshops for utilizing the refuse, so as not to throw away such things as pieces of lumber, sawdust and iron scraps that are turned out in the course of production, but make the most of them. This is very important.

Second, I should like to refer to the strengthening of the cost-accounting system in the field of construction. The cost-accounting system should be strengthened in such a way as, above all, to give the workers more material incentives and stimulate their productive zeal. Along with this, the contracting system should also be strengthened. Many shortcomings exist so far in this respect.

Since the cost-accounting system in the building organizations has not been established properly, no clear-cut limits of responsibility have been drawn between the truster organizations and the constructors, and this causes considerable difficulties to the financial activities of the enterprises. We should, therefore, take every possible measure to strengthen the cost-accounting system and the contracting system in the field of construction.

Third, personnel in building organizations and enterprises should be armed with the ideology of the working class. In order to correctly carry out all the above-mentioned tasks and bring about innovation in construction, all workers, technicians, office employees and leading personnel of the building organizations and enterprises should be thoroughly armed with Marxist-Leninist ideology in accordance with the spirit of the April Plenary Meeting of the Party Central Committee.

How can our construction workers—the builders of socialism—build socialism without arming themselves with socialist ideology? You are honourable socialist builders. So you cannot fulfil your tasks if you retain the backward feudal or capitalist ideologies. Being socialist builders, we should necessarily arm ourselves with socialist ideology.

Backward, conservative ideologies are the main obstacle in the domain of construction now. We must all fight against them. Conservatism hampers progress everywhere, and holds back the advancing workers. We must wage an intense struggle against conservatism, and thus completely overcome the wrong ideological tendency of sticking to outmoded building methods and bring about a turn in construction work.

Last, I call, through this conference, on all the builders, workers, technicians and office employees to become profoundly conscious of the necessity for innovating construction work now, with new methods, and to come forward for its realization in the struggle for victoriously carrying out the huge capital construction to build socialism. I am firmly convinced that you will fulfil this task with honour.

TASKS OF THE PARTY ORGANIZATIONS IN NORTH PYONGAN PROVINCE

Speech Delivered at a Party Conference of North Pyongan Province

April 7, 1956

I am attending the Party conference of North Pyongan Province by decision of the Political Committee of the Party Central Committee. First, I offer congratulations, on behalf of the Central Committee of the Party, to the Party organizations in North Pyongan Province and to the representatives attending this conference on the great achievements in their work.

In the past period the North Pyongan provincial Party organization, under the leadership of the Party Central Committee, has correctly acquitted itself of its work in the main. As was also pointed out in the report on the work of the Provincial Party Committee, the North Pyongan provincial Party organization has scored great successes in the work of uniting the entire Party members and working masses around the Party Central Committee, bringing home to the Party members and working people the lines and policies set forth by the Party Central Committee and mobilizing them to the struggle to carry through the Party's policies. We consider that, during the period under review, the provincial Party organization has assured unity of action and ideological cohesion of the Party ranks through a vigorous struggle against all manifestations of wrong tendencies inside and outside the Party, and that it has given Party guidance satisfactorily on the whole to the building of socialism in all political, economic and cultural spheres.

It must be admitted that, while it has scored these successes, the provincial Party organization also has many shortcomings in its work.

I should like to remark on some important tasks confronting the North Pyongan provincial Party organization, on the basis of the contents of the report the Party Central Committee received from the North Pyongan Provincial Party Committee on its work, and of what has been discussed at this conference.

1. ON THE ORGANIZATIONAL AND IDEOLOGICAL STRENGTHENING OF THE PARTY ORGANIZATION

(1) CONCERNING THE ORGANIZATIONAL WORK OF THE PARTY

As everyone knows, our Party adopted the line of expanding the Communist Party beyond its narrow limits to attain to a mass scale, by admitting a larger number of advanced elements from among the workers, peasants and working intellectuals, in conformity with the specific situation created in our country after liberation. Thus, our Party merged with the New Democratic Party, which was a petty bourgeois party, and developed into the Workers' Party of Korea, a mass political party.

This organizational line of the Party was most correct. Because in the Korean revolution, the question of who would come out victorious depended on who won over the broad masses —our working class or the propertied classes. The development of our Party into the Workers' Party of Korea at that time fully accorded with the requirements of the Korean revolution and represented a step of decisive significance for leading the revolution in our country along the right path.

The North Pyongan provincial Party organization, too, under the guidance of the Party centre, has in the main correctly carried out the work of developing the Party into a mass political party, so it now has 128,157 Party members under it. This is a graphic illustration of the provincial Party organization's adherence in its activities to the organizational line of the Party Central Committee.

However, there are also many shortcomings in the organizational work of the provincial Party organization.

Since the Second Party Congress to this day, the North Pyongan provincial Party organization has expelled 18,000 Party members. This figure seems very big to me. It signifies that an average of 2,250 members were driven out of the Party every year. What does this mean? It means that Party members were recruited at random and expelled at random. Accordingly, the Party's organizational work and the work of Party building have not been conducted on a sound basis.

Since the Party is an organized detachment and not an inn, it is unreasonable to admit people and expel them in such a disorderly manner. If a person is admitted to the Party without a careful examination, along the formalities prescribed in the Party Rules, of whether he is qualified for membership or without helping him to make adequate preparations in advance to be worthy of becoming a Party member, and if an enrolled Party member is expelled thoughtlessly on the pretext that he is not up to the standard, the sound growth of the Party organization is impossible. How is it possible to expel 15 per cent of the total Party membership in eight years when it is not a case of purging the Party? The matter has been seriously mismanaged. That was the result of the irresponsibility of the provincial Party organization in its work of increasing Party membership.

Everyone is glad when he is admitted to the Party, but is sure to feel aggrieved if he is expelled from it. Why should we breed disaffected elements like this for no reason? If a comrade were not yet qualified to join the Party, it would have been rather better to make him wait a little longer until he got more education. Then, he would not have felt himself aggrieved but would have tried harder to qualify himself for Party membership.

Because the work was not handled this way, those expelled from the Party may possibly have turned into disaffected elements, at best, and, at worst, into hostile elements. You have done a really reckless thing. This is similar to the action of Ho Ga I who played havoc with the Party.

Following the retreat, Ho Ga I, holding a post in the Party centre, penalized large numbers of Party members. In those days, 450,000 out of the total Party membership of 600,000 were disciplined. Even those who had temporarily buried their Party cards to avoid the enemy's eyes, were subjected to punishment. This was an act of disrupting and liquidating the Party. The North Pyongan provincial Party organization does not seem to have shaken off the evil aftermath of such practices yet.

To prevent this sort of thing, it is necessary, first of all, to be prudent in recruiting Party members. When the draft of the Rules was discussed, some comrades suggested that the term of probationary membership be made longer or that the number of endorsers be increased. That, too, deserves consideration. But the question does not lie here. It is more important for the primary, county and provincial Party organizations to make good preparations for enrolling new Party members. One cannot become a good Party member all by himself even if the probationary term is long. When admitting people to the Party, you ought to accept tested people through the procedure of individual enrolment after giving them education for a year or two, carefully studying the candidates for membership, giving them assignments and training them in the work, bringing them to a thorough understanding of the Party Programme and Rules and explaining the Party's lines and policies to them patiently. This alone will make it possible to prevent impure elements, chance elements and egoists from entering our Party. Once people have been admitted to the Party, it is wrong to expel them because of a slight error.

Our Party is an organized vanguard of the working class

and all the working masses of our country. How is it possible for the Party organization, which leads the revolution and the popular masses, to enrol Party members at random and then kick them out lightly because they are not as desired? Once admitted, a Party member must be educated perseveringly so as not to commit mistakes, and even when he has committed mistakes, he should be helped to correct them and become a more faithful member of the Party.

The Party must always treat its members as a parent would do in bringing up his children. There is no parent who, bringing up his children, does not take scrupulous care to prevent them from going astray. It is quite natural that he always keeps a lookout over his children lest they should go to the river and be drowned, be run over by a vehicle in the street, or tell a lie.

The organizational work of the Party, too, must be done precisely in this way. It is necessary to understand the character, thoughts, merits and demerits of Party members well, and always look after them with care, so that they may not commit grave mistakes. The Party must bring its lines and policies to the knowledge of its members and correct shortcomings in their work in good time. If one has a weakness for wine, advice should be given to him against heavy drinking and he should be admonished against immoral conduct; if he is liable to be influenced by bourgeois ideology, he should be given help in advance to keep him from falling under such influence. In this way, the Party organization must see that none of its members takes a wrong path, and must look after every member with warm affection at all times.

If a Party member, even when given advice, does not heed it but continues to follow the wrong path, he should not be left alone but be given more positive help so that he can get out of his rut. For instance, when a family member falls ill, he should be given proper medicine after diagnosis is made as to whether he has caught cold or developed an internal disorder. Similarly, when a Party member has made a mistake, the cause of the mistake must be traced and an effective, comradely assistance be given to him to rectify the mistake. When a man falls ill, efforts must be made to cure him. If, instead, anyone were to assume that the man is no good, and stuff him into a straw sack and leave him in the public cemetery, everyone would object and reproach such conduct.

It is a fundamental attitude of our Party towards its members to give them comradely education to remedy shortcomings in their thought or conduct. The North Pyongan provincial Party organization has expelled a large number of members from the Party since the Second Party Congress up to now. And this can only mean that the Party organization has failed to treat its members in a parental manner and conducted the organizational work of the Party carelessly and imprudently.

In order to remedy the shortcomings mentioned above, it is necessary for the North Pyongan provincial Party organization to improve the organizational work of the Party and strengthen the work of the organizational departments of the provincial, city and county Party committees.

The Party committees at all levels should not just occupy themselves with rush campaigns, but should always direct their main efforts to the organizational and ideological work of the Party. The leading body of the Party, therefore, should always pay close attention to the work and life of its members and give them proper guidance and help, seeing whether the members or cadres of the Party are working well, and if not, what the reason is, whether they are active or passive in their work, if they are intent on Party studies or not, and so on. Of course, this does not mean that organizational work should be conducted by detective methods as it was done by Pak Yong Bin. Detective methods were used by the Japanese detectives and police. Our provincial, city and county Party committees must not handle their organizational work in this way. And organizational work can by no means be replaced by the registration of Party membership cards or the compilation of penalty statistics.

The organizational department of the Party must keep the Party members under control, educate them and always have a good grasp of their thinking, organize and guide them in their work and conduct. This is fundamental to the organizational work of the Party. The organizational work of the North Pyongan provincial Party organization, however, leaves much to be desired in this respect. This is why I deem it essential for the organizational departments of the Party committees of various levels to further improve and strengthen their work in future in line with what has been mentioned here.

Now I should like to say a few words about the guidance of the Party in both the administrative and economic institutions.

The speakers pointed out that the provincial Party committee and other Party organs at different levels had failed to give concrete Party guidance to the activities of the government bodies, economic institutions and cultural establishments. In my opinion, too, this seems true.

As you know, our Party is the political leader of our people, the leader that guides the country and the people along the path of happiness. The Party plays an organizing and guiding role in all spheres of our life—politics, economy, culture, etc. Under the guidance of the Party, the government bodies, economic institutions, cultural establishments and social organizations implement the Party's lines and policies among the masses. It goes without saying that mismanagement of work by the government bodies, economic institutions and cultural establishments will greatly impede the implementation of the Party's lines and policies. And yet, some Party organs still neglect guidance of the work of the government bodies, economic institutions and cultural establishments.

Some time ago the centre carried out an intensive inspection of the work of the North Pyongan Provincial People's Committee, in the course of which a lot of shortcomings were revealed. Nevertheless, the North Pyongan Provincial Party Committee does not feel itself seriously responsible, from the Party standpoint, for the grave defects manifested in the work of the government body, claiming that everything went wrong due to one person, the chairman of the Provincial People's Committee. This is wrong. Such a tendency implies an attitude on the part of the Party to dodge its political responsibility for the work of government bodies.

It is a very wrong working attitude for the Party organ to remain indifferent towards the work of the government bodies and, especially, to criticize their work behind their backs, instead of giving them guidance and help.

If things went wrong with the work of the North Pyongan Provincial People's Committee, that ought to be considered a failure of the North Pyongan Provincial Party Committee in giving proper guidance in the work of the government body. Experience shows that where the provincial or county people's committees did not do a good job, the Party organizations had in many cases connived at their faults or joined them in doing injustices or, at best, failed to provide effective Party guidance. Even in this best case, things are very serious. Yet, some Party functionaries are wont to think that whenever the work of the government bodies and economic and cultural establishments has gone badly, it is attributable to the poor work on the part of the officials at those bodies and establishments, and that the Party functionaries are not to blame for it. If things are evaluated in this way, will there be any Party member willing to work at an administrative body? Just as the Party members who work at the Party organs are members of the Workers' Party, so the Party members who work at factories, schools, co-operatives, and government bodies are members of the same Workers' Party. There is no difference between them in carrying out the Party's lines and policies, though their domains of activity are different. Can only the work of the functionaries in Party organs be considered to be work for the Party and that of the Party members in the government bodies and economic and cultural establishments not? Absolutely not. Both are work for the Party and for the revolution. We must have a clear understanding of this.

Success in the activities of government bodies and all the economic and cultural establishments rests upon the enthusiasm and sense of responsibility of the Party members and the role of the Party organizations in their respective domains. Then how can the functionaries of the Party organs just sit around appraising or finding fault with the activities of Party members in government bodies and economic and cultural establishments? They must not do so. The provincial, city and county Party committees must always show scrupulous care for the activities of government bodies and economic and cultural establishments, and give intensified guidance to them.

By saying that the Party organs must give responsible leadership to the activities of government bodies, we do not mean on any account that they should snatch away their jobs and rule the roost. Guidance of the work of the government bodies by the Party means making the Party's lines and policies correctly understood through the medium of the Party group of the respective body, organizing and mobilizing the Party members in that body to the struggle for carrying through the Party's policies.

In its guidance of economic establishments, too, the Provincial Party Committee is only working superficially, failing to delve into the processes of production at factories and enterprises. The question of how the working people are faring and working and how production is proceeding should be a matter of day-to-day concern for the Party and the object of its guidance. Even if the responsible workers have made a tour of factories in a car, or if provincial or county Party committees have called meetings and dealt with questions of production, this does not necessarily mean that everything is right with the work of guidance. The question lies not only in the discussion and adoption of decisions at meetings but also in organizing the execution of what has been decided, and in guiding and checking on the execution. Nevertheless, some Party organizations are still guiding economic construction in a very perfunctory way.

The main reason for such a perfunctory guidance of the economic work lies in the Party functionaries' lack of economic knowledge. Because they do not know about the economy, quite a few functionaries are even reluctant to go to factories for guidance. So all the leading Party functionaries must acquire knowledge of the economy. To learn is always a good thing. The prestige of the chairman of a provincial Party committee or county Party committee will not suffer because he learns something he did not know. Some chairmen of agricultural co-operative may not know as much as workteam leaders or individual co-operative members about agro-technique or about advanced methods of farming. If a chairman does not know about wide-row sowing, he must learn from a workteam leader or a co-operative member who does know about it. While he is being taught he may be a pupil, but when he puts it into practice after having learned it, he is a leading functionary.

Another thing that must be emphasized is the strengthening of collective leadership in the work of Party and government bodies at all levels.

There is a saying, "Putting their heads together, three shoemakers are wiser than *Chuko Liang*." And "Pooling their resources, three blind men can read a letter," is also a common saying. These proverbs tell us what great power collective wisdom can display in work.

The provincial, city, and county Party committees and people's committees are all organs of collective leadership. And to ensure collective leadership effectively, it is necessary, first of all, to form committees well. The committees at all levels in the Party and government bodies must be composed of competent workers who are loyal to the Party and the state, and must comprise workers, peasants, economic workers, technicians and cultural workers, too. Only then can the committees advance good creative opinions and form correct judgments on various matters. Suppose a group of people who know nothing about the economy and technology gather together to discuss economic and technological problems. What good opinion can they ever put forth? Of course, they cannot.

Collective leadership does not mean sitting together and holding a meeting where recognized "authorities" make speeches and prepared resolutions are passed. It means discussing and settling every problem with positive participation of all members of the leading body, relying on the creativeness of the broad masses, giving the fullest scope to everyone's abilities and talents, and preventing any arbitrary handling of affairs on the basis of any individual's opinions and assertions.

In this regard, too, the North Pyongan Provincial Party Committee seems to have shortcomings in its work. Plenary meetings of the Provincial Party Committee have been convened few and far between and in many cases they were replaced by meetings of the standing committee. And the work of the Provincial Party Auditing Commission has been dealt with by only a few members of the commission who live in Sinuiju. This proves that collective leadership is not yet thoroughly exercised in the work of the provincial Party organization. I think it necessary for the Party organizations at all levels in the province to bring about decisive improvement in collective leadership in the future.

(2) CONCERNING THE PARTY'S CADRE MANAGEMENT

In my opinion, cadre management, too, is not handled properly in the North Pyongan provincial Party organization. Especially, it appears that some people have a wrong attitude towards the intellectuals.

As the principal of the Sonchon Senior Middle School said in his speech, the role of intellectuals in general, teachers in particular, is underestimated; they are looked at through coloured glasses; and due solicitude and concern are not directed to them. This contravenes our Party's policy towards the intellectuals.

The Party Central Committee has always emphasized that the right attitude should be taken towards the intellectuals, especially those who were educated under Japanese imperialism and served it. We raised this problem already in the early days when the Workers' Party as a mass political party was founded.

Some people speak ill of the intellectuals for having served the Japanese imperialists in the past. They reproach them indiscriminately without making distinctions as to whether they served the Japanese imperialists faithfully or served them against their will, only to earn a living. This is wrong.

We must not see in the same light all the intellectuals who served the Japanese imperialists, the landlords or capitalists in the past, but must make distinctions among them. Because some of the old intellectuals, as agents of Japanese imperialism, betrayed the country and the people and held government posts by currying favour with the Japanese imperialists, the landlords or capitalists, willingly helping those scoundrels in their acts of exploitation, but the absolute majority of the intellectuals served with the firms or educational establishments—organs of the Japanese imperialists—out of the necessity of earning a living, although they had no intention to help Japanese imperialism.

As for the first kind of intellectuals, they were and are the targets of our people's hatred and our people's enemies. Almost all of those fellows are by now no longer in our ranks. Afraid of being punished for their past crimes, they took flight to the side of the enemy immediately after liberation.

As for the absolute majority of old intellectuals, they served the Japanese imperialists, the landlords or capitalists against their will to escape starvation, for in the pre-liberation days there were neither a people's power and Party, nor sufficient conditions to awaken and inspire their national and class consciousness so that they might serve the people. Indeed, the fact itself that they served Japanese imperialism is not commendable in any case. But there was no other alternative for them under the circumstances of those days.

It was after the emergence of our Party and the establishment of the people's power after liberation that a radical change took place in the situation. Since then, our intellectuals—teachers, engineers and artists — under the guidance of our Party have been able to dedicate, at their respective posts, all their knowledge and talents to the upbuilding of the country on the side of the working class. They have not only cast off the shameful fetters of imperialism, landlords and capitalists, but also have become people who, as reliable allies of the workers and peasants, are engaged in worthwhile brain work for the building of a new society and the happiness of the working people.

Thus, a change has taken place today in the position of the intellectuals of our country and in their character. So, unconditional, indiscriminate rejection of old intellectuals is very wrong.

After liberation many good comrades joined our Party from among the old intellectuals. The emblem of our Party, with the design of a sickle, a hammer and a writing brush, symbolizes the character of the Party well. This indicates the firm unity of the working class with the peasants and working intellectuals.

Under the guidance of the Party, the intellectuals outside it, not to speak of those admitted to it, are also working faithfully for the country and the people.

In the early period of the Fatherland Liberation War many of the teachers of our higher educational institutions such as Kim Il Sung University, Kim Chaek Polytechnical Institute, Pyongyang Normal College, etc., went down as far as the Rakdong-gang River area as members of the political workers' group to work in the southern half, in the wake of the People's Army that was advancing, repelling the enemy invasion. No small number of them were old intellectuals. They not only fulfilled their assigned tasks creditably in the southern half, but, even in the difficult period of retreat, they all came back to Chagang Province, hiking over rugged paths thousands of *ri* long across mountains and rivers—with tightened belts, in straw sandals and with the aid of walking sticks.

In the difficult years of the war, our many engineers and assistant engineers worked day and night for victory amid hails of enemy bombs and in a sea of flames, to rehabilitate factories and keep up production and wartime transport. They devoted all their energies and talents to the struggle for the Party and the country.

Even when the schools were lost in the U.S. imperialists' bombings, our people's teachers were not daunted in the least but kept on teaching their pupils out on mountains or in the fields, in dugout class-rooms or at their homes. Thus, they never discontinued the education of the younger generation even for a moment.

What more can we ask of the intellectuals? And what more must they do to be loyal to the Party and the country? If it had not been for the intellectuals, we would have been unable to run factories, railways and schools. Have they rendered services to the Party and the Government? Certainly, they have. They have rendered great services. Why should they be kept at a distance, suspected and left out in the cold? Since the intellectuals are loyal to the Party and serving the country and the revolution, they naturally ought to be loved, respected, educated properly, and always be given warm care. This is our Party's attitude towards the intellectuals.

It seems that some people think as if the old intellectuals must and will be elbowed out of the way when new intellectuals come forward. Such a notion is absolutely wrong. We must give more concern to the old intellectuals and help them patiently in their ideological remoulding. We should thus see to it that all the intellectuals work with greater enthusiasm and faith for the country and the people.

According to the speech made by the principal of the Sonchon Senior Middle School, it seems that intellectuals everywhere are often taken to task for having "intellectual inclinations." That is mistaken. Survivals of old ideology may be found in anybody. You should not blame intellectuals and molest them for their having survivals of old petty-bourgeois ideology, but should correct them kindly.

There is a Korean saying: "In ten years even mountains and rivers will change." And much more, how can men, particularly the intellectuals who are sensitive to things new, have remained unchanged under the people's power? For ten years since liberation, they have been educated by the Party and tested and steeled in the revolutionary struggle and have turned into people's intellectuals armed with the ideas of the working class.

Therefore, it runs counter to our Party's policy towards

the intellectuals to suspect them for no reason, to give them a wide berth, not to promote them to proper positions and not to learn from their knowledge. That is a wrong attitude which tends to make ignoramuses of our Party and the working class. Such an attitude can never be tolerated in our Party.

Workers should learn knowledge and technology from the intellectuals, and the intellectuals should learn organization and revolutionary spirit from the workers. Only when the workers, peasants and working intellectuals are firmly united, help each other and join efforts under the guidance of our Party, can all our work proceed with greater success.

(3) ON ERADICATING DOGMATISM AND FORMALISM IN PARTY WORK

Dogmatism and formalism persist in the work of the Party organizations in North Pyongan Province. Dogmatism and formalism are extremely harmful to our work. We are also going to raise this problem at the Party Congress as an important matter.

Yesterday, the chief of the propaganda department of the Taegwan County Party Committee said in his speech that he had had much trouble to propagandize about the agricultural co-operative movement, because he had committed dogmatic and formalistic errors. According to him, the peasants of his locality would not listen to him when he introduced them to the experiences of the Soviet Union and China in the agricultural co-operative movement, and the experiences acquired in other parts of the country. It was not until he told them about the experiences of the co-operatives in mountainous areas like theirs that they nodded approval. This is a good example showing that when introducing the experiences of the advanced countries or putting Marxist-Leninist principles into practice, one must always apply them creatively to fit in with the specific realities of his country, of his locality or village.

Some people do not have a correct idea of what is meant by

dogmatism. Dogmatism is nothing special. It implies, briefly, an attitude of applying general propositions as they are, or of mechanically copying from the things of others, without taking account of the specific conditions of one's own reality. To speak figuratively, it means swallowing others' things whole.

Let us take a familiar example. A mother rearing a baby has to feed food to the baby with due regard to its growth. Has the baby cut its teeth? If it has, how many? It will not do to feed the baby without taking account of this. When feeding chestnuts to her baby that has not yet got any teeth, she must mash them beforehand, and if the baby has a few teeth, she must slice them into small pieces. If the baby has many teeth, she may feed them to it whole. Suppose a baby with no teeth were given whole chestnuts, it would have an attack of indigestion or stomach troubles, and its health would be injured.

Likewise, dogmatism and formalism are liable to bring grave consequences in the accomplishment of the revolution. That is why we oppose dogmatism and formalism.

It is beyond doubt that when we build a socialist society, the people will come to live a plentiful, happy life. This is a truth. Even this truth, however, can actually be carried to effect in our life only when we apply the Marxist-Leninist principles on socialist construction in a creative way to suit the realities of Korea.

Some comrades, worried that the speed of co-operativization is too fast in the agricultural co-operative movement of our country, insist on going at a somewhat slower rate as in other countries. What is the need for us to go slow when our country has the conditions and possibilities for speedy advance, just because other countries are slow in agricultural co-operativization? There is no need of doing so.

In the Soviet Union, the collective-farm movement only entered the stage of full-scale collectivization over ten years after the revolution, and it took about five years more to complete it basically. That pace, I think, was suited to the specific circumstances in the Soviet Union at that time. In the People's Democracies in Europe, too, the agricultural co-operative movement is proceeding at a much slower rate than in our country. In the northern half of our country, this movement has progressed at a rapid pace in the postwar period. By the end of 1955, 49 per cent of all peasant households had joined the agricultural co-operatives, and as of the end of February this year, 65.6 per cent had joined.

The low rate of co-operativization in the People's Democracies in Europe does not mean that the Communists of those countries do not know how to speed up the agricultural co-operative movement; it is ascribable to the specific political and economic conditions in those countries.

What, then, is at the bottom of such a rapid development of the agricultural co-operative movement in our country?

First, the social forces in the rural areas of our country that oppose the agricultural co-operative movement are quite meagre, due to the thoroughgoing agrarian reform carried out under the guidance of our Party after liberation, to the consistent policy thereafter of restricting the rich farmers, and to the further weakening of their force during the Fatherland Liberation War.

Second, our peasants, fettered to feudal land relations for a long time in the past, not only had the bitter experience of being relentlessly exploited by the Japanese imperialists and the landlords, but also have the precious revolutionary tradition of struggle against them for land, rice and freedom, and have been politically tempered and awakened in the 10 years of struggle for creating a new life after liberation, particularly in the course of the Fatherland Liberation War.

Third, such traditional forms of joint labour as oxen-sharing teams, labour-exchanging teams, etc., were further developed and popularized in our countryside during the war, under conditions in which manpower and draught animals were short; especially the co-operatives organized on an experimental basis in the past period demonstrated vast advantages, greatly inspiring and encouraging the peasants to take the road of co-operativization.

Fourth, our Party, with its correct policy, has always firmly convinced the entire people that the instructions of the Party are unfailingly right, and is correctly leading and guiding the socialist transformation of agriculture by properly applying the Marxist-Leninist theory of agricultural co-operativization and the experiences of other countries to the realities of our country.

All these are the major conditions which have led the peasants actively to join agricultural co-operatives. Also, the swift development of our country's industry in the postwar years has furnished the material basis for rapid strengthening and progress of agricultural co-operatives at present, not only in quantity but also in quality.

It is very wrong to try artificially to slow down the speed of the agricultural co-operative movement without taking into consideration these historical, social and economic conditions, and dampening the enthusiasm of our peasants who are aspiring to socialism, just because co-operativization is going on at a slow rate in other countries. This is shocking dogmatism and formalism.

Our task is therefore to complete agricultural co-operativization in the near future without vacillation, and the propaganda work should also be oriented to this end.

I should like to cite another instance of dogmatism and formalism. Some people think they ought to apply foreign methods even in holding a meeting. The dogmatists, hearing that meetings are held briefly in the Soviet Union, insist that we must also make our meetings brief. This is wrong. It has already been nearly 40 years since the Soviet people succeeded in their revolution. It has been only 10 years since our liberation. How can a 10-year-old boy be treated just like a 40-year-old grown-up? If people are well prepared, we can conduct a meeting briefly. In general, our people fall behind the Soviet people in their levels of awareness, culture and knowledge. If the Soviet comrades take three days to have a meeting, we will have to spend, if necessary, even 5-6 days.

The aim of a meeting lies not in sitting together at one place, but is, first of all, to educate all the participants so that they may have a thorough understanding of the essence of the questions taken up at the meeting and may put them into practice. The meeting is a good school. If a meeting is conducted briefly, after the Soviet style, under our conditions in which the people's level is low, the participants may not grasp well what the meeting has discussed and decided upon, and how.

No success can be expected if, as the formalists insist, people get together, make some glib speeches, clap their hands in applause, cheer and then disperse, or if they merely jot down a few words in their notebooks at the meeting.

Dogmatism and formalism are doing considerable harm to our work of education and teaching as well. Workers in this field seem to think little, and in extreme cases not at all, about what help the subjects they are teaching will be of to the accomplishment of our revolution.

In teaching the history of the Communist Party of the Soviet Union, too, they do not give priority to and lay stress on the questions essential for the revolution in our country today, but just teach it in generalities. What is more serious, they deal little with the questions of our country, questions concerning the Korean revolution.

In our educational and teaching work today, questions essential for the solution of our immediate tasks are handled very carelessly, or not at all, although matters far removed from the practical activities of our people are treated. We must eradicate such defects without delay.

The educational and teaching work ought to be conducted in conformity to the realities of our country in close connection with our revolutionary tasks, so that it may be of practical help to carrying out the Korean revolution.

2. ON STRENGTHENING THE PARTY GUIDANCE OF ECONOMIC AND CULTURAL CONSTRUCTION

(1) CONCERNING INDUSTRY

North Pyongan Province is a province whose relative importance is very great in the industry of our country. It has power plants, chemical factories, ore and coal mines, and light industry factories as well. Also, the province accounts for a large part of the machine-building industry of our country. It has all the major industrial branches, except the metallurgical industry.

In other words, North Pyongan Province has important assets for the economic development of our country. This is why the Central Committee of our Party and the Government of the Republic give great concern to, and expect much from, North Pyongan Province.

This means that the North Pyongan provincial Party organization bears a heavy responsibility to the Party and the state for the development of industry.

a) Electric Industry

As you know, the Supung Hydroelectric Power Station is producing half of the total electric power output in our country. This power station is the biggest of its kind in the East. If it stops working, many of the industrial enterprises in our country will come to a standstill, and the people's life will be greatly affected. We must therefore make every effort to ensure normal production of electricity at the Supung Hydroelectric Power Station.

Not long ago, there was a serious accident that a runner of a turbine was damaged due to negligence in repairs and checkups on the part of the workers at this power station, causing hindrance to production and construction throughout the country for over 50 days.

The North Pyongan provincial Party organization must direct attention, from the Party standpoint, to strengthening the repair work and checkups in the power station, to ensuring quality in the assembly of generators, and to making timely repairs when a breakdown occurs.

And the Party organizations and the workers of the power station must fully rehabilitate its damaged installations at an early date, and run the power station in a cultured way.

b) Machine-building Industry

North Pyongan Province has a big share of our country's machine-building industry. It has major machine-building plants such as the Pukjung Machine Plant, Rakwon Machine Plant, Kusong Mining Machinery Plant and Kusong Machine-tool Plant as well as the Unsan Tool Factory, Factory No. 76, Kujang Railway Factory, etc., now under construction. It is impossible for us to strengthen the material and technical foundations of our national economy without developing the machine-building industry. Only a developed machine-building industry makes it possible to equip industry, agriculture, transport, communications and all other branches of the national economy with new technique, eliminate the colonial lopsidedness in industry, and lay the basis of socialist industrialization.

Our country is rich in natural resources—iron, gold, silver, copper, etc. But it will be impossible for us to make effective use of them for the economic development of our country unless we have our own machine-building industry. If the machine-building industry is not developed, we will not be able to process ores even if they are mined, nor manufacture necessary goods, and we will have no alternative but to export crude ores to foreign countries and, in return, import living necessaries and machinery and even machine parts. It is intolerable for us to export crude ores to foreign countries while importing even very simple machines and their accessories from abroad. We have not yet overcome this weak point.

If we continue, as at present, to mine ores and sell them to foreign countries as they are, then nothing but hollow caves will remain in our country. That will mean we are sinning seriously against our descendants.

To overcome such weakness in our country's economy, we must establish the base of the machine-building industry and consolidate it. If we have a powerful machine-building industry of our own and turn out various kinds of machines in large quantities, we will be able to use our country's resources more effectively. Then wealth, not hollow caves, will be left us.

Yesterday, a play "Maize Is King of Dry-field Grain Crops" was performed on the stage of this conference hall. I think it necessary to put forward the slogan: "Machine-building Industry Is King of Industry." Machinery is required everywhere. It is badly needed not only in industry but also in agriculture. Provided we have machinery, nothing will be impossible for us, and work will also become very easy. In fixing the roads too, when the machine-building industry is developed, there will be no need to do it by the method used at present, the method of women carrying a few stones in small wash-basins; all we will need to do is to remove earth with bulldozers, bring gravel by trucks and level the roadbeds with rollers. Furthermore, if plenty of cement is produced and the roads are paved with it, or they are paved with asphalt, there will be no need to repair them for several years.

That is why our Party set about building some machine factories, including the Huichon Machine Plant, even in the difficult years of war with a view to developing the machine-building industry. Today these factories are already turning out quite a number of machines.

Had our Party failed to take steps to establish a base of the machine-building industry in those days, the Huichon Machine Plant would now find itself starting construction, with its design barely finished.

Syngman Rhee spends the so-called U.S. "aid" to purchase Western sweets, but we, overcoming temporary difficulties, are doing everything we can to build up industry with a view to laying a solid economic foundation of the country and providing everlasting happiness to the masses of the people. The measures taken by the Party Central Committee for the development of the machine-building industry were correct.

The provincial Party organization must correctly understand the Party's policy and struggle for its thorough implementation. Active help should be given to complete in due time those machine factories now under construction or to be built in the future, and the scale of existing machine factories should be expanded to turn out a wider variety of products.

The important task ahead for the development of the machine-building industry is to raise the utilization rate of machine tools. At present, the utilization rate of machinery at machine factories is very low. The result of the recent checkup made by the chief of the Engineering Industry Bureau and Cabinet advisors has shown that the operation rate of machines at the Pukjung and Rakwon Machine Plants is no more than 44 per cent. There are various shortcomings: the failure of the casting shop to provide materials fast enough due to the poor organization of work, lack of balance in the distribution of labour power and in the arrangement of machines, etc.

For example, in the production of pumps, the small machines for intermediate processes stand idle after working one shift only, while the large machine tools are working in three shifts. Why not make full use of those small machines? Of course, irrationality exists in setting assignments under the plans, too. Assignments should be given in such a way as to use those small machines for making simple machines, machine parts, items of daily use, etc. Is it not better to produce even animal-drawn weeders rather than keep machines standing idle?

Who is to blame for it? In my opinion, the manager, the chief engineer, and the primary Party organization are to blame. Yesterday, the manager of the Rakwon Machine Plant made a lengthy speech boasting of their pump manufacturing, but did not say a single word about raising the operation rate of machines. Even if the state only assigned the plant to make pumps, the manager ought to see to it that the small machines, when they are not worked, be geared to the production of other kinds of items. Yet the leading personnel of the Rakwon Machine Plant have already grown puffed-up, thinking as if the manufacture of pumps were something great, while leaving out of account the question of raising the operation rate of machines. We cannot rest content with our machine-building industry making pumps at best. This is just an initial success. There are still no grounds for being complacent.

The Party organizations, therefore, must give proper education to those impudent persons who are carried away by an initial success, and help them produce modern machines by raising the utilization rate of machines and showing creativeness.

The same is true of the Kusong Mining Machinery Plant. Although the manager of the plant boasts of the fulfilment of the plan, all the plant can produce at present is mine cars. What is there to be so proud of in the production of mere mine cars with such excellent machines? Now we are in urgent need of drilling machines, winches, rock drills, etc. It is necessary to switch over to the production of such items.

The Unsan Tool Factory must mass-produce a greater variety of tools such as drills, taps, dies, cutters, and jigs and wood-working machines. To this end, measures must be taken to complete capital construction at the factory soon.

It is also important to raise the quality of products in the machine-building industry. The Party organizations must wage a struggle against the practice of inflicting enormous losses on the state at machine-building plants by turning out lots of rejects owing to technical mismanagement and lack of discipline and order in production. An important task confronting the Party organizations in guiding production is to eliminate rejects, raise labour productivity and reduce production costs. The Party organizations must give intensified guidance to industry so that this task can be fulfilled successfully.

Another important thing in the machine-building industry is to master technology and raise workers' technical level steadily.

Now, when advanced technology is being rapidly introduced into production and construction, it is most important for the workers to master technology. No matter how good a machine may be, it is impossible to operate it and turn out good-quality products without possessing advanced technique.

The Party organizations must see to it that the Party members set examples in introducing advanced technique and must ensure the training of a large number of mechanical engineers and assistant engineers.

We have recently made a tour of some industrial districts in North Pyongan Province, and thought it was necessary to establish a higher specialized technological school in the Kusong area. We must discuss this problem further and translate it into practice. In accordance with the Party's line of intensifying technical education, the North Pyongan provincial Party organization must correctly carry out the work of reorganizing some senior middle schools in the province into specialized technical schools.

With the purpose of raising the technical standard of workers and office employees, technical education must be developed through various forms of education such as evening specialized technical schools, technical training courses, training centres for skilled workers, etc., and especially efforts must be made for training designers in large numbers.

c) Mining Industry

The Cholsan Mine has an important place in obtaining foreign currency. Now, the level of mechanization at this mine cannot be regarded as high. Therefore, this mine should first of all raise its level of mechanization.

The Taeyudong Mine has a considerable share of the total gold production of our country. Now is the time for selling gold. It would be good for us to mine more gold and sell it before the ruin of the capitalist countries. We must not just indulge in boasting of our abundance of gold, but mine more gold quickly and sell it, using the returns for the construction of factories. To increase gold production, the prospecting work should be intensified and, particularly, measures be taken to carry on deep mining extensively. Also, the extraction rate should be raised by improving ore-dressing, and various measures be taken to mechanize conveyance, a labour-consuming work.

Further, advanced mining methods should be widely introduced to improve work in the coal mines and increase coal output.

Though our country has huge coal deposits, we are short of coal and spend precious foreign currency to buy a large amount of coal from foreign countries every year. This results from backward methods in coal mining and a slow pace in the rehabilitation of collieries. We must mine more good-quality coal to meet the internal demand.

Many people were reported frozen to death in Seoul last winter because of lack of fuel. We intend to send coal to our compatriots in the southern half as a gift, with a view to lessening their sufferings. Some time ago we discussed this problem at the Political Committee of the Party Central Committee. If we are to supply coal to Seoul in the future, the present coal output is not enough.

Coal mining should be mechanized and advanced mining methods should be introduced on an extensive scale to increase coal output sharply. And heading excavation should be kept ahead to develop the work of coal mining in a far-sighted way.

d) Chemical Industry

There is the Chongsu Chemical Factory in North Pyongan Province which is of national importance. This factory must turn out more carbide of good quality. It constitutes an important source of foreign currency. At present the price of carbide in foreign markets is 500 rubles per ton, which is equivalent to the price of two and a half tons of millet.

The Party organizations in the province should pay close attention to the Chongsu Chemical Factory, and particularly must see to it that the problem of manufacturing chemical fibres from carbide is solved by drawing scholars extensively into the research work for the manufacture of new kinds of products.

e) Light Industry

One of the major tasks confronting our Party now is to turn out large quantities of fabrics, footwear and other items of daily use and processed foodstuffs for improving the people's life extremely deteriorated in the war. The people lost all their furniture and clothing in the war, but those things have not yet been replenished in full. Therefore, we must produce more daily necessaries than before the war by rapidly developing light industry.

The light industry factories in North Pyongan Province have quite a lot of work to do. The Kusong Textile Mill fulfilled its production plan, but it must not rest on its laurels for it. It must strive to increase output and reduce production costs by cutting down the standard of materials consumption per unit.

And the Pakchon and Nyongbyon Silk Mills must produce large quantities of diverse silk fabrics. The quality of silks produced at these mills is better than in prewar years, but their output is smaller.

The quality of silk goods and woolen stuff produced at the Pakchon and Nyongbyon Silk Mills and the Sinuiju Woolen Textile Mill should be further improved and their output increased.

It should be an important fighting task of the Party organizations to raise the quality of products and cut their production costs in the sphere of light industry.

Now I want to speak about the paper industry. The Sinuiju

Paper Mill is an excellent plant. The equipment of the mill is good as such and its buildings can also be made nice with a little more rehabilitation. The factory has the conditions for producing a large quantity of paper in the future.

However, it is very uneconomical to use timber as raw material in the paper industry as in the Kilju Pulp Mill. It is therefore advisable to make paper with the pulp made on their own from straw, maize and other grain stalks, instead of bringing pulp from Kilju.

North Pyongan Province is abundant in grain stalks, as agriculture holds a big share in production in this province. How good it is to eat rice and make paper from the straw! The workers of the paper mill should also take measures for raising the quality of paper and for producing high-grade paper. Students complain of the paper produced at the Sinuiju Paper Mill because ink spreads on it. The workers of this mill must listen to the voices of the consumers and strive to remedy defects.

Then, the Sinuiju Pulp Mill must solve the important task of making artificial pulp from reeds. We are now rehabilitating a rayon spinning mill in Chongjin. This mill is to produce rayon yarn and staple fibre by using the artificial pulp turned out at the Sinuiju Pulp Mill as raw material. This work is of great importance in our country where timber is in short supply. So the Party Central Committee expects much of the Sinuiju Pulp Mill. During our visit to this mill, we saw the sample of the rayon of which the Japanese had already succeeded in the experimental production. There is no reason why we cannot do what the Japanese have done.

In order to supply raw materials to the Sinuiju Pulp Mill, it is necessary to expand the reed fields in the Ryongampo area and strengthen the work of tending them. The Party organizations in the province should unfold a fight to raise the per-unit-area yield in the reed fields.

f) Industries Run by the Province and the Co-operative Organizations

Some functionaries of the Party organizations and local government bodies have the wrong tendency to consider the producers' co-operatives or the industry run by the province not to be an industry.

The industries run by the province and co-operative organizations all represent the socialist economy. The industry run by co-operative organizations has come into being as a result of the reorganization of the small-commodity economy along socialist lines by drawing the urban handicraftsmen into the co-operative economy, and the province-run industry is a part of the state industry, which produces articles of daily necessity by enlisting local resources. Proper guidance and much assistance are needed for the province-run industry and producers' co-operatives.

The Party organizations should guide the producers' co-operatives toward producing large quantities of good-quality daily necessaries, mainly through effective use of local material sources. It is also necessary for the producers' co-operatives to produce large quantities of building materials and fittings needed in construction.

In the present conditions when state industry has not yet achieved an overall development, it is of great advantage to the development of the national economy and the improvement of the people's living standards that the producers' co-operatives and province-run industry put stress on those branches which are not covered by state industry, mainly on the production of daily necessaries for the people and building materials.

As you can see from this, industry in North Pyongan Province has great potentials. In guiding economic work, it is important for the Party organizations in the province to ensure proper utilization of these potentials.

And every possible means should be applied for the introduction of mechanization and for economizing labour power.

At present we have a great shortage of labour. As many young people went to the front, and many people have gone to work in industry and construction, the countryside is very short of manpower. In addition, rural manpower consists mostly of women and old people. At present, therefore, our countryside cannot meet the growing demand of industry for labour power.

As a step towards solving this question, the Party Central Committee has raised the saving of labour power as a combat task for the entire Party. Today it can be said that precisely he who saves labour power is a man of strong Party spirit and is faithful in state affairs.

The basic way of saving labour is to raise productivity by mechanizing labour-consuming processes of operation and organizing work rationally. If we waste labour power, neither industry nor agriculture can be developed. Nevertheless, the decision of the Presidium of the Party Central Committee on saving labour power has not yet been brought home to the factory Party organizations, and the practice of wasting huge amounts of labour power persists at some factories and enterprises.

Also, the struggle for the mechanization of work is lukewarm on construction sites, and thoroughgoing measures have not been taken for employing the labour of family dependents. What advantage can there be in using the labour of dependents? Employment of the labour of family dependents is good in that it covers the shortage of manpower and results in a saving of food for the state. Extensive enlistment of the labour of family dependents in production and construction will lead to improvement in the living standards of the workers and office employees and to the solution of the housing problem as well. Now we are building a large number of houses, yet we are still in need of them. Some comrades seem to think that dwellings come from Heaven. Those who believe in Jesus may expect that, but we do not believe in Jesus.

Large-scale housing construction requires an enormous sum of money and lots of equipment and materials. And we cannot build dwellings alone at present. We have to build schools and many factories, too. Where can we get such a great deal of equipment and materials? If we use the labour of family dependents, the housing problem can be eased that much, since several persons from one family go to work.

Therefore, every enterprise should pose the saving of labour as a foremost task. We can ask for foreign aid in other things, but how can we turn to foreign countries for labour power? Technical assistance is, of course, another question.

Another important thing is to use local materials in restoring and constructing factories and enterprises.

Our building workers make no effort to utilize good stones which they have in abundance within their reach, but instead bring bricks from distant places. Adobe, for instance, could be made locally, and yet they only sit and wail, insisting that they cannot undertake construction because they have no bricks. Such practice must be stopped.

Selection of proper sites for erecting factories and other buildings is also very important. In building a munitions factory making military shoes in Sakju, for instance, it was not built near the township but at a place far from the county seat, beyond a mountain, on the plea of maintaining secrecy. This caused losses to the state in many respects. Had this factory been built in the Sakju county seat, there would have been no need of laying electric wires across the mountain and building a road, and of motorcars running long distance consuming much gasoline. Now this factory is even asking for the construction of a railway. What a great loss this is! Had it been built in the township of Sakju, it would have been possible to employ the labour of family dependents. As it has been built on the other side of the mountain, it has become difficult to do so.

What is more serious, the planning of urban construction was left out of consideration. If the factory had been built in Sakju, the township would have become more prosperous. Though this is attributable to the mistake made by the Munitions Production Bureau, the County Party Committee and the County People's Committee also failed to act properly as masters.

The masters of the county are the chairmen of the County People's Committee and the County Party Committee. As they failed to fulfil properly their duties as masters, the factory was built beyond the mountain, a road leading to it had to be built and raw materials and products transported by trucks. Also, a primary school had to be built there. Is that all? The wives of the factory workers have come to suffer great inconveniences in going to the market for shopping.

As you see, it is not infrequently the case that great losses are incurred by undertaking economic construction without reckoning seriously with everything.

Yet, this does not mean, of course, that all factories should be built in the vicinity of towns. However, what great secret is there about a shoe factory that forbids its building in the township?

Control should be intensified over the construction of factories and towns. Factories, dwellings or public buildings must be built according to the plans of urban construction, with due consideration for various conditions—electricity, waterworks, sewerage, railways, roads, communications and others. In particular, designs should be so drawn up as to enable the existing facilities to be fully utilized.

In some localities, such wrong practices are observed as building many temporary houses in a disorderly way on the nearby farmland, while setting aside spacious vacant lots in the centre of the town for the future construction of multistorey buildings in the county seat.

In Kusong, too, though they have funds and are provided with all other conditions, the Engineering Industry Bureau and Ministry of Light Industry are erecting makeshift buildings or one-storey houses anywhere they please at random, neglecting the town planning. The Kusong County Party Committee and County People's Committee, exercising strict control over the workers in this field, should see to it that they build multistorey houses in town, not allowing them to build houses outside it. Managers of the Kusong Textile Mill and Machine Plant say that the building of two-storey houses involves difficulties, for it entails more building expenditures. True, there will be a variety of difficulties in obtaining materials. But it is not economical to build one-storey houses, for it requires lots of tiles and large sites.

At present, building materials are somewhat insufficient, but large quantities of materials will be put out beginning next year. Party control should be tightened so as to carry on urban construction in a far-sighted, methodical way, not in a make-shift, disorderly manner.

(2) CONCERNING AGRICULTURE

The report went into details on agriculture, and a full debate was made by many comrades.

The most important task confronting agriculture today is to increase grain production. For higher grain output, it is necessary to raise the per-unit-area yield of dry-field crops decisively.

The area of dry fields is larger than that of paddies in our country. In North Pyongan Province, too, of the total 280,000 *chongbo* of cultivated land, only 80,000 *chongbo* is paddyfields and the rest is all dry fields. It is therefore impossible to raise the grain harvest without increasing the yields of dry-field crops.

Maize, of all dry-field grain crops, is especially high-yielding. The Party organizations and government bodies should pay close attention to the expansion of the area under maize.

According to the debates, kaoliang yields more than maize in an area like Uiju County. Of course, it would be better for such a district to cultivate much kaoliang in line with the principle of the right crop on the right soil for higher crop yields.

Further, it is important to increase the utilization of land for an increased harvest of grain. Land should be used to the full by means of raising two crops or inter-row crops wherever possible, whether in paddies or dry fields.

Besides, backward farming methods should be abolished and advanced methods should be actively introduced.

Grain output in North Pyongan Province in 1955 was far less than that in the prewar year 1949. We are told that a few agricultural co-operatives had an increased harvest last year, but that is nothing to boast of. Much effort is still required in order to reach the prewar level throughout the province.

As everyone knows, the food situation was good before the war and, accordingly, rice was not expensive. But now the price of rice is high due to the shortage of food grains, and this causes us a lot of trouble.

Grain output in North Pyongan Province should surpass the prewar level of 590,000 tons within the next few years, and the provincial Party organization should wage an active struggle for it. This year's target figure of grain output is 470,000 tons, and this is very small. But this, of course, does not mean that the province should produce 590,000 tons right away this year. In my opinion, North Pyongan Province can turn out more than 560,000 tons in 1957-58, and it must do so without fail. Though the supply of chemical fertilizer to the peasants by the state is still insufficient, from 1958 on it will be possible to supply them with plenty of it. And by that time, much will be done in the way of irrigation projects, farmland will also be further expanded, mechanization of agriculture will be accelerated, and a big stride will be made in agricultural co-operativization, too. In this way many problems will be solved.

However, we cannot merely sit and wait for that time to come. We must make full use of the existing potentialities to produce more grain.

Here it is necessary above all to make effective use of the farm machines at our disposal. Farm machines play a very important role in saving rural labour power and increasing the harvest. Last year, in an area like South Pyongan Province, animal-drawn weeders were kept idle in warehouses. If the case is similar in North Pyongan Province too, it would do well to put an end to it at an early date.

Further. Irrigation and river projects should be carried out through an all-people movement. In carrying on irrigation projects, we should undertake many small-scale projects, not just go in for large-scale ones. Since the state cannot undertake all the irrigation projects, large and small, two to three co-operatives need to join efforts and build small-scale reservoirs or pumping stations to enlarge irrigated areas. At the same time, farmland should be protected from floods through a well-organized river improvement work.

We should also ensure the timely repairs and proper management of existing irrigation facilities such as reservoirs and pumping stations.

And agricultural co-operatives should strive for the expansion of the land under cultivation. It should likewise be made a very important task in the future to turn the tidelands on the west coast into farmland.

Another problem that is important in developing agriculture is to strengthen and develop the agricultural co-operatives organizationally and economically.

Organizational strengthening of the agricultural co-operative means forming its management board with model, advanced workers, according to the genuinely democratic will of the co-operative members, managing and running the co-operative in accordance with the will of its members, and enhancing the organizational role of the Party and social organizations in the co-operative.

Economic strengthening of the agricultural co-operative means increasing its income by all possible means to improve the life of its members and consolidate its economic foundation.

To improve the living standards of the co-operative members, it is necessary to increase their income. The state will help the agricultural co-operative members to increase their real income by appropriately regulating the procurement prices of agricultural produce and by systematically reducing the prices of daily necessities.

To prepare instruments of production well, step up irrigation and river improvements, and secure enough fertilizers and seeds is all a work aimed at strengthening the economic foundation of the co-operatives. This kind of work is very important for the development of the co-operatives.

To strengthen the agricultural co-operatives organizationally and economically, the Party organizations must delve deep into their work and give a live leadership.

It must be borne in mind that, with the formation of co-operatives, the responsibility of the Party for the peasants' life has become incomparably greater than in the days of individual farming. The success or failure of the co-operatives rests entirely on the work of the Party organizations. Therefore, the Party organizations must make every effort to consolidate the agricultural co-operatives.

The Party organizations should continue boldiy to push ahead with the agricultural co-operative movement. Only two years have passed since we started the agricultural co-operative movement, but the peasants have already become convinced, through their experience, of the far greater advantage of the co-operative farming over the individual farming.

The Party organizations must strengthen the economic foundation of the co-operatives that have already been organized and thus lead the broader sections of peasants to join them.

(3) CONCERNING THE FISHING INDUSTRY

North Pyongan Province now plays the biggest role in the fishing industry on the West Sea of our country. The West Sea is rich in fish, especially in tasty, high-grade fish. The gizzard shad caught in the West Sea is so famous that the saying goes: "The smell of broiling gizzard shad makes the daughter-in-law change her mind when she is about to go away."

The fishing industry on the West Sea, however, is not developed and remains in a very backward state. The Ministry of Fishing Industry and the local government bodies have been criticized several times by the Political Committee on account of their failure to develop the fishing industry on the West Sea.

The problem of developing the fishing industry on the

West Sea will be taken up as an important question at the Third Party Congress too, and this problem will also be raised as an important task in working out the Five-Year Plan.

The main shortcoming in the fishing industry on the West Sea is that the backward methods of fishing have not yet been improved and there is no daring and activity in the work. Workers in this sphere said that they could not catch fish because they had no angle-net boats. So the state made the boats and delivered them. Nevertheless, their work has not yet improved. After all, the question lies not in angle-net boats but in the fact that our workers do not struggle to make full use of every condition and potentiality for a big catch of fish.

The Chinese are making good hauls on the West Sea; and why can we not catch fish on that same sea? The fishing workers on the West Sea still lack courage. In order to develop the fishing industry on the West Sea, there must be a great change in work and positive, creative efforts are required of the Party organizations and members.

There is no insurmountable difficulty nor unconquerable fortress before our Party members. We have boats, motors and nets.

The question lies in whether our fishing workers and Party organizations rise up or not to innovate the fishing industry on the West Sea. On the West Sea there must be decisive switchover to deep-sea fishing.

The Five-Year Plan envisages the extension of fishing bases around Ryongampo and Tasa-do Island. The Party organizations in North Pyongan Province must ensure preparatory work for carrying out this task and guarantee its successful fulfilment.

(4) CONCERNING EDUCATIONAL WORK

The Presidium of the Party Central Committee adopted last February a decision on improving and strengthening the work of school education.

It seems, however, that this decision has not yet been conveyed in full to all Party organizations in North Pyongan Province. The decision of the Presidium of the Party Central Committee should be made known to the Party organizations at all levels and to the Party members at an early date after this conference and, on that basis, steps should be taken for overall improvement of educational work.

The task of intensifying educational work is posed ever more urgently with the advance of socialist construction in the northern half.

How great our yearnings were towards the Soviet Union, the socialist state, when we were waging an underground revolutionary struggle in the past! After the triumph of the October Socialist Revolution in Russia, the Korean working class, especially the youth, felt a very strong yearning for socialism. Today that socialism is being realized precisely in our country.

In order to build a socialist society, the source of exploitation must be done away with and socialist production relations be established and, moreover, the material and technical foundations of socialism must be firmly laid and the consciousness of the people be remoulded along socialist lines. Only then can we say that socialist construction has been completed. Take an example. If an agricultural co-operative is just organized, and then neither technique is developed nor the work of remoulding its members' consciousness is conducted, it cannot become a fully socialist economy.

Socialism cannot be built by slogans or eloquent speeches; it can only be built by the creative activities of the working people equipped with socialist consciousness and high-level technology. The more all the members of society are awakened politically and ideologically and the higher their cultural and technical standards become, the more the construction of socialist society will be accelerated.

I do not intend to make a lengthy explanation of the great significance of the remoulding of people's ideological consciousness and of the enhancement of their cultural and technical attainments in promoting socialist construction. Only I want to say a few words about our teachers educating millions of the younger generation in new science and technology and in socialist ideology, and about the work of guiding school education.

Fifty thousand teachers are engaged in the education of the new, younger generation at schools of various levels in our country today. Their mission is really great and their responsibility is very heavy.

To educate the students in socialism, it is most important for teachers to arm themselves firmly with socialist ideological consciousness. To teach "One-Thousand Characters," one must not only know "One-Thousand Characters" but must, in fact, know more. Teachers must shake themselves free from the survivals of outdated ideology that still remain in them, and raise their level of ideological consciousness. This is essential for attaining a qualitative rise in the work of education and teaching at schools. The Party organizations at various levels must pay special attention to the work of raising the qualifications of teachers, who play an important part in the socialist construction of our country, and of training them politically and ideologically.

Further. Keen attention should be paid to treating teachers well socially and improving their living standards. This is to enable them to settle down to educational work and dedicate all their energies and talents to bringing up the children and youth into socialist builders who are loyal to the Party and the revolution and who have knowledge and skills. As a comrade said in his speech, it is wrong to be interested only in working the teachers hard without looking after them.

Not long ago, the Presidium of the Party Central Committee discussed the question of giving better material treatment to the teachers. When we were waging the trying war, it was impossible for us to raise such a matter, but we are now in a position gradually to solve this question as the country's economic situation improves.

The Party organizations at all levels should intensify the guidance of school education, and give concrete assistance to the teachers. Now, in North Pyongan Province, the Party's guidance in this sphere leaves much to be desired.

Some time ago I visited Kaechon County and found that the County Party Committee was overly neglecting its guidance of educational work. The fact is that functionaries of the County Party Committee do not visit schools until towards July, when they receive directives from the higher Party organization on the work of preparing for the new school-year. They know absolutely nothing about whether the teachers were giving instruction correctly, what methods they were applying in educating the pupils, or how the work of schools was going. The North Pyongan Provincial Party Committee also leaves this work entirely in the care of the educational department, and only when the new school-year comes around does it show a little attention to the question of constructing school buildings. This is the way it is "guiding" educational work. This is a glaring mistake.

The Minister of Education, who has recently made a tour of North Pyongan Province to inspect the work of some schools, says that the province has firmer material foundations for strengthening the work of schools than other provinces. What, then, is lacking there? All that is lacking is the proper guidance of educational work by the Party organizations, Ministry of Education and local people's committees.

Now let me speak briefly about intensifying technical education. This will also be raised at the forthcoming Third Party Congress as one of the important tasks.

Today the most urgent problem in the socialist construction of our country is to train technical personnel. Following the war, many factories have been built, machines are being turned out, and agriculture has also been co-operativized and is advancing along socialist lines in our country. In the northern half of the Republic, we will lay the basis of socialist industrialization before long and, furthermore, will have to equip agriculture, the fishing industry and all other branches of the national economy with modern technology. Only then will there be laid the material and technical foundations of socialist society, far more developed than capitalist society. This means a great change in the development of the productive forces in our country. The greatest difficulty we have to tide over in effecting this change is the dearth of technical personnel. Unless the problem of technical talent is solved, it is impossible to take a single step forward.

That is why the Party Central Committee has long since posed this problem as an important one, and particularly, last year, it saw to it that the Supreme People's Assembly adopted a relevant law on the intensification of technical education. And in line with the policy adopted by the Party and the Government, a large number of senior middle schools have been reorganized into specialized schools, and the possibility of receiving technical education at the technical refresher courses has been provided for those junior middle school graduates who are unable to go to schools of higher level.

And what is the present state of affairs? In many cases, the work is carried on in a perfunctory manner and is not on the right track. First of all, refresher courses have not been distributed properly. Agricultural refresher courses have been set up in factory districts, and children of workers are enrolled in them. Most of them are youngsters under 15 years of age, and it would be hardly possible for the young children of workers to engage in farming away from their homes. And in my opinion, there seems to be no need of taking the trouble of sending workers' children to the countryside, in the light of the prospects of our country's development. It will be advisable to see that they, too, become workers in the wake of their parents.

Some refresher course students do not clearly understand why they are attending the course. As was confirmed during our visit to Kaechon County some time ago, it is often the case that the students regard the refresher course as a place where they receive education preparatory to entering schools of higher level. As the students say, it is not a refresher course but a "review course." According to the Minister of Education, in North Pyongan Province, too, the refresher courses have been turned into "review courses."

Many agricultural co-operatives have been organized in our countryside now. In order to further consolidate them and increase their production, the old-fashioned, handicraft technique must be replaced by new technique, and this requires large numbers of technical personnel in the countryside. The agricultural refresher courses attached to the junior middle schools in the rural districts aim precisely at solving this problem. We do not ask much of the agricultural refresher courses. If, in one year's intensive study, the students are taught such simple technical matters as the methods of manuring and cultivating crops, knowledge of soil, methods of using agricultural chemicals, knowledge of damage by blight and noxious insects and rudimentary skills in handling farm machinery, as well as advanced methods of farming, they will be able to work efficiently when they go to agricultural co-operatives.

If the agricultural co-operatives only draw on the old experience in farming, they cannot make progress. We do not reject experience in general. Good experience can make for advancement, but the empiricism that is manifested in shortsightedness, narrowness and sticking to old experience impedes advance in work. Herein lie the significance of the establishment of technical refresher courses and the reason why the senior middle schools have been reorganized into specialized technical schools. By running specialized technological schools and refresher courses on industrial technique in industrial districts and by effectively running specialized agricultural schools and refresher courses on agro-technique in the countryside, we must bring up technicians and skilled personnel in large numbers.

More than 14,000 assistant agronomists are needed if we are to assign only one to every agricultural co-operative now. And if only a few agro-technicians including those in silk culture and livestock breeding are to be allocated to every provincial and county people's committee, we need several thousands of them. If we train technicians at a snail's pace as at present, the problem would not be solved even in ten years.

Taking into account such a situation, the curricula of

schools at all levels, under the general educational system, should also be revised in the future with an eye to imparting basic knowledge of production technology to the pupils. Only then is it possible to achieve a successful, early solution of the problem of technical talent, a matter of urgency everywhere—factories, mines, rural areas, fishing villages, and construction sites.

* * *

In conclusion, I should like to touch briefly on the need of improving explanatory and propaganda work on the perspectives of the development of our country's national economy and the difficulties confronting us.

Some people seem to wonder why the people's living conditions do not improve in spite of the great achievements in economic construction. We have done much and the results are enormous, indeed. But, as you all know, after the truce we were obliged to improve the people's living standards rapidly, while giving priority to the rehabilitation and expansion of the ravaged factories, mines, railways, etc., because the war damage was so serious. We are rehabilitating industry not merely to its former state but on the basis of new technology, and are proceeding along the lines of abolishing the old weak points of colonial industry, and establishing an independent industry. Hence our Party has adhered to the principle of giving priority to the development of heavy industry, and has made great efforts to build the base of the machine-building industry which was formerly non-existent in our country. We have used, and are still now using, our domestic resources and the aid from fraternal countries mainly for this purpose. Such being the situation, it is understandable that the people's life can hardly be improved in a day.

Nevertheless, although we are now in needy circumstances, our life has, in fact, become far better than during the war or immediately after the truce. This is due to the fact that our Party, giving priority to the rehabilitation and development of heavy industry, simultaneously ensured the rapid development of light industry and agriculture to improve the people's living conditions. Particularly, now that the foundation of our heavy industry has been laid to a certain extent as a result of its rapid growth, there is no doubt that in the future our life will improve more rapidly than ever.

We must carry on propaganda correctly about the line pursued by the Party and the results attained, and about our life today and its prospects. Falsehood and exaggeration in propaganda could possibly produce harmful effects on the mobilization of the broad popular masses to socialist construction.

For example, the peasants should also be given a correct understanding of the situation which prevents an enough supply of fertilizers. Instead of just saying in sweet-sounding words that the chemical industry has developed, we should acquaint them well with the fact that the most severely damaged fertilizer plants are now under reconstruction, that fertilizer cannot gush forth at once in a stream, like a surging flood in the rainy season, but that it will presumably become possible to supply enough fertilizer beginning 1958, after the factories are fully restored by hard work.

At the same time, the reason why we cannot supply a sufficient amount of food grains to the workers, office employees and other sections of the population at present, and why the market price of rice is still high, should be correctly explained to them. It must be frankly explained to the workers that this problem can be solved only when they produce and supply a large quantity of farm machinery, fertilizer and consumer goods to the countryside, thereby enabling the peasants to produce an abundance of grain, and that until then the food situation may remain difficult to a certain degree.

The same can be said of the problem of cloth. We are now turning out more fabrics than in prewar days. Then why is the problem of cloth so acute? That is due to the fact that the demand for cloth is immensely big because the people lost everything, even mattresses, quilts and clothes in the U.S. imperialists' barbarous bombing during the war. I hear that some say the price of fabrics is high, but the problem would not be solved even if the price were lowered. The price of cloth has been set fairly in view of the purchasing power of the population at present. It will be possible to sharply reduce the price of cloth and solve the problem of fabrics completely only when plenty of cloth is produced by rapidly developing the textile and other branches of light industry on the basis of accelerating the priority development of heavy industry. Our propaganda should also give a clear explanation of this.

Thus, our propaganda should be frank and clear and should tell the truth as it is. The people will then overcome every difficulty and advance valiantly with firm confidence in the prospects ahead, and will devote all their energies to the struggle for their own happiness and for the country's prosperity and development.

Today things are going very well with us, and we have the promise of a brighter future. In contrast, the situation in south Korea is gloomy indeed, and its people are groaning in the slough of hunger and poverty. We have the responsibility for relieving our south Korean compatriots from such a miserable plight.

In order to carry into effect the country's peaceful reunification programme, outlined by the Party and the Government, we have to further consolidate the socialist economic foundations in the northern half of the Republic and further improve the people's life. As days go by, the people in the southern half, yearning for the land of bliss in the northern half, will curse the living hell of the southern half and, rallying firmly around our Party, will come out bravely in the national-salvation struggle against the U.S. imperialists' colonial plunder and the Syngman Rheeites' traitorous rule, the source of all their misery and distress.

The socialist economic foundations being laid solidly in the northern half constitute not only the material basis for the country's reunification but will serve as a decisive guarantee for the successful rehabilitation of the economy and the rapid improvement of the people's life in south Korea after reunification. Socialist construction in the northern half, therefore, instills a great hope not only in the people of the northern half but also in the people of the southern half, and will prove a strong impetus impelling the latter to rise in a just struggle.

All the Party organizations, Party members and working people in North Pyongan Province are today greeting the Third Party Congress, which is of great significance in our Party's life, with high labour achievements. After the Party Congress, they should all be mobilized, following the path indicated by the Congress, to the fulfilment of the already set assignments of the Three-Year National Economic Plan ahead of schedule and to the material and ideological preparations for going over to carrying out a Five-Year National Economic Plan in the future.

I am convinced that the Party organizations and Party members in North Pyongan Province, under the guidance of the Party Central Committee, will fulfil this honourable revolutionary task with credit.

KIM IL SUNG, Selected Works (I)

Second Edition

The Democratic People's Republic of Korea